Beneath the Moon

Witchcraft and Moon Magic for a Deeper Practice

Beneath the Moon

Witchcraft and Moon Magic for a Deeper Practice

Rachel Patterson

MOON BOOKS
Winchester, UK
Washington, USA

JOHN HUNT PUBLISHING

First published by Moon Books, 2021
Moon Books is an imprint of John Hunt Publishing Ltd., No. 3 East Street, Alresford
Hampshire SO24 9EE, UK
office@jhpbooks.net
www.johnhuntpublishing.com
www.moon-books.net

For distributor details and how to order please visit the 'Ordering' section on our website.

ISBN: 978 1 78535 579 0
978 1 78535 5806 (ebook)
Library of Congress Control Number: 2020940139

A CIP catalogue record for this book is available from the British Library.

Design: Matthew Greenfield

UK: Printed and bound by CPI Group (UK) Ltd, Croydon, CR0 4YY
Printed in North America by CPI GPS partners

Contents

Who am I?

I am a witch ... have been for a very long time. I am also a working wife and mother who has been lucky enough to write and have published a book, or twenty! I love to learn, I love to study and have done so from books, online resources, schools and wonderful mentors over the years and continue to learn every day, but I have learnt the most from getting outside and doing it.

I am High Priestess of the Kitchen Witch Coven and an Elder at the online Kitchen Witch School. My craft is a combination of old religion Witchcraft, Kitchen Witchery, Hedge Witchery and folk magic. My heart is that of a Kitchen Witch. I like to laugh, bake and eat cake.

My website and personal blog: www.rachelpatterson.co.uk
Facebook: www.facebook.com/rachelpattersonbooks
Email: kitchenwitchhearth@yahoo.com

I also have regular blogs on:
Witches & Pagans – www.witchesandpagans.com/pagan–paths–blogs/hedge–witch.html
Patheos Pagan – www.patheos.com/blogs/beneaththeMoon
Moon Books – www.johnhuntpublishing.com/Moon–books/

Kitchen Witch School website and blog: www.kitchenwitchhearth.net
www.facebook.com/kitchenwitchuk

MY BOOKS

Kitchen Witchcraft Series
Spells & Charms
Garden Magic
Crystal Magic
The Element of Earth

Pagan Portals
Kitchen Witchcraft
Hoodoo Folk Magic
Moon Magic
Meditation
The Cailleach
Animal Magic
Sun Magic

Other Moon Books
The Art of Ritual
Witchcraft … into the Wilds
Grimoire of a Kitchen Witch
A Kitchen Witch's World of Magical Foods
A Kitchen Witch's World of Magical Plants & Herbs
Arc of the Goddess (co–written with Tracey Roberts)
Moon Books Gods & Goddesses Colouring Book (Patterson family)
Practically Pagan: An Alternative Guide to Cooking

Llewellyn
Curative Magic
Flower Magic Oracle deck

A detailed and in-depth practical guide for working with the magic of the Moon.

Delve into the magic of the Moon

How to work with this book

I have tried to squeeze as much information about Moon magic between these pages as I could. Although I have touched on the science stuff, the focus is on working magic. You can read through the book from cover to cover and I will be chuffed to bits if you do. However, the book is designed to work from many angles. My primary goal was to write a book that had all the Moon magic information in one place for each different phase of the Moon. Whether you are looking to work with a new Moon, waning Moon or the Moon in Scorpio (for instance) you will find a section on each. Those sections contain magical properties, correspondences, some rituals and meditations and items to work with for that phase. It can also be used as a reference guide.

My Witchcraft is a mixed bag, I have taken workings, ideas and methods from many different pathways over the years. Although these days I tend to work with deities from ancient Britain and the Celts, I have worked with gods and goddesses from various pantheons. I do so, with the utmost respect for each culture. Please do bear in mind that manners and respect count for a lot, physically and spiritually. Work with this book in a way that suits you, work your magic in a way that suits you, walk your pathway in a way that suits you, it is your journey.

Why work with the Moon?

She is so powerful and affects not only our moods and emotions but can also provide us with the power to work very successful magic. Living, playing and working in tune with her rhythms can change your life and the way you look at the world. She will help you to connect not only with her magic but your own, your intuition and every thread that wraps its way through this big ole world of ours. She has the power to transform your life, you have the power within you to do the same…

You can work with the guidelines I have set out here, and there are magical prompts that make sense such as a waxing Moon bringing things to you and a waning Moon taking them away. But if you work regularly yourself and tune in to her you will find your own way and what works for you. Let her be your guide.

If you find yourself in a real jam on the new Moon and need to release something but can't wait until the waning Moon, re-word your spell. All it takes is a bit of creative writing.

Moon Science

Why is the Moon so important? Why do we work with the Moon and how come it has so much power over us and the planet? As a witch one of the first things I was taught was to create a Moon diary and work with the phases of the Moon for spell work and to notice how each phase affected me and my emotions; a Moon diary is an excellent way of introducing yourself to Moon magic and see exactly what each phase means to you.

But why? How did this fascination with the Moon come about and what on earth does it all mean? Hopefully I have touched on some of the answers to those questions within this book, but whatever the reason, the Moon is a beautiful and powerful source of magic available for us to tap into.

The science bit

The clever science bods reckon that when the Earth was in its infancy there was no Moon at all *gasp*…then on some undetermined date a rogue planet smashed into the Earth like a cosmic game of pool, and this caused the rogue planet to be obliterated and knocked a chunk off the side of the Earth too. This all created a huge cloud of planet debris. The cloud rose upwards and eventually squished together into large particles that orbited the Earth, as time went on the particles all joined forces with each other and eventually et voila...the Moon was formed.

Apparently, using some clever gadget, they can also measure the age of lunar rock and they know it is about 4.6 billion years old. The Moon is 238,900 miles away from the Earth and is 2,160 miles in diameter, that is about one eightieth of the Earth's mass. The Moon itself has one sixth of the Earth's gravity – that explains the astronauts doing the funny slow–motion Moon walk.

The Moon takes about 27.3 days to spin once around on its own axis which is about the same time as it takes for the Moon to complete on orbit of the Earth. Which means the Moon is synchronized with the Earth, so we only ever see the same face of the Moon at all times. What is called the 'dark side' of the Moon i.e. the far side, has only ever been seen from spacecraft.

What we see of the Moon and what shape it is depends on the amount of illuminated Moon and is relative to the position of the Moon in relation to the Earth and the Sun. When the Sun is directly behind us, we see the full face of the Moon as the Moon is directly in front of us. When the Moon is dark, on the new Moon, the Moon is directly between the Earth and the Sun, the light of the Sun only illuminates the far side of the Moon, which we can't see.

The Moon orbits around the Earth at a whacking 2,300 miles an hour.

It is the gravitational pull from the Moon on the Earth that causes the tides of the oceans. Where the ocean faces the Moon, the pull is strongest and where the ocean faces away from the Moon the pull is weakest. These gravitational pulls cause bulges of water on the oceans, these bulges cause the high tides. As the Earth rotates the bulges move, one always facing the Moon and the other always opposite. The rotation of the Earth and the combined forces of gravity are the main factors in creating two high tides and two low tides every day.

The lumpy surface of the Moon is made up from lots of scars

created by objects that hit the Moon. Some of the largest scars are 1,500 miles across. At some point in its history the craters were filled with lava, these are the dark areas you can see on the surface of the Moon and are referred to as 'maria' (a Latin word meaning 'seas').

If we didn't have the Moon controlling the spin of the earth, we would not be able to live on our planet.

No one has yet discovered a man in the Moon or that there is any evidence it was made from cheese...

Moon magic history

Since man has walked on this planet, I suspect he has always looked to the stars at night and it wouldn't have taken him very long to work out that the Moon had regular phases. Not only would man have worked with the seasons, but he would also have needed to pay attention to the Moon. On a dark/new Moon it would have been pretty black at night so his hunting would have been done during the day. However, on the nights of the full Moon he would have been able to track nocturnal animals to bop on the head for his supper. Finding food was one of his top priorities so the light of the Moon would have been very important.

Watching the Moon was a guide to the changing of the seasons. They were learning about how the planet worked and trying to predict the weather and the tides to allow them to grow more successful crops to keep them alive.

Roll forward in time just a tad, OK maybe more than just a tad...those clever Babylonians were also looking to the stars and creating the principles of astrology (somewhere in the region of 3,500 years ago). They understood astronomy and worked with the phases to create a calendar for planting, harvesting and religious festivals.

By around 1,000BC the Babylonians had created planetary omens, giving each planet a name and characteristics that it controlled. The twelve–sign zodiac came into being around 600BC with the first known record of a horoscope dating back to April 410BC.

The Roman and Greek astronomers were a bit sniffy about astrology, but the public had other ideas and astrology grew in popularity.

By the beginning of the Middle Ages astrologers were struggling because of the rise of Christianity, it just wasn't their thing…but those Crusaders brought back the idea from the Middle East and it became fashionable again.

Then in the 1600s the elliptical solar system was discovered kind of putting a dampener on astrology again, but it didn't disappear for long. Just after the end of World War I daily newspapers started to carry astrology columns and it has been with us ever since.

It has also been suggested that some of the greatest minds, such as Sir Isaac Newton, studied astrology and many members of royalty and important public figures over the years have employed astrologers as counselors. Nostradamus is one of the most well–known, and of course Queen Elizabeth I consulted John Dee. Napoleon was said to have astrologers on hand for advice.

Astrology is based on the positions of ten planets, including the Sun and the Moon but not including the Earth because the Earth is the centre or starting point for the positions of the other planets. We really do like to think we are the centre of the universe…which we aren't…sorry. When the Moon travels through the different signs (the Sun does too), that sign influences the magic of the Moon.

I think it is a combination of factors that make the Moon phases a key part in working magic. It is the huge power that the Moon commands in controlling the oceans along with the history of our ancestors and how important it was for them and their well–being, all with a bit of astrology thrown in too. It is also about cycles; our whole lives work in cycles, think about it… the main one obviously being the cycle of birth, life and death and if you work with that idea the added bonus of reincarnation and doing the whole circus again…and again…But we also work in cycles of years and months and weeks and days, the whole calendar system is a set of cycles and all tied in with the cycles of the Moon. Women will probably feel this more than men, but it isn't exclusive, the menstrual cycle usually works on a monthly basis too. I say women will feel it more because we have the whole physical ovaries thing, but I do wholeheartedly believe that men are affected by the cycles as well. A lot of women will also notice that their menstrual cycles are aligned with the Moon phases. I always encourage everyone no matter what gender to keep a Moon diary; it can be quite enlightening to see how the phases affect your moods and mindset.

I have found that the full Moon brings the most power, but I also love working with the new Moon because it brings such a fresh and bright energy for new beginnings. The waning Moon I don't work with as much, unless I need to get rid of something…

Moon magic is a huge subject and one that I am looking forward to delving into and sharing more with you…

Moon gender?

I see the Moon as female and the Sun as male and that is the case for a lot of Pagans. However not all cultures see it that way and some don't assign a gender at all. The Moon has a lot of feminine connections including controlling water and our emotions. Whereas the Sun is often associated with more masculine attributes such as power, strength and energy (but then the roles can easily be reversed). The Moon also follows a twenty–eight–day cycle much as a woman does with her menstruation cycle.

Different cultures will also have a lot of stories, some involving the Moon being male and some female.

The Sun was seen as a stable life giver, it provides light and heat. Whereas the Moon appeared in the dark sky as a shape shifter, always changing shape or not there at all, it is full of mystery. The Moon was seen perhaps as a cycle of destruction, growth and rebirth, linked to fertility even. The powerful Sun took on the masculine role and the mysterious Moon the female characteristics.

Mythology on the Sun and the Moon often sees them as siblings or partners, stories woven to tell of their chase across the skies, never to catch each other. The Sun god usually riding in his chariot drawn by various animals depending on the culture. As a child I was taught nursery rhymes that claimed there was a man living in the Moon. The Polynesians believe it to be a woman in the Moon with her child. The Selish Indians believe the Moon shows the image of a toad. Some see the image of an old man carrying a bundle of sticks on his back. Some see a giant or a hunchback. In some areas of East Asian and Japan the Moon is thought to hold the image of a rabbit. In India the Moon is seen as a pair of hands. Scandinavians see a girl and boy holding a bucket of water (ala the Jack and Jill nursery rhyme). I think this is a case of going with what works for you, do some research, look at different cultures but ultimately the choice is yours and it doesn't need to have a gender at all.

Moon rise

Just as the Sun has a rise time, so does the Moon. The Moon rise is the moment when the upper edge of the Moon touches the horizon. This also coincides with the time of high tide.

As a general rule this is a guide to the Moon rise times, bear in mind that these are affected by daylight saving time and your time zone:

- New Moon will rise near Sunrise.
- First quarter Moon rises close to noon.
- Full Moon rises around Sunset.

- Last quarter Moon rises close to midnight.

Moon energy

There is energy in all things, by working in tune with the ebb and flow of the Moon's energy we can literally go with the flow. It makes life so much easier than fighting against the tide. It will just be a case of working out how the Moon affects you and how best you can fall in line with it. Although the general idea is the structure of: New positive upwards energy for waxing and then releasing or letting go with the waning, for example. It is a personal experience so it may be different for you. Work with it, play around with it and fashion your own schedule.

Esbat

The word 'esbat' is used a lot in Pagan circles, but what does it actually mean? It seems to be used more often for a full Moon ritual, but I think it is much broader than that. It can be purely a coven meeting, a group of like–minded people getting together to celebrate something other than a sabbat, for group healing or just to learn from each other. It also seems to cover new Moon rituals in some circles. The word 'esbat' may come from the old French "s'esbattre" meaning 'to frolic, to enjoy oneself'. Quite a few descriptions to choose from. It seems the most popular use is for a full Moon ritual, but it can be used for new Moon rituals or just general coven knees ups. Personally, I am going to adopt it so that I can officially frolic...

Working with the Moon Phases

In this section I work through each of the phases of the Moon and include information to guide you and also some suggested rituals and craft working. One word about the dark and new Moon before we get started. Most Moon calendars will show eight phases of the Moon; new, waxing crescent, first quarter, waxing gibbous, full, waning gibbous, third quarter and waning crescent (balsamic). They don't often mention the dark Moon because they call it the 'new Moon'. Technically this is correct, but for magical purpose I like to separate the two. I feel the dark Moon has a different magic all to its own, separate from the new Moon. For the purpose of this book and for magical workings I have separated the dark Moon and the new Moon, referring to the new Moon when we see the first slither in the sky, before it reaches the first crescent. It is entirely up to you if you want to work with the dark Moon as the new Moon, trust your intuition.

Which way round?

The waxing and waning Moons show in the sky as different facing crescent shapes. Think about the triple goddess Moon sign:

In the Northern Hemisphere the first shape looks like a backwards 'C', this is the waxing Moon i.e. leading up to the full

Moon in the centre. The waning Moon will be opposite, the side that looks like a forward facing 'C'. In the Southern Hemisphere it will be reversed.

Triple Goddess

I don't want to delve too much into this subject (that's a whole other book in itself...). However, the triple Moon symbol of crescent, full and crescent is often recognized as that of the triple goddess. The waxing crescent being the maiden, the full Moon being the mother and the waning crescent as the crone goddess. I do feel there is a stage missing and I prefer to have the quadruple goddess. The waxing crescent as the maiden, the full Moon as the mother, the waning Moon as the matriarch and the dark Moon as the crone. In our modern times I believe the gap between mother and crone is too large and needs the addition of the matriarch (some call this stage the Queen). It also echoes the four seasons as well; spring is maiden, summer is mother, autumn is matriarch and winter is crone. You can work with any of the goddesses on any of the Moon phases, but I often find it helps to tie in one that corresponds to the Moon phase. Not essential, but something to think about to add to the layers of your Moon magic.

The idea of a triple goddess may just be a modern one, some suggest that Robert Graves promoted the idea in his book, The White Goddess, in 1948. Although there is some evidence that triple goddesses can be found much earlier in history, albeit perhaps not in the format we recognize as maiden, mother, crone. Some triple goddesses have been recorded as sisters or three 'faces' of one goddess. However, for the purpose of this book and for Moon magic in general, if you want to work with the phases of the Moon in connection with the types of goddess then I find it works really well. Let's not get too complicated here, *if it ain't broke, don't fix it.*

NEW MOON

The slightest glimpse of pale Moon light
A slip of new Moon up in the sky bright
New beginnings, inspiration, hopes and dreams
The new Moon magic with a manifesting theme

After the dark skies, when you can just see the first slither of the Moon in the sky.

New Moon Magic

New beginnings, new adventures, new projects, anything new really, changes and opportunities. Inspiration, hope, manifesting, intentions, planning creating and wishes. Potential, dreams, anything is possible, ideas and intuition, good luck and protection. This is the phase you should use for acknowledging those plans you want to start. Write lists, plot, plan and scheme. Get all those ideas down on paper and formulate, clarify and start making contact. Get everything organized ready to roll out later. This is a time to do the ground work.

- Write down all the goals and desires you have. Stand outside under the new Moon and read the list aloud. Leave the list outside to charge with the Moon energy, or inside on a window sill. Then place the list on your altar.

- Create a mind map of plans. Take a clean sheet of paper and write your goal in the centre, then just jot down any words or thoughts on the paper, connected with that goal. Don't think too hard, just let the words hit the paper. You can make sense of it afterwards.
- Meditate sitting under the Moon, outside if you have a safe place, or inside by a window. Just sit quietly and focus on the Moon and the phase she is in. Ask her what guidance she has for you.
- Clean and clear your altar and sacred space.
- Work on decorating or tidying up your book of shadows.

New Moon Abundance Cheque Spell

On every new Moon I work an abundance cheque spell. I have been doing this regularly for several years now and it has never let me down. Work on the new Moon as this helps boost the magic of bringing positive energy and prosperity towards you.

You will need:

A blank cheque – this can be from your own cheque book, but I prefer to download one from the internet, just do a search for "abundance cheque" and you will get lots of options and designs to print off.
A pen – I like to use green as this is a colour associated with money
A pinch of cocoa powder
A coin

On your cheque in the space where it says 'pay to the order of' write your own name.

Where it has space for the amount to be paid write 'paid in full' both in the figures box and the line for words. For the date write *'now'*. Sign it *'The Universe'*. Sprinkle a pinch of cocoa powder into the centre of the cheque. Say:

Abundance, power of cocoa, draw money to me
I ask the Universe for prosperity I can see

Then fold the cheque, bringing the paper edge towards you, folding the paper a couple of times over. Folding the cheque towards you brings in the action of drawing money to you. Folding it away from you will send money out, don't do that! Once it is folded neatly, draw a £ or $ sign on the top of the folded paper. Hold it in both hands and visualise money coming to you and your bank account being full. Then pop it in a safe place with the coin placed on top.

Keep it there for the whole month, then on the next new Moon you can dispose of the cheque either by burning it or throwing it away as it will have worked its magic. Then you can write a new one for the coming month.

New Moon Colours

You must work with the colours that you associate with this Moon phase, but here are my suggestions:

- Green
- Orange
- White

Plants for the New Moon

You can work with any plants that you feel drawn to, but these are my suggestions. Also check out the food section for herbs, spices and foods that can also work in incense blends or spell workings:

Comfrey

(Symphytum officinale)

Comfrey Magical Properties:

Money, travel, protection, healing, hex breaking, bringing

together
Ruling planet – Saturn
Sign – Capricorn
Element – Water
Gender – Feminine

Cypress

(Cupressus sempervirens)
Cypress Magical Properties:
Release, binding, grief, protection, healing
Ruling planet – Saturn
Sign – Aquarius
Element – Earth
Gender – Feminine

Jasmine

(Jasminum grandiflorum, Jasminum officinale, Jasminum odoratissimum)
Jasmine Magical Properties:
Dreams, money, love, meditation, lust
Ruling planet – Moon, Venus
Sign – Cancer
Element – Water
Gender – Feminine

Myrrh

(Commiphora myrrha)
Myrrh Magical Properties:
Protection, purification, healing, Crone, Underworld, courage
Ruling planet – Mars, Sun
Sign – Aries, Aquarius
Element – Water
Gender – Feminine

Nettle

(Urtica dioica)

Nettle Magical Properties:

Healing, protection, lust, money, exorcism.

Ruling planet – Mars

Sign – Scorpio, Aries

Element – Fire

Gender – Masculine

Oak

(Quercus alba, Quercus robur, Quercus petraea)

Oak Magical Properties:

Healing, health, protection, money, fertility, luck, strength, vitality, power

Ruling planet – Sun, Jupiter, Mars

Sign – Sagittarius

Element – Fire, Water

Gender – Masculine

Rue

(Ruta graveolens)

Rue Magical Properties:

Protection, health, healing, purification, balance, clarity, anxiety, hex breaking

Ruling planet – Mars, Sun

Sign – Leo

Element – Fire

Gender – Masculine

New Moon incense and oil blends:

Use equal quantities of each ingredient, or experiment to find a blend that you like. If you are creating a loose incense (rather than an essential oil mix) and the blend doesn't include a resin or woody component you might like to add one in to help it burn longer.

- Jasmine, lemon, lavender
- Sandalwood, myrrh, honey
- Copal, sandalwood, rose, myrrh

New Moon Body Care – Body Powder

Pamper yourself with this all over body powder to bring in the energy of the New Moon.

2 tablespoons baking soda
5 tablespoons arrowroot or corn starch
3 teaspoons of powdered dried jasmine flowers
3 teaspoons of powdered dried nettle leaves
8 drops jasmine essential oil
4 drops cypress essential oil

Mix the essential oil with the dried herbs and allow it to dry. Then combine with the baking soda and arrowroot/corn starch.

New Moon Foods, Herbs and Spices

This phase is all about new beginnings so with regard to food it is an excellent time to start a new way of eating (notice I avoid the word 'diet'). It is also about changes, opportunities and inspiration so how about trying a new food that you have not eaten before? Keep your foods light and not too heavy, no big ole stodgy puddings. Definitely eat seasonally and connect with the produce of the moment. Some of these foods can also be used in incense blends or spell working.

Bay

(Laurus nobilis)
Bay Magical Properties:
Protection, purification, strength, power, healing, creativity, spirituality, psychic powers
Ruling planet – Sun

Element – Fire
Gender – Masculine

Basil

(Ocimum basilicum)

Basil Magical Properties:

Wealth, money, prosperity, love, exorcism, protection, happiness, peace
Ruling planet – Mars
Sign – Scorpio
Element – Fire
Gender – masculine

Cardamom

(Elettaria cardamomum)

Cardamom Magical Properties:

Love, passion, clarity, uplifting, protection
Ruling planet – Venus & Mars
Element – Water
Gender – Feminine

Chamomile

(Chameamelum nobile, Anthemis nobilis)

Chamomile Magical Properties:

Sleep, dreams, love, calm, money, relaxation, purification, balancing
Ruling planet – Sun
Sign – Leo
Element – Water
Gender – Masculine

Cherry

(Prunus avium/cerasus)

Cherry Magical Properties:

Love, fertility, divination, beginnings
Ruling planet – Venus
Element – Water, Air
Gender – Feminine

Chillies

(capsicum)
Chillies Magical Properties:
Creativity, energy, power, protection, passion, hex breaking
Ruling planet – Mars
Element – Fire
Gender – Masculine

Cinnamon

(Cinnamomum zeylanicum, Cinnamomum verum)
Cinnamon Magical Properties:
Success, healing, power, psychic powers, protection, love, focus, lust, spirituality, changes
Ruling planet – Sun
Element – Fire
Gender – Masculine

Eggs

Eggs Magical Properties:
Fertility, creation, life, new beginnings, divination
Element – Water, Earth, Air, Fire
Gender – Masculine/Feminine

Lamb

Lamb Magical Properties:
Caring, nurture, new life, beginnings, spring, fertility
Element – Fire, Earth
Gender – Masculine

Nutmeg

(Myristica fragrans)

Nutmeg Magical Properties:

Money, luck, fidelity, protection

Ruling planet – Jupiter

Sign – Sagittarius

Element – Fire

Gender – Masculine

Orange

(Citrus × sinensis)

Orange Magical Properties:

Love, happiness, uplifting, generosity, purification, clarity, energy, fidelity

Ruling planet – Sun

Element – Fire

Gender – Masculine

Paprika

(Capsicum annuum)

Paprika Magical Properties:

Creativity, energy

Ruling planet – Mars

Element – Fire

Gender –Masculine

Pasta

Pasta Magical Properties:

Psychic powers, protection, communication, creativity

Ruling planet – Mercury

Element – Earth

Gender – Masculine

Peach

(Prunus persica)

Peach Magical Properties:

Love, fertility, spirituality, wishes, longevity

Ruling planet – Venus

Element – Water, Air

Gender – Feminine

Pomegranate

(Punica granatum)

Pomegranate Magical Properties:

Growth, fertility, wishes, death, rebirth, new beginnings

Ruling planet – Mercury

Element – Fire, Earth

Gender – Masculine

Sage

(salvia officinalis)

Sage Magical Properties:

Protection, wishes, wisdom, purification, stimulating, intuition, abundance, success.

Ruling planet – Jupiter

Element – Air

Gender – Masculine

Tomato

(Solanum lycopersicum)

Tomato Magical Properties:

Love, passion, protection, creativity

Ruling planet – Venus

Element – Water

Gender – Feminine

Vanilla

(Vanilla planifolia)

Vanilla Magical Properties:

Love, spirituality, sex magic, passion, creativity

Ruling planet – Venus

Element – Water, Air

Gender – Feminine

Walnut

(Juglans regia)

Walnut Magical Properties:

Wishes, mental powers, clarity, fertility

Ruling planet – Sun

Element – Fire

Gender – Masculine

Wheat

(Triticum spp.)

Wheat Magical Properties:

Prosperity, rebirth, abundance, wishes

Ruling planet – Venus

Element – Earth

Gender – Feminine

Yogurt

Yogurt Magical Properties:

Spirituality, creativity, depression

Ruling planet – Moon

Element – Water, Air

Gender – Feminine

New Moon Recipe – Cheese Biscuits

150g/5.3 oz strong cheddar cheese (finely grated)

100g/3 ½ oz plain flour

50g/1.7 oz butter
1/2 teaspoon paprika
1 egg yolk
You may need a tablespoon of water

Crumble the butter into the flour (I do this in a food mixer) until it resembles breadcrumbs.

Add in the cheese, egg yolk and paprika.

Knead together to form a dough, you may need a little water.

Wrap the dough in cling film and pop in the refrigerator for half an hour.

Preheat the oven to 180C/350F/Gas 4.

Roll the dough out to about 2mm, on a flat surface dusted with flour.

Cut circles with a pastry cutter and pop them on a baking sheet lined with baking parchment.

Bake for 10 minutes, turn them over and bake for a further 5 minutes.

Options: You can change the flavour and intent by adding a teaspoon of dried herbs to the mix.

New Moon Teas

Herbal teas can be purchased in tea bag form or ready–made loose blends and there are some fantastic brands out there. However, I have also purchased herbal teas that tasted like sweepings from the factory floor. Check the ingredients when purchasing ready–made herbal teas, make sure they include only the items that the tea is supposed to taste of. Some companies bulk out with cheaper items. Herbal tea is very easy to make if you grow fresh herbs or if you have a supply of dried herbs and dried fruits. Experiment with different flavours. The basic rule is one or two teaspoons of dried herbs to a mug full of boiling water, brew for at least five minutes then strain. If you are using fresh herbs you may need a slightly larger quantity. Herbal tea can be drunk hot (obviously), left and poured over ice as a cold drink or even used as a hair rinse. Drop it into your bath water or add to a bucket of hot water and use as a floor or surface wash.

Please be careful and make sure you have identified the herbs you use correctly. Never ingest herbs that you are not sure about. Always check with a qualified practitioner if you are on medication, have health problems or are pregnant.

I have given some of my favourite recipes here, adjust the amounts of each ingredient to suit your own taste. If the blend isn't sweet enough you can add a teaspoon of sugar or honey.

Fresh start tea:
Pomegranate
Cherry
Rosemary

Opportuni–tea:
Cinnamon
Apple
Clove

Potential tea:
Coffee! Seriously, ditch the tea bags for a moment. Nothing gives you more potential than a good cup of coffee.

Crystals for the New Moon

You can work with any crystals that you feel drawn to, but these are my suggestions:

Amethyst

Amethyst magical properties:

Peace, protection, success, good luck, hidden knowledge, legal issues, spirituality, contentment, soothing, relaxation, calm, hope, patience, transformation, changes, breaking patterns, grounding, guilt, overcoming addictions, business matters, judgement, clarity, courage, travel, psychic protection, sleep, anxiety, focus, understanding, happiness, justice, intuition, inspiration, channeling, meditation

Energy: Receptive
Element: Water
Planet: Jupiter, Neptune
Zodiac: Pisces, Scorpio, Sagittarius
Birthstone: February

Aquamarine

Aquamarine magical properties:

Calming, soothing, serenity, sea magic, travel, intuition, wisdom, creativity, compassion, relaxation, truth, secrets, clarity, enlightenment, reasoning, flexibility, moderation, judgement, tolerance, order, spirituality, psychic abilities, peace, purification

Energy: Receptive
Element: Water
Planet: Moon, Neptune
Zodiac: Pisces, Aquarius
Birthstone: March

Citrine

Citrine magical properties:

Happiness, joy, Sun magic, negative energy, optimism, abundance, depression, stress, success, wealth, healing, intuition, creativity, confidence, changes, self–esteem, protection, psychic powers, fears, clarity, stamina, nightmares

Energy: Projective
Element: Fire
Planet: Sun, Jupiter
Zodiac: Scorpio
Birthstone: November

Labradorite

Labradorite magical properties

Transformation, cleansing, breaking patterns, potential, psychic abilities, intuition, confidence, spirituality, focus, protection, imagination, relaxation, soothing, energy, healing, stress, anxiety, luck, abundance, success, decisions, trust, changes, strength, courage, self–confidence, inspiration, perseverance, journeying, clarity, insight, meditation, depression, jealousy, grounding

Energy	Projective
Element	Water
Planet	Earth, Moon, Uranus
Zodiac	Aquarius, Sagittarius, Scorpio, Leo

Moldavite

Moldavite magical properties:

Transformation, changes, spiritual development, intuition, growth, healing, love, Otherworld communication, astral travel

Energy	Projective
Element	Fire
Planet	Uranus
Zodiac	Aquarius

Moonstone

Moonstone magical properties

New beginnings, Moon magic, intuition, calming, psychic abilities, balance, harmony, wishes, cleansing, uplifting, hope, meditation, emotions, love, divination, spirituality, wealth, truth, healing, sensuality, insight, peace, wisdom, communication, confidence, abundance, prosperity, dreams, fertility, travel

Energy	Receptive
Element	Water
Planet	Moon
Zodiac	Cancer, Libra, Scorpio

Birthstone June, September

Quartz (clear)

Quartz (clear) magical properties

Purification, cleansing, healing, calming, emotions, strength, support, spirituality, energy, balance, psychic abilities, motivation, uplifting, decisions, anxiety, divine connection, amplifying, focus, meditation, manifestation, channelling, protection, negative energy, clarity, wisdom, concentration, learning, spirit work, communication, astral travel, divination, dreams, harmony

Energy Projective, Receptive
Planet Sun, Moon
Element Fire, Water
Zodiac Leo, Gemini, Capricorn

Quartz (smoky)

Quartz (smoky) magical properties

Grounding, centring, focus, negative energy, decisions, cooperation, creativity, emotions, depression, anxiety, jealousy, nature, protection, calming, manifestation, wishes, divination, meditation, insight, guidance, uplifting, fears, relaxation, releasing, abundance, luck, prosperity

Energy Receptive
Element Earth
Planet Saturn, Jupiter
Zodiac Capricorn, Sagittarius

New Moon Meditation

Find a place where you won't be disturbed and make yourself comfortable. If you have a safe place to sit outside at night time then it would be perfect to do so, otherwise indoors is just fine. Close your eyes and focus on your breathing, deep breaths in and deep breaths out.

As your world around you dissipates you find yourself standing inside a stone columned temple. Pillars around you and a stone wall behind you. Above your head is open to the sky.

It is dark and the deep indigo blue sky is scattered with stars.

You cannot see a Moon of any kind, but the air feels static with possibilities and new energy.

Investigate the temple; running along the back wall is a ledge set out as an altar with candles, tapers and bowls of herbs and spices. Dishes sit filled with sweet smelling incense on top of smouldering charcoal.

In front of the altar are piles of brightly coloured cushions.

You sit comfortably in front of the central altar.

Take a fresh candle from the side and light it with a taper. Place it on the altar in front of you.

Take a handful of herbs and spices and add them to the charcoal, do you recognize any of them?

Breathe in the scent from the incense and watch the smoke as it swirls and twists into the air.

Now sit and watch the flame of your candle as it flickers.

Open your mind to new ideas, projects and possibilities. What would you love to start? Is there anything you have always wanted to do, to learn, to create or to follow?

Take some time and sit quietly, allow the ideas to come into your mind.

When you are ready, get up and head to the other side of the temple.

Laid out in front of you is a large garden. Lit by flaming torches lining each side, stretching out into the far distance.

To one side you notice a large wooden planter, a trowel and a big pile of compost with what looks like several jars filled with different seeds.

Plunge your hands into the soil, feel the strong connection to the earth.

Start filling the planter with the soil, use your hands or the trowel.

When it is full, pick up each of the jars of seed in turn. Look carefully at them and choose whichever one you are most drawn to.

Take a few seeds out and press them gently into the soil. Sprinkle another handful of soil on top.

You notice a large watering can and use it now to water in the seeds.

Sit quietly in the darkness and take a few moments to send out a blessing to the newly planted seeds. When you are ready, walk back to the altar and snuff out your candle.

Slowly and gently come back to this reality. Open your eyes and wriggle your fingers and toes. Have something to eat and drink and write down any important notes.

New Moon Ritual for New Ideas

This ritual script is to help you plant new seeds of ideas, to find your inspiration and open up new ideas and opportunities.

You will need:

Representations for the four quarters, if using
Central candle for deity, if using
Matches or lighter
Safe holders for the candles, if using
Something to eat and drink

For the spell:

Two brown or white candles (to represent new ideas, opportunities or projects)
One green, orange or white candle (to represent fertility, success and prosperity)
One candle of any colour (to represent you)
Essential oil such as cinnamon, basil or mint in an oil burner
A pebble or crystal tumble stone

Safe holders for the candles

Cast the circle
Walking deosil (clockwise) around the circle.

With the power of the Moon
I cast this circle to attune
Magic creating a boundary to last
This Moon circle is now cast

Call the quarters
Facing North

I call upon the element of earth
May you bring your energy of grounding and stability to this rite
Earth, I welcome you

Facing East

I call upon the element of air
May you bring your energy of intellect and inspiration to this rite
Air, I welcome you

Facing South

I call upon the element of fire,
May you bring your energy of passion and power to this rite
Fire, I welcome you

Facing West

I call upon the element of water,
May you bring your energy of emotions and cleansing to this rite
Water, I welcome you

Deity
Facing centre

I call upon the powerful and wise goddess Hestia
And ask that you bring the energy of new beginnings, inspiration and manifesting to this rite.
Hestia, I honour your presence

Spell work: This spell works with the power of the new Moon to bring things to you. Place one of the brown candles in the centre of your altar or sacred space. Put the green candle to the right and your personal candle to the left. Place your essential oil burner with the oil in, in front of the central candle. Lay the second brown candle on its side in front of the oil burner and the pebble or crystal in front of that. Take the pebble or crystal and hold it in your hand whilst you work with the candles.

Light the personal candle and sit quietly focusing on the flame, say:

Flame of fire, burning bright
Bring to me clarity of sight
To see opportunities and inspiration before me
Make it so

Next light the green candle and focus on the flame, say:

Opportunities, inspiration and new ideas open up to me
Avenues, projects and ventures, let me see
Make it so

Sit quietly and visualise new ideas and opportunities opening up to you and how happy and excited you would be when this happens.

Light the brown candle and say:

New ideas, new ventures, fresh inspiration for me
Make it so

Now snuff out the candles. Relight them each night and repeat the words for three nights. On the last night allow them to burn out. Carry the pebble or stone with you or place it on your altar to allow the energy to flow.

Feast: Eat and drink something to celebrate your ritual and to help you ground. Sprinkle some of the drink and food onto the earth after the ritual as an offering to deity.

Deity

I thank the powerful and wise goddess Hestia
For bringing the energy of new beginnings, inspiration and manifesting to this rite.
Hestia, I honour you and ask that your energy continue with me as long as is needed.
With blessings and thanks, I bid you farewell

Release the quarters
Facing West

I thank the element of water,
For bringing your energy of emotions and cleansing to this rite
Water, I bid you farewell

Facing South

I thank the element of fire,
For bringing your energy of passion and power to this rite
Fire, I bid you farewell

Facing East

I thank the element of air
For bringing your energy of intellect and inspiration to this rite
Air, I bid you farewell

Facing North

I thank the element of earth
For bringing your energy of grounding and stability to this rite
Earth, I bid you farewell

Close the circle
Walking widdershins (anti clockwise) around the circle

I thank the power of the Moon
I uncast this circle but stay in tune
Magic unties the boundary to last
This Moon circle is now uncast

New Moon Tarot Cards

Tarot cards and oracle cards can be used as a focal point for meditation or as a key component to spell work. These cards are particularly associated with this Moon phase but trust your intuition about which ones to use.

New beginnings: The Fool, The Emperor, The World, The Chariot, The Hermit, Death, The Sun, Two of Pentacles, Ten of Swords, Ace of Wands, Knight of Wands, Four of Cups, Eight of Cups.

New business/project success: The Magician, The Sun, Ace of Wands, The Empress, Seven of Pentacles.

Changes: Wheel of Fortune, The Magician, Hanged Man, Death, The Tower, Judgement, The World, Knight of

Swords, Eight of Wands.

Opportunities: The Magician, Wheel of Fortune, The Devil, The Star, The World, Knight of Cups, Seven of Cups.

Inspiration, ideas and creativity: The Magician, The Moon, The Star, The Fool, The Empress, The World, The Hierophant, Temperance, Ace of Cups, Ace of Wands, Queen of Wands, Page of Cups, Knight of Cups.

Dreams: The Star, The Moon, Ace of Cups, HighPriestess.

Intuition: The High Priestess, The Devil,The Moon.

Potential: The Fool.

New Moon Deities

Trust your intuition when working with deities, but please do your research before you call upon any of them. Make sure you know their history, personality and story before you work with them. Here are my suggestions for deities to work with for this Moon phase:

Hekate – Greek goddess of the dark Moon. She covers new beginnings and magic of all kinds. She walks the ancient roads and pathways, particularly associated with crossroads, those where three roads cross. She forms a triad with Persephone and Demeter, she being the Crone aspect. She guards the spirit world and wields power over all realms. She is one seriously intimidating goddess, but wise beyond words. Call upon her for: Moon magic, witchcraft, herb magic, necromancy, protection, prosperity, new beginnings, decisions, mysteries, knowledge, learning, inner work, shadow work.

Hestia – Greek goddess of the hearth and home she is also a fire goddess. Her Roman equivalent is Vesta. The Greeks did not have statues of this goddess as it was believed she didn't take human form, instead she appeared as the flames of fire in the hearth. Hestia was the first born of the Olympian goddesses. She is absolutely about new beginnings and the start of all things. This goddess is the ultimate super housekeeper and home maker, with added omnipotence. Call upon her for: Home life, domesticity, fire magic, devotion, wishes, manifesting, unity, new beginnings, spirituality, blessings.

Ilmatar/Luonnotar – A Finnish–Ugrian creation goddess of the air whose duck laid eggs on her knee. The eggs fell and the whites became the Moon, the yolks the Sun and the shell pieces became the stars. She is goddess of the crescent Moon. Call upon her for: New beginnings, creativity, inspiration, traditions, fertility, nature, the arts, magic.

Levana – A Roman goddess of childbirth. Her name derives from the Latin 'levare' which means to raise or lift. She is present at the birth of every child. Call upon her for: New beginnings, protection of children, childbirth.

Ma'at – Egyptian goddess of the crescent Moon, order and balance. Think 'strict school headmistress', she dishes out the justice as she sees fit, whether you are a deity or a mere mortal. Her name translates as 'truth/that which is straight'. If you are looking for balance between work and home life or any kind of justice, Ma'at should be on your speed dial. Call upon her for: Justice, balance, freedom, new beginnings, morals, organisation, law, promises, fairness, truth, oaths, harmony, honesty.

Neith/Nit – Egyptian goddess of the crescent Moon and domesticity. She has an eclectic list of duties including war, hunting and weaving. She is also considered to be the personification of the primordial waters of creation. Call upon her for: Home, marriage, protection, feminine energy, hunting, war, creativity, new beginnings.

Parvati – Hindu goddess of the crescent Moon. Oh, this goddess has all the feminine wiles and knows how to use them. She is maiden to the Mother Durga and Crone Kali. She can charm the secrets out of the trees. Call upon her for: Power, creativity, new beginnings, victory, feminine energy, beauty, charm, secrets, the arts, fertility, cleansing,devotion.

Isis – Egyptian goddess Queen of Egypt. She is looked upon as Mother Moon, Queen of Sorcery and the life force within the river Nile. Isis taught her people useful skills, those they would need to survive and flourish, no being high up in the sky for this one, she got down with her subjects (very practical woman). Call upon her for: Magic, dreams, divination, harvest, perspective, love, spirituality, faithfulness, destiny, revitalisation, fulfilment, inner beauty, rebirth, feminine energy, knowledge, motherhood, healing, changes, manifesting.

Andraste – a warrior goddess of Britain – she was invoked by Queen Boadicea/Boudicca. Call upon her for: Strength, courage, warrior, victory, battle, guidance, inspiration,honour.

Ishtar – Babylonian goddess of the full Moon, also known as Inanna in Sumeria. A goddess of love, sex and war (pretty much covers it all then) she is a bit of a floozy, taking many lovers to bed (I don't judge). Call upon her for: Love, passion, sexuality, fertility, womanhood, independence, insight, inspiration, wishes

Anu – a Mesopotamian/Sumerian sky god viewed as Father of the gods and ruler of the heavens, the stars and the spirits. Call upon him for: Goals, wishes,spirituality.

WAXING CRESCENT MOON

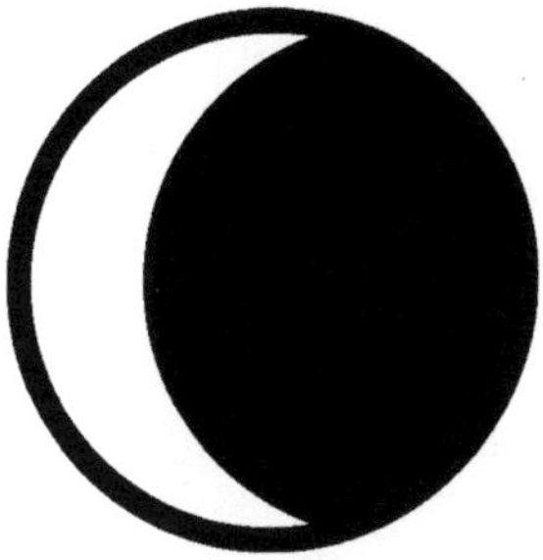

A waxing crescent up in the sky above
To help increase, inspire and grow that which we love
Intentions, determination and wishes made
Building upon plans that are already laid

Bigger than a slither but not yet a quarter.

Waxing Crescent Moon Magic

Increasing, knowledge, prosperity, abundance, attraction, creativity, inspiration, motivation, friendships, healing, luck, love, power, business, career, fertility, communication, healing and legal matters. Exploring, courage, flourishing, moving forwards and growth. Manifesting, visualising, intentions, wishes, faith and determination. Start work on projects and add to your intentions made on the new Moon. Bring in new things, new people and add to your life. The energy is beginning to rise. This is the phase for building…

- Write down all the goals and desires you have. Stand outside under the Moon and read the list aloud. Leave the list outside to charge with Moon energy, or inside on a window sill. Then place the list on your altar.

- Ask the Moon for an unexpected gift. Stand under her and put in the request. Don't be specific, the Moon knows better than you do, what you need.
- Pop your magical tools out under the waxing Moon light to cleanse and re–charge. Outside if you have somewhere safe, or on a window sill where the Moon can be seen.
- Meditate sitting under the Moon, outside if you have a safe place, or inside by a window. Just sit quietly and focus on the Moon and the phase she is in. Ask her what guidance she has for you.
- Work with a long–term money spell, plan out your finances.

Waxing Crescent Moon Colours

You must work with the colours that you associate with this Moon phase, but here are my suggestions:

- Orange
- Pink
- Blue

Plants for the Waxing Crescent Moon

You can work with any plants that you feel drawn to, but these are my suggestions. Also check out the food section for herbs, spices and foods that can also work in incense blends or spell workings:

Bergamot

(Monarda didyma, Mondarda fistulosa)

Bergamot Magical Properties:

Abundance, meditation, sleep, dreams, clarity, friendship

Sign – Gemini, Libra

Element – Air

Gender – Feminine

Cedar

(Cedrus spp)

Cedar Magical Properties:

Purification, money, protection, Goddess

Ruling planet – Sun, Jupiter

Sign – Sagittarius

Element – Fire

Gender – Masculine

Cypress

(Cupressus sempervirens)

Cypress Magical Properties:

Release, binding, grief, protection, healing

Ruling planet – Saturn

Sign – Aquarius

Element – Earth

Gender – Feminine

Honeysuckle

(Lonicera caprifolium, Lonicera japonica, Lonicera periclymenum)

Honeysuckle Magical Properties:

Prosperity, psychic powers, protection, balance, lust, meditation, memory

Ruling planet – Jupiter

Sign – Gemini, Cancer

Element – Earth

Gender – Masculine

Hyacinth

(Hyacinthus orientalis)

Hyacinth Magical Properties:

Love, happiness, peace, sleep, nightmares, abundance

Ruling planet – Venus

Element – Water
Gender – Feminine

Juniper

(Juniperus communes)
Juniper Magical Properties:
Love, exorcism, healing, protection, justice, stolen items, purification, psychic powers, clarity
Ruling planet – Sun, Jupiter, Moon
Sign – Aries
Element – Fire
Gender – Masculine

Myrrh

(Commiphora myrrha)
Myrrh Magical Properties:
Protection, purification, healing, Crone, Underworld, courage
Ruling planet – Mars, Sun
Sign – Aries, Aquarius
Element – Water
Gender – Feminine

Pine

(Pinus)
Pine Magical Properties:
Centring, focus, Dragon magic, protection, truth, abundance, purification, fertility, healing
Ruling planet – Mars, Saturn
Sign – Capricorn
Element – Air, Fire
Gender – Masculine

Sandalwood

(White Sandalwood – Santalum album)

Sandalwood (White) Magical Properties:
Death rites, purification, wishes, psychic powers
Ruling planet – Moon, Mercury
Sign – Sagittarius, Virgo
Element – Water

Waxing Crescent Moon Incense and Oil Blends

Use equal quantities of each ingredient, or experiment to find a blend that you like. If you are creating a loose incense (rather than an essential oil mix) and the blend doesn't include a resin or woody component you might like to add one in to help it burn longer.

- Lavender, basil, pine, nutmeg
- Juniper, cedar, pine, eucalyptus
- Thyme, sandalwood, myrrh

Waxing Crescent Moon Body Care – Body Spritz

Spray all over for a lovely refreshing and hydrating scent.
You will need:

75ml/2 ½ fl oz distilled water, or you could use rose water
2 tablespoons aloe vera juice or gel (this isn't essential but helps make the spray more hydrating)
8 drops pine essential oil
7 drops juniper essential oil
10 drops honeysuckle essential oil

Combine everything together and pour into a sterilised spray bottle. This will keep for up to six months. Shake well before use.

Waxing Crescent Moon Foods, Herbs and Spices

On the waxing crescent Moon work with foods that feed your soul, boost your strength and engage your spirit. Explore new foods, spicy menus and ingredients that excite your taste buds. Use spices and herbs to boost your immune system and ramp up the flavour in your recipes. Be daring! Some of these foods can also be used in incense blends or spell working.

Basil

(Ocimum basilicum)

Basil Magical Properties:

Wealth, money, prosperity, love, exorcism, protection, happiness, peace

Ruling planet – Mars

Element – Fire

Gender – masculine

Bean

(Phaseolus spp)

Beans Magical Properties:

Wisdom, divination, prosperity

Ruling planet – Mercury

Element – Air

Gender – Masculine

Broccoli

(Brassica oleracea)

Broccoli Magical Properties:

Strength, protection

Ruling planet – Moon

Element – Water

Gender – Feminine

Carrot

(Daucus carota)

Carrot Magical Properties:

Clarity, fertility, passion

Ruling planet – Mars
Element – Fire
Gender – Masculine

Chicken

Chicken Magical Properties:
Healing, divination, prosperity, luck, fertility
Element – Fire
Gender – feminine

Cinnamon

(Cinnamomum zeylanicum, Cinnamomum verum)
Cinnamon Magical Properties:
Success, healing, power, psychic powers, protection, love, focus, lust, spirituality, changes
Ruling planet – Sun
Sign – Aries
Element – Fire
Gender – Masculine

Coriander

(Coriandrum sativum)
Coriander Magical Properties:
Health, healing, peace, love, release, wealth, protection, negativity
Ruling planet – Mars
Sign – Aries
Element – Fire
Gender – Masculine

Corn/Cornmeal

(Zea mays)
Corn Magical Properties:
Abundance, luck, prosperity, offerings, fertility

Ruling planet – Sun
Element – Fire, Earth
Gender – Feminine

Fennel

(Foeniculum vulgare)
Fennel Magical Properties:
Purification, protection, healing
Ruling planet – Mercury
Element – Fire
Gender – Masculine

Fish

Fish Magical Properties:
Fertility, Prosperity, Abundance, healing, emotions, cleansing, purification
Element – Water
Gender – Feminine

Garlic

(Allium sativum)
Garlic Magical Properties:
Healing, protection, hex breaking, negative energies, lust, strength, courage, depression
Ruling planet – Mars
Element – Fire
Gender – Masculine

Ginger

(Zingiber officinale)
Ginger Magical Properties:
Healing, power, love, passion, success, prosperity, protection
Ruling planet – Mars
Element – Fire

Gender – Masculine

Honey

Honey Magical Properties:

Happiness, healing, love, prosperity, passion, spirituality, faerie

Element – Water, Earth

Gender – Feminine

Onions

(Allium cepa)

Onion Magical Properties:

Passion, fertility

Ruling planet – Mars

Element – Fire

Gender – Masculine

Rosemary

(Rosemarinus officinalis)

Rosemary Magical Properties:

Protection, love, lust, mental powers, exorcism, purification, healing, sleep

Ruling planet – Sun

Sign – Aries

Element – Fire

Gender – Masculine

Sweet Potato

(Ipomoea batatas)

Sweet Potato Magical Properties:

Love, passion

Ruling planet – Venus

Element – Earth, Water

Gender – Feminine

Thyme

(Thymus vulgaris, Thymus serpyllum)

Thyme Magical Properties:

Healing, health, peace, psychic powers, love, purification, courage, releasing, sleep, beauty

Ruling planet – Venus

Element – Water

Gender – Feminine

Turmeric

(Cucurma longa)

Turmeric Magical Properties:

Purification, protection, peace

Ruling planet – Mars

Element – Fire, Air

Gender – Feminine

Waxing Crescent Moon Recipe – Honey Cookies

Can't stop eating these…

2 heaped tablespoons honey
1 tablespoon milk (any kind)
1 teaspoon bicarbonate soda
100g/3.5 oz butter, softened
75g/2.6 oz light brown sugar
175g6.1 oz plain/all–purpose flour

Preheat your oven to 180C/350F/Gas 4. Line two baking trays with baking parchment.

Put the honey and milk into a bowl and microwave for 30 seconds. Or place them in a small pan over a low heat and warm gently. When hot add the bicarbonate of soda and whisk until frothy.

In a separate bowl, cream the butter and sugar until light and fluffy.

Add the honey mixture and stir.

Then add the flour and mix until combined.

Roll the dough into walnut sized balls and pop them on the baking tray, flattening them slightly, leave space as they will spread.

Bake for 10 minutes.

Leave to cool on the trays.

Waxing Crescent Moon Teas

Herbal teas can be purchased in tea bag form or ready–made loose blends and there are some fantastic brands out there. However, I have also purchased herbal teas that tasted like sweepings from the factory floor. Check the ingredients when purchasing ready–made herbal teas, make sure they include only the items that the tea is supposed to taste of. Some companies bulk out with cheaper items. Herbal tea is very easy to make if you grow fresh herbs or if you have a supply of dried herbs and dried fruits. Experiment with different flavours. The basic rule is one or two teaspoons of dried herbs to a mug full of boiling water, brew for at least five minutes then strain. If you are using fresh herbs you may need a slightly larger quantity. Herbal tea can be drunk hot (obviously), left and poured over ice as a cold drink or even used as a hair rinse. Drop it into your bath water or add to a bucket of hot water and use as a floor or surface wash.

Please be careful and make sure you have identified the herbs you use correctly. Never ingest herbs that you are not sure about. Always check with a qualified practitioner if you are on medication, have health problems or are pregnant.

I have given some of my favourite recipes here, adjust the amounts of each ingredient to suit your own taste. If the blend isn't sweet enough you can add a teaspoon of sugar or honey.

Prosperi–tea:

Nutmeg
Apple
Ginger
Honey

Communication tea:

Black tea, milk and sugar – A good ole fashioned cuppa, always gets people talking.

Wish upon a cup of tea:
Peace
Sage

Crystals for the Waxing Crescent Moon

You can work with any crystals that you feel drawn to, but these are my suggestions:

Agate (banded)

Agate (banded) magical properties

Perception, wisdom, balance, spirituality, goodwill, peace, memory, concentration, stamina, truth, clarity, honesty, courage, protection, calming, sleep, dreams, strength, longevity, nature, love, anti–stress, energy

Energy: Projective
Element: Fire
Planet: Mercury
Zodiac: Gemini

Amber

Amber magical properties:

Manifesting, energy, beauty, Sun magic, power, wishes, intellect, clarity, wisdom, balance, purification, protection, psychic abilities, healing, calm, patience, love, sensuality, good luck, marriage, abundance, success, vitality, joy, sexuality, cleansing, stress, harmony, creativity

Energy: Projective
Element: Fire, Spirit
Planet: Sun
Zodiac: Leo

Amethyst

Amethyst magical properties

Peace, protection, success, good luck, hidden knowledge, legal issues, spirituality, contentment, soothing, relaxation, calm, hope, patience, transformation, changes, breaking patterns, grounding, guilt, overcoming addictions, business matters, judgement, clarity, courage, travel, psychic protection, sleep, anxiety, focus, understanding, happiness, justice, intuition, inspiration, channelling, meditation

Energy: Receptive
Element: Water
Planet: Jupiter, Neptune
Zodiac: Pisces, Scorpio, Sagittarius
Birthstone: February

Amazonite

Amazonite magical properties

Courage, soothing, bravery, calming, determination, focus, clarity, insight, self–confidence, self–assurance, respect, grace, intuition, understanding, balance, communication, creativity, inspiration, spirituality, success, luck, money, stress relief, energy, worries, fears

Energy: Receptive
Element: Earth
Planet: Saturn
Zodiac: Virgo, Pisces

Aragonite

Aragonite magical properties:

Balance, insight, grounding, peace, meditation, understanding, connections, family, friendship, calming, emotional balance, energy, releasing, stabilizing, spiritual development, concentration, flexibility, tolerance, patience, acceptance, support, stress relief

Energy: Projective, Receptive
Element: Earth
Planet: Sun, Earth
Zodiac: Virgo, Capricorn

Carnelian

Carnelian magical properties

Grounding, protection, calm, concentration, confidence, self–worth, success, courage, creativity, negative energy, direction, control, organisation, opportunity, planning, psychic protection, jealousy, hate, harmony, depression, doubt, patience, stability, vitality, motivation, stamina, passion, truth, love, faith, honesty, trust, luck, abundance

Energy: Projective
Element: Fire
Planet: Sun
Zodiac: Taurus, Leo
Birthstone: May, June, July, August

Citrine

Citrine magical properties:

Happiness, joy, Sun magic, negative energy, optimism, abundance, depression, stress, success, wealth, healing, intuition, creativity, confidence, changes, self–esteem, protection, psychic powers, fears, clarity, stamina, nightmares

Energy: Projective
Element: Fire

Planet: Sun, Jupiter
Zodiac: Scorpio
Birthstone: November

Malachite

Malachite magical properties

Changes, transformation, clarity, emotions, protection, support, healing, peace, travel, fears, growth, creativity, renewal, energy, wealth, money, opportunity, abundance, new beginnings, finances, success, business, focus, strength, wisdom, releasing, prosperity, breaking barriers, psychic abilities, manifestation, soothing, stress, love, power

Energy Receptive
Element Earth
Planet Venus
Zodiac Capricorn, Scorpio

Quartz (rose)

Quartz (rose) magical properties

Love, happiness, emotions, spirituality, growth, fears, healing, sexuality, passion, calming, soothing, stress, depression, sleep, luck, wisdom, inspiration, success, intuition, grounding, balance, prosperity, self–esteem, harmony, trust, jealousy, gossip, beauty, peace, cleansing, fertility

Energy Receptive
Element Earth, Water
Planet Venus, Moon
Zodiac Taurus

Tiger's eye

Tiger's eye magical properties

Amplification, balance, harmony, releasing, fears, anxiety, courage, strength, self–confidence, focus, creativity, optimism, self–worth, protection, psychic abilities, healing, wealth, money, opportunity, abundance, prosperity, luck, success, commitment, determination, support, clarity, vitality, motivation, grounding, patience

Energy	Projective
Element	Fire, Earth
Planet	Sun
Zodiac	Leo, Capricorn

Tourmaline

Tourmaline magical properties

Calming, harmony, balance, insight, spirituality, protection, negative energy, transformation, courage, grounding, fears, creativity, understanding, power, motivation, commitment, patience, stability, releasing, emotions, anxiety, strength, happiness, protection, relaxation, friendship, astral travel

Energy	Receptive (pink, green, blue, black, watermelon)
	Projective (watermelon, red)
Element	Water (pink, blue, watermelon)
	Fire (watermelon, red)
	Earth (green, black)
Planet	Venus, Mars
Zodiac	Libra
Birthstone	October

Waxing Crescent Moon Meditation

Find a place where you won't be disturbed and make yourself comfortable. If you have a safe place to sit outside at night time then it would be perfect to do so, otherwise indoors is just fine. Close your eyes and focus on your breathing, deep breaths in and deep breaths out.

As your world around you dissipates you find yourself standing inside a stone columned temple. Pillars around you and a stone wall behind you. Above your head is open to the sky.

It is dark and the deep indigo blue sky is scattered with stars.

You can just see the slither of waxing crescent Moon hanging in the sky.

Investigate the temple; running along the back wall is a ledge set out as an altar with candles, tapers and bowls of herbs and spices. Dishes sit filled with sweet smelling incense on top of smouldering charcoal.

In front of the altar are piles of brightly coloured cushions.

You sit comfortably in front of the central altar.

Take a fresh candle from the side and light it with a taper. Place it on the altar in front of you.

Take a handful of herbs and spices and add them to the charcoal, do you recognize any of them?

Breathe in the scent from the incense and watch the smoke as it swirls and twists into the air.

Now sit and watch the flame of your candle as it flickers.

Sit quietly and think about ideas and projects that you may have already thought about but that need a bit of a push. What can you do to manifest new things, more things or give growth to areas in your life?

When you are ready, get up and head to the other side of the temple.

Laid out in front of you is a large garden. Lit by flaming torches lining each side, stretching out into the far distance.

A large wooden planter sits to one side, freshly planted with seeds. Beside it is a watering can, pick up the can and water the soil.

Sit quietly in the darkness and look out over the garden.

What do you see growing in the light of the torches? Can you see or hear any wildlife? Sit for a while…take some time to look and listen.

When you are ready, walk back to the temple and over to the altar and snuff out your candle.

Slowly and gently come back to this reality. Open your eyes and wriggle your fingers and toes. Have something to eat and drink and write down any important notes.

Waxing Crescent Moon Ritual for Manifesting Prosperity

This ritual is all about bringing abundance and wealth to you, get your manifesting power on!

You will need:

Representations for the four quarters, if using
Central candle for deity, if using
Matches or lighter
Safe holders for the candles, if using
Something to eat and drink

For the spell:

A white candle
Four green, gold or orange candles
A compass (or compass app on your phone)
A gold or silver coin

Cast the circle
Walking deosil (clockwise) around the circle.

With the power of the Moon
I cast this circle to attune
Magic creating a boundary to last
This Moon circle is now cast

Call the quarters
Facing North

I call upon the element of earth
May you bring your energy of grounding and stability to this rite
Earth, I welcome you

Facing East

I call upon the element of air
May you bring your energy of intellect and inspiration to this rite
Air, I welcome you

Facing South

I call upon the element of fire,
May you bring your energy of passion and power to this rite
Fire, I welcome you

Facing West

I call upon the element of water,
May you bring your energy of emotions and cleansing to this rite
Water, I welcome you

Deity
Facing centre

I call upon the fruitful and practical goddess Ops
And ask that you bring the energy of abundance, prosperity and manifesting to this rite.
Ops, I honour your presence

Spell work: The white candle represents you and 'the all'. Green uses colour magic to represent prosperity and money. The compass is used to find the directions but also symbolises your own direction in life. The coin does what is says…it represents money and prosperity.

We will be working with the four compass directions; North, South, East and West these all have meaning:

North – finances, stability and material matters
East – intellect and inspiration
South – passion and energy
West – Emotions, intuition and releasing

Place your white candle in the centre of a safe level space. Use your compass (or compass app) to ascertain the four directions of North, South, East and West. Place a green candle at each of the four directions, in a square around the main white candle. Place the coin between the white candle and the green candle in the North. Light the white candle. Say this chant or one of your own, three times out loud. At the end of each chant turn the coin over.

Drawing magic from the waxing crescent Moon
Bring to me, fresh opportunities and new money soon
As I turn this gold/silver coin around
Prosperity and financial security to me in abounds

Then starting with the green candle in the North, light all four saying at each direction:

Waxing crescent Moon money arrive in from the North
Waxing crescent Moon money blow in from the East
Waxing crescent Moon money blast in from the South
Waxing crescent Moon money wash in from the West

Sit quietly watching the flames and visualise money flowing to you and doors opening for new opportunities. Finish by saying *"make it so"*. Extinguish the candles and pop the coin in your purse.

Feast: Eat and drink something to celebrate your ritual and to help you ground. Sprinkle some of the drink and food onto the earth after the ritual as an offering to deity.

Deity

I thank the fruitful and practical goddess Ops
For bringing the energy of abundance, prosperity and manifesting to this rite.
Ops, I honour you and ask that your energy continue with me as long as is needed.
With blessings and thanks, I bid you farewell

Release the quarters
Facing West

I thank the element of water,
For bringing your energy of emotions and cleansing to this rite
Water, I bid you farewell

Facing South

I thank the element of fire,
For bringing your energy of passion and power to this rite
Fire, I bid you farewell

Facing East

I thank the element of air
For bringing your energy of intellect and inspiration to this rite
Air, I bid you farewell

Facing North

I thank the element of earth
For bringing your energy of grounding and stability to this rite
Earth, I bid you farewell

Close the circle
Walking widdershins (anti clockwise) around the circle

I thank the power of the Moon
I uncast this circle but stay in tune
Magic unties the boundary to last
This Moon circle is now uncast

Waxing Crescent Moon tarot cards

Tarot cards and oracle cards can be used as a focal point for meditation or as a key component to spell work. These cards are particularly associated with this Moon phase but trust your intuition about which ones to use.

Growth: The Empress, The Hermit.

Knowledge and Wisdom: The Hermit, High Priestess, The Moon, The Magician, The Hierophant, Wheel of Fortune, Two of Pentacles, Ace of Swords, Page of Pentacles.

Prosperity and money: Wheel of Fortune, Ten of Pentacles, Knight of Pentacles, Page of Pentacles, Six of Pentacles, Ace of Pentacles, Two of Pentacles, Four of Pentacles, Queen of Pentacles.

Fertility: The Sun, The Fool, The Empress, Ten of Cups, Ace of Wands.

Communication: The Magician, Page of Swords.

Healing and good health: Strength, The World, The Magician, The Sun, The Star, The Empress, The Chariot, Judgement, Three of Cups.

Courage and strength: The Star, Strength, The Chariot, The Fool, Ace of Swords, Knight of Swords, Seven of Wands, Nine of Wands.

Abundance: The Empress, The Star, The World, Ace of Pentacles, Six of Pentacles, Nine of Pentacles, Ace of Cups.

Waxing Crescent Moon Deities

Trust your intuition when working with deities, but please do your research before you call upon any of them. Make sure you know their history, personality and story before you work with them. Here are my suggestions for deities to work with for this Moon phase:

Anuket – Egyptian goddess of the crescent Moon. She is responsible for the annual flooding of the river Nile. She watches over agriculture and all food growth along with wealth and prosperity. Call upon her for: Wealth, prosperity, growth, fertility, nourishment, contentment.

Hekate – Greek goddess of the dark Moon. She covers new beginnings and magic of all kinds. She walks the ancient roads and pathways, particularly associated with crossroads, those where three roads cross. She forms a triad with Persephone and Demeter, she being the Crone aspect. She guards the spirit world and wields power over all realms. She is one seriously intimidating goddess, but wise beyond words. Call upon her for: Moon magic, witchcraft, herb magic, necromancy, protection, prosperity, new beginnings, decisions, mysteries, knowledge, learning, inner work, shadow work.

Ops – Roman goddess of the full Moon and agriculture. If you are after abundance and prosperity, then Ops is your 'go to' goddess. She can also teach you all kinds of practical skills to gain that abundance for yourself. Ain't nothing in this life for free! Call upon her for: Fertility, abundance, wealth, nurturing, prosperity, opportunity,growth.

Sin/Nanna – Sumerian Moon god with a long flowing beard sometimes depicted as being made of lapis lazuli. He rode upon a winged bull. He was represented by the number thirty, the days in a lunar month. Nanna is the Sumerian name for the Moon god, which may mean just the full Moon phase. 'Sin' being the name given to the crescent Moon. Call upon him for: Moon magic, fertility, prosperity, growth.

Aine – an Irish goddess of summer and the Moon, she looks after livestock and crops. She is also known as a Fairy Queen and a Sun goddess. Associated with midsummer/Litha and Lughnasadh. Call upon her for: Love, protection, fertility, wealth, sovereignty, Moon magic, Sun magic, fairy magic.

Asherah – Ancient West Semitic goddess, often referred to as Queen of the Gods. Also known as 'She who walks on the sea' or 'holiness'. You will find her name in the Old Testament she is consort of Yahweh. Asherah is a goddess of the sea. Call upon her for: Divine wisdom, feminine energy, feminine issues, strength, self–esteem, self–confidence, courage, kindness, love, divination, insight, justice, fertility, compassion, healing, nurturing.

Cerridwen – Welsh goddess usually shown hunched over her cauldron filled with Awen (inspiration and wisdom). Generally seen as the crone aspect of the triad with Blodeuwedd and Arianrhod. A goddess of the Moon she covers death, rebirth, magic and divination of all kinds. Also, one of the five goddesses of Avalon. Call upon Cerridwen for: Inspiration, creativity, wisdom, death, rebirth, divination, prophecy, spiritual transformation, justice, fertility, luck.

Chang–O – Chinese goddess of the Moon. Banished from heaven along with her husband, destined to be mere mortals. Chang–O took a double dose of immortality pill, without sharing with her husband (rude). She floated up to the Moon, leaving her husband behind. Call upon her for: Love, partnership, courage, power, fertility, growth, manifesting, belief, self–confidence, new beginnings, transformation.

Demeter – Ancient Greek goddess of the full Moon. She is an Olympian goddess of agriculture, harvest and fertility. Featuring in the Eleusinian mysteries alongside her daughter Persephone. She forms a triad with Persephone and Hecate, Demeter taking on the mother role. Equivalent to the Roman goddess Ceres. Call upon her for: Abundance, harvest, mysteries, fertility, marriage, relationships, life and death, rebirth, justice, grief, suffering, parenthood.

Diana – Goddess of the Moon, hunter and Roman Queen of Witches. She is queen of the open skies and may also have been worshipped as a Sun goddess as well as the Moon. Call upon her for: Fertility, abundance, harvest, protection, children, nurturing, hunting, childbirth.

Epona – Celtic/Saxon/Gaulish goddess of horses. Ancient Britains gave her the title 'Rigantona' which translates as Great Queen. Call upon her for: Protection, animals, love, fertility, providence, leadership, authority.

Freyja/Freya – although not called a Moon goddess, many of her attributes connect her with both the Full and Dark Moons. A Norse goddess of love, beauty, war and fertility. She leads souls of dead warriors to the Otherworld. She rides a chariot driven by two cats, so she must be powerful to get cats to do what they are told! Call upon her for: Love, beauty, fertility, war, dearth, happiness, sex, sensuality, inspiration.

Ilmatar/Luonnotar – A Finnish–Ugrian creation goddess of the air whose duck laid eggs on her knee. The eggs fell and the whites became the Moon, the yolks the Sun and the shell pieces became the stars. She is goddess of the crescent Moon. Call upon her for: New beginnings, creativity, inspiration, traditions, fertility, nature, the arts, magic.

Inanna – Sumerian goddess of the full Moon and the stars, also known as Ishtar in Babylon. She is Queen of heaven and earth. She has a reputation for being a little bit saucy which led her to be linked to fertility rituals. She does look after her followers, dishing out the rules and keeping them safe. Call upon her for: Love, fertility, warrior, strength, courage, seduction, sensuality, protection, justice.

Ishtar – Babylonian goddess of the full Moon, also known as Inanna in Sumeria. A goddess of love, sex and war (pretty much covers it all then) she is a bit of a floozy, taking many lovers to bed (I don't judge). Call upon her for: Love, passion, sexuality, fertility, womanhood, independence, insight, inspiration, wishes.

Ixchel – Mayan goddess of the Moon, weaving, water and childbirth. Mother of all Mayan deities she rules over life and death and bears the title of 'Keeper of Souls'. Her name translates as 'Lady Rainbow'. She spends her time constantly changing from a beautiful young woman into an old crone, it must be both exhausting and confusing. Call upon her for: Weather magic, fertility, health, healing, childbirth, water magic, rainbow magic, control, power, choices, assertion, self–confidence.

Kuan Yin – Chinese/Buddhist goddess of mercy who is probably one of the most chilled out and relaxed deities ever. This beautiful goddess hears all your prayers and responds to each and every request for help. She needs some kind of medal... Call upon her for: Kindness, magic, health, healing, fertility, children, sympathy, support, suffering, encouragement, enlightenment, spirituality, protection.

Lucina – Roman goddess of light. She also covers childbirth. Possibly later merged with Juno and/or Diana. She may even have been converted, becoming St Lucy. An ancient bronze mask believed to depict Juno Lucina shows her with a tiny crescent Moon engraved on her forehead. Call upon her for: Charity, protection, health, healing, kindness, banishing, fertility, well–being.

Ops – Roman goddess of the full Moon and agriculture. If you are after abundance and prosperity, then Ops is your 'go to' goddess. She can also teach you all kinds of practical skills to gain that abundance for yourself. Ain't nothing in this life for free! Call upon her for: Fertility, abundance, wealth, nurturing, prosperity, opportunity, growth.

Parvati – Hindu goddess of the crescent Moon. Oh, this goddess has all the feminine wiles and knows how to use them. She is maiden to the Mother Durga and Crone Kali. She can charm the secrets out of the trees. Call upon her for: Power, creativity, new beginnings, victory, feminine energy, beauty, charm, secrets, the arts, fertility, cleansing, devotion.

Rhiannon – if you aren't singing the Fleetwood Mac song right now, you need to... A Welsh goddess and great Queen of Wales. She brings peace, comfort and patience. If you are looking for magical enchantments, then she has a bounty of them. Call upon her for: Patience, comfort, peace, magic, movement, relaxation, communication, fertility, leadership, spirit work, motivation, dream work.

Sin/Nanna – Sumerian Moon god with a long flowing beard sometimes depicted as being made of lapis lazuli. He rode upon a winged bull. He was represented by the number thirty, the days in a lunar month. Nanna is the Sumerian name for the Moon god, which may mean just the full Moon phase. 'Sin' being the name given to the crescent Moon. Call upon him for: Moon magic, fertility, prosperity, growth.

Vesta – Roman goddess of the crescent Moon, the hearth and home. She rules domesticity with a flip of the feather duster and a whip of her apron. She keeps the house and family running like clockwork. She is known as Hestia in Greece. Call upon her for: Home, family, relationships, harmony, peace, love, fertility, fire magic, spirituality.

FIRST QUARTER MOON

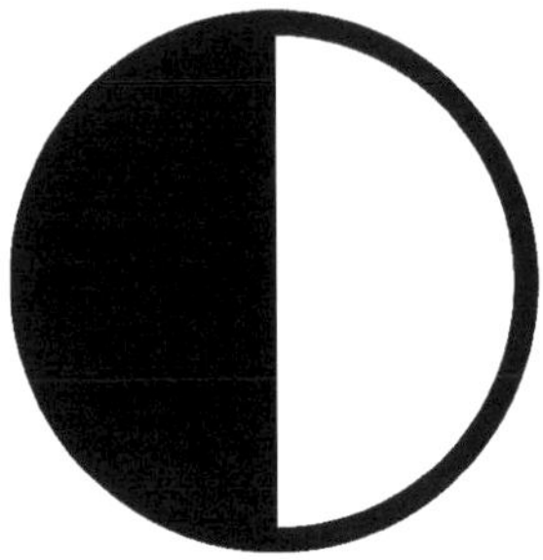

The first quarter Moon hanging up in the sky
Shining down upon our challenges, drawing magic from high
Moving things forward, making it fast
Run like the wind, this energy will last

As the name suggests, this is when a quarter of the Moon can be seen. Although it looks like half the Moon as we can only see one side of the globe. This is the moment when the Moon has reached its first quarter orbit around the Earth. Sometimes called a half Moon because that's what we can see.

First Quarter Moon Magic

Challenges, confidence, courage, manifesting, commitment, visualization, imagination, growth, self–healing, intuition, psychic abilities, spirituality, emotions, abundance, creativity, health, beauty, self–esteem, self–love, family, fertility, luck, love, friendships, luck, motivation, protection, success, wishes and actions. Work with elemental magic.

This is where ambition takes centre stage. Use magic to draw things toward you and attract those that you want and need. Take those project plans and really make some progress with them. Focus your energy and move things forward. Tap into the growing abundant energy of the first quarter Moon phase and get some action happening. Run like the wind!

- Write down all the goals and desires you have. Stand outside under the Moon and read the list aloud. Leave the list outside to charge with the Moon energy, or inside on a window sill. Then place the list on your altar.
- Meditate sitting under the Moon, outside if you have a safe place, or inside by a window. Just sit quietly and focus on the Moon and the phase she is in. Ask her what guidance she has for you.
- Do a tarot or oracle card reading to check for any stumbling blocks or blockages that might hamper your new projects.
- Pop your ritual tools out under the Moon if you have a safe place outside to cleanse and recharge. Or put them on a windowsill indoors so that the Moonlight can shine on them.
- Sort your magical herb and crystals, tidy them up and make sure they are all labelled and organized.

First Quarter Moon Colours

You must work with the colours that you associate with this Moon phase, but here are my suggestions:

- Yellow
- Purple
- Blue

Plants for the First Quarter Moon

You can work with any plants that you feel drawn to, but these are my suggestions. Also check out the food section for herbs, spices and foods that can also work in incense blends or spell workings:

Alexanders

(Smyrnium olusatrum)

Alexanders Magical Properties:

Sea magic, intuition, emotions, cleansing, releasing

Element – Water

Gender – Masculine

Ash

(Fraxinus excelsior or F. americana)

Ash Magical Properties:

Protection, prosperity, dispels negativity, improves health, sea magic, dreams, love, intuition.

Ruling planet – Sun and Neptune

Element – Fire and Water

Gender – Masculine

Beech

(Fagus sylvatica)

Beech Magical Properties:

Wishes, creativity, spirituality, divination, luck, success

Ruling planet – Saturn

Sign – Sagittarius

Element – Air and Earth

Gender – Feminine

Benzoin

(Styrax benzoin)

Benzoin Magical Properties:

Prosperity, purification, calming, confidence, love, lust

Ruling planet – Sun, Venus

Sign – Capricorn

Element – Air

Gender – Masculine

Cleavers

(Galium aparine)

Cleavers Magical Properties:

Commitment, tenacity, relationships, love, binding

Ruling planet – Saturn

Element – Fire

Gender – Feminine

Dandelion

(Taraxacum officinale)

Dandelion Magical Properties:

Wishes, divination, love, abundance, psychic powers

Ruling planet –Jupiter

Sign – Taurus

Element – Air

Gender – Masculine

Elder

(Sambucus nigra/Canadensis)

Elder Magical Properties:

Protection, healing, faeries, purification, intuition, exorcism, hex breaking, rebirth

Ruling planet – Venus

Sign – Sagittarius, Aquarius, Libra

Element – Water

Gender – Feminine

Hazel

(Corylus spp. avellana, Corylus cornuta)

Hazel Magical Properties:

Fertility, wishes, love, protection, luck, wisdom, divination, healing, inspiration, prosperity

Ruling planet – Sun

Element – Air

Gender – Masculine

Rowan

(Sorbus acuparia)

Rowan Magical Properties:

Psychic powers, power, success, protection, love, spirituality, faeries, divination, healing, inspiration

Ruling planet – Sun, Mercury

Sign – Sagittarius

Element – Fire

Gender – Masculine

Sandalwood

(White Sandalwood – Santalum album)

Sandalwood (White) Magical Properties:

Death rites, purification, wishes, psychic powers

Ruling planet – Moon, Mercury

Sign – Sagittarius, Virgo

Element – Water

Sunflower

(Helianthus annuus)

Sunflower Magical Properties:

Wishes, fertility, truth, integrity, luck, protection, loyalty, happiness

Ruling planet – Sun

Sign – Leo

Element – Fire

Gender – Masculine

Violet

(Viola odorata)

Violet Magical Properties:

Love, lust, peace, healing, protection, commitment, death

and rebirth
Ruling planet – Venus
Sign – Cancer, Libra
Element – Water
Gender – Feminine

Willow

(Salix alba, Salix fragilis)
Willow Magical Properties:
Love, protection, healing, cleansing, wishes, release, inspiration, intuition
Ruling planet – Moon
Sign – Pisces
Element – Water
Gender – Feminine

First Quarter Incense and Oils

Use equal quantities of each ingredient, or experiment to find a blend that you like. If you are creating a loose incense (rather than an essential oil mix) and the blend doesn't include a resin or woody component you might like to add one in to help it burn longer.

- Benzoin, black pepper, cinnamon
- Sandalwood, violet, sage
- Sunflower, cinnamon, sage

First Quarter Moon Body Care – Perfume Oil

Keep this in a roll–on bottle or jar to dab onto your skin.

You will need:

10ml/0.3 fl oz base oil such as almond or jojoba
6 drops sandalwood essential oil

4 drops cinnamon essential oil
2 drops black pepper essential oil

Combine the base oil with the essential oils. Shake the bottle before use.

First Quarter Moon Foods, Herbs and Spices

Keep with the seasonal foods that feed your soul and excite your palate. But don't forget to give yourself a treat every now and then, choose something that sparks your imagination. Keep menus inspiring and be creative.

Almond

(Prunus dulcis)
Almond Magical Properties:
Love, prosperity, treasure, intuition, psychic powers, passion
Ruling planet – Mercury
Element – Air
Gender – Masculine

Black Pepper

(Piper nigrum)
Black Pepper Magical Properties:
Protection, exorcism, jealousy, negativity, strength, confidence, gossip
Ruling planet – Mars
Element – Fire
Gender – Masculine

Cinnamon

(Cinnamomum zeylanicum, Cinnamomum verum)
Cinnamon Magical Properties:
Success, healing, power, psychic powers, protection, love, focus, lust, spirituality, changes

Ruling planet – Sun
Element – Fire
Gender – Masculine

Fennel

(Foeniculum vulgare)
Fennel Magical Properties:
Purification, protection, healing
Ruling planet – Mercury
Element – Fire
Gender – Masculine

Peach

(Prunus persica)
Peach Magical Properties:
Love, fertility, spirituality, wishes, longevity
Ruling planet – Venus
Element – Water, Air
Gender – Feminine

Pomegranate

(Punica granatum)
Pomegranate Magical Properties:
Growth, fertility, wishes, death, rebirth, new beginnings
Ruling planet – Mercury
Element – Fire, Earth
Gender – Masculine

Sage

(salvia officinalis)
Sage Magical Properties:
Protection, wishes, wisdom, purification, stimulating, intuition, abundance, success.
Ruling planet – Jupiter

Element – Air
Gender – Masculine

Turkey

Turkey Magical Properties:
Motivation, clarity, focus, celebration
Element – Fire, Air
Gender – Masculine

Walnut

(Juglans regia)
Walnut Magical Properties:
Wishes, mental powers, clarity, fertility
Ruling planet – Sun
Element – Fire
Gender – Masculine

Wheat

(Triticum spp.)
Wheat Magical Properties:
Prosperity, rebirth, abundance, wishes
Ruling planet – Venus
Element – Earth
Gender – Feminine

First Quarter Moon Recipe – Almond Crescent Cookies

These are perfect, shaped like the crescent Moon and very delicious.

225g/8 oz butter, softened
160g/5.6 oz sugar
1 teaspoon vanilla extract
1 teaspoon almond extract
375g/13.2 oz plain/all–purpose flour

100g/3.5 oz ground almonds
Possibly a teaspoon or two of water
Icing/powdered sugar for dusting

Preheat your oven to 180C/350F/Gas 4.

Line a baking sheet with baking parchment.

Beat the butter and sugar together until light and fluffy.

Stir in the vanilla and almond extracts.

Add the flour and almond flour, mix to combine.

The dough will be crumbly. If it is very crumbly and won't hold together add a teaspoon of water.

Take tablespoons of the dough and roll into small balls, shape into a crescent. Place on the baking sheet.

Bake for 15–20 minutes until golden.

Dust with icing sugar.

Options:

Replace the almond extract with orange extract or rose water.

Add a teaspoon of mixed spice or ground cinnamon.

First Quarter Moon Teas

Herbal teas can be purchased in tea bag form or ready–made loose blends and there are some fantastic brands out there. However, I have also purchased herbal teas that tasted like sweepings from the factory floor. Check the ingredients when purchasing ready–made herbal teas, make sure they include only the items that the tea is supposed to taste of. Some companies bulk out with cheaper items. Herbal tea is very easy to make if you grow fresh herbs or if you have a supply of dried herbs and dried fruits. Experiment with different flavours. The basic rule is one or two teaspoons of dried herbs to a mug full of boiling water, brew for at least five minutes then strain. If you are using fresh herbs you may need a slightly larger quantity. Herbal tea can be drunk hot (obviously), left and poured over ice as a cold drink or even used as a hair rinse. Drop it into your bath water or add to a bucket of hot water and use as a floor or surface wash.

Please be careful and make sure you have identified the herbs you use correctly. Never ingest herbs that you are not sure about. Always check with a qualified practitioner if you are on medication, have health problems or are pregnant.

I have given some of my favourite recipes here, adjust the amounts of each ingredient to suit your own taste. If the blend isn't sweet enough you can add a teaspoon of sugar or honey.

Confidence tea:
Fennel
Thyme

Get Creative tea:
Vanilla
Honey
Milk
More of a warming hot milk than a tea, heat a mug of milk and add a dash of vanilla and a spoonful of honey.

Manifest it tea:
Beer or wine.

OK this isn't actually tea, or coffee or any kind of hot beverage…

Hops and grapes are both excellent for all kinds of manifesting. Just one glass though, coz we don't want you 'manifesting' that everyone in the whole world is your best mate…

Crystals for the First Quarter Moon

You can work with any crystals that you feel drawn to, but these are my suggestions:

Agate (moss)

Agate (moss) magical properties

Nature, happiness, prosperity, wealth, longevity, friendship, success, abundance, healing, renewal, fertility, creativity, confidence, strength, love, beginnings, self–esteem, communication, emotions, stress, releasing, hope, trust, depression, growth, finances, cleansing, support, peace, stability, fears, luck, divination

Energy	Receptive
Element	Earth
Planet	Moon
Zodiac	Virgo, Gemini

Amber

Amber magical properties:

Manifesting, energy, beauty, Sun magic, power, wishes, intellect, clarity, wisdom, balance, purification, protection, psychic abilities, healing, calm, patience, love, sensuality, good luck, marriage, abundance, success, vitality, joy, sexuality, cleansing, stress, harmony, creativity

Energy:	Projective
Element:	Fire, Spirit
Planet:	Sun
Zodiac:	Leo

Aventurine (green)

Aventurine (green) magical properties

Balance, decisions, motivation, leadership, dreams, visualisation, creativity, luck, money, anxiety, calm, opportunities, happiness, adventure, love, courage, truth, comfort, support, healing, peace, connection, perception, intellect, psychic abilities

Energy:	Projective
Element:	Air
Planet:	Mercury, Mars
Zodiac:	Aries

Carnelian

Carnelian magical properties

Grounding, protection, calm, concentration, confidence, self–worth, success, courage, creativity, negative energy, direction, control, organisation, opportunity, planning, psychic protection, jealousy, hate, harmony, depression, doubt, patience, stability, vitality, motivation, stamina, passion, truth, love, faith, honesty, trust, luck, abundance

Energy: Projective
Element: Fire
Planet: Sun
Zodiac: Taurus, Leo
Birthstone: May, June, July, August

Citrine

Citrine magical properties:

Happiness, joy, Sun magic, negative energy, optimism, abundance, depression, stress, success, wealth, healing, intuition, creativity, confidence, changes, self–esteem, protection, psychic powers, fears, clarity, stamina, nightmares

Energy: Projective
Element: Fire
Planet: Sun, Jupiter
Zodiac: Scorpio
Birthstone: November

Fluorite

Fluorite magical properties

Magic, imagination, discernment, aptitude, psychic protection, protection, purification, calming, relaxation, tension, anxiety, organisation, structure, challenges, declutter, releasing, support, breaking patterns, intuition, confidence, reassurance, comforting, communication, balance, spirituality, decisions, manifestation, peace, meditation, grounding, healing, cleansing, channelling, past life work, fairy realm, amplifying, memory, power, emotions, depression, stability

Energy: Projective
Element: Water, Air
Planet: Neptune
Zodiac: Scorpio, Aquarius, Pisces

Goldstone

Goldstone magical properties

Ambition, luck, goals, determination, persistence, achievements, success, calm, emotions, energy, enthusiastic, confidence, self–belief, inner self, personal development, possibilities, courage, direction, clarity, uplifting, optimism, protection, deflects negative energy, knowledge, perception, manifestation, creativity, faith, energy flow, spirituality, abundance, wealth, grounding, perspective, ambition, drive, ingenuity, money, generosity, willpower, goals, emotions, divination (see also copper for additional magical properties)

Energy: Receptive/Projective
Element: Fire, Earth
Planet: Jupiter, Venus
Zodiac: Sagittarius

Labradorite

Labradorite magical properties

Transformation, cleansing, breaking patterns, potential, psychic abilities, intuition, confidence, spirituality, focus, protection, imagination, relaxation, soothing, energy, healing, stress, anxiety, luck, abundance, success, decisions, trust, changes, strength, courage, self–confidence, inspiration, perseverance, journeying, clarity, insight, meditation, depression, jealousy, grounding

Energy Projective
Element Water

Planet	Earth, Moon, Uranus
Zodiac	Aquarius, Sagittarius, Scorpio, Leo

Lapis lazuli

Lapis lazuli magical properties

Protection, manifestation, meditation, psychic protection, problem solving, knowledge, clarity, decisions, memory, spirituality, peace, energy, organisation, concentration, stress, luck, negative energy, wealth, abundance, success, love, confidence, truth, renewal, intellect, wisdom, leadership, legal issues, sleep, anxiety, harmony, understanding

Energy	Receptive
Element	Water
Planet	Venus, Jupiter
Zodiac	Sagittarius

Malachite

Malachite magical properties

Changes, transformation, clarity, emotions, protection, support, healing, peace, travel, fears, growth, creativity, renewal, energy, wealth, money, opportunity, abundance, new beginnings, finances, success, business, focus, strength, wisdom, releasing, prosperity, breaking barriers, psychic abilities, manifestation, soothing, stress, love, power

Energy	Receptive
Element	Earth
Planet	Venus
Zodiac	Capricorn, Scorpio

Moonstone

Moonstone magical properties

New beginnings, Moon magic, intuition, calming, psychic abilities, balance, harmony, wishes, cleansing, uplifting, hope, meditation, emotions, love, divination, spirituality, wealth, truth, healing, sensuality, insight, peace, wisdom, communication, confidence, abundance, prosperity, dreams, fertility, travel

Energy	Receptive
Element	Water
Planet	Moon
Zodiac	Cancer, Libra, Scorpio
Birthstone	June, September

Pebble/hag stone

Pebble/hag stone magical properties

Protection, fairy magic, nightmares, dreams, healing, fertility, manifestation, negative energy

Energy	Projective
Element	Earth, Water
Planet	Earth

Pyrite

Pyrite magical properties

Releasing, breaking patterns, clarity, protection, support, decisions, growth, success, inspiration, grounding, vitality, learning, perception, memory, wisdom, psychic abilities, healing, cleansing, prosperity, wealth, abundance, luck, strength, motivation, manifestation, finances, energy, Sun magic, power, focus, perseverance, confidence, divination, communication, self–confidence, meditation

Energy	Projective
Element	Fire
Planet	Mars, Sun
Zodiac	Leo

Quartz (clear)

Quartz (clear) magical properties

Purification, cleansing, healing, calming, emotions, strength, support, spirituality, energy, balance, psychic abilities, motivation, uplifting, decisions, anxiety, divine connection, amplifying, focus, meditation, manifestation, channelling, protection, negative energy, clarity, wisdom, concentration, learning, spirit work, communication, astral travel, divination, dreams, harmony

Energy	Projective, Receptive
Planet	Sun, Moon
Element	Fire, Water
Zodiac	Leo, Gemini, Capricorn

Quartz (smoky)

Quartz (smoky) magical properties

Grounding, centring, focus, negative energy, decisions, cooperation, creativity, emotions, depression, anxiety, jealousy, nature, protection, calming, manifestation, wishes, divination, meditation, insight, guidance, uplifting, fears, relaxation, releasing, abundance, luck, prosperity

Energy	Receptive
Element	Earth
Planet	Saturn, Jupiter
Zodiac	Capricorn, Sagittarius

Rhodochrosite

Rhodochrosite magical properties

Power, potential, strength, confidence, healing, new beginnings, breaking barriers, releasing, joy, happiness, creativity, determination, manifestation, prosperity, abundance, love, emotions, peace, renewal, connection, balance, spirituality, harmony, energy

Energy	Projective
Element	Fire
Planet	Mars, Jupiter
Zodiac	Scorpio, Leo

Serpentine

Serpentine magical properties

Meditation, peace, clarity, nature, fairy magic, emotions, calming, protection, negative energy, love, prosperity, manifestation, psychic protection, success, cleansing

Energy:	Projective
Element:	Fire
Planet:	Saturn
Zodiac:	Gemini

Silver

Silver magical properties

Healing, communication, cleansing, energy, intuition, stability, spirituality, patience, perseverance, Moon magic, negative energy, protection, balance, psychic abilities, manifestation, wealth, prosperity, abundance, travel, dreams, emotions, purification, love, peace, astral travel

Energy	Receptive
Element	Water
Planet	Moon
Zodiac	Cancer

First Quarter Moon Meditation

Find a place where you won't be disturbed and make yourself comfortable. If you have a safe place to sit outside at night time then it would be perfect to do so, otherwise indoors is just fine. Close your eyes and focus on your breathing, deep breaths in and deep breaths out.

As your world around you dissipates you find yourself standing inside a stone columned temple. Pillars around you and a stone wall behind you. Above your head is open to the sky.

It is dark and the deep indigo blue sky is scattered with stars.

You can see the first quarter crescent of the Moon hanging in the

sky.

Investigate the temple; running along the back wall is a ledge set out as an altar with candles, tapers and bowls of herbs and spices. Dishes sit filled with sweet smelling incense on top of smouldering charcoal.

In front of the altar are piles of brightly coloured cushions.

You sit comfortably in front of the central altar.

Take a fresh candle from the side and light it with a taper. Place it on the altar in front of you.

Take a handful of herbs and spices and add them to the charcoal, do you recognize any of them?

Breathe in the scent from the incense and watch the smoke as it swirls and twists into the air.

Now sit and watch the flame of your candle as it flickers.

Sit quietly and think about your own self–confidence. Draw deep from the energy around you, from the flames of the candles and the incense smoke. Allow that energy to permeate your body and fill you with confidence. Confidence in your own abilities, confidence in your skills to manifest and succeed. Confidence in yourself completely.

When you are ready, get up and head to the other side of the temple.

Laid out in front of you is a large garden. Lit by flaming torches lining each side, stretching out into the far distance.

A large wooden planter sits to one side. If you look closely you can see the surface of the soil has been disturbed slightly. It seems that seeds are beginning to sprout from below the soil.

Beside it is a watering can, pick up the can and water the soil.

Sit quietly in the darkness and look out over the garden.

What do you see growing in the light of the torches? Can you see or hear any wildlife? Sit for a while…take some time to look and listen.

When you are ready, walk back to the temple and over to the altar and snuff out your candle.

Slowly and gently come back to this reality. Open your eyes and wriggle your fingers and toes. Have something to eat and drink and write down any important notes.

First Quarter Moon Ritual for Confidence

We all need a bit of a confidence boost on occasion, this ritual will help give your self–confidence and self–esteem a big ole kick in the butt.

You will need:

Representations for the four quarters, if using
Central candle for deity, if using
Matches or lighter
Safe holders for the candles, if using
Something to eat and drink

For the spell:

A large mirror
A crystal or pebble, one that represents confidence to you (I suggest moonstone, labradorite, jasper, bloodstone, or moss agate)
A candle, colour of your choosing, one that best represents confidence to you

Cast the circle
Walking deosil (clockwise) around the circle.

With the power of the Moon
I cast this circle to attune
Magic creating a boundary to last
This Moon circle is now cast

Call the quarters
Facing North

I call upon the element of earth
May you bring your energy of grounding and stability to this rite
Earth, I welcome you

Facing East

I call upon the element of air
May you bring your energy of intellect and inspiration to this rite
Air, I welcome you

Facing South

I call upon the element of fire,
May you bring your energy of passion and power to this rite
Fire, I welcome you

Facing West

I call upon the element of water,
May you bring your energy of emotions and cleansing to this rite
Water, I welcome you

Deity
Facing centre

I call upon the kind and loving goddess Asherah
And ask that you bring the energy of self–confidence, self–esteem and strength to this rite.
Asherah, I honour your presence

Spell work: Place the mirror in front of you. Light your candle and place it in front of the mirror. Sit or stand behind the candle so that you can see yourself, at least your face but preferably your whole body. Hold the pebble, crystal or piece of jewellery in your hands. Look in the mirror, take in the reflection of yourself, see the candle flame and feel the energy from the item you are holding in your hands.

Say:

Magic of the first quarter Moon
Boost my self–confidence and do it soon
Beauty, wisdom and self–esteem come my way
I gain more confidence each and every day
Make it so

Blow a kiss into your hands, aimed at the pebble or crystal.

Snuff out the candle and carry the pebble or crystal with you. Hold the item each time you feel the need for some confidence.

Feast: Eat and drink something to celebrate your ritual and to help you ground. Sprinkle some of the drink and food onto the earth after the ritual as an offering to deity.

Deity

I thank the kind and loving goddess Asherah
For bringing the energy of self–confidence, self–esteem and strength to this rite.
Asherah, I honour you and ask that your energy continue with me as long as is needed.
With blessings and thanks, I bid you farewell

Release the quarters
Facing West
I thank the element of water,
For bringing your energy of emotions and cleansing to this rite
Water, I bid you farewell

Facing South

I thank the element of fire,
For bringing your energy of passion and power to this rite
Fire, I bid you farewell

Facing East

I thank the element of air
For bringing your energy of intellect and inspiration to this rite
Air, I bid you farewell

Facing North

I thank the element of earth
For bringing your energy of grounding and stability to this rite
Earth, I bid you farewell

Close the circle
Walking widdershins (anti clockwise) around the circle

I thank the power of the Moon
I uncast this circle but stay in tune
Magic unties the boundary to last
This Moon circle is now uncast

First Quarter Moon tarot cards

Tarot cards and oracle cards can be used as a focal point for meditation or as a key component to spell work. These cards are particularly associated with this Moon phase but trust your intuition about which ones to use.

Challenges: The Magician, Queen of Swords, Two of Wands.
Confidence: The Emperor, The Chariot.

Courage and strength: The Star, Strength, The Chariot, The Fool, Ace of Swords, Knight of Swords, Seven of Wands, Nine of Wands.

Abundance: The Empress, The Star, The World, Ace of Pentacles, Six of Pentacles, Nine of Pentacles, Ace of Cups.

Intuition: The High Priestess, The Devil, The Moon.

Inspiration, ideas and creativity: The Magician, The Moon, The Star, The Fool, The Empress, The World, The Hierophant, Temperance, Ace of Cups, Ace of Wands, Queen of Wands, Page of Cups, Knight of Cups.

Action/to set things in motion: The Chariot, The Empress, Ace of Wands, Eight of Wands.

First Quarter Moon Deities

Trust your intuition when working with deities, but please do your research before you call upon any of them. Make sure you know their history, personality and story before you work with them. Here are my suggestions for deities to work with for this Moon phase:

Anuket – Egyptian goddess of the crescent Moon. She is responsible for the annual flooding of the river Nile. She watches over agriculture and all food growth along with wealth and prosperity. Call upon her for: Wealth, prosperity, growth, fertility, nourishment, contentment.

Asherah – Ancient West Semitic goddess, often referred to as Queen of the Gods. Also known as 'She who walks on the sea' or 'holiness'. You will find her name in the Old Testament she is consort of Yahweh. Asherah is a goddess of the sea. Call upon her for: Divine wisdom, feminine energy, feminine issues, strength, self–esteem, self– confidence, courage, kindness, love, divination, insight, justice, fertility, compassion, healing, nurturing.

Chang–O – Chinese goddess of the Moon. Banished from heaven along with her husband, destined to be mere mortals.

Chang–O took a double dose of immortality pill, without sharing with her husband (rude). She floated up to the Moon, leaving her husband behind. Call upon her for: Love, partnership, courage, power, fertility, growth, manifesting, belief, self–confidence, new beginnings, transformation.

Hera – Greek Olympian Queen of gods, she covers marriage, childbirth and looking after women (she's got her hands full then). Although she can help when called upon, she has a jealous side and can be vengeful particularly when infidelity is involved. Call upon her for: Love, humour, forgiveness, romance, creativity, marriage, strength, courage, self–confidence, jealousy.

Ixchel – Mayan goddess of the Moon, weaving, water and childbirth. Mother of all Mayan deities she rules over life and death and bears the title of 'Keeper of Souls'. Her name translates as 'Lady Rainbow'. She spends her time constantly changing from a beautiful young woman into an old crone, it must be both exhausting and confusing. Call upon her for: Weather magic, fertility, health, healing, childbirth, water magic, rainbow magic, control, power, choices, assertion, self–confidence.

Kali/Kali Ma – Hindu goddess of time, change and destruction and the Divine Mother. She has blue black skin, red eyes and four arms. Often seen with skulls hanging around her neck. This is a real kick butt, no messing kind of gal. She is a forceful destroyer but brings rebirth with it, she is the cycle of destruction and creation. Call upon her for: Death and rebirth, cycles, time, happiness, courage, hope, change, cleansing, transformation, destruction, fear, knowledge, creativity.

Neith/Nit – Egyptian goddess of the crescent Moon and domesticity. She has an eclectic list of duties including war, hunting and weaving. She is also considered to be the personification of the primordial waters of creation. Call upon her for: Home, marriage, protection, feminine energy, hunting, war, creativity, new beginnings.

Parvati – Hindu goddess of the crescent Moon. Oh, this goddess has all the feminine wiles and knows how to use them. She is maiden to the Mother Durga and Crone Kali. She can charm the secrets out of the trees. Call upon her for: Power, creativity, new beginnings, victory, feminine energy, beauty, charm, secrets, the arts, fertility, cleansing, devotion.

Sin/Nanna – Sumerian Moon god with a long flowing beard sometimes depicted as being made of lapis lazuli. He rode upon a winged bull. He was represented by the number thirty, the days in a lunar month. Nanna is the Sumerian name for the Moon god, which may mean just the full Moon phase. 'Sin' being the name given to the crescent Moon. Call upon him for: Moon magic, fertility, prosperity, growth.

Ops – Roman goddess of the full Moon and agriculture. If you are after abundance and prosperity, then Ops is your 'go to' goddess. She can also teach you all kinds of practical skills to gain that abundance for yourself. Ain't nothing in this life for free! Call upon her for: Fertility, abundance, wealth, nurturing, prosperity, opportunity, growth.

Venus – Roman goddess of love, passion and sexuality. This goddess has more va va voom than she needs, so she likes to share it around. She also covers gardens and spring within her remit. Equivalent to the Greek Aphrodite. Call upon her for: Love, passion, sexuality, romance, beauty, self–esteem, happiness, relationships, charm, the arts.

WAXING GIBBOUS MOON

The waxing gibbous Moon shining so bright
Moving things forward with a strong guiding light
Build and rebuild with a growing energy push
Creativity, potential and commitment with a great rush

Not quite full...but getting there. Waxing means that the visible Moon we see is getting bigger. Gibbous refers to the shape which is larger than the semi–circle that we saw at the first quarter but smaller than a full circle.

Waxing Gibbous Moon Magic

Adjustments, stamina, commitment, refining, editing, reevaluate, determination, changes, potential, patience, go with the flow, organization, focus, clarity, goals, persistence, stamina, reviewing and openness. Honing, effort, energy, routines, building and re–building.

And that final push of effort...we are heading to the full Moon energy, so this is the last bit of effort to use the waxing energy to move things forward. Add to what you have been working with. Build on the plans, be creative and put the final touches to make things happen.

Write down all the goals and desires you have. Stand outside under the Moon and read the list aloud. Leave the list outside to charge with the Moon energy, or inside on a window sill. Then place the list on your altar.

Meditate sitting under the Moon, outside if you have a safe place, or inside by a window. Just sit quietly and focus on the Moon and the phase she is in. Ask her what guidance she has for you.

Create a mind map of how you would like your life to be and what you need do to achieve it. Take a clean sheet of paper and write your goal in the centre, then just jot down any words or thoughts on the paper, connected with that goal. Don't think too hard, just let the words hit the paper. You can make sense of it afterwards.

Waxing Gibbous Moon Colours

You must work with the colours that you associate with this Moon phase, but here are my suggestions:

- Blue
- Red
- Orange

Plants for the Waxing Gibbous Moon

You can work with any plants that you feel drawn to, but these are my suggestions. Also check out the food section for herbs, spices and foods that can also work in incense blends or spell workings:

Cleavers

(Galium aparine)

Cleavers Magical Properties:

Commitment, tenacity, relationships, love, binding

Ruling planet – Saturn

Element – Fire

Gender – Feminine

Coltsfoot

(Tussilago farfara)

Coltsfoot Magical Properties:

Visions, love, energy, health, tranquillity, peace

Ruling planet – Venus

Sign – Taurus

Element – Water

Gender – Feminine

Cramp Bark (Guelder rose)

(Viburnum opulus)

Cramp Bark Magical Properties:

Relaxing, meditation, stress, tension, anxiety, healing, rebirth, protection

Element – Earth

Gender – Feminine

Elder

(Sambucus nigra/Canadensis)

Elder Magical Properties:

Protection, healing, faeries, purification, intuition, exorcism, hex breaking, rebirth

Ruling planet – Venus

Sign – Sagittarius, Aquarius, Libra

Element – Water

Gender – Feminine

Elm

(Ulmus campestris)

Elm Magical Properties:

Love, balance, luck, energy, psychic powers

Ruling planet – Saturn, Mercury

Element – Water

Gender – Feminine

Pansy

(Viola tricolor)

Pansy Magical Properties:

Love, rain magic, focus, rebirth

Ruling planet – Saturn, Venus

Element – Water

Gender – Feminine

Plantain

(Plantago spp. Lanceolata, Plantago major, Plantago media)

Plantain Magical Properties:

Strength, protection, healing, energy, courage

Ruling planet – Venus

Sign – Capricorn

Element – Earth

Gender – Feminine

Poppy

(Papaver spp)

Poppy Magical Properties:

Love, sleep, money, luck, fertility, rebirth, grief

Ruling planet – Moon, Mars, Venus

Sign – Capricorn

Element – Water

Gender – Feminine

Primrose

(Primula vulgaris)

Primrose Magical Properties:

Love, protection, faeries, changes, growth

Ruling planet – Venus

Element – Earth

Gender – Feminine

Rose

(Rosa spp)

Rose Magical Properties:

Love, psychic powers, healing, luck, protection, peace, mysteries, knowledge, dreams, friendship, death and rebirth, abundance

Ruling planet – Venus, Moon

Sign – Pisces

Element – Water

Gender – Feminine

Scullcap

(Scutellaria)

Scullcap Magical Properties:

Faithfulness, restoring, prosperity, stress, peace

Ruling planet – Saturn

Sign – Virgo

Element – Water

Gender – Feminine

Tansy

(Tanacetum vulgare)

Tansy Magical Properties:

Health, longevity, rebirth, cleansing, protection, travel

Ruling planet – Venus

Sign – Gemini

Element – Water

Gender – Feminine

Violet

(Viola odorata)

Violet Magical Properties:

Love, lust, peace, healing, protection, commitment, death and rebirth

Ruling planet – Venus
Sign – Cancer, Libra
Element – Water
Gender – Feminine

Yew

(Taxus baccata)
Yew Magical Properties:
Death and rebirth, transformation, astral travel, ancient knowledge, knowledge
Ruling planet – Saturn, Mercury
Element – Water, Earth
Gender – Feminine

Waxing Gibbous Moon Incense and Oils

Use equal quantities of each ingredient, or experiment to find a blend that you like. If you are creating a loose incense (rather than an essential oil mix) and the blend doesn't include a resin or woody component you might like to add one in to help it burn longer.

- Rose, grapefruit, orange
- Primrose, pansy, tansy
- Cinnamon, poppy, rose

Waxing Gibbous Moon Body Care – Body Oil

Massage this scented oil into the skin or dab at your pulse points.

You will need:

3 tablespoons base oil such as almond or jojoba
12 drops rose essential oil
8 drops grapefruit essential oil

Mix the oils together. Store in an airtight bottle for up to three months.

Waxing Gibbous Moon Foods, Herbs and Spices

Eat foods that give you strength of body, mind and soul. Be open to new tastes and keep experimenting with your menus and recipes. Some of these foods can also be used in incense blends or spell working.

Baking Powder/Soda

Baking Powder/Soda Magical Properties:
Energy, magic
Element – Air

Cashew

(Anacardium occidentale)
Cashew Magical Properties:
Prosperity, energy
Ruling planet – Sun
Element – Fire, Earth
Gender – Feminine

Chillies

(capsicum)
Chillies Magical Properties:
Creativity, energy, power, protection, passion, hex breaking
Ruling planet – Mars
Element – Fire
Gender – Masculine

Cinnamon

(Cinnamomum zeylanicum, Cinnamomum verum)
Cinnamon Magical Properties:

Success, healing, power, psychic powers, protection, love, focus, lust, spirituality, changes
Ruling planet – Sun
Element – Fire
Gender – Masculine

Coffee

(coffea)
Coffee Magical Properties:
Energy, clarity, divination
Ruling planet – Mars
Element – Fire, Water
Gender – Feminine

Curry

Curry Magical Properties:
Energy, passion
Ruling planet – Mars
Element – Fire
Gender – Masculine

Grapefruit

(Citrus paradise)
Grapefruit Magical Properties:
Happiness, spirit work, purification, depression, energy
Ruling planet – Jupiter, Sun
Element – Fire, Water
Gender – Feminine

Horseradish

(Armoracia rusticana)
Horseradish Magical Properties:
Protection, energy, purification, passion
Ruling planet – Mars

Element – Fire
Gender – Masculine

Lime

(Citrus aurantifolia)
Lime Magical Properties:
Purification, love, healing, protection, energy
Ruling planet –Sun
Element – Fire
Gender – Masculine

Orange

(Citrus × sinensis)
Orange Magical Properties:
Love, happiness, uplifting, generosity, purification, clarity, energy, fidelity
Ruling planet – Sun
Element – Fire
Gender – Masculine

Paprika

(Capsicum annuum)
Paprika Magical Properties:
Creativity, energy
Ruling planet – Mars
Element – Fire
Gender –Masculine

Potato

(Solanum tuberosum L)
Potato Magical Properties:
Energy, magic, grounding, prosperity, healing
Ruling planet – Moon
Element – Earth

Gender – Feminine

Saffron

(Crocus sativus)
Saffron Magical Properties:
Happiness, energy, psychic powers, healing, fertility
Ruling planet – Sun
Element – Fire
Gender – Masculine

Sesame

(Sesamum indicum)
Sesame Magical Properties:
Prosperity, protection, energy, strength, secrets
Ruling planet – Sun
Element – Fire, Earth
Gender – Masculine

Waxing Gibbous Moon Recipe – Saffron and chocolate chip cake

Saffron gives quite a distinctive earthy taste and it works well paired with chocolate in this cake.

170g/6oz butter, softened
100ml/3.5 fl oz milk (any kind)
¼ teaspoon saffron threads
300g/10 ½ oz plain/all–purpose flour
2 teaspoons baking powder
½ teaspoon salt
115g/4 oz plain yogurt
240g/8 ½ oz sugar
3 large eggs
1 teaspoon vanilla extract
125g/4 ½ oz plain chocolate chips

Tablespoon demerara sugar

Preheat your oven to 180C/350F/Gas 4.

Butter and flour a 9″ x 5″ loaf tin.

In a small saucepan warm the milk and saffron, bring it to a simmer and then remove from the heat, leave to cool for ten minutes.

Mix the flour, baking powder and salt together.

Stir the yogurt and vanilla extract into the milk.

In a separate bowl whisk the butter and sugar together until light and fluffy.

Add in the eggs a little at a time, alternate with the flour and milk mixture. Mix until combined.

Fold in the chocolate chips.

Spoon into the pan. Sprinkle the demerara sugar over the top.

Bake in the oven for 60 to 70 minutes.

Waxing Gibbous Moon Teas

Herbal teas can be purchased in tea bag form or ready–made loose blends and there are some fantastic brands out there. However, I have also purchased herbal teas that tasted like sweepings from the factory floor. Check the ingredients when purchasing ready–made herbal teas, make sure they include only the items that the tea is supposed to taste of. Some companies bulk out with cheaper items. Herbal tea is very easy to make if you grow fresh herbs or if you have a supply of dried herbs and dried fruits. Experiment with different flavours. The basic rule is one or two teaspoons of dried herbs to a mug full of boiling water, brew for at least five minutes then strain. If you are using fresh herbs you may need a slightly larger quantity. Herbal tea can be drunk hot (obviously), left and poured over ice as a cold drink or even used as a hair rinse. Drop it into your bath water or add to a bucket of hot water and use as a floor or surface wash.

Please be careful and make sure you have identified the

herbs you use correctly. Never ingest herbs that you are not sure about. Always check with a qualified practitioner if you are on medication, have health problems or are pregnant.

I have given some of my favourite recipes here, adjust the amounts of each ingredient to suit your own taste. If the blend isn't sweet enough you can add a teaspoon of sugar or honey.

Ch..ch..changes tea:
Black tea
Cinnamon
Orange

Determination tea:
Rosemary
Ginger

Energy boost tea:
Chocolate
Chillies
You can either make a tea using cocoa nibs and chilli flakes or make a milk based hot chocolate and add some chilli flakes.

Crystals for the Waxing Gibbous Moon

You can work with any crystals that you feel drawn to, but these are my suggestions:

Amber

Amber magical properties:
Manifesting, energy, beauty, Sun magic, power, wishes, intellect, clarity, wisdom, balance, purification, protection, psychic abilities, healing, calm, patience, love, sensuality, good luck, marriage, abundance, success, vitality, joy, sexuality, cleansing, stress, harmony, creativity

Energy: Projective
Element: Fire, Spirit
Planet: Sun
Zodiac: Leo

Amethyst

Amethyst magical properties

Peace, protection, success, good luck, hidden knowledge, legal issues, spirituality, contentment, soothing, relaxation, calm, hope, patience, transformation, changes, breaking patterns, grounding, guilt, overcoming addictions, business matters, judgement, clarity, courage, travel, psychic protection, sleep, anxiety, focus, understanding, happiness, justice, intuition, inspiration, channelling, meditation

Energy: Receptive
Element: Water
Planet: Jupiter, Neptune
Zodiac: Pisces, Scorpio, Sagittarius
Birthstone: February

Bloodstone

Bloodstone magical properties:

Organisation, adaptability, anxiety, clarity, concentration, renewal, energy, self–confidence, connection, calm, protection, breaking barriers, selfishness, mysticism, insight, spirituality, truth, intuition, creativity, guidance, strength, healing, victory, wealth, money, power, invisibility, deception, negative energy, divine connection, past life, dreams

Energy: Projective
Element: Fire, Earth
Planet: Mars
Zodiac: Aries, Pisces, Scorpio
Birthstone: February, March

Calcite (orange)

Calcite (orange) magical properties

Amplification, energy, protection, grounding, centring, purification, peace, calm, emotions, balance, fear, depression, problems, power, potential, breaking patterns, changes, inspiration, creativity, positive energy, wealth, abundance, leadership, perseverance, finances, confidence, determination, money, opportunities, clarity, productivity, release

Energy: Receptive
Element: Earth
Planet: Sun
Zodiac: Cancer

Citrine

Citrine magical properties:

Happiness, joy, Sun magic, negative energy, optimism, abundance, depression, stress, success, wealth, healing, intuition, creativity, confidence, changes, self–esteem, protection, psychic powers, fears, clarity, stamina, nightmares

Energy: Projective
Element: Fire
Planet: Sun, Jupiter
Zodiac: Scorpio
Birthstone: November

Garnet

Garnet magical properties

Organisation, warrior spirit, protection, love, commitment, passion, sexuality, sensuality, attraction, depression, spiritual healing, success, self–confidence, energy, inspiration, perception, strength, survival, fear, courage, clarity, challenges, past life work, truth, compassion, deflecting negative energy, gossip, ambition, motivation, goals, purification, cleansing, balance, inner strength, self–empowerment, creativity, confidence, meditation, spirit work, nightmares, journeying, abundance, support

Energy: Projective
Element: Fie
Planet: Mars
Zodiac: Aries, Virgo, Capricorn, Leo, Aquarius
Birthstone: January

Goldstone

Goldstone magical properties

Ambition, luck, goals, determination, persistence, achievements, success, calm, emotions, energy, enthusiastic, confidence, self–belief, inner self, personal development, possibilities, courage, direction, clarity, uplifting, optimism, protection, deflects negative energy, knowledge, perception, manifestation, creativity, faith, energy flow, spirituality, abundance, wealth, grounding, perspective, ambition, drive, ingenuity, money, generosity, willpower, goals, emotions, divination (see also copper for additional magical properties)

Energy: Receptive/Projective
Element: Fire, Earth
Planet: Jupiter, Venus
Zodiac: Sagittarius

Labradorite

Labradorite magical properties

Transformation, cleansing, breaking patterns, potential, psychic abilities, intuition, confidence, spirituality, focus, protection, imagination, relaxation, soothing, energy, healing, stress, anxiety, luck, abundance, success, decisions, trust, changes, strength, courage, self–confidence, inspiration, perseverance, journeying, clarity, insight, meditation, depression, jealousy, grounding

Energy Projective

Element	Water
Planet	Earth, Moon, Uranus
Zodiac	Aquarius, Sagittarius, Scorpio, Leo

Lepidolite

Lepidolite magical properties

Transformation, soothing, calming, stress, happiness, changes, emotions, psychic abilities, spirituality, depression, divination, connection, strength, uplifting, luck, hope, balance, peace, sleep, harmony, decisions, addiction, releasing, trust, goals, optimism, patience, dreams, opportunities, support, love

Energy	Receptive
Element	Water
Planet	Jupiter, Neptune
Zodiac	Libra

Malachite

Malachite magical properties

Changes, transformation, clarity, emotions, protection, support, healing, peace, travel, fears, growth, creativity, renewal, energy, wealth, money, opportunity, abundance, new beginnings, finances, success, business, focus, strength, wisdom, releasing, prosperity, breaking barriers, psychic abilities, manifestation, soothing, stress, love, power

Energy	Receptive
Element	Earth
Planet	Venus
Zodiac	Capricorn, Scorpio

Obsidian (black)

Obsidian (black) magical properties

Truth, healing, clarity, illusions, breaking barriers, integrity, grounding, centring, strength, courage, protection, cleansing, meditation, stress, calming, relaxation, depression, anxiety, wealth, luck, focus, emotions, power, determination, success, patience, perseverance, releasing, spirit work, spirituality, challenges, past life work, divination

Energy	Projective
Element	Fire, Earth, Water
Planet	Saturn, Jupiter
Zodiac	Sagittarius

Petrified wood

Petrified wood magical properties

Stability, grounding, calming, anxiety, fears, meditation, determination, decisions, strength, courage, patience, transformation, perseverance, success, luck, emotions, wisdom, past life work, insight, leadership

Energy	Receptive
Element	Earth, Spirit
Planet	Earth, Sun
Zodiac	All

Quartz (clear)

Quartz (clear) magical properties

Purification, cleansing, healing, calming, emotions, strength, support, spirituality, energy, balance, psychic abilities, motivation, uplifting, decisions, anxiety, divine connection, amplifying, focus, meditation, manifestation, channelling, protection, negative energy, clarity, wisdom, concentration, learning, spirit work, communication, astral travel, divination, dreams, harmony

Energy	Projective, Receptive
Planet	Sun, Moon
Element	Fire, Water
Zodiac	Leo, Gemini, Capricorn

Rhodochrosite

Rhodochrosite magical properties

Power, potential, strength, confidence, healing, new beginnings, breaking barriers, releasing, joy, happiness, creativity, determination, manifestation, prosperity, abundance, love, emotions, peace, renewal, connection, balance, spirituality, harmony, energy

Energy	Projective
Element	Fire
Planet	Mars, Jupiter
Zodiac	Scorpio, Leo

Rhodonite

Rhodonite magical properties

Protection, renewal, emotions, strength, soothing, clarity, happiness, love, balance, harmony, decisions, confidence, spirituality, peace, energy, passion, optimism, changes, vitality, anxiety, travel, psychic abilities, self–confidence, trust, calming, relaxation, patience, determination, releasing, stress, negative energy

Energy	Projective
Element	Fire
Planet	Mars, Venus
Zodiac	Taurus

Tiger's eye

Tiger's eye magical properties

Amplification, balance, harmony, releasing, fears, anxiety, courage, strength, self–confidence, focus, creativity, optimism, self–worth, protection, psychic abilities, healing, wealth, money, opportunity, abundance, prosperity, luck, success, commitment, determination, support, clarity, vitality, motivation, grounding, patience

Energy	Projective
Element	Fire, Earth

Planet	Sun
Zodiac	Leo, Capricorn

Waxing Gibbous Moon Meditation

Find a place where you won't be disturbed and make yourself comfortable. If you have a safe place to sit outside at night time then it would be perfect to do so, otherwise indoors is just fine. Close your eyes and focus on your breathing, deep breaths in and deep breaths out.

As your world around you dissipates you find yourself standing inside a stone columned temple. Pillars around you and a stone wall behind you. Above your head is open to the sky.

It is dark and the deep indigo blue sky is scattered with stars.

You can see the large crescent of the waxing gibbous Moon hanging in the sky.

Investigate the temple; running along the back wall is a ledge set out as an altar with candles, tapers and bowls of herbs and spices. Dishes sit filled with sweet smelling incense on top of smouldering charcoal.

In front of the altar are piles of brightly coloured cushions.

You sit comfortably in front of the central altar.

Take a fresh candle from the side and light it with a taper. Place it on the altar in front of you.

Take a handful of herbs and spices and add them to the charcoal, do you recognize any of them?

Breathe in the scent from the incense and watch the smoke as it swirls and twists into the air.

Now sit and watch the flame of your candle as it flickers.

Sit quietly and look closely at the altar and the items on it. There are many things; candles, vases of fresh flowers, herbs, spices, dishes and jars. A fire has also been lit in an alcove to one side.

Think about any changes you could or should make in your life to create a better, happier, easier and/or more productive situation. What changes, no matter how small could you make to allow your goals and desires to manifest?

When you are ready, get up and head to the other side of the temple.

Laid out in front of you is a large garden. Lit by flaming torches lining each side, stretching out into the far distance.

A large wooden planter sits to one side, to your delight when you reach the planter it is full of fresh green seedlings. Small stems and leaves unfurled, sprouting above the soil.

Beside it is a watering can, pick up the can and water the soil.

Sit quietly in the darkness and look out over the garden.

What do you see growing in the light of the torches? Can you see or hear any wildlife? Sit for a while…take some time to look and listen.

When you are ready, walk back to the temple and over to the altar and snuff out your candle.

Slowly and gently come back to this reality. Open your eyes and wriggle your fingers and toes. Have something to eat and drink and write down any important notes.

Waxing Gibbous Moon Ritual for Transformation

You will need:

Representations for the four quarters, if using
Central candle for deity, if using
Matches or lighter
Safe holders for the candles, if using
Something to eat and drink

For the spell:

Image or photograph of a frog (you can visualise this, but it helps to have a focal point)
A white or light coloured candle
A black or dark coloured candle

Ground cinnamon

Cast the circle

Walking deosil (clockwise) around the circle.

With the power of the Moon
I cast this circle to attune
Magic creating a boundary to last
This Moon circle is now cast

Call the quarters

Facing North

I call upon the element of earth
May you bring your energy of grounding and stability to this rite
Earth, I welcome you

Facing East

I call upon the element of air
May you bring your energy of intellect and inspiration to this rite
Air, I welcome you

Facing South

I call upon the element of fire,
May you bring your energy of passion and power to this rite
Fire, I welcome you

Facing West

I call upon the element of water,
May you bring your energy of emotions and cleansing to this rite
Water, I welcome you

Deity

Facing centre

I call upon the Queen of Magic, the goddess Isis
And ask that you bring the energy of change, transition and transformation to this rite.
Isis, I honour your presence

Spell work: Set your image of the frog in front of you where you can see it properly. Pop the candles in front of the image, the black on the left and the white to your right. Get the image of the frog in your mind. Now light the black candle and say:

Magic of frog from the fairy tale
Change is a journey that will not fail
Transformation with a kiss
Work this magic, it will not miss

Sprinkle some cinnamon on the candle (carefully). Now snuff out the black candle.

Light the white candle. Repeat the chant, then sprinkle the white candle with cinnamon.

Sit quietly focusing on the image of the frog and visualise the transformation that you want to occur.

When you are ready snuff out the candle.

Dispose of the black candle. You can leave the white candle and the image of the frog on your altar. If you need a reminder or a boost to your journey relight the white candle.

Feast: Eat and drink something to celebrate your ritual and to help you ground. Sprinkle some of the drink and food onto the earth after the ritual as an offering to deity.

Deity

I thank the Queen of Magic, the goddess Isis

For bringing the energy of change, transition and transformation to this rite.
Isis, I honour you and ask that your energy continue with me as long as is needed.
With blessings and thanks, I bid you farewell

Release the quarters

Facing West

I thank the element of water,
For bringing your energy of emotions and cleansing to this rite
Water, I bid you farewell

Facing South

I thank the element of fire,
For bringing your energy of passion and power to this rite
Fire, I bid you farewell

Facing East

I thank the element of air
For bringing your energy of intellect and inspiration to this rite
Air, I bid you farewell

Facing North

I thank the element of earth
For bringing your energy of grounding and stability to this rite
Earth, I bid you farewell

Close the circle

Walking widdershins (anti clockwise) around the circle

I thank the power of the Moon
I uncast this circle but stay in tune
Magic unties the boundary to last
This Moon circle is now uncast

Waxing Gibbous Moon Tarot Cards

Tarot cards and oracle cards can be used as a focal point for meditation or as a key component to spell work. These cards are particularly associated with this Moon phase but trust your intuition about which ones to use.

Commitment: The Lovers, Three of Pentacles, Three of Wands, Two of Cups.

Courage and strength: The Star, Strength, The Chariot, The Fool, Ace of Swords, Knight of Swords, Seven of Wands, Nine of Wands.

Changes: Wheel of Fortune, The Magician, Hanged Man, Death, The Tower, Judgement, The World, Knight of Swords, Eight of Wands.

Potential: The Fool.

Opportunities: The Magician, Wheel of Fortune, The Devil, The Star, The World, Knight of Cups, Seven of Cups.

Power: The Emperor, The Chariot, Strength, Temperance, Ace of Swords.

Waxing Gibbous Moon Deities

Trust your intuition when working with deities, but please do your research before you call upon any of them. Make sure you know their history, personality and story before you work with them. Here are my suggestions for deities to work with for this Moon phase:

Anu – a Mesopotamian/Sumerian sky god viewed as Father of the gods and ruler of the heavens, the stars and the spirits. Call upon him for: Goals, wishes, spirituality.

Asherah – Ancient West Semitic goddess, often referred to as Queen of the Gods. Also known as 'She who walks on the sea' or 'holiness'. You will find her name in the Old Testament she is consort of Yahweh. Asherah is a goddess of the sea. Call upon her for: Divine wisdom, feminine energy, feminine issues, strength, self–esteem, self–confidence, courage, kindness, love, divination, insight, justice, fertility, compassion, healing, nurturing.

Hathor – Egyptian goddess of the Moon, associated with the dark Moon. Goddess of the Underworld but also ruler of the sky. She is a mother to all Egyptians. Definitely packing a powerful punch of feminine energy having given birth to the universe, she must have been exhausted. Call upon her for: Love, feminine energy, beauty, sexuality, happiness, romance, music, the arts, protection (primarily for women).

Isis – Egyptian goddess Queen of Egypt. She is looked upon as Mother Moon, Queen of Sorcery and the life force within the river Nile. Isis taught her people useful skills, those they would need to survive and flourish, no being high up in the sky for this one, she got down with her subjects (very practical woman). Call upon her for: Magic, dreams, divination, harvest, perspective, love, spirituality, faithfulness, destiny, revitalisation, fulfilment, inner beauty, rebirth, feminine energy, knowledge, motherhood, healing, changes, manifesting.

Juno – A Roman goddess, mother of all the gods. She protects Rome and all things feminine. She is a goddess of marriage, women and young girls. She is a strong, confident business woman, she definitely has a modern approach to being a deity. Her Greek equivalent is Hera. Call upon her for: Romance, love, relationships, marriage, protection, leadership, time, feminine energy, safety, happiness.

Luna – Roman goddess of the Moon. Depicted as a beautiful woman with the power to ease childbirth and bring about love. She carries a very strong feminine energy. If you want an answer to a problem, then call upon this lovely lady to bring you the answer in your dreams, it is her speciality. Her Greek equivalent is Selene. Call upon her for: Feminine energy, water magic, safety, travel, intuition, blue Moon magic, protection, illusion, truth, love, psychic abilities, dreams, solutions.

Neith/Nit – Egyptian goddess of the crescent Moon and domesticity. She has an eclectic list of duties including war, hunting and weaving. She is also considered to be the personification of the primordial waters of creation. Call upon her for: Home, marriage, protection, feminine energy, hunting, war, creativity, new beginnings.

Parvati – Hindu goddess of the crescent Moon. Oh, this goddess has all the feminine wiles and knows how to use them. She is maiden to the Mother Durga and Crone Kali. She can charm the secrets out of the trees. Call upon her for: Power, creativity, new beginnings, victory, feminine energy, beauty, charm, secrets, the arts, fertility, cleansing, devotion.

Rhiannon – if you aren't singing the Fleetwood Mac song right now, you need to… A Welsh goddess and great Queen of Wales. She brings peace, comfort and patience. If you are looking for magical enchantments, then she has a bounty of them. Call upon her for: Patience, comfort, peace, magic, movement, relaxation, communication, fertility, leadership, spirit work, motivation, dream work.

FULL MOON

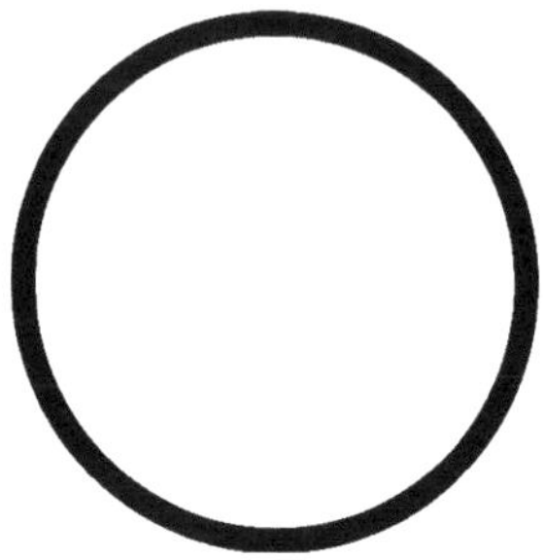

Beautiful globe in the sky all aglow
The full Moon energy with magic in tow
Whatever you want, whatever you need
Full Moon power helps you manifest with speed

In her full power showing a big ole beautiful circle of silvery light. This is when the Sun and the Moon are aligned on opposite sides of the Earth. Although it is a full Moon for a fleeting moment, we can still see what appears to be a full Moon a day before and after the point of the full Moon.

Full Moon Magic

Fulfilment, divination, celebrations, commitments, renewal, psychic abilities, truth, manifesting, abundance, power, wisdom, confidence, spell working of all kinds.

Results, gratitude, encouragement, blessings, anxiety, energy, success, social, relationships, communication, love, wildness, chaos, review, forgiveness and emotions. The energy of the Moon is at its peak, use the power of the full Moon for whatever you need. This is also a good time to give thanks and blessings for all that you have.

- Pop your magical and divination tools and any crystals

that correspond to the Moon outside to cleanse and recharge in the full Moon light. If you don't have a safe space outside, pop them on a window sill inside.
- Recharge your own energy by Moon bathing or performing a Drawing Down of the Moon.
- Use the full Moon energy to work some divination.
- The full Moon is perfect for manifesting your desires. Stand outside and send the Moon your wishes. Write them on a slip of paper and leave it to charge in the full Moon light.
- The full Moon brings clarity, sit quietly in her light and allow her to shine some insight into your life.
- Meditate sitting under the Moon, outside if you have a safe place, or inside by a window. Just sit quietly and focus on the Moon and the phase she is in. Ask her what guidance she has for you.

Full Moon Colours

You must work with the colours that you associate with this Moon phase, but here are my suggestions:

- White
- Purple
- Silver
- Red

Plants for the Full Moon

You can work with any plants that you feel drawn to, but these are my suggestions. Also check out the food section for herbs, spices and foods that can also work in incense blends or spell workings:

Bergamot

(Mentha citrate)

Bergamot (Orange) Magical Properties:

Money, uplifting, success, Sun magic, banishing, purification
Planet – Mercury, Sun
Sign – Virgo, Aquarius
Element – Air
Gender – Masculine

Hyssop

(Hyssopus officinalis)
Hyssop Magical Properties:
Purification, protection, healing
Ruling planet – Jupiter, Moon
Sign – Cancer
Element – Fire
Gender – Masculine

Jasmine

(Jasminum grandiflorum, Jasminum officinale, Jasminum odoratissimum)
Jasmine Magical Properties:
Dreams, money, love, meditation, lust
Ruling planet – Moon, Venus
Sign – Cancer
Element – Water
Gender – Feminine

Myrtle

(Myrtaceae communis)
Myrtle Magical Properties:
Love, protection, money
Ruling planet – Venus, Moon
Sign – Taurus
Element – Water
Gender – Feminine

Rose

(Rosa spp)

Rose Magical Properties:

Love, psychic powers, healing, luck, protection, peace, mysteries, knowledge, dreams, friendship, death and rebirth, abundance

Ruling planet – Venus, Moon

Sign – Pisces

Element – Water

Gender – Feminine

Sandalwood

(White Sandalwood – Santalum album)

(Red Sandalwood – Pterocarpus santalinus)

Sandalwood (Red) Magical Properties:

Meditation, love

Ruling planet – Venus, Jupiter

Sign – Sagittarius, Virgo

Element – Water

Gender – Feminine

Sandalwood (White)

Magical Properties:

Death rites, purification, wishes, psychic powers

Ruling planet – Moon, Mercury

Sign – Sagittarius, Virgo

Element – Water

Gender – Feminine

Yarrow

(Achillea millefolium)

Yarrow Magical Properties:

Psychic powers, love, courage, exorcism, dreams, peace, happiness, divination, protection.

Ruling planet – Venus
Element – Water
Gender – Feminine

Full Moon Incense and Oil Blends

Use equal quantities of each ingredient, or experiment to find a blend that you like. If you are creating a loose incense (rather than an essential oil mix) and the blend doesn't include a resin or woody component you might like to add one in to help it burn longer.

- Frankincense, sandalwood, rose petals
- Sandalwood, eucalyptus, mugwort, jasmine
- Myrrh, rose, lemon, camphor, jasmine

Full Moon Body Care – Body Butter

A nice blend of body butter to impart the energy of the full Moon, use as you would a moisturiser.

225g/8 oz shea butter or cocoa butter (or a mixture of both)
110g/4 oz coconut oil
110g/4 oz carrier oil such as almond or jojoba
10 drops of rose essential oil
8 drops jasmine essential oil
4 drops vanilla essential oil

Put the butters, coconut oil and carrier oils into a bowl over a pan of simmering water. Stir continuously until all the ingredients are melted. Remove from the heat and allow to cool slightly. Add in your essential oils. Put the mixture in the fridge to cool for about an hour, it should still be soft but starting to harden around the edges. Now whisk the mixture for about ten minutes, until it is light and fluffy. This is best done using an electric mixer. Spoon into glass jars and seal with lids.

Put back into the fridge to set for about fifteen to twenty minutes.

Full Moon Foods, Herbs and Spices

Bring on the feast! The full Moon is all about celebrating and being extravagant. Big rich foods that are packed full of flavour. Splurge, and treat yourself. Big hearty dishes and lots of warming spices. Remember to treat yourself to dessert with plenty of cake and of course chocolate. Some of these foods can also be used in incense blends or spell working.

Basil

(Ocimum basilicum)

Basil Magical Properties:

Wealth, money, prosperity, love, exorcism, protection, happiness, peace

Ruling planet – Mars

Element – Fire

Gender – masculine

Black pepper

(Piper nigrum)

Black Pepper Magical Properties:

Protection, exorcism, jealousy, negativity, strength, confidence, gossip

Ruling planet – Mars

Element – Fire

Gender – Masculine

Cabbage

(Brassica oleracea/var.)

Cabbage Magical Properties:

Moon magic, protection, prosperity, fertility, love

Ruling planet – Moon

Element – Water
Gender – Feminine

Cake

Cake Magical Properties:
Happiness, ritual, rites of passage, offerings, celebration, grounding
Element – Earth
Gender – Feminine

Cauliflower

(Brassica oleracea)
Cauliflower Magical Properties:
Emotions, Moon magic, protection
Ruling planet – Moon
Element – Water
Gender – Feminine

Cheese

Cheese Magical Properties:
Success, happiness
Ruling planet –Saturn
Element – Earth, Air
Gender – Masculine

Chillies

(capsicum)
Chillies Magical Properties:
Creativity, energy, power, protection, passion, hex breaking
Ruling planet – Mars
Element – Fire
Gender – Masculine

Chocolate

(Theobroma cacao)

Chocolate Magical Properties:

Prosperity, positive energy, happiness, love

Ruling planet – Mars

Element – Fire

Gender – Feminine

Cinnamon

(Cinnamomum zeylanicum, Cinnamomum verum)

Cinnamon Magical Properties:

Success, healing, power, psychic powers, protection, love, focus, lust, spirituality, changes

Ruling planet – Sun

Element – Fire

Gender – Masculine

Eggs

Eggs Magical Properties:

Fertility, creation, life, new beginnings, divination

Element – Water, Earth, Air, Fire

Gender – Masculine/Feminine

Fish

Fish Magical Properties:

Fertility, Prosperity, Abundance, healing, emotions, cleansing, purification

Element – Water

Gender – Feminine

Garlic

(Allium sativum)

Garlic Magical Properties:

Healing, protection, hex breaking, negative energies, lust,

strength, courage, depression
Ruling planet – Mars
Element – Fire
Gender – Masculine

Mint

(Mentha spp, Mentha aquatic, Mentha piperita)
Mint Magical Properties:
Money, healing, exorcism, protection, cleansing, calming
Ruling planet – Mercury, Venus
Element – Air
Gender – Masculine

Oregano

(Origanum vulgare)
Oregano Magical Properties:
Ruling planet – Mars, Venus, Mercury
Sign – Gemini
Element – Air
Gender – Masculine

Pasta

Pasta Magical Properties:
Psychic powers, protection, communication, creativity
Ruling planet – Mercury
Element – Earth
Gender – Masculine

Potato

(Solanum tuberosum L)
Potato Magical Properties:
Energy, magic, grounding, prosperity, healing
Ruling planet – Moon
Element – Earth

Gender – Feminine

Thyme

(Thymus vulgaris, Thymus serpyllum)

Thyme Magical Properties:

Healing, health, peace, psychic powers, love, purification, courage, releasing, sleep, beauty

Ruling planet – Venus

Element – Water

Gender – Feminine

Tomato

(Solanum lycopersicum)

Tomato Magical Properties:

Love, passion, protection, creativity

Ruling planet – Venus

Element – Water

Gender – Feminine

Vanilla

(Vanilla planifolia)

Vanilla Magical Properties:

Love, spirituality, sex magic, passion, creativity

Ruling planet – Venus

Element – Water, Air

Gender – Feminine

Full Moon Recipe – Chocolate Bundt Cake

This is an easy cake mix that turns out to look quite grand. It can also be made vegan if you use plant–based milk. If you don't have a bundt tin you can use a cake tin but pop a small china or metal ramekin in the centre.

350g/12.3 oz plain/all–purpose flour

400g/14 oz sugar
120g/4.2 oz cocoa powder
2 teaspoons baking powder
1 teaspoon baking/bicarbonate soda
½ teaspoon salt
240ml/8 fl oz milk (any kind)
240ml/8 fl oz water
180ml/6 fl oz vegetable oil
4 tablespoons white vinegar
2 teaspoons vanilla extract
100g chocolate (plain or milk)

Preheat your oven to 180C/350F/Gas 4.

Spray a bundt cake tin with oil and dust with flour.

In a bowl mix the flour, cocoa powder, sugar, salt, baking powder and baking soda.

Add the milk, water, oil, vanilla and vinegar – whisk to combine.

Pour into the prepared pan and bake for 45 minutes.

Allow to cool in the tin before turning out.

Melt the chocolate in a bowl over a pan of simmering water and drizzle over the top of the cake.

Full Moon Herbal Teas

Herbal teas can be purchased in tea bag form or ready–made loose blends and there are some fantastic brands out there. However, I have also purchased herbal teas that tasted like sweepings from the factory floor. Check the ingredients when purchasing ready–made herbal teas, make sure they include only the items that the tea is supposed to taste of. Some companies bulk out with cheaper items. Herbal tea is very easy to make if you grow fresh herbs or if you have a supply of dried herbs and dried fruits. Experiment with different flavours. The basic rule is one or two teaspoons of dried herbs to a mug full of boiling water, brew for at least five minutes then strain. If you are using fresh herbs you may need a slightly larger quantity. Herbal tea can be drunk hot (obviously), left and poured over ice as a cold drink or even used as a hair rinse. Drop it into your bath water or add to a bucket of hot water and use as a floor or surface wash.

Please be careful and make sure you have identified the herbs you use correctly. Never ingest herbs that you are not sure about. Always check with a qualified practitioner if you are on medication, have health problems or are pregnant.

I have given some of my favourite recipes here, adjust the amounts of each ingredient to suit your own taste. If the blend isn't sweet enough you can add a teaspoon of sugar or honey.

Psychic tea:
Star anise
Bay
Thyme

With thanks, gratitude tea:
Lavender
Lemon

Curb those emotions tea:
Cucumber
Lemon

Crystals for the Full Moon

You can work with any crystals you feel drawn to, but these are my suggestions:

Agate (moss)

Agate (moss) magical properties

Nature, happiness, prosperity, wealth, longevity, friendship, success, abundance, healing, renewal, fertility, creativity, confidence, strength, love, beginnings, self–esteem, communication, emotions, stress, releasing, hope, trust, depression, growth, finances, cleansing, support, peace, stability, fears, luck, divination

Energy Receptive
Element Earth
Planet Moon
Zodiac Virgo, Gemini

Amethyst

Amethyst magical properties

Peace, protection, success, good luck, hidden knowledge, legal issues, spirituality, contentment, soothing, relaxation, calm, hope, patience, transformation, changes, breaking patterns, grounding, guilt, overcoming addictions, business matters, judgement, clarity, courage, travel, psychic protection, sleep, anxiety, focus, understanding, happiness, justice, intuition, inspiration, channelling, meditation

Energy: Receptive
Element: Water
Planet: Jupiter, Neptune
Zodiac: Pisces, Scorpio, Sagittarius
Birthstone: February

Amazonite

Amazonite magical properties

Courage, soothing, bravery, calming, determination, focus, clarity, insight, self–confidence, self–assurance, respect, grace, intuition, understanding, balance, communication, creativity, inspiration, spirituality, success, luck, money, stress relief, energy, worries, fears

Energy: Receptive
Element: Earth
Planet: Saturn

Zodiac: Virgo, Pisces

Chrysocolla

Chrysocolla magical properties

Wisdom, peace, patience, love, soothing, intuition, energy, calming, emotions, fear, strength, clarity, balance, negative energy, insight, releasing, spirituality, psychic abilities, guilt, divine, harmony, communication, meditation

Energy: Receptive
Element: Water
Planet: Venus
Zodiac: Taurus

Quartz (clear)

Quartz (clear) magical properties

Purification, cleansing, healing, calming, emotions, strength, support, spirituality, energy, balance, psychic abilities, motivation, uplifting, decisions, anxiety, divine connection, amplifying, focus, meditation, manifestation, channelling, protection, negative energy, clarity, wisdom, concentration, learning, spirit work, communication, astral travel, divination, dreams, harmony

Energy Projective, Receptive
Planet Sun, Moon
Element Fire, Water
Zodiac Leo, Gemini, Capricorn

Jade

Jade magical properties

Purification, harmony, friendship, luck, protection, clarity, manifestation, peace, courage, wealth, longevity, wisdom, prosperity, love, renewal, fertility, uplifting, calming, confidence, truth, psychic abilities, spirit work, dreams, past life work, healing, abundance, finances, creativity, manifestation, emotions

Energy	Receptive
Element	Water
Planet	Venus, Neptune
Zodiac	Pisces, Libra, Gemini, Taurus, Aries
Birthstone	March

Kyanite

Kyanite magical properties

Balance, harmony, calming, connection, psychic abilities, healing, communication, grounding, transformation, meditation, relaxation, luck, growth, leadership, new beginnings, clarity, decisions, stability, truth, vitality, abundance, spirituality, channelling, understanding, dreams

Energy	Receptive
Element	Water
Planet	Jupiter, Venus, Mars
Zodiac	Aries, Libra, Taurus

Moonstone

Moonstone magical properties

New beginnings, Moon magic, intuition, calming, psychic abilities, balance, harmony, wishes, cleansing, uplifting, hope, meditation, emotions, love, divination, spirituality, wealth, truth, healing, sensuality, insight, peace, wisdom, communication, confidence, abundance, prosperity, dreams, fertility, travel

Energy	Receptive
Element	Water
Planet	Moon
Zodiac	Cancer, Libra, Scorpio
Birthstone	June, September

Opal

Opal magical properties

Inspiration, change, creativity, imagination, releasing, spirituality, invisibility, emotions, dream work, visualization, appreciation, astral projection, power, psychic abilities, past life work

Energy	Projective, Receptive
Element	Earth, Air, Fire, Water
Planet	Mercury
Zodiac	Cancer, Libra, Pisces, Scorpio
Birthstone	October, April

Quartz (smoky)

Quartz (smoky) magical properties

Grounding, centring, focus, negative energy, decisions, cooperation, creativity, emotions, depression, anxiety, jealousy, nature, protection, calming, manifestation, wishes, divination, meditation, insight, guidance, uplifting, fears, relaxation, releasing, abundance, luck, prosperity

Energy	Receptive
Element	Earth
Planet	Saturn, Jupiter
Zodiac	Capricorn, Sagittarius

Selenite

Selenite magical properties

Clarity, psychic protection, cleansing, balance, stability, emotions, divine, connections, spirituality, psychic abilities, spirit work, protection, healing, breaking barriers, decisions, intuition, meditation, money, success, love

Energy	Receptive
Element	Water
Planet	Moon
Zodiac	Cancer

Silver

Silver magical properties

Healing, communication, cleansing, energy, intuition, stability, spirituality, patience, perseverance, Moon magic, negative energy, protection, balance, psychic abilities, manifestation, wealth, prosperity, abundance, travel, dreams, emotions, purification, love, peace, astral travel

Energy	Receptive
Element	Water
Planet	Moon
Zodiac	Cancer

Full Moon Meditation

Find a place where you won't be disturbed and make yourself comfortable. If you have a safe place to sit outside at night time then it would be perfect to do so, otherwise indoors is just fine. Close your eyes and focus on your breathing, deep breaths in and deep breaths out.

As your world around you dissipates you find yourself standing inside a stone columned temple. Pillars around you and a stone wall behind you. Above your head is open to the sky.

It is dark and the deep indigo blue sky is scattered with stars.

A large, glowing full Moon hangs in the sky, shining her light down.

Investigate the temple; running along the back wall is a ledge set out as an altar with candles, tapers and bowls of herbs and spices. Dishes sit filled with sweet smelling incense on top of smouldering charcoal.

In front of the altar are piles of brightly coloured cushions.

You sit comfortably in front of the central altar.

Take a fresh candle from the side and light it with a taper. Place it on the altar in front of you.

Take a handful of herbs and spices and add them to the charcoal, do

you recognize any of them?

Breathe in the scent from the incense and watch the smoke as it swirls and twists into the air.

Now sit and watch the flame of your candle as it flickers.

Sit quietly and count your blessings.

Even very small positives in your life count.

Spend some time and see just how many blessings you have.

When you are ready, get up and head to the other side of the temple.

Laid out in front of you is a large garden. Lit by flaming torches lining each side, stretching out into the far distance.

A large wooden planter sits to one side, it is full of green leafy plants, growing strongly. You notice a dish of plant food beside the planter, pick up a handful and sprinkle it around the plants.

Beside it is a watering can, pick up the can and water the soil.

Sit quietly in the darkness and look out over the garden.

What do you see growing in the light of the torches? Can you see or hear any wildlife? Sit for a while…take some time to look and listen.

Look up at the full Moon and send her your thanks for all that you have.

When you are ready, walk back to the temple and over to the altar and snuff out your candle.

Slowly and gently come back to this reality. Open your eyes and wriggle your fingers and toes. Have something to eat and drink and write down any important notes.

Full Moon Ritual for Gratitude

We ask for a lot, and it is only fair that every so often we give thanks and blessings for all that we have. And a little thanks now and then to deity, the Universe or whatever guiding light you make your requests to is only good manners.

You will need:

Representations for the four quarters, if using
Central candle for deity, if using
Matches or lighter
Safe holders for the candles, if using
Something to eat and drink

For the spell:

A white candle
A silver or white candle
A divination tool of your choice

Cast the circle
Walking deosil (clockwise) around the circle.

With the power of the Moon
I cast this circle to attune
Magic creating a boundary to last
This Moon circle is now cast

Call the quarters
Facing North

I call upon the element of earth
May you bring your energy of grounding and stability to this rite
Earth, I welcome you

Facing East

I call upon the element of air
May you bring your energy of intellect and inspiration to this rite
Air, I welcome you

Facing South

I call upon the element of fire,
May you bring your energy of passion and power to this rite
Fire, I welcome you

Facing West

I call upon the element of water,
May you bring your energy of emotions and cleansing to this rite
Water, I welcome you

Deity
Facing centre

I call upon the fair and honest goddess Ma'at
And ask that you bring the energy of balance, fairness and truth to this rite.
Ma'at, I honour your presence

Spell work
Light the white candle. Sit quietly in front of the candle and focus on the flame. Think about all the blessings you have and the things you are thankful for in your life. No matter how small, really count each and every one of your blessings.

Now light the silver candle.

Stand up and hold your arms in the air and look to the skies, say:

I give my thanks for all the blessings I see
I give my thanks for all that is provided for me
My dreams, my hopes, all that I need
Any guidance given, I will whole heartedly heed
With heartfelt blessings from me

Allow the candles to burn out. As the full Moon is an excellent time to work with divination, use your divination tool now to do a reading to see what guidance you are given.

Feast: Eat and drink something to celebrate your ritual and to help you ground. Sprinkle some of the drink and food onto the earth after the ritual as an offering to deity.

Deity

I thank the fair and honest goddess Ma'at
For bringing the energy of balance, fairness and truth to this rite.
Ma'at, I honour you and ask that your energy continue with me as long as is needed.
With blessings and thanks, I bid you farewell

Release the quarters
Facing West

I thank the element of water,
For bringing your energy of emotions and cleansing to this rite
Water, I bid you farewell

Facing South

I thank the element of fire,
For bringing your energy of passion and power to this rite
Fire, I bid you farewell

Facing East

I thank the element of air
For bringing your energy of intellect and inspiration to this rite
Air, I bid you farewell

Facing North

I thank the element of earth
For bringing your energy of grounding and stability to this rite
Earth, I bid you farewell

Close the circle
Walking widdershins (anti clockwise) around the circle

I thank the power of the Moon
I uncast this circle but stay in tune
Magic unties the boundary to last
This Moon circle is now uncast

Full Moon tarot cards

Tarot cards and oracle cards can be used as a focal point for meditation or as a key component to spell work. These cards are particularly associated with this Moon phase but trust your intuition about which ones to use.

Commitment: The Lovers, Three of Pentacles, Three of Wands, Two of Cups.
Magic: The Magician, The High Priestess, The Moon.
Power: The Emperor, The Chariot, Strength, Temperance, Ace of Swords.
Goals: The Emperor, The Chariot, Strength.
Emotions: The Empress, Queen of Cups.
Love: The Lovers, Knight of Cups, The Star, Two of Cups, Ace of Cups, Four of Wands
Abundance: The Empress, The Star, The World, Ace of Pentacles, Six of Pentacles, Nine of Pentacles, Ace of Cups.
Inspiration, ideas and creativity: The Magician, The Moon, The Star, The Fool, The Empress, The World, The Hierophant,

Temperance, Ace of Cups, Ace of Wands, Queen of Wands, Page of Cups, Knight of Cups.

Full Moon Deities

Trust your intuition when working with deities, but please do your research before you call upon any of them. Make sure you know their history, personality and story before you work with them. Here are my suggestions for deities to work with for this Moon phase:

Arianrhod – Welsh goddess of the Moon. She forms the triple goddess triad with Blodeuwedd and Cerridwen. Her name translates as 'silver disc', she is often referred to as Goddess of the Silver Wheel. Arianrhod guides the dead to the other side and rules the sky and the sea as well as the Moon. She can shapeshift into an owl. She is also known as one of the goddesses of Avalon. Call upon her for: Moon magic, dream work, psychic abilities, divination, past lives, reincarnation, other realms, feminine power, retribution, karma.

Asherah – Ancient West Semitic goddess, often referred to as Queen of the Gods. Also known as 'She who walks on the sea' or 'holiness'. You will find her name in the Old Testament she is consort of Yahweh. Asherah is a goddess of the sea. Call upon her for: Divine wisdom, feminine energy, feminine issues, strength, self–esteem, self–confidence, courage, kindness, love, divination, insight, justice, fertility, compassion, healing, nurturing.

Chang–O – Chinese goddess of the Moon. Banished from heaven along with her husband, destined to be mere mortals. Chang–O took a double dose of immortality pill, without sharing with her husband (rude). She floated up to the Moon, leaving her husband behind. Call upon her for: Love, partnership, courage, power, fertility, growth, manifesting, belief, self–confidence, new beginnings, transformation.

Coyolxauhqui – Aztec Moon goddess. Her name translates as 'painted with bells'. Apparently in most images she is wearing bells on her cheeks, which must be terribly uncomfortable. When the full Moon rises you can see the bells as rosy red. In a bit of a misunderstanding Coyolxauhqui had her head cut off, which was flung up into the sky, where it became the Moon. Call upon her for: Moon magic, family issues, balance, differences.

Demeter – Ancient Greek goddess of the full Moon. She is an Olympian goddess of agriculture, harvest and fertility. Featuring in the Eleusinian mysteries alongside her daughter Persephone. She forms a triad with Persephone and Hecate, Demeter taking on the mother role. Equivalent to the Roman goddess Ceres. Call upon her for: Abundance, harvest, mysteries, fertility, marriage, relationships, life and death, rebirth, justice, grief, suffering, parenthood.

Freyja/Freya – although not called a Moon goddess, many of her attributes connect her with both the Full and Dark Moons. A Norse goddess of love, beauty, war and fertility. She leads souls of dead warriors to the Otherworld. She rides a chariot driven by two cats, so she must be powerful to get cats to do what they are told! Call upon her for: Love, beauty, fertility, war, dearth, happiness, sex, sensuality, inspiration.

Hera – Greek Olympian Queen of gods, she covers marriage, childbirth and looking after women (she's got her hands full then). Although she can help when called upon, she has a jealous side and can be vengeful particularly when infidelity is involved. Call upon her for: Love, humour, forgiveness, romance, creativity, marriage, strength, courage, self–confidence, jealousy.

Inanna – Sumerian goddess of the full Moon and the stars, also known as Ishtar in Babylon. She is Queen of heaven and earth. She has a reputation for being a little bit saucy which led her to be linked to fertility rituals. She does look after her followers, dishing out the rules and keeping them safe. Call upon her for: Love, fertility, warrior, strength, courage, seduction, sensuality, protection, justice.

Ishtar – Babylonian goddess of the full Moon, also known as Inanna in Sumeria. A goddess of love, sex and war (pretty much covers it all then) she is a bit of a floozy, taking many lovers to bed (I don't judge). Call upon her for: Love, passion, sexuality, fertility, womanhood, independence, insight, inspiration, wishes.

Luna – Roman goddess of the Moon. Depicted as a beautiful woman with the power to ease childbirth and bring about love. She carries a very strong feminine energy. If you want an answer to a problem, then call upon this lovely lady to bring you the answer in your dreams, it is her speciality. Her Greek equivalent is Selene. Call upon her for: Feminine energy, water magic, safety, travel, intuition, blue Moon magic, protection, illusion, truth, love, psychic abilities, dreams, solutions.

Ma'at – Egyptian goddess of the crescent Moon, order and balance. Think 'strict school headmistress', she dishes out the justice as she sees fit, whether you are a deity or a mere mortal. Her name translates as 'truth/that which is straight'. If you are looking for balance between work and home life or any kind of justice, Ma'at should be on your speed dial. Call upon her for: Justice, balance, freedom, new beginnings, morals, organisation, law, promises, fairness, truth, oaths, harmony, honesty.

Mama Quilla/Killa– Incan goddess of the full Moon, she cried silver tears. Lunar eclipses were said to be caused by a serpent or animal attacking Mama Quilla (ouch). She also covers marriage and the menstrual cycle. She is known as 'Mother Moon' and is responsible for the passage of time. Call upon her for: Time, Moon magic, feminine issues, protection of women, marriage, relationships, truth, deceit.

Mani – From the Norse pantheon, son of the giant Mundilfore. Mani is the god of the Moon and brother to the Sun goddess Sol. Mani controls the phases of the Moon and guides it across the skies. He also helps humans learn to tell the time and date. Mani and Sol are both chased endlessly by a pair of wolves, who will catch and devour them at Ragnarok (the end of the world), let's hope they never get caught... Call upon him for: Moon magic, Moon phases, time.

Ops – Roman goddess of the full Moon and agriculture. If you are after abundance and prosperity, then Ops is your 'go to' goddess. She can also teach you all kinds of practical skills to gain that abundance for yourself. Ain't nothing in this life for free! Call upon her for: Fertility, abundance, wealth, nurturing, prosperity, opportunity, growth.

WANING GIBBOUS MOON

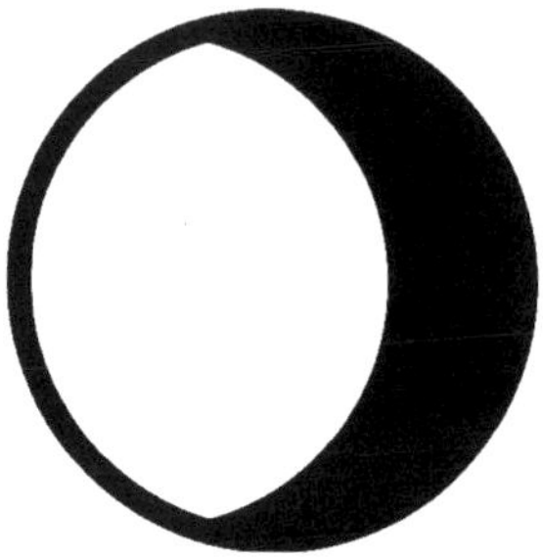

She is starting to move, slipping from sight
The waning gibbous Moon helps release with her might
Release, separate, banish and let go
Tie up loose ends, get ready to throw

Still quite full looking but no longer a full circle, it is on the wane flowing from full downwards. Sometimes referred to as disseminating. Waning because it is getting smaller and gibbous because the shape is larger than a semicircle but smaller than a full circle.

Waning Gibbous Moon Magic

Relax, acceptance, re–group, cleansing, repelling, reversing, curses, protection, sharing, wisdom and experience. Breaking habits, letting go of negative emotions and attachments, removing and releasing. Release, separate, remove anything that no longer serves you (people, situations, problems, addictions, cycles, stress and negative emotions). Get rid of old patterns, negative situations, toxic friendships and closing down projects. Bring in protection. Tie up all those loose ends. Work with banishing spells. Basically, this is the phase to chuck everything out that serves you no purpose...go on...get rid of it!

- Write a list of all the bad habits and negative cycles in your life that you want to get rid of. Take the list and stand outside under the waning Moon, read the list out loud. Either leave your list outside to weather and break apart or burn the list.
- Work any weight loss spells on the waning Moon to tap into the releasing energy.
- Let go of toxic relationships, cut the cords and let it go…
- Work magic to reduce your debts and loans.
- Make endings and burn negative energies to allow yourself to move forward.
- Cleanse and purify your home on a waning Moon to help release negative energy that might be trapped.
- Take a cleansing bath or shower with added oils and herbs to release any negative energy you might be holding on to.
- Reversing spells can be worked on a waning Moon. Undo any spells that didn't work or are causing chaos.
- Meditate sitting under the Moon, outside if you have a safe place, or inside by a window. Just sit quietly and focus on the Moon and the phase she is in. Ask her what guidance she has for you.

Waning Gibbous Moon Colours

You must work with the colours that you associate with this Moon phase, but here are my suggestions:

- White
- Black
- Pale blue

Plants for the Waning Gibbous Moon

You can work with any plants that you feel drawn to, but these are my suggestions. Also check out the food section for herbs, spices and foods that can also work in incense blends or spell workings:

Cypress

(Cupressus sempervirens)

Cypress Magical Properties:

Release, binding, grief, protection, healing

Ruling planet – Saturn

Sign – Aquarius

Element – Earth

Gender – Feminine

Eucalyptus

(Eucalyptus spp)

Eucalyptus Magical Properties:

Moon magic, Sun magic, divination, dreams, healing, purification

Ruling planet – Moon, Sun

Element – Water, Air

Gender – Feminine

Frankincense

Frankincense Magical Properties:

Purification, spirituality, relaxation, focus, love, abundance

Ruling planet – Sun

Sign – Aries, Leo, Aquarius

Element – Fire

Gender – Masculine

Hyssop

(Hyssopus officinalis)

Hyssop Magical Properties:

Purification, protection, healing

Ruling planet – Jupiter, Moon

Sign – Cancer

Element – Fire

Gender – Masculine

Jasmine

(Jasminum grandiflorum, Jasminum officinale, Jasminum odoratissimum)

Jasmine Magical Properties:

Dreams, money, love, meditation, lust

Ruling planet – Moon, Venus

Sign – Cancer

Element – Water

Gender – Feminine

Myrtle

(Myrtaceae communis)

Myrtle Magical Properties:

Love, protection, money

Ruling planet – Venus, Moon

Sign – Taurus

Element – Water

Gender – Feminine

Sandalwood

(White Sandalwood – Santalum album)

Sandalwood (White) Magical Properties:

Death rites, purification, wishes, psychic powers

Ruling planet – Moon, Mercury

Sign – Sagittarius, Virgo

Element – Water

Gender – Feminine

Yarrow

(Achillea millefolium)

Yarrow Magical Properties:

Psychic powers, love, courage, exorcism, dreams, peace, happiness, divination, protection.

Ruling planet – Venus

Element – Water
Gender – Feminine

Waning Gibbous Moon Incense and Oils

Use equal quantities of each ingredient, or experiment to find a blend that you like. If you are creating a loose incense (rather than an essential oil mix) and the blend doesn't include a resin or woody component you might like to add one in to help it burn longer.

- Mint, orange, cypress
- Frankincense, star anise, sage
- Rose, lime, mint, lemon

Waning Gibbous Moon Body Care – Body Scrub

Scoop some out into your hand and massage into the skin, then rinse off. It clears out the skin pores and leaves your skin soft.

You will need:

1 tablespoon oats
2 tablespoons base oil such as almond or jojoba
1 teaspoon dried mint
5 drops frankincense essential oils
3 drops lemon essential oil
2 drops rosemary essential oil

Grind the oats and dried herbs/flowers to a powder in a pestle and mortar, blender or use the end of a rolling pin in a dish.

Mix the essential oils with the base oil.

Combine it all together to form a paste.

Store in an airtight jar for up to three months.

Waning Gibbous Moon Foods, Herbs and Spices

Leftovers time, work with what you have in the fridge or cupboards and eat up what you have left from the full Moon feasts. Keep it simple, fresh and cleansing. Soups are excellent to eat on this Moon phase along with plenty of fresh fruit. Some of these foods can also be used in incense blends or spell working.

Bay

(Laurus nobilis)

Bay Magical Properties:

Protection, purification, strength, power, healing, creativity, spirituality, psychic powers

Ruling planet – Sun

Sign – Aries, Leo

Element – Fire

Gender – Masculine

Bean

(Phaseolus spp)

Beans Magical Properties:

Wisdom, divination, prosperity

Ruling planet – Mercury

Element – Air

Gender – Masculine

Coriander

(Coriandrum sativum)

Coriander Magical Properties:

Health, healing, peace, love, release, wealth, protection, negativity

Ruling planet – Mars

Element – Fire

Gender – Masculine

Fish

Fish Magical Properties:

Fertility, Prosperity, Abundance, healing, emotions, cleansing, purification

Element – Water

Gender – Feminine

Lemon

(Citrus x lemon)

Lemon Magical Properties:

Purification, Moon magic, happiness, decisions, uplifting, love, protection, friendship, fidelity

Ruling planet – Moon

Element – Water

Gender – Feminine

Lime

(Citrus aurantifolia)

Lime Magical Properties:

Purification, love, healing, protection, energy

Ruling planet –Sun

Element – Fire

Gender – Masculine

Marjoram

(Origanum majorana)

Marjoram Magical Properties:

Love, happiness, health, protection, marriage, grief

Ruling planet – Mercury

Sign – Aries, Capricorn

Element – Air

Gender – Masculine

Mint

(Mentha spp, Mentha aquatic, Mentha piperita)

Mint Magical Properties:
Money, healing, exorcism, protection, cleansing, calming
Ruling planet – Mercury, Venus
Element – Air
Gender – Masculine

Orange

(Citrus × sinensis)
Orange Magical Properties:
Love, happiness, uplifting, generosity, purification, clarity, energy, fidelity
Ruling planet – Sun
Element – Fire
Gender – Masculine

Parsley

(Petroselinum crispum, Petrselinum sativum)
Parsley Magical Properties:
Protection, purification, lust, happiness, fertility, spirit work
Ruling planet – Mercury
Element – Air
Gender – Masculine

Pasta

Pasta Magical Properties:
Psychic powers, protection, communication, creativity
Ruling planet – Mercury
Element – Earth
Gender – Masculine

Rice

(Oryza spp)
Rice Magical Properties:
Prosperity, fertility, protection, rain, grounding, stability

Ruling planet – Sun
Element – Air, Earth
Gender – Masculine

Rosemary

(Rosemarinus officinalis)
Rosemary Magical Properties:
Protection, love, lust, mental powers, exorcism, purification, healing, sleep
Ruling planet – Sun
Element – Fire
Gender – Masculine

Sage

(salvia officinalis)
Sage Magical Properties:
Protection, wishes, wisdom, purification, stimulating, intuition, abundance, success.
Ruling planet – Jupiter
Element – Air
Gender – Masculine

Star Anise

(Illicum verum)
Star Anise Magical Properties:
Luck, psychic powers, purification, protection, dreams, spirituality, sleep
Ruling planet – Jupiter
Element – Air
Gender – Masculine

Waning Gibbous Moon Recipe – Lemon Pound Cake

A simple recipe with a delicious result. It can also be made vegan by using vegan butter/margarine and plant–based milk.

112g/4 oz butter
200g/7 oz sugar
2 teaspoons vanilla extract
Zest of 3 lemons
275g/9.7 oz plain/all–purpose flour
3 teaspoons baking powder
1/2 teaspoon salt
240ml/8 fl oz buttermilk (add a tablespoon of lemon juice to your regular/plant–based milk to create buttermilk)
120g/4.2 oz icing/powdered sugar
1 to 1 ½ tablespoons lemon juice

Preheat your oven to 180C/350F/Gas 4.

Cream the butter and sugar together until light and fluffy then add the vanilla and lemon zest.

In a separate bowl mix the flour, baking powder and salt. Then add this to the butter and sugar mixture.

Stir the buttermilk into the other ingredients and mix until combined (the batter will be thick).

Grease a 9x5″ loaf pan and line with baking parchment.

Spoon your batter into the pan and level the top.

Bake in the oven for 40 minutes, then cover the top with tin foil and bake for a further 20 minutes.

Once the cake is cool mix the icing sugar with the lemon juice, slowly a bit at a time (you might not need all of it) and drizzle over the top.

Options:

Add lime or orange instead of lemon.

Replace the lemon with a teaspoon of vanilla extract.

Add a teaspoon of dried rosemary or thyme.

Replace the lemon with a teaspoon of cinnamon or mixed spice.

Waning Gibbous Moon Teas

Herbal teas can be purchased in tea bag form or ready–made loose blends and there are some fantastic brands out there. However, I have also purchased herbal teas that tasted like sweepings from the factory floor. Check the ingredients when purchasing ready–made herbal teas, make sure they include only the items that the tea is supposed to taste of. Some companies bulk out with cheaper items. Herbal tea is very easy to make if you grow fresh herbs or if you have a supply of dried herbs and dried fruits. Experiment with different flavours. The basic rule is one or two teaspoons of dried herbs to a mug full of boiling water, brew for at least five minutes then strain. If you are using fresh herbs you may need a slightly larger quantity. Herbal tea can be drunk hot (obviously), left and poured over ice as a cold drink or even used as a hair rinse. Drop it into your bath water or add to a bucket of hot water and use as a floor or surface wash.

Please be careful and make sure you have identified the herbs you use correctly. Never ingest herbs that you are not sure about. Always check with a qualified practitioner if you are on medication, have health problems or are pregnant.

I have given some of my favourite recipes here, adjust the amounts of each ingredient to suit your own taste. If the blend isn't sweet enough you can add a teaspoon of sugar or honey.

And relax…tea:
Chamomile, yep it is that simple

Knowledge tea:
Sage
Lemon
Apple

Let it go, releasing tea:
Thyme

Fennel

You can add to the releasing energy by making this with coconut water

Crystals for the Waning Gibbous Moon

You can work with any crystals you feel drawn to, but these are my suggestions:

Amazonite

Amazonite magical properties

Courage, soothing, bravery, calming, determination, focus, clarity, insight, self–confidence, self–assurance, respect, grace, intuition, understanding, balance, communication, creativity, inspiration, spirituality, success, luck, money, stress relief, energy, worries, fears

Energy: Receptive
Element: Earth
Planet: Saturn
Zodiac: Virgo, Pisces

Black tourmaline

Black tourmaline magical properties:

Understanding, self–confidence, psychic abilities, dispel negative energy, fears, grief, concentration, communication, relaxation, compassion, serenity, balance, transformation, healing, strength, tolerance, protection, grounding

Energy: Receptive
Element: Earth
Planet: Venus, Mars
Zodiac: Libra
Birthstone: October

Bloodstone

Bloodstone magical properties:

Organisation, adaptability, anxiety, clarity, concentration, renewal, energy, self–confidence, connection, calm, protection, breaking barriers, selfishness, mysticism, insight, spirituality, truth, intuition, creativity, guidance, strength, healing, victory, wealth, money, power, invisibility, deception, negative energy, divine connection, past life, dreams

Energy:	Projective
Element:	Fire, Earth
Planet:	Mars
Zodiac:	Aries, Pisces, Scorpio
Birthstone:	February, March

Citrine

Citrine magical properties:

Happiness, joy, Sun magic, negative energy, optimism, abundance, depression, stress, success, wealth, healing, intuition, creativity, confidence, changes, self–esteem, protection, psychic powers, fears, clarity, stamina, nightmares

Energy:	Projective
Element:	Fire
Planet:	Sun, Jupiter
Zodiac:	Scorpio
Birthstone:	November

Obsidian

Obsidian magical properties

Truth, healing, clarity, illusions, breaking barriers, integrity, grounding, centring, strength, courage, protection, cleansing, meditation, stress, calming, relaxation, depression, anxiety, wealth, luck, focus, emotions, power, determination, success, patience, perseverance, releasing, spirit work, spirituality, challenges, past life work, divination

Energy	Projective
Element	Fire, Earth, Water
Planet	Saturn, Jupiter

Zodiac	Sagittarius

Obsidian (snowflake)

Obsidian (snowflake) magical properties

Grounding, protection, birth & death, rebirth, connection, challenges, past life work, dispel negative energy, releasing, healing, centering, scrying

Energy	Projective
Element	Fire
Planet	Saturn, Jupiter
Zodiac	Sagittarius

Quartz (clear)

Quartz (clear) magical properties

Purification, cleansing, healing, calming, emotions, strength, support, spirituality, energy, balance, psychic abilities, motivation, uplifting, decisions, anxiety, divine connection, amplifying, focus, meditation, manifestation, channelling, protection, negative energy, clarity, wisdom, concentration, learning, spirit work, communication, astral travel, divination, dreams, harmony

Energy	Projective, Receptive
Planet	Sun, Moon
Element	Fire, Water
Zodiac	Leo, Gemini, Capricorn

Quartz (smoky)

Quartz (smoky) magical properties

Grounding, centring, focus, negative energy, decisions, cooperation, creativity, emotions, depression, anxiety, jealousy, nature, protection, calming, manifestation, wishes, divination, meditation, insight, guidance, uplifting, fears, relaxation, releasing, abundance, luck, prosperity

Energy	Receptive

Element	Earth
Planet	Saturn, Jupiter
Zodiac	Capricorn, Sagittarius

Waning Gibbous Moon Meditation

Find a place where you won't be disturbed and make yourself comfortable. If you have a safe place to sit outside at night time then it would be perfect to do so, otherwise indoors is just fine. Close your eyes and focus on your breathing, deep breaths in and deep breaths out.

As your world around you dissipates you find yourself standing inside a stone columned temple. Pillars around you and a stone wall behind you. Above your head is open to the sky.

It is dark and the deep indigo blue sky is scattered with stars.

You can see the large crescent of the waning gibbous Moon hanging in the sky.

Investigate the temple; running along the back wall is a ledge set out as an altar with candles, tapers and bowls of herbs and spices. Dishes sit filled with sweet smelling incense on top of smouldering charcoal.

In front of the altar are piles of brightly coloured cushions.

You sit comfortably in front of the central altar.

Take a fresh candle from the side and light it with a taper. Place it on the altar in front of you.

Take a handful of herbs and spices and add them to the charcoal, do you recognize any of them?

Breathe in the scent from the incense and watch the smoke as it swirls and twists into the air.

Now sit and watch the flame of your candle as it flickers.

Sit quietly and think about what you would like to let go of. Old feelings and emotions that are unhealthy, that you have held on to. Negative emotions or feelings you don't want or need.

Take a pinch of herbs from the dishes on the altar, one pinch for each feeling, memory, thought or emotion you would like to release. Throw the herbs into the fire and watch them burn away. Repeat as many times as you need to. Once you are done, take a moment to think about positive memories, fill the void you have created with happy vibes.

When you are ready, get up and head to the other side of the temple.

Laid out in front of you is a large garden. Lit by flaming torches lining each side, stretching out into the far distance.

A large wooden planter sits to one side. It is filled with large plants but they appear to have too many side shoots and won't produce strong fruits if not sorted. Carefully pinch out the side shoots, leaving the main stronger ones to grow and bear fruit. Throw the pinched outside shoots onto the ground.

Beside it is a watering can, pick up the can and water the soil.

Sit quietly in the darkness and look out over the garden.

What do you see growing in the light of the torches? Can you see or hear any wildlife? Sit for a while…take some time to look and listen.

When you are ready, walk back to the temple and over to the altar and snuff out your candle.

Slowly and gently come back to this reality. Open your eyes and wriggle your fingers and toes. Have something to eat and drink and write down any important notes.

Waning Gibbous Ritual for Releasing

To enable good things to come our way, we need to have a clear out. Allowing negative energy and bad cycles to fester is not good. This ritual will help you let it all go, paving the way for new and positive energy to flow right in.

You will need:

Representations for the four quarters, if using
Central candle for deity, if using
Matches or lighter

Safe holders for candles, if using
Smudge bundle or incense for cleansing and purifying (I suggest sage, rosemary, mint or mugwort)
If you don't want to use smoke, this is a perfect time to work with Moon water instead.

For the spell:

A black or dark coloured candle
Slips of paper
Pen
Dried herbs, such as bay, eucalyptus, hyssop, jasmine, marjoram or sage.
A cauldron or fireproof dish
Piece of board, thick card or tile – something you don't mind being ruined!

Cast the circle

Walking deosil (clockwise) around the circle.

With the power of the Moon
I cast this circle to attune
Magic creating a boundary to last
This Moon circle is now cast

Call the quarters

Facing North

I call upon the element of earth
May you bring your energy of grounding and stability to this rite
Earth, I welcome you

Facing East

I call upon the element of air

May you bring your energy of intellect and inspiration to this rite
Air, I welcome you

Facing South

I call upon the element of fire,
May you bring your energy of passion and power to this rite
Fire, I welcome you

Facing West

I call upon the element of water,
May you bring your energy of emotions and cleansing to this rite
Water, I welcome you

Deity
Facing centre

I call upon the powerful and destructive goddess Kali Ma
And ask that you bring the energy of transformation, releasing and cleansing to this rite.
Kali Ma, I honour your presence

Spell work: Start this spell work by lighting your smudge bundle or incense. Waft the smoke all over your body, start at your feet, work up each leg, your torso, each arm, your hands, your neck and over your head. If you are using Moon water, sprinkle droplets of water instead.

As you smudge, say:

Purifying magic, power of the Moon
Align my energy, bring me in tune
Cleanse my energy, allow it to flow
Moon magic power make it so

Light your candle. Place your board, card or tile in front of you. Write the first thing, bad habit, emotion, feeling you want to release onto a slip of paper. Place the slip on the board. Carefully take the candle and drip some wax onto the paper. As you do so, visualise that energy leaving you, let go of it, release it and allow it to flow into the wax. Say:

Candle wax allowed to flow
Negative energy let it go

Write on another slip of paper (the same as before or another situation/emotion if you need to) Place that paper on top of the last one and drip more wax on top. Repeat the chant. Keep going with this process until you feel you are finished. Placing each slip of paper on top of the last and melting more wax on top. When you feel you are finished, say:

All that no longer serves is now released from me
Replaced with happy and positive energy
Make it so

Snuff out the candle. Throw the paper/wax pile into the trash or if you have a bonfire or hearth fire it can be burnt.

Feast: Eat and drink something to celebrate your ritual and to help you ground. Sprinkle some of the drink and food onto the earth after the ritual as an offering to deity.

Deity

I thank the powerful and destructive goddess Kali Ma
For bringing the energy of transformation, releasing and cleansing to this rite.
Kali Ma, I honour you and ask that your energy continue with me as long as is needed.

With blessings and thanks, I bid you farewell

Release the quarters

Facing West

I thank the element of water,
For bringing your energy of emotions and cleansing to this rite
Water, I bid you farewell

Facing South

I thank the element of fire,
For bringing your energy of passion and power to this rite
Fire, I bid you farewell

Facing East

I thank the element of air
For bringing your energy of intellect and inspiration to this rite
Air, I bid you farewell

Facing North

I thank the element of earth
For bringing your energy of grounding and stability to this rite
Earth, I bid you farewell

Close the circle

Walking widdershins (anti clockwise) around the circle

I thank the power of the Moon
I uncast this circle but stay in tune
Magic unties the boundary to last
This Moon circle is now uncast

Waning Gibbous Moon Tarot Cards

Tarot cards and oracle cards can be used as a focal point for meditation or as a key component to spell work. These cards are particularly associated with this Moon phase but trust your intuition about which ones to use.

Knowledge and Wisdom: The Hermit, High Priestess, The Moon, The Magician, The Hierophant, Wheel of Fortune, Two of Pentacles, Ace of Swords, Page of Pentacles.
Emotions: The Empress, Queen of Cups.
Decisions: Justice, The Hermit, The Star, The Lovers, The Hanged Man, The Devil, Judgement, Two of Pentacles, Two of Swords, Seven of Swords, King of Swords, Seven of Cups.
Overcoming obstacles: The Chariot, Strength, Death, Temperance, Ace of Swords, Six of Swords, Six of Wands, Three of Cups.
Releasing: Hanged Man, Death, The Devil, The Tower, Four of Swords, Six of Swords.
Bad habits, to overcome: Strength, Temperance, Judgement, The World.

Waning Gibbous Moon Deities

Trust your intuition when working with deities, but please do your research before you call upon any of them. Make sure you know their history, personality and story before you work with them. Here are my suggestions for deities to work with for this Moon phase:

Artemis – Greek goddess associated with the crescent Moon, she is goddess of the hunt and rules over forest and animals. Artemis protects those in childbirth and young girls. She is a strong, independent virgin goddess. Usually depicted holding a bow and arrow. Call upon her for: Warrior, strength, courage, night magic, protection, independence, defence, justice, nature.

Athene/Athena – Greek goddess of weaving, a trait often connected with the Moon. She is a goddess of wisdom and a full–on warrior gal complete with protection, defence and all the hero stuff. Her skills also cover cunning, metal work and weapons. Basically, don't mess with her. Call upon Athene for: protection, courage, leadership, victory, discipline, control, wisdom, defence, cunning.

Epona – Celtic/Saxon/Gaulish goddess of horses. Ancient Britains gave her the title 'Rigantona' which translates as Great Queen. Call upon her for: Protection, animals, love, fertility, providence, leadership, authority.

Hekate – Greek goddess of the dark Moon. She covers new beginnings and magic of all kinds. She walks the ancient roads and pathways, particularly associated with crossroads, those where three roads cross. She forms a triad with Persephone and Demeter, she being the Crone aspect. She guards the spirit world and wields power over all realms. She is one seriously intimidating goddess, but wise beyond words. Call upon her for: Moon magic, witchcraft, herb magic, necromancy, protection, prosperity, new beginnings, decisions, mysteries, knowledge, learning, inner work, shadow work.

Kali/Kali Ma – Hindu goddess of time, change and destruction and the Divine Mother. She has blue black skin, red eyes and four arms. Often seen with skulls hanging around her neck. This is a real kick butt, no messing kind of gal. She is a forceful destroyer but brings rebirth with it, she is the cycle of destruction and creation. Call upon her for: Death and rebirth, cycles, time, happiness, courage, hope, change, cleansing, transformation, destruction, fear, knowledge, creativity.

Kuan Yin – Chinese/Buddhist goddess of mercy who is probably one of the most chilled out and relaxed deities ever. This beautiful goddess hears all your prayers and responds to each and every request for help. She needs some kind of medal…

Call upon her for: Kindness, magic, health, healing, fertility, children, sympathy, support, suffering, encouragement, enlightenment, spirituality, protection.

Lucina – Roman goddess of light. She also covers childbirth. Possibly later merged with Juno and/or Diana. She may even have been converted, becoming St Lucy. An ancient bronze mask believed to depict Juno Lucina shows her with a tiny crescent Moon engraved on her forehead. Call upon her for: Charity, protection, health, healing, kindness, banishing, fertility, well–being.

Luna – Roman goddess of the Moon. Depicted as a beautiful woman with the power to ease childbirth and bring about love. She carries a very strong feminine energy. If you want an answer to a problem, then call upon this lovely lady to bring you the answer in your dreams, it is her speciality. Her Greek equivalent is Selene. Call upon her for: Feminine energy, water magic, safety, travel, intuition, blue Moon magic, protection, illusion, truth, love, psychic abilities, dreams, solutions.

Parvati – Hindu goddess of the crescent Moon. Oh, this goddess has all the feminine wiles and knows how to use them. She is maiden to the Mother Durga and Crone Kali. She can charm the secrets out of the trees. Call upon her for: Power, creativity, new beginnings, victory, feminine energy, beauty, charm, secrets, the arts, fertility, cleansing, devotion.

Rhiannon – if you aren't singing the Fleetwood Mac song right now, you need to… A Welsh goddess and great Queen of Wales. She brings peace, comfort and patience. If you are looking for magical enchantments, then she has a bounty of them. Call upon her for: Patience, comfort, peace, magic, movement, relaxation, communication, fertility, leadership, spirit work, motivation, dream work.

THIRD QUARTER MOON

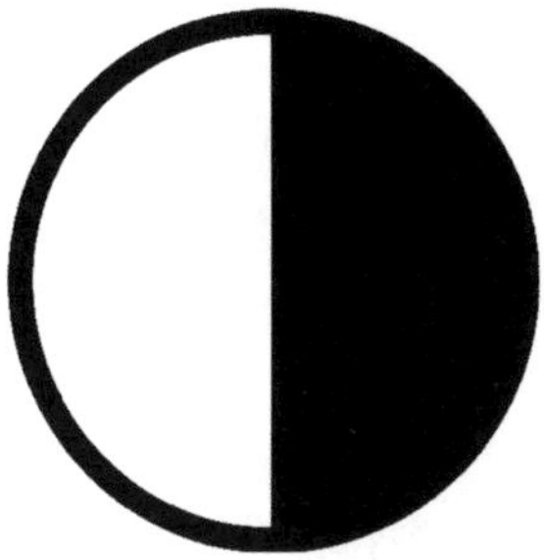

Third quarter Moon as she is slipping away
Balance, adjust and keep negative energy at bay
Break bad habits and get set to release
Clear out the old so that you may now find peace

The Moon is now only showing a quarter of its face, heading to dark. This phase occurs when the opposite half of the Moon is illuminated, compared to the first quarter Moon. And like the first quarter, we actually see what looks like half the Moon.

Third Quarter Moon Magic

Re–evaluate, balance, re–orientate, let go, adjustments, challenges, decreasing, forgiveness, cleansing, purification, emotions, decisions, break habits, reduce, reflection, self–care, rest, release and directions. Really tie up all those loose ends, finish things completely and tidy up. Break negative patterns and release…

- As well as emotional de–cluttering, clear out your physical space too. Sort through cupboards and closets and donate unwanted items to charity.
- Look at your life closely and see what no longer serves you, you may need to cut some ties.

- Write down all the things you want to release and let go of. Stand outside under the Moon and read the list aloud. Leave the list outside to charge with the Moon energy, or inside on a window sill. Then place the list on your altar.
- Create a mind map of how you would like your life to be and what you need to release to achieve it. Take a clean sheet of paper and write your goal in the centre, then just jot down any words or thoughts on the paper, connected with that goal. Don't think too hard, just let the words hit the paper. You can make sense of it afterwards.
- Meditate sitting under the Moon, outside if you have a safe place, or inside by a window. Just sit quietly and focus on the Moon and the phase she is in. Ask her what guidance she has for you.

Third Quarter Moon Colours

You must work with the colours that you associate with this Moon phase, but here are my suggestions:

- White
- Pale blue
- Pink

Plants for the Third Quarter Moon

You can work with any plants that you feel drawn to, but these are my suggestions. Also check out the food section for herbs, spices and foods that can also work in incense blends or spell workings:

Alexanders

(Smyrnium olusatrum)
Alexanders Magical Properties:
Sea magic, intuition, emotions, cleansing, releasing
Element – Water

Gender – Masculine

Alyssum

(Alyssum spp. & Lobularia spp)

Alyssum Magical Properties:

Protection, Maiden magic, peace, calming, balance, spirituality

Element – Air

Gender – Feminine

Birch

(Betula pendula, Betula pubescens, Betula lenta, Betula alba)

Birch Magical Properties:

Purification, protection, exorcism, new beginnings, courage, fertility, love, release

Ruling planet – Venus, Moon, Jupiter

Sign – Sagittarius

Element – Water, Air

Gender – Feminine

Carnation

(Dianthus carphyllus)

Carnation Magical Properties:

Healing, strength, protection, release, courage

Ruling planet – Sun

Element – Fire

Gender – Masculine

Celandine

(Chelidonium majus)

Celandine Magical Properties:

Happiness, protection, release, escape, legal matters

Ruling planet – Sun

Element – Fire

Gender – Masculine

Cypress

(Cupressus sempervirens)

Cypress Magical Properties:

Release, binding, grief, protection, healing

Ruling planet – Saturn

Sign – Aquarius

Element – Earth

Gender – Feminine

Elm

(Ulmus campestris)

Elm Magical Properties:

Love, balance, luck, energy, psychic powers

Ruling planet – Saturn, Mercury

Element – Water

Gender – Feminine

Holly

(Ilex aquifolium, Ilex opaca)

Holly Magical Properties:

Protection, luck, dreams, balance, success

Ruling planet – Mars, Saturn

Element – Fire

Gender – Masculine

Honeysuckle

(Lonicera caprifolium, Lonicera japonica, Lonicera periclymenum)

Honeysuckle Magical Properties:

Prosperity, psychic powers, protection, balance, lust, meditation, memory

Ruling planet – Jupiter

Sign – Gemini, Cancer

Element – Earth

Gender – Masculine

Lungwort

(Pulmonaria officinalis)

Lungwort Magical Properties:

Healing, cleansing, releasing, calming

Ruling planet – Mercury

Sign – Taurus, Pisces

Element – Earth

Gender – Masculine

Patchouli

(Pogostemon)

Patchouli Magical Properties:

Grounding, Earth magic, prosperity, money, protection, sex magic, balance, calm

Ruling planet – Saturn

Sign – Virgo

Element – Earth

Gender – Feminine

Rue

(Ruta graveolens)

Rue Magical Properties:

Protection, health, healing, purification, balance, clarity, anxiety, hex breaking

Ruling planet – Mars, Sun

Sign – Leo

Element – Fire

Gender – Masculine

Self–Heal/All Heal

(Prunella vulgaris)

Self–Heal Magical Properties:

Releasing, cleansing, spirituality, stress, calming, clarity, protection
Ruling planet – Venus
Element – Water
Gender – Feminine

Willow

(Salix alba, Salix fragilis)
Willow Magical Properties:
Love, protection, healing, cleansing, wishes, release, inspiration, intuition
Ruling planet – Moon
Sign – Pisces
Element – Water
Gender – Feminine

Witch Hazel

(Hamamelis virginiea)
Witch Hazel Magical Properties:
Protection, divining, balance, grief
Ruling planet – Sun, Saturn
Sign – Capricorn
Element – Fire
Gender – Masculine

Woodruff

(Asperula odorata, Galium odoratum)
Woodruff Magical Properties:
Protection, money, balance, justice
Ruling planet – Mars
Element – Fire
Gender – Masculine

Third Quarter Moon Incense and Oils

Use equal quantities of each ingredient, or experiment to find a blend you like. If you are creating a loose incense (rather than an essential oil mix) and the blend doesn't include a resin or woody component you might like to add one in to help it burn longer.

- Honeysuckle, cypress, lemon
- Thyme, lemon, cinnamon
- Patchouli, lemon, thyme

Third Quarter Moon Body Care – Bath Melts

Add a melt to your warm bath or use in the shower.

Makes 10 melts.

You will need:

50g/2 oz shea nut butter
50g/2 oz cocoa butter
2 tablespoons solid coconut oil
10 drops patchouli essential oil
6 drops honeysuckle essential oil
4 drops cypress essential oil

Melt the shea butter and cocoa butter in a bowl over a pan of simmering water. Add the coconut oil and stir. Add the essential oils and mix together. Pour into mini cupcake moulds. Leave to cool and set. Keep in the fridge for up to three months.

Third Quarter Moon Foods, Herbs and Spices

Feeling a big sluggish or perhaps you have overeaten? This is a good phase to look at your food intake and maybe make some changes. It doesn't have to be a huge dramatic change, in fact I wouldn't recommend that, take baby steps at first. This is about making sure you have balance in your diet.

Chamomile

(Chameamelum nobile, Anthemis nobilis)

Chamomile Magical Properties:

Sleep, dreams, love, calm, money, relaxation, purification, balancing

Ruling planet – Sun

Sign – Leo

Element – Water

Gender – Masculine

Chives

(Allium schoenoprasum)

Chives Magical Properties:

Exorcism, negative energy, bad habits, protection

Ruling planet – Mars

Element – Fire

Gender – Masculine

Cinnamon

(Cinnamomum zeylanicum, Cinnamomum verum)

Cinnamon Magical Properties:

Success, healing, power, psychic powers, protection, love, focus, lust, spirituality, changes

Ruling planet – Sun

Element – Fire

Gender – Masculine

Coriander

(Coriandrum sativum)

Coriander Magical Properties:

Health, healing, peace, love, release, wealth, protection, negativity

Ruling planet – Mars

Element – Fire

Gender – Masculine

Dates

(Phoenix dactylifera)

Dates Magical Properties:

Spirituality, death & rebirth, offerings

Ruling planet – Sun

Element – Air

Gender – Feminine

Dill

(Anethum graveolens)

Dill Magical Properties:

Protection, love, lust, money, jealousy, balance, clarity, knowledge, magic

Ruling planet –Mercury

Sign – Cancer, Gemini, Leo

Element – Fire

Gender – Masculine

Lemon

(Citrus x lemon)

Lemon Magical Properties:

Purification, Moon magic, happiness, decisions, uplifting, love, protection, friendship, fidelity

Ruling planet – Moon

Element – Water

Gender – Feminine

Liquorice

(Glycyrrhiza glabra)

Liquorice Magical Properties:

Love, passion, balance

Ruling planet – Venus, Mercury

Element – Earth, Water
Gender – Feminine

Mushrooms

Mushrooms Magical Properties:
Strength, courage, magic, balance
Ruling planet – Moon
Element – Earth
Gender – Feminine

Oysters

Oyster Magical Properties:
Passion, balance
Ruling planet – Moon
Element – Water
Gender – Masculine & feminine

Plum

(Prunus spp)
Plum Magical Properties:
Love, spirituality, relaxation, passion, longevity, wisdom, rebirth
Ruling planet – Venus
Element – Water, Air
Gender – Feminine

Pomegranate

(Punica granatum)
Pomegranate Magical Properties:
Growth, fertility, wishes, death, rebirth, new beginnings
Ruling planet – Mercury
Element – Fire, Earth
Gender – Masculine

Thyme

(Thymus vulgaris, Thymus serpyllum)

Thyme Magical Properties:

Healing, health, peace, psychic powers, love, purification, courage, releasing, sleep, beauty

Ruling planet – Venus

Element – Water

Gender – Feminine

Turkey

Turkey Magical Properties:

Motivation, clarity, focus, celebration

Element – Fire, Air

Gender – Masculine

Wheat

(Triticum spp.)

Wheat Magical Properties:

Prosperity, rebirth, abundance, wishes

Ruling planet – Venus

Element – Earth

Gender – Feminine

Third Quarter Moon Recipe – Plum Cake

This is a fabulous recipe that you can adapt to suit most fruits. Rhubarb, apple, peach and apricot all work well too.

300g/10 ½ oz plums or a fruit of your choice
Juice of ½ lemon or lime
165g/5.8 oz self–raising flour
175g/6.1 oz butter, softened
175g/6.1 oz sugar
3 large eggs
2 teaspoons vanilla extract

For the topping:
25g/0.9oz butter
2 tablespoons self–raising flour
1 tablespoon sugar
1 teaspoon ground ginger or cinnamon

Preheat your oven to 180C/350F/Gas 4. Grease and line a 23cm square baking tin with baking parchment.

Prepare your fruit by de–stoning and chopping into bite size pieces. Place the fruit in a bowl and add the lemon or lime juice then stir.

In a separate bowl whisk the flour, butter, sugar, eggs and vanilla extract.

Fold in half the fruit.

Spoon into the tin, spread evenly.

Sprinkle the remaining fruit over the top.

For the topping: Rub the butter into the flour, stir in the sugar and ginger or cinnamon. Sprinkle over the cake mixture.

Bake for 40–50 minutes.

Third Quarter Moon Teas

Herbal teas can be purchased in tea bag form or ready–made loose blends and there are some fantastic brands out there. However, I have also purchased herbal teas that tasted like sweepings from the factory floor. Check the ingredients when purchasing ready–made herbal teas, make sure they include only the items that the tea is supposed to taste of. Some companies bulk out with cheaper items. Herbal tea is very easy to make if you grow fresh herbs or if you have a supply of dried herbs and dried fruits. Experiment with different flavours. The basic rule is one or two teaspoons of dried herbs to a mug full of boiling water, brew for at least five minutes then strain. If you are using fresh herbs you may need a slightly larger quantity. Herbal tea can be drunk hot (obviously), left and poured over ice as a cold drink or even used as a hair rinse. Drop it into your bath water or add to a bucket of hot water and use as a floor or surface wash.

Please be careful and make sure you have identified the herbs you use correctly. Never ingest herbs that you are not sure about. Always check with a qualified practitioner if you are on medication, have health problems or are pregnant.

I have given some of my favourite recipes here, adjust the amounts of each ingredient to suit your own taste. If the blend isn't sweet enough you can add a teaspoon of sugar or honey.

It's all about the balance tea:
Liquorice
Mint

Decisions, decisions tea:
Black tea
Lemon

Take on the challenge tea:
Thyme
Black pepper

Crystals for the Third Quarter Moon

You can work with any crystals you feel drawn to, but these are my suggestions:

Agate (banded)

Agate (banded) magical properties

Perception, wisdom, balance, spirituality, goodwill, peace, memory, concentration, stamina, truth, clarity, honesty, courage, protection, calming, sleep, dreams, strength, longevity, nature, love, anti–stress, energy

Energy: Projective
Element: Fire

Planet: Mercury

Amber

Amber magical properties:

Manifesting, energy, beauty, Sun magic, power, wishes, intellect, clarity, wisdom, balance, purification, protection, psychic abilities, healing, calm, patience, love, sensuality, good luck, marriage, abundance, success, vitality, joy, sexuality, cleansing, stress, harmony, creativity

Energy: Projective
Element: Fire, Spirit
Planet: Sun
Zodiac: Leo

Aventurine (green)

Aventurine (green) magical properties

Balance, decisions, motivation, leadership, dreams, visualisation, creativity, luck, money, anxiety, calm, opportunities, happiness, adventure, love, courage, truth, comfort, support, healing, peace, connection, perception, intellect, psychic abilities

Energy: Projective
Element: Air
Planet: Mercury, Mars
Zodiac: Aries

Carnelian

Carnelian magical properties

Grounding, protection, calm, concentration, confidence, self–worth, success, courage, creativity, negative energy, direction, control, organisation, opportunity, planning, psychic protection, jealousy, hate, harmony, depression, doubt, patience, stability, vitality, motivation, stamina, passion, truth, love, faith, honesty, trust, luck, abundance

Energy: Projective

Element: Fire
Planet: Sun
Zodiac: Taurus, Leo
Birthstone: May, June, July, August

Chrysoprase

Chrysoprase magical properties

Courage, strength, wisdom, releasing, selfishness, imagination, happiness, success, balance, break barriers, protection, truth, healing, luck, prosperity, marriage, negative energy, transformation, love

Energy: Receptive
Element: Earth
Planet: Venus
Zodiac: Taurus, Cancer

Fluorite

Fluorite magical properties

Magic, imagination, discernment, aptitude, psychic protection, protection, purification, calming, relaxation, tension, anxiety, organisation, structure, challenges, declutter, releasing, support, breaking patterns, intuition, confidence, reassurance, comforting, communication, balance, spirituality, decisions, manifestation, peace, meditation, grounding, healing, cleansing, channelling, past life work, fairy realm, amplifying, memory, power, emotions, depression, stability

Energy: Projective
Element: Water, Air
Planet: Neptune
Zodiac: Scorpio, Aquarius, Pisces

Garnet

Garnet magical properties

Organisation, warrior spirit, protection, love, commitment,

passion, sexuality, sensuality, attraction, depression, spiritual healing, success, self–confidence, energy, inspiration, perception, strength, survival, fear, courage, clarity, challenges, past life work, truth, compassion, deflecting negative energy, gossip, ambition, motivation, goals, purification, cleansing, balance, inner strength, self–empowerment, creativity, confidence, meditation, spirit work, nightmares, journeying, abundance, support

Energy: Projective
Element: Fie
Planet: Mars
Zodiac: Aries, Virgo, Capricorn, Leo, Aquarius
Birthstone: January

Goldstone

Goldstone magical properties

Ambition, luck, goals, determination, persistence, achievements, success, calm, emotions, energy, enthusiastic, confidence, self–belief, inner self, personal development, possibilities, courage, direction, clarity, uplifting, optimism, protection, deflects negative energy, knowledge, perception, manifestation, creativity, faith, energy flow, spirituality, abundance, wealth, grounding, perspective, ambition, drive, ingenuity, money, generosity, willpower, goals, emotions, divination (see also copper for additional magical properties)

Energy: Receptive/Projective
Element: Fire, Earth
Planet: Jupiter, Venus
Zodiac: Sagittarius

Kyanite

Kyanite magical properties

Balance, harmony, calming, connection, psychic abilities, healing, communication, grounding, transformation, meditation, relaxation, luck, growth, leadership, new beginnings, clarity, decisions, stability, truth, vitality, abundance, spirituality, channelling, understanding, dreams

Energy	Receptive
Element	Water
Planet	Jupiter, Venus, Mars
Zodiac	Aries, Libra, Taurus

Lepidolite

Lepidolite magical properties

Transformation, soothing, calming, stress, happiness, changes, emotions, psychic abilities, spirituality, depression, divination, connection, strength, uplifting, luck, hope, balance, peace, sleep, harmony, decisions, addiction, releasing, trust, goals, optimism, patience, dreams, opportunities, support, love

Energy	Receptive
Element	Water
Planet	Jupiter, Neptune
Zodiac	Libra

Moonstone

Moonstone magical properties

New beginnings, Moon magic, intuition, calming, psychic abilities, balance, harmony, wishes, cleansing, uplifting, hope, meditation, emotions, love, divination, spirituality, wealth, truth, healing, sensuality, insight, peace, wisdom, communication, confidence, abundance, prosperity, dreams, fertility, travel

Energy	Receptive
Element	Water
Planet	Moon
Zodiac	Cancer, Libra, Scorpio
Birthstone	June, September

Obsidian (black)

Obsidian (black) magical properties

Truth, healing, clarity, illusions, breaking barriers, integrity, grounding, centring, strength, courage, protection, cleansing, meditation, stress, calming, relaxation, depression, anxiety, wealth, luck, focus, emotions, power, determination, success, patience, perseverance, releasing, spirit work, spirituality, challenges, past life work, divination

Energy	Projective
Element	Fire, Earth, Water
Planet	Saturn, Jupiter
Zodiac	Sagittarius

Petrified Wood

Petrified Wood magical properties

Stability, grounding, calming, anxiety, fears, meditation, determination, decisions, strength, courage, patience, transformation, perseverance, success, luck, emotions, wisdom, past life work, insight, leadership

Energy	Receptive
Element	Earth, Spirit
Planet	Earth, Sun
Zodiac	All

Quartz (rose)

Quartz (rose) magical properties

Love, happiness, emotions, spirituality, growth, fears, healing, sexuality, passion, calming, soothing, stress, depression, sleep, luck, wisdom, inspiration, success, intuition, grounding, balance, prosperity, self–esteem, harmony, trust, jealousy, gossip, beauty, peace, cleansing, fertility

Energy	Receptive
Element	Earth, Water
Planet	Venus, Moon

Zodiac	Taurus

Rhodochrosite

Rhodochrosite magical properties

Power, potential, strength, confidence, healing, new beginnings, breaking barriers, releasing, joy, happiness, creativity, determination, manifestation, prosperity, abundance, love, emotions, peace, renewal, connection, balance, spirituality, harmony, energy

Energy	Projective
Element	Fire
Planet	Mars, Jupiter
Zodiac	Scorpio, Leo

Sodalite

Sodalite magical properties

Creativity, communication, peace, friendship, clarity, truth, connection, knowledge, wisdom, emotions, balance, divination, psychic abilities, cleansing, confidence, fears, love, intuition, decisions, perseverance, anxiety, insight, organisation, self–esteem, releasing, understanding, harmony, learning, dreams, meditation

Energy	Receptive
Element	Water
Planet	Jupiter, Venus
Zodiac	Sagittarius

Tiger's eye

Tiger's eye magical properties

Amplification, balance, harmony, releasing, fears, anxiety, courage, strength, self–confidence, focus, creativity, optimism, self–worth, protection, psychic abilities, healing, wealth, money, opportunity, abundance, prosperity, luck, success, commitment, determination, support, clarity, vitality, motivation, grounding

Energy Projective
Element Fire, Earth
Planet Sun
Zodiac Leo, Capricorn

Unakite

Unakite magical properties

Love, happiness, growth, wealth, success, harmony, decisions, support, balance, emotions, stability, confidence, strength, anxiety, nature, courage, transformation, releasing, spirituality

Energy Receptive
Element Fire, Water
Planet Mars, Venus, Pluto
Zodiac Scorpio

Third Quarter Moon Meditation

Find a place where you won't be disturbed and make yourself comfortable. If you have a safe place to sit outside at night time then it would be perfect to do so, otherwise indoors is just fine. Close your eyes and focus on your breathing, deep breaths in and deep breaths out.

As your world around you dissipates you find yourself standing inside a stone columned temple. Pillars around you and a stone wall behind you. Above your head is open to the sky.

It is dark and the deep indigo blue sky is scattered with stars.

You can see a waning crescent shape Moon hanging in the sky.

Investigate the temple; running along the back wall is a ledge set out as an altar with candles, tapers and bowls of herbs and spices. Dishes sit filled with sweet smelling incense on top of smouldering charcoal.

In front of the altar are piles of brightly coloured cushions.

You sit comfortably in front of the central altar.

Take a fresh candle from the side and light it with a taper. Place it

on the altar in front of you.

Take a handful of herbs and spices and add them to the charcoal, do you recognize any of them?

Breathe in the scent from the incense and watch the smoke as it swirls and twists into the air.

Now sit and watch the flame of your candle as it flickers.

You notice a pile of kindling wood set out beside the fire. Pick up some of the pieces, break each one in half. Each one represents a bad habit or cycle you want to break. Throw the broken pieces into the flames of the fire and watch them burn.

Repeat as many times as you need. Then take a moment to think about your good habits and what positive cycles you can replace the bad ones with.

When you are ready, get up and head to the other side of the temple.

Laid out in front of you is a large garden. Lit by flaming torches lining each side, stretching out into the far distance.

A large wooden planter sits to one side. It is filled with tall green blossoming plants. Each one is covered in beautiful flowers. Take a moment to breath in the scent.

Beside it is a watering can, pick up the can and water the soil.

You notice a snail making its way across the planter, pick it up and put it on the garden path.

Sit quietly in the darkness and look out over the garden.

What do you see growing in the light of the torches? Can you see or hear any wildlife? Sit for a while…take some time to look and listen.

When you are ready, walk back to the temple and over to the altar and snuff out your candle.

Slowly and gently come back to this reality. Open your eyes and wriggle your fingers and toes. Have something to eat and drink and write down any important notes.

Third Quarter Moon Ritual to break bad habits

We all have them; we all repeat them. Bad habits and negative cycles are very easy to fall into, getting out of them is a little trickier. This ritual will help you break the chain.

You will need:

Representations for the four quarters, if using
Central candle for deity, if using
Matches or lighter
Safe holders for the candles, if using
Something to eat and drink

For the spell:

Black or dark coloured candle
A piece of thread long enough to tie around the candle
Essential oil such as thyme or fennel
Tarot card such as Strength, Temperance, Judgement, The World
Crystal such as smoky quartz, aragonite, malachite, tourmaline or tiger's eye

Cast the circle

Walking deosil (clockwise) around the circle.

With the power of the Moon
I cast this circle to attune
Magic creating a boundary to last
This Moon circle is now cast

Call the quarters

Facing North

I call upon the element of earth

May you bring your energy of grounding and stability to this rite
Earth, I welcome you

Facing East

I call upon the element of air
May you bring your energy of intellect and inspiration to this rite
Air, I welcome you

Facing South

I call upon the element of fire,
May you bring your energy of passion and power to this rite
Fire, I welcome you

Facing West

I call upon the element of water,
May you bring your energy of emotions and cleansing to this rite
Water, I welcome you

Deity
Facing centre

I call upon the wise and knowledgeable god Thoth
And ask that you bring the energy of balance, judgement and magic to this rite.
Thoth, I honour your presence

Spell work: Dress your candle with essential oil. Traditionally If you are doing a spell that is getting rid of something, rub oil from the centre upward to the top and then from the centre down to the bottom. Place your candle safely in front of you and put the crystal in front of that. Pop the tarot card behind the candle as a focal point. Tie the piece of thread around the candle, as you do so, say:

Threads of bad habits tie me down
Time to let go and change around
Fire will burn and let it go
Break the cycle and make it so

As you tie the thread think about the bad habit or cycle that you want to let go of or break.

Light the candle and watch the flame.

As the flame reaches the thread and burns through it visualise yourself breaking free from negative cycles and habits.

Once the thread has burnt you can snuff the candle and dispose of the left over.

Focus on the tarot card and take hold of the crystal in your hand and visualise yourself setting new, positive and healthy cycles and habits.

Keep the crystal with you as a reminder.

Feast: Eat and drink something to celebrate your ritual and to help you ground. Sprinkle some of the drink and food onto the earth after the ritual as an offering to deity.

Deity

I thank the wise and knowledgeable god Thoth

For bringing the energy of balance, judgement and magic to this rite.

Thoth, I honour you and ask that your energy continue with me as long as is needed.

With blessings and thanks, I bid you farewell

Release the quarters

Facing West

I thank the element of water,
For bringing your energy of emotions and cleansing to this rite
Water, I bid you farewell

Facing South

I thank the element of fire,
For bringing your energy of passion and power to this rite
Fire, I bid you farewell

Facing East

I thank the element of air
For bringing your energy of intellect and inspiration to this rite
Air, I bid you farewell

Facing North

I thank the element of earth
For bringing your energy of grounding and stability to this rite
Earth, I bid you farewell

Close the circle
Walking widdershins (anti clockwise) around the circle

I thank the power of the Moon
I uncast this circle but stay in tune
Magic unties the boundary to last
This Moon circle is now uncast

Third Quarter Moon Tarot Cards

Tarot cards and oracle cards can be used as a focal point for meditation or as a key component to spell work. These cards are particularly associated with this Moon phase but trust your intuition about which ones to use.

Balance: The Lovers, Justice, Temperance, Two of Swords, Four of Wands, Two of Cups.
Releasing: Hanged Man, Death, The Devil, The Tower, Four of Swords, Six of Swords.
Changes: Wheel of Fortune, The Magician, Hanged Man, Death, The Tower, Judgement, The World, Knight of Swords, Eight of Wands.
Challenges: The Magician, Queen of Swords, Two of Wands.
Decisions: Justice, The Hermit, The Star, The Lovers, The Hanged Man, The Devil, Judgement, Two of Pentacles, Two of Swords, Seven of Swords, King of Swords, Seven of Cups.
Overcoming obstacles: The Chariot, Strength, Death, Temperance, Ace of Swords, Six of Swords, Six of Wands, Three of Cups.
Bad habits, to overcome: Strength, Temperance, Judgement, The World.

Third Quarter Moon Deities

Trust your intuition when working with deities, but please do your research before you call upon any of them. Make sure you know their history, personality and story before you work with them. Here are my suggestions for deities to work with for this Moon phase:

Coyolxauhqui – Aztec Moon goddess. Her name translates as 'painted with bells'. Apparently in most images she is wearing bells on her cheeks, which must be terribly uncomfortable. When the full Moon rises you can see the bells as rosy red. In a bit of a misunderstanding Coyolxauhqui had her head cut off, which was flung up into the sky, where it became the Moon. Call upon her for: Moon magic, family issues, balance, differences.

Hekate – Greek goddess of the dark Moon. She covers new beginnings and magic of all kinds. She walks the ancient roads and pathways, particularly associated with crossroads, those where three roads cross. She forms a triad with Persephone and Demeter, she being the Crone aspect. She guards the spirit world and wields power over all realms. She is one seriously intimidating goddess, but wise beyond words. Call upon her for: Moon magic, witchcraft, herb magic, necromancy, protection, prosperity, new beginnings, decisions, mysteries, knowledge, learning, inner work, shadow work.

Hera – Greek Olympian Queen of gods, she covers marriage, childbirth and looking after women (she's got her hands full then). Although she can help when called upon, she has a jealous side and can be vengeful particularly when infidelity is involved. Call upon her for: Love, humour, forgiveness, romance, creativity, marriage, strength, courage, self–confidence, jealousy.

Kali/Kali Ma – Hindu goddess of time, change and destruction and the Divine Mother. She has blue black skin, red eyes and four arms. Often seen with skulls hanging around her neck. This is a real kick butt, no messing kind of gal. She is a forceful destroyer but brings rebirth with it, she is the cycle of destruction and creation. Call upon her for: Death and rebirth, cycles, time, happiness, courage, hope, change, cleansing, transformation, destruction, fear, knowledge, creativity.

Ma'at – Egyptian goddess of the crescent Moon, order and balance. Think 'strict school headmistress', she dishes out the justice as she sees fit, whether you are a deity or a mere mortal. Her name translates as 'truth/that which is straight'. If you are looking for balance between work and home life or any kind of justice, Ma'at should be on your speed dial. Call upon her for: Justice, balance, freedom, new beginnings, morals, organisation, law, promises, fairness, truth, oaths, harmony, honesty.

Parvati – Hindu goddess of the crescent Moon. Oh, this goddess has all the feminine wiles and knows how to use them. She is maiden to the Mother Durga and Crone Kali. She can charm the secrets out of the trees. Call upon her for: Power, creativity, new beginnings, victory, feminine energy, beauty, charm, secrets, the arts, fertility, cleansing, devotion.

Thoth – Egyptian ibis headed Moon god. He is a seriously studious dude. God of writing and wisdom he is considered to be one of the most important gods of ancient Egypt (he didn't let it go to his head though). Call upon him for: Knowledge, Moon magic, wisdom, learning, intellect, meditation, logic, reason, magic, secrets, balance, judgement.

WANING CRESCENT MOON

Waning crescent Moon up on high
Slowly slipping down, right out of the sky
Forgive, forget, release and let loose
Break up that which no longer serves any use

You will now only see a crescent Moon in the sky, waning because it is getting smaller, heading towards the dark Moon. The Sun illuminates less than half of the visible part of the Moon. Sometimes referred to as a balsamic Moon, balsamic comes from the from Latin balsamum, meaning soothing or restorative.

Waning Crescent Moon Magic

Soothing, healing, acceptance, rest, recuperate, forgiveness, closure, reflection, surrender, hope, dreams, rest, break bad habits and endings. Tie up loose ends from the last Moon cycle, seriously...don't mess about, get those things done and dusted! The waning crescent energy can really give a boost to releasing and breaking negative cycles, jump onboard.

- Write down all the goals and desires you have to end or release things. Stand outside under the Moon and read the list aloud. Leave the list outside to charge with the Moon energy, or inside on a window sill. Then place the list on your altar.

- Meditate sitting under the Moon, outside if you have a safe place, or inside by a window. Just sit quietly and focus on the Moon and the phase she is in. Ask her what guidance she has for you.
- Create a mind map of what you can do to help heal yourself and to create a better life environment. Take a clean sheet of paper and write your goal in the centre, then just jot down any words or thoughts on the paper, connected with that goal. Don't think too hard, just let the words hit the paper. You can make sense of it afterwards.
- Meditate sitting under the Moon, outside if you have a safe place, or inside by a window. Just sit quietly and focus on the Moon and the phase she is in. Ask her what guidance she has for you.

Waning Crescent Moon Colours

You must work with the colours that you associate with this Moon phase, but here are my suggestions:

- Blue
- Pale green
- Pale yellow

Plants for the Waning Crescent Moon

You can work with any plants that you feel drawn to, but these are my suggestions. Also check out the food section for herbs, spices and foods that can also work in incense blends or spell workings:

Anemone

(Anemone pulsatilla)

Anemone Magical Properties:

Protection, healing, health

Ruling planet – Mars
Element – Fire
Gender – Masculine

Angelica

(Angelica archangelica)
Angelica Magical Properties:
Protection, healing, exorcism, divination, prosperity, luck, hex breaking, courage
Ruling planet – Sun, Venus
Sign – Gemini, Cancer, Leo, Libra
Element – Fire
Gender – Masculine

Ash

(Fraxinus excelsior or F. americana)
Ash Magical Properties:
Protection, prosperity, dispels negativity, improves health, sea magic, dreams, love, intuition.
Ruling planet – Sun and Neptune
Element – Fire and Water
Gender – Masculine

Burdock

(Arctium lappa)
Burdock Magical Properties:
Protection, healing, cleansing
Ruling planet – Venus
Sign – Leo, Libra
Element – Water
Gender – Feminine

Carnation

(Dianthus carphyllus)

Carnation Magical Properties:

Healing, strength, protection, release, courage
Ruling planet – Sun
Element – Fire
Gender – Masculine

Comfrey

(Symphytum officinale)
Comfrey Magical Properties:
Money, travel, protection, healing, hex breaking, bringing together
Ruling planet – Saturn
Sign – Capricorn
Element – Water
Gender – Feminine

Dock

(Rumex spp. Crispus, R. obtusifolius)
Dock Magical Properties:
Money, healing, fertility, cleansing, love, purification
Ruling planet – Jupiter
Element – Air
Gender – Masculine

Elder

(Sambucus nigra/Canadensis)
Elder Magical Properties:
Protection, healing, faeries, purification, intuition, exorcism, hex breaking, rebirth
Ruling planet – Venus
Sign – Sagittarius, Aquarius, Libra
Element – Water
Gender – Feminine

Feverfew

(Tanacetum parthenium, Chrysanthemum parthenium)

Feverfew Magical Properties:

Protection, peace, health, purification

Ruling planet – Venus

Sign – Aries, Sagittarius, Libra

Element – Water

Gender – Masculine

Hyssop

(Hyssopus officinalis)

Hyssop Magical Properties:

Purification, protection, healing

Ruling planet – Jupiter, Moon

Sign – Cancer

Element – Fire

Gender – Masculine

Juniper

(Juniperus communes)

Juniper Magical Properties:

Love, exorcism, healing, protection, justice, stolen items, purification, psychic powers, clarity

Ruling planet – Sun, Jupiter, Moon

Sign – Aries

Element – Fire

Gender – Masculine

Lungwort

(Pulmonaria officinalis)

Lungwort Magical Properties:

Healing, cleansing, releasing, calming

Ruling planet – Mercury

Sign – Taurus, Pisces

Element – Earth
Gender – Masculine

Mugwort

(Artemisia vulgaris)
Mugwort Magical Properties:
Strength, psychic powers, protection, dreams, healing, astral travel, feminine energy, cleansing
Ruling planet – Venus, Moon
Sign – Cancer
Element – Earth
Gender – Feminine

Myrrh

(Commiphora myrrha)
Myrrh Magical Properties:
Protection, purification, healing, Crone, Underworld, courage
Ruling planet – Mars, Sun
Sign – Aries, Aquarius
Element – Water
Gender – Feminine

Nettle

(Urtica dioica)
Nettle Magical Properties:
Healing, protection, lust, money, exorcism.
Ruling planet – Mars
Sign – Scorpio, Aries
Element – Fire
Gender – Masculine

Pine

(Pinus)
Pine Magical Properties:

Centring, focus, Dragon magic, protection, truth, abundance, purification, fertility, healing
Ruling planet – Mars, Saturn
Sign – Capricorn
Element – Air, Fire
Gender – Masculine

Rue

(Ruta graveolens)
Rue Magical Properties:
Protection, health, healing, purification, balance, clarity, anxiety, hex breaking
Ruling planet – Mars, Sun
Sign – Leo
Element – Fire
Gender – Masculine

Tansy

(Tanacetum vulgare)
Tansy Magical Properties:
Health, longevity, rebirth, cleansing, protection, travel
Ruling planet – Venus
Sign – Gemini
Element – Water
Gender – Feminine

Violet

(Viola odorata)
Violet Magical Properties:
Love, lust, peace, healing, protection, commitment, death and rebirth
Ruling planet – Venus
Sign – Cancer, Libra
Element – Water

Gender – Feminine

Waning Crescent Moon Incense and Oils

Use equal quantities of each ingredient, or experiment to find a blend you like. If you are creating a loose incense (rather than an essential oil mix) and the blend doesn't include a resin or woody component you might like to add one in to help it burn longer.

- Fennel, mint, lime
- Bay, myrrh, pine
- Rosemary, thyme, fennel, juniper

Waning Crescent Moon Body Care – Bath salts

Add a couple of tablespoons of these bath salts to your bath.

You will need:

450g/16 oz sea salt
225g/8 oz Epsom salt
4 drops myrrh essential oil
2 drops fennel essential oil
1 teaspoon of dried nettle leaves, ground

Mix together, keep in an air–tight jar.

Waning Crescent Moon Foods, Herbs and Spices

Eat foods that heal and soothe not just your body but your mind and soul too. Be kind to yourself and your body. Break bad habits if you have gotten into them. But most importantly this is a phase to eat foods that make you feel good. Some of these foods can also be used in incense blends or spell working.

Bay

(Laurus nobilis)

Bay Magical Properties:

Protection, purification, strength, power, healing, creativity, spirituality, psychic powers

Ruling planet – Sun

Element – Fire

Gender – Masculine

Beer

Beer Magical Properties:

Dreams, purification, offerings

Ruling planet – Mars

Element – Fire

Gender – Masculine (got to be really?)

Coriander

(Coriandrum sativum)

Coriander Magical Properties:

Health, healing, peace, love, release, wealth, protection, negativity

Ruling planet – Mars

Element – Fire

Gender – Masculine

Cucumber

(Cucumis sativus)

Cucumber Magical Properties:

Fertility, emotions, chastity, meditation, spirituality, purification, healing

Ruling planet – Moon

Element – Water

Gender – Feminine

Fennel

(Foeniculum vulgare)

Fennel Magical Properties:

Purification, protection, healing

Ruling planet – Mercury

Element – Fire

Gender – Masculine

Fish

Fish Magical Properties:

Fertility, Prosperity, Abundance, healing, emotions, cleansing, purification

Element – Water

Gender – Feminine

Garlic

(Allium sativum)

Garlic Magical Properties:

Healing, protection, hex breaking, negative energies, lust, strength, courage, depression

Ruling planet – Mars

Element – Fire

Gender – Masculine

Hazelnut

(Corylus)

Hazelnut Magical Properties:

Protection, psychic powers, wisdom, fertility, Faerie, Healing

Ruling planet – Sun, Mercury

Element – Air

Gender – Feminine/Masculine

Lime

(Citrus aurantifolia)

Lime Magical Properties:

Purification, love, healing, protection, energy

Ruling planet –Sun
Element – Fire
Gender – Masculine

Melon

Melon Magical Properties:
Love, chaos, healing, purification
Ruling planet – Moon
Element – Water
Gender – Feminine

Mint

(Mentha spp, Mentha aquatic, Mentha piperita)
Mint Magical Properties:
Money, healing, exorcism, protection, cleansing, calming
Ruling planet – Mercury, Venus
Element – Air
Gender – Masculine

Rosemary

(Rosemarinus officinalis)
Rosemary Magical Properties:
Protection, love, lust, mental powers, exorcism, purification, healing, sleep
Ruling planet – Sun
Element – Fire
Gender – Masculine

Star Anise

(Illicum verum)
Star Anise Magical Properties:
Luck, psychic powers, purification, protection, dreams, spirituality, sleep
Ruling planet – Jupiter

Element – Air
Gender – Masculine

Thyme

(Thymus vulgaris, Thymus serpyllum)
Thyme Magical Properties:
Healing, health, peace, psychic powers, love, purification, courage, releasing, sleep, beauty
Ruling planet – Venus
Element – Water
Gender – Feminine

Waning Crescent Moon Recipe – Orange Rosemary Cupcakes

Rosemary sounds weird in a sweet dish, but it really works. This recipe makes a large batch (24) of cupcakes so it is perfect for family gatherings or rituals.

350g plain/all–purpose flour
2 tablespoons orange zest
1 teaspoon finely chopped fresh rosemary leaves
2 ½ teaspoons baking powder
½ teaspoon salt
225g butter, softened
300g sugar
3 eggs
1 teaspoon vanilla extract
140ml/5 fl oz milk (any kind)
250g icing/powdered sugar
30ml warm water

Preheat your oven to 180C/350F/Gas 4.

Pop paper cases into two muffin trays.

Mix together the flour, orange zest, rosemary, baking powder and salt.

In a separate bowl whisk the butter and sugar until light and fluffy.

Add the eggs, one at a time, whisking between each addition.

Stir in the vanilla extract.

Now add the flour mixture, alternate with the milk a few spoonfuls at a time. Beating between each, until combined.

Spoon the batter into the cupcake cases.

Bake for 20 to 25 minutes.

Cool.

Make the icing by stirring the warm water into the icing sugar a little at a time (you may not need all the water). Stir until smooth. Spoon onto the top of the cupcakes.

Options:

Replace the orange zest with lime or lemon.

Use orange juice instead of water when mixing the icing.

Waning Crescent Moon Teas

Herbal teas can be purchased in tea bag form or ready–made loose blends and there are some fantastic brands out there. However, I have also purchased herbal teas that tasted like sweepings from the factory floor. Check the ingredients when purchasing ready–made herbal teas, make sure they include only the items that the tea is supposed to taste of. Some companies bulk out with cheaper items. Herbal tea is very easy to make if you grow fresh herbs or if you have a supply of dried herbs and dried fruits. Experiment with different flavours. The basic rule is one or two teaspoons of dried herbs to a mug full of boiling water, brew for at least five minutes then strain. If you are using fresh herbs you may need a slightly larger quantity. Herbal tea can be drunk hot (obviously), left and poured over ice as a cold drink or even used as a hair rinse. Drop it into your bath water or add to a bucket of hot water and use as a floor or surface wash.

Please be careful and make sure you have identified the

herbs you use correctly. Never ingest herbs that you are not sure about. Always check with a qualified practitioner if you are on medication, have health problems or are pregnant.

I have given some of my favourite recipes here, adjust the amounts of each ingredient to suit your own taste. If the blend isn't sweet enough you can add a teaspoon of sugar or honey.

Healing tea:
Mint
Rose
Ginger

Soothing tea:
Mint
Blueberry

Forgiveness tea:
Lemon
Marjoram
Orange

Waning Crescent Moon Crystals

You can work with any crystals you feel drawn to, but these are my suggestions:

Amethyst

Amethyst magical properties

Peace, protection, success, good luck, hidden knowledge, legal issues, spirituality, contentment, soothing, relaxation, calm, hope, patience, transformation, changes, breaking patterns, grounding, guilt, overcoming addictions, business matters, judgement, clarity, courage, travel, psychic protection, sleep, anxiety, focus, understanding, happiness, justice, intuition, inspiration, channelling, meditation

Energy: Receptive
Element: Water
Planet: Jupiter, Neptune
Zodiac: Pisces, Scorpio, Sagittarius
Birthstone: February

Bloodstone

Bloodstone magical properties:

Organisation, adaptability, anxiety, clarity, concentration, renewal, energy, self–confidence, connection, calm, protection, breaking barriers, selfishness, mysticism, insight, spirituality, truth, intuition, creativity, guidance, strength, healing, victory, wealth, money, power, invisibility, deception, negative energy, divine connection, past life, dreams

Energy: Projective
Element: Fire, Earth
Planet: Mars
Zodiac: Aries, Pisces, Scorpio
Birthstone: February, March

Hematite

Hematite magical properties

Grounding, money, decisions, manifestation, finances, healing, focus, clarity, stability, protection, balance, divination, problem solving, emotions, self–esteem, productivity, doubt, anxiety, communication, strength

Energy: Projective
Element: Fire, Earth
Planet: Saturn
Zodiac: Aries, Aquarius

Kyanite

Kyanite magical properties

Balance, harmony, calming, connection, psychic abilities,

healing, communication, grounding, transformation, meditation, relaxation, luck, growth, leadership, new beginnings, clarity, decisions, stability, truth, vitality, abundance, spirituality, channelling, understanding, dreams

Energy Receptive
Element Water
Planet Jupiter, Venus, Mars
Zodiac Aries, Libra, Taurus

Labradorite

Labradorite magical properties

Transformation, cleansing, breaking patterns, potential, psychic abilities, intuition, confidence, spirituality, focus, protection, imagination, relaxation, soothing, energy, healing, stress, anxiety, luck, abundance, success, decisions, trust, changes, strength, courage, self–confidence, inspiration, perseverance, journeying, clarity, insight, meditation, depression, jealousy, grounding

Energy Projective
Element Water
Planet Earth, Moon, Uranus
Zodiac Aquarius, Sagittarius, Scorpio, Leo

Larimar

Larimar magical properties

Peace, clarity, healing, inspiration, spirituality, understanding, calming, soothing, uplifting, emotions, fears, depression, patience, creativity, love, communication, friendship, guidance, happiness, decisions, relaxation, meditation, wisdom, divine, harmony

Energy: Receptive
Element: Water/Fire/Spirit
Planet: Neptune
Zodiac: Pisces

Lepidolite

Lepidolite magical properties

Transformation, soothing, calming, stress, happiness, changes, emotions, psychic abilities, spirituality, depression, divination, connection, strength, uplifting, luck, hope, balance, peace, sleep, harmony, decisions, addiction, releasing, trust, goals, optimism, patience, dreams, opportunities, support, love

Energy	Receptive
Element	Water
Planet	Jupiter, Neptune
Zodiac	Libra

Malachite

Malachite magical properties

Changes, transformation, clarity, emotions, protection, support, healing, peace, travel, fears, growth, creativity, renewal, energy, wealth, money, opportunity, abundance, new beginnings, finances, success, business, focus, strength, wisdom, releasing, prosperity, breaking barriers, psychic abilities, manifestation, soothing, stress, love, power

Energy	Receptive
Element	Earth
Planet	Venus
Zodiac	Capricorn, Scorpio

Obsidian (black)

Obsidian (black) magical properties

Truth, healing, clarity, illusions, breaking barriers, integrity, grounding, centring, strength, courage, protection, cleansing, meditation, stress, calming, relaxation, depression, anxiety, wealth, luck, focus, emotions, power, determination, success, patience, perseverance, releasing, spirit work, spirituality, challenges, past life work, divination

Energy	Projective

Element Fire, Earth, Water
Planet Saturn, Jupiter
Zodiac Sagittarius

Pyrite

Pyrite magical properties

Releasing, breaking patterns, clarity, protection, support, decisions, growth, success, inspiration, grounding, vitality, learning, perception, memory, wisdom, psychic abilities, healing, cleansing, prosperity, wealth, abundance, luck, strength, motivation, manifestation, finances, energy, Sun magic, power, focus, perseverance, confidence, divination, communication, self–confidence, meditation

Energy Projective
Element Fire
Planet Mars, Sun
Zodiac Leo

Selenite

Selenite magical properties

Clarity, psychic protection, cleansing, balance, stability, emotions, divine, connections, spirituality, psychic abilities, spirit work, protection, healing, breaking barriers, decisions, intuition, meditation, money, success, love

Energy Receptive
Element Water
Planet Moon
Zodiac Cancer

Sugilite

Sugilite magical properties

Spirituality, wisdom, clarity, insight, courage, truth, passion, inspiration, healing, strength, channelling, psychic abilities, amplification, confidence, focus, love, emotions, releasing, calming, peace, protection, connection, balance, understanding, stress

Energy	Receptive
Element	Water
Planet	Mercury, Jupiter
Zodiac	Virgo

Tiger's eye

Tiger's eye magical properties

Amplification, balance, harmony, releasing, fears, anxiety, courage, strength, self–confidence, focus, creativity, optimism, self–worth, protection, psychic abilities, healing, wealth, money, opportunity, abundance, prosperity, luck, success, commitment, determination, support, clarity, vitality, motivation, grounding, patience

Energy	Projective
Element	Fire, Earth
Planet	Sun
Zodiac	Leo, Capricorn

Waning Crescent Moon Meditation

Find a place where you won't be disturbed and make yourself comfortable. If you have a safe place to sit outside at night time then it would be perfect to do so, otherwise indoors is just fine. Close your eyes and focus on your breathing, deep breaths in and deep breaths out.

As your world around you dissipates you find yourself standing inside a stone columned temple. Pillars around you and a stone wall behind you. Above your head is open to the sky.

It is dark and the deep indigo blue sky is scattered with stars.

You can see the crescent of the waning Moon hanging in the sky.

Investigate the temple; running along the back wall is a ledge set out as an altar with candles, tapers and bowls of herbs and

spices. Dishes sit filled with sweet smelling incense on top of smouldering charcoal.

In front of the altar are piles of brightly coloured cushions.

You sit comfortably in front of the central altar.

Take a fresh candle from the side and light it with a taper. Place it on the altar in front of you.

Take a handful of herbs and spices and add them to the charcoal, do you recognize any of them?

Breathe in the scent from the incense and watch the smoke as it swirls and twists into the air.

Now sit and watch the flame of your candle as it flickers.

You notice a large jug set on the altar with a small glass beside it. Pour yourself a drink, what does it taste like?

Sit quietly and allow the liquid to fill your body from the inside. Healing and soothing every part of you. Take as many sips as you like.

When you are ready, get up and head to the other side of the temple.

Laid out in front of you is a large garden. Lit by flaming torches lining each side, stretching out into the far distance.

A large wooden planter sits to one side. It is overflowing with plants heavily laden with ripe fruits. Cascading over the sides of the planter. Pick one of the fruits and bite into it. What does it taste like?

Sit eating the fruit, allow it to nourish, heal and soothe your body, spirit and soul.

Sit quietly in the darkness and look out over the garden.

What do you see growing in the light of the torches? Can you see or hear any wildlife? Sit for a while…take some time to look and listen.

When you are ready, walk back to the temple and over to the altar and snuff out your candle.

Slowly and gently come back to this reality. Open your eyes and wriggle your fingers and toes. Have something to eat and drink and write down any important notes.

Waning Crescent Moon Ritual for Healing

Whether it is physical, mental or emotional, we all suffer at times. This ritual will help the healing energy to flow.

You will need:

Representations for the four quarters, if using
Central candle for deity, if using
Matches or lighter
Safe holders for the candles, if using

For the spell:

A photograph of the person who requires healing
Dried mint leaves
A blue candle (or a colour that you associate with healing)
A pin or sharp object to carve into the candle

Cast the circle
Walking deosil (clockwise) around the circle.

With the power of the Moon
I cast this circle to attune
Magic creating a boundary to last
This Moon circle is now cast

Call the quarters
Facing North

I call upon the element of earth
May you bring your energy of grounding and stability to this rite
Earth, I welcome you

Facing East

I call upon the element of air
May you bring your energy of intellect and inspiration to this rite
Air, I welcome you

Facing South

I call upon the element of fire,
May you bring your energy of passion and power to this rite
Fire, I welcome you

Facing West

I call upon the element of water,
May you bring your energy of emotions and cleansing to this rite
Water, I welcome you

Deity
Facing centre

I call upon the compassionate and merciful goddess Kuan Yin
And ask that you bring the energy of health and healing to this rite.
Kuan Yin, I honour your presence

Spell work: Carefully carve the name of the person that needs healing (or just their initials) into the candle. Light the candle. Place the photograph of the person that needs healing in front of the candle. Sprinkle the dried mint leaves onto the photograph and say:

Universe please provide
Healing energy by my side
Send it now, please direct through me

As is your will, so mote it be
Allow the candle to burn out.

Leave the photograph on your altar and sprinkle with more dried herbs as needed.

Feast: Eat and drink something to celebrate your ritual and to help you ground. Sprinkle some of the drink and food onto the earth after the ritual as an offering to deity.

Deity

I thank the compassionate and merciful goddess Kuan Yin
For bringing the energy of health and healing to this rite.
Kuan Yin, I honour you and ask that your energy continue with me as long as is needed.
With blessings and thanks, I bid you farewell

Release the quarters

Facing West

I thank the element of water,
For bringing your energy of emotions and cleansing to this rite
Water, I bid you farewell

Facing South

I thank the element of fire,
For bringing your energy of passion and power to this rite
Fire, I bid you farewell

Facing East

I thank the element of air
For bringing your energy of intellect and inspiration to this rite

Air, I bid you farewell

Facing North

I thank the element of earth
For bringing your energy of grounding and stability to this rite
Earth, I bid you farewell

Close the circle
Walking widdershins (anti clockwise) around the circle

I thank the power of the Moon
I uncast this circle but stay in tune
Magic unties the boundary to last
This Moon circle is now uncast

Waning Crescent Moon Tarot Cards

Tarot cards and oracle cards can be used as a focal point for meditation or as a key component to spell work. These cards are particularly associated with this Moon phase but trust your intuition about which ones to use.

Healing and good health: Strength, The World, The Magician, The Sun, The Star, The Empress, The Chariot, Judgement, Three of Cups.
Dreams: The Star, The Moon, Ace of Cups, High Priestess
Emotions: The Empress, Queen of Cups.
Releasing: Hanged Man, Death, The Devil, The Tower, Four of Swords, Six of Swords.
Bad habits, to overcome: Strength, Temperance, Judgement, The World.

Waning Crescent Moon Deities

Trust your intuition when working with deities, but please do your research before you call upon any of them. Make sure you know their history, personality and story before you work with them. Here are my suggestions for deities to work with for this Moon phase:

Asherah – Ancient West Semitic goddess, often referred to as Queen of the Gods. Also known as 'She who walks on the sea' or 'holiness'. You will find her name in the Old Testament she is consort of Yahweh. Asherah is a goddess of the sea. Call upon her for: Divine wisdom, feminine energy, feminine issues, strength, self–esteem, self–confidence, courage, kindness, love, divination, insight, justice, fertility, compassion, healing, nurturing.

Cybele/Kybele –Phrygian goddess of the Underworld and associated with the dark Moon. Worshipped in ancient Greece and found in Romany mythology. Some associate her with the Greek/Minoan goddess Rhea. She is known as mother of the gods. Associated with mountains, caves, nature and wild animals particularly hawks, lions and bees. Call upon her for: Love, victory, strength, relationships, humour, healing, health, fun, stability.

Hera – Greek Olympian Queen of gods, she covers marriage, childbirth and looking after women (she's got her hands full then). Although she can help when called upon, she has a jealous side and can be vengeful particularly when infidelity is involved. Call upon her for: Love, humour, forgiveness, romance, creativity, marriage, strength, courage, self–confidence, jealousy.

Isis – Egyptian goddess Queen of Egypt. She is looked upon as Mother Moon, Queen of Sorcery and the life force within the river Nile. Isis taught her people useful skills, those they would need to survive and flourish, no being high up in the sky for this one, she got down with her subjects (very practical woman). Call upon her for: Magic, dreams, divination, harvest, perspective, love, spirituality, faithfulness, destiny, revitalisation, fulfilment, inner beauty, rebirth, feminine energy, knowledge, motherhood, healing, changes, manifesting.

Ixchel – Mayan goddess of the Moon, weaving, water and childbirth. Mother of all Mayan deities she rules over life and death and bears the title of 'Keeper of Souls'. Her name translates as 'Lady Rainbow'. She spends her time constantly changing from a beautiful young woman into an old crone, it must be both exhausting and confusing. Call upon her for: Weather magic, fertility, health, healing, childbirth, water magic, rainbow magic, control, power, choices, assertion, self–confidence.

Kali/Kali Ma – Hindu goddess of time, change and destruction and the Divine Mother. She has blue black skin, red eyes and four arms. Often seen with skulls hanging around her neck. This is a real kick butt, no messing kind of gal. She is a forceful destroyer but brings rebirth with it, she is the cycle of destruction and creation. Call upon her for: Death and rebirth, cycles, time, happiness, courage, hope, change, cleansing, transformation, destruction, fear, knowledge, creativity.

Kuan Yin – Chinese/Buddhist goddess of mercy who is probably one of the most chilled out and relaxed deities ever. This beautiful goddess hears all your prayers and responds to each and every request for help. She needs some kind of medal… Call upon her for: Kindness, magic, health, healing, fertility, children, sympathy, support, suffering, encouragement, enlightenment, spirituality, protection.

Lucina – Roman goddess of light. She also covers childbirth. Possibly later merged with Juno and/or Diana. She may even have been converted, becoming St Lucy. An ancient bronze mask believed to depict Juno Lucina shows her with a tiny crescent Moon engraved on her forehead. Call upon her for: Charity, protection, health, healing, kindness, banishing, fertility, well–being.

Luna – Roman goddess of the Moon. Depicted as a beautiful woman with the power to ease childbirth and bring about love. She carries a very strong feminine energy. If you want an answer to a problem, then call upon this lovely lady to bring you the answer in your dreams, it is her speciality. Her Greek equivalent is Selene. Call upon her for: Feminine energy, water magic, safety, travel, intuition, blue Moon magic, protection, illusion, truth, love, psychic abilities, dreams, solutions.

DARK MOON

The skies are dark, deep and black
The dark Moon allows us to seek that which we lack
Turn inward, it is a time to seek rest
Reflect on the inner work that suits you best

The two or three days when the sky is dark and you cannot see the Moon at all, hence the term 'dark'. Often considered to be part of the new Moon phase, but I like to keep them separate. I think the dark Moon has a magic all of its own. The Moon is actually facing fully the Sun, showing its dark side to the earth (must be a Darth Vader joke here somewhere). This phase has also been referred to as the 'dead Moon'.

Dark Moon Magic

Contemplation, inner work, rejuvenation, beauty, health, personal improvement, planning, plotting and looking ahead. A time of introspection, self–analysis and reflection. This is really 'you' time, make the most of looking after and doing things for yourself. Relax, rest and recuperate. Meditate, contemplate and just 'be'. It is a total introvert time of the Moon. Clear your head, get some clarity and gain some perspective. It is kind of like a quiet peaceful pause, before the whole Moon cycle starts again.

This phase is represented as the crone aspect of the goddess.

The wise woman full of knowledge and magical mystery. The dark Moon provides an opportunity for introspection and inner work. It also allies nicely with shadow work. Some choose not to work magic on the dark Moon, but I have found it to be very successful especially if it focuses on personal growth and insight. Look to divination and mediation for insight into your inner self. Take time to really see yourself how others do and to take stock of how you treat other people and yourself. Why you act and react as you do.

- The dark Moon is a good time to give thanks. Take a look back on the previous month and see what worked and what didn't.
- Be thankful for what you have. Maybe offer up a little blessing to the Moon for everything that she does.
- The dark Moon is a good phase to spend some quality alone time. Do what makes you happy.
- Meditate sitting under the Moon, outside if you have a safe place, or inside by a window. Just sit quietly and focus on the Moon and the phase she is in. Ask her what guidance she has for you.

Dark Moon Colours

You must work with the colours that you associate with this Moon phase, but here are my suggestions:

- Black
- Dark purple
- Dark blue

Plants for the Dark Moon

You can work with any plants that you feel drawn to, but these are my suggestions. Also check out the food section for herbs, spices and foods that can also work in incense blends or spell workings:

Ash

(Fraxinus excelsior or F. americana)

Ash Magical Properties:

Protection, prosperity, dispels negativity, improves health, sea magic, dreams, love, intuition.

Ruling planet – Sun and Neptune

Element – Fire and Water

Gender – Masculine

Benzoin

(Styrax benzoin)

Benzoin Magical Properties:

Prosperity, purification, calming, confidence, love, lust

Ruling planet – Sun, Venus

Sign – Capricorn

Element – Air

Gender – Masculine

Burdock

(Arctium lappa)

Burdock Magical Properties:

Protection, healing, cleansing

Ruling planet – Venus

Sign – Leo, Libra

Element – Water

Gender – Feminine

Cypress

(Cupressus sempervirens)

Cypress Magical Properties:

Release, binding, grief, protection, healing

Ruling planet – Saturn

Sign – Aquarius

Element – Earth

Gender – Feminine

Dandelion

(Taraxacum officinale)

Dandelion Magical Properties:

Wishes, divination, love, abundance, psychic powers

Ruling planet –Jupiter

Sign – Taurus

Element – Air

Gender – Masculine

Dittany

Dictamnus albus

Dittany Magical Properties:

Fire, Samhain

Ruling planet –Moon

Element – Fire

Gender – Feminine

Elder

(Sambucus nigra/Canadensis)

Elder Magical Properties:

Protection, healing, faeries, purification, intuition, exorcism, hex breaking, rebirth

Ruling planet – Venus

Sign – Sagittarius, Aquarius, Libra

Element – Water

Gender – Feminine

Frankincense

Frankincense Magical Properties:

Purification, spirituality, relaxation, focus, love, abundance

Ruling planet – Sun

Sign – Aries, Leo, Aquarius

Element – Fire
Gender – Masculine

Hawthorn

(Crataegus oxacantha/monogyna)
Hawthorn Magical Properties:
Happiness, fertility, love, protection, purification, forgiveness, faeries, hope
Ruling planet – Mars, Venus
Sign – Sagittarius
Element – Fire
Gender – Masculine

Hazel

(Corylus spp. avellana, Corylus cornuta)
Hazel Magical Properties:
Fertility, wishes, love, protection, luck, wisdom, divination, healing, inspiration, prosperity
Ruling planet – Sun
Element – Air
Gender – Masculine

Heather

(Calluna spp, Erica spp, vulgaris)
Heather Magical Properties:
Luck, protection, cleansing, ghosts, rain, spirit, love, friendship, faeries, dreams, shape shifting
Ruling planet – Venus
Element – Water
Gender – Feminine

Jasmine

(Jasminum grandiflorum, Jasminum officinale, Jasminum

odoratissimum)
Jasmine Magical Properties:
Dreams, money, love, meditation, lust
Ruling planet – Moon, Venus
Sign – Cancer
Element – Water
Gender – Feminine

Mugwort

(Artemisia vulgaris)
Mugwort Magical Properties:
Strength, psychic powers, protection, dreams, healing, astral travel, feminine energy, cleansing
Ruling planet – Venus, Moon
Sign – Cancer
Element – Earth
Gender – Feminine

Myrrh

(Commiphora myrrha)
Myrrh Magical Properties:
Protection, purification, healing, Crone, Underworld, courage
Ruling planet – Mars, Sun
Sign – Aries, Aquarius
Element – Water
Gender – Feminine

Oak

(Quercus alba, Quercus robur, Quercus petraea)
Oak Magical Properties:
Healing, health, protection, money, fertility, luck, strength, vitality, power
Ruling planet – Sun, Jupiter, Mars
Sign – Sagittarius

Element – Fire, Water
Gender – Masculine

Patchouli

(Pogostemon)
Patchouli Magical Properties:
Grounding, Earth magic, prosperity, money, protection, sex magic, balance, calm
Ruling planet – Saturn
Sign – Virgo
Element – Earth
Gender – Feminine

Sandalwood

(White Sandalwood – Santalum album)
(Red Sandalwood – Pterocarpus santalinus)
Sandalwood (Red) Magical Properties:
Meditation, love
Ruling planet – Venus, Jupiter
Sign – Sagittarius, Virgo
Element – Water
Gender – Feminine
Sandalwood (White) Magical Properties:
Death rites, purification, wishes, psychic powers
Ruling planet – Moon, Mercury
Sign – Sagittarius, Virgo
Element – Water
Gender – Feminine

Saint John's Wort

(Hypericum perforatum)
Saint John's Wort Magical Properties:
Protection, health, strength, love, divination, happiness, abundance, truth

Ruling planet – Sun
Sign – Aquarius, Libra
Element – Fire
Gender – Masculine

Scullcap

(Scutellaria)
Scullcap Magical Properties:
Faithfulness, restoring, prosperity, stress, peace
Ruling planet – Saturn
Sign – Virgo
Element – Water
Gender – Feminine

Tansy

(Tanacetum vulgare)
Tansy Magical Properties:
Health, longevity, rebirth, cleansing, protection, travel
Ruling planet – Venus
Sign – Gemini
Element – Water
Gender – Feminine

Thistle

(Carduus spp)
Thistle Magical Properties:
Protection, healing, exorcism, hex breaking, spirit
Ruling planet – Mars, Jupiter
Element – Fire
Gender – Masculine

Willow

(Salix alba, Salix fragilis)

Willow Magical Properties:

Love, protection, healing, cleansing, wishes, release, inspiration, intuition

Ruling planet – Moon

Sign – Pisces

Element – Water

Gender – Feminine

Woodruff

(Asperula odorata, Galium odoratum)

Woodruff Magical Properties:

Protection, money, balance, justice

Ruling planet – Mars

Element – Fire

Gender – Masculine

Dark Moon Herbs – the 'deadly' ones

All of these are toxic in some way or even poisonous so please never take any of them internally and handle with care. Wash your hands after touching them or better still wear gloves. Don't eat them. Don't drink them. Don't smoke them. Don't burn them.

Enough of the 'do nots' because what you can do is add them to witch bottles, medicine pouches, meditate with them or pop them under candles and lots of other uses that I am sure you can come up with. If you are worried about working with darker herbs you can bring in some balance by using colour magic or mixing them with tamer herbs. Or choose the dark Moon herbs that are not toxic.

Belladonna

(Atropa belladonna)

Belladonna or as I know it, Deadly Nightshade is a perennial herbaceous plant – the whole plant is extremely TOXIC (the Romans used it as poison).

ALWAYS wear gloves when handling belladonna, always make sure if you use it in a medicine pouch that it is securely wrapped so that nothing can get out – this plant is DEADLY poisonous.

Belladonna Magical Properties:

Astral travel, baneful spells, Crone magic

Ruling planet – Saturn, Mars

Element – Water

Gender – Feminine

Datura

(Datura stramonium)

This plant is TOXIC.

It does work well in protection and hex breaking spell work but also in dream work – you DO NOT have to eat it, just use it in medicine pouches.

Datura Magical Properties:

Protection, feminine energy, hex breaking, dreams

Ruling planet – Saturn, Venus

Element – Water

Gender – Feminine

Dragons blood (you can burn this one with no ill effect)

(Daemonorops draco, Daemonorops propinquos)

Dragon's Blood Magical Properties:

Power, protection, love, happiness, dragon magic

Ruling planet – Mars

Sign – Aries

Element – Fire

Gender – Masculine

Foxglove

(Digitalis purpurea)

Foxglove is poisonous…do not ingest.
Foxglove Magical Properties:
Protection, gossip, faeries, divination
Ruling planet – Venus, Saturn
Element – Water
Gender – Feminine

Mandrake

(Mandragora officinale)
It's poisonous…enough said.
Mandrake Magical Properties:
Protection, love, prosperity
Ruling planet – Mercury
Sign – Taurus, Cancer, Virgo
Element – Fire
Gender – Masculine

Rue

(Ruta graveolens)
Rue Magical Properties:
Protection, health, healing, purification, balance, clarity, anxiety, hex breaking
Ruling planet – Mars, Sun
Sign – Leo
Element – Fire
Gender – Masculine

Solomon's Seal

(Polygonatum officinale)
Solomon's Seal Magical Properties:
Wisdom, knowledge, protection, exorcism, success, Elementals, purification
Ruling planet – Saturn
Sign – Capricorn

Element – Water
Gender – Feminine

Tobacco (obviously you can smoke and burn this one, but it does have health warnings)

(Nicotiana spp)
CAUTION: this plant is poisonous, but then you knew that already
Tobacco Magical Properties:
Purification, travel, protection
Ruling planet – Mars
Element – Fire
Gender – Masculine

Valerian

(Valeriana officinalis)
Valerian Magical Properties:
Protection, purification, love, sleep, peace, animal spirit, stress
Ruling planet – Venus, Jupiter
Sign – Virgo
Element – Water, Earth
Gender – Feminine

Wormwood

(Artemisia absinthium)
Wormwood Magical Properties:
Vengeance, attack magic, protection, divination, dreams, meditation, psychic powers
Ruling planet – Mars, Moon
Sign – Cancer, Scorpio
Element – Fire
Gender – Masculine

Dark Moon Incense and Oil Blends

Use equal quantities of each ingredient, or experiment to create a blend you like. If you are creating a loose incense (rather than an essential oil mix) and the blend doesn't include a resin or woody component you might like to add one in to help it burn longer.

- Myrrh, bay, frankincense
- Sandalwood, patchouli, myrrh, jasmine, lemon
- Dragon's blood, patchouli, myrrh

Dark Moon Body Care – Bath Infusion

Add the infusion to your bath water, as a foot bath, or add to a bucket of warm water for a floor or surface wash.

You will need:

500ml/16 fl oz water
5 drops patchouli essential oil
5 drops frankincense essential oil
1 tablespoon sea salt
2 tablespoons dried rosemary

Boil the water then pour over the dried herbs/flowers. Leave to infuse for ten minutes.

In a separate bowl add the essential oils to the salt and mix to a paste.

Strain the herb/flower water.

Add the oil and salt paste to the strained water infusion.

Stir until the salt has dissolved.

Dark Moon Foods, Herbs and Spices

On the dark Moon we welcome the dark goddess; this is a

powerful phase of the Moon and a time for inner work. It is suggested that this time is one of fasting, but I would recommend just keeping things light and healthy and make sure you drink plenty of fluids. Some of these foods can also be used in incense blends or spell working.

Apple

(Pyrus spp)

Apple Magical Properties:

Love, healing, clarity, knowledge, abundance, spirit work

Ruling planet – Venus

Element – Water

Gender – Feminine

Bay

(Laurus nobilis)

Bay Magical Properties:

Protection, purification, strength, power, healing, creativity, spirituality, psychic powers

Ruling planet – Sun

Element – Fire

Gender – Masculine

Blackberries

(Rubus fruticosus)

Blackberries Magical Properties:

Prosperity, protection, fertility, Faerie

Ruling planet – Venus

Element – Water, Fire, Earth

Gender – Feminine

Fennel

(Foeniculum vulgare)

Fennel Magical Properties:

Healing, purification, protection, courage, confidence, fertility, initiation

Ruling planet – Mercury

Sign – Leo, Virgo, Aquarius

Element – Fire

Gender – Masculine

Garlic

(Allium sativum)

Garlic Magical Properties:

Healing, protection, hex breaking, negative energies, lust, strength, courage, depression

Ruling planet – Mars

Element – Fire

Gender – Masculine

Ginger

(Zingiber officinale)

Ginger Magical Properties:

Healing, power, love, passion, success, prosperity, protection

Ruling planet – Mars

Element – Fire

Gender – Masculine

Nutmeg

(Myristica fragrans)

Nutmeg Magical Properties:

Money, luck, fidelity, protection

Ruling planet – Jupiter

Element – Fire

Gender – Masculine

Paprika

(Capsicum annuum)

Paprika Magical Properties:
Creativity, energy
Ruling planet – Mars
Element – Fire
Gender –Masculine

Pomegranate

(Punica granatum)
Pomegranate Magical Properties:
Growth, fertility, wishes, death, rebirth, new beginnings
Ruling planet – Mercury
Element – Fire, Earth
Gender – Masculine

Rosemary

(Rosemarinus officinalis)
Rosemary Magical Properties:
Protection, love, lust, mental powers, exorcism, purification, healing, sleep
Ruling planet – Sun
Element – Fire
Gender – Masculine

Sage

(salvia officinalis)
Sage Magical Properties:
Protection, wishes, wisdom, purification, stimulating, intuition, abundance, success.
Ruling planet – Jupiter
Element – Air
Gender – Masculine

Star Anise

(Illicum verum)

Star Anise Magical Properties:
Luck, psychic powers, purification, protection, dreams, spirituality, sleep
Ruling planet – Jupiter
Element – Air
Gender – Masculine

Thyme

(Thymus vulgaris, Thymus serpyllum)
Thyme Magical Properties:
Healing, health, peace, psychic powers, love, purification, courage, releasing, sleep, beauty
Ruling planet – Venus
Element – Water
Gender – Feminine

Dark Moon Recipe – Nutmeg Cake

This is a bit of a weird recipe, but trust me, it makes for an unusual, but delicious cake with a soft spongey top and a crunchy, almost biscuit base.

300g/10 ½ oz self–raising flour
340g/12 oz brown sugar
125g/4.4 oz butter, cold
2 teaspoons mixed spice
1 teaspoon baking powder
2 teaspoons ground nutmeg
1 egg
227 ml/8 fl oz milk

Preheat your oven to 180C/350F/Gas 4. Line a 23cm/8" baking tin with baking parchment.

In a large bowl, mix together the flour, sugar, mixed spice and one teaspoon of the ground nutmeg.

Rub the butter into the flour mix with your fingertips (I do this in the food mixer), until it resembles breadcrumbs.

Spoon just under half of this mixture into the base of your baking tin and spread evenly (don't push it down too firmly).

Add the baking powder to the other half of the flour mix and put to one side for now.

In a separate bowl, whisk the egg and milk together then add the other teaspoon of nutmeg.

Add the wet ingredients into the remaining flour mixture and combine.

Pour over the base and pop the cake tin into the oven. Bake for 45 minutes.

Dark Moon Teas

Herbal teas can be purchased in tea bag form or ready–made loose blends and there are some fantastic brands out there. However, I have also purchased herbal teas that tasted like sweepings from the factory floor. Check the ingredients when purchasing ready–made herbal teas, make sure they include only the items that the tea is supposed to taste of. Some companies bulk out with cheaper items. Herbal tea is very easy to make if you grow fresh herbs or if you have a supply of dried herbs and dried fruits. Experiment with different flavours. The basic rule is one or two teaspoons of dried herbs to a mug full of boiling water, brew for at least five minutes then strain. If you are using fresh herbs you may need a slightly larger quantity. Herbal tea can be drunk hot (obviously), left and poured over ice as a cold drink or even used as a hair rinse. Drop it into your bath water or add to a bucket of hot water and use as a floor or surface wash.

Please be careful and make sure you have identified the herbs you use correctly. Never ingest herbs that you are not sure about. Always check with a qualified practitioner if you are on medication, have health problems or are pregnant.

I have given some of my favourite recipes here, adjust the

amounts of each ingredient to suit your own taste. If the blend isn't sweet enough you can add a teaspoon of sugar or honey.

Inner work:
Hot chocolate (made with any kind of milk)
Pinch of cardamom

Love yourself:
Hot milk (any kind)
Ginger
Honey
Cinnamon

Past Lives tea:
Star anise
Cinnamon
Clove
Ginger

Crystals for the Dark Moon

You can work with any crystals you feel drawn to, but these are my suggestions:

Apache tear

Apache tear magical properties

Grief, releasing, blockages, peace, acceptance, forgiveness, balance, emotions, change, insight, clarity, success, hope, healing, grounding, protection, meditation, dispel negative energy

Energy: Projective
Element: Fire
Planet: Saturn, Jupiter
Zodiac: Aries, Capricorn
Birthstone: November

Chrysocolla

Chrysocolla magical properties

Wisdom, peace, patience, love, soothing, intuition, energy, calming, emotions, fear, strength, clarity, balance, negative energy, insight, releasing, spirituality, psychic abilities, guilt, divine, harmony, communication, meditation

Energy: Receptive
Element: Water
Planet: Venus
Zodiac: Taurus

Fluorite

Fluorite magical properties

Magic, imagination, discernment, aptitude, psychic protection, protection, purification, calming, relaxation, tension, anxiety, organisation, structure, challenges, declutter, releasing, support, breaking patterns, intuition, confidence, reassurance, comforting, communication, balance, spirituality, decisions, manifestation, peace, meditation, grounding, healing, cleansing, channelling, past life work, fairy realm, amplifying, memory, power, emotions, depression, stability

Energy: Projective
Element: Water, Air
Planet: Neptune
Zodiac: Scorpio, Aquarius, Pisces

Jasper (red)

Jasper (red) magical properties

General: Protection, balance, stability, healing, grounding, stress, peace, happiness, confidence, fears, comfort, relaxation, release, beauty, astral travel, motivation, determination, energy, focus, prosperity, organisation, honesty, trust

Zodiac Scorpio, Aries, Virgo
Birthstone August

Energy Projective
Element Fire
Planet Mars

Jet

Jet magical properties

Protection, fears, dispel negative energy, psychic attacks, depression, solutions, psychic abilities, past life work, support, grief, divination

Energy Receptive
Element Earth, Spirit
Planet Saturn
Zodiac Capricorn

Labradorite

Labradorite magical properties

Transformation, cleansing, breaking patterns, potential, psychic abilities, intuition, confidence, spirituality, focus, protection, imagination, relaxation, soothing, energy, healing, stress, anxiety, luck, abundance, success, decisions, trust, changes, strength, courage, self–confidence, inspiration, perseverance, journeying, clarity, insight, meditation, depression, jealousy, grounding

Energy Projective
Element Water
Planet Earth, Moon, Uranus
Zodiac Aquarius, Sagittarius, Scorpio, Leo

Obsidian

Obsidian magical properties

Truth, healing, clarity, illusions, breaking barriers, integrity, grounding, centring, strength, courage, protection, cleansing, meditation, stress, calming, relaxation, depression, anxiety, wealth, luck, focus, emotions, power, determination, success, patience, perseverance, releasing, spirit work, spirituality, challenges, past life work, divination

Energy	Projective
Element	Fire, Earth, Water
Planet	Saturn, Jupiter
Zodiac	Sagittarius

Selenite

Selenite magical properties

Clarity, psychic protection, cleansing, balance, stability, emotions, divine, connections, spirituality, psychic abilities, spirit work, protection, healing, breaking barriers, decisions, intuition, meditation, money, success, love

Energy	Receptive
Element	Water
Planet	Moon
Zodiac	Cancer

Dark Moon Meditation

Find a place where you won't be disturbed and make yourself comfortable. If you have a safe place to sit outside at night time then it would be perfect to do so, otherwise indoors is just fine. Close your eyes and focus on your breathing, deep breaths in and deep breaths out.

As your world around you dissipates you find yourself standing inside a stone columned temple. Pillars around you and a stone wall behind you. Above your head is open to the sky.

It is dark and the deep indigo blue sky is scattered with stars.

There is no visible Moon in the sky, the air feels fresh and clear.

Investigate the temple; running along the back wall is a ledge set out as an altar with candles, tapers and bowls of herbs and spices. But there are no candles lit, the altar sits in darkness other than a slight glow from the dishes filled with sweet smelling incense

on top of smouldering charcoal.

In front of the altar are piles of brightly coloured cushions.

You sit comfortably in front of the central altar.

Take a fresh candle from the side and light it with a taper. Place it on the altar in front of you.

Take a handful of herbs and spices and add them to the charcoal, do you recognize any of them?

Breathe in the scent from the incense and watch the smoke as it swirls and twists into the air.

Now sit and watch the flame of your candle as it flickers.

Sit quietly and contemplate.

Really look inwards.

This is your time…

When you are ready, get up and head to the other side of the temple.

Laid out in front of you is a large garden. Lit by flaming torches lining each side, stretching out into the far distance.

A large wooden planter sits to one side. It is filled with plants that have gone over. Having grown and fruited, they now lie withered. Pull out the plants, put each one in a pile on the ground. These will be made into compost.

Sit quietly in the darkness and look out over the garden.

What do you see growing in the light of the torches? Can you see or hear any wildlife? Sit for a while…take some time to look and listen.

When you are ready, walk back to the temple and over to the altar and snuff out your candle.

Slowly and gently come back to this reality. Open your eyes and wriggle your fingers and toes. Have something to eat and drink and write down any important notes.

Dark Moon Ritual for dream work

We can learn a lot from our dreams. When you first wake, jot down any images, symbols or words that you dreamt about.

Later on, go back to your notes and see what it means to you. I believe our dreams are personal and the images will mean something specific to each individual. This ritual and the dream jar can also be used to help increase your psychic abilities.

You will need:

Representations for the four quarters, if using
Central candle for deity, if using
Matches or lighter
Safe holders for the candles, if using
Something to eat and drink

For the spell:

Empty jam jar or bottle and lid
A crystal chip or small tumble stone such as selenite, red jasper, obsidian or labradorite
Dried pasta
Herbs such as thyme, star anise, rosemary, bay, wormwood or valerian
A small feather
Incense of your choice (or essential oil in a burner if you prefer, if you don't want to use incense or oil you could just light a candle and use the flame)
Any other small items you associated with dreams and astral travel

Cast the circle
Walking deosil (clockwise) around the circle.

With the power of the Moon
I cast this circle to attune
Magic creating a boundary to last
This Moon circle is now cast

Call the quarters

Facing North

I call upon the element of earth
May you bring your energy of grounding and stability to this rite
Earth, I welcome you

Facing East

I call upon the element of air
May you bring your energy of intellect and inspiration to this rite
Air, I welcome you

Facing South

I call upon the element of fire,
May you bring your energy of passion and power to this rite
Fire, I welcome you

Facing West

I call upon the element of water,
May you bring your energy of emotions and cleansing to this rite
Water, I welcome you

Deity

Facing centre

I call upon the patient and peaceful goddess Rhiannon
And ask that you bring the energy of dream work, peace and communication to this rite.
Rhiannon, I honour your presence

Spell work

We are going to create a dream bottle that will hopefully help you seek guidance and assistance with your inner work, through the dream world.

Take your clean jam jar or bottle and hold it over the smoke of your incense. Allow the smoke to waft inside the jar. Say:

Cleanse, clear and purify
So mote it be

Now take each item that you have to fill the jar.

Hold each one in your hand and say:

Rhiannon, goddess of the dark
Charge this item with a spark
Prophetic dreams and guidance be mine
Imbue this ingredient with the magic of time

Layer up the jar with all the items in turn, charging each one with energy and saying the chant each time.

You don't have to fill the jar right up to the top, sometimes it is good to leave a space for the energy to move.

When you feel it is ready, pop the lid on.

Hold the jar in both hands and say:

This is my dream jar, now done
The magic begins on the downing of the Sun

Pop the jar beside your bed and let it work its dream magic. Keep a journal beside your bed to write down notes when you awake.

Feast: Eat and drink something to celebrate your ritual and to help you ground. Sprinkle some of the drink and food onto the earth after the ritual as an offering to deity.

Deity

I thank the patient and peaceful goddess Rhiannon
For bringing the energy of dream work, peace and communication to this rite.
Rhiannon, I honour you and ask that your energy continue with me as long as is needed.
With blessings and thanks, I bid you farewell

Release the quarters
Facing West

I thank the element of water,
For bringing your energy of emotions and cleansing to this rite
Water, I bid you farewell

Facing South

I thank the element of fire,
For bringing your energy of passion and power to this rite
Fire, I bid you farewell

Facing East

I thank the element of air
For bringing your energy of intellect and inspiration to this rite
Air, I bid you farewell

Facing North

I thank the element of earth
For bringing your energy of grounding and stability to this rite
Earth, I bid you farewell

Close the circle

Walking widdershins (anti clockwise) around the circle

I thank the power of the Moon
I uncast this circle but stay in tune
Magic unties the boundary to last
This Moon circle is now uncast

Dark Moon Spell Craft – Flying Ointment

One of the most well–known uses for baneful plants was for flying ointments. A salve that was made by adding plant matter to fat which was then rubbed on the body to induce an hallucination that allowed the person to believe they were flying. This is not a recommended course of action, really it isn't – slathering your skin with poisonous ingredients is not wise. If you want an out of body experience then please do try the method of astral projection, it is so much safer and doesn't involve covering yourself in deadly animal fat.

Many stories are told of witches creating magic potions that would allow them to fly and the ingredients were said to be mixed with the fat from plump human babies ... Do remember that our ancestors were wary of anyone that appeared to be different or have magical abilities – and that included the herbalists who could cure illness and disease. They also liked to sit and gossip, in fact a lot of people still do.

Historians have found details on flying ointments that included herbs from the nightshade family such as belladonna, datura, mandrake and henbane with the addition of less poisonous, but still dangerous plants like mugwort and poppies.

The practice of using hallucinogenic plants isn't restricted to witches. The history of their use goes back thousands of years and includes Shamanic and Native American tribes whose rituals included experiencing trance journeys.

I believe that if you study hard and work at your Craft then you can reach a trance state for journeying without the need to endanger your health or your life messing about with poisons, but that is purely my own point of view.

You can, however, create a salve or an incense to help create a good atmosphere for astral travel or Otherworld journeys without the use of poisonous or hallucinogenic plants. Play around with some of your favourite herbs and spices or use those that are particularly associated with astral travel, psychic abilities, meditation or the Otherworld such as: Bay, beech, benzoin, black pepper, blackthorn, borage, chamomile, cinnamon, dandelion, eucalyptus, fennel, fenugreek, frankincense, jasmine, juniper, marigold, myrrh, mugwort, parsley, pine, rose, white and red sandalwood, star anise, thyme and yarrow.

Or you could create a medicine pouch which includes baneful plants, that way you benefit from their spirit rather than choking on fumes from burning them.

Dark Moon Tarot Cards

Tarot cards and oracle cards can be used as a focal point for meditation or as a key component to spell work. These cards are particularly associated with this Moon phase but trust your intuition about which ones to use.

Courage and strength: The Star, Strength, The Chariot, The Fool, Ace of Swords, Knight of Swords, Seven of Wands, Nine of Wands.

Inspiration, ideas and creativity: The Magician, The Moon, The Star, The Fool, The Empress, The World, The Hierophant, Temperance, Ace of Cups, Ace of Wands, Queen of Wands, Page of Cups, Knight of Cups.

Knowledge and Wisdom: The Hermit, High Priestess, The Moon, The Magician, The Hierophant, Wheel of Fortune, Two of Pentacles, Ace of Swords, Page of Pentacles.

Opportunities: The Magician, Wheel of Fortune, The Devil,

The Star, The World, Knight of Cups, Seven of Cups.

Intuition: The High Priestess, The Devil, The Moon.

Growth: The Empress, The Hermit.

Goals: The Emperor, The Chariot, Strength.

Dark Moon Deities

Trust your intuition when working with deities, but please do your research before you call upon any of them. Make sure you know their history, personality and story before you work with them. Here are my suggestions for deities to work with for this Moon phase:

Blodeuwedd – Welsh goddess, who has a connection with the Moon, and death and reincarnation (aspects of the Dark Moon). Her name translates as 'flower face' as she was created out of plants by magicians, who then later changed her into an owl (it was a whole punishment betrayal thing). As a maiden she forms part of the triad with Arianrhod and Cerridwen. A goddess of spring and one of the five goddesses of Avalon. Call upon her for: Beauty (temporary), spring, reincarnation, transformation, betrayal, manipulation, strength, power, love, wisdom, innocence.

Cerridwen – Welsh goddess usually shown hunched over her cauldron filled with Awen (inspiration and wisdom). Generally seen as the crone aspect of the triad with Blodeuwedd and Arianrhod. A goddess of the Moon she covers death, rebirth, magic and divination of all kinds. Also, one of the five goddesses of Avalon. Call upon Cerridwen for: Inspiration, creativity, wisdom, death, rebirth, divination, prophecy, spiritual transformation, justice, fertility, luck.

Cybele/Kybele –Phrygian goddess of the Underworld and associated with the dark Moon. Worshipped in ancient Greece and found in Romany mythology. Some associate her with the Greek/Minoan goddess Rhea. She is known as mother of the gods. Associated with mountains, caves, nature and wild animals particularly hawks, lions and bees. Call upon her for: Love, victory, strength, relationships, humour, healing, health, fun, stability.

Ereshkigal – A Sumerian Queen of the Underworld and in her aspect as the Crone is goddess of the Dark Moon. An excellent goddess to work with to seek your shadow side. She is a powerful deity. Call upon her for: Shadow work, justice, power, love, wisdom.

Freyja/Freya – although not called a Moon goddess, many of her attributes connect her with both the Full and Dark Moons. A Norse goddess of love, beauty, war and fertility. She leads souls of dead warriors to the Otherworld. She rides a chariot driven by two cats, so she must be powerful to get cats to do what they are told! Call upon her for: Love, beauty, fertility, war, dearth, happiness, sex, sensuality, inspiration.

Hathor – Egyptian goddess of the Moon, associated with the dark Moon. Goddess of the Underworld but also ruler of the sky. She is a mother to all Egyptians. Definitely packing a powerful punch of feminine energy having given birth to the universe, she must have been exhausted. Call upon her for: Love, feminine energy, beauty, sexuality, happiness, romance, music, the arts, protection (primarily for women).

Hekate – Greek goddess of the dark Moon. She covers new beginnings and magic of all kinds. She walks the ancient roads and pathways, particularly associated with crossroads, those where three roads cross. She forms a triad with Persephone and Demeter, she being the Crone aspect. She guards the spirit world and wields power over all realms. She is one seriously intimidating goddess, but wise beyond words. Call upon her for: Moon magic, witchcraft, herb magic, necromancy, protection, prosperity, new beginnings, decisions, mysteries, knowledge, learning, inner work, shadow work.

Kali/Kali Ma – Hindu goddess of time, change and

destruction and the Divine Mother. She has blue black skin, red eyes and four arms. Often seen with skulls hanging around her neck. This is a real kick butt, no messing kind of gal. She is a forceful destroyer but brings rebirth with it, she is the cycle of destruction and creation. Call upon her for: Death and rebirth, cycles, time, happiness, courage, hope, change, cleansing, transformation, destruction, fear, knowledge, creativity.

Nephthys – Egyptian goddess of the dark Moon, the dead, darkness and the shadows. She is the dark to the light of Isis. Call upon her for: Death and rebirth, night magic, protection, shadow work, grief, spirit work, devotion, reincarnation, power, magic.

Rhiannon – if you aren't singing the Fleetwood Mac song right now, you need to… A Welsh goddess and great Queen of Wales. She brings peace, comfort and patience. If you are looking for magical enchantments, then she has a bounty of them. Call upon her for: Patience, comfort, peace, magic, movement, relaxation, communication, fertility, leadership, spirit work, motivation, dream work.

Thoth – Egyptian ibis headed Moon god. He is a seriously studious dude. God of writing and wisdom he is considered to be one of the most important gods of ancient Egypt (he didn't let it go to his head though). Call upon him for: Knowledge, Moon magic, wisdom, learning, intellect, meditation, logic, reason, magic, secrets, balance, judgement.

Shadow Work

I wonder why the dark is often feared so much, it is just the absence of light…

We need dark to balance with the light, too much of one can overpower. Shadows are cast by the light. Don't fear them, seek them out and they become light.

Recognising those shadow areas of your personality can really help you. You don't have to stop or change your complete personality in the process. Just by recognizing those characteristics of yourself that you don't like is a good start. Being aware of them can help you to understand why you do things or even react to certain people. We often resent people that act in a way that mirrors our own behaviour...think about it.

It took me a long time to learn that not everyone will act or react in the way I wanted or expected them to. I used to get very angry and 'knee jerk' react in situations because people didn't do what I thought they should. I often felt let down or disappointed. But it was my lesson to learn, not theirs. I still feel let down on occasion, but I don't let it affect me as much anymore. We are all unique and we all have our own individual ways. Just because someone does something differently does not make it wrong. This was a lesson learnt in my own shadow work journey.

Shadow work is about peering into the dark and seeking out the negative aspects of your psyche and breaking the cycles of bad habits. It takes time, in fact I think once you start it is ongoing and it takes courage and determination. The dark Moon phase is an excellent time to work with your shadow.

Working with the Lunar Year

Each monthly Moon has a name and these are different in each culture, region, country, faith or religion – many, many different names but usually they refer to the season, the weather or what the people are up to at that time of the year. A lot of our ancestors didn't record time using a calendar, they would work with the phases of the Moon, the Sun and seasons.

If you would like to work with names for each month then find a set that suits you, perhaps link it to your area or the particular pathway that you follow, for instance the Native Americans have several different sets of names depending on the tribe or the Japanese have beautiful Moon names and the Celtic culture has its own set of names too.

I prefer to work with names that suit where I live so although they are lovely, I don't work with American Moon names because they don't all fit with me living in the UK so I tend to work with more Celtic/folk lore names. If you don't like any that you find what about making up your own names to suit your area and seasons?

I have included some that I know of but there are more, you will also find that different cultures might have similar or the same Moon names but they are transposed or shifted by a month or two – it all depends on the seasons and where you are in the world.

Each month also has its own particular Moon energy that you can use to tie in with your Moon magic. I have included my own correspondences; see how you feel each month and create a list of your own.

JANUARY

In all honesty January is probably my least favourite month. The festivities are over, no one has any money and it is a long time until pay day. Add to that the weather which is usually pretty awful. Over the years I have learnt to accept it as a restful month, quiet and contemplative before the preparation for new growth, plans and schemes in February and March. It has taken time but now I try to embrace the quiet, new energy and make it a month of organization. Clearing away that which didn't serve me in the previous year and making lists (I do love a good list) of ideas and inspirations that come to me.

I tend to work a lot with meditation and divination in January to gain insight and ideas for the coming months. Look within and really 'see' what needs to be done, sorted, tweaked or re–balanced to create the life you want.

Use the energy of this month to strengthen your connection to the divine. Clear your altar and give it a good clean remembering to dust all the items you removed as well. Lay out a fresh altar cloth and use your intuition to replace items. Spend some time each day, even just a few moments to re–connect with the divine in whatever form you work with. Ask them to send you insight and inspiration for the year ahead.

My recommendation is to take this month slowly. Most of us ate too much last month and it would probably have been an incredibly hectic month. Take your time getting back into routine (I love a good routine too).

January Magical Energy

Sluggish, below the surface; beginning and conceiving, protection, reversing spells. Conserving energy by working on personal problems. Getting your various bodies to work smoothly together for the same goals. Work towards your aspirations, new projects, bringing balance to your life and your emotions and bring in some clarity. Inner work, creativity, aspirations, balance, clarity, truth, divination, spiritual connections and enlightenment.

Colours: White, violet, black
Sign: Capricorn
Element: Water
Season: Winter

January Moon Names

Wolf Moon, Quiet Moon, Snow Moon, Cold Moon, Chaste Moon, Disting Moon, Old Moon, Hard Time Moon, Dwarf Seal Moon, Holiday Moon, Cooking Moon, Ice Moon, Moon after Yule, Winter Moon, Stay Home Moon, After Yule Moon and Moon of Little Winter.

The Wolf Moon name comes from wolves tending to howl more often at this time. I wonder if it was because of the lack of food in January? It also seems that wolves may howl more on a full Moon because they have more light to see by. Disting Moon – Dating back to the Middle Ages, 'distin' was a festival often held on January 25 to prepare for the return of spring. After Yule Moon or Æftera Geól is the Anglo–Saxon name for the month after Yule.

Plants to work with for January

These are my suggested herbs to work with that correspond with the energy of this month. But, trust your intuition and the supplies that you have in your cupboards.

Alyssum

(Alyssum spp. & Lobularia spp)
Alyssum Magical Properties:
Protection, Maiden magic, peace, calming, balance, spirituality

Element – Air
Gender – Feminine

Betony (Wood)

(Stachys betonica, Betonica officinalis)
Betony Magical Properties:
Love, purification, clarity, protection, anti–intoxication, nightmares, anti–depression, memory, stress relief
Ruling planet – Jupiter
Sign – Gemini, Sagittarius
Element – Fire
Gender – Masculine

Birch

(Betula pendula, Betula pubescens, Betula lenta, Betula alba)
Birch Magical Properties:
Purification, protection, exorcism, new beginnings, courage, fertility, love, release
Ruling planet – Venus, Moon, Jupiter
Sign – Sagittarius
Element – Water, Air
Gender – Feminine

Crocus

(Crocus vemus)
Crocus Magical Properties:
Love, happiness, hope, visions, blessings, new beginnings
Ruling planet – Venus
Sign – Aquarius
Element – Water
Gender – Feminine

Holly

(Ilex aquifolium, Ilex opaca)

Holly Magical Properties:

Protection, luck, dreams, balance, success

Ruling planet – Mars, Saturn

Element – Fire

Gender – Masculine

Honeysuckle

(Lonicera caprifolium, Lonicera japonica, Lonicera periclymenum)

Honeysuckle Magical Properties:

Prosperity, psychic powers, protection, balance, lust, meditation, memory

Ruling planet – Jupiter

Sign – Gemini, Cancer

Element – Earth

Gender – Masculine

Horehound

(Marrubium vulgare)

Horehound Magical Properties:

Exorcism, protection, healing, clarity, peace, love

Ruling planet – Mercury

Sign –Scorpio

Element – Air

Gender – Masculine

Juniper

(Juniperus communes)

Juniper Magical Properties:

Love, exorcism, healing, protection, justice, stolen items, purification, psychic powers, clarity

Ruling planet – Sun, Jupiter, Moon

Sign – Aries

Element – Fire

Gender – Masculine

Lavender

(Lavendula officinale or Lavendula vera)

Lavender Magical Properties:

Happiness, peace, love, protection, sleep, clarity, faeries, strength

Ruling planet – Mercury

Sign – Leo, Gemini

Element – Air

Gender – Masculine

Patchouli

(Pogostemon)

Patchouli Magical Properties:

Grounding, Earth magic, prosperity, money, protection, sex magic, balance, calm

Ruling planet – Saturn

Sign – Virgo

Element – Earth

Gender – Feminine

Rue

(Ruta graveolens)

Rue Magical Properties:

Protection, health, healing, purification, balance, clarity, anxiety, hex breaking

Ruling planet – Mars, Sun

Sign – Leo

Element – Fire

Gender – Masculine

Witch Hazel

(Hamamelis virginiea)

Witch Hazel Magical Properties:
Protection, divining, balance, grief
Ruling planet – Sun, Saturn
Sign – Capricorn
Element – Fire
Gender – Masculine

Woodruff

(Asperula odorata, Galium odoratum)
Woodruff Magical Properties:
Protection, money, balance, justice
Ruling planet – Mars
Element – Fire
Gender – Masculine

Foods, Herbs and Spices to work with for January

Whether you chose to include the foods in a recipe for the table or add them to spell work, here is my suggested list of foods to work with for the energy of this month.

Basil

(Ocimum basilicum)
Basil Magical Properties:
Wealth, money, prosperity, love, exorcism, protection, happiness, peace
Ruling planet – Mars
Sign – Scorpio
Element – Fire
Gender – masculine

Bay

(Laurus nobilis)
Bay Magical Properties:
Protection, purification, strength, power, healing, creativity,

spirituality, psychic powers
Ruling planet – Sun
Element – Fire
Gender – Masculine

Black Pepper

(Piper nigrum)
Black Pepper Magical Properties:
Protection, exorcism, jealousy, negativity, strength, confidence, gossip
Ruling planet – Mars
Element – Fire
Gender – Masculine

Cardamom

(Elettaria cardamomum)
Cardamom Magical Properties:
Love, passion, clarity, uplifting, protection
Ruling planet – Venus & Mars
Element – Water
Gender – Feminine

Cinnamon

(Cinnamomum zeylanicum, Cinnamomum verum)
Cinnamon Magical Properties:
Success, healing, power, psychic powers, protection, love, focus, lust, spirituality, changes
Ruling planet – Sun
Element – Fire
Gender – Masculine

Clove

(Eugenia carophyllus, Syzygium aromaticum, Caryophyllus aromaticus)

Clove Magical Properties:

Love, money, exorcism, clarity, protection, abundance, repels negativity, prevents gossip, stress relief, truth

Ruling planet – Jupiter

Element – Fire

Gender – Masculine

Coriander

(Coriandrum sativum)

Coriander Magical Properties:

Health, healing, peace, love, release, wealth, protection, negativity

Ruling planet – Mars

Sign – Aries

Element – Fire

Gender – Masculine

Cumin

(Cumimum cyminum)

Cumin Magical Properties:

Exorcism, protection, anti–theft, fidelity, lust, peace, love, abundance, success

Ruling planet – Mars

Element – Fire

Gender – Masculine

Dill

(Anethum graveolens)

Dill Magical Properties:

Protection, love, lust, money, jealousy, balance, clarity, knowledge, magic

Ruling planet –Mercury

Sign – Cancer, Gemini, Leo

Element – Fire

Gender – Masculine

Fennel

(Foeniculum vulgare)

Fennel Magical Properties:

Purification, protection, healing

Ruling planet – Mercury

Element – Fire

Gender – Masculine

Garlic

(Allium sativum)

Garlic Magical Properties:

Healing, protection, hex breaking, negative energies, lust, strength, courage, depression

Ruling planet – Mars

Element – Fire

Gender – Masculine

Ginger

(Zingiber officinale)

Ginger Magical Properties:

Healing, power, love, passion, success, prosperity, protection

Ruling planet – Mars

Element – Fire

Gender – Masculine

Marjoram

(Origanum majorana)

Marjoram Magical Properties:

Love, happiness, health, protection, marriage, grief

Ruling planet – Mercury

Element – Air

Gender – Masculine

Mint

(Mentha spp, Mentha aquatic, Mentha piperita)

Mint Magical Properties:

Money, healing, exorcism, protection, cleansing, calming

Ruling planet – Mercury, Venus

Element – Air

Gender – Masculine

Mustard

(Brassica juncea, Brassica nigra, Sinapis hirta)

Mustard Magical Properties:

Clarity, psychic abilities, protection, astral travel, faith, success

Ruling planet – Mars

Element – Fire

Gender – Masculine

Nutmeg

(Myristica fragrans)

Nutmeg Magical Properties:

Money, luck, fidelity, protection

Ruling planet – Jupiter

Sign – Sagittarius

Element – Fire

Gender – Masculine

Parsley

(Petroselinum crispum, Petrselinum sativum)

Parsley Magical Properties:

Protection, purification, lust, happiness, fertility, spirit work

Ruling planet – Mercury

Element – Air

Gender – Masculine

Rosemary

(Rosemarinus officinalis)

Rosemary Magical Properties:

Protection, love, lust, mental powers, exorcism, purification, healing, sleep

Ruling planet – Sun

Element – Fire

Gender – Masculine

Sage

(salvia officinalis)

Sage Magical Properties:

Protection, wishes, wisdom, purification, stimulating, intuition, abundance, success.

Ruling planet – Jupiter

Element – Air

Gender – Masculine

Star Anise

(Illicum verum)

Star Anise Magical Properties:

Luck, psychic powers, purification, protection, dreams, spirituality, sleep

Ruling planet – Jupiter

Element – Air

Gender – Masculine

Turmeric

(Cucurma longa)

Turmeric Magical Properties:

Purification, protection, peace

Ruling planet – Mars

Element – Fire, Air

Gender – Feminine

Crystals to work with in January

As always, go with your intuition and what you have in your collection when working with crystals. The list below is my suggestion of crystals that work particularly well with the energy of this month.

Agate (moss)

Agate (moss) magical properties

Nature, happiness, prosperity, wealth, longevity, friendship, success, abundance, healing, renewal, fertility, creativity, confidence, strength, love, beginnings, self–esteem, communication, emotions, stress, releasing, hope, trust, depression, growth, finances, cleansing, support, peace, stability, fears, luck, divination

Energy	Receptive
Element	Earth
Planet	Moon
Zodiac	Virgo, Gemini

Amber

Amber magical properties:

Manifesting, energy, beauty, Sun magic, power, wishes, intellect, clarity, wisdom, balance, purification, protection, psychic abilities, healing, calm, patience, love, sensuality, good luck, marriage, abundance, success, vitality, joy, sexuality, cleansing, stress, harmony, creativity

Energy:	Projective
Element:	Fire, Spirit
Planet:	Sun
Zodiac:	Leo

Fluorite

Fluorite magical properties

Magic, imagination, discernment, aptitude, psychic protection,

protection, purification, calming, relaxation, tension, anxiety, organisation, structure, challenges, declutter, releasing, support, breaking patterns, intuition, confidence, reassurance, comforting, communication, balance, spirituality, decisions, manifestation, peace, meditation, grounding, healing, cleansing, channelling, past life work, fairy realm, amplifying, memory, power, emotions, depression, stability

Energy: Projective
Element: Water, Air
Planet: Neptune
Zodiac: Scorpio, Aquarius, Pisces

Garnet

Garnet magical properties

Organisation, warrior spirit, protection, love, commitment, passion, sexuality, sensuality, attraction, depression, spiritual healing, success, self–confidence, energy, inspiration, perception, strength, survival, fear, courage, clarity, challenges, past life work, truth, compassion, deflecting negative energy, gossip, ambition, motivation, goals, purification, cleansing, balance, inner strength, self–empowerment, creativity, confidence, meditation, spirit work, nightmares, journeying, abundance, support

Energy: Projective
Element: Fie
Planet: Mars
Zodiac: Aries, Virgo, Capricorn, Leo, Aquarius
Birthstone: January

Hematite

Hematite magical properties

Grounding, money, decisions, manifestation, finances, healing, focus, clarity, stability, protection, balance, divination, problem solving, emotions, self–esteem, productivity, doubt, anxiety, communication, strength

Energy:	Projective
Element:	Fire, Earth
Planet:	Saturn
Zodiac:	Aries, Aquarius

Kyanite

Kyanite magical properties

Balance, harmony, calming, connection, psychic abilities, healing, communication, grounding, transformation, meditation, relaxation, luck, growth, leadership, new beginnings, clarity, decisions, stability, truth, vitality, abundance, spirituality, channelling, understanding, dreams

Energy	Receptive
Element	Water
Planet	Jupiter, Venus, Mars
Zodiac	Aries, Libra, Taurus

Malachite

Malachite magical properties

Changes, transformation, clarity, emotions, protection, support, healing, peace, travel, fears, growth, creativity, renewal, energy, wealth, money, opportunity, abundance, new beginnings, finances, success, business, focus, strength, wisdom, releasing, prosperity, breaking barriers, psychic abilities, manifestation, soothing, stress, love, power

Energy	Receptive
Element	Earth
Planet	Venus
Zodiac	Capricorn, Scorpio

Quartz (clear)

Quartz (clear) magical properties

Purification, cleansing, healing, calming, emotions, strength, support, spirituality, energy, balance, psychic abilities, motivation, uplifting, decisions, anxiety, divine connection, amplifying, focus, meditation, manifestation, channelling, protection, negative energy, clarity, wisdom, concentration, learning, spirit work, communication, astral travel, divination, dreams, harmony

Energy	Projective, Receptive
Planet	Sun, Moon
Element	Fire, Water
Zodiac	Leo, Gemini, Capricorn

Rhodonite

Rhodonite magical properties

Protection, renewal, emotions, strength, soothing, clarity, happiness, love, balance, harmony, decisions, confidence, spirituality, peace, energy, passion, optimism, changes, vitality, anxiety, travel, psychic abilities, self–confidence, trust, calming, relaxation, patience, determination, releasing, stress, negative energy

Energy	Projective
Element	Fire
Planet	Mars, Venus
Zodiac	Taurus

Selenite

Selenite magical properties

Clarity, psychic protection, cleansing, balance, stability, emotions, divine, connections, spirituality, psychic abilities, spirit work, protection, healing, breaking barriers, decisions, intuition, meditation, money, success, love

Energy	Receptive
Element	Water
Planet	Moon
Zodiac	Cancer

Sugilite

Sugilite magical properties

Spirituality, wisdom, clarity, insight, courage, truth, passion, inspiration, healing, strength, channelling, psychic abilities, amplification, confidence, focus, love, emotions, releasing, calming, peace, protection, connection, balance, understanding, stress

Energy	Receptive
Element	Water
Planet	Mercury, Jupiter
Zodiac	Virgo

Sunstone

Sunstone magical properties

Sun magic, power, decisions, leadership, strength, happiness, inspiration, love, luck, stability, clarity, energy, stress, depression, emotions, optimism, perseverance, intuition, fears, self–esteem, self–confidence, healing, balance, harmony, abundance, prosperity, opportunities, peace, protection

Energy	Projective
Element	Fire
Planet	Sun
Zodiac	Leo

Tiger's eye

Tiger's eye magical properties

Amplification, balance, harmony, releasing, fears, anxiety, courage, strength, self–confidence, focus, creativity, optimism, self–worth, protection, psychic abilities, healing, wealth, money, opportunity, abundance, prosperity, luck, success, commitment, determination, support, clarity, vitality, motivation, grounding, patience

Energy	Projective
Element	Fire, Earth

Planet	Sun
Zodiac	Leo, Capricorn

Turquoise

Turquoise magical properties

Purification, negative energy, protection, balance, relaxation, emotions, stress, spirituality, energy, depression, clarity, wisdom, understanding, psychic abilities, insight, intuition, past life work, communication, wealth, abundance, finances, prosperity, luck, decisions, friendship, uplifting, meditation, love, harmony

Energy	Receptive
Element	Earth
Planet	Venus, Neptune
Zodiac	Sagittarius, Pisces, Aquarius
Birthstone	December

Moon Deities to work with in January

Here you will find my suggestions on some of the Moon deities to work with that align with the energies of this month. Trust your intuition and be guided by the deities that may also make themselves known to you.

Chang–O – Chinese goddess of the Moon. Banished from heaven along with her husband, destined to be mere mortals. Chang–O took a double dose of immortality pill, without sharing with her husband (rude). She floated up to the Moon, leaving her husband behind. Call upon her for: Love, partnership, courage, power, fertility, growth, manifesting, belief, self–confidence, new beginnings, transformation.

Coyolxauhqui – Aztec Moon goddess. Her name translates as 'painted with bells'. Apparently in most images she is wearing bells on her cheeks, which must be terribly uncomfortable. When the full Moon rises you can see the bells as rosy red. In a bit of a misunderstanding Coyolxauhqui had her head cut off, which was flung up into the sky, where it became the Moon. Call upon her for: Moon magic, family issues, balance, differences

Hekate – Greek goddess of the dark Moon. She covers new beginnings and magic of all kinds. She walks the ancient roads and pathways, particularly associated with crossroads, those where three roads cross. She forms a triad with Persephone and Demeter, she being the Crone aspect. She guards the spirit world and wields power over all realms. She is one seriously intimidating goddess, but wise beyond words. Call upon her for: Moon magic, witchcraft, herb magic, necromancy, protection, prosperity, new beginnings, decisions, mysteries, knowledge, learning, inner work, shadow work.

Hestia – Greek goddess of the hearth and home she is also a fire goddess. Her Roman equivalent is Vesta. The Greeks did not have statues of this goddess as it was believed she didn't take human form, instead she appeared as the flames of fire in the hearth. Hestia was the first born of the Olympian goddesses. She is absolutely about new beginnings and the start of all things. This goddess is the ultimate super housekeeper and home maker, with added omnipotence. Call upon her for: Home life, domesticity, fire magic, devotion, wishes, manifesting, unity, new beginnings, spirituality, blessings.

Ilmatar/Luonnotar – A Finnish–Ugrian creation goddess of the air whose duck laid eggs on her knee. The eggs fell and the whites became the Moon, the yolks the Sun and the shell pieces became the stars. She is goddess of the crescent Moon. Call upon her for: New beginnings, creativity, inspiration, traditions, fertility, nature, the arts, magic.

Levana – A Roman goddess of childbirth. Her name derives from the Latin 'levare' which means to raise or lift. She is present at the birth of every child. Call upon her for: New beginnings, protection of children, childbirth.

Ma'at – Egyptian goddess of the crescent Moon, order and balance. Think 'strict school headmistress', she dishes out the justice as she sees fit, whether you are a deity or a mere mortal. Her name translates as 'truth/that which is straight'. If you are looking for balance between work and home life or any kind of justice, Ma'at should be on your speed dial. Call upon her for: Justice, balance, freedom, new beginnings, morals, organisation, law, promises, fairness, truth, oaths, harmony, honesty.

Neith/Nit – Egyptian goddess of the crescent Moon and domesticity. She has an eclectic list of duties including war, hunting and weaving. She is also considered to be the personification of the primordial waters of creation. Call upon her for: Home, marriage, protection, feminine energy, hunting, war, creativity, new beginnings.

Parvati – Hindu goddess of the crescent Moon. Oh, this goddess has all the feminine wiles and knows how to use them. She is maiden to the Mother Durga and Crone Kali. She can charm the secrets out of the trees. Call upon her for: Power, creativity, new beginnings, victory, feminine energy, beauty, charm, secrets, the arts, fertility, cleansing, devotion.

Thoth – Egyptian ibis headed Moon god. He is a seriously studious dude. God of writing and wisdom he is considered to be one of the most important gods of ancient Egypt (he didn't let it go to his head though). Call upon him for: Knowledge, Moon magic, wisdom, learning, intellect, meditation, logic, reason, magic, secrets, balance, judgement.

World celebration days

I have given some dates and a little information on celebrations from around the world that take place during January. A lot of them were based on Moon phases. I apologise for any errors but history is a fickle thing and calendars have changed over the years...

Rome

1st January – A Roman festival where vows were offered

to Juno and Janus, presents were exchanged as a token of friendship. Dates, figs and honey were sealed in white jars and offered to Janus.

Fortuna – A Roman day of sacrifices which were given to Fortuna to bring a year of luck and abundance.

11th – 15th January – The festival of Carmentalia in honour of Carmenta and the Camenae, Roman nymphs of inspiration and prophecy.

11th January – The Roman day of Juturnalia, Juturna was given sacrifices on this day.

12th January – The Roman festival of Compitalia held to honour the spirits of the crossroads and to mark the end of the winter planting season. Each member of the household would hang a woollen doll in the household shrine and give garlic to the Lares (gods of the household). Neighbours would also share honey cakes.

15th January – Roman 'Feast of the Ass' … this festival was to mark the event in which Vesta was saved by a donkey.

Guatemala

1st January – A Guatemalan festival where the water from five sacred coconuts is drunk and used to fertilise the ground, women officiate the ceremony and guard the coconuts overnight then dedicate them to The Goddess before the coconut milk is drunk.

Egypt

2nd January – offerings are made to celebrate the coming of Isis from Phoenicia.

7th January – a day to celebrate the Decrees of Sekhmet that were put forward at the end of the reign of Ra.

30th January – Amun in the festival of raising heaven, the day of bringing branches of the ished tree (sacred tree of the Sun god Iunu) including the ceremony of filling the sacred eye of Iunu.

Sumeria

2nd January – a white candle is lit the previous night at Sunset to burn throughout the night and extinguished the next morning to celebrate the birth of Inanna.

Greece

5th January – Kore/Persephone – people spent the night in a temple singing to the Alexandria after which a statue, a wooden idol is brought into the inner temple and carried around seven times in honour of the story of Persephone.

31st January – Hekate– make offerings to this Moon goddess on the last night of the month, preferably at a crossroads.

Italy

6th January – Ancient Italian festival of Befana. An old hag figure, Befana, flies around the world on a broomstick, landing on the roof of a house and descending down the chimney where she delivered sweets and presents to children that have been good, or coal to those that haven't. They story goes that La Befana was approached by the Three Wise Men who asked her to direct them to the stable where baby Jesus had been born. La Befana was too busy doing the housework and declined. But then she realised she may have made a mistake and gathered up a bag of gifts and set off to search for the baby Jesus. Although she followed the star, she was unable to find the stable, so she continues to travel the world searching every house for Jesus. The arrival on 6th January of La Befana marks the end of the festive holiday season in July and is celebrated with feasting.

Norse

Freya – the first Monday after January 6th was called Old Saxons Plough Monday, the day when men returned to the plough (or their daily work). The farm labourers would draw a plough from door to door of the parish and solicit plough money.

The Queen of their celebration was Bessie, a caricature of Freya. Those dragging the plough would dress as white mummers covered with flowers and ribbons.

19th January – Norse festival of Thor.

January Full Moon – Minor feast honouring Thor, the protector of Midgard. During this time, the height of the Storm season, Thor's power is invoked to drive back the frost Jotuns so that spring may return to Midgard.

Hindu

16th January – Hindu festival of Ganesha.

Jan/Feb – The Hindu celebration of Vasant Panchami for the birthday of the goddess Saraswati. This festival is celebrated on the 5th day of the bright fortnight of the lunar month of Magha (which falls during Jan/Feb). This celebration also welcomes the beginning of the spring season.

Mid Jan – Lord Krishna – the celebration of Lohri falls in mid-January marking the end of the coldest month of the year and a time when Lord Krishna manifests himself.

Christian

20th January – a night to dream of your future husband… aided by a nod to St Agnes before you sleep.

FEBRUARY

This is a bit of an unpredictable month. The weather never knows what it is doing. The first signs of spring are making an effort (depending where you are in the world of course) and then the snow dumps on top of them. But the signs of the earth beginning to awaken are there...somewhere. The year spreads open before us full of potential even if we need to wrap up warm in seventeen layers of clothing.

February contains St Valentine's Day and Lupercalia so there is definitely an air of love and fertility whizzing about. February always feels like the start of the turning point, although it is not yet spring February sees the beginnings of new growth and even (hopefully) a few Sunnier days. The beginning of February brings the festival of Imbolc which is traditionally sacred to the goddess Brighid. This is the month where we celebrate the maiden awaiting the return of her Sun god. Open up pathways to allow the positive energy in. It is a time for renewal, new beginnings and a good 'ole clear out, spring clean, sort clutter (physically, mentally and spiritually) and smudge, smudge, smudge...

It is also the time of year for lambs to be bouncing around the fields and to celebrate that spring is on its way, prepare for growth and renewal of all kinds and keep an eye out for the first spring flowers.

February Magical Energy

Love, passion and fertility – fertility of all kinds not just bouncing babies, it covers new projects, plans and ways of looking at things. Energy working toward the surface; purification, growth, healing. Loving the self. Accepting responsibility for past errors, forgiving yourself and making future plans. Dedications, initiations, astral travel work, personal power, problem solving and friendship issues. Success, personal protection, divination, aspirations and balance of emotions. Clarity, truth and spiritual connections.

Colours: Light blue, violet, pale green, pink
Sign: Aquarius
Element: Earth
Season: Spring

February Moon Names

Ice Moon, Storm Moon, Horning Moon, Hunger Moon, Starvation Moon, Wild Moon, Red and Cleansing Moon, Quickening Moon, Solmonath, Budding Moon, Snow Moon, Bone Moon, Long Day Moon, Seal Pup Moon, Trapper's Moon, Tree Moon, Little Famine Moon and Big Winter Moon.

Snow Moon because the heaviest snow often falls in February. Hunger Moon may have been because of the lack of food. Bone Moon refers to the lack of food and the necessity to gnaw on whatever bones there were and to eat bone marrow soup.

Solmonath is the Anglo–Saxon name for February, It has been suggested this was the month of cakes (I am liking February more and more), the cakes were offered to the gods. However, further research also suggests that 'sol' was more likely to mean 'mud', so February is the muddy month (yep, that makes sense too). Or maybe the 'plow month'. More research…and it appears that 'sol' translated also means 'hearthcake', so I am sticking with the month of cakes.

Full Moon in February

Once every nineteen years February does not have a full Moon. So, in 2018 there was no full Moon, the time before that was 1999 and afterwards in 2037 and so on. This is true for most parts of the planet although in some places such as eastern Australia and eastern Asia the full Moon often just sneaks into February 1st.

The Greek astronomer Meton discovered this phenomenon. February is the only month in which this can happen. The lunar cycle being roughly 29.5 days on average, but with February only having 28 or 29 (on a leap year) days it creates this weird occurrence.

Plants to work with in February

These are my suggested herbs to work with that correspond with the energy of this month. But, trust your intuition and the supplies that you have in your cupboards.

Birch

(Betula pendula, Betula pubescens, Betula lenta, Betula alba)
Birch Magical Properties:
Purification, protection, exorcism, new beginnings, courage, fertility, love, release
Ruling planet – Venus, Moon, Jupiter
Sign – Sagittarius
Element – Water, Air
Gender – Feminine

Dock

(Rumex spp. Crispus, R. obtusifolius)
Dock Magical Properties:
Money, healing, fertility, cleansing, love, purification
Ruling planet – Jupiter
Element – Air
Gender – Masculine

Frankincense

Frankincense Magical Properties:
Purification, spirituality, relaxation, focus, love, abundance
Ruling planet – Sun
Sign – Aries, Leo, Aquarius

Element – Fire
Gender – Masculine

Hawthorn

(Crataegus oxacantha/monogyna)
Hawthorn Magical Properties:
Happiness, fertility, love, protection, purification, forgiveness, faeries, hope
Ruling planet – Mars, Venus
Sign – Sagittarius
Element – Fire
Gender – Masculine

Hazel

(Corylus spp. avellana, Corylus cornuta)
Hazel Magical Properties:
Fertility, wishes, love, protection, luck, wisdom, divination, healing, inspiration, prosperity
Ruling planet – Sun
Element – Air
Gender – Masculine

Hyssop

(Hyssopus officinalis)
Hyssop Magical Properties:
Purification, protection, healing
Ruling planet – Jupiter, Moon
Sign – Cancer
Element – Fire
Gender – Masculine

Juniper

(Juniperus communes)
Juniper Magical Properties:

Love, exorcism, healing, protection, justice, stolen items, purification, psychic powers, clarity

Ruling planet – Sun, Jupiter, Moon

Sign – Aries

Element – Fire

Gender – Masculine

Mistletoe

(Viscum album, Phoradendron leucarpum, Phoradendron flavescens)

Caution: Mistletoe is poisonous – do not ingest.

Mistletoe Magical Properties:

Fertility, protection, love, health, dreams

Ruling planet – Sun

Sign – Leo

Element – Air

Gender – Masculine

Myrrh

(Commiphora myrrha)

Myrrh Magical Properties:

Protection, purification, healing, Crone, Underworld, courage

Ruling planet – Mars, Sun

Sign – Aries, Aquarius

Element – Water

Gender – Feminine

Pine

(Pinus)

Pine Magical Properties:

Centring, focus, Dragon magic, protection, truth, abundance, purification, fertility, healing

Ruling planet – Mars, Saturn

Sign – Capricorn

Element – Air, Fire
Gender – Masculine

Poppy

(Papaver spp)
Poppy Magical Properties:
Love, sleep, money, luck, fertility, rebirth, grief
Ruling planet – Moon, Mars, Venus
Sign – Capricorn
Element – Water
Gender – Feminine

Rose

(Rosa spp)
Rose Magical Properties:
Love, psychic powers, healing, luck, protection, peace, mysteries, knowledge, dreams, friendship, death and rebirth, abundance
Ruling planet – Venus, Moon
Sign – Pisces
Element – Water
Gender – Feminine

Rowan

(Sorbus acuparia)
Rowan Magical Properties:
Psychic powers, power, success, protection, love, spirituality, faeries, divination, healing, inspiration
Ruling planet – Sun, Mercury
Sign – Sagittarius
Element – Fire
Gender – Masculine

Rue

(Ruta graveolens)

Rue Magical Properties:

Protection, health, healing, purification, balance, clarity, anxiety, hex breaking

Ruling planet – Mars, Sun

Sign – Leo

Element – Fire

Gender – Masculine

Vervain

(Verbena officinalis)

Vervain Magical Properties:

Protection, love, purification, peace, sleep, healing, money, inspiration, shape shifting

Ruling planet – Venus

Sign – Gemini

Element – Earth

Gender – Feminine

Foods, Herbs and Spices to work with in February

Whether you chose to include the foods in a recipe for the table or add them to spell work, here is my suggested list of foods to work with for the energy of this month.

Avocado

(Persea americana)

Avocado Magical Properties:

Beauty, passion, love, fertility

Ruling planet – Venus

Element – Earth

Gender – Feminine

Basil

(Ocimum basilicum)

Basil Magical Properties:

Wealth, money, prosperity, love, exorcism, protection, happiness, peace

Ruling planet – Mars

Element – Fire

Gender – masculine

Bay

(Laurus nobilis)

Bay Magical Properties:

Protection, purification, strength, power, healing, creativity, spirituality, psychic powers

Ruling planet – Sun

Sign – Aries, Leo

Element – Fire

Gender – Masculine

Cabbage

(Brassica oleracea/var.)

Cabbage Magical Properties:

Moon magic, protection, prosperity, fertility, love

Ruling planet – Moon

Element – Water

Gender – Feminine

Cherry

(Prunus avium/cerasus)

Cherry Magical Properties:

Love, fertility, divination, beginnings

Ruling planet – Venus

Element – Water, Air

Gender – Feminine

Cinnamon

(Cinnamomum zeylanicum, Cinnamomum verum)

Cinnamon Magical Properties:

Success, healing, power, psychic powers, protection, love, focus, lust, spirituality, changes

Ruling planet – Sun

Element – Fire

Gender – Masculine

Cucumber

(Cucumis sativus)

Cucumber Magical Properties:

Fertility, emotions, chastity, meditation, spirituality, purification, healing

Ruling planet – Moon

Element – Water

Gender – Feminine

Fennel

(Foeniculum vulgare)

Fennel Magical Properties:

Purification, protection, healing

Ruling planet – Mercury

Element – Fire

Gender – Masculine

Fish

Fish Magical Properties:

Fertility, Prosperity, Abundance, healing, emotions, cleansing, purification

Element – Water

Gender – Feminine

Figs

(Ficus carica)

Figs Magical Properties:

Meditation, love, fertility, divination

Ruling planet – Jupiter

Element – Air, Fire

Gender – Masculine/Feminine

Ginger

(Zingiber officinale)

Ginger Magical Properties:

Healing, power, love, passion, success, prosperity, protection

Ruling planet – Mars

Element – Fire

Gender – Masculine

Leeks

(Allium ampeloprasum)

Leeks Magical Properties:

Purification, protection, love

Ruling planet – Mars

Element – Fire

Gender – Masculine

Lime

(Citrus aurantifolia)

Lime Magical Properties:

Purification, love, healing, protection, energy

Ruling planet –Sun

Element – Fire

Gender – Masculine

Melon

Melon Magical Properties:

Love, chaos, healing, purification
Ruling planet – Moon
Element – Water
Gender – Feminine

Olives

(Olea europaea)
Olives Magical Properties:
Spirituality, integrity, passion, fertility, healing, peace, protection, luck
Ruling planet – Sun
Element – Fire, Air
Gender – Masculine

Peach

(Prunus persica)
Peach Magical Properties:
Love, fertility, spirituality, wishes, longevity
Ruling planet – Venus
Element – Water, Air
Gender – Feminine

Rosemary

(Rosemarinus officinalis)
Rosemary Magical Properties:
Protection, love, lust, mental powers, exorcism, purification, healing, sleep
Ruling planet – Sun
Sign – Aries
Element – Fire
Gender – Masculine

Strawberry

(Fragaria spp)

Strawberry Magical Properties:
Love, fertility, romance, luck, success
Ruling planet – Venus
Element – Water, Earth
Gender – Feminine

Thyme

(Thymus vulgaris, Thymus serpyllum)
Thyme Magical Properties:
Healing, health, peace, psychic powers, love, purification, courage, releasing, sleep, beauty
Ruling planet – Venus
Sign – Gemini, Taurus, Libra
Element – Water
Gender – Feminine

Crystals to work with in February

As always, go with your intuition and what you have in your collection when working with crystals. The list below is my suggestion of crystals that work particularly well with the energy of this month.

Agate (moss)

Agate (moss) magical properties
Nature, happiness, prosperity, wealth, longevity, friendship, success, abundance, healing, renewal, fertility, creativity, confidence, strength, love, beginnings, self–esteem, communication, emotions, stress, releasing, hope, trust, depression, growth, finances, cleansing, support, peace, stability, fears, luck, divination

Energy	Receptive
Element	Earth
Planet	Moon
Zodiac	Virgo, Gemini

Amber

Amber magical properties:

Manifesting, energy, beauty, Sun magic, power, wishes, intellect, clarity, wisdom, balance, purification, protection, psychic abilities, healing, calm, patience, love, sensuality, good luck, marriage, abundance, success, vitality, joy, sexuality, cleansing, stress, harmony, creativity

Energy: Projective
Element: Fire, Spirit
Planet: Sun
Zodiac: Leo

Aventurine (green)

Aventurine (green) magical properties

Balance, decisions, motivation, leadership, dreams, visualisation, creativity, luck, money, anxiety, calm, opportunities, happiness, adventure, love, courage, truth, comfort, support, healing, peace, connection, perception, intellect, psychic abilities

Energy: Projective
Element: Air
Planet: Mercury, Mars
Zodiac: Aries

Chrysoprase

Chrysoprase magical properties

Courage, strength, wisdom, releasing, selfishness, imagination, happiness, success, balance, break barriers, protection, truth, healing, luck, prosperity, marriage, negative energy, transformation, love

Energy: Receptive
Element: Earth
Planet: Venus
Zodiac: Taurus, Cancer

Fluorite

Fluorite magical properties

Magic, imagination, discernment, aptitude, psychic protection, protection, purification, calming, relaxation, tension, anxiety, organisation, structure, challenges, declutter, releasing, support, breaking patterns, intuition, confidence, reassurance, comforting, communication, balance, spirituality, decisions, manifestation, peace, meditation, grounding, healing, cleansing, channelling, past life work, fairy realm, amplifying, memory, power, emotions, depression, stability

Energy: Projective
Element: Water, Air
Planet: Neptune
Zodiac: Scorpio, Aquarius, Pisces

Larimar

Larimar magical properties

Peace, clarity, healing, inspiration, spirituality, understanding, calming, soothing, uplifting, emotions, fears, depression, patience, creativity, love, communication, friendship, guidance, happiness, decisions, relaxation, meditation, wisdom, divine, harmony

Energy: Receptive
Element: Water/Fire/Spirit
Planet: Neptune
Zodiac: Pisces

Malachite

Malachite magical properties

Changes, transformation, clarity, emotions, protection, support, healing, peace, travel, fears, growth, creativity, renewal, energy, wealth, money, opportunity, abundance, new beginnings, finances, success, business, focus, strength, wisdom, releasing, prosperity, breaking barriers, psychic abilities, manifestation, soothing, stress, love, power

Energy	Receptive
Element	Earth
Planet	Venus
Zodiac	Capricorn, Scorpio

Moonstone

Moonstone magical properties

New beginnings, Moon magic, intuition, calming, psychic abilities, balance, harmony, wishes, cleansing, uplifting, hope, meditation, emotions, love, divination, spirituality, wealth, truth, healing, sensuality, insight, peace, wisdom, communication, confidence, abundance, prosperity, dreams, fertility, travel

Energy	Receptive
Element	Water
Planet	Moon
Zodiac	Cancer, Libra, Scorpio
Birthstone	June, September

Pebble/Hag stone

Pebble/hag stone magical properties

Protection, fairy magic, nightmares, dreams, healing, fertility, manifestation, negative energy

Energy	Projective
Element	Earth, Water
Planet	Earth

Quartz (clear)

Quartz (clear) magical properties

Purification, cleansing, healing, calming, emotions, strength, support, spirituality, energy, balance, psychic abilities, motivation, uplifting, decisions, anxiety, divine connection, amplifying, focus, meditation, manifestation, channelling, protection, negative energy, clarity, wisdom, concentration, learning, spirit work, communication, astral travel, divination, dreams, harmony

Energy	Projective, Receptive
Planet	Sun, Moon
Element	Fire, Water
Zodiac	Leo, Gemini, Capricorn

Quartz (rose)

Quartz (rose) magical properties

Love, happiness, emotions, spirituality, growth, fears, healing, sexuality, passion, calming, soothing, stress, depression, sleep, luck, wisdom, inspiration, success, intuition, grounding, balance, prosperity, self–esteem, harmony, trust, jealousy, gossip, beauty, peace, cleansing, fertility

Energy	Receptive
Element	Earth, Water
Planet	Venus, Moon
Zodiac	Taurus

Selenite

Selenite magical properties

Clarity, psychic protection, cleansing, balance, stability, emotions, divine, connections, spirituality, psychic abilities, spirit work, protection, healing, breaking barriers, decisions, intuition, meditation, money, success, love

Energy	Receptive
Element	Water
Planet	Moon
Zodiac	Cancer

Sugilite

Sugilite magical properties

Spirituality, wisdom, clarity, insight, courage, truth, passion, inspiration, healing, strength, channelling, psychic abilities, amplification, confidence, focus, love, emotions, releasing, calming, peace, protection, connection, balance, understanding, stress

Energy	Receptive
Element	Water
Planet	Mercury, Jupiter
Zodiac	Virgo

Sunstone

Sunstone magical properties

Sun magic, power, decisions, leadership, strength, happiness, inspiration, love, luck, stability, clarity, energy, stress, depression, emotions, optimism, perseverance, intuition, fears, self–esteem, self–confidence, healing, balance, harmony, abundance, prosperity, opportunities, peace, protection

Energy	Projective
Element	Fire
Planet	Sun
Zodiac	Leo

Turquoise

Turquoise magical properties

Purification, negative energy, protection, balance, relaxation, emotions, stress, spirituality, energy, depression, clarity, wisdom, understanding, psychic abilities, insight, intuition, past life work, communication, wealth, abundance, finances, prosperity, luck, decisions, friendship, uplifting, meditation, love, harmony

Energy	Receptive
Element	Earth
Planet	Venus, Neptune
Zodiac	Sagittarius, Pisces, Aquarius
Birthstone	December

Moon Deities to work with in February

Here you will find my suggestions on some of the Moon deities to work with that align with the energies of this month. Trust your intuition and be guided by the deities that may also make themselves known to you.

Aine – an Irish goddess of summer and the Moon, she looks after livestock and crops. She is also known as a Fairy Queen and a Sun goddess. Associated with midsummer/Litha and Lughnasadh. Call upon her for: Love, protection, fertility, wealth, sovereignty, Moon magic, Sun magic, fairy magic.

Asherah – Ancient West Semitic goddess, often referred to as Queen of the Gods. Also known as 'She who walks on the sea' or 'holiness'. You will find her name in the Old Testament she is consort of Yahweh. Asherah is a goddess of the sea. Call upon her for: Divine wisdom, feminine energy, feminine issues, strength, self–esteem, self–confidence, courage, kindness, love, divination, insight, justice, fertility, compassion, healing, nurturing.

Blodeuwedd – Welsh goddess, who has a connection with the Moon, and death and reincarnation (aspects of the Dark Moon). Her name translates as 'flower face' as she was created out of plants by magicians, who then later changed her into an owl (it was a whole punishment betrayal thing). As a maiden she forms part of the triad with Arianrhod and Cerridwen. A goddess of spring and one of the five goddesses of Avalon. Call upon her for: Beauty (temporary), spring, reincarnation, transformation, betrayal, manipulation, strength, power, love, wisdom, innocence.

Chang–O – Chinese goddess of the Moon. Banished from heaven along with her husband, destined to be mere mortals. Chang–O took a double dose of immortality pill, without sharing with her husband (rude). She floated up to the Moon, leaving her husband behind. Call upon her for: Love, partnership, courage, power, fertility, growth, manifesting, belief, self–confidence, new beginnings, transformation.

Cybele/Kybele –Phrygian goddess of the Underworld and associated with the dark Moon. Worshipped in ancient Greece and found in Romany mythology. Some associate her with the Greek/Minoan goddess Rhea. She is known as mother of the gods. Associated with mountains, caves, nature and wild animals particularly hawks, lions and bees. Call upon her for: Love, victory, strength, relationships, humour, healing, health, fun, stability.

Epona – Celtic/Saxon/Gaulish goddess of horses. Ancient Britains gave her the title 'Rigantona' which translates as Great Queen. Call upon her for: Protection, animals, love, fertility, providence, leadership, authority.

Ereshkigal – A Sumerian Queen of the Underworld and in her aspect as the Crone is goddess of the Dark Moon. An excellent goddess to work with to seek your shadow side. She is a powerful deity. Call upon her for: Shadow work, justice, power, love, wisdom.

Freyja/Freya – although not called a Moon goddess, many of her attributes connect her with both the Full and Dark Moons. A Norse goddess of love, beauty, war and fertility. She leads souls of dead warriors to the Otherworld. She rides a chariot driven by two cats, so she must be powerful to get cats to do what they are told! Call upon her for: Love, beauty, fertility, war, dearth, happiness, sex, sensuality, inspiration.

Hathor – Egyptian goddess of the Moon, associated with the dark Moon. Goddess of the Underworld but also ruler of the sky. She is a mother to all Egyptians. Definitely packing a powerful punch of feminine energy having given birth to the universe, she must have been exhausted. Call upon her for: Love, feminine energy, beauty, sexuality, happiness, romance, music, the arts, protection (primarily for women).

Hera – Greek Olympian Queen of gods, she covers marriage, childbirth and looking after women (she's got her hands full then). Although she can help when called upon, she has a jealous side and can be vengeful particularly when infidelity is involved. Call upon her for: Love, humour, forgiveness, romance, creativity, marriage, strength, courage, self–confidence, jealousy.

Inanna – Sumerian goddess of the full Moon and the stars, also known as Ishtar in Babylon. She is Queen of heaven and earth. She has a reputation for being a little bit saucy which led her to be linked to fertility rituals. She does look after her followers, dishing out the rules and keeping them safe. Call upon her for: Love, fertility, warrior, strength, courage, seduction, sensuality, protection, justice.

Ishtar – Babylonian goddess of the full Moon, also known as Inanna in Sumeria. A goddess of love, sex and war (pretty much covers it all then) she is a bit of a floozy, taking many lovers to bed (I don't judge). Call upon her for: Love, passion, sexuality, fertility, womanhood, independence, insight, inspiration, wishes.

Isis – Egyptian goddess Queen of Egypt. She is looked upon as Mother Moon, Queen of Sorcery and the life force within the river Nile. Isis taught her people useful skills, those they would need to survive and flourish, no being high up in the sky for this one, she got down with her subjects (very practical woman). Call upon her for: Magic, dreams, divination, harvest, perspective, love, spirituality, faithfulness, destiny, revitalisation, fulfilment, inner beauty, spirituality, rebirth, feminine energy, knowledge, motherhood, healing, changes, manifesting.

Juno – A Roman goddess, mother of all the gods. She protects Rome and all things feminine. She is a goddess of marriage, women and young girls. She is a strong, confident business woman, she definitely has a modern approach to being a deity. Her Greek equivalent is Hera. Call upon her for: Romance, love, relationships, marriage, protection, leadership, time, feminine energy, safety, happiness.

Luna – Roman goddess of the Moon. Depicted as a beautiful woman with the power to ease childbirth and bring about love. She carries a very strong feminine energy. If you want an answer to a problem, then call upon this lovely lady to bring you the answer in your dreams, it is her speciality. Her Greek equivalent is Selene. Call upon her for: Feminine energy, water magic, safety, travel, intuition, blue Moon magic, protection, illusion, truth, love, psychic abilities, dreams, solutions.

Venus – Roman goddess of love, passion and sexuality. This goddess has more va va voom than she needs, so she likes to share it around. She also covers gardens and spring within her remit. Equivalent to the Greek Aphrodite. Call upon her for: Love, passion, sexuality, romance, beauty, self–esteem, happiness, relationships, charm, the arts.

Vesta – Roman goddess of the crescent Moon, the hearth and home. She rules domesticity with a flip of the feather duster and a whip of her apron. She keeps the house and family running like clockwork. She is known as Hestia in Greece. Call upon her for: Home, family, relationships, harmony, peace, love, fertility, fire magic, spirituality.

World celebration days

I have given some dates and a little information on celebrations from around the world that take place during February. A lot of them were based on Moon phases. I apologise for any errors but history is a fickle thing and calendars have changed over the years…

Pagan

Imbolc – 1st/2nd February. The beginnings of Spring. When the earth begins to stir and life begins to awaken. This festival is also known sometimes as Candlemas. This festival is one dedicated to the Maiden aspect of the Goddess and it is usually attributed to the Goddess Brighid (also called Bride or Brigit).

Hindu

Maha Shivarati is a festival in honour of Lord Shiva and falls on the 13th or 14th day of the Hindu month of Maagha. It usually occurs in February or March. It is celebrated during the night and day that comes just before the new Moon. Prayers and rituals are held dedicated to Lord Shiva.

Thaipusam is an important festival observed by the Hindus of southern India during the Tamil month of Thai (January – February). Outside of India, it is celebrated mainly by the Tamil speaking community settled in Malaysia, Singapore, South Africa, Sri Lanka and elsewhere around the world.

Thaipusam is dedicated to the Hindu god Murugan, the son of Shiva and Parvati. Murugan is also known as Kartikeya, Subramaniam, Sanmukha, Shadanana, Skanda and Guha. It is believed that on this day, Goddess Parvati presented a lance to Lord Murgan to vanquish the demon army of Tarakasura and combat their evil deeds. Therefore, Thaipusam is a celebration of the victory of good over evil.

Maha Shivratri – The night of the worship of Lord Shiva, occurs on the 14th night of the new Moon during the dark half of the month of Phalguna. It falls on a Moonless February night, when Hindus offer special prayer to the lord of destruction. Shivratri (Sanskrit 'ratri' = night) is the night when he is said to have performed the Tandava Nritya or the dance of primordial creation, preservation and destruction. The festival is observed for one day and one night only.

Greek

1st February – Demeter/ Persephone – Celebrating the return of Persephone to her mother Demeter after her descent into the Otherworld.

11th–13th February – Anthesteria was held annually for three days (11th–13th) in the month of Anthesterion (February–March). Although its name indicates a Festival of Flowers (anthos), the festival focused primarily on opening the new wine and on placating the spirits of the dead. On the evening of the first day, called Pithoigia (Jar–opening), casks of the previous vintage were taken to the sanctuary of Dionysus in the Marshes and libations were offered to the god of wine and sampled by the entire household. The rooms and the drinking vessels were adorned with spring flowers, as were also the children over three years of age. The second day, named Choes (Pitchers), was a time of merrymaking. The people dressed themselves gaily, some in the disguise of the mythical personages in the suite of Dionysus, and paid a round of visits to their acquaintances. The primary activity of the day was a drinking competition, in which participants sat at separate tables and competed in silence at draining a chous (a five–litre container) of wine. Slaves had a share as well. Miniature choes were given to children as toys, and "first Choes" was a rite of passage.

Diasia – A great festival celebrated in Athens in honour of Zeus. The whole town took part, the wealthier citizens offered victims whilst the poorer classes burned incense accompanied by plenty of feasting and a fair.

Christianity

Celebrating St Brighid's Day and the Christian celebration of Candlemas all with the theme of recognising and welcoming the first day of spring, new beginnings and new initiations.

2nd February – The Virgin Mary – Day of the Holy Virgin Mary when candles are lit.

14th February – St Valentine – A descendant of Lupercalia perhaps, in the middle of February names of willing young ladies were put in a box and shaken up, each young suitor would draw out one at random, the girl thus won to remain his companion whilst the festivities lasted.

Egypt

1st February – Egyptian festival of Ptah; day of return of the image of the deity in the festival 'Amun–in–the–festival–of–raising–heaven'.

26th February – Mut – A powerful, protective and primordial vulture goddess of Egypt, later in her lioness form also the wife of the god Amun of Karnak and mother of the Moon god Khonsu. Every High Priestess Queen of Egypt wore the vulture goddess Mut as a head dress to signify their spiritual development, opening of the third eye and blending of her head with the goddess of life and death herself.

Rome

2nd February – Februa – An old Roman custom of burning candles to the goddess Februa, mother of Marsh to scare away evil spirits.

15th February – Lupa, the She Wolf/Faunus/Inuus – The Lupercalia was celebrated to worship the she–wolf who suckled Romulus & Remus. It started with a group of specially appointed priests gathering at the Lupercal, a cave at the bottom of the Palatine Hill. The priests would offer a sacrifice a goat and anoint the Lupercii (young male participants) on their foreheads with the blood. The blood was wiped away with milk by other priests, and the young men laughed at them. The Lupercii them skinned the sacrificed goat and ripped the hide into strips which they tied around their naked waists. They then got drunk and ran around Rome striking everyone they met with goatskin thongs. Young women who were touched in this manner were thought to be specially blessed, especially in regards to fertility and procreation.

Lupercalia was a very ancient festival and may have originally been a festival for purification and fertility in honour of either Faunus or Inuus.

Feralia – The Feralia was the closing festival of the Parentalia.

During the Feralia, families would picnic at the tombs of their deceased family members and give libations to the dearly departed. It was believed that the shades of the dead could walk upon the earth above their graves during Feralia.

February 22nd – Caristia – also known as the Cara Cognatio, was held to honour Concordia. During this festival family members would gather in the home and feast together and then make offerings to the household deities and settle arguments.

27th February – Equirria – This festival involved racing horses to honour Mars. It was held in the Campus Martius or the Campus Martialis on the Caelian Hill if the Campus Martius was flooded. The Equirria was said to have been founded by Romulus.

5–17th February – The Fornacalia was held in honour of bread, and the ovens used to dry grains. This festival was movable and could have been held any time between February 5th and February 17th.

Quirinalia on February 17 – The Quirinalia was a festival of Quirinus, and it signalled the end of the Fornacalia. It was also known as the "Feast of Fools".

13–21st February – Parentalia – This festival honoured the Di Manes. It began at dawn on February 13th with private ceremonies and ended with the public Feralia on February 21st. During the Parentalia every temple was closed, marriages were forbidden to take place, magistrates were not allowed to wear anything signifying their office, and all Romans were expected to give offerings to the deceased at the necropolis located outside the city walls.

February 23rd – Terminalia – On this day, landowners would honour the boundaries of their land at the boundary markers and the god Terminus. Rome's public boundary stone in the temple of Jupiter Optimus Maximus was also honoured. Garlands were placed over the boundary stones, and altars were built near them. Offerings of grain and honey were given by the children, and the adults would offer wine and pig blood. Everyone was dressed in white and were required to keep silent throughout the offerings. A picnic feast was held at the end of the ritual.

Amburbium – This ritual was held in Rome to clean and purify the city and everything in it. The actual date changed from year to year, though it was usually held after the ides.

Norse

Disting – Norse festival of the Idises, when the effects of winter are beginning to lessen and the world prepares itself for spring. Disting is characterised by preparing the land for planting. In ancient times, Disting was the time when the cattle were counted and one's wealth was tallied; thus, making it a festival of prosperity as well. It was said that new calves born during Disting were a sign of great abundance for the coming year.

Valisblot – Many modern Asatruar celebrate Valisblot, or Vali's Feast, even though there is no historical precedent for associating Odin's youngest son with this festival; other than the name Vali associated with "Valentine." The hero Svenfjotli, son of Sigimund, was reputed to have been born at this time, and often blots are drunk to him as well.

Babylonian

21st February – Anunitu, the heavenly one was a Babylonian goddess with one fish between her legs and one across her breasts. This was a day of celebration in her honour.

China

23rd February – Birthday of the Chinese God of Wealth.

MARCH

Spring is in the air! Hopefully... You can begin to feel the change. The earth is waking properly albeit that some parts of the globe may still be covered in snow, but the Sun is gaining in strength. As the month progresses, we will start to see and feel that spring air. Plants, animals and humans are feeling those familiar stirrings...ooh err. Everything is fresh, new and young.

March heralds the arrival of spring and the celebration of the Spring Equinox. Dark and light are equal on the equinox, so it always represents a time of finding balance for me.

And of course, with Ostara/the spring equinox being in March we get to celebrate new life and new beginnings in the form of chocolate...who could argue with that?

Mother Earth is awakening and feeling the first joys of spring, join in the celebrations and revel in the new and exciting energy. It is a time to plant new seeds, not just in the garden but within your life as well, a time to bring in the inspiration and make wonderful plans for new schemes and adventures.

I know you don't really want to hear this but...think 'spring cleaning' too, not just the house but a whole magical spring clean that includes clearing out old habits and past worries too.

This is the time of the Maiden; young, excitable and literally full of the joys of spring.

March Magical Energy

Energy breaks into the open; growing, prospering, exploring. New beginnings; balance of light and dark. Breaking illusions. Seeing the truth in your life however much it may hurt. Rebirth, renewal, new life, growth and balance. Fertility (not just babies but new projects and ideas as well). Reconciliation, resolving issues and conflicts, protection, self–control and communication.

Colours: Pink, pale green, pale blue, yellow, white, lilac
Sign: Pisces
Element: Earth
Season: Spring

March Moon Names

Storm Moon, Seed Moon, Moon of Winds, Plow/Plough Moon, Worm Moon, Hrethmonath, Lentzinmanoth, Lenten/Lengthening Moon, Sap Moon, Crow Moon, Snow Bird Moon, Sore Eye Moon, Sleeping Moon, Big Famine Moon, Wind Moon and Moon of the Snowblind.

The Worm Moon name is because the ground begins to soften in March and the earthworm casts start appearing.

The name Sap Moon comes from the time of year when the maple sap begins to flow.

Sore Eye Moon – long days watching the glare of the Sun on the snow gives you sore eyes.

Hrethmonath is Anglo Saxon for purifying or cleansing month. Hertha is an old word for earth and the name of the great Earth Mother Goddess. Lentzinmanoth translates as 'spring month'. Lenten moon means the last full moon of winter.

Plants to work with in March

These are my suggested herbs to work with that correspond with the energy of this month. But, trust your intuition and the supplies that you have in your cupboards.

Birch

(Betula pendula, Betula pubescens, Betula lenta, Betula alba)

Birch Magical Properties:

Purification, protection, exorcism, new beginnings, courage, fertility, love, release

Ruling planet – Venus, Moon, Jupiter

Sign – Sagittarius

Element – Water, Air
Gender – Feminine

Bluebell/Harebell

(Campanula rotundifolia, Hyacinthoides non–scripta)
Bluebell Heart Magical Properties:
Truth, shape shifting, protection, healing
Ruling planet – Mercury
Element – Water
Gender – Feminine

Cornflower/Batchelor's Buttons

(Centaurea cyanus)
Cornflower/Batchelor's Buttons Magical Properties:
Love, psychic powers, protection, fertility, abundance, Faeries
Ruling planet – Venus, Saturn
Element – Water, Earth
Gender – Feminine

Cyclamen

(Cyclamen spp)
Cyclamen Magical Properties:
Happiness, self–esteem, protection, fertility, love, lust, nightmares
Ruling planet – Venus
Element – Water
Gender – Feminine

Hawthorn

(Crataegus oxacantha/monogyna)
Hawthorn Magical Properties:
Happiness, fertility, love, protection, purification, forgiveness, faeries, hope
Ruling planet – Mars, Venus

Sign – Sagittarius
Element – Fire
Gender – Masculine

Hazel

(Corylus spp. avellana, Corylus cornuta)
Hazel Magical Properties:
Fertility, wishes, love, protection, luck, wisdom, divination, healing, inspiration, prosperity
Ruling planet – Sun
Element – Air
Gender – Masculine

Honesty

(Lunaria spp)
Honesty Magical Properties:
Money, monsters, truth
Ruling planet – Moon
Element – Earth
Gender – Feminine

Horsetail

(Equisetum arvense, Equisetum telmateia)
Horsetail Magical Properties:
Fertility, snakes, longevity, strength, cleansing
Ruling planet – Saturn
Element – Earth
Gender – Feminine

Pine

(Pinus)
Pine Magical Properties:
Centring, focus, Dragon magic, protection, truth, abundance, purification, fertility, healing

Ruling planet – Mars, Saturn
Sign – Capricorn
Element – Air, Fire
Gender – Masculine

Primrose

(Primula vulgaris)
Primrose Magical Properties:
Love, protection, faeries, changes, growth
Ruling planet – Venus
Element – Earth
Gender – Feminine

Saint John's Wort

(Hypericum perforatum)
Saint John's Wort Magical Properties:
Protection, health, strength, love, divination, happiness, abundance, truth
Ruling planet – Sun
Sign – Aquarius, Libra
Element – Fire
Gender – Masculine

Snapdragon

(Antirrhinum majus)
Snapdragon Magical Properties:
Dragon magic, divination, Elementals, protection, hexes, truth, sleep, nightmares
Ruling planet – Mars
Sign – Gemini
Element – Fire
Gender – Masculine

Sunflower

(Helianthus annuus)

Sunflower Magical Properties:

Wishes, fertility, truth, integrity, luck, protection, loyalty, happiness

Ruling planet – Sun

Sign – Leo

Element – Fire

Gender – Masculine

Sweetpea

(Lathyrus odoratus)

Sweetpea Magical Properties:

Courage, strength, friendship, peace, happiness, truth, spirituality, psychic abilities, protection, sleep

Ruling planet – Venus, Moon, Mercury

Element – Water

Gender – Feminine

Foods, Herbs and Spices to work with in March

Whether you chose to include the foods in a recipe for the table or add them to spell work, here is my suggested list of foods to work with for the energy of this month.

Artichoke (Globe)

(Cynara cardunculus /scolymus)

Artichoke Magical Properties:

Protection, growth, passion, strength, courage

Ruling planet – Mars

Element – Fire

Gender – Masculine/Feminine

Cabbage

(Brassica oleracea/var.)

Cabbage Magical Properties:
Moon magic, protection, prosperity, fertility, love
Ruling planet – Moon
Element – Water
Gender – Feminine

Carrot

(Daucus carota)
Carrot Magical Properties:
Clarity, fertility, passion
Ruling planet – Mars
Element – Fire
Gender – Masculine

Clove

(Eugenia carophyllus, Syzygium aromaticum, Caryophyllus aromaticus)
Clove Magical Properties:
Love, money, exorcism, clarity, protection, abundance, repels negativity, prevents gossip, stress relief, truth
Ruling planet – Jupiter
Element – Fire
Gender – Masculine

Cranberry

(Vaccinium oxycoccos)
Cranberry Magical Properties:
Protection, emotions, communication
Ruling planet – Mars
Element – Water, Fire
Gender – Feminine

Eggs

Eggs Magical Properties:

Fertility, creation, life, new beginnings, divination
Element – Water, Earth, Air, Fire
Gender – Masculine/Feminine

Fennel

(Foeniculum vulgare)
Fennel Magical Properties:
Purification, protection, healing
Ruling planet – Mercury
Element – Fire
Gender – Masculine

Mustard

(Brassica juncea, Brassica nigra, Sinapis hirta)
Mustard Magical Properties:
Clarity, psychic abilities, protection, astral travel, faith, success
Ruling planet – Mars
Element – Fire
Gender – Masculine

Parsley

(Petroselinum crispum, Petrselinum sativum)
Parsley Magical Properties:
Protection, purification, lust, happiness, fertility, spirit work
Ruling planet – Mercury
Element – Air
Gender – Masculine

Pasta

Pasta Magical Properties:
Psychic powers, protection, communication, creativity
Ruling planet – Mercury
Element – Earth

Gender – Masculine

Pomegranate

(Punica granatum)

Pomegranate Magical Properties:

Growth, fertility, wishes, death, rebirth, new beginnings

Ruling planet – Mercury

Element – Fire, Earth

Gender – Masculine

Rice

(Oryza spp)

Rice Magical Properties:

Prosperity, fertility, protection, rain, grounding, stability

Ruling planet – Sun

Element – Air, Earth

Gender – Masculine

Spinach

(Spinacia oleracea)

Spinach Magical Properties:

Passion, fertility, strength

Ruling planet – Jupiter

Element – Earth

Gender – Feminine

Walnut

(Juglans regia)

Walnut Magical Properties:

Wishes, mental powers, clarity, fertility

Ruling planet – Sun

Element – Fire

Gender – Masculine

Crystals to work with in March

As always, go with your intuition and what you have in your collection when working with crystals. The list below is my suggestion of crystals that work particularly well with the energy of this month.

Agate (moss)

Agate (moss) magical properties

Nature, happiness, prosperity, wealth, longevity, friendship, success, abundance, healing, renewal, fertility, creativity, confidence, strength, love, beginnings, self–esteem, communication, emotions, stress, releasing, hope, trust, depression, growth, finances, cleansing, support, peace, stability, fears, luck, divination

Energy	Receptive
Element	Earth
Planet	Moon
Zodiac	Virgo, Gemini

Agate (blue lace)

Agate (blue lace) magical properties

Mediation, spirituality, uplifting, calming, peace, communication, emotions, support, optimism, happiness, protection, cleansing, healing, prosperity, longevity, strength, courage, clarity, success, patience, truth, stress, relaxation, creativity, justice, travel, renewal, understanding, soothing, trust

Energy	Receptive
Element	Water
Planet	Mercury
Zodiac	Gemini

Celestite

Celestite magical properties

Divine, spirit work, love, clarity, decisions, meditation,

communication, peace, dreams, stress, healing, astral travel, calming, uplifting, harmony, happiness, spirituality

Energy: Receptive
Element: Air, Water
Planet: Neptune, Venus
Zodiac: Gemini

Chrysocolla

Chrysocolla magical properties

Wisdom, peace, patience, love, soothing, intuition, energy, calming, emotions, fear, strength, clarity, balance, negative energy, insight, releasing, spirituality, psychic abilities, guilt, divine, harmony, communication, meditation

Energy: Receptive
Element: Water
Planet: Venus
Zodiac: Taurus

Fluorite

Fluorite magical properties

Magic, imagination, discernment, aptitude, psychic protection, protection, purification, calming, relaxation, tension, anxiety, organisation, structure, challenges, declutter, releasing, support, breaking patterns, intuition, confidence, reassurance, comforting, communication, balance, spirituality, decisions, manifestation, peace, meditation, grounding, healing, cleansing, channelling, past life work, fairy realm, amplifying, memory, power, emotions, depression, stability

Energy: Projective
Element: Water, Air
Planet: Neptune
Zodiac: Scorpio, Aquarius, Pisces

Howlite

Howlite magical properties

Understanding, wisdom, connection, truth, meditation, focus, stress, anxiety, calm, strength, peace, releasing, emotions, selfishness, communication, creativity, inspiration, motivation, concentration, support, patience, relaxation, courage, past life work, astral travel

Energy: Projective
Element: Earth
Planet: Moon, Earth
Zodiac: Gemini, Virgo

Kyanite

Kyanite magical properties

Balance, harmony, calming, connection, psychic abilities, healing, communication, grounding, transformation, meditation, relaxation, luck, growth, leadership, new beginnings, clarity, decisions, stability, truth, vitality, abundance, spirituality, channelling, understanding, dreams

Energy Receptive
Element Water
Planet Jupiter, Venus, Mars
Zodiac Aries, Libra, Taurus

Larimar

Larimar magical properties

Peace, clarity, healing, inspiration, spirituality, understanding, calming, soothing, uplifting, emotions, fears, depression, patience, creativity, love, communication, friendship, guidance, happiness, decisions, relaxation, meditation, wisdom, divine, harmony

Energy: Receptive
Element: Water/Fire/Spirit
Planet: Neptune

Zodiac: Pisces

Moonstone

Moonstone magical properties

New beginnings, Moon magic, intuition, calming, psychic abilities, balance, harmony, wishes, cleansing, uplifting, hope, meditation, emotions, love, divination, spirituality, wealth, truth, healing, sensuality, insight, peace, wisdom, communication, confidence, abundance, prosperity, dreams, fertility, travel

Energy Receptive
Element Water
Planet Moon
Zodiac Cancer, Libra, Scorpio
Birthstone June, September

Pyrite

Pyrite magical properties

Releasing, breaking patterns, clarity, protection, support, decisions, growth, success, inspiration, grounding, vitality, learning, perception, memory, wisdom, psychic abilities, healing, cleansing, prosperity, wealth, abundance, luck, strength, motivation, manifestation, finances, energy, Sun magic, power, focus, perseverance, confidence, divination, communication, self–confidence, meditation

Energy Projective
Element Fire
Planet Mars, Sun
Zodiac Leo

Quartz (rose)

Quartz (rose) magical properties

Love, happiness, emotions, spirituality, growth, fears, healing, sexuality, passion, calming, soothing, stress, depression, sleep, luck, wisdom, inspiration, success, intuition, grounding, balance, prosperity, self–esteem, harmony, trust, jealousy, gossip, beauty, peace, cleansing, fertility

Energy	Receptive
Element	Earth, Water
Planet	Venus, Moon
Zodiac	Taurus

Sodalite

Sodalite magical properties

Creativity, communication, peace, friendship, clarity, truth, connection, knowledge, wisdom, emotions, balance, divination, psychic abilities, cleansing, confidence, fears, love, intuition, decisions, perseverance, anxiety, insight, organisation, self–esteem, releasing, understanding, harmony, learning, dreams, meditation

Energy	Receptive
Element	Water
Planet	Jupiter, Venus
Zodiac	Sagittarius

Turquoise

Turquoise magical properties

Purification, negative energy, protection, balance, relaxation, emotions, stress, spirituality, energy, depression, clarity, wisdom, understanding, psychic abilities, insight, intuition, past life work, communication, wealth, abundance, finances, prosperity, luck, decisions, friendship, uplifting, meditation, love, harmony

Energy	Receptive
Element	Earth
Planet	Venus, Neptune
Zodiac	Sagittarius, Pisces, Aquarius
Birthstone	December

Moon Deities to work with in March

Here you will find my suggestions on some of the Moon deities to work with that align with the energies of this month. Trust your intuition and be guided by the deities that may also make themselves known to you.

Anuket – Egyptian goddess of the crescent Moon. She is responsible for the annual flooding of the river Nile. She watches over agriculture and all food growth along with wealth and prosperity. Call upon her for: Wealth, prosperity, growth, fertility, nourishment, contentment.

Chang–O – Chinese goddess of the Moon. Banished from heaven along with her husband, destined to be mere mortals. Chang–O took a double dose of immortality pill, without sharing with her husband (rude). She floated up to the Moon, leaving her husband behind. Call upon her for: Love, partnership, courage, power, fertility, growth, manifesting, belief, self–confidence, new beginnings, transformation.

Luna – Roman goddess of the Moon. Depicted as a beautiful woman with the power to ease childbirth and bring about love. She carries a very strong feminine energy. If you want an answer to a problem, then call upon this lovely lady to bring you the answer in your dreams, it is her speciality. Her Greek equivalent is Selene. Call upon her for: Feminine energy, water magic, safety, travel, intuition, blue Moon magic, protection, illusion, truth, love, psychic abilities, dreams, solutions.

Ma'at – Egyptian goddess of the crescent Moon, order and balance. Think 'strict school headmistress', she dishes out the justice as she sees fit, whether you are a deity or a mere mortal. Her name translates as 'truth/that which is straight'. If you are looking for balance between work and home life or any kind of justice, Ma'at should be on your speed dial. Call upon her for: Justice, balance, freedom, new beginnings, morals, organisation, law, promises, fairness, truth, oaths, harmony, honesty.

Mama Quila/Killa– Incan goddess of the full Moon, she cried silver tears. Lunar eclipses were said to be caused by a serpent or animal attacking Mama Quilla (ouch). She also covers marriage and the menstrual cycle. She is known as 'Mother Moon' and is responsible for the passage of time. Call upon her for: Time, Moon magic, feminine issues, protection of women, marriage, relationships, truth, deceit.

Ops – Roman goddess of the full Moon and agriculture. If you are after abundance and prosperity, then Ops is your 'go to' goddess. She can also teach you all kinds of practical skills to gain that abundance for yourself. Ain't nothing in this life for free! Call upon her for: Fertility, abundance, wealth, nurturing, prosperity, opportunity, growth.

Parvati – Hindu goddess of the crescent Moon. Oh, this goddess has all the feminine wiles and knows how to use them. She is maiden to the Mother Durga and Crone Kali. She can charm the secrets out of the trees. Call upon her for: Power, creativity, new beginnings, victory, feminine energy, beauty, charm, secrets, the arts, fertility, cleansing, devotion.

Rhiannon – if you aren't singing the Fleetwood Mac song right now, you need to... A Welsh goddess and great Queen of Wales. She brings peace, comfort and patience. If you are looking for magical enchantments, then she has a bounty of them. Call upon her for: Patience, comfort, peace, magic, movement, relaxation, communication, fertility, leadership, spirit work, motivation, dream work.

Sin/Nanna – Sumerian Moon god with a long flowing beard sometimes depicted as being made of lapis lazuli. He rode upon a winged bull. He was represented by the number thirty, the days in a lunar month. Nanna is the Sumerian name for the Moon god, which may mean just the full Moon phase. 'Sin' being the name given to the crescent Moon. Call upon him for: Moon magic, fertility, prosperity, growth.

Vesta – Roman goddess of the crescent Moon, the hearth and home. She rules domesticity with a flip of the feather duster and a whip of her apron. She keeps the house and family running like clockwork. She is known as Hestia in Greece. Call upon her for: Home, family, relationships, harmony, peace, love, fertility, fire magic, spirituality.

World celebration days

I have given some dates and a little information on celebrations from around the world that take place during March. A lot of them were based on Moon phases. I apologise for any errors but history is a fickle thing and calendars have changed over the years…

Ancient Egypt

21st March – Festival of restructuring of the heavens.

5th March – Isis – The festival of the ship of Isis held in recognition of her being patroness of navigation and inventor of the sail.

25th/27th March – Renenutet – Harvest offering to the Egyptian deity Renenutet.

Pagan

20th–22nd March – spring equinox, Ostara. Ostara is a celebration of the Spring Equinox; the signs of spring should be well under way and new planting of crops and flowers should be happening. It is a time when day and night are equal. Spring is sprung!

Rome

1st March – The Matronalia – A festival celebrated by Roman matrons, the anniversary of the foundation of the temple of Juno Lucina on the Esquiline. In the house's prayers were offered for a prosperous wedlock, the women received presents from the men and waited on the slaves. In the temple of the Goddess women and girls prayed to her and brought pious offerings.

Vesta – On every 1st March the Vestal fire was rekindled only by a burning glass or the method of friction by boring a piece of wood from a fruit tree. The withered laurel was withdrawn from the Vestal hearth so that Vesta may show herself dressed in fresh leaves.

7th March – Junonalia – This day honoured Juno with a procession of 27 girls accompanying a statue of Juno carved out of a cypress tree.

15th March – Anna Parenna – The festival for Anna Parenna, "goddess of the returning year" was held each year on the first day of the ancient year. Traditionally, Romans would cross the Tiber and "go abroad" into Etruria and have picnics in flimsy tents or huts made of branches. Both men and women would drink as much alcohol as they could, for it was thought that one would live for as many years as cups of alcohol one could drink on this day. Once finished with the picnic and drinking the Romans would wander back to their homes in Rome.

Guild Festival – Guilds whose members practiced the arts of Minerva had a festival on this day. This was mainly a Plebeian festival and was celebrated at Minerva's temple in Rome. Weapons used for war were purified during this festival.

16–17th March – Festival of Bacchus – This festival was held to honour Bacchus in order to convince the god to give a good grape harvest later that year. It was originally a Greek festival held to honour Dionysus.

17th March – Liberalia — Liberalia was a fertility festival celebrated in rural areas and was held in honour of Liber Pater and Libera. Most towns created a large phallus and carted it through the countryside and into the town centre where it stayed until the beginning of the next month. The phallus was decorated by a virtuous woman with flowers, which ensured a good crop at the next harvest. Masks were also hung on fences, and crude songs were Sung during the procession.

19th –23rd March – Minerva – The Greater Quinquatrus was a festival for Minerva as a Goddess of the Arts. The first day of the festival was dedicated to the arts, and those who practiced them would give Minerva sacrifices at her temple on the Aventine.

Mars/Nerine – On 23rd March there was a festival of Mars and Nerine, the Sabine goddess who was identified with Athena/ Minerva or Aphrodite.

Luna – The Italian goddess of the Moon had in Rome an ancient sanctuary on the Aventine in which as Goddess of the month she received worship on the last day of March (which was the first month of the old Roman year).

Hindu

Holi is the Hindu festival of colours, it celebrates a good harvest, fertility and the triumph of good over evil. Every year it is celebrated on the day after the full Moon in early March. It is also time for spring harvest. Colour powders and dyes are thrown at one another creating a huge festival of colour.

Nyepi – Nyepi is New Year's Day in Bali; Nyepi is a day of celebration and of silence – a day to remember not only oneself but also the state of the universe before creation. Usually Nyepi falls in mid–March. Following the Hindu lunar calendar, Nyepi begins the Saka year in the month of Chaitra (March). In India the Saka calendar begins with purnima or full Moon, but in Bali it starts with amavasya or Moonless night. Nyepi begins with Fast and Silence. Even as Bali celebrates Nyepi, life stands still and quietude descends on this one of its kind 'Day of Silence'. The Balinese Hindus believe that before ushering in the New Year, one should meditate for self–introspection, which can be achieved by observing a fast, and maintaining silence with very little movement inside the house and none at all outside– virtually closing the gates, switching off light and fire for the day.

Navaratri – Navaratri ("nava" + "ratri") literally means "nine nights." This ritual is observed twice a year, in spring and in autumn. "Vasanta Navaratri" or Spring Navaratri is nine days of fast and worship that Hindus undertake during spring every year during which the devout Hindu seeks the blessings of the Mother Goddess. "The Divine Mother or Devi is worshipped during the Vasanta Navaratri. This occurs during the spring. She is worshipped by Her own command.

Ramnavami – Ramnavami or the birthday of Lord Rama falls on the 9th day of the bright fortnight of the month of Chaitra (March–April). In Honour of Lord Rama Ramnavami is one of the most important festivals of the Hindus, particularly the Vaishnava sect of the Hindus. On this auspicious day, devotees repeat the name of Rama with every breath and vow to lead a righteous life. People pray to attain the final beatitude of life through intense devotion towards Rama and invoke him for his blessings and protection.

Greek

15th March – Week long purification for the Rites of Kybele on 22nd March begins initiated by a process of reed bearers.

16th March – Mounykhion – In honour of Artemis the Moon goddess and lady of the beasts. Procession of people carrying small round cakes Amphiphontes in which small torches were stuck. These were offered to Artemis. Some say the cake was called Amphiphon which can mean 'shining by double light' as they were offered when the Sun and the Moon were both visible. In ancient times a she goat was sacrificed.

Artemis – Artemis' favourite animal was held all over Greece to be the hind, from this sacred animal the month which the other Greeks called Artemision (March–April) was named by the Athenians Elaphe–bolion and held her festival as goddess of game and hunting at which cakes in the shape of deer were offered up.

22nd March – Kybele – After a week of fasting and purification the festival properly begins.

The Gardens of Adonis (the dying or dead lover of Astarte/ Aphrodite/Venus were baskets or pots filled with earth in which wheat, barley, lettuce, fennel and flowers were sown and tended for eight days (usually by women).

25th March – Hilaria – "Day of Joy" This festival honoured Attis and was primarily a festival for the followers of his cult. Several smaller festivals connected to the Hilaria were held on the preceding days, such as the Dies Sanguinis ("day of blood") on March 24, and the Day of Mourning on March 23.

Bendis – Bendis was a goddess of the Moon amongst the Thracians; she had power over heaven and earth and also identified with the Greek Artemis, Hecate and Persephone. A public festival was instituted called the Bendideia at which there were torch races and a procession.

Hecate/Artemis/Selene/Diana – Hot cross buns are always associated with Easter and Good Friday but they were around long before Christianity. Greeks offered to Apollo, Diana, Hecate and the Moon cakes with 'horns' called a 'bous', the cross symbolised the four quarters of the Moon. Wheaten cakes marked with a cross have been eaten at the Spring Festival by many cultures dating far back and indeed they were eaten wherever Diana was worshipped and her festival occurred at this time.

Dionysian festival – Greek Dionysian festival known as Great Dionysia or City Dionysia. This festival is highly significant as the origin of dramatic tragedy and comedy. The Great Dionysia is thought to have been founded, or at least revived, by the tyrant Pisistratus (c. 530 BCE). It was held in Athens at the end of March, when the city was once again full of visitors after the winter. The festival honoured Dionysus Eleuthereus, who was said to have been introduced into Athens from the village of Eleuterae.

Babylon

Tiamat – The Babylonians celebrated the spring equinox during which the Epic of the Creation of the World was recited twice and probably a series of rituals carried out.

Mesopotamia

31st March – Mammitu was the Goddess of Fate responsible for fixing of destinies. This was a time when the King of Mesopotamia would have his fortune read from a chart and be told what destiny awaited him and the kingdom for the year to come.

Christian

Good Friday, a day to pay honour to Mary Magdalene.

Europe

The Corn Mother – During the European ritual of the Corn Mother and Corn Daughter the last sheaf of corn, called the Corn Mother is made up into the shape of a woman by the oldest married woman in the village, the finest ears are plucked out of it and made into a wreath which twined with flowers is carried on the head of the prettiest girl in the village. On Easter Eve the grain is rubbed out of it by a seven–year–old girl and scattered amongst the young corn. Here the fertilising power of the Corn Mother is brought out by scattering seed taken from her body among the new corn and her influence over animal life is indicated by placing the straw in a manger.

APRIL

April can be a bit hit and miss with the weather, but it is (usually and hopefully) most definitely spring. Plants are starting to really come alive, the seeds planted at the spring equinox are making good headway and the weather is (she says again hopefully) a bit warmer.

We are working off the back of the spring equinox and heading towards Beltane, everything is alive and buzzing with energy. I think the equinox always brings about changes of one kind or another (in my experience anyway), it is a time to clear out the old and that which has not worked and to bring in new projects, new ventures and new ways of thinking, make changes that bring in the positive. It is so easy to get caught in a cycle of destructive or unhealthy action, now is the time to break free (yep I am singing now…). Sometimes we end up taking on too much and finding our entire life is out of balance and it has a ripple effect, like dropping a pebble into a still pool, the ripples from one tiny stone can have a huge effect on everything else. The equinox gives us an opportunity to re–balance and use all the energy that Beltane brings with it to put those changes into action.

Take a step back…take a really good look at your life and see where you can make changes to bring it back into alignment, to give a good balance between work, friends, family, play and 'you' time. Even little changes are a start and can lead onto bigger ones.

April Magical Energy

Put energy into creating and producing; return balance to all areas of your life. Change, transformation, self–confidence, self–reliance, take advantage of opportunities, build on projects that are already underway. Spring clean not just your home, but your spiritual and emotional areas as well. Set new plans, work on new projects and put things into motion to create a better life. Work on temper and emotional flare ups and selfishness.

Colours: Red, gold, green
Sign: Aries
Element: Earth
Season: Spring

April Moon Names

Growing Moon, Hare Moon, Seed or planting Moon, Planters Moon, and Budding trees Moon, Eostremonath, Pink Moon, Snow Melt Moon, Egg Moon, Frog Moon, New Shoots Moon, Peony Moon, Wild Cat Moon and Green Grass Moon.

Pink Moon refers to the appearance of wild ground phlox or moss pink, one of the first spring flowers to show. Eostremonath is the Anglo–Saxon name for April. Translates as Eostres month.

Plants to work with in April

These are my suggested herbs to work with that correspond with the energy of this month. But, trust your intuition and the supplies that you have in your cupboards.

Beech

(Fagus sylvatica)
Beech Magical Properties:
Wishes, creativity, spirituality, divination, luck, success
Ruling planet – Saturn
Sign – Sagittarius
Element – Air and Earth
Gender – Feminine

Benzoin

(Styrax benzoin)

Benzoin Magical Properties:
Prosperity, purification, calming, confidence, love, lust
Ruling planet – Sun, Venus
Sign – Capricorn
Element – Air
Gender – Masculine

Bergamot

(Monarda didyma, Mondarda fistulosa)
Bergamot Magical Properties:
Abundance, meditation, sleep, dreams, clarity, friendship
Sign – Gemini, Libra
Element – Air
Gender – Feminine

Clover

(Trifolium pratense, Trifolium repens)
Clover Magical Properties:
Luck, money, protection, love, fidelity, exorcism, success
Ruling planet – Mercury
Sign – Aries
Element – Air
Gender – Masculine

Holly

(Ilex aquifolium, Ilex opaca)
Holly Magical Properties:
Protection, luck, dreams, balance, success
Ruling planet – Mars, Saturn
Element – Fire
Gender – Masculine

Lemon Balm

(Melissa officinalis)

Lemon Balm Magical Properties:
Success, healing, anti–depression, memory, love, anxiety
Ruling planet – Moon & Venus
Sign – Cancer
Element – Water
Gender – Feminine

Lily of the Valley

(Convallaria majalis)
Lily of the Valley Magical Properties:
Happiness, cleansing, success, faeries, divination, magic
Ruling planet – Mercury
Sign – Pisces
Element – Air
Gender – Masculine

Primrose

(Primula vulgaris)
Primrose Magical Properties:
Love, protection, faeries, changes, growth
Ruling planet – Venus
Element – Earth
Gender – Feminine

Rowan

(Sorbus acuparia)
Rowan Magical Properties:
Psychic powers, power, success, protection, love, spirituality, faeries, divination, healing, inspiration
Ruling planet – Sun, Mercury
Sign – Sagittarius
Element – Fire
Gender – Masculine

Solomon's Seal

(Polygonatum officinale)

Solomon's Seal Magical Properties:

Wisdom, knowledge, protection, exorcism, success, Elementals, purification

Ruling planet – Saturn

Sign – Capricorn

Element – Water

Gender – Feminine

Foods, Herbs and Spices to work with in April

Whether you chose to include the foods in a recipe for the table or add them to spell work, here is my suggested list of foods to work with for the energy of this month.

Bay

(Laurus nobilis)

Bay Magical Properties:

Protection, purification, strength, power, healing, creativity, spirituality, psychic powers

Ruling planet – Sun

Element – Fire

Gender – Masculine

Black Pepper

(Piper nigrum)

Black Pepper Magical Properties:

Protection, exorcism, jealousy, negativity, strength, confidence, gossip

Ruling planet – Mars

Element – Fire

Gender – Masculine

Cheese

Cheese Magical Properties:

Success, happiness

Ruling planet –Saturn

Element – Earth, Air

Gender – Masculine

Chillies

(capsicum)

Chillies Magical Properties:

Creativity, energy, power, protection, passion, hex breaking

Ruling planet – Mars

Element – Fire

Gender – Masculine

Cinnamon

(Cinnamomum zeylanicum, Cinnamomum verum)

Cinnamon Magical Properties:

Success, healing, power, psychic powers, protection, love, focus, lust, spirituality, changes

Ruling planet – Sun

Element – Fire

Gender – Masculine

Cumin

(Cumimum cyminum)

Cumin Magical Properties:

Exorcism, protection, anti–theft, fidelity, lust, peace, love, abundance, success

Ruling planet – Mars

Element – Fire

Gender – Masculine

Ginger

(Zingiber officinale)

Ginger Magical Properties:

Healing, power, love, passion, success, prosperity, protection

Ruling planet – Mars

Element – Fire

Gender – Masculine

Paprika

(Capsicum annuum)

Paprika Magical Properties:

Creativity, energy

Ruling planet – Mars

Element – Fire

Gender –Masculine

Pasta

Pasta Magical Properties:

Psychic powers, protection, communication, creativity

Ruling planet – Mercury

Element – Earth

Gender – Masculine

Tomato

(Solanum lycopersicum)

Tomato Magical Properties:

Love, passion, protection, creativity

Ruling planet – Venus

Element – Water

Gender – Feminine

Vanilla

(Vanilla planifolia)

Vanilla Magical Properties:

Love, spirituality, sex magic, passion, creativity
Ruling planet – Venus
Element – Water, Air
Gender – Feminine

Yogurt

Yogurt Magical Properties:
Spirituality, creativity, depression
Ruling planet – Moon
Element – Water, Air
Gender – Feminine

Crystals to work with in April

As always, go with your intuition and what you have in your collection when working with crystals. The list below is my suggestion of crystals that work particularly well with the energy of this month.

Agate (moss)

Agate (moss) magical properties

Nature, happiness, prosperity, wealth, longevity, friendship, success, abundance, healing, renewal, fertility, creativity, confidence, strength, love, beginnings, self–esteem, communication, emotions, stress, releasing, hope, trust, depression, growth, finances, cleansing, support, peace, stability, fears, luck, divination

Energy	Receptive
Element	Earth
Planet	Moon
Zodiac	Virgo, Gemini

Aventurine (green)

Aventurine (green) magical properties

Balance, decisions, motivation, leadership, dreams, visualisation, creativity, luck, money, anxiety, calm, opportunities, happiness, adventure, love, courage, truth, comfort, support, healing, peace, connection, perception, intellect, psychic abilities

Energy: Projective
Element: Air
Planet: Mercury, Mars
Zodiac: Aries

Calcite (orange)

Calcite (orange) magical properties

Amplification, energy, protection, grounding, centring, purification, peace, calm, emotions, balance, fear, depression, problems, power, potential, breaking patterns, changes, inspiration, creativity, positive energy, wealth, abundance, leadership, perseverance, finances, confidence, determination, money, opportunities, clarity, productivity, release

Energy: Receptive
Element: Earth
Planet: Sun
Zodiac: Cancer

Carnelian

Carnelian magical properties

Grounding, protection, calm, concentration, confidence, self–worth, success, courage, creativity, negative energy, direction, control, organisation, opportunity, planning, psychic protection, jealousy, hate, harmony, depression, doubt, patience, stability, vitality, motivation, stamina, passion, truth, love, faith, honesty, trust, luck, abundance

Energy: Projective
Element: Fire
Planet: Sun
Zodiac: Taurus, Leo
Birthstone: May, June, July, August

Citrine

Citrine magical properties:

Happiness, joy, Sun magic, negative energy, optimism, abundance, depression, stress, success, wealth, healing, intuition, creativity, confidence, changes, self–esteem, protection, psychic powers, fears, clarity, stamina, nightmares

Energy: Projective
Element: Fire
Planet: Sun, Jupiter
Zodiac: Scorpio
Birthstone: November

Garnet

Garnet magical properties

Organisation, warrior spirit, protection, love, commitment, passion, sexuality, sensuality, attraction, depression, spiritual healing, success, self–confidence, energy, inspiration, perception, strength, survival, fear, courage, clarity, challenges, past life work, truth, compassion, deflecting negative energy, gossip, ambition, motivation, goals, purification, cleansing, balance, inner strength, self–empowerment, creativity, confidence, meditation, spirit work, nightmares, journeying, abundance, support

Energy: Projective
Element: Fie
Planet: Mars
Zodiac: Aries, Virgo, Capricorn, Leo, Aquarius
Birthstone: January

Goldstone

Goldstone magical properties

Ambition, luck, goals, determination, persistence, achievements, success, calm, emotions, energy, enthusiastic, confidence, self–belief, inner self, personal development, possibilities, courage, direction, clarity, uplifting, optimism, protection, deflects negative energy, knowledge, perception, manifestation, creativity, faith, energy flow, spirituality, abundance, wealth, grounding, perspective, ambition, drive, ingenuity, money, generosity, willpower, goals, emotions, divination (see also copper for additional magical properties)

Energy: Receptive/Projective
Element: Fire, Earth
Planet: Jupiter, Venus
Zodiac: Sagittarius

Labradorite

Labradorite magical properties

Transformation, cleansing, breaking patterns, potential, psychic abilities, intuition, confidence, spirituality, focus, protection, imagination, relaxation, soothing, energy, healing, stress, anxiety, luck, abundance, success, decisions, trust, changes, strength, courage, self–confidence, inspiration, perseverance, journeying, clarity, insight, meditation, depression, jealousy, grounding

Energy Projective
Element Water
Planet Earth, Moon, Uranus
Zodiac Aquarius, Sagittarius, Scorpio, Leo

Lepidolite

Lepidolite magical properties

Transformation, soothing, calming, stress, happiness, changes, emotions, psychic abilities, spirituality, depression, divination, connection, strength, uplifting, luck, hope, balance, peace, sleep, harmony, decisions, addiction, releasing, trust, goals, optimism, patience, dreams, opportunities, support, love

Energy Receptive
Element Water

Planet	Jupiter, Neptune
Zodiac	Libra

Malachite

Malachite magical properties

Changes, transformation, clarity, emotions, protection, support, healing, peace, travel, fears, growth, creativity, renewal, energy, wealth, money, opportunity, abundance, new beginnings, finances, success, business, focus, strength, wisdom, releasing, prosperity, breaking barriers, psychic abilities, manifestation, soothing, stress, love, power

Energy	Receptive
Element	Earth
Planet	Venus
Zodiac	Capricorn, Scorpio

Rhodocrosite

Rhodochrosite magical properties

Power, potential, strength, confidence, healing, new beginnings, breaking barriers, releasing, joy, happiness, creativity, determination, manifestation, prosperity, abundance, love, emotions, peace, renewal, connection, balance, spirituality, harmony, energy

Energy	Projective
Element	Fire
Planet	Mars, Jupiter
Zodiac	Scorpio, Leo

Rhodonite

Rhodonite magical properties

Protection, renewal, emotions, strength, soothing, clarity, happiness, love, balance, harmony, decisions, confidence, spirituality, peace, energy, passion, optimism, changes, vitality, anxiety, travel, psychic abilities, self–confidence, trust, calming, relaxation, patience, determination, releasing, stress, negative energy

Energy	Projective
Element	Fire
Planet	Mars, Venus
Zodiac	Taurus

Sodalite

Sodalite magical properties

Creativity, communication, peace, friendship, clarity, truth, connection, knowledge, wisdom, emotions, balance, divination, psychic abilities, cleansing, confidence, fears, love, intuition, decisions, perseverance, anxiety, insight, organisation, self–esteem, releasing, understanding, harmony, learning, dreams, meditation

Energy	Receptive
Element	Water
Planet	Jupiter, Venus
Zodiac	Sagittarius

Tiger's eye

Tiger's eye magical properties

Amplification, balance, harmony, releasing, fears, anxiety, courage, strength, self–confidence, focus, creativity, optimism, self–worth, protection, psychic abilities, healing, wealth, money, opportunity, abundance, prosperity, luck, success, commitment, determination, support, clarity, vitality, motivation, grounding, patience

Energy	Projective
Element	Fire, Earth
Planet	Sun
Zodiac	Leo, Capricorn

Moon Deities to work with in April

Here you will find my suggestions on some of the Moon deities to work with that align with the energies of this month. Trust your intuition and be guided by the deities that may also make themselves known to you.

Asherah – Ancient West Semitic goddess, often referred to as Queen of the Gods. Also known as 'She who walks on the sea' or 'holiness'. You will find her name in the Old Testament she is consort of Yahweh. Asherah is a goddess of the sea. Call upon her for: Divine wisdom, feminine energy, feminine issues, strength, self–esteem, self–confidence, courage, kindness, love, divination, insight, justice, fertility, compassion, healing, nurturing.

Cerridwen – Welsh goddess usually shown hunched over her cauldron filled with Awen (inspiration and wisdom). Generally seen as the crone aspect of the triad with Blodeuwedd and Arianrhod. A goddess of the Moon she covers death, rebirth, magic and divination of all kinds. Also, one of the five goddesses of Avalon. Call upon Cerridwen for: Inspiration, creativity, wisdom, death, rebirth, divination, prophecy, spiritual transformation, justice, fertility, luck.

Chang–O – Chinese goddess of the Moon. Banished from heaven along with her husband, destined to be mere mortals. Chang–O took a double dose of immortality pill, without sharing with her husband (rude). She floated up to the Moon, leaving her husband behind. Call upon her for: Love, partnership, courage, power, fertility, growth, manifesting, belief, self–confidence, new beginnings, transformation.

Hera – Greek Olympian Queen of gods, she covers marriage, childbirth and looking after women (she's got her hands full then). Although she can help when called upon, she has a jealous side and can be vengeful particularly when infidelity is involved. Call upon her for: Love, humour, forgiveness, romance, creativity, marriage, strength, courage, self–confidence, jealousy.

Ilmatar/Luonnotar – A Finnish–Ugrian creation goddess of the air whose duck laid eggs on her knee. The eggs fell and the whites became the Moon, the yolks the Sun and the shell pieces became the stars. She is goddess of the crescent Moon. Call upon her for: New beginnings, creativity, inspiration, traditions, fertility, nature, the arts, magic.

Isis – Egyptian goddess Queen of Egypt. She is looked upon as Mother Moon, Queen of Sorcery and the life force within the river Nile. Isis taught her people useful skills, those they would need to survive and flourish, no being high up in the sky for this one, she got down with her subjects (very practical woman). Call upon her for: Magic, dreams, divination, harvest, perspective, love, spirituality, faithfulness, destiny, revitalisation, fulfilment, inner beauty, spirituality, rebirth, feminine energy, knowledge, motherhood, healing, changes, manifesting.

Ixchel – Mayan goddess of the Moon, weaving, water and childbirth. Mother of all Mayan deities she rules over life and death and bears the title of 'Keeper of Souls'. Her name translates as 'Lady Rainbow'. She spends her time constantly changing from a beautiful young woman into an old crone, it must be both exhausting and confusing. Call upon her for: Weather magic, fertility, health, healing, childbirth, water magic, rainbow magic, control, power, choices, assertion, self–confidence.

Kali/Kali Ma – Hindu goddess of time, change and destruction and the Divine Mother. She has blue black skin, red eyes and four arms. Often seen with skulls hanging around her neck. This is a real kick butt, no messing kind of gal. She is a forceful destroyer but brings rebirth with it, she is the cycle of destruction and creation. Call upon her for: Death and rebirth, cycles, time, happiness, courage, hope, change, cleansing, transformation, destruction, fear, knowledge, creativity.

Ops – Roman goddess of the full Moon and agriculture. If you are after abundance and prosperity, then Ops is your 'go to' goddess. She can also teach you all kinds of practical skills to gain that abundance for yourself. Ain't nothing in this life for free! Call upon her for: Fertility, abundance, wealth, nurturing, prosperity, opportunity, growth.

Parvati – Hindu goddess of the crescent Moon. Oh, this goddess has all the feminine wiles and knows how to use them. She is maiden to the Mother Durga and Crone Kali. She can charm the secrets out of the trees. Call upon her for: Power, creativity, new beginnings, victory, feminine energy, beauty, charm, secrets, the arts, fertility, cleansing, devotion.

World celebration days

I have given some dates and a little information on celebrations from around the world that take place during April. A lot of them were based on Moon phases. I apologise for any errors but history is a fickle thing and calendars have changed over the years…

Rome

1st April – Venus/Fortuna/Concordia – The goddess Concordia was invoked with Venus and Fortuna by married women at the Veneralia on 1st April. At the time when Venus was worshipped the first day of the month was a festival in her honour and it was customary to play all sorts of pranks to do her veneration. Fortuna Virilis:

This festival was celebrated by women who wished to improve their relationships with the men in their lives. Also, a festival during which select women or Rome gave Venus' statue its yearly ritual bath.

4th April – Megalesia/Cybele – The Megalesia was a festival in honour of the Magna Mater (Cybele) celebrated annually on 4th April with processions and games. The Megalesia – Festival of the Great Mother. The festival began with a ceremonial offering of herbs at the temple of Magna Mater followed by her priests carrying her cult statue through Rome, accompanied by tambourine and cymbal players. The priests were blood stained by wounds inflicted upon themselves. During the festival there were games in the Circus Maximus, theatre performances, sacrifices, and feasts. The last day of Megalesia featured horse racing.

12th – 19th April – Ceres – The Cerealia were games introduced at the founding of the temple of Ceres. This was a private religious festival dedicated to Ceres. There were a few public festivities as well, including a chariot race and public games that doubled as the closing of the Megalesia. During these festivities all participants were required to wear white. Private rituals usually included an offering of milk, honey, and wine to Ceres.

15th April – Fordicalia/Tellus Mater – The Italian deity of mother earth was held on 15th April to ensure plenty during the year and was celebrated under the management of the pontifices and the Vestal Virgins. During this festival a pregnant cow was sacrificed to Tellus Mater, "Mother Earth", who was considered to be pregnant with seeds. The unborn calf was taken to the Grand Vesta in Rome, where the priestess of Vesta burned it in Vesta's sacred flame (considered to be the flame of the earth). The ashes of the burned foetus were kept safe for later use during the Parilia.

21st April – Pales – Festivals for Pales, goddess of herds. During these festivals, ritualistic cleansing of sheep/cattle pens and animals would take place. The shepherd would sweep out the pens and smudge the animals and pens with burning sulphur. In the evening, the animals were sprinkled with water, and their pens were decorated with garlands. Fires were started, and in were thrown olives, horse blood, beanstalks without pods, and the ashes from the Fordicalia fires. Men and beasts jumped over the fire three times to purify themselves further, and to bring them protection from anything that might harm them (wolves, sickness, starvation, etc.). After the animals were put back into their pens the shepherds would offer non–blood sacrifices of grain, cake millet, and warm milk to Pales. The Parilia took place on the same day as the traditional day for the founding of Rome.

23rd April – Venus – There were two Vinalia festivals, on 23rd April when the wine from the previous year was broached and a libation from it poured on the soil and 19th August. Both festivals are associated with the worship of Venus who as the goddess of gardens had vineyards also under her protection. It was also a special day for prostitutes, who paid homage to Venus.

25th April – Robigalia – A festival intended to protect corn from blight. During Robigalia, in a special grove outside of the city walls, offerings were given to Robiga. Rust coloured dogs and sheep were also sacrificed to him at the 5th milestone along the Via Claudia in order to ask for his help in keeping blight and mildew from entering the city limits.

28th April – 3rd May – Flora – Originally a Sabine goddess of the spring and of flowers and blossoms to whom prayers were offered for the prospering of the ripe fruits of the fields and trees. She was also regarded as a goddess of the flower of youth and its pleasures. The Floralia was a theatrical feast and one of unrestrained merriment. There were many theatrical performances largely consisting of lewd farces called mimes. The people were regaled during the games with porridge, pease and lentils. Animals with great fertility (rabbits, goats, etc.) were released into the country. Women were encouraged to wear brightly coloured clothing, and wear flowers as garlands and in their hair during Floralia to honour Flora. The Floralia was also regarded as a festival for prostitutes.

End of April – Feriae Latinae – "Feast of the Latin League". This festival honoured Jupiter Latiaris and was one of the festivals appropriated from the Latins. It was held at Jupiter's temple on the Alban Mount. During the Feriae Latinae milk and other agricultural foods were offered to Jupiter. A white cow that had never worked was sacrificed and eaten by representatives from all of the cities in the Latin League. The trees in the area were decorated with human–shaped puppets dangling from the branches. The Feriae Latinae was a one–day festival, but if anything went wrong the whole thing had to be repeated until it went perfectly. The feast was followed by two days of public games.

Egypt

1st April – Egyptian festival of Renenutet also identified as the birthday of Nepri (personification of grain).

10th April – Adoration of the Egyptian god Anubis.

11th April – Egyptian festival of Min, a 4–day festival at the New Moon according to the great festival list in the temple for Ramesses III at Medinet Habu.

Greece

6th April – Delphinia – A festival celebrated in various towns in Greece in honour of Apollo surnamed Delphinius. He was assumed to be a wrathful god, so it was thought necessary to appease him, seven boys and seven girls carried olive branches bound with white wool into the Delphinium.

15th – 19th April – Demeter – The Thesmophoria was a festival to Demeter as the founder of agriculture and the civic rite of marriage.

Asia

7th April – Guan Yin – Guan Yin is one of the most popular and well–known female goddess in Asia and probably in the world. Guan Yin is the Bodhisattva of Great Compassion in Mahayana Buddhism and also worshiped by Taoists. 7th April is acknowledged as her birthday. In most Buddhist monasteries, there is a Guan Yin hall dedicated to her. There are also many temples dedicated to her and they are usually known as Guan Yin Temple with her sculpture occupying the central shrine.

These temples can have Buddhist or Taoist origins. There are also sintuas (shrines) dedicated in her honour where the spirit of Guan Yin is manifested through a spirit medium. Devotees pray to Guan Yin for help during crisis, for protection during difficult times of their lives and also as a sign of respect to her. While Guan yin reaches out to help all beings, her ultimate aim is to help them towards their enlightenment.

Hindu

15th April – Baishakh – In mid–April, the Bengalis usher in the new year with the Poila Baishakh celebrations, the Assamese in the northeast with Bihu festivals, and the Tamils in the South with Puthandu. Around this time, Hindus in Punjab get agog with Baisakhi, the springtime harvest festival marking the beginning of their new year, and the people of Kerala in the south of India welcome their new year – Vishu.

Akshaya Tritiya – Hindus believe in the theory of "mahurats" or auspicious timings in every step in life – be it to begin a new venture or making an important purchase. Akshaya Tritiya is one such momentous occasion, which is considered one of the most auspicious days of the Hindu Calendar. It is believed, any meaningful activity started on this day would be fruitful. Akshaya Tritiya falls on the third day of the bright half of Vaishakh month (April–May), when the Sun and Moon are in exaltation; they are simultaneously at their peak of brightness, which happens only once every year. Akshaya Tritiya, also known as "Akha Teej", is traditionally the birthday of Lord Parasurama, the sixth incarnation of Lord Vishnu. People conduct special Pujas on this day, bathe in holy rivers, and make a charity, offer barley in a sacred fire, and worship Lord Ganesha & Devi Lakshmi on this day.

Norse

22nd April – 1st May – Walpurgis/Thrimilci – The festival of

Walpurgis, a Norse night both of revelry and darkness. The nine nights of April 22 to April 30 are venerated as remembrance of the All Father's self–sacrifice upon the World Tree Yggdrasil. It was on the ninth night (April 30, Walpurgisnacht) that he be held the Runes, grasped them, and ritually died for an instant. At that moment, all the Light in the 9 worlds is extinguished and utter Chaos reigns. At the final stroke of midnight, the Light returns in dazzling brilliance, and the bale–fires are lit. On Walpurgisnacht, the dead have full sway upon the earth; it is the ending night of the Wild Hunt. May 1 is the festival of Thrimilci; the beginning of Summer. Thrimilci is a festival of joy and fertility, much like Ostara; however, most of the Northern World is finally escaping from the snow at this time.

Pagan

30th April – St Walpurga – On Walpurgis night was the eve of May Day, when the old pagan world of witches was supposed to hold high revelry on certain high places. St Walpurga was a Sussex (UK) born woman saint who immigrated to Germany. Walpurg is an old Teutonic name for the Earth Mother.

MAY

The magic of May and Beltane – and so begins the active part of the year, the earth is sending forth new life, the sap is rising, the birds are singing and growth is all around us.

This month is all about passion, power and raw energy, the fertility of new life and growth and the union of male and female energy in whatever form…getting naked optional… The male and female energy is a traditional reflection of the god and goddess but in today's enlightened society let's go with unions of all kinds, no matter what flavour you are.

Everything you do in this month will bring you closer to your goals; use the energy that is all around you to focus your intent. Work with May's powerful, bawdy, raucous energy. Although it is not just about the animal instincts, this month also brings the magical properties of abundance and growth. It is time to work some magic to increase your bank balance and improve your health.

1st May is Beltane or May Day and it is all about that va va voom passion, jump on board and get carried away with the fiery energy and make it work for you.

Don't forget to show some love for Mother Earth too…

May Magical Energy

Full creating energy; propagation and intuition. Contact with faeries and other supernatural beings. Strengthen connection with supernatural protectors and beings around you. Power flowing from nature. Work magic concerning your career or a new job, making changes or furthering your education. Light up the fire (or a candle) and read some flame or smoke divination for guidance. Do some planting rituals or spells to set the seeds for future projects. Workings for fertility whether it is the pitter patter of tiny feet or new projects will be on fire if set in motion this month. Hold an abundance ritual or work with abundance spells – not just for material wealth but spiritual and emotional too.

Colours: Green, brown, pink, orange, red
Sign: Taurus
Element: Fire
Season: Summer

May Moon Names

Hare Moon, Merry or Dyad Moon, Flower Moon, Frogs Return Moon, Thrilmilcmonath, Sproutkale, Winnemanoth, Planting Moon, Dragon Moon, Panther Moon, Milk Moon, Idle Moon, Goose Moon, Mother's Moon, Bright Moon and Moon when the ponies shed.

Flower Moon because of the flowers that arrive. Dyad Moon because 'dyad' is an old word meaning 'pair', I suspect this reflects the balance of the Sun of the Moon. The Anglo–Saxons called this month Thrilmilcmonath, which translates as thrice–milk month' which refers to three yields of milk. Winnemanoth, translates as "joy month," and was the Frankish name.

Plants to work with in May

These are my suggested herbs to work with that correspond with the energy of this month. But, trust your intuition and the supplies that you have in your cupboards.

African Violet

(Saintpaulia ionantha)
African Violet Magical Properties:
Protection, spirituality, blessings, happiness.
Ruling planet – Venus
Element – Water
Gender – Feminine

Alexanders

(Smyrnium olusatrum)

Alexanders Magical Properties:

Sea magic, intuition, emotions, cleansing, releasing

Element – Water

Gender – Masculine

Ash

(Fraxinus excelsior or F. americana)

Ash Magical Properties:

Protection, prosperity, dispels negativity, improves health, sea magic, dreams, love, intuition.

Ruling planet – Sun and Neptune

Element – Fire and Water

Gender – Masculine

Beech

(Fagus sylvatica)

Beech Magical Properties:

Wishes, creativity, spirituality, divination, luck, success

Ruling planet – Saturn

Sign – Sagittarius

Element – Air and Earth

Gender – Feminine

Camellia

(Camellia japonica)

Camellia Magical Properties:

Abundance, prosperity, spirituality

Ruling planet – Moon

Element – Water

Gender – Feminine

Cornflower/Batchelor's Buttons

(Centaurea cyanus)

Cornflower/Batchelor's Buttons Magical Properties:

Love, psychic powers, protection, fertility, abundance, Faeries

Ruling planet – Venus, Saturn

Element – Water, Earth

Gender – Feminine

Elder

(Sambucus nigra/Canadensis)

Elder Magical Properties:

Protection, healing, faeries, purification, intuition, exorcism, hex breaking, rebirth

Ruling planet – Venus

Sign – Sagittarius, Aquarius, Libra

Element – Water

Gender – Feminine

Frankincense

Frankincense Magical Properties:

Purification, spirituality, relaxation, focus, love, abundance

Ruling planet – Sun

Sign – Aries, Leo, Aquarius

Element – Fire

Gender – Masculine

Heliotrope

(Heliotropium spp)

Heliotrope Magical Properties:

Dreams, spirituality, exorcism, protection, forgiveness, abundance

Ruling planet – Sun

Sign – Leo

Element – Fire

Gender – Masculine

Orchid

(Orchidaceae)

Orchid Magical Properties:

Spirituality, love, abundance

Ruling planet – Venus

Element – Water

Gender – Feminine

Rowan

(Sorbus acuparia)

Rowan Magical Properties:

Psychic powers, power, success, protection, love, spirituality, faeries, divination, healing, inspiration

Ruling planet – Sun, Mercury

Sign – Sagittarius

Element – Fire

Gender – Masculine

Self Heal/All Heal

(Prunella vulgaris)

Self Heal Magical Properties:

Releasing, cleansing, spirituality, stress, calming, clarity, protection

Ruling planet – Venus

Element – Water

Gender – Feminine

Sweetpea

(Lathyrus odoratus)

Sweetpea Magical Properties:

Courage, strength, friendship, peace, happiness, truth, spirituality, psychic abilities, protection, sleep

Ruling planet – Venus, Moon, Mercury
Element – Water
Gender – Feminine

Willow

(Salix alba, Salix fragilis)
Willow Magical Properties:
Love, protection, healing, cleansing, wishes, release, inspiration, intuition
Ruling planet – Moon
Sign – Pisces
Element – Water
Gender – Feminine

Foods, Herbs and Spices to work with in May

Whether you chose to include the foods in a recipe for the table or add them to spell work, here is my suggested list of foods to work with for the energy of this month.

Almond

(Prunus dulcis)
Almond Magical Properties:
Love, prosperity, treasure, intuition, psychic powers, passion
Ruling planet – Mercury
Element – Air
Gender – Masculine

Banana

(Musa spp.)
Banana Magical Properties:
Prosperity, spirituality
Ruling planet – Mars
Element – Air
Gender – Masculine

Bay

(Laurus nobilis)

Bay Magical Properties:

Protection, purification, strength, power, healing, creativity, spirituality, psychic powers

Ruling planet – Sun

Element – Fire

Gender – Masculine

Butter

Butter Magical Properties:

Peace, spirituality, Faerie

Ruling planet – Moon

Element – Earth

Gender – Feminine

Cinnamon

(Cinnamomum zeylanicum, Cinnamomum verum)

Cinnamon Magical Properties:

Success, healing, power, psychic powers, protection, love, focus, lust, spirituality, changes

Ruling planet – Sun

Element – Fire

Gender – Masculine

Cucumber

(Cucumis sativus)

Cucumber Magical Properties:

Fertility, emotions, chastity, meditation, spirituality, purification, healing

Ruling planet – Moon

Element – Water

Gender – Feminine

Grapes

(Vitis vinifera)

Grapes Magical Properties:

Spiritual, fertility, Moon magic

Ruling planet – Moon

Element – Air, Water

Gender – Feminine

Honey

Honey Magical Properties:

Happiness, healing, love, prosperity, passion, spirituality, faerie

Element – Water, Earth

Gender – Feminine

Milk

Milk Magical Properties:

Feminine power, goddess energy, Moon magic, nurturing, offerings, love, spirituality, Faeries

Ruling planet – Moon

Element – Water

Gender – Feminine

Mustard

(Brassica juncea, Brassica nigra, Sinapis hirta)

Mustard Magical Properties:

Clarity, psychic abilities, protection, astral travel, faith, success

Ruling planet – Mars

Element – Fire

Gender – Masculine

Parsley

(Petroselinum crispum, Petrselinum sativum)

Parsley Magical Properties:
Protection, purification, lust, happiness, fertility, spirit work
Ruling planet – Mercury
Element – Air
Gender – Masculine

Star Anise

(Illicum verum)
Star Anise Magical Properties:
Luck, psychic powers, purification, protection, dreams, spirituality, sleep
Ruling planet – Jupiter
Element – Air
Gender – Masculine

Vanilla

(Vanilla planifolia)
Vanilla Magical Properties:
Love, spirituality, sex magic, passion, creativity
Ruling planet – Venus
Element – Water, Air
Gender – Feminine

Crystals to work with in May

As always, go with your intuition and what you have in your collection when working with crystals. The list below is my suggestion of crystals that work particularly well with the energy of this month.

Amethyst

Amethyst magical properties
Peace, protection, success, good luck, hidden knowledge, legal issues, spirituality, contentment, soothing, relaxation, calm, hope, patience, transformation, changes, breaking patterns,

grounding, guilt, overcoming addictions, business matters, judgement, clarity, courage, travel, psychic protection, sleep, anxiety, focus, understanding, happiness, justice, intuition, inspiration, channeling, meditation

Energy: Receptive
Element: Water
Planet: Jupiter, Neptune
Zodiac: Pisces, Scorpio, Sagittarius
Birthstone: February

Bloodstone

Bloodstone magical properties:

Organisation, adaptability, anxiety, clarity, concentration, renewal, energy, self–confidence, connection, calm, protection, breaking barriers, selfishness, mysticism, insight, spirituality, truth, intuition, creativity, guidance, strength, healing, victory, wealth, money, power, invisibility, deception, negative energy, divine connection, past life, dreams

Energy: Projective
Element: Fire, Earth
Planet: Mars
Zodiac: Aries, Pisces, Scorpio
Birthstone: February, March

Chrysocolla

Chrysocolla magical properties

Wisdom, peace, patience, love, soothing, intuition, energy, calming, emotions, fear, strength, clarity, balance, negative energy, insight, releasing, spirituality, psychic abilities, guilt, divine, harmony, communication, meditation

Energy: Receptive
Element: Water
Planet: Venus
Zodiac: Taurus

Citrine

Citrine magical properties:

Happiness, joy, Sun magic, negative energy, optimism, abundance, depression, stress, success, wealth, healing, intuition, creativity, confidence, changes, self–esteem, protection, psychic powers, fears, clarity, stamina, nightmares

Energy: Projective
Element: Fire
Planet: Sun, Jupiter
Zodiac: Scorpio
Birthstone: November

Fluorite

Fluorite magical properties

Magic, imagination, discernment, aptitude, psychic protection, protection, purification, calming, relaxation, tension, anxiety, organisation, structure, challenges, declutter, releasing, support, breaking patterns, intuition, confidence, reassurance, comforting, communication, balance, spirituality, decisions, manifestation, peace, meditation, grounding, healing, cleansing, channelling, past life work, fairy realm, amplifying, memory, power, emotions, depression, stability

Energy: Projective
Element: Water, Air
Planet: Neptune
Zodiac: Scorpio, Aquarius, Pisces

Goldstone

Goldstone magical properties

Ambition, luck, goals, determination, persistence, achievements, success, calm, emotions, energy, enthusiastic, confidence, self–belief, inner self, personal development, possibilities, courage, direction, clarity, uplifting, optimism, protection, deflects negative energy, knowledge, perception, manifestation, creativity, faith, energy flow, spirituality, abundance, wealth, grounding, perspective, ambition, drive, ingenuity, money, generosity, willpower, goals, emotions, divination (see also copper for additional magical properties)

Energy: Receptive/Projective
Element: Fire, Earth
Planet: Jupiter, Venus
Zodiac: Sagittarius

Garnet

Garnet magical properties

Organisation, warrior spirit, protection, love, commitment, passion, sexuality, sensuality, attraction, depression, spiritual healing, success, self–confidence, energy, inspiration, perception, strength, survival, fear, courage, clarity, challenges, past life work, truth, compassion, deflecting negative energy, gossip, ambition, motivation, goals, purification, cleansing, balance, inner strength, self–empowerment, creativity, confidence, meditation, spirit work, nightmares, journeying, abundance, support

Energy: Projective
Element: Fie
Planet: Mars
Zodiac: Aries, Virgo, Capricorn, Leo, Aquarius
Birthstone: January

Kyanite

Kyanite magical properties

Balance, harmony, calming, connection, psychic abilities, healing, communication, grounding, transformation, meditation, relaxation, luck, growth, leadership, new beginnings, clarity, decisions, stability, truth, vitality, abundance, spirituality, channelling, understanding, dreams

Energy Receptive

Element	Water
Planet	Jupiter, Venus, Mars
Zodiac	Aries, Libra, Taurus

Labradorite

Labradorite magical properties

Transformation, cleansing, breaking patterns, potential, psychic abilities, intuition, confidence, spirituality, focus, protection, imagination, relaxation, soothing, energy, healing, stress, anxiety, luck, abundance, success, decisions, trust, changes, strength, courage, self–confidence, inspiration, perseverance, journeying, clarity, insight, meditation, depression, jealousy, grounding

Energy	Projective
Element	Water
Planet	Earth, Moon, Uranus
Zodiac	Aquarius, Sagittarius, Scorpio, Leo

Lapis lazuli

Lapis lazuli magical properties

Protection, manifestation, meditation, psychic protection, problem solving, knowledge, clarity, decisions, memory, spirituality, peace, energy, organisation, concentration, stress, luck, negative energy, wealth, abundance, success, love, confidence, truth, renewal, intellect, wisdom, leadership, legal issues, sleep, anxiety, harmony, understanding

Energy	Receptive
Element	Water
Planet	Venus, Jupiter
Zodiac	Sagittarius

Moonstone

Moonstone magical properties

New beginnings, Moon magic, intuition, calming, psychic

abilities, balance, harmony, wishes, cleansing, uplifting, hope, meditation, emotions, love, divination, spirituality, wealth, truth, healing, sensuality, insight, peace, wisdom, communication, confidence, abundance, prosperity, dreams, fertility, travel

Energy	Receptive
Element	Water
Planet	Moon
Zodiac	Cancer, Libra, Scorpio
Birthstone	June, September

Quartz (rose)

Quartz (rose) magical properties

Love, happiness, emotions, spirituality, growth, fears, healing, sexuality, passion, calming, soothing, stress, depression, sleep, luck, wisdom, inspiration, success, intuition, grounding, balance, prosperity, self–esteem, harmony, trust, jealousy, gossip, beauty, peace, cleansing, fertility

Energy	Receptive
Element	Earth, Water
Planet	Venus, Moon
Zodiac	Taurus

Rhodochrosite

Rhodochrosite magical properties

Power, potential, strength, confidence, healing, new beginnings, breaking barriers, releasing, joy, happiness, creativity, determination, manifestation, prosperity, abundance, love, emotions, peace, renewal, connection, balance, spirituality, harmony, energy

Energy	Projective
Element	Fire
Planet	Mars, Jupiter
Zodiac	Scorpio, Leo

Selenite

Selenite magical properties

Clarity, psychic protection, cleansing, balance, stability, emotions, divine, connections, spirituality, psychic abilities, spirit work, protection, healing, breaking barriers, decisions, intuition, meditation, money, success, love

Energy	Receptive
Element	Water
Planet	Moon
Zodiac	Cancer

Sunstone

Sunstone magical properties

Sun magic, power, decisions, leadership, strength, happiness, inspiration, love, luck, stability, clarity, energy, stress, depression, emotions, optimism, perseverance, intuition, fears, self–esteem, self–confidence, healing, balance, harmony, abundance, prosperity, opportunities, peace, protection

Energy	Projective
Element	Fire
Planet	Sun
Zodiac	Leo

Turquoise

Turquoise magical properties

Purification, negative energy, protection, balance, relaxation, emotions, stress, spirituality, energy, depression, clarity, wisdom, understanding, psychic abilities, insight, intuition, past life work, communication, wealth, abundance, finances, prosperity, luck, decisions, friendship, uplifting, meditation, love, harmony

Energy	Receptive
Element	Earth
Planet	Venus, Neptune

Zodiac	Sagittarius, Pisces, Aquarius
Birthstone	December

Moon Deities to work with in May

Here you will find my suggestions on some of the Moon deities to work with that align with the energies of this month. Trust your intuition and be guided by the deities that may also make themselves known to you.

Anu – a Mesopotamian/Sumerian sky god viewed as Father of the gods and ruler of the heavens, the stars and the spirits. Call upon him for: Goals, wishes, spirituality.

Anuket – Egyptian goddess of the crescent Moon. She is responsible for the annual flooding of the river Nile. She watches over agriculture and all food growth along with wealth and prosperity. Call upon her for: Wealth, prosperity, growth, fertility, nourishment, contentment.

Demeter – Ancient Greek goddess of the full Moon. She is an Olympian goddess of agriculture, harvest and fertility. Featuring in the Eleusinian mysteries alongside her daughter Persephone. She forms a triad with Persephone and Hecate, Demeter taking on the mother role. Equivalent to the Roman goddess Ceres. Call upon her for: Abundance, harvest, mysteries, fertility, marriage, relationships, life and death, rebirth, justice, grief, suffering, parenthood.

Diana – Goddess of the Moon, hunter and Roman Queen of Witches. She is queen of the open skies and may also have been worshipped as a Sun goddess as well as the Moon. Call upon her for: Fertility, abundance, harvest, protection, children, nurturing, hunting, childbirth.

Hestia – Greek goddess of the hearth and home she is also a fire goddess. Her Roman equivalent is Vesta. The Greeks did not have statues of this goddess as it was believed she didn't take human form, instead she appeared as the flames of fire in the hearth. Hestia was the first born of the Olympian goddesses. She is absolutely about new beginnings and the start of all things. This goddess is the ultimate super housekeeper and home maker, with added omnipotence. Call upon her for: Home life, domesticity, fire magic, devotion, wishes, manifesting, unity, new beginnings, spirituality, blessings.

Isis – Egyptian goddess Queen of Egypt. She is looked upon as Mother Moon, Queen of Sorcery and the life force within the river Nile. Isis taught her people useful skills, those they would need to survive and flourish, no being high up in the sky for this one, she got down with her subjects (very practical woman). Call upon her for: Magic, dreams, divination, harvest, perspective, love, spirituality, faithfulness, destiny, revitalisation, fulfilment, inner beauty, spirituality, rebirth, feminine energy, knowledge, motherhood, healing, changes, manifesting.

Kuan Yin – Chinese/Buddhist goddess of mercy who is probably one of the most chilled out and relaxed deities ever. This beautiful goddess hears all your prayers and responds to each and every request for help. She needs some kind of medal... Call upon her for: Kindness, magic, health, healing, fertility, children, sympathy, support, suffering, encouragement, enlightenment, spirituality, protection.

Luna – Roman goddess of the Moon. Depicted as a beautiful woman with the power to ease childbirth and bring about love. She carries a very strong feminine energy. If you want an answer to a problem, then call upon this lovely lady to bring you the answer in your dreams, it is her speciality. Her Greek equivalent is Selene. Call upon her for: Feminine energy, water magic, safety, travel, intuition, blue Moon magic, protection, illusion, truth, love, psychic abilities, dreams, solutions.

Ops – Roman goddess of the full Moon and agriculture. If you are after abundance and prosperity, then Ops is your 'go to' goddess. She can also teach you all kinds of practical skills to gain that abundance for yourself. Ain't nothing in this life for free! Call upon her for: Fertility, abundance, wealth, nurturing, prosperity, opportunity, growth.

Vesta – Roman goddess of the crescent Moon, the hearth and home. She rules domesticity with a flip of the feather duster and a whip of her apron. She keeps the house and family running like clockwork. She is known as Hestia in Greece. Call upon her for: Home, family, relationships, harmony, peace, love, fertility, fire magic, spirituality.

World celebration days

I have given some dates and a little information on celebrations from around the world that take place during May. A lot of them were based on Moon phases. I apologise for any errors but history is a fickle thing and calendars have changed over the years…

Pagan

Beltane – 1st May. Beltane heralds the coming of summer and is a festival of fertility. The seeds are sown the plant and crops are all growing, the Earth is fertile. Our ancestors would have transferred their livestock from their winter shelter to the fields and pastures, at this time the animals would have been driven between the Beltane bonfire to cleanse and purge them from evil spirits and to bring fertility.

Danu/Danann – The Tuatha Dea Danann came to Ireland on Monday the calends of May, in ships. The Tuatha Dea Danann signifies the people of the Goddess Danu or Danann, who was the Mother of Gods.

Maeve – A strong Celtic goddess, it is for Maeve that the hawthorn was named May or May–thorn. She became the goddess of Beltane in whose honour the May queen was crowned. She is often referred to as Queen Mab/Maeve of the Faeries.

8th May – Flora – A popular Cornish (UK) festival was held annually on 8th May called 'the Furrey' said to have been derived from the Roman Floralia in honour of the goddess Flora. People would parade the streets with garlands of flowers and dance. The name Furrey is possibly derived from the Latin word feria meaning fair or holy day.

Rome

Bona Dea – The Good Goddess was an Italian goddess supposed to preside over the earth and all the blessings which spring from it, the anniversary of the foundation of her temple was held on the 1st May when prayers were offered to her for averting earthquakes.

Flora – Roman youths would apparently go into the fields and spend the kalends of May in dancing and singing in honour of Flora, goddess of fruits and flowers. The Romans welcomed the month of May be dedicating the month to Flora. Roman children made images of Flora and decorated them with flowers on this day.

9th, 11th, 13th May – Lemuria is a private series of rites held to ward off the Lemures. For the rite, the pater familia got up at Midnight wearing clothes without knots and washed his hands with pure water. He would then walk through the household without looking backwards, making the mano fico sign with his hand, spitting black beans out of his mouth and repeating a prayer nine times. After he was done, he would again wash his hands and would then make noise using instruments made of brass. It was thought that the Lemures would collect the beans instead of the souls of the living and would be scared away by the noise. At the end of the rite he should again say a chant nine times and then look backwards to ensure that the Lemures were gone.

15th May – Sacrifice Day for the Tiber River – On this day the Vestal Virgins made a sacrifice to the Tiber River to convince it to bring a steady supply of water to the city of Rome for the rest of the growing season.

29th May – Ambarvalia – This purification festival was held to honour Ceres and Dea Dia. During the festival participants would walk around their fields to convince the gods to bless the growing plants.

Full Moon – Vesta – Where the sacred fire of the Moon is tended by Vestal priestesses, they were also responsible for rain rituals. The Vestal Virgins performed a ceremony at the May full Moon to regular the water supply.

Hindu

Parasurama Jayanti – Lord Parasurama, also known as the "axe–wielding Rama," was the sixth avatar of Vishnu, whose main objective was to deliver the world from the oppression of the Kshatriya rulers or unrighteous kings who strayed from the path of dharma. Parasurama Jayanti or the birthday of Lord Parasurama is a major festival for the Brahmin or the Hindu priest class. On this day, devotees' worship Parasurama and observe a ritual fast in his honour.

11th day – Ekadasi in Sanskrit means 'the Eleventh Day,' which occurs twice in a lunar month – once each on the 11th days of the bright and dark fortnight respectively. Known as the 'Day of Lord Vishnu,' it is a very auspicious time in the Hindu calendar and an important day to fast. According to the Hindu scriptures, Ekadasi and the movement of the Moon has a direct correlation with the human mind. It is believed that during Ekadasi, our mind attains maximum efficiency giving the brain a better capacity to concentrate. Spiritual seekers are said to devote the two monthly days of Ekadasi in extreme worship and meditation owing to its favourable influence on the mind. Religious reasons aside, these fortnightly fasts helps the body and its organs get respite from dietary irregularities and over indulgences. Lord Krishna says that if a person fasts on Ekadasi, "I shall burn all sins. This day is the most meritorious day to kill all sins."

Norse

30th May – Einherjar – Minor modern Asatru festival honouring the warriors who fell during battle and who ascended to Valhalla's halls.

Christian

31st May – Virgin Mary – The feast of Our Lady Queen of Heaven kept on 31st May. Bread or cake was offered to the Virgin Mary on this day.

Egyptian

New Moon – Egyptian Festival of the Valley was celebrated at the May new Moon. This was the greatest festival of the Theban necropolis, when the image of Amun of Karnak on the east bank at Thebes was brought to the temples for the cult of individual kings on the west bank – a distinctive feature of this festival was the presentation of great quantities of flowers – this would have been a time for each family to feast with their dead, and the architecture and decoration of tomb–chapels at Thebes reflect such festive banquets

Greek

Thargelia was a Greek festival of Apollo held in Athens on the 6th and 7th of Thargelion (late May). It was both a vegetation festival and a ritual expiation of communal guilt. The first day of the festival featured the cathartic rite of the pharmakos (scapegoat). One or two persons, male or female, were selected to be a scapegoat. They were usually criminals or outcasts, but occasionally an important person would sacrifice himself or herself for the city. The scapegoat was fed, led through town, and then expelled from the city. In times of severe calamity, the scapegoat might be thrown off a cliff, cast into the sea, or sacrificed on a funeral pyre. The rite of the pharmakos cleansed the town and prepared for the new harvest.

JUNE

Following on from the Beltane theme of celebrating life, this month is also about the abundance of beauty on our planet and all that she provides for us. The longest day and the shortest night of the year arrives in June. This is a time to celebrate the completion of the cycle that began at the winter solstice – the Sun is at the height of its power and although hopefully the hot days of summer are yet to come this is the point when the year starts to wane.

Connect to this moment by taking time to stop, be still and look back over the past few months, celebrate your achievements and acknowledge your failures, make sense of your actions and learn from them. Focus now on what you want to nurture and develop during the coming months.

June Magical Energy

Full but restful energy; protect, strengthen and prevent. A time of light; Earth tides are turning. Decision making, taking responsibility for present happenings. Work on personal inconsistencies. Strengthen and reward yourself for your positive traits. Celebrate, clarity, reflect, focus, nurture and develop.

Colours: Orange, gold, green
Sign: Gemini
Element: Fire
Season: Summer

June Moon Names

Mead Moon, Moon of Horses, Lovers Moon, Strong Sun Moon, Honey Moon, Aerra Litha, Brachmanoth, Strawberry Moon, Rose Moon, Lotus Moon, Windy Moon, Flower Moon, Full Leaf Moon and Moon of Making Fat.

Strawberry Moon because the strawberries are in full season – it all makes perfect sense really. Aerra Litha/Forelitha the Saxon name for June which translates as 'fulfilment of the moon before the sun relents'. Brachmanoth meaning 'break month' from the Franks.

Plants to work with in June

These are my suggested herbs to work with that correspond with the energy of this month. But, trust your intuition and the supplies that you have in your cupboards.

Blackthorn (Sloe)

(Prunus spinosa)
Blackthorn Magical Properties:
Protection, exorcism, divination, healing
Ruling planet – Saturn and Mars
Sign – Scorpio
Element – Fire
Gender – Masculine

Carnation

(Dianthus carphyllus)
Carnation Magical Properties:
Healing, strength, protection, release, courage
Ruling planet – Sun
Element – Fire
Gender – Masculine

Daisy

(Chrysanthemum leucanthemum, Bellis Perennis)
Daisy Magical Properties:
Love, lust, protection, happiness, dreams, strength, courage
Ruling planet – Venus
Sign – Cancer, Taurus

Element – Water
Gender – Feminine

Delphinium/Larkspur

(Delphinium spp)
Delphinium Magical Properties:
Protection, midsummer, faeries, dragons.
Ruling planet – Venus
Element – Water
Gender – Feminine

Dragon's blood

(Daemonorops draco, Daemonorops propinquos)
Dragon's Blood Magical Properties:
Power, protection, love, happiness, dragon magic
Ruling planet – Mars
Sign – Aries
Element – Fire
Gender – Masculine

Horsetail

(Equisetum arvense, Equisetum telmateia)
Horsetail Magical Properties:
Fertility, snakes, longevity, strength, cleansing
Ruling planet – Saturn
Element – Earth
Gender – Feminine

Lavender

(Lavendula officinale or Lavendula vera)
Lavender Magical Properties:
Happiness, peace, love, protection, sleep, clarity, faeries, strength
Ruling planet – Mercury

Sign – Leo, Gemini
Element – Air
Gender – Masculine

Mugwort

(Artemisia vulgaris)
Mugwort Magical Properties:
Strength, psychic powers, protection, dreams, healing, astral travel, feminine energy, cleansing
Ruling planet – Venus, Moon
Sign – Cancer
Element – Earth
Gender – Feminine

Oak

(Quercus alba, Quercus robur, Quercus petraea)
Oak Magical Properties:
Healing, health, protection, money, fertility, luck, strength, vitality, power
Ruling planet – Sun, Jupiter, Mars
Sign – Sagittarius
Element – Fire, Water
Gender – Masculine

Pennyroyal

(Mentha/Mamentha pulegium)
Pennyroyal Magical Properties:
Strength, protection, peace, initiation, Goddess, business
Ruling planet – Mars, Venus
Sign – Scorpio, Libra
Element – Fire
Gender – Masculine

Plantain

(Plantago spp. Lanceolata, Plantago major, Plantago media)

Plantain Magical Properties:

Strength, protection, healing, energy, courage

Ruling planet – Venus

Sign – Capricorn

Element – Earth

Gender – Feminine

Saint John's Wort

(Hypericum perforatum)

Saint John's Wort Magical Properties:

Protection, health, strength, love, divination, happiness, abundance, truth

Ruling planet – Sun

Sign – Aquarius, Libra

Element – Fire

Gender – Masculine

Sweetpea

(Lathyrus odoratus)

Sweetpea Magical Properties:

Courage, strength, friendship, peace, happiness, truth, spirituality, psychic abilities, protection, sleep

Ruling planet – Venus, Moon, Mercury

Element – Water

Gender – Feminine

Foods, Herbs and Spices to work with in June

Whether you chose to include the foods in a recipe for the table or add them to spell work, here is my suggested list of foods to work with for the energy of this month.

Artichoke (Globe)

(Cynara cardunculus /scolymus)

Artichoke Magical Properties:

Protection, growth, passion, strength, courage

Ruling planet – Mars

Element – Fire

Gender – Masculine/Feminine

Bay

(Laurus nobilis)

Bay Magical Properties:

Protection, purification, strength, power, healing, creativity, spirituality, psychic powers

Ruling planet – Sun

Element – Fire

Gender – Masculine

Black Pepper

(Piper nigrum)

Black Pepper Magical Properties:

Protection, exorcism, jealousy, negativity, strength, confidence, gossip

Ruling planet – Mars

Element – Fire

Gender – Masculine

Broccoli

(Brassica oleracea)

Broccoli Magical Properties:

Strength, protection

Ruling planet – Moon

Element – Water

Gender – Feminine

Chestnut (sweet)

(Castanea var.)

Chestnut Magical Properties:

Strength, success, prosperity, abundance, fertility

Ruling planet – Jupiter

Element – Fire

Gender – Masculine

Garlic

(Allium sativum)

Garlic Magical Properties:

Healing, protection, hex breaking, negative energies, lust, strength, courage, depression

Ruling planet – Mars

Element – Fire

Gender – Masculine

Lemon

(Citrus x lemon)

Lemon Magical Properties:

Purification, Moon magic, happiness, decisions, uplifting, love, protection, friendship, fidelity

Ruling planet – Moon

Element – Water

Gender – Feminine

Mushrooms

Mushrooms Magical Properties:

Strength, courage, magic, balance

Ruling planet – Moon

Element – Earth

Gender – Feminine

Pine nut

(Pinus spp)

Pine nut Magical Properties:

Happiness, strength, centring, dragon magic, protection, hospitality

Ruling planet – Mars, Saturn

Element – Air

Gender – Masculine

Pork

Pork Magical Properties:

Strength, fertility, prosperity, luck, longevity

Element – Fire

Gender – Masculine

Raspberry

(Rubus spp.)

Raspberry Magical Properties:

Love, protection, strength

Ruling planet – Venus

Element – Water, Earth

Gender – Feminine

Sesame

(Sesamum indicum)

Sesame Magical Properties:

Prosperity, protection, energy, strength, secrets

Ruling planet – Sun

Element – Fire, Earth

Gender – Masculine

Spinach

(Spinacia oleracea)

Spinach Magical Properties:

Passion, fertility, strength
Ruling planet – Jupiter
Element – Earth
Gender – Feminine

Sunflower Seeds

(Helianthus annuus)
Sunflower Seeds Magical Properties:
Fertility, Sun magic, strength, courage, happiness, prosperity, confidence
Ruling planet – Sun
Element – Fire
Gender – Masculine

Tea

(Camellia sinensis)
Tea Magical Properties:
Meditation, courage, strength, prosperity
Ruling planet – Sun
Element – Fire
Gender – Masculine

Crystals to work with in June

As always, go with your intuition and what you have in your collection when working with crystals. The list below is my suggestion of crystals that work particularly well with the energy of this month.

Agate (blue lace)

Agate (blue lace) magical properties
Mediation, spirituality, uplifting, calming, peace, communication, emotions, support, optimism, happiness, protection, cleansing, healing, prosperity, longevity, strength, courage, clarity, success, patience, truth, stress, relaxation, creativity, justice,

travel, renewal, understanding, soothing, trust

Energy	Receptive
Element	Water
Planet	Mercury
Zodiac	Gemini

Fluorite

Fluorite magical properties

Magic, imagination, discernment, aptitude, psychic protection, protection, purification, calming, relaxation, tension, anxiety, organisation, structure, challenges, declutter, releasing, support, breaking patterns, intuition, confidence, reassurance, comforting, communication, balance, spirituality, decisions, manifestation, peace, meditation, grounding, healing, cleansing, channelling, past life work, fairy realm, amplifying, memory, power, emotions, depression, stability

Energy:	Projective
Element:	Water, Air
Planet:	Neptune
Zodiac:	Scorpio, Aquarius, Pisces

Hematite

Hematite magical properties

Grounding, money, decisions, manifestation, finances, healing, focus, clarity, stability, protection, balance, divination, problem solving, emotions, self–esteem, productivity, doubt, anxiety, communication, strength

Energy:	Projective
Element:	Fire, Earth
Planet:	Saturn
Zodiac:	Aries, Aquarius

Labradorite

Labradorite magical properties

Transformation, cleansing, breaking patterns, potential, psychic abilities, intuition, confidence, spirituality, focus, protection, imagination, relaxation, soothing, energy, healing, stress, anxiety, luck, abundance, success, decisions, trust, changes, strength, courage, self–confidence, inspiration, perseverance, journeying, clarity, insight, meditation, depression, jealousy, grounding

Energy	Projective
Element	Water
Planet	Earth, Moon, Uranus
Zodiac	Aquarius, Sagittarius, Scorpio, Leo

Lapis lazuli

Lapis lazuli magical properties

Protection, manifestation, meditation, psychic protection, problem solving, knowledge, clarity, decisions, memory, spirituality, peace, energy, organisation, concentration, stress, luck, negative energy, wealth, abundance, success, love, confidence, truth, renewal, intellect, wisdom, leadership, legal issues, sleep, anxiety, harmony, understanding

Energy	Receptive
Element	Water
Planet	Venus, Jupiter
Zodiac	Sagittarius

Lepidolite

Lepidolite magical properties

Transformation, soothing, calming, stress, happiness, changes, emotions, psychic abilities, spirituality, depression, divination, connection, strength, uplifting, luck, hope, balance, peace, sleep, harmony, decisions, addiction, releasing, trust, goals, optimism, patience, dreams, opportunities, support, love

Energy	Receptive
Element	Water

Planet	Jupiter, Neptune
Zodiac	Libra

Petrified wood

Petrified wood magical properties

Stability, grounding, calming, anxiety, fears, meditation, determination, decisions, strength, courage, patience, transformation, perseverance, success, luck, emotions, wisdom, past life work, insight, leadership

Energy	Receptive
Element	Earth, Spirit
Planet	Earth, Sun
Zodiac	All

Pyrite

Pyrite magical properties

Releasing, breaking patterns, clarity, protection, support, decisions, growth, success, inspiration, grounding, vitality, learning, perception, memory, wisdom, psychic abilities, healing, cleansing, prosperity, wealth, abundance, luck, strength, motivation, manifestation, finances, energy, Sun magic, power, focus, perseverance, confidence, divination, communication, self–confidence, meditation

Energy	Projective
Element	Fire
Planet	Mars, Sun
Zodiac	Leo

Quartz (clear)

Quartz (clear) magical properties

Purification, cleansing, healing, calming, emotions, strength, support, spirituality, energy, balance, psychic abilities, motivation, uplifting, decisions, anxiety, divine connection, amplifying, focus, meditation, manifestation, channelling, protection, negative energy, clarity, wisdom, concentration, learning, spirit work, communication, astral travel, divination, dreams, harmony

Energy	Projective, Receptive
Planet	Sun, Moon
Element	Fire, Water
Zodiac	Leo, Gemini, Capricorn

Quartz (smoky)

Quartz (smoky) magical properties

Grounding, centring, focus, negative energy, decisions, cooperation, creativity, emotions, depression, anxiety, jealousy, nature, protection, calming, manifestation, wishes, divination, meditation, insight, guidance, uplifting, fears, relaxation, releasing, abundance, luck, prosperity

Energy	Receptive
Element	Earth
Planet	Saturn, Jupiter
Zodiac	Capricorn, Sagittarius

Rhodonite

Rhodonite magical properties

Protection, renewal, emotions, strength, soothing, clarity, happiness, love, balance, harmony, decisions, confidence, spirituality, peace, energy, passion, optimism, changes, vitality, anxiety, travel, psychic abilities, self–confidence, trust, calming, relaxation, patience, determination, releasing, stress, negative energy

Energy	Projective
Element	Fire
Planet	Mars, Venus
Zodiac	Taurus

Selenite

Selenite magical properties

Clarity, psychic protection, cleansing, balance, stability, emotions, divine, connections, spirituality, psychic abilities, spirit work, protection, healing, breaking barriers, decisions, intuition, meditation, money, success, love

Energy	Receptive
Element	Water
Planet	Moon
Zodiac	Cancer

Sunstone

Sunstone magical properties

Sun magic, power, decisions, leadership, strength, happiness, inspiration, love, luck, stability, clarity, energy, stress, depression, emotions, optimism, perseverance, intuition, fears, self–esteem, self–confidence, healing, balance, harmony, abundance, prosperity, opportunities, peace, protection

Energy	Projective
Element	Fire
Planet	Sun
Zodiac	Leo

Turquoise

Turquoise magical properties

Purification, negative energy, protection, balance, relaxation, emotions, stress, spirituality, energy, depression, clarity, wisdom, understanding, psychic abilities, insight, intuition, past life work, communication, wealth, abundance, finances, prosperity, luck, decisions, friendship, uplifting, meditation, love, harmony

Energy	Receptive
Element	Earth
Planet	Venus, Neptune

Zodiac	Sagittarius, Pisces, Aquarius
Birthstone	December

Unakite

Unakite magical properties

Love, happiness, growth, wealth, success, harmony, decisions, support, balance, emotions, stability, confidence, strength, anxiety, nature, courage, transformation, releasing, spirituality

Energy	Receptive
Element	Fire, Water
Planet	Mars, Venus, Pluto
Zodiac	Scorpio

Moon Deities to work with in June

Here you will find my suggestions on some of the Moon deities to work with that align with the energies of this month. Trust your intuition and be guided by the deities that may also make themselves known to you.

Andraste – a warrior goddess of Britain – she was invoked by Queen Boadicea/Boudicca. Call upon her for: Strength, courage, warrior, victory, battle, guidance, inspiration, honour.

Anu – a Mesopotamian/Sumerian sky god viewed as Father of the gods and ruler of the heavens, the stars and the spirits. Call upon him for: Goals, wishes, spirituality.

Artemis – Greek goddess associated with the crescent Moon, she is goddess of the hunt and rules over forest and animals. Artemis protects those in childbirth and young girls. She is a strong, independent virgin goddess. Usually depicted holding a bow and arrow. Call upon her for: Warrior, strength, courage, night magic, protection, independence, defence, justice, nature.

Asherah – Ancient West Semitic goddess, often referred to as Queen of the Gods. Also known as 'She who walks on the sea' or 'holiness'. You will find her name in the Old Testament she is consort of Yahweh. Asherah is a goddess of the sea. Call upon her for: Divine wisdom, feminine energy, feminine issues, strength, self–esteem, self–confidence, courage, kindness, love, divination, insight, justice, fertility, compassion, healing, nurturing.

Athene/Athena – Greek goddess of weaving, a trait often connected with the Moon. She is a goddess of wisdom and a full–on warrior gal complete with protection, defence and all the hero stuff. Her skills also cover cunning, metal work and weapons. Basically, don't mess with her. Call upon Athene for: protection, courage, leadership, victory, discipline, control, wisdom, defence, cunning.

Blodeuwedd – Welsh goddess, who has a connection with the Moon, and death and reincarnation (aspects of the Dark Moon). Her name translates as 'flower face' as she was created out of plants by magicians, who then later changed her into an owl (it was a whole punishment betrayal thing). As a maiden she forms part of the triad with Arianrhod and Cerridwen. A goddess of spring and one of the five goddesses of Avalon. Call upon her for: Beauty (temporary), spring, reincarnation, transformation, betrayal, manipulation, strength, power, love, wisdom, innocence.

Cybele/Kybele –Phrygian goddess of the Underworld and associated with the dark Moon. Worshipped in ancient Greece and found in Romany mythology. Some associate her with the Greek/Minoan goddess Rhea. She is known as mother of the gods. Associated with mountains, caves, nature and wild animals particularly hawks, lions and bees. Call upon her for: Love, victory, strength, relationships, humour, healing, health, fun, stability.

Hekate – Greek goddess of the dark Moon. She covers new beginnings and magic of all kinds. She walks the ancient roads and pathways, particularly associated with crossroads, those where three roads cross. She forms a triad with Persephone and Demeter, she being the Crone aspect. She guards the spirit world and wields power over all realms. She is one seriously intimidating goddess, but wise beyond words. Call upon her for: Moon magic, witchcraft, herb magic, necromancy, protection, prosperity, new beginnings, decisions, mysteries, knowledge, learning, inner work, shadow work.

Hera – Greek Olympian Queen of gods, she covers marriage, childbirth and looking after women (she's got her hands full then). Although she can help when called upon, she has a jealous side and can be vengeful particularly when infidelity is involved. Call upon her for: Love, humour, forgiveness, romance, creativity, marriage, strength, courage, self–confidence, jealousy.

Inanna – Sumerian goddess of the full Moon and the stars, also known as Ishtar in Babylon. She is Queen of heaven and earth. She has a reputation for being a little bit saucy which led her to be linked to fertility rituals. She does look after her followers, dishing out the rules and keeping them safe. Call upon her for: Love, fertility, warrior, strength, courage, seduction, sensuality, protection, justice.

World celebration days

I have given some dates and a little information on celebrations from around the world that take place during June. A lot of them were based on Moon phases. I apologise for any errors but history is a fickle thing and calendars have changed over the years…

Pagan

Summer Solstice/Mid–Summer/Litha – 20–23rd June. Litha is the summer solstice, it is midsummer – the longest day and the shortest night of the year. The Sun is at the height of its power, and although we hope that there are lots more days of summer to follow for a while, this is the point when the year starts to wane. Solstice is a time to stand still, to stop and take stock of our lives and what we are doing, to celebrate what we have achieved and to acknowledge our failures, make sense of our actions and learn from them.

5th June – The Sheela–na–Gig/Damhnaid/Gobnet – The female saint Damhnaid (possibly Domnu) had a place of worship in Ballyvourney in Cork, Ireland where she was known as Gobnet. The bushes around the site were garnished with rags tied on by devotees. Near there was the Holy Well, the branches there also hung with rags. The ritual consisted of devotees going four times around the cairn and saying seven prayers at each round. The Pattern or festival day of Saint Gobnatt was 5th June. The beggars then assembled and exhibited a sheela, the image of a woman, the female genital. Gyg is the name in Norse for giantess or goddess.

Greece

7th June – Callynteria & Plynteria – Feasts of adorning and cleansing were held on two days as a service of atonement held in Athens. The Erechtheum, sanctuary of Athena was cleansed, the images unclothed and garments washed and the images purified.

12th June – Scirophoria – An annual festival at the time of threshing, priests and priestesses from the temples of Athena, Poseidon and Helios marched to the place known as Skiron under the large white umbrella, the umbrella symbolised protection of the soil from the Sun.

14th June – Diipolia – A Greek festival held in Athens to honour Zeus as protector of the city. It was also called Buphonia from the sacrificed ox connected with it. A labouring ox was led to the altar of Zeus in the Acropolise which was strewn with wheat and barley. As soon as the ox touched the consecrated grain, he was punished by a blow on the neck from an axe delivered by a priest who instantly threw away the axe and ran…In his absence the axe was brought to judgement and condemned as a thing polluted by murder to be thrown in the sea. To kill a labouring ox the trusty helper of man was forbidden by custom. In the exceptional sacrifice of one at this festival.

Heras – A Greek 'day of all heras'. A hera is one who in the course of an earthly life has reached that single goal, achieving full communion with the Mother of all Things. A hera was often a guardian of a temple, community of village. (A hero was the male equivalent).

Rome

Vestalia – The Vestalia a festival in honour of Vesta was observed in Rome on 9th June. Banquets were prepared and meat sent to the Vestals to be offered to the gods, millstones were decorated with garlands as well as the donkeys that worked them. The matrons of the town walked barefoot in procession to the temple to ask for their households to be blessed and to make offerings. The millers and bakers all took the day off work.

11th June – Matralia – Matralia was a festival held in honour of Mater Matua. During the festival statues of the goddess were decorated with garlands and gifts by women who had been married once and cakes cooked in clay pots were offered to the goddess. Only one female slave was allowed into the temple on this day, the one chosen to be ritually slapped on the head.

Juno – The festival of Juno Moneta was held; Juno was believed to be the great guardian of the female sex.

27th June – Initium Aestatis – This Roman festival celebrated the first day of summer and is sacred to Aestas.

Norse

9th June – Sigurdsblot – Norse festival honouring Sigurd (Sigifrith or Siegfreid), the great hero who slayed the dragon Fafnir and won back the treasure of the Rhine.

Baldur – The god Baldur is said to have been sacrificed at this time, but is reborn at Jul; the hero Sigurd was also said to have been slain by treachery at Midsummer by his blood–brothers Hagan and Gunthur (Gundahar).

Egypt

15th June – Hapy & Amun – Offerings made to the Egyptian deities Hapy & Amun to secure a good flood.

30th June – Eve of the Egyptian Hathor festival at Thebes.

Buddhist

Vesak day is a Buddhist holiday commemorating the birth, enlightenment and death of the historical Shakyamuni Gautam Buddha. As there are diverse Buddhist cultures around the world, Vesak day is celebrated on different days by different traditions. On Vesak day, Buddhists visit monasteries to offer their prayers and to attend sermons led by Buddhist Venerables. Buddhist prayers often extend beyond themselves to pray for world peace and harmony. They also perform rituals such as the bathing of the Buddha; A symbolic act to commemorate the devas and spirits who made offerings to the Buddha at the time of his birth. During the Vesak Day period, monasteries are decorated with Buddhist flags and flowers while vegetarian restaurants offer promotions as people abstain from meat as an act of compassion. Many Buddhist will also make donations to charity organizations and to free animals that are captured for human consumption.

Yoruban

Odunde Festival – Odunde means "Happy New Year" in the language of the Yoruba people of Nigeria. A celebration of the African new year, the Odunde Festival centres on a vibrant procession where participants make offerings of flowers and fruit to the River Goddess Oshun.

JULY

In the summertime when the weather is hot… What we often refer to as the height of summer, flowers are blooming the skies are blue there's not a cloud in the sky to spoil the view (July is full of song words) and hopefully it is warm.

Spend as much time outside as you can, I like to eat my lunch out in the garden and most of us love to spend our evenings sitting the garden. Just relaxing and listening to the sound of the birds and neighbours mowing their lawns.

Keep saving those flower petals and any seeds that start to appear, dry them and put them away for spell work later in the year.

July Magical Energy

Relaxed energy; preparing, succeeding. Dream work, divination, and meditation on goals and plans especially spiritual ones. Work with nature.

Colours: Silver, blue, grey
Sign: Cancer
Element: Fire
Season: Summer

July Moon Names

Hay Moon, Wort Moon, Moon of Claiming, Moon of Blood, Blessing Moon, Maedmonat, Hewimanoth, Fallow Moon, Buck Moon, Afterlitha Moon and Thunder Moon. The Buck Moon name comes from deer, this is the time when their antlers are in full growth.

Thunder Moon – because of the frequent thunderstorms. Maedmonath meaning 'meadow or mead month', an Anglo Saxon name. Hewimanoth/Hegmonath meaning 'hay month', another Anglo Saxon name. Afterlitha/Æftera Liđa is the Anglo Saxon name and translates as after Litha.

Plants to work with in July

These are my suggested herbs to work with that correspond with the energy of this month. But, trust your intuition and the supplies that you have in your cupboards.

Ash

(Fraxinus excelsior or F. americana)

Ash Magical Properties:

Protection, prosperity, dispels negativity, improves health, sea magic, dreams, love, intuition.

Ruling planet – Sun and Neptune

Element – Fire and Water

Gender – Masculine

Bergamot

(Monarda didyma, Mondarda fistulosa)

Bergamot Magical Properties:

Abundance, meditation, sleep, dreams, clarity, friendship

Sign – Gemini, Libra

Element – Air

Gender – Feminine

Cramp Bark (Guelder rose)

(Viburnum opulus)

Cramp Bark Magical Properties:

Relaxing, meditation, stress, tension, anxiety, healing, rebirth, protection

Element – Earth

Gender – Feminine

Datura

(Datura stramonium)

This plant is TOXIC.

Datura Magical Properties:

Protection, feminine energy, hex breaking, dreams

Ruling planet – Saturn, Venus

Element – Water

Gender – Feminine

Eucalyptus

(Eucalyptus spp)

Eucalyptus Magical Properties:

Moon magic, Sun magic, divination, dreams, healing, purification

Ruling planet – Moon, Sun

Element – Water, Air

Gender – Feminine

Frankincense

Frankincense Magical Properties:

Purification, spirituality, relaxation, focus, love, abundance

Ruling planet – Sun

Sign – Aries, Leo, Aquarius

Element – Fire

Gender – Masculine

Heather

(Calluna spp, Erica spp, vulgaris)

Heather Magical Properties:

Luck, protection, cleansing, ghosts, rain, spirit, love, friendship, faeries, dreams, shape shifting

Ruling planet – Venus

Element – Water

Gender – Feminine

Heliotrope

(Heliotropium spp)

Heliotrope Magical Properties:

Dreams, spirituality, exorcism, protection, forgiveness, abundance

Ruling planet – Sun

Sign – Leo

Element – Fire

Gender – Masculine

Holly

(Ilex aquifolium, Ilex opaca)

Holly Magical Properties:

Protection, luck, dreams, balance, success

Ruling planet – Mars, Saturn

Element – Fire

Gender – Masculine

Honeysuckle

(Lonicera caprifolium, Lonicera japonica, Lonicera periclymenum)

Honeysuckle Magical Properties:

Prosperity, psychic powers, protection, balance, lust, meditation, memory

Ruling planet – Jupiter

Sign – Gemini, Cancer

Element – Earth

Gender – Masculine

Jasmine

(Jasminum grandiflorum, Jasminum officinale, Jasminum odoratissimum)

Jasmine Magical Properties:

Dreams, money, love, meditation, lust

Ruling planet – Moon, Venus
Sign – Cancer
Element – Water
Gender – Feminine

Rose

(Rosa spp)

Rose Magical Properties:

Love, psychic powers, healing, luck, protection, peace, mysteries, knowledge, dreams, friendship, death and rebirth, abundance

Ruling planet – Venus, Moon
Sign – Pisces
Element – Water
Gender – Feminine

Rowan

(Sorbus acuparia)

Rowan Magical Properties:

Psychic powers, power, success, protection, love, spirituality, faeries, divination, healing, inspiration

Ruling planet – Sun, Mercury
Sign – Sagittarius
Element – Fire
Gender – Masculine

Sandalwood

(Red Sandalwood – Pterocarpus santalinus)

Sandalwood (Red) Magical Properties:

Meditation, love

Ruling planet – Venus, Jupiter
Sign – Sagittarius, Virgo
Element – Water
Gender – Feminine

Foods, Herbs and Spices to work with in July

Whether you chose to include the foods in a recipe for the table or add them to spell work, here is my suggested list of foods to work with for the energy of this month.

Chamomile

(Chameamelum nobile, Anthemis nobilis)

Chamomile Magical Properties:

Sleep, dreams, love, calm, money, relaxation, purification, balancing

Ruling planet – Sun

Sign – Leo

Element – Water

Gender – Masculine

Cinnamon

(Cinnamomum zeylanicum, Cinnamomum verum)

Cinnamon Magical Properties:

Success, healing, power, psychic powers, protection, love, focus, lust, spirituality, changes

Ruling planet – Sun

Element – Fire

Gender – Masculine

Cumin

(Cumimum cyminum)

Cumin Magical Properties:

Exorcism, protection, anti–theft, fidelity, lust, peace, love, abundance, success

Ruling planet – Mars

Element – Fire

Gender – Masculine

Dates

(Phoenix dactylifera)

Dates Magical Properties:

Spirituality, death & rebirth, offerings

Ruling planet – Sun

Element – Air

Gender – Feminine

Ginger

(Zingiber officinale)

Ginger Magical Properties:

Healing, power, love, passion, success, prosperity, protection

Ruling planet – Mars

Element – Fire

Gender – Masculine

Horseradish

(Armoracia rusticana)

Horseradish Magical Properties:

Protection, energy, purification, passion

Ruling planet – Mars

Element – Fire

Gender – Masculine

Lettuce

(Lactuca sativa)

Lettuce Magical Properties:

Fertility, meditation, astral travel, calm

Ruling planet – Moon

Element – Water

Gender – neutral

Plum

(Prunus spp)

Plum Magical Properties:

Love, spirituality, relaxation, passion, longevity, wisdom, rebirth

Ruling planet – Venus

Element – Water, Air

Gender – Feminine

Sage

(salvia officinalis)

Sage Magical Properties:

Protection, wishes, wisdom, purification, stimulating, intuition, abundance, success.

Ruling planet – Jupiter

Element – Air

Gender – Masculine

Star Anise

(Illicum verum)

Star Anise Magical Properties:

Luck, psychic powers, purification, protection, dreams, spirituality, sleep

Ruling planet – Jupiter

Element – Air

Gender – Masculine

Tea

(Camellia sinensis)

Tea Magical Properties:

Meditation, courage, strength, prosperity

Ruling planet – Sun

Element – Fire

Gender – Masculine

Crystals to work with in July

As always, go with your intuition and what you have in your collection when working with crystals. The list below is my suggestion of crystals that work particularly well with the energy of this month.

Agate (blue lace)

Agate (blue lace) magical properties

Mediation, spirituality, uplifting, calming, peace, communication, emotions, support, optimism, happiness, protection, cleansing, healing, prosperity, longevity, strength, courage, clarity, success, patience, truth, stress, relaxation, creativity, justice, travel, renewal, understanding, soothing, trust

Energy	Receptive
Element	Water
Planet	Mercury
Zodiac	Gemini

Amethyst

Amethyst magical properties

Peace, protection, success, good luck, hidden knowledge, legal issues, spirituality, contentment, soothing, relaxation, calm, hope, patience, transformation, changes, breaking patterns, grounding, guilt, overcoming addictions, business matters, judgement, clarity, courage, travel, psychic protection, sleep, anxiety, focus, understanding, happiness, justice, intuition, inspiration, channeling, meditation

Energy:	Receptive
Element:	Water
Planet:	Jupiter, Neptune
Zodiac:	Pisces, Scorpio, Sagittarius
Birthstone:	February

Celestite

Celestite magical properties

Divine, spirit work, love, clarity, decisions, meditation, communication, peace, dreams, stress, healing, astral travel, calming, uplifting, harmony, happiness, spirituality

Energy: Receptive
Element: Air, Water
Planet: Neptune, Venus
Zodiac: Gemini

Fluorite

Fluorite magical properties

Magic, imagination, discernment, aptitude, psychic protection, protection, purification, calming, relaxation, tension, anxiety, organisation, structure, challenges, declutter, releasing, support, breaking patterns, intuition, confidence, reassurance, comforting, communication, balance, spirituality, decisions, manifestation, peace, meditation, grounding, healing, cleansing, channelling, past life work, fairy realm, amplifying, memory, power, emotions, depression, stability

Energy: Projective
Element: Water, Air
Planet: Neptune
Zodiac: Scorpio, Aquarius, Pisces

Howlite

Howlite magical properties

Understanding, wisdom, connection, truth, meditation, focus, stress, anxiety, calm, strength, peace, releasing, emotions, selfishness, communication, creativity, inspiration, motivation, concentration, support, patience, relaxation, courage, past life work, astral travel

Energy: Projective
Element: Earth

Planet: Moon, Earth
Zodiac: Gemini, Virgo

Kyanite

Kyanite magical properties

Balance, harmony, calming, connection, psychic abilities, healing, communication, grounding, transformation, meditation, relaxation, luck, growth, leadership, new beginnings, clarity, decisions, stability, truth, vitality, abundance, spirituality, channelling, understanding, dreams

Energy	Receptive
Element	Water
Planet	Jupiter, Venus, Mars
Zodiac	Aries, Libra, Taurus

Labradorite

Labradorite magical properties

Transformation, cleansing, breaking patterns, potential, psychic abilities, intuition, confidence, spirituality, focus, protection, imagination, relaxation, soothing, energy, healing, stress, anxiety, luck, abundance, success, decisions, trust, changes, strength, courage, self–confidence, inspiration, perseverance, journeying, clarity, insight, meditation, depression, jealousy, grounding

Energy	Projective
Element	Water
Planet	Earth, Moon, Uranus
Zodiac	Aquarius, Sagittarius, Scorpio, Leo

Larimar

Larimar magical properties

Peace, clarity, healing, inspiration, spirituality, understanding, calming, soothing, uplifting, emotions, fears, depression, patience, creativity, love, communication, friendship, guidance, happiness, decisions, relaxation, meditation, wisdom, divine, harmony

Energy: Receptive
Element: Water/Fire/Spirit
Planet: Neptune
Zodiac: Pisces

Moonstone

Moonstone magical properties

New beginnings, Moon magic, intuition, calming, psychic abilities, balance, harmony, wishes, cleansing, uplifting, hope, meditation, emotions, love, divination, spirituality, wealth, truth, healing, sensuality, insight, peace, wisdom, communication, confidence, abundance, prosperity, dreams, fertility, travel

Energy Receptive
Element Water
Planet Moon
Zodiac Cancer, Libra, Scorpio
Birthstone June, September

Obsidian (black)

Obsidian (black) magical properties

Truth, healing, clarity, illusions, breaking barriers, integrity, grounding, centring, strength, courage, protection, cleansing, meditation, stress, calming, relaxation, depression, anxiety, wealth, luck, focus, emotions, power, determination, success, patience, perseverance, releasing, spirit work, spirituality, challenges, past life work, divination

Energy Projective
Element Fire, Earth, Water
Planet Saturn, Jupiter
Zodiac Sagittarius

Quartz (clear)

Quartz (clear) magical properties

Purification, cleansing, healing, calming, emotions, strength, support, spirituality, energy, balance, psychic abilities, motivation, uplifting, decisions, anxiety, divine connection, amplifying, focus, meditation, manifestation, channelling, protection, negative energy, clarity, wisdom, concentration, learning, spirit work, communication, astral travel, divination, dreams, harmony

Energy	Projective, Receptive
Planet	Sun, Moon
Element	Fire, Water
Zodiac	Leo, Gemini, Capricorn

Quartz (smoky)

Quartz (smoky) magical properties

Grounding, centring, focus, negative energy, decisions, cooperation, creativity, emotions, depression, anxiety, jealousy, nature, protection, calming, manifestation, wishes, divination, meditation, insight, guidance, uplifting, fears, relaxation, releasing, abundance, luck, prosperity

Energy	Receptive
Element	Earth
Planet	Saturn, Jupiter
Zodiac	Capricorn, Sagittarius

Turquoise

Turquoise magical properties

Purification, negative energy, protection, balance, relaxation, emotions, stress, spirituality, energy, depression, clarity, wisdom, understanding, psychic abilities, insight, intuition, past life work, communication, wealth, abundance, finances, prosperity, luck, decisions, friendship, uplifting, meditation, love, harmony

Energy	Receptive
Element	Earth
Planet	Venus, Neptune
Zodiac	Sagittarius, Pisces, Aquarius
Birthstone	December

Moon Deities to work with in July

Here you will find my suggestions on some of the Moon deities to work with that align with the energies of this month. Trust your intuition and be guided by the deities that may also make themselves known to you.

Anu – a Mesopotamian/Sumerian sky god viewed as Father of the gods and ruler of the heavens, the stars and the spirits. Call upon him for: Goals, wishes, spirituality.

Arianrhod – Welsh goddess of the Moon. She forms the triple goddess triad with Blodeuwedd and Cerridwen. Her name translates as 'silver disc', she is often referred to as Goddess of the Silver Wheel. Arianrhod guides the dead to the other side and rules the sky and the sea as well as the Moon. She can shapeshift into an owl. She is also known as one of the goddesses of Avalon. Call upon her for: Moon magic, dream work, psychic abilities, divination, past lives, reincarnation, other realms, feminine power, retribution, karma.

Hestia – Greek goddess of the hearth and home she is also a fire goddess. Her Roman equivalent is Vesta. The Greeks did not have statues of this goddess as it was believed she didn't take human form, instead she appeared as the flames of fire in the hearth. Hestia was the first born of the Olympian goddesses. She is absolutely about new beginnings and the start of all things. This goddess is the ultimate super housekeeper and home maker, with added omnipotence. Call upon her for: Home life, domesticity, fire magic, devotion, wishes, manifesting, unity, new beginnings, spirituality, blessings.

Isis – Egyptian goddess Queen of Egypt. She is looked upon as Mother Moon, Queen of Sorcery and the life force within the river Nile. Isis taught her people useful skills, those they would need to survive and flourish, no being high up on the sky for this one, she got down with her subjects (very practical woman). Call upon her for: Magic, dreams, divination, harvest, perspective, love, spirituality, faithfulness, destiny, revitalisation, fulfilment, inner beauty, spirituality, rebirth, feminine energy, knowledge, motherhood, healing, changes, manifesting.

Kuan Yin – Chinese/Buddhist goddess of mercy who is probably one of the most chilled out and relaxed deities ever. This beautiful goddess hears all your prayers and responds to each and every request for help. She needs some kind of medal… Call upon her for: Kindness, magic, health, healing, fertility, children, sympathy, support, suffering, encouragement, enlightenment, spirituality, protection.

Luna – Roman goddess of the Moon. Depicted as a beautiful woman with the power to ease childbirth and bring about love. She carries a very strong feminine energy. If you want an answer to a problem, then call upon this lovely lady to bring you the answer in your dreams, it is her speciality. Her Greek equivalent is Selene. Call upon her for: Feminine energy, water magic, safety, travel, intuition, blue Moon magic, protection, illusion, truth, love, psychic abilities, dreams, solutions.

Rhiannon – if you aren't singing the Fleetwood Mac song right now, you need to… A Welsh goddess and great Queen of Wales. She brings peace, comfort and patience. If you are looking for magical enchantments, then she has a bounty of them. Call upon her for: Patience, comfort, peace, magic, movement, relaxation, communication, fertility, leadership, spirit work, motivation, dream work.

Selene – From ancient Greece, she is a Titan Moon goddess, sister of Helios (the Sun). She drives a silver chariot drawn by two white horses, across the sky each night. The Roman equivalent is

Luna. Call upon her for: Moon magic, dream work, sleep, Moon phases, magic, divination, sensuality.

Thoth – Egyptian ibis headed Moon god. He is a seriously studious dude. God of writing and wisdom he is considered to be one of the most important gods of ancient Egypt (he didn't let it go to his head though). Call upon him for: Knowledge, Moon magic, wisdom, learning, intellect, meditation, logic, reason, magic, secrets, balance, judgement.

Vesta – Roman goddess of the crescent Moon, the hearth and home. She rules domesticity with a flip of the feather duster and a whip of her apron. She keeps the house and family running like clockwork. She is known as Hestia in Greece. Call upon her for: Home, family, relationships, harmony, peace, love, fertility, fire magic, spirituality.

World celebration days

I have given some dates and a little information on celebrations from around the world that take place during July. A lot of them were based on Moon phases. I apologise for any errors but history is a fickle thing and calendars have changed over the years…

Moon Landing

On 20th July 1969, the space craft Apollo 11 carrying Neil Armstrong, Buzz Aldrin and Michael Collins landed on the Moon. Armstrong was the first to step out and walk on the surface of the Moon, followed by Buzz Aldrin. Poor old Michael Collins remained alone in the craft until they returned.

Egypt

19th July – the Feast of Thoth

25th July – the Feast of Anket, welcoming the rise in water levels of the river Nile.

28th July – festival of the goddess of weaving, Hedjihotep.

19th July – Every year during the second month of the floods came an Egyptian festival, for eleven days the capital celebrated the feast of Opet. Amun and his spouse Mut accompanied the god Khonsu in a ceremonial time of divine emergence, giving the crowds a glimpse of the triad of three great gods.

24th July – Isis–Neith – A feast of lamps was celebrated in Egypt in honour of Isis–Neith. The ceremony took place in an under chapel beneath the temple. Lamps were carried in procession around the coffin of Osiris.

27th July – Hatshepsut – Festival of Queen of Egypt and Priestess Hatshepsut, the only ruling female Pharaoh of Egypt who fostered exploration and the arts and cultivated government by peaceful means.

Hindu

Guru Purnima – The full Moon day in the Hindu month of Ashad (July–August) is observed as the auspicious day of Guru Purnima, a day sacred to the memory of the great sage Maharshi Veda Vyasa. All Hindus are indebted to this ancient saint who edited the four Vedas, wrote the 18 Puranas, Mahabharata and the Srimad Bhagavatam. Vyasa even taught Dattatreya, who is regarded as the Guru of Gurus. On this day, all spiritual aspirants and devotees worship Vyasa in honour of his divine personage and all disciples perform a 'puja' of their respective spiritual preceptor or 'Gurudevs'. This day is of deep significance to the farmers, for it heralds the setting in of the much–needed rains, as the advent of cool showers usher in fresh life in the fields. It is a good time to begin your spiritual lessons. Traditionally, spiritual seekers commence to intensify their spiritual 'sadhana' from this day. The period 'Chaturmas' ("four months") begins from this day. In the past, wandering spiritual masters and their disciples used to settle down at a place to study and discourse on the Brahma Sutras composed by Vyasa, and engage themselves in Vedantic discussions.

Rome

1st July – middle of July – Rosalia – The Romans loved roses and used them whenever they could for festivals and special occasions. The feast of roses, the Rosalia was a common event and held on dates ranging from 1st July to the middle of the month.

7th July – Nonae Caprotinae – "Nones of the Wild Fig", also called "Feast of the Serving Women". This festival was held to honour Juno Caprotina, and a sacrifice was given to her under a wild fig tree. It also celebrates the serving women who helped free the city of Rome from the Gauls.

Parilia/Palilia – Festivals for Pales, goddess of herds. During these festivals, ritualistic cleansing of sheep/cattle pens and animals would take place. The shepherd would sweep out the pens and smudge the animals and pens with burning sulphur. In the evening, the animals were sprinkled with water, and their pens were decorated with garlands. Fires were started, and in were thrown olives, horse blood, beanstalks without pods, and the ashes from the Fordicalia fires. Men and beasts jumped over the fire three times to purify themselves further, and to bring them protection from anything that might harm them (wolves, sickness, starvation, etc.). After the animals were put back into their pens the shepherds would offer non–blood sacrifices of grain, cake millet, and warm milk to Pales. The festival in April was for smaller livestock, while the one in July was for larger animals.

23rd July – Neptunalia – This festival celebrated Neptune as the god of irrigation. During the festival, participants would sit under arbours made from leaves. They would ask Neptune to continue supplying them with fresh water during the heat of the summer and early autumn. Salacia was also worshipped during the Neptunalia.

25th July – Furrinalia – This festival venerated all those who searched for underground water sources. In Rome's early days it was a festival that took place in a grove on the Janiculum, and honoured the goddess Furrina.

Salacia – A Roman goddess of salt water and often regarded as wife to Neptune. A festival where boughs were erected, possibly to bring blessings of sufficient water.

Greece

4th July – Aphrodisia – Greek festival in honour of Aphrodite, sacrifice of the dove, myrtle tree, sea shells and roses. Dancing and athletic games.

12th July – Kronia – A harvest festival in honour of the god of agriculture Kronos.

6th – 13th July – Ludi Apollinares – "Games of Apollo". These games were first held in 212 BCE to celebrate Apollo as a god of healing (especially during war) and lasted for a single day (July 13). They were gradually expanded to eight days, with two days reserved for theatre performances, two days for games in the circus, and the remaining days for markets and fairs. Apollo was given sacrifices during the Ludi Apollinares, and all participants were expected to wear garlands while attending the events.

The Great Panathenaia – This took place in July at the height of the summer heat when the need for rain was the greatest; the day of the festival was the birthday of the goddess Athena.

Aphrodite – At Alexandria the rites consisted of a huge pageant of the wedding of Adonis and Aphrodite.

Athena – The Panathenaea, festivals in honour of the patroness of Athens were first called Atheneaea. Originally, they were observed on one day but were eventually extended. Four young virgins were yearly chosen from noble houses who then had to spend several months at the temple of Athena and take part in the services. Two of them had the task of commencing the cloak which the women of Athens wove and presented to the Goddess. The other two on the night of the festival received from the priestess of Athena certain coffers with unknown contents which they carried in procession on their heads to a grotto beside the temple of Aphrodite of the gardens, receiving something in exchange which they carried to the temple. Athena's procession garment was white and embroidered in gold with the achievements of the goddess. Her garment was hung upon the sail of a ship that was built for the procession which upon reaching Athena's statue was placed upon her; the statue was then laid on a bed of flowers.

28th July – Pythias – Greek festival of Pythias, mother of Pythagoras.

Adonia – During this moveable festival a household's female members would climb onto the roof of the house and plant the "Garden of Adonis". These gardens contained fast–growing plants. For eight days the women would tend to the plants, and then neglect. After the plants had died the women would mourn for them. There was also a sacred play portraying the wedding of Adonis and Venus held during the Adonia and was probably based on a Greek tradition. The last part of the festival involved making effigies of Adonis and placing them into coffins.

Christianity

26th July – Festival of St Anne, Mother of the Virgin Mary.

Norse

31st July – 1st August – Lithasblot – Norse harvest festival; giving thanks to Urda (Ertha) for her bounty. Often alms are given to the unfortunate at this time, or loaves in the shape of the fylfot (the Sun–wheel, which fell into regrettable disrepute during the dark times of the Second World War when the symbol was perverted as a symbol of chaos and darkness). Lithasblot has long been associated with ceremonial magic and magical workings.

AUGUST

The height of summer (or hopefully) and the beginning of the harvests. Lughnasadh or Lammas arrives – 31st July/1st August (pronounced loo–nah–sah). A time to celebrate the first harvest, we give thanks to the Earth for its bounty and beauty. Lughnasadh is associated with bread as grain is one of the first crops of the year to be harvested.

August Magical Energy:

Energy into harvesting; gathering, appreciating. Vitality, health, friendships. Count your blessings.

Colours: Yellow, gold
Sign: Leo
Element: Air
Season: Autumn

August Moon Names

Corn Moon, Barley Moon, Dispute Moon, Wedmonath, Wyrtmonath, Harvest Moon, Crane Moon, Red Berries Moon, Dry Moon, Wheat Cut Moon, Lynx Moon, Grain Moon, Sturgeon Moon, Hungry Ghost Moon and Moon when cherries turn black.

Sturgeon Moon is from the Great Lakes and Lake Champlain, when the sturgeon are easy catch. Wedmonath and Weodmonath both mean 'weed month' or 'the fulfilment of the month of weeds' from Anglo Saxon. Wyrtmonath translates as wort moon or herb moon in Anglo Saxon. Hungry Ghost Moon comes from the Chinese tradition that the gates of hell open in August and the hungry ghosts roam the earth seeking food and mischief.

Plants to work with in August

These are my suggested herbs to work with that correspond

with the energy of this month. But, trust your intuition and the supplies that you have in your cupboards.

Bergamot

(Monarda didyma, Mondarda fistulosa)
Bergamot Magical Properties:
Abundance, meditation, sleep, dreams, clarity, friendship
Sign – Gemini, Libra
Element – Air
Gender – Feminine

Carnation

(Dianthus carphyllus)
Carnation Magical Properties:
Healing, strength, protection, release, courage
Ruling planet – Sun
Element – Fire
Gender – Masculine

Coltsfoot

(Tussilago farfara)
Coltsfoot Magical Properties:
Visions, love, energy, health, tranquillity, peace
Ruling planet – Venus
Sign – Taurus
Element – Water
Gender – Feminine

Elm

(Ulmus campestris)
Elm Magical Properties:
Love, balance, luck, energy, psychic powers
Ruling planet – Saturn, Mercury
Element – Water

Gender – Feminine

Heather

(Calluna spp, Erica spp, vulgaris)

Heather Magical Properties:

Luck, protection, cleansing, ghosts, rain, spirit, love, friendship, faeries, dreams, shape shifting

Ruling planet – Venus

Element – Water

Gender – Feminine

Hyssop

(Hyssopus officinalis)

Hyssop Magical Properties:

Purification, protection, healing

Ruling planet – Jupiter, Moon

Sign – Cancer

Element – Fire

Gender – Masculine

Lemon Balm

(Melissa officinalis)

Lemon Balm Magical Properties:

Success, healing, anti–depression, memory, love, anxiety

Ruling planet – Moon & Venus

Sign – Cancer

Element – Water

Gender – Feminine

Passion Flower

(Passiflora)

Passion Flower Magical Properties:

Love, calm, peace, sleep, friendship

Ruling planet – Venus

Element – Water
Gender – Feminine

Plantain

(Plantago spp. Lanceolata, Plantago major, Plantago media)
Plantain Magical Properties:
Strength, protection, healing, energy, courage
Ruling planet – Venus
Sign – Capricorn
Element – Earth
Gender – Feminine

Rose

(Rosa spp)
Rose Magical Properties:
Love, psychic powers, healing, luck, protection, peace, mysteries, knowledge, dreams, friendship, death and rebirth, abundance
Ruling planet – Venus, Moon
Sign – Pisces
Element – Water
Gender – Feminine

Sweetpea

(Lathyrus odoratus)
Sweetpea Magical Properties:
Courage, strength, friendship, peace, happiness, truth, spirituality, psychic abilities, protection, sleep
Ruling planet – Venus, Moon, Mercury
Element – Water
Gender – Feminine

Tansy

(Tanacetum vulgare)

Tansy Magical Properties:
Health, longevity, rebirth, cleansing, protection, travel
Ruling planet – Venus
Sign – Gemini
Element – Water
Gender – Feminine

Foods, Herbs and Spices to work with in August

Whether you chose to include the foods in a recipe for the table or add them to spell work, here is my suggested list of foods to work with for the energy of this month.

Chillies

(capsicum)
Chillies Magical Properties:
Creativity, energy, power, protection, passion, hex breaking
Ruling planet – Mars
Element – Fire
Gender – Masculine

Coffee

(coffea)
Coffee Magical Properties:
Energy, clarity, divination
Ruling planet – Mars
Element – Fire, Water
Gender – Feminine

Grapefruit

(Citrus paradise)
Grapefruit Magical Properties:
Happiness, spirit work, purification, depression, energy
Ruling planet – Jupiter, Sun
Element – Fire, Water

Gender – Feminine

Horseradish

(Armoracia rusticana)

Horseradish Magical Properties:

Protection, energy, purification, passion

Ruling planet – Mars

Element – Fire

Gender – Masculine

Lemon

(Citrus x lemon)

Lemon Magical Properties:

Purification, Moon magic, happiness, decisions, uplifting, love, protection, friendship, fidelity

Ruling planet – Moon

Element – Water

Gender – Feminine

Lime

(Citrus aurantifolia)

Lime Magical Properties:

Purification, love, healing, protection, energy

Ruling planet –Sun

Element – Fire

Gender – Masculine

Orange

(Citrus × sinensis)

Orange Magical Properties:

Love, happiness, uplifting, generosity, purification, clarity, energy, fidelity

Ruling planet – Sun

Element – Fire

Gender – Masculine

Paprika

(Capsicum annuum)

Paprika Magical Properties:

Creativity, energy

Ruling planet – Mars

Element – Fire

Gender –Masculine

Passion Fruit

(Passiflora edulis)

Passion Fruit Magical Properties:

Love, peace, friendship, meditation, dreams

Ruling planet – Venus

Element – Water

Gender – Feminine

Potato

(Solanum tuberosum L)

Potato Magical Properties:

Energy, magic, grounding, prosperity, healing

Ruling planet – Moon

Element – Earth

Gender – Feminine

Rosemary

(Rosemarinus officinalis)

Rosemary Magical Properties:

Protection, love, lust, mental powers, exorcism, purification, healing, sleep

Ruling planet – Sun

Sign – Aries

Element – Fire

Gender – Masculine

Saffron

(Crocus sativus)

Saffron Magical Properties:

Happiness, energy, psychic powers, healing, fertility

Ruling planet – Sun

Element – Fire

Gender – Masculine

Sesame

(Sesamum indicum)

Sesame Magical Properties:

Prosperity, protection, energy, strength, secrets

Ruling planet – Sun

Element – Fire, Earth

Gender – Masculine

Crystals to work with in August

As always, go with your intuition and what you have in your collection when working with crystals. The list below is my suggestion of crystals that work particularly well with the energy of this month.

Agate (moss)

Agate (moss) magical properties

Nature, happiness, prosperity, wealth, longevity, friendship, success, abundance, healing, renewal, fertility, creativity, confidence, strength, love, beginnings, self–esteem, communication, emotions, stress, releasing, hope, trust, depression, growth, finances, cleansing, support, peace, stability, fears, luck, divination

Energy Receptive

Element Earth

Planet Moon
Zodiac Virgo, Gemini

Amber

Amber magical properties:

Manifesting, energy, beauty, Sun magic, power, wishes, intellect, clarity, wisdom, balance, purification, protection, psychic abilities, healing, calm, patience, love, sensuality, good luck, marriage, abundance, success, vitality, joy, sexuality, cleansing, stress, harmony, creativity

Energy: Projective
Element: Fire, Spirit
Planet: Sun
Zodiac: Leo

Bloodstone

Bloodstone magical properties:

Organisation, adaptability, anxiety, clarity, concentration, renewal, energy, self–confidence, connection, calm, protection, breaking barriers, selfishness, mysticism, insight, spirituality, truth, intuition, creativity, guidance, strength, healing, victory, wealth, money, power, invisibility, deception, negative energy, divine connection, past life, dreams

Energy: Projective
Element: Fire, Earth
Planet: Mars
Zodiac: Aries, Pisces, Scorpio
Birthstone: February, March

Labradorite

Labradorite magical properties

Transformation, cleansing, breaking patterns, potential, psychic abilities, intuition, confidence, spirituality, focus, protection, imagination, relaxation, soothing, energy, healing, stress, anxiety, luck, abundance, success, decisions, trust, changes, strength, courage, self–confidence, inspiration, perseverance, journeying, clarity, insight, meditation, depression, jealousy, grounding

Energy Projective
Element Water
Planet Earth, Moon, Uranus
Zodiac Aquarius, Sagittarius, Scorpio, Leo

Larimar

Larimar magical properties

Peace, clarity, healing, inspiration, spirituality, understanding, calming, soothing, uplifting, emotions, fears, depression, patience, creativity, love, communication, friendship, guidance, happiness, decisions, relaxation, meditation, wisdom, divine, harmony

Energy: Receptive
Element: Water/Fire/Spirit
Planet: Neptune
Zodiac: Pisces

Malachite

Malachite magical properties

Changes, transformation, clarity, emotions, protection, support, healing, peace, travel, fears, growth, creativity, renewal, energy, wealth, money, opportunity, abundance, new beginnings, finances, success, business, focus, strength, wisdom, releasing, prosperity, breaking barriers, psychic abilities, manifestation, soothing, stress, love, power

Energy Receptive
Element Earth
Planet Venus
Zodiac Capricorn, Scorpio

Pyrite

Pyrite magical properties

Releasing, breaking patterns, clarity, protection, support, decisions, growth, success, inspiration, grounding, vitality, learning, perception, memory, wisdom, psychic abilities, healing, cleansing, prosperity, wealth, abundance, luck, strength, motivation, manifestation, finances, energy, Sun magic, power, focus, perseverance, confidence, divination, communication, self–confidence, meditation

Energy	Projective
Element	Fire
Planet	Mars, Sun
Zodiac	Leo

Quartz (clear)

Quartz (clear) magical properties

Purification, cleansing, healing, calming, emotions, strength, support, spirituality, energy, balance, psychic abilities, motivation, uplifting, decisions, anxiety, divine connection, amplifying, focus, meditation, manifestation, channelling, protection, negative energy, clarity, wisdom, concentration, learning, spirit work, communication, astral travel, divination, dreams, harmony

Energy	Projective, Receptive
Planet	Sun, Moon
Element	Fire, Water
Zodiac	Leo, Gemini, Capricorn

Rhodochrosite

Rhodochrosite magical properties

Power, potential, strength, confidence, healing, new beginnings, breaking barriers, releasing, joy, happiness, creativity, determination, manifestation, prosperity, abundance, love, emotions, peace, renewal, connection, balance, spirituality, harmony, energy

Energy	Projective
Element	Fire
Planet	Mars, Jupiter
Zodiac	Scorpio, Leo

Sodalite

Sodalite magical properties

Creativity, communication, peace, friendship, clarity, truth, connection, knowledge, wisdom, emotions, balance, divination, psychic abilities, cleansing, confidence, fears, love, intuition, decisions, perseverance, anxiety, insight, organisation, self–esteem, releasing, understanding, harmony, learning, dreams, meditation

Energy	Receptive
Element	Water
Planet	Jupiter, Venus
Zodiac	Sagittarius

Sunstone

Sunstone magical properties

Sun magic, power, decisions, leadership, strength, happiness, inspiration, love, luck, stability, clarity, energy, stress, depression, emotions, optimism, perseverance, intuition, fears, self–esteem, self–confidence, healing, balance, harmony, abundance, prosperity, opportunities, peace, protection

Energy	Projective
Element	Fire
Planet	Sun
Zodiac	Leo

Turquoise

Turquoise magical properties

Purification, negative energy, protection, balance, relaxation, emotions, stress, spirituality, energy, depression, clarity, wisdom, understanding, psychic abilities, insight, intuition, past life work, communication, wealth, abundance, finances, prosperity, luck, decisions, friendship, uplifting, meditation, love, harmony

Energy	Receptive
Element	Earth
Planet	Venus, Neptune
Zodiac	Sagittarius, Pisces, Aquarius
Birthstone	December

Moon Deities to work with in August

Here you will find my suggestions on some of the Moon deities to work with that align with the energies of this month. Trust your intuition and be guided by the deities that may also make themselves known to you.

Asherah – Ancient West Semitic goddess, often referred to as Queen of the Gods. Also known as 'She who walks on the sea' or 'holiness'. You will find her name in the Old Testament she is consort of Yahweh. Asherah is a goddess of the sea. Call upon her for: Divine wisdom, feminine energy, feminine issues, strength, self–esteem, self–confidence, courage, kindness, love, divination, insight, justice, fertility, compassion, healing, nurturing.

Cybele/Kybele –Phrygian goddess of the Underworld and associated with the dark Moon. Worshipped in ancient Greece and found in Romany mythology. Some associate her with the Greek/Minoan goddess Rhea. She is known as mother of the gods. Associated with mountains, caves, nature and wild animals particularly hawks, lions and bees. Call upon her for: Love, victory, strength, relationships, humour, healing, health, fun, stability.

Hathor – Egyptian goddess of the Moon, associated with the dark Moon. Goddess of the Underworld but also ruler of the sky. She is a mother to all Egyptians. Definitely packing a powerful punch of feminine energy having given birth to the universe, she must have been exhausted. Call upon her for: Love, feminine energy, beauty, sexuality, happiness, romance, music, the arts, protection (primarily for women).

Isis – Egyptian goddess Queen of Egypt. She is looked upon as Mother Moon, Queen of Sorcery and the life force within the river Nile. Isis taught her people useful skills, those they would need to survive and flourish, no being high up in the sky for this one, she got down with her subjects (very practical woman). Call upon her for: Magic, dreams, divination, harvest, perspective, love, spirituality, faithfulness, destiny, revitalisation, fulfilment, inner beauty, spirituality, rebirth, feminine energy, knowledge, motherhood, healing, changes, manifesting.

Ixchel – Mayan goddess of the Moon, weaving, water and childbirth. Mother of all Mayan deities she rules over life and death and bears the title of 'Keeper of Souls'. Her name translates as 'Lady Rainbow'. She spends her time constantly changing from a beautiful young woman into an old crone, it must be both exhausting and confusing. Call upon her for: Weather magic, fertility, health, healing, childbirth, water magic, rainbow magic, control, power, choices, assertion, self–confidence.

Juno – A Roman goddess, mother of all the gods. She protects Rome and all things feminine. She is a goddess of marriage, women and young girls. She is a strong, confident business woman, she definitely has a modern approach to being a deity. Her Greek equivalent is Hera. Call upon her for: Romance, love, relationships, marriage, protection, leadership, time, feminine energy, safety, happiness.

Kuan Yin – Chinese/Buddhist goddess of mercy who is probably one of the most chilled out and relaxed deities ever. This beautiful goddess hears all your prayers and responds to each and every request for help. She needs some kind of medal... Call upon her for: Kindness, magic, health, healing, fertility, children, sympathy, support, suffering, encouragement, enlightenment, spirituality, protection.

Lucina – Roman goddess of light. She also covers childbirth. Possibly later merged with Juno and/or Diana. She may even have been converted, becoming St Lucy. An ancient bronze mask believed to depict Juno Lucina shows her with a tiny crescent Moon engraved on her forehead. Call upon her for: Charity, protection, health, healing, kindness, banishing, fertility, well–being.

Luna – Roman goddess of the Moon. Depicted as a beautiful woman with the power to ease childbirth and bring about love. She carries a very strong feminine energy. If you want an answer to a problem, then call upon this lovely lady to bring you the answer in your dreams, it is her speciality. Her Greek equivalent is Selene. Call upon her for: Feminine energy, water magic, safety, travel, intuition, blue Moon magic, protection, illusion, truth, love, psychic abilities, dreams, solutions.

Neith/Nit – Egyptian goddess of the crescent Moon and domesticity. She has an eclectic list of duties including war, hunting and weaving. She is also considered to be the personification of the primordial waters of creation. Call upon her for: Home, marriage, protection, feminine energy, hunting, war, creativity, new beginnings.

World celebration days

I have given some dates and a little information on celebrations from around the world that take place during August. A lot of them were based on Moon phases. I apologise for any errors but history is a fickle thing and calendars have changed over the years...

Pagan

Lughnasadh or Lammas – 31st July/1st August. A time to celebrate the first harvest, we give thanks to the Earth for its bounty and beauty. Lughnasadh is associated with bread as grain is one of the first crops of the year to be harvested.

Blodeuwedd – In some parts of Britain it became customary to set a bonfire in a wagon wheel on a hilltop at Lushnasadh. When the wheel was glowing red it would be bowled down the hilltop as the community watched. It was to symbolise the descent of the Sun from its midsummer height, this festival was also associated with the marriage of Lugh to Blodeuwedd.

Macha – The annual fair of Macha was held at Armagh in Ireland to commemorate Queen Macha of the Golden Hair who had founded a palace there. The Three Machas were also associated with this feast.

Rome

Beginning on 13th August, the ancient Romans held a week–long festival dedicated to the goddess Diana. They would pray to her to bring a good harvest and keep the storms at bay. Offerings of fruit and vines were left for her in the woods or at crossroads. Fires and candles were lit in her honour on 15th August.

Demeter and Ceres – The Roman festivals of late summer open the Mysteries of Life, a cycle which spans a quarter of the year. They celebrate the Goddess as the source of all life, creatrix and sustainer of the cycles of existence through which the soul moves.

Diana – The Festival of Torches was held on 15th August in honour of the goddess Diana where torches were hung in her groves.

25th August – Ops (meaning abundance) was the old Italian goddess of fertility, sowing and reaping and on the 25th August, she had a festival, the Opeconsiva which only the Vestals and one of the pontifices could attend because her shrine in Regia was so tiny.

Greece

7th August – Karneia (Carneia) – Festival in honour of Apollo held in the Greek city of Sparta.

13th August – marks a great festival for the Greek goddess Hecate, Moon goddess and her descendant Diana. The goddess' aid is sought to avert storms which might injure the coming harvest.

23rd August – This day is dedicated to the Greek Genia of Personal Fate. The threads of Moira draw all things in life together. Her symbols are the wheel and the scales. A day to examine the direction of your soul and make resolutions for the future.

Nemesis – The Greeks celebrated a festival called the Nemesia in memory of those departed as the goddess Nemesis was supposed to defend the relics and memory of the dead from all insult.

Mid–August – Pamboeotia – Dedicated to Zeus Panemeros and Athena.

Egypt

4th August – Festival of the Dead, a Sunset ceremony.

19th August – procession of Hera to Neith.

23rd August – Great feast of the Netjeru (gods and goddesses).

15th August – Offerings made to Egyptian deities Hapy & Amun to secure a good flood.

19th August – Wag and Thoth festival according to the great festival list in the temple for Ramesses III.

22nd August – Great procession of the Egyptian god Osiris.

29th August – Great festivals were held to celebrate the anniversary of the birth of Hathor. Before dawn the priestesses would bring Hathor's image out onto the terrace to expose it to the rays of the rising Sun. Followed by much rejoicing, song and plenty of alcohol.

Buddhist

3rd August – Guan Yin Enlightenment Day – Guan Yin is the Bodhisattva of Great Compassion in Mahayana Buddhism and also worshiped by Taoists. The Bodhisattva was introduced into China via the Silk Road and initially, Guan Yin was presented in male form. As Buddhism became localized in China, Guan Yin was subsequently transformed into Chinese female form. By the Song dynasty, Guan Yin evolved into a female bodhisattva in white robes that we see today. The male Guan Yin continues to be depicted albeit less frequently. The bodhisattva's gender is unproblematic to devotees as Guan Yin will manifest in any form to reach out or to help suffering beings.

China

14th August – 12th September – Hungry Ghosts Festival – The Chinese believe that on the 7th lunar month of each year, spirits of the deceased return to the human realm for a month. The seventh month is sometimes referred to as the ghost month and the festival is commonly known as the "hungry ghost festival. Many people avoid important events during the 7th month. Activities to avoid include moving to new homes, weddings, and opening ceremony of new businesses.

Christian

The Virgin Mary – 22nd August marks the Irish Octave of the Feast of the Assumption, the Immaculate Heart of the Blessed Virgin Mary.

Hindu

Teej – The Hindu festival of Teej is marked by fasting of women who pray to Lord Shiva and Goddess Parvati seeking their blessings for marital bliss. It is a three–day festival that occurs on the third day of 'Shukla Paksha' or bright fortnight of the Moon in the Hindu month of Shravana or Sawan, which falls during the Indian monsoon season, i.e., July – August. While ritual fasting is central to Teej, the festival is marked by colourful celebrations, especially by the womenfolk, who enjoy swing rides, song and dance. Swings are often hung from trees or placed in the courtyard of homes and decked with flowers. Young girls and married women apply mehendi or henna tattoos on this auspicious occasion. Women wear beautiful saris and adorn themselves with jewellery and visit temples to offer their special prayers to goddess Parvati. A special sweet called 'ghewar' is prepared and distributed as Prasad or divine offering.

Manasa – the Snake Goddess – Ma Manasa Devi, the snake goddess, is worshipped by Hindus, mainly for the prevention and cure of snakebites and infectious diseases like smallpox and chicken pox as well as for prosperity and fertility. She stands for both 'destruction' and 'regeneration', almost akin to a snake shedding its skin and being reborn. The idol of the goddess is depicted as a graceful lady with her body, adorned with snakes and sitting on a lotus or standing on a snake, under a hooded canopy of seven cobras. She is often seen as 'the one-eyed goddess', and sometimes portrayed with her son Astika on her lap. During the monsoon season, Goddess Manasa is worshiped, mainly in the eastern Indian states of Bengal, Assam, Jharkand, and Orissa, throughout the months of June, July and August (Ashar – Shravan), a time when the snakes leave their nesting ground and come out into the open and become active. In Bangladesh, the Manasa and Ashtanaag Puja is a month-long affair spanning July and August. Devotees pay obeisance to goddess Manasa and perform various 'pujas' or rituals to appease her. Special 'murtis' or statues of the goddess are sculpted, various sacrifices made, and prayers chanted. In some places, worshippers are seen to pierce their bodies, poisonous snakes are displayed on the altar, and live shows depicting the life and legends of Manasa Devi are performed.

Raksha Bandhan Festival – The chaste bond of love between a brother and a sister is one of the deepest and noblest of human emotions. 'Raksha Bandhan' or 'Rakhi' is a special occasion to celebrate this emotional bonding by tying a holy thread around the wrist. This thread, which pulsates with sisterly love and sublime sentiments, is rightly called the 'Rakhi'. It means 'a bond of protection', and Raksha Bandhan signifies that the strong must protect the weak from all that's evil. The ritual is observed on the full Moon day of the Hindu month of Shravan, on which sisters tie the sacred Rakhi string on their brothers' right wrists, and pray, for their long life. Rakhis are ideally made of silk with gold and silver threads, beautifully crafted embroidered sequins, and studded with semi–precious stones. This ritual not only strengthens the bond of love between brothers and sisters, but also transcends the confines of the family. When a Rakhi is tied on the wrists of close friends and neighbours, it underscores the need for a harmonious social life, where every individual co–exist peacefully as brothers and sisters. All members of the community commit to protect each other and the society.

SEPTEMBER

September is a month full of harvesting and we start to see the first signs of autumn. We still get warm Sunny days, but the morning and evening air carries the chill of autumn with it. September also brings the autumn equinox, a time of change. Mother Earth is making her final push of the summer to provide her bounty before the balance shifts at the equinox.

A month of hearth and home, preparing and storing. Cooking, baking and preserving to fill the store cupboards for the winter ahead. The harvest is being brought in, just as the plants are sending out their seeds for the cycle of life to begin again.

September is a pivotal point where we say our thankyous to summer and start to make preparation for the coming winter, it is a transitional month.

September Magical Energy

Rest after labour; balance of light and dark. Organise. De–clutter. Reap what you have sown. Clean and straighten up physical, mental, emotional and spiritual clutter – have an autumn clean. Take stock of your life in general and any projects you have been working with. Check your daily routine and make sure you have a good work/home/you time balance. This is a perfect time to make adjustments. Let go of things that no longer serve you. Give gratitude for what you have and then ask for re–balance or re–fuelling or increasing.

Colours: Brown, yellow green, yellow
Sign: Virgo
Element: Air
Season: Autumn

September Moon Names

Harvest Moon, Wine Moon (sounds like an excuse to party), Singing/Song Moon, Witumanoth, Haligonath, Gerstmonath, Mulberry Moon, Harpoon Moon, Chrysanthemum Moon, Fruit Moon, Corn Moon, Spiderweb on the ground at dawn Moon, Barley Moon, Yellow Leaf Moon and Moon when deer paw the Earth. Corn Moon from, yep you guessed it – when the corn is ready for harvest.

Barley Moon for the same reason. Harvest Moon – because in the Northern hemisphere that is exactly what is happening in this month. The Harvest Moon name is also associated with the full Moon closest to the autumn equinox.

Haligmonath – from the Anglo–Saxon calendar, an old English word meaning 'holy month' considered holy perhaps because of all the bounty we receive from Mother Earth. Witumanoth meaning wood month. Gerstmonath meaning 'grist month', grist being ground up grain.

Plants to work with for September

These are my suggested herbs to work with that correspond with the energy of this month. But, trust your intuition and the supplies that you have in your cupboards.

Alexanders

(Smyrnium olusatrum)

Alexanders Magical Properties:

Sea magic, intuition, emotions, cleansing, releasing

Element – Water

Gender – Masculine

Agrimony

(Agrimonia eupatoria or procera)

Agrimony Magical Properties:

Dispels negativity, reverses spells, aids spiritual healing,

cleanses the aura, brings sleep, happiness, luck, love, protection
Ruling planet – Jupiter
Sign – Cancer, Sagittarius
Element – Air
Gender – Masculine

Cramp Bark (Guelder rose)

(Viburnum opulus)
Cramp Bark Magical Properties:
Relaxing, meditation, stress, tension, anxiety, healing, rebirth, protection
Element – Earth
Gender – Feminine

Dock

(Rumex spp. Crispus, R. obtusifolius)
Dock Magical Properties:
Money, healing, fertility, cleansing, love, purification
Ruling planet – Jupiter
Element – Air
Gender – Masculine

Elm

(Ulmus campestris)
Elm Magical Properties:
Love, balance, luck, energy, psychic powers
Ruling planet – Saturn, Mercury
Element – Water
Gender – Feminine

Honeysuckle

(Lonicera caprifolium, Lonicera japonica, Lonicera periclymenum)

Honeysuckle Magical Properties:

Prosperity, psychic powers, protection, balance, lust, meditation, memory

Ruling planet – Jupiter

Sign – Gemini, Cancer

Element – Earth

Gender – Masculine

Geranium

(Pelargonium maculatum/P.odoratissimum/Hortorum)

Geranium Magical Properties:

Protection, fertility, love, socialise, aura cleansing

Ruling planet – Venus

Sign – Pisces

Element – Water

Gender – Feminine

Lungwort

(Pulmonaria officinalis)

Lungwort Magical Properties:

Healing, cleansing, releasing, calming

Ruling planet – Mercury

Sign – Taurus, Pisces

Element – Earth

Gender – Masculine

Patchouli

(Pogostemon)

Patchouli Magical Properties:

Grounding, Earth magic, prosperity, money, protection, sex magic, balance, calm

Ruling planet – Saturn

Sign – Virgo

Element – Earth

Gender – Feminine

Rue

(Ruta graveolens)

Rue Magical Properties:

Protection, health, healing, purification, balance, clarity, anxiety, hex breaking

Ruling planet – Mars, Sun

Sign – Leo

Element – Fire

Gender – Masculine

Self Heal/All Heal

(Prunella vulgaris)

Self Heal Magical Properties:

Releasing, cleansing, spirituality, stress, calming, clarity, protection

Ruling planet – Venus

Element – Water

Gender – Feminine

Tansy

(Tanacetum vulgare)

Tansy Magical Properties:

Health, longevity, rebirth, cleansing, protection, travel

Ruling planet – Venus

Sign – Gemini

Element – Water

Gender – Feminine

Witch Hazel

(Hamamelis virginiea)

Witch Hazel Magical Properties:

Protection, divining, balance, grief

Ruling planet – Sun, Saturn
Sign – Capricorn
Element – Fire
Gender – Masculine

Foods, Herbs and Spices to work with for September

Whether you chose to include the foods in a recipe for the table or add them to spell work, here is my suggested list of foods to work with for the energy of this month.

Asparagus

(Asparagus officinalis)
Asparagus Magical Properties:
Passion, sex, cleansing, healing
Ruling planet – Mars, Jupiter
Element – Fire
Gender – Masculine (well it wouldn't be anything else really would it?)

Chamomile

(Chameamelum nobile, Anthemis nobilis)
Chamomile Magical Properties:
Sleep, dreams, love, calm, money, relaxation, purification, balancing
Ruling planet – Sun
Sign – Leo
Element – Water
Gender – Masculine

Dill

(Anethum graveolens)
Dill Magical Properties:
Protection, love, lust, money, jealousy, balance, clarity, knowledge, magic

Ruling planet –Mercury
Sign – Cancer, Gemini, Leo
Element – Fire
Gender – Masculine

Fish

Fish Magical Properties:
Fertility, Prosperity, Abundance, healing, emotions, cleansing, purification
Element – Water
Gender – Feminine

Ginger

(Zingiber officinale)
Ginger Magical Properties:
Healing, power, love, passion, success, prosperity, protection
Ruling planet – Mars
Element – Fire
Gender – Masculine

Gravy

Gravy Magical Properties:
Calming, emotions, healing, cleansing, purification
Ruling planet – Moon
Element – Water
Gender – Feminine

Liquorice

(Glycyrrhiza glabra)
Liquorice Magical Properties:
Love, passion, balance
Ruling planet – Venus, Mercury
Element – Earth, Water
Gender – Feminine

Mint

(Mentha spp, Mentha aquatic, Mentha piperita)

Mint Magical Properties:

Money, healing, exorcism, protection, cleansing, calming

Ruling planet – Mercury, Venus

Element – Air

Gender – Masculine

Mushrooms

Mushrooms Magical Properties:

Strength, courage, magic, balance

Ruling planet – Moon

Element – Earth

Gender – Feminine

Oysters

Oyster Magical Properties:

Passion, balance

Ruling planet – Moon

Element – Water

Gender – Masculine & feminine

Plum

(Prunus spp)

Plum Magical Properties:

Love, spirituality, relaxation, passion, longevity, wisdom, rebirth

Ruling planet – Venus

Element – Water, Air

Gender – Feminine

Salt

Salt Magical Properties:

Cleansing, purification, protection

Ruling planet – Earth
Element – Earth
Gender – Feminine

Water

Water Magical Properties:
Emotions, cleansing, purification
Ruling planet – Moon
Element – Water
Gender – Feminine

Crystals to work with for September

As always, go with your intuition and what you have in your collection when working with crystals. The list below is my suggestion of crystals that work particularly well with the energy of this month.

Agate (blue lace)

Agate (blue lace) magical properties
Mediation, spirituality, uplifting, calming, peace, communication, emotions, support, optimism, happiness, protection, cleansing, healing, prosperity, longevity, strength, courage, clarity, success, patience, truth, stress, relaxation, creativity, justice, travel, renewal, understanding, soothing, trust

Energy	Receptive
Element	Water
Planet	Mercury
Zodiac	Gemini

Amber

Amber magical properties:
Manifesting, energy, beauty, Sun magic, power, wishes, intellect, clarity, wisdom, balance, purification, protection, psychic abilities, healing, calm, patience, love, sensuality, good luck,

marriage, abundance, success, vitality, joy, sexuality, cleansing, stress, harmony, creativity

Energy: Projective
Element: Fire, Spirit
Planet: Sun
Zodiac: Leo

Amethyst

Amethyst magical properties

Peace, protection, success, good luck, hidden knowledge, legal issues, spirituality, contentment, soothing, relaxation, calm, hope, patience, transformation, changes, breaking patterns, grounding, guilt, overcoming addictions, business matters, judgement, clarity, courage, travel, psychic protection, sleep, anxiety, focus, understanding, happiness, justice, intuition, inspiration, channelling, meditation

Energy: Receptive
Element: Water
Planet: Jupiter, Neptune
Zodiac: Pisces, Scorpio, Sagittarius
Birthstone: February

Fluorite

Fluorite magical properties

Magic, imagination, discernment, aptitude, psychic protection, protection, purification, calming, relaxation, tension, anxiety, organisation, structure, challenges, declutter, releasing, support, breaking patterns, intuition, confidence, reassurance, comforting, communication, balance, spirituality, decisions, manifestation, peace, meditation, grounding, healing, cleansing, channelling, past life work, fairy realm, amplifying, memory, power, emotions, depression, stability

Energy: Projective
Element: Water, Air

Planet: Neptune
Zodiac: Scorpio, Aquarius, Pisces

Garnet

Garnet magical properties

Organisation, warrior spirit, protection, love, commitment, passion, sexuality, sensuality, attraction, depression, spiritual healing, success, self–confidence, energy, inspiration, perception, strength, survival, fear, courage, clarity, challenges, past life work, truth, compassion, deflecting negative energy, gossip, ambition, motivation, goals, purification, cleansing, balance, inner strength, self–empowerment, creativity, confidence, meditation, spirit work, nightmares, journeying, abundance, support

Energy: Projective
Element: Fie
Planet: Mars
Zodiac: Aries, Virgo, Capricorn, Leo, Aquarius
Birthstone: January

Hematite

Hematite magical properties

Grounding, money, decisions, manifestation, finances, healing, focus, clarity, stability, protection, balance, divination, problem solving, emotions, self–esteem, productivity, doubt, anxiety, communication, strength

Energy: Projective
Element: Fire, Earth
Planet: Saturn
Zodiac: Aries, Aquarius

Kyanite

Kyanite magical properties

Balance, harmony, calming, connection, psychic abilities,

healing, communication, grounding, transformation, meditation, relaxation, luck, growth, leadership, new beginnings, clarity, decisions, stability, truth, vitality, abundance, spirituality, channelling, understanding, dreams

Energy	Receptive
Element	Water
Planet	Jupiter, Venus, Mars
Zodiac	Aries, Libra, Taurus

Labradorite

Labradorite magical properties

Transformation, cleansing, breaking patterns, potential, psychic abilities, intuition, confidence, spirituality, focus, protection, imagination, relaxation, soothing, energy, healing, stress, anxiety, luck, abundance, success, decisions, trust, changes, strength, courage, self–confidence, inspiration, perseverance, journeying, clarity, insight, meditation, depression, jealousy, grounding

Energy	Projective
Element	Water
Planet	Earth, Moon, Uranus
Zodiac	Aquarius, Sagittarius, Scorpio, Leo

Rhodonite

Rhodonite magical properties

Protection, renewal, emotions, strength, soothing, clarity, happiness, love, balance, harmony, decisions, confidence, spirituality, peace, energy, passion, optimism, changes, vitality, anxiety, travel, psychic abilities, self–confidence, trust, calming, relaxation, patience, determination, releasing, stress, negative energy

Energy	Projective
Element	Fire
Planet	Mars, Venus

Zodiac Taurus

Selenite

Selenite magical properties

Clarity, psychic protection, cleansing, balance, stability, emotions, divine, connections, spirituality, psychic abilities, spirit work, protection, healing, breaking barriers, decisions, intuition, meditation, money, success, love

Energy Receptive
Element Water
Planet Moon
Zodiac Cancer

Sugilite

Sugilite magical properties

Spirituality, wisdom, clarity, insight, courage, truth, passion, inspiration, healing, strength, channelling, psychic abilities, amplification, confidence, focus, love, emotions, releasing, calming, peace, protection, connection, balance, understanding, stress

Energy Receptive
Element Water
Planet Mercury, Jupiter
Zodiac Virgo

Turquoise

Turquoise magical properties

Purification, negative energy, protection, balance, relaxation, emotions, stress, spirituality, energy, depression, clarity, wisdom, understanding, psychic abilities, insight, intuition, past life work, communication, wealth, abundance, finances, prosperity, luck, decisions, friendship, uplifting, meditation, love, harmony

Energy Receptive

Element	Earth
Planet	Venus, Neptune
Zodiac	Sagittarius, Pisces, Aquarius
Birthstone	December

Moon Deities to work with for September

Here you will find my suggestions on some of the Moon deities to work with that align with the energies of this month. Trust your intuition and be guided by the deities that may also make themselves known to you.

Coyolxauhqui – Aztec Moon goddess. Her name translates as 'painted with bells'. Apparently in most images she is wearing bells on her cheeks, which must be terribly uncomfortable. When the full Moon rises you can see the bells as rosy red. In a bit of a misunderstanding Coyolxauhqui had her head cut off, which was flung up into the sky, where it became the Moon. Call upon her for: Moon magic, family issues, balance, differences.

Hestia – Greek goddess of the hearth and home she is also a fire goddess. Her Roman equivalent is Vesta. The Greeks did not have statues of this goddess as it was believed she didn't take human form, instead she appeared as the flames of fire in the hearth. Hestia was the first born of the Olympian goddesses. She is absolutely about new beginnings and the start of all things. This goddess is the ultimate super housekeeper and home maker, with added omnipotence. Call upon her for: Home life, domesticity, fire magic, devotion, wishes, manifesting, unity, new beginnings, spirituality, blessings.

Demeter – Ancient Greek goddess of the full Moon. She is an Olympian goddess of agriculture, harvest and fertility. Featuring in the Eleusinian mysteries alongside her daughter Persephone. She forms a triad with Persephone and Hecate, Demeter taking on the mother role. Equivalent to the Roman goddess Ceres. Call upon her for: Abundance, harvest, mysteries, fertility, marriage, relationships, life and death, rebirth, justice, grief, suffering, parenthood.

Diana – Goddess of the Moon, hunter and Roman Queen of Witches. She is queen of the open skies and may also have been worshipped as a Sun goddess as well as the Moon. Call upon her for: Fertility, abundance, harvest, protection, children, nurturing, hunting, childbirth.

Isis – Egyptian goddess Queen of Egypt. She is looked upon as Mother Moon, Queen of Sorcery and the life force within the river Nile. Isis taught her people useful skills, those they would need to survive and flourish, no being high up on the sky for this one, she got down with her subjects (very practical woman). Call upon her for: Magic, dreams, divination, harvest, perspective, love, spirituality, faithfulness, destiny, revitalisation, fulfilment, inner beauty, spirituality, rebirth, feminine energy, knowledge, motherhood, healing, changes, manifesting.

Kali/Kali Ma – Hindu goddess of time, change and destruction and the Divine Mother. She has blue black skin, red eyes and four arms. Often seen with skulls hanging around her neck. This is a real kick butt, no messing kind of gal. She is a forceful destroyer but brings rebirth with it, she is the cycle of destruction and creation. Call upon her for: Death and rebirth, cycles, time, happiness, courage, hope, change, cleansing, transformation, destruction, fear, knowledge, creativity.

Ma'at – Egyptian goddess of the crescent Moon, order and balance. Think 'strict school headmistress', she dishes out the justice as she sees fit, whether you are a deity or a mere mortal. Her name translates as 'truth/that which is straight'. If you are looking for balance between work and home life or any kind of justice, Ma'at should be on your speed dial. Call upon her for: Justice, balance, freedom, new beginnings, morals, organisation, law, promises, fairness, truth, oaths, harmony, honesty.

Parvati – Hindu goddess of the crescent Moon. Oh, this goddess has all the feminine wiles and knows how to use them.

She is maiden to the Mother Durga and Crone Kali. She can charm the secrets out of the trees. Call upon her for: Power, creativity, new beginnings, victory, feminine energy, beauty, charm, secrets, the arts, fertility, cleansing, devotion.

Rhiannon – if you aren't singing the Fleetwood Mac song right now, you need to… A Welsh goddess and great Queen of Wales. She brings peace, comfort and patience. If you are looking for magical enchantments, then she has a bounty of them. Call upon her for: Patience, comfort, peace, magic, movement, relaxation, communication, fertility, leadership, spirit work, motivation, dream work.

Thoth – Egyptian ibis headed Moon god. He is a seriously studious dude. God of writing and wisdom he is considered to be one of the most important gods of ancient Egypt (he didn't let it go to his head though). Call upon him for: Knowledge, Moon magic, wisdom, learning, intellect, meditation, logic, reason, magic, secrets, balance, judgement.

World celebration days

I have given some dates and a little information on celebrations from around the world that take place during September. A lot of them were based on Moon phases. I apologise for any errors but history is a fickle thing and calendars have changed over the years…

China

The Chinese Moon Festival or Mid–Autumn Festival falls on the 15th day of the 8th month according to the Chinese lunar calendar (mid to end September, sometimes the beginning of October).

The ancient Chinese recognized that the movement of the Moon related to the changes in season and thereby agricultural production. This is their festival to say thank you to the Moon and celebrate the harvest. On the day of the festival families gather to offer sacrifices to the Moon (not human ones), they eat

Moon cakes and send blessings to the family and friends that live elsewhere. The day is also filled with dancing dragons, lanterns and lions. Personally, I don't think you can ever get enough dancing dragons. Moon cakes are round to symbolize family, happiness and longevity. It is more of a cookie than a cake and has various fillings inside and patterns on top. The traditional filling is; five kernels, lotus seed paste, sweet bean paste, jujube paste and egg yolk. But more modern twists have been added such as shredded coconut, orange, olive seeds and even savoury versions filled with sausage meat. The Moon goddess, Chang–O is recognized at this festival. Altars are set outdoors and in homes, facing the full Moon. Photographs of Chang–O and the Jade Rabbit, her companion, are sent up into the air. She brings devotion for relationships and brings prosperity and growth for the coming year.

28th September – Birthday of the Monkey God – The Monkey God is one of the most popular characters in Chinese culture and is worshiped as a Taoist Deity. The Monkey God was born from a rock left behind from goddess Nuwa's creation of the universe. After being conditioned by natural forces, the Monkey God emerged from this piece of rock.

12th September – Birthday of Ksitigarbha Bodhisattva – The Bodhisattva of Great Aspiration is one of the most well–known Bodhisattva in Chinese Mahayana Buddhism. He is also known as Di Zhang Wang Pusa in Chinese and commonly translated as Earth Store Bodhisattva. The Bodhisattva is also commonly worshipped in Taoist temples especially at the ancestral halls. The Bodhisattva is known for his great vow to help beings in all realms to gain enlightenment before he would become a Buddha. He is also tasked to teach the Dharma to all beings during the time between the passing of the historical Buddha (Gautama Buddha) and the arrival of Maitreya Buddha.

Greece

5th September – Genesia – Greek festival in honour of the dead.

13th/15th September – 21st/22nd September – Eleusinia Mysteries – This ancient Greek festival was held by those of the Eleusinian religion based on the myth of Demeter and Kore (Persephone).

Proerosia – A festival which involved praying to Demeter for a good harvest before they begin ploughing and sowing.

Rome

4th – 19th September – Ludi Romani / Ludi Magni – "Roman Games" or "Great Games". The Ludi Romani were held in honour of Jupiter Optimus Maximus. They were originally held only on September 13 but were gradually expanded until they were held over 16 days by the time of the Empire. The Ludi Romani began with a solemn procession from Jupiter's temple on the Capitoline to the Circus Maximus. Sacrifices were made to Jupiter, and circus performances were given.

13th September – Epulum Iovis – "Feast of Jupiter". This feast was attended by senators and high–ranking magistrates during the Ludi Romani and Ludi Plebeii. It started with the sacrifice of a white cow and ritual cakes to honour Jupiter, and possibly Juno and Minerva.

30th September – Meditrinalia – During this festival fruits were offered to Meditrina as a goddess of medicine.

Australia

Of course, for Australia September is the beginning of spring.

Japan

Higan is a week of services for Buddhist followers in Japan. The spend time over the equinox remembering those that have passed over and visit their graves to clean and decorate them. The word higan means 'other shore' and relates to the spirits of the dead.

Christianity

Michaelmas is the feast of Michael and All Angels and falls on 29th September.

8th September – The birth of the Virgin Mary is celebrated.

Pagan

Mabon is a modern pagan term referring to the autumn equinox. Usually somewhere around 20/21/22nd September. It celebrates the harvest and the onset of autumn. This is the second harvest, where our ancestors would have been storing away food to last the cold winter months. This is the time of year when we give thanks to the Sun and all that is has helped provide for us and we welcome in the dark half of the year.

Hindu

Ananta Chaturthi is the last day of the Ganesh Chaturthi festival. It is the tenth day after Ganesh Chaturthi which falls on the 14th day of the sixth month of the Hindu calendar. Statues of the Hindu god Ganesha will have been set up in the home and on the last day they are taken to the local water (ocean, river, lake) and immersed. This ends the ten–day long festival in honour of Ganesh and Lord Vishnu to bring prosperity and wealth. Usually the festival starts at the end of August and finishes ten days later in September.

1st September is the festival of Radha–An (one of Laskshmi's incarnations) – her body was dressed with flowers and jewellery and then worshipped.

16th/17th September – Vishwakarma Puja – Vishwakarma is the presiding deity of all craftsmen and architects. Son of Brahma, he is the divine draftsman of the whole universe, and the official builder of all the gods' palaces. Hindus widely regard Vishwakarma as the god of architecture and engineering, and September 16 or 17 every year is celebrated as Vishwakarma Puja — a resolution time for workers and craftsmen to increase productivity and gain divine inspiration for creating novel products. This occasion in a way also marks the start of the festive season that culminates in Diwali.

Mahalakshmi or Varalakshmi Vrata – This is a special vrata or fast dedicated to Hindu Goddess 'Mahalakshmi,' or as the name implies 'Great Lakshmi' (maha = great). Lakshmi is the presiding deity of wealth, prosperity, light, wisdom, fortune, fertility, generosity and courage. According to the lunar calendar of North India, the Mahalakshmi Vrata fast is observed for 16 days in a row between Bhadrapad Shukla Ashtami and Ashwin Krishna Ashtami, i.e., commencing on the 8th day of the bright fortnight of the month of Bhadra and ending on the 8th day of the dark fortnight of the following month Ashwin, which corresponds to September – October of the international calendar.

Ganesha Chaturthi – The great Ganesha festival, also known as 'Vinayak Chaturthi' or 'Vinayaka Chavithi' is celebrated by Hindus around the world as the birthday of Lord Ganesha. It is observed during the Hindu month of Bhadra (mid–August to mid–September) and the grandest and most elaborate of them, especially in the western India state of Maharashtra, lasts for 10 days, ending on the day of 'Ananta Chaturdashi'.

Pitri–Paksha – The annual ancestor–worship or 'Pitri–Paksha' is a period that is observed during the dark half of the Hindu month of 'Ashwin.' This period of 15 days is set aside by the Hindus for the remembrance of their ancestors. During this fortnight, Hindus donate food to the hungry in the hope that their ancestors will also be thus fed. It is this time that Hindus throughout the world reflect on the contributions their forefathers made to their present life, and the cultural norms, traditions and values they set for us in order to make our lives better. (Dates vary each year during Sep/Oct).

Durga Puja – The ceremonial worship of the mother goddess is one of the most important festivals of India. While the rituals entails ten days of fast, feast and worship, the last four days –

Saptami, Ashtami, Navami and Dashami – are celebrated with much gaiety and grandeur in India and abroad, especially in Bengal, where the ten–armed goddess. Durga Puja is celebrated every year in the Hindu month of Ashwin (September–October) and commemorates Prince Rama's invocation of the goddess before going to war with the demon king Ravana.

Worldwide

In 2014 a worldwide celebration began in honour of the goddess and her followers. It is now held annually on the first Sunday of September every year. Events are held across the globe.

Santeria

The Orisha Yemaya has a feast day in her honour held on 7th September.

The Orisha Oshun has a feast day in her honour held on 8th September.

Catholic

The Catholic church observe a feast day on 15th September for Our Lady of Sorrows, a name given to the Virgin Mary.

Mesopotamian

September 27th is the Day of Willows a Mesopotamian festival to honour the goddess Astarte.

Egypt

13th September – Festival of lighting the fires of Neith.

OCTOBER

Obviously, October is particularly special because of Samhain (Hallowmas/All Hallows) at the end of the month. It is a period between times. The leaves are changing, and the air is crisp and clear as the dark nights begin to draw in.

The veil between the worlds is said to be thinner at this time. Remember those that have gone before you and honour your ancestors.

October lends itself to drama and atmosphere. It is a good excuse to make the most of this time by overloading on the witchy decorations.

If you can work some magic outside, then even better. Get a fire going and plenty of candles on the dark evenings. The October full Moon is an especially good time to work divination of all kinds.

Scrying outside under the Moon is perfect. It doesn't need to be fancy, a cauldron or dish filled with water or even an old bucket will do. Drop a silver coin into the water or sprinkle on a handful of herbs to help with the images. Allow the light of the full Moon to shine on the surface.

October is also a good month to work protection spells or create protection amulets and pouches. There are several things to focus on with this full Moon such as bringing energy back into whatever you are doing and finding a way to balance your feelings, emotions and what goes on in your everyday life.

Also take a moment to look at how you have been over the past few weeks...what negative energy have you been putting out into the world? What have you not done that you should have?

Recognise and acknowledge those issues, actions and feelings and then...let them go...allow the full Moon energy to remove them from you. Then re–focus and put plans into action to bring heap loads of positive energy into your life, be thankful for what you have and move forward with a leap in your step and a song in your heart...well OK maybe not quite that musically dramatic but you get the idea.

Leave out a plate of food and drink for the spirits on All Hallows Eve. Decorate your altar with pumpkins, squashes, apples, pomegranates, marigolds and chrysanthemums along with autumn leaves, nuts, seeds and corn dollies.

'Tis the season of the witch.

October Magical energy

To let go; inner cleansing. Karma and reincarnation. Justice and balance. Inner harmony. Introspection and reflection. Work candle magic, past life work and astral projection. Mirror spells are particularly good this month.

Protection, inner work, removing obstacles, transition, changes, transformation and uncrossing.

Divination, meditation, fire magic, spirit work, sex magic and faery magic all lend themselves to the energy of this month.

Colours: Dark blue green, orange, black, autumn colours
Sign: Libra
Element: Air
Season: Autumn

October Moon Names

Falling Leaf Moon, The Blood Moon, Hunter's Moon, Moon when the Gopher looks back, Travellers' Moon, Blackberry Moon, Seed Fall Moon and Kindly Moon, Harvest Moon, Shedding Moon, Winterfylleth, Windermanoth, Ten Colds Moon, Ice Moon, Blackberry Moon and Moon of the changing seasons.

Falling Leaf Moon – which is obvious, as this is the time when the leaves start to fall.

The Blood Moon – this name refers to the time of the year

when animals were slaughtered to provide food for the winter. Hunter's Moon or Hunter's Moon – time to hunt and lay in store for provisions over the winter. Gopher looks back – the gopher is looking behind him at lost summer days.

Winterfylleth an old English/Anglo Saxon name meaning 'winter filling' which referred to preparations made for the coming of winter. Windermanoth meaning 'vintage month'.

Plants to work with for October

These are my suggested herbs to work with that correspond with the energy of this month. But, trust your intuition and the supplies that you have in your cupboards.

Ash

(Fraxinus excelsior or F. americana)

Ash Magical Properties:

Protection, prosperity, dispels negativity, improves health, sea magic, dreams, love, intuition.

Ruling planet – Sun and Neptune

Element – Fire and Water

Gender – Masculine

Belladonna

(Atropa belladonna)

Belladonna or as I know it, Deadly Nightshade is a perennial herbaceous plant – the whole plant is extremely TOXIC (the Romans used it as poison).

ALWAYS wear gloves when handling belladonna, always make sure if you use it in a medicine pouch that it is securely wrapped so that nothing can get out – this plant is DEADLY poisonous.

Belladonna Magical Properties:

Astral travel, baneful spells, Crone magic

Ruling planet – Saturn, Mars

Element – Water
Gender – Feminine

Dittany

Dictamnus albus
Dittany Magical Properties:
Fire, Samhain
Ruling planet –Moon
Element – Fire
Gender – Feminine

Elder

(Sambucus nigra/Canadensis)
Elder Magical Properties:
Protection, healing, faeries, purification, intuition, exorcism, hex breaking, rebirth
Ruling planet – Venus
Sign – Sagittarius, Aquarius, Libra
Element – Water
Gender – Feminine

Fern

(Pteridophyte)
Fern Magical Properties:
Spirit work, Underworld, Faerie, protection, love, invisibility
Ruling planet – Mercury
Sign – Taurus, Pisces
Element – Air
Gender – Masculine

Heather

(Calluna spp, Erica spp, vulgaris)
Heather Magical Properties:
Luck, protection, cleansing, ghosts, rain, spirit, love,

friendship, faeries, dreams, shape shifting
Ruling planet – Venus
Element – Water
Gender – Feminine

Myrrh

(Commiphora myrrha)
Myrrh Magical Properties:
Protection, purification, healing, Crone, Underworld, courage
Ruling planet – Mars, Sun
Sign – Aries, Aquarius
Element – Water
Gender – Feminine

Morning Glory

(Convolvulaceae, Impomoea)
Morning Glory Magical Properties:
Divination, astral travel, psychic powers
Ruling planet – Sun, Neptune
Element – Air
Gender – Masculine

Mugwort

(Artemisia vulgaris)
Mugwort Magical Properties:
Strength, psychic powers, protection, dreams, healing, astral travel, feminine energy, cleansing
Ruling planet – Venus, Moon
Sign – Cancer
Element – Earth
Gender – Feminine

Periwinkle

(Vinca minor)

Periwinkle Magical Properties:

Money, protection, love, lust, mental powers, Goddess, purification, spirit

Ruling planet – Venus

Element – Water

Gender – Feminine

Thistle

(Carduus spp)

Thistle Magical Properties:

Protection, healing, exorcism, hex breaking, spirit

Ruling planet – Mars, Jupiter

Element – Fire

Gender – Masculine

Willow

(Salix alba, Salix fragilis)

Willow Magical Properties:

Love, protection, healing, cleansing, wishes, release, inspiration, intuition

Ruling planet – Moon

Sign – Pisces

Element – Water

Gender – Feminine

Foods, Herbs and Spices to work with for October

Whether you chose to include the foods in a recipe for the table or add them to spell work, here is my suggested list of foods to work with for the energy of this month.

Almond

(Prunus dulcis)

Almond Magical Properties:

Love, prosperity, treasure, intuition, psychic powers, passion

Ruling planet – Mercury
Element – Air
Gender – Masculine

Apple

(Pyrus spp)
Apple Magical Properties:
Love, healing, clarity, knowledge, abundance, spirit work
Ruling planet – Venus
Element – Water
Gender – Feminine

Bay

(Laurus nobilis)
Bay Magical Properties:
Protection, purification, strength, power, healing, creativity, spirituality, psychic powers
Ruling planet – Sun
Element – Fire
Gender – Masculine

Cinnamon

(Cinnamomum zeylanicum, Cinnamomum verum)
Cinnamon Magical Properties:
Success, healing, power, psychic powers, protection, love, focus, lust, spirituality, changes
Ruling planet – Sun
Element – Fire
Gender – Masculine

Grapefruit

(Citrus paradise)
Grapefruit Magical Properties:
Happiness, spirit work, purification, depression, energy

Ruling planet – Jupiter, Sun
Element – Fire, Water
Gender – Feminine

Parsley

(Petroselinum crispum, Petrselinum sativum)
Parsley Magical Properties:
Protection, purification, lust, happiness, fertility, spirit work
Ruling planet – Mercury
Element – Air
Gender – Masculine

Pasta

Pasta Magical Properties:
Psychic powers, protection, communication, creativity
Ruling planet – Mercury
Element – Earth
Gender – Masculine

Saffron

(Crocus sativus)
Saffron Magical Properties:
Happiness, energy, psychic powers, healing, fertility
Ruling planet – Sun
Element – Fire
Gender – Masculine

Sage

(salvia officinalis)
Sage Magical Properties:
Protection, wishes, wisdom, purification, stimulating, intuition, abundance, success.
Ruling planet – Jupiter
Element – Air

Gender – Masculine

Star Anise

(Illicum verum)

Star Anise Magical Properties:

Luck, psychic powers, purification, protection, dreams, spirituality, sleep

Ruling planet – Jupiter

Element – Air

Gender – Masculine

Thyme

(Thymus vulgaris, Thymus serpyllum)

Thyme Magical Properties:

Healing, health, peace, psychic powers, love, purification, courage, releasing, sleep, beauty

Ruling planet – Venus

Sign – Gemini, Taurus, Libra

Element – Water

Gender – Feminine

Crystals to work with for October

As always, go with your intuition and what you have in your collection when working with crystals. The list below is my suggestion of crystals that work particularly well with the energy of this month.

Bloodstone

Bloodstone magical properties:

Organisation, adaptability, anxiety, clarity, concentration, renewal, energy, self–confidence, connection, calm, protection, breaking barriers, selfishness, mysticism, insight, spirituality, truth, intuition, creativity, guidance, strength, healing, victory, wealth, money, power, invisibility, deception, negative energy, divine connection, past life, dreams

Energy: Projective
Element: Fire, Earth
Planet: Mars
Zodiac: Aries, Pisces, Scorpio
Birthstone: February, March

Fluorite

Fluorite magical properties

Magic, imagination, discernment, aptitude, psychic protection, protection, purification, calming, relaxation, tension, anxiety, organisation, structure, challenges, declutter, releasing, support, breaking patterns, intuition, confidence, reassurance, comforting, communication, balance, spirituality, decisions, manifestation, peace, meditation, grounding, healing, cleansing, channelling, past life work, fairy realm, amplifying, memory, power, emotions, depression, stability

Energy: Projective
Element: Water, Air
Planet: Neptune
Zodiac: Scorpio, Aquarius, Pisces

Garnet

Garnet magical properties

Organisation, warrior spirit, protection, love, commitment, passion, sexuality, sensuality, attraction, depression, spiritual healing, success, self–confidence, energy, inspiration, perception, strength, survival, fear, courage, clarity, challenges, past life work, truth, compassion, deflecting negative energy, gossip, ambition, motivation, goals, purification, cleansing, balance, inner strength, self–empowerment, creativity, confidence, meditation, spirit work, nightmares, journeying, abundance, support

Energy: Projective

Element:	Fie
Planet:	Mars
Zodiac:	Aries, Virgo, Capricorn, Leo, Aquarius
Birthstone:	January

Labradorite

Labradorite magical properties

Transformation, cleansing, breaking patterns, potential, psychic abilities, intuition, confidence, spirituality, focus, protection, imagination, relaxation, soothing, energy, healing, stress, anxiety, luck, abundance, success, decisions, trust, changes, strength, courage, self–confidence, inspiration, perseverance, journeying, clarity, insight, meditation, depression, jealousy, grounding

Energy	Projective
Element	Water
Planet	Earth, Moon, Uranus
Zodiac	Aquarius, Sagittarius, Scorpio, Leo

Lepidolite

Lepidolite magical properties

Transformation, soothing, calming, stress, happiness, changes, emotions, psychic abilities, spirituality, depression, divination, connection, strength, uplifting, luck, hope, balance, peace, sleep, harmony, decisions, addiction, releasing, trust, goals, optimism, patience, dreams, opportunities, support, love

Energy	Receptive
Element	Water
Planet	Jupiter, Neptune
Zodiac	Libra

Malachite

Malachite magical properties

Changes, transformation, clarity, emotions, protection, support, healing, peace, travel, fears, growth, creativity, renewal, energy, wealth, money, opportunity, abundance, new beginnings, finances, success, business, focus, strength, wisdom, releasing, prosperity, breaking barriers, psychic abilities, manifestation, soothing, stress, love, power

Energy	Receptive
Element	Earth
Planet	Venus
Zodiac	Capricorn, Scorpio

Obsidian (black)

Obsidian magical properties

Truth, healing, clarity, illusions, breaking barriers, integrity, grounding, centring, strength, courage, protection, cleansing, meditation, stress, calming, relaxation, depression, anxiety, wealth, luck, focus, emotions, power, determination, success, patience, perseverance, releasing, spirit work, spirituality, challenges, past life work, divination

Energy	Projective
Element	Fire, Earth, Water
Planet	Saturn, Jupiter
Zodiac	Sagittarius

Petrified wood

Petrified wood magical properties

Stability, grounding, calming, anxiety, fears, meditation, determination, decisions, strength, courage, patience, transformation, perseverance, success, luck, emotions, wisdom, past life work, insight, leadership

Energy	Receptive
Element	Earth, Spirit
Planet	Earth, Sun
Zodiac	All

Tourmaline

Tourmaline magical properties

Calming, harmony, balance, insight, spirituality, protection, negative energy, transformation, courage, grounding, fears, creativity, understanding, power, motivation, commitment, patience, stability, releasing, emotions, anxiety, strength, happiness, protection, relaxation, friendship, astral travel

Energy	Receptive (pink, green, blue, black, watermelon)
	Projective (watermelon, red)
Element	Water (pink, blue, watermelon)
	Fire (watermelon, red)
	Earth (green, black)
Planet	Venus, Mars
Zodiac	Libra
Birthstone	October

Turquoise

Turquoise magical properties

Purification, negative energy, protection, balance, relaxation, emotions, stress, spirituality, energy, depression, clarity, wisdom, understanding, psychic abilities, insight, intuition, past life work, communication, wealth, abundance, finances, prosperity, luck, decisions, friendship, uplifting, meditation, love, harmony

Energy	Receptive
Element	Earth
Planet	Venus, Neptune
Zodiac	Sagittarius, Pisces, Aquarius
Birthstone	December

Unakite

Unakite magical properties

Love, happiness, growth, wealth, success, harmony, decisions, support, balance, emotions, stability, confidence, strength, anxiety, nature, courage, transformation, releasing, spirituality

Energy	Receptive
Element	Fire, Water
Planet	Mars, Venus, Pluto
Zodiac	Scorpio

Moon Deities to work with for October

Here you will find my suggestions on some of the Moon deities to work with that align with the energies of this month. Trust your intuition and be guided by the deities that may also make themselves known to you.

Arianrhod – Welsh goddess of the Moon. She forms the triple goddess triad with Blodeuwedd and Cerridwen. Her name translates as 'silver disc', she is often referred to as Goddess of the Silver Wheel. Arianrhod guides the dead to the other side and rules the sky and the sea as well as the Moon. She can shapeshift into an owl. She is also known as one of the goddesses of Avalon. Call upon her for: Moon magic, dream work, psychic abilities, divination, past lives, reincarnation, other realms, feminine power, retribution, karma.

Blodeuwedd – Welsh goddess, who has a connection with the Moon, and death and reincarnation (aspects of the Dark Moon). Her name translates as 'flower face' as she was created out of plants by magicians, who then later changed her into an owl (it was a whole punishment betrayal thing). As a maiden she forms part of the triad with Arianrhod and Cerridwen. A goddess of spring and one of the five goddesses of Avalon. Call upon her for: Beauty (temporary), spring, reincarnation, transformation, betrayal, manipulation, strength, power, love, wisdom, innocence.

Cerridwen – Welsh goddess usually shown hunched over her cauldron filled with Awen (inspiration and wisdom). Generally seen as the crone aspect of the triad with Blodeuwedd and

Arianrhod. A goddess of the Moon she covers death, rebirth, magic and divination of all kinds. Also, one of the five goddesses of Avalon. Call upon Cerridwen for: Inspiration, creativity, wisdom, death, rebirth, divination, prophecy, spiritual transformation, justice, fertility, luck.

Coyolxauhqui – Aztec Moon goddess. Her name translates as 'painted with bells'. Apparently in most images she is wearing bells on her cheeks, which must be terribly uncomfortable. When the full Moon rises you can see the bells as rosy red. In a bit of a misunderstanding Coyolxauhqui had her head cut off, which was flung up into the sky, where it became the Moon. Call upon her for: Moon magic, family issues, balance, differences.

Hekate – Greek goddess of the dark Moon. She covers new beginnings and magic of all kinds. She walks the ancient roads and pathways, particularly associated with crossroads, those where three roads cross. She forms a triad with Persephone and Demeter, she being the Crone aspect. She guards the spirit world and wields power over all realms. She is one seriously intimidating goddess, but wise beyond words. Call upon her for: Moon magic, witchcraft, herb magic, necromancy, protection, prosperity, new beginnings, decisions, mysteries, knowledge, learning, inner work, shadow work.

Isis – Egyptian goddess Queen of Egypt. She is looked upon as Mother Moon, Queen of Sorcery and the life force within the river Nile. Isis taught her people useful skills, those they would need to survive and flourish, no being high up in the sky for this one, she got down with her subjects (very practical woman). Call upon her for: Magic, dreams, divination, harvest, perspective, love, spirituality, faithfulness, destiny, revitalisation, fulfilment, inner beauty, spirituality, rebirth, feminine energy, knowledge, motherhood, healing, changes, manifesting.

Kali/Kali Ma – Hindu goddess of time, change and destruction and the Divine Mother. She has blue black skin, red eyes and four arms. Often seen with skulls hanging around her neck. This is a real kick butt, no messing kind of gal. She is a forceful destroyer but brings rebirth with it, she is the cycle of destruction and creation. Call upon her for: Death and rebirth, cycles, time, happiness, courage, hope, change, cleansing, transformation, destruction, fear, knowledge, creativity.

Ma'at – Egyptian goddess of the crescent Moon, order and balance. Think 'strict school headmistress', she dishes out the justice as she sees fit, whether you are a deity or a mere mortal. Her name translates as 'truth/that which is straight'. If you are looking for balance between work and home life or any kind of justice, Ma'at should be on your speed dial. Call upon her for: Justice, balance, freedom, new beginnings, morals, organisation, law, promises, fairness, truth, oaths, harmony, honesty.

Parvati – Hindu goddess of the crescent Moon. Oh, this goddess has all the feminine wiles and knows how to use them. She is maiden to the Mother Durga and Crone Kali. She can charm the secrets out of the trees. Call upon her for: Power, creativity, new beginnings, victory, feminine energy, beauty, charm, secrets, the arts, fertility, cleansing, devotion.

Thoth – Egyptian ibis headed Moon god. He is a seriously studious dude. God of writing and wisdom he is considered to be one of the most important gods of ancient Egypt (he didn't let it go to his head though). Call upon him for: Knowledge, Moon magic, wisdom, learning, intellect, meditation, logic, reason, magic, secrets, balance, judgement.

World Celebration Days

I have given some dates and a little information on celebrations from around the world that take place during October. A lot of them were based on Moon phases. I apologise for any errors, but history is a fickle thing and calendars have changed over the years…

Vietnam

In the port town of Hoi An in Vietnam they celebrate the full Moon each month with a festival. They pay respects to their ancestors and make offerings at altars, burning fake money to bring prosperity and luck. In the temple's monks hold candlelit ceremonies and the fishermen out on the water honour the goddess of the sea. Cardboard lanterns are lit and floated on the river to bring happiness, luck and love. Games are played and lots of festival food is eaten.

China

Festival of High Places – Chinese festival for good luck.

13th October – 11th November – Nine Emperor Gods – The first 9 days of the 9th lunar month is the Nine Emperor Festival and the most visible signs of this festival are devotees dressed in white with a yellow cloth tied around their waist. The Nine Emperors are generally thought to be 9 stars around the Big dipper and children of female deity, Dou Mu. Seven of the stars are visible while two are invisible stars.

Greece

1st October is the nineth day of nine days celebrating the Eleusinian Mysteries and was devoted to 'the pourings of plenty' in liquid form.

Thesmorphia – This ancient Greek festival honours the goddess Demeter and is held on 11th–13th October. It coincided with the time of autumn planting. A procession of women only went from Athens up to the Thesmorphorion (probably on the hillside of the Pnyx) and camped there away from the men for three days. The women were said to have fasted but particularly avoided pomegranate seeds.

7th October – Oschophoria – Dedicated to Dionysos, a procession led by two men dressed as women in commemoration of the two youths whom Theseus disguised as maidens to protect the other maidens. They carry vine branches still bearing grapes and the procession starts at the temple of Dionysus and arrives at the shrine of Athena Skira to recall both Theseus' return and the death of Dionysus by which he is reborn.

Pyanepsia – The rite involved hanging a mixture of pulses and a branch of olive or laurel on the gate of the temple of Apollo. The Athenian hero Theseus was said to have begun this ritual to thank Apollo and commemorate his victory over the Minotaur. Children carry a wand of laurel and go from house to house singing. Gifts are given to the children which they exchange for the wands to bring the household good luck.

11th – 13th October – Thesmophoria – A three day festival in various parts of Greece. Women participating in the autumn sowing festival had to fast and observe their chastity for several days. Married women would take supplies up to the top of the hill Thesmorphorion for two nights. They would build shelters made with plants.

The second day they would fast. On the third day there would be a torch light procession to celebrate Demeter and her search for Persephone. A feast was then held and offerings to Demeter made in the hope of a good harvest.

Apaturia – Apaturia was a Greek festival celebrated in Athens and nearly all other Ionian towns. Apaturia is unique among Greek festivals in being associated with a particular social group: the phratry, or brotherhood. The name probably means festival of "common relationship." The phratries celebrated Apaturia annually for three days in the month of Pyanopsion (October–November). The main function of the festival was to enrol new phratry members, who thereby acquired a title to citizenship. The first day of the festival, Dorpia (Dinner), featured an evening meal. The central ritual of the second day, Anarrhysis (Drawing Back [of animals' necks]), was sacrifice to Zeus Phratrios and Athena Phratria.

Egypt

The Egyptian goddess Isis had two great festivals, one in the spring and the other in autumn often the autumn one began on 31st October and ran for four days. The celebration consisted of a passion play.

4th October – festival of Hathor (Het–Hert).

7th October – feast day of Ma'at.

9th October – Festival for Amun according to the festival list of Thutmose III at Elephantine.

Jewish

Shemini Atzeret / Simchat Torah – 4–6th October is a Jewish holiday that marks the day after the end of Sukkot. Many religious Jews observe a rota of weekly readings from the Torah which allows them to read it through from Genesis to Deuteronomy on a yearly basis. Simchat Torah means "Rejoicing in the Torah" and is the day when this annual cycle of rereading the Torah ends and starts anew.

Hindu

Mid October Navaratri is celebrated by Hindus as a nine day festival of music and dance to honour the female divine in the forms of Durga, Lakshmi and Saraswati.

Mahalaya – Mahalaya is an auspicious occasion observed seven days before the Durga Puja, and heralds the advent of Durga, the goddess of supreme power. It is a kind of invocation or invitation to the mother goddess to descend on earth – "Jago Tumi Jago". This is done through the chanting of mantras and singing devotional songs.

Nava–ratri – "Nava–ratri" literally means "nine nights." This festival is observed twice a year, once in the beginning of summer and again at the onset of winter. During Navaratri, we invoke the energy aspect of God in the form of the universal mother, commonly referred to as "Durga," which literally means the remover of miseries of life. She is also referred to as "Devi" (goddess) or "Shakti" (energy or power). It is this energy, which helps God to proceed with the work of creation, preservation and destruction.

Lakshmi – On the full Moon night following Dusshera or Durga Puja, Hindus worship Lakshmi ceremonially at home, pray for her blessings, and invite neighbours to attend the puja. It is believed that on this full Moon night the goddess herself visits the homes and replenishes the inhabitants with wealth.

Karwa Chauth – 'Karwa Chauth' is a ritual of fasting observed by married Hindu women seeking the longevity, well–being and prosperity of their husbands. This festival comes 9 days before Diwali on 'kartik ki chauth', i.e., on the fourth day of the new Moon immediately after Dusshera, in the month of 'Karthik' (October–November).

Dhanteras – The festival of Dhanteras falls in the month of Kartik (Oct–Nov) on the thirteenth day of the dark fortnight. This auspicious day is celebrated two days before the festival of lights, Diwali. On Dhanteras, Lakshmi – the Goddess of wealth – is worshiped to provide prosperity and well–being. It is also the day for celebrating wealth, as the word 'Dhan' literally means wealth and 'Tera' comes from the date 13th.

Deepawali or Diwali – Certainly the biggest and the brightest of all Hindu festivals. It is the festival of lights (deep = light and avali = ạ row i.e., a row of lights) that is marked by four days of celebration. Each of the four days in the festival of Diwali is separated by a different tradition, but what remains true and constant is the celebration of life, its enjoyment and goodness. Historically, the origin of Diwali can be traced back to ancient India, when it was probably an important harvest festival. Each day of Diwali has its own tale, legend, and myth to tell.

Rome

Fontinalia – October 13 To Fons or Fontus, god of fountains, springs, and wells. Fountains and wellheads around the city of Rome were decorated with garlands.

4th October – Ieiunium Cereris – "Fast of Ceres". This fast was held to honour Ceres. It was originally held every five years but was held every year by the time of the Empire.

5th October – Mania – These festivals were held to placate the Manes. It was believed that on these days the Mundus, the passageway to the underworld, was open and the spirits of the dead were free to roam the earth.

11th October – Meditrinalia – This agricultural festival was sacred to Meditrina and to Jupiter and had something to do with the year's new wine.

13th October – Fontinalia – "Feast of the Source". During this festival garlands were thrown into springs and on top of wells to honour Fons.

15th October – Ludi Capitolini – "Capitoline Games". The Ludi Capitolini were games held in honour of Jupiter Capitolini and was only celebrated by his priests. They may have originally been held to honour Jupiter Feretrius.

15th October – Roman festival of Mars, God of War.

Pagan

31st October/1st November marks the sabbat of Samhain. When the veil between the worlds is thin and we celebrate and remember those that have gone before us. It also marks the third and last harvest of the year. At this point in the year our ancestors would have taken their cattle and livestock to be slaughtered and then preserved to last them over the coming dark winter months.

For witches Samhain also marks the end of the old year and the beginning of the new.

Norse

29th October – 2nd November – Winternights – The beginning of the winter season for the Northern folk. Remembrance of the dead and one's ancestors were made during this feast. Winternights was a ceremony of wild abandon and it marked the end of the summer season of commerce and travel and the beginning of the winter season of hunting. Much divination was done during Winternights to foretell the fates of those entering the coming year. It was said that if one sat on a barrow–mound (grave) all night long on Winternights, one would have full divinatory, shamanic (galdr and seith), and bardic (skaldr) powers . . . that is, if one retained one's sanity. Winternights marked the beginning of the Wild Hunt, which would continue until Walpurgisnacht. This festival corresponds roughly to the Celtic Samhain, and the modern American festival of Halloween, although the darker aspects of the festival are not as pronounced among the Norse people.

NOVEMBER

Crackling fires, rustling, crunchy piles of leaves to kick up as you walk through them and crisp cold air brrr… The days are shorter, and the darkness arrives in the late afternoon rather than the evening. Stay warm with big bowls of steaming chilli, close the curtains, light the fire and the candles and settle in for the evening. It is a time for home comforts.

There is a quietness and a feel for the need of safety. We hurry home through the darkness seeking the lights and safety of our homes. November has a slightly eerie feel to it, perhaps it is the haunt of the Wild Hunt? Remember that the Wild Hunt is not out to harm you, just to have a fun, wild time. Go with the energy and enjoy yourself…just don't get lost out there.

November is a time for remembering, reaffirming relationships and giving thanks. This is the month where beautiful fireworks fill the skies and we gather around bonfires.

Remembrance Day where we pay homage to those that fought in wars for us. Thanksgiving Day is celebrated in America and although I don't celebrate in the UK this marks the lead up and preparation for Yule and Christmas. I don't ever need an excuse to make a pumpkin pie either ...

For me November is also a time to work with deity, take the time to connect and see what you can discover. Whether you choose to work with a new deity or re–affirm the connection with one close to you. Remember to always do some research first before starting to work with a deity that is new to you. Learn about their history, life story and characteristics, be as prepared as you can before you meet them.

November Magical Energy

Take root, prepare. Transformation. Strengthen communication with the deity who seems closest to you. Clearing, freedom, release and relief. Protection, inner work and visualisation. Banishing, psychic work and divination. Plan new projects and manifest wishes. Honour your ancestors. Bring balance and justice. Remove blockages and be ambitious.

Colours: Grey, deep green, dark blue
Sign: Scorpio
Element: Water
Season: Winter

November Moon Names

Snow Moon, Dark Moon, Fog Moon, Beaver Moon, Mourning Moon, Hunters Moon, Blotmanoth, Herbistmanoth, Mad Moon, Moon of Storms, Mourning Moon, Darkest Depths Moon, Frosty Moon, White Moon, Hunters Moon, Sassafras Moon, Freezing Mist Moon and Moon when deer shed antlers.

Beaver Moon – the name is given because it is time to set beaver traps before the water freezes over or perhaps because the beavers are preparing for winter. The furs were used to keep people warm over winter.

Moon when deer shed antlers is self–explanatory but it will depend on where you are in the world and all sorts of other environment factors.

Blotmanoth an Anglo–Saxon word meaning 'blood month', November was the month they slaughtered the weak animals to store away for winter. Herbistmanoth meaning 'harvest month'.

Plants to work with for November

These are my suggested herbs to work with that correspond with the energy of this month. But, trust your intuition and the supplies that you have in your cupboards.

Aloe

(Aloe vera)

Aloe Magical Properties:
Luck, protection, calming, Moon magic, psychic abilities
Ruling planet – Moon, Saturn
Sign – Sagittarius
Element – Water
Gender – Feminine

Bergamot

(Monarda didyma, Mondarda fistulosa)
Bergamot Magical Properties:
Abundance, meditation, sleep, dreams, clarity, friendship
Sign – Gemini, Libra
Element – Air
Gender – Feminine

Bladder wrack

(Fucus vesiculosus)
Bladder wrack Magical Properties:
Protection, sea magic, money, psychic powers, weather magic
Ruling planet – Moon
Sign – Pisces
Element – Water
Gender – Feminine

Borage

(Borage officinalis)
Borage Magical Properties:
Psychic powers, courage, protection, happiness, peace
Ruling planet – Jupiter
Sign – Leo, Aquarius
Element – Air
Gender – Masculine

Elm

(Ulmus campestris)

Elm Magical Properties:

Love, balance, luck, energy, psychic powers

Ruling planet – Saturn, Mercury

Element – Water

Gender – Feminine

Grass

(Graminoids)

Grass Magical Properties:

Protection, psychic powers, knot magic, abundance

Element – Earth

Juniper

(Juniperus communes)

Juniper Magical Properties:

Love, exorcism, healing, protection, justice, stolen items, purification, psychic powers, clarity

Ruling planet – Sun, Jupiter, Moon

Sign – Aries

Element – Fire

Gender – Masculine

Marigold

(Calendula officinalis)

Marigold Magical Properties:

Psychic powers, dreams, protection, luck, happiness, gossip

Ruling planet – Sun

Sign – Leo

Element – Fire

Gender – Masculine

Mugwort

(Artemisia vulgaris)

Mugwort Magical Properties:

Strength, psychic powers, protection, dreams, healing, astral travel, feminine energy, cleansing

Ruling planet – Venus, Moon

Sign – Cancer

Element – Earth

Gender – Feminine

Rowan

(Sorbus acuparia)

Rowan Magical Properties:

Psychic powers, power, success, protection, love, spirituality, faeries, divination, healing, inspiration

Ruling planet – Sun, Mercury

Sign – Sagittarius

Element – Fire

Gender – Masculine

Sandalwood

(White Sandalwood – Santalum album)

Sandalwood (White) Magical Properties:

Death rites, purification, wishes, psychic powers

Ruling planet – Moon, Mercury

Sign – Sagittarius, Virgo

Element – Water

Gender – Feminine

Wormwood

(Artemisia absinthium)

Wormwood Magical Properties:

Vengeance, attack magic, protection, divination, dreams, meditation, psychic powers

Ruling planet – Mars, Moon
Sign – Cancer, Scorpio
Element – Fire
Gender – Masculine

Yarrow

(Achillea millefolium)
Yarrow Magical Properties:
Psychic powers, love, courage, exorcism, dreams, peace, happiness, divination, protection.
Ruling planet – Venus
Element – Water
Gender – Feminine

Yew

(Taxus baccata)
Yew Magical Properties:
Death and rebirth, transformation, astral travel, ancient knowledge, knowledge
Ruling planet – Saturn, Mercury
Element – Water, Earth
Gender – Feminine

Foods, Herbs and Spices to work with for November

Whether you chose to include the foods in a recipe for the table or add them to spell work, here is my suggested list of foods to work with for the energy of this month.

Almond

(Prunus dulcis)
Almond Magical Properties:
Love, prosperity, treasure, intuition, psychic powers, passion
Ruling planet – Mercury
Element – Air

Gender – Masculine

Bay

(Laurus nobilis)

Bay Magical Properties:

Protection, purification, strength, power, healing, creativity, spirituality, psychic powers

Ruling planet – Sun

Element – Fire

Gender – Masculine

Chives

(Allium schoenoprasum)

Chives Magical Properties:

Exorcism, negative energy, bad habits, protection

Ruling planet – Mars

Element – Fire

Gender – Masculine

Cinnamon

(Cinnamomum zeylanicum, Cinnamomum verum)

Cinnamon Magical Properties:

Success, healing, power, psychic powers, protection, love, focus, lust, spirituality, changes

Ruling planet – Sun

Element – Fire

Gender – Masculine

Coriander

(Coriandrum sativum)

Coriander Magical Properties:

Health, healing, peace, love, release, wealth, protection, negativity

Ruling planet – Mars

Element – Fire

Hazelnut

(Corylus)

Hazelnut Magical Properties:

Protection, psychic powers, wisdom, fertility, Faerie, Healing

Ruling planet – Sun, Mercury

Element – Air

Gender – Feminine/Masculine

Mustard

(Brassica juncea, Brassica nigra, Sinapis hirta)

Mustard Magical Properties:

Clarity, psychic abilities, protection, astral travel, faith, success

Ruling planet – Mars

Element – Fire

Gender – Masculine

Pasta

Pasta Magical Properties:

Psychic powers, protection, communication, creativity

Ruling planet – Mercury

Element – Earth

Gender – Masculine

Saffron

(Crocus sativus)

Saffron Magical Properties:

Happiness, energy, psychic powers, healing, fertility

Ruling planet – Sun

Element – Fire

Gender – Masculine

Sage

(salvia officinalis)

Sage Magical Properties:

Protection, wishes, wisdom, purification, stimulating, intuition, abundance, success.

Ruling planet – Jupiter

Element – Air

Gender – Masculine

Soya Bean

(Glycine max)

Soya Bean Magical Properties:

Fertility, passion, prosperity, luck, psychic powers, spirituality

Ruling planet – Moon

Element – Earth

Gender – Feminine

Crystals to work with for November

As always, go with your intuition and what you have in your collection when working with crystals. The list below is my suggestion of crystals that work particularly well with the energy of this month.

Chrysocolla

Chrysocolla magical properties

Wisdom, peace, patience, love, soothing, intuition, energy, calming, emotions, fear, strength, clarity, balance, negative energy, insight, releasing, spirituality, psychic abilities, guilt, divine, harmony, communication, meditation

Energy: Receptive
Element: Water
Planet: Venus
Zodiac: Taurus

Citrine

Citrine magical properties:

Happiness, joy, Sun magic, negative energy, optimism, abundance, depression, stress, success, wealth, healing, intuition, creativity, confidence, changes, self–esteem, protection, psychic powers, fears, clarity, stamina, nightmares

Energy: Projective
Element: Fire
Planet: Sun, Jupiter
Zodiac: Scorpio
Birthstone: November

Kyanite

Kyanite magical properties

Balance, harmony, calming, connection, psychic abilities, healing, communication, grounding, transformation, meditation, relaxation, luck, growth, leadership, new beginnings, clarity, decisions, stability, truth, vitality, abundance, spirituality, channelling, understanding, dreams

Energy Receptive
Element Water
Planet Jupiter, Venus, Mars
Zodiac Aries, Libra, Taurus

Labradorite

Labradorite magical properties

Transformation, cleansing, breaking patterns, potential, psychic abilities, intuition, confidence, spirituality, focus, protection, imagination, relaxation, soothing, energy, healing, stress, anxiety, luck, abundance, success, decisions, trust, changes, strength, courage, self–confidence, inspiration, perseverance, journeying, clarity, insight, meditation, depression, jealousy, grounding

Energy Projective

Element	Water
Planet	Earth, Moon, Uranus
Zodiac	Aquarius, Sagittarius, Scorpio, Leo

Lepidolite

Lepidolite magical properties

Transformation, soothing, calming, stress, happiness, changes, emotions, psychic abilities, spirituality, depression, divination, connection, strength, uplifting, luck, hope, balance, peace, sleep, harmony, decisions, addiction, releasing, trust, goals, optimism, patience, dreams, opportunities, support, love

Energy	Receptive
Element	Water
Planet	Jupiter, Neptune
Zodiac	Libra

Malachite

Malachite magical properties

Changes, transformation, clarity, emotions, protection, support, healing, peace, travel, fears, growth, creativity, renewal, energy, wealth, money, opportunity, abundance, new beginnings, finances, success, business, focus, strength, wisdom, releasing, prosperity, breaking barriers, psychic abilities, manifestation, soothing, stress, love, power

Energy	Receptive
Element	Earth
Planet	Venus
Zodiac	Capricorn, Scorpio

Moonstone

Moonstone magical properties

New beginnings, Moon magic, intuition, calming, psychic abilities, balance, harmony, wishes, cleansing, uplifting, hope, meditation, emotions, love, divination, spirituality, wealth, truth, healing, sensuality, insight, peace, wisdom, communication, confidence, abundance, prosperity, dreams, fertility, travel

Energy	Receptive
Element	Water
Planet	Moon
Zodiac	Cancer, Libra, Scorpio
Birthstone	June, September

Quartz (clear)

Quartz (clear) magical properties

Purification, cleansing, healing, calming, emotions, strength, support, spirituality, energy, balance, psychic abilities, motivation, uplifting, decisions, anxiety, divine connection, amplifying, focus, meditation, manifestation, channelling, protection, negative energy, clarity, wisdom, concentration, learning, spirit work, communication, astral travel, divination, dreams, harmony

Energy	Projective, Receptive
Planet	Sun, Moon
Element	Fire, Water
Zodiac	Leo, Gemini, Capricorn

Rhodonite

Rhodonite magical properties

Protection, renewal, emotions, strength, soothing, clarity, happiness, love, balance, harmony, decisions, confidence, spirituality, peace, energy, passion, optimism, changes, vitality, anxiety, travel, psychic abilities, self–confidence, trust, calming, relaxation, patience, determination, releasing, stress, negative energy

Energy	Projective
Element	Fire
Planet	Mars, Venus
Zodiac	Taurus

Selenite

Selenite magical properties

Clarity, psychic protection, cleansing, balance, stability, emotions, divine, connections, spirituality, psychic abilities, spirit work, protection, healing, breaking barriers, decisions, intuition, meditation, money, success, love

Energy	Receptive
Element	Water
Planet	Moon
Zodiac	Cancer

Sodalite

Sodalite magical properties

Creativity, communication, peace, friendship, clarity, truth, connection, knowledge, wisdom, emotions, balance, divination, psychic abilities, cleansing, confidence, fears, love, intuition, decisions, perseverance, anxiety, insight, organisation, self–esteem, releasing, understanding, harmony, learning, dreams, meditation

Energy	Receptive
Element	Water
Planet	Jupiter, Venus
Zodiac	Sagittarius

Sugilite

Sugilite magical properties

Spirituality, wisdom, clarity, insight, courage, truth, passion, inspiration, healing, strength, channelling, psychic abilities, amplification, confidence, focus, love, emotions, releasing, calming, peace, protection, connection, balance, understanding, stress

Energy	Receptive
Element	Water
Planet	Mercury, Jupiter

Zodiac	Virgo

Turquoise

Turquoise magical properties

Purification, negative energy, protection, balance, relaxation, emotions, stress, spirituality, energy, depression, clarity, wisdom, understanding, psychic abilities, insight, intuition, past life work, communication, wealth, abundance, finances, prosperity, luck, decisions, friendship, uplifting, meditation, love, harmony

Energy	Receptive
Element	Earth
Planet	Venus, Neptune
Zodiac	Sagittarius, Pisces, Aquarius
Birthstone	December

Moon Deities to work with for November

Here you will find my suggestions on some of the Moon deities to work with that align with the energies of this month. Trust your intuition and be guided by the deities that may also make themselves known to you.

Anu – a Mesopotamian/Sumerian sky god viewed as Father of the gods and ruler of the heavens, the stars, and the spirits. Call upon him for: Goals, wishes, spirituality.

Arianrhod – Welsh goddess of the Moon. She forms the triple goddess triad with Blodeuwedd and Cerridwen. Her name translates as 'silver disc', she is often referred to as Goddess of the Silver Wheel. Arianrhod guides the dead to the other side and rules the sky and the sea as well as the Moon. She can shapeshift into an owl. She is also known as one of the goddesses of Avalon. Call upon her for: Moon magic, dream work, psychic abilities, divination, past lives, reincarnation, other realms, feminine power, retribution, karma.

Blodeuwedd – Welsh goddess, who has a connection with the Moon, and death and reincarnation (aspects of the Dark Moon). Her name translates as 'flower face' as she was created out of plants by magicians, who then later changed her into an owl (it was a whole punishment betrayal thing). As a maiden she forms part of the triad with Arianrhod and Cerridwen. A goddess of spring and one of the five goddesses of Avalon. Call upon her for: Beauty (temporary), spring, reincarnation, transformation, betrayal, manipulation, strength, power, love, wisdom, innocence.

Cerridwen – Welsh goddess usually shown hunched over her cauldron filled with Awen (inspiration and wisdom). Generally seen as the crone aspect of the triad with Blodeuwedd and Arianrhod. A goddess of the Moon she covers death, rebirth, magic, and divination of all kinds. Also, one of the five goddesses of Avalon. Call upon Cerridwen for: Inspiration, creativity, wisdom, death, rebirth, divination, prophecy, spiritual transformation, justice, fertility, luck.

Chang–O – Chinese goddess of the Moon. Banished from heaven along with her husband, destined to be mere mortals. Chang–O took a double dose of immortality pill, without sharing with her husband (rude). She floated up to the Moon, leaving her husband behind. Call upon her for: Love, partnership, courage, power, fertility, growth, manifesting, belief, self–confidence, new beginnings, transformation.

Hekate – Greek goddess of the dark Moon. She covers new beginnings and magic of all kinds. She walks the ancient roads and pathways, particularly associated with crossroads, those where three roads cross. She forms a triad with Persephone and Demeter, she being the Crone aspect. She guards the spirit world and wields power over all realms. She is one seriously intimidating goddess, but wise beyond words. Call upon her for: Moon magic, witchcraft, herb magic, necromancy, protection, prosperity, new beginnings, decisions, mysteries, knowledge, learning, inner work, shadow work.

Kali/Kali Ma – Hindu goddess of time, change and destruction and the Divine Mother. She has blue black skin, red eyes and four arms. Often seen with skulls hanging around her neck. This is a real kick butt, no messing kind of gal. She is a forceful destroyer but brings rebirth with it, she is the cycle of destruction and creation. Call upon her for: Death and rebirth, cycles, time, happiness, courage, hope, change, cleansing, transformation, destruction, fear, knowledge, creativity.

Luna – Roman goddess of the Moon. Depicted as a beautiful woman with the power to ease childbirth and bring about love. She carries a very strong feminine energy. If you want an answer to a problem, then call upon this lovely lady to bring you the answer in your dreams, it is her speciality. Her Greek equivalent is Selene. Call upon her for: Feminine energy, water magic, safety, travel, intuition, blue Moon magic, protection, illusion, truth, love, psychic abilities, dreams, solutions.

Nephthys – Egyptian goddess of the dark Moon, the dead, darkness, and the shadows. She is the dark to the light of Isis. Call upon her for: Death and rebirth, night magic, protection, shadow work, grief, spirit work, devotion, reincarnation, power, magic.

Rhiannon – if you aren't singing the Fleetwood Mac song right now, you need to… A Welsh goddess and great Queen of Wales. She brings peace, comfort, and patience. If you are looking for magical enchantments then she has a bounty of them. Call upon her for: Patience, comfort, peace, magic, movement, relaxation, communication, fertility, leadership, spirit work, motivation, dream work.

World Celebration Days

I have given some dates and a little information on celebrations from around the world that take place during November. A lot of them were based on Moon phases. I apologise for any errors but history is a fickle thing and calendars have changed over the years…

Rome

1st November – Pomona – This festival was held to honour the goddess Pomona.

4th – 17th November – Ludi Plebeii – "Plebeian Games". This set of games was established in 220 BCE to honour Jupiter. They were opened with a procession of Rome's magistrates and priests that wound from the Capitoline through the Forum along the via sacra to the Circus Maximus. The first week of the games was set aside for plays and other types of theatre. The last three days were reserved for athletic events, and events in the Circus Maximus.

13th November – Roman festival of Jupiter.

29th November – Saturnia – This festival honoured the sons of Saturn: Jupiter, Neptune, and Pluto.

Egypt

Hathor – Festival for Hathor, according to the great festival list in the temple for Ramesses III at Medinet Habu.

Isis – The autumn festival of Isis lasted from three to five days.

18th November – Start of the Khoiak ceremonies in honour of Osiris.

Babylon

6th November – Birthday of Tiamat.

France

10th November – Goddess of Reason Festival. The Goddess of Reason's themes are logic, reasoning, learning and the conscious mind. Her symbols are a crown of oak leaves (representing the seat of the divine). While this lady had no other specific designation other than the Goddess of Reason, She dispenses the power of knowledge to those who seek Her. The French honoured this Goddess with celebrations at Notre Dame, the world's most acclaimed centre of scholarship. Traditionally, the women depicting Her wore a blue robe and red cap, then were crowned in laurel at the end of a processional. "During the French Revolution, on 10 November 1793, a Goddess of Reason (most likely representing Sophia (wisdom) was proclaimed by the French Convention at the suggestion of Chaumette. As personification for the Goddess, Sophie Momoro, wife of the printer Antoine–François Momoro, was chosen. The Goddess was celebrated in Notre Dame de Paris (She was put on the high altar in the Cathedral).

Christianity

25th November – St Catherine of Sinai celebrated on this day, a Christian version of Nemesis, Goddess of the Wheel of Fate.

Hawaii

Makahiki – The Makahiki festival punctuated the yearly farming cycle in ancient Hawai`i. Celebrating harvest and Lono, the Hawaiian god associated with rain and fecundity, Makahiki marked a temporary halt to activities of war and occasioned lesser changes in many other daily routines. For religious reasons that coincided with seasonal weather, activities such as deep–sea fishing – associated with Ku, the god of war – were kapu, or prohibited, during Makahiki. Beginning in late October or early November when the Pleiades constellation was first observed rising above the horizon at Sunset, the Makahiki period continued for four months, through the time of rough seas, high winds, storms and heavy rains. Makahiki was a time to gather and pay tithes to chiefs who redistributed the gifts of the land, a time to cease farming labours and a time to feast and enjoy competitive games.

Hindu

Skanda Sashti – Skanda Sashti is observed on the sixth day of the bright fortnight of the Tamil month of Aippasi (October – November). This day is dedicated to the second son of Lord Shiva – Lord Subramanya, also known as Kartikeya, Kumaresa, Guha, Murugan, Shanmukha and Velayudhan, who on this day, is believed to have annihilated the mythical demon Taraka. On this day, elaborate festivals are held with grandeur in South India. In many places the festival commences six days before the Sashti day and concludes on the day of the Sashti.

Bhai Dooj – After the celebrations of Diwali, sisters all over India get ready for 'Bhai Dooj' – when sisters celebrate their love by putting an auspicious tilak or a vermilion mark on the forehead of their brothers and perform an aarti of him by showing him the light of the holy flame as a mark of love and protection from evil forces. Sisters are lavished with gifts, goodies and blessings from their brothers. Bhai Dooj comes every year on the fifth and last day of Diwali, which falls on a new Moon night. The name 'Dooj' means the second day after the new Moon, the day of the festival, and 'Bhai' means brother.

Chhath Puja – Chhath Puja also called Dala Puja is a Hindu festival popular in the Northern and Eastern Indian states of Bihar and Jharkhand and even Nepal. The word 'Chhath' has its origin in 'sixth' as it is celebrated on the 6th day or 'Shasthi' of the lunar fortnight of Kartik (October – November) in the Hindu calendar – six days after Diwali, the festival of lights. Chhath is mainly characterized by riverside rituals in which the Sun God or Surya is worshiped, giving it the name of 'Suryasasthi.'

DECEMBER

I will admit I am a total festive season fanatic, in fact if I am honest our Yule celebrations usually start around 1st November (don't judge). This time is not about shopping and material things, but it is about the existing positive energy of the season. Spending time with family and friends. Wishing compliments of the season to strangers and bringing festive cheer wherever you go.

December hosts the winter solstice, the ending of the darker nights and the very slow beginnings of the greater light. This is a celebration of the returning Sun, albeit that it will take a long while to arrive!

December Magical Energy

To endure, die, be reborn; Earth tides turning. Darkness. Personal alchemy. Spiritual paths. Introspection. Purification. Meditation. Reach out to friends and family, the lonely and needy. Revitalisation. Divination. Relaxation and reflection.

Creating prosperity and setting goals for new projects and ventures. Planning for the future.

Being thankful and gratitude rituals. Peace, harmony and love. Bringing in happiness. Work prosperity magic and a bit of the passion stuff too.

Colours: Red, white, black, green, silver and gold
Sign: Sagittarius
Element: Water
Season: Winter

December Moon Names

Cold Moon, Oak Moon, Wolf Moon, Moon of Long Nights, Long Nights Moon, Aerra Geola, Wintermonat, Heilagmanoth,

Big Winter Moon, Dark Night Moon, Bitter Moon, Peach Moon, Younger Hard Time Moon and Moon of popping trees. Cold Moon because…well, it is pretty cold!

Moon of Long Nights could refer to the full Moon closest to the winter solstice. Aerra Geola/Foreyule an Anglo–Saxon name meaning 'before Yule', or more accurately 'moon before the sun wheels' i.e. the winter solstice. Heilagmanoth meaning 'holy month'.

Plants to work with for December

These are my suggested herbs to work with that correspond with the energy of this month. But, trust your intuition and the supplies that you have in your cupboards.

Alyssum

(Alyssum spp. & Lobularia spp)

Alyssum Magical Properties:

Protection, Maiden magic, peace, calming, balance, spirituality

Element – Air

Gender – Feminine

Borage

(Borage officinalis)

Borage Magical Properties:

Psychic powers, courage, protection, happiness, peace

Ruling planet – Jupiter

Sign – Leo, Aquarius

Element – Air

Gender – Masculine

Frankincense

Frankincense Magical Properties:

Purification, spirituality, relaxation, focus, love, abundance

Ruling planet – Sun

Sign – Aries, Leo, Aquarius
Element – Fire
Gender – Masculine

Horehound

(Marrubium vulgare)
Horehound Magical Properties:
Exorcism, protection, healing, clarity, peace, love
Ruling planet – Mercury
Sign –Scorpio
Element – Air
Gender – Masculine

Hyacinth

(Hyacinthus orientalis)
Hyacinth Magical Properties:
Love, happiness, peace, sleep, nightmares, abundance
Ruling planet – Venus
Element – Water
Gender – Feminine

Lavender

(Lavendula officinale or Lavendula vera)
Lavender Magical Properties:
Happiness, peace, love, protection, sleep, clarity, faeries, strength
Ruling planet – Mercury
Sign – Leo, Gemini
Element – Air
Gender – Masculine

Meadowsweet

(Spiraea filipendula, Filipendula ulmaria, Spirea ulmaria)
Meadowsweet Magical Properties:

Peace, happiness, love
Ruling planet – Jupiter
Sign – Gemini, Pisces
Element – Air
Gender – Masculine

Pennyroyal

(Mentha/Mamentha pulegium)
Pennyroyal Magical Properties:
Strength, protection, peace, initiation, Goddess, business
Ruling planet – Mars, Venus
Sign – Scorpio, Libra
Element – Fire
Gender – Masculine

Sweetpea

(Lathyrus odoratus)
Sweetpea Magical Properties:
Courage, strength, friendship, peace, happiness, truth, spirituality, psychic abilities, protection, sleep
Ruling planet – Venus, Moon, Mercury
Element – Water
Gender – Feminine

Vervain

(Verbena officinalis)
Vervain Magical Properties:
Protection, love, purification, peace, sleep, healing, money, inspiration, shape shifting
Ruling planet – Venus
Sign – Gemini
Element – Earth
Gender – Feminine

Violet

(Viola odorata)

Violet Magical Properties:

Love, lust, peace, healing, protection, commitment, death and rebirth

Ruling planet – Venus

Sign – Cancer, Libra

Element – Water

Gender – Feminine

Yarrow

(Achillea millefolium)

Yarrow Magical Properties:

Psychic powers, love, courage, exorcism, dreams, peace, happiness, divination, protection.

Ruling planet – Venus

Element – Water

Gender – Feminine

Foods, Herbs and Spices to work with for December

Whether you chose to include the foods in a recipe for the table or add them to spell work, here is my suggested list of foods to work with for the energy of this month.

Basil

(Ocimum basilicum)

Basil Magical Properties:

Wealth, money, prosperity, love, exorcism, protection, happiness, peace

Ruling planet – Mars

Sign – Scorpio

Element – Fire

Gender – masculine

Blueberries

(Vaccinium Cyanococcus)

Blueberries Magical Properties:

Calm, peace, protection, passion, fertility

Ruling planet – Moon

Element – Earth, water

Gender – Feminine

Butter

Butter Magical Properties:

Peace, spirituality, Faerie

Ruling planet – Moon

Element – Earth

Gender – Feminine

Cake

Cake Magical Properties:

Happiness, ritual, rites of passage, offerings, celebration, grounding

Element – Earth

Gender – Feminine

Cheese

Cheese Magical Properties:

Success, happiness

Ruling planet –Saturn

Element – Earth, Air

Gender – Masculine

Chocolate

(Theobroma cacao)

Chocolate Magical Properties:

Prosperity, positive energy, happiness, love

Ruling planet – Mars

Element – Fire
Gender – Feminine

Cumin

(Cumimum cyminum)
Cumin Magical Properties:
Exorcism, protection, anti–theft, fidelity, lust, peace, love, abundance, success
Ruling planet – Mars
Element – Fire
Gender – Masculine

Honey

Honey Magical Properties:
Happiness, healing, love, prosperity, passion, spirituality, faerie
Element – Water, Earth
Gender – Feminine

Orange

(Citrus × sinensis)
Orange Magical Properties:
Love, happiness, uplifting, generosity, purification, clarity, energy, fidelity
Ruling planet – Sun
Element – Fire
Gender – Masculine

Poppy seeds

(Papaver spp)
Poppy Magical Properties:
Love, sleep, money, luck, fertility, rebirth, grief
Ruling planet – Moon, Mars, Venus
Sign – Capricorn

Element – Water
Gender – Feminine

Saffron

(Crocus sativus)
Saffron Magical Properties:
Happiness, energy, psychic powers, healing, fertility
Ruling planet – Sun
Element – Fire
Gender – Masculine

Thyme

(Thymus vulgaris, Thymus serpyllum)
Thyme Magical Properties:
Healing, health, peace, psychic powers, love, purification, courage, releasing, sleep, beauty
Ruling planet – Venus
Element – Water
Gender – Feminine

Turmeric

(Cucurma longa)
Turmeric Magical Properties:
Purification, protection, peace
Ruling planet – Mars
Element – Fire, Air
Gender – Feminine

Wine

Wine Magical Properties:
Spirituality, offerings, happiness, love
Ruling planet – Moon (white wine)
Element – Earth, Fire
Gender – Feminine

Crystals to work with for December

As always, go with your intuition and what you have in your collection when working with crystals. The list below is my suggestion of crystals that work particularly well with the energy of this month.

Agate (blue lace)

Agate (blue lace) magical properties

Mediation, spirituality, uplifting, calming, peace, communication, emotions, support, optimism, happiness, protection, cleansing, healing, prosperity, longevity, strength, courage, clarity, success, patience, truth, stress, relaxation, creativity, justice, travel, renewal, understanding, soothing, trust

Energy	Receptive
Element	Water
Planet	Mercury
Zodiac	Gemini

Agate (moss)

Agate (moss) magical properties

Nature, happiness, prosperity, wealth, longevity, friendship, success, abundance, healing, renewal, fertility, creativity, confidence, strength, love, beginnings, self–esteem, communication, emotions, stress, releasing, hope, trust, depression, growth, finances, cleansing, support, peace, stability, fears, luck, divination

Energy	Receptive
Element	Earth
Planet	Moon
Zodiac	Virgo, Gemini

Amethyst

Amethyst magical properties

Peace, protection, success, good luck, hidden knowledge, legal issues, spirituality, contentment, soothing, relaxation, calm, hope, patience, transformation, changes, breaking patterns, grounding, guilt, overcoming addictions, business matters, judgement, clarity, courage, travel, psychic protection, sleep, anxiety, focus, understanding, happiness, justice, intuition, inspiration, channeling, meditation

Energy: Receptive
Element: Water
Planet: Jupiter, Neptune
Zodiac: Pisces, Scorpio, Sagittarius
Birthstone: February

Fluorite

Fluorite magical properties

Magic, imagination, discernment, aptitude, psychic protection, protection, purification, calming, relaxation, tension, anxiety, organisation, structure, challenges, declutter, releasing, support, breaking patterns, intuition, confidence, reassurance, comforting, communication, balance, spirituality, decisions, manifestation, peace, meditation, grounding, healing, cleansing, channelling, past life work, fairy realm, amplifying, memory, power, emotions, depression, stability

Energy: Projective
Element: Water, Air
Planet: Neptune
Zodiac: Scorpio, Aquarius, Pisces

Howlite

Howlite magical properties

Understanding, wisdom, connection, truth, meditation, focus, stress, anxiety, calm, strength, peace, releasing, emotions, selfishness, communication, creativity, inspiration, motivation, concentration, support, patience, relaxation, courage, past life work, astral travel

Energy: Projective
Element: Earth
Planet: Moon, Earth
Zodiac: Gemini, Virgo

Larimar

Larimar magical properties

Peace, clarity, healing, inspiration, spirituality, understanding, calming, soothing, uplifting, emotions, fears, depression, patience, creativity, love, communication, friendship, guidance, happiness, decisions, relaxation, meditation, wisdom, divine, harmony

Energy: Receptive
Element: Water/Fire/Spirit
Planet: Neptune
Zodiac: Pisces

Lepidolite

Lepidolite magical properties

Transformation, soothing, calming, stress, happiness, changes, emotions, psychic abilities, spirituality, depression, divination, connection, strength, uplifting, luck, hope, balance, peace, sleep, harmony, decisions, addiction, releasing, trust, goals, optimism, patience, dreams, opportunities, support, love

Energy Receptive
Element Water
Planet Jupiter, Neptune
Zodiac Libra

Rhodochrosite

Rhodochrosite magical properties

Power, potential, strength, confidence, healing, new beginnings, breaking barriers, releasing, joy, happiness, creativity, determination, manifestation, prosperity, abundance, love, emotions, peace, renewal, connection, balance, spirituality, harmony, energy

Energy	Projective
Element	Fire
Planet	Mars, Jupiter
Zodiac	Scorpio, Leo

Rhodonite

Rhodonite magical properties

Protection, renewal, emotions, strength, soothing, clarity, happiness, love, balance, harmony, decisions, confidence, spirituality, peace, energy, passion, optimism, changes, vitality, anxiety, travel, psychic abilities, self–confidence, trust, calming, relaxation, patience, determination, releasing, stress, negative energy

Energy	Projective
Element	Fire
Planet	Mars, Venus
Zodiac	Taurus

Quartz (rose)

Quartz (rose) magical properties

Love, happiness, emotions, spirituality, growth, fears, healing, sexuality, passion, calming, soothing, stress, depression, sleep, luck, wisdom, inspiration, success, intuition, grounding, balance, prosperity, self–esteem, harmony, trust, jealousy, gossip, beauty, peace, cleansing, fertility

Energy	Receptive
Element	Earth, Water
Planet	Venus, Moon
Zodiac	Taurus

Sunstone

Sunstone magical properties

Sun magic, power, decisions, leadership, strength, happiness, inspiration, love, luck, stability, clarity, energy, stress, depression, emotions, optimism, perseverance, intuition, fears, self–esteem, self–confidence, healing, balance, harmony, abundance, prosperity, opportunities, peace, protection

Energy	Projective
Element	Fire
Planet	Sun
Zodiac	Leo

Tourmaline

Tourmaline magical properties

Calming, harmony, balance, insight, spirituality, protection, negative energy, transformation, courage, grounding, fears, creativity, understanding, power, motivation, commitment, patience, stability, releasing, emotions, anxiety, strength, happiness, protection, relaxation, friendship, astral travel

Energy	Receptive (pink, green, blue, black, watermelon)
	Projective (watermelon, red)
Element	Water (pink, blue, watermelon)
	Fire (watermelon, red)
	Earth (green, black)
Planet	Venus, Mars
Zodiac	Libra
Birthstone	October

Moon Deities to work with for December

Here you will find my suggestions on some of the Moon deities to work with that align with the energies of this month. Trust your intuition and be guided by the deities that may also make themselves known to you.

Andraste – a warrior goddess of Britain – she was invoked by Queen Boadicea/Boudicca. Call upon her for: Strength, courage, warrior, victory, battle, guidance, inspiration, honour.

Anu – a Mesopotamian/Sumerian sky god viewed as Father of the gods and ruler of the heavens, the stars, and the spirits. Call upon him for: Goals, wishes, spirituality.

Freyja/Freya – although not called a Moon goddess, many of her attributes connect her with both the Full and Dark Moons. A Norse goddess of love, beauty, war, and fertility. She leads souls of dead warriors to the Otherworld. She rides a chariot driven by two cats, so she must be powerful to get cats to do what they are told! Call upon her for: Love, beauty, fertility, war, dearth, happiness, sex, sensuality, inspiration.

Hathor – Egyptian goddess of the Moon, associated with the dark Moon. Goddess of the Underworld but also ruler of the sky. She is a mother to all Egyptians. Definitely packing a powerful punch of feminine energy having given birth to the universe, she must have been exhausted. Call upon her for: Love, feminine energy, beauty, sexuality, happiness, romance, music, the arts, protection (primarily for women).

Hestia – Greek goddess of the hearth and home she is also a fire goddess. Her Roman equivalent is Vesta. The Greeks did not have statues of this goddess as it was believed she didn't take human form, instead she appeared as the flames of fire in the hearth. Hestia was the first born of the Olympian goddesses. She is absolutely about new beginnings and the start of all things. This goddess is the ultimate super house keeper and home maker, with added omnipotence.

Call upon her for: Home life, domesticity, fire magic, devotion, wishes, manifesting, unity, new beginnings, spirituality, blessings.

Isis – Egyptian goddess Queen of Egypt. She is looked upon as Mother Moon, Queen of Sorcery, and the life force within the river Nile. Isis taught her people useful skills, those they would need to survive and flourish, no being high up in the sky for this one, she got down with her subjects (very practical woman). Call upon her for: Magic, dreams, divination, harvest, perspective, love, spirituality, faithfulness, destiny, revitalisation, fulfilment, inner beauty, spirituality, rebirth, feminine energy, knowledge, motherhood, healing, changes, manifesting.

Juno – A Roman goddess, mother of all the gods. She protects Rome and all things feminine. She is a goddess of marriage, women, and young girls. She is a strong, confident business woman, she definitely has a modern approach to being a deity. Her Greek equivalent is Hera. Call upon her for: Romance, love, relationships, marriage, protection, leadership, time, feminine energy, safety, happiness.

Kuan Yin – Chinese/Buddhist goddess of mercy who is probably one of the most chilled out and relaxed deities ever. This beautiful goddess hears all your prayers and responds to each and every request for help. She needs some kind of medal… Call upon her for: Kindness, magic, health, healing, fertility, children, sympathy, support, suffering, encouragement, enlightenment, spirituality, protection.

Rhiannon – if you aren't singing the Fleetwood Mac song right now, you need to… A Welsh goddess and great Queen of Wales. She brings peace, comfort, and patience. If you are looking for magical enchantments then she has a bounty of them. Call upon her for: Patience, comfort, peace, magic, movement, relaxation, communication, fertility, leadership, spirit work, motivation, dream work.

Vesta – Roman goddess of the crescent Moon, the hearth and home. She rules domesticity with a flip of the feather duster and a whip of her apron. She keeps the house and family running like clockwork. She is known as Hestia in Greece. Call upon her for: Home, family, relationships, harmony, peace, love, fertility, fire magic, spirituality.

World Celebration Dates

I have given some dates and a little information on celebrations from around the world that take place during December. A lot of them were based on Moon phases. I apologise for any errors but history is a fickle thing and calendars have changed over the years…

Celtic/Pagan

2nd December – festival to celebrate the goddess Arianrhod.

20th–22nd December – Yule/Winter Solstice. Yule is the Winter Solstice; it marks the shortest day and the longest night of the year. This is in celebration of having survived halfway through the winter (this holiday is sometimes called "Midwinter celebrations"). This was especially significant in northern European countries, where it was not always certain that food storage would last through winter months. To many societies, Winter Solstice also symbolized the earth's regeneration or rebirth. From this day forward, the days would continually grow longer as Sunlight increased.

Ancient Egypt

1st December – Festival of Nehebkau. The Beginning of Eternity festival.

8th December – Feast of Neith.

21st December – Feast of Isis (Aset).

31st December – Feast of Sekhmet.

Hindu

2nd December – Hindu festival of Shiva.

Rome

5th December – Faunalia – A rural festival held in honour of Faunus that involved eating, drinking, dancing, and sacrifices.

11th December – Septimontia / Septimontium: This festival was held to honour the Seven Hills of Rome, either all of them together, or just the earliest enclosed part (inside the Servian

Wall, which enclosed parts of the Caelian, Esquiline, Palatine, and Velian hills). During the festival sacrifices were made somewhere on each hill.

17th – 24th December – Saturnalia – An ancient Roman festival to honour the deity Saturn. The celebrations began with a sacrifice at the temple of Saturn and was followed by banquets, exchanging of gifts and general partying. Masters would serve their slaves at the table and much general merriment was had by all. It was a festival of light leading towards the winter solstice and the renewal of the coming year.

18th December – Eponalia – This festival honoured Epona. The Romans would celebrate on this day by giving all the horses, donkeys, and mules a day of rest.

Divalia – The Divalia honoured the goddess Angerona in rites so secret that even the statue of the goddess had to be gagged to keep the details secret.

Greece

15th December – Greek festival of Alcyone.

Special Moons

Throughout the year there are new and full Moons that take on a special appearance, such as the blue Moon and the super Moon. Each one is unique and deserves a little bit of extra attention as they bring some special magic with them.

Blue Moon

Generally, a blue Moon is considered to be the second full Moon in a calendar month. Although originally a blue Moon was categorized as the third full Moon in a season that has four full Moons. Usually there are only three full Moons in a season. The season being the period between a solstice and an equinox or vice versa. Are you still with me? The idea of the blue Moon being the second in a calendar month seems to be a modern idea that surfaced during the 1940s due to incorrect information being published. And as happens in these cases, the misinformation was repeated and the idea seems to have become accepted over the original definition.

We all know the phrase 'once in a blue Moon' which relates to the occurrence being infrequent but where did the term come from? There is no definite answer that I am aware of, only suggestions. In old English the word 'betrayer' translates as 'belewe' which may have evolved over time to become 'blue'. The term 'betrayer' was used for the extra full Moon that didn't fit into the usual pattern of twelve. Apparently, some research has shown that in the 16th Century the term 'blue Moon' translates as 'absurd' and in the 18th Century 'blue Moon' meant 'never'. During the 19th Century we started to see actual blue tinges to the Moon caused mainly by natural and man mage disasters affecting the atmosphere and causing the full Moon to appear blue in colour.

The magical energy of a blue Moon is a bit special. It is

ramped up and super charged. For me this is the time to ask for something out of the ordinary, something you wouldn't normally request because it might be a bit far–fetched. Play on the idea of 'once in a blue Moon' and run with it. Definitely a Moon for dreams and wishes. Give it time to work though, blue Moon magic can take time, even up to the next blue Moon to work, but know that it is ticking away in the background the whole time. It is good for long term projects.

Blue Moon spell tips and activities:

- Be clear about your intentions, show the blue Moon that you really want this and that your will is strong for the goal.
- Take a cleansing ritual bath with the energy of the blue Moon in the skies.
- Talk to the blue Moon, tell it what you want or need.
- Write a petition asking the blue Moon energy to remove all the things in your life that no longer serve you, leave it out under the Moonlight and then burn it the following day.
- Dance or bathe in the blue Moon light.
- Pick leaves, berries, seeds and flowers on the blue Moon and dry them for magical use, they will have an extra boost of energy.
- Pop a silver coin in your pocket, stand outside under the blue Moon and turn the coin over. Take the coin and place it on your altar to bring you good luck and fortune.
- The blue Moon is a super fertile energy, work spells for fertility.
- Work with colour magic and the energy of blue; wisdom, faith, trust, honesty, peace and healing are some of the intents covered by the colour blue.
- Cleanse and recharge all your magical tools and crystals.

Sidhe Moon

If we have a second full Moon in a calendar month then it stands to reason that we may also have a second new Moon in a calendar month too. This second new Moon is often referred to as a sidhe (pronounced 'shee') or fairy Moon. It is believed by some to be an Otherworldly Moon.

Sidhe Moon spell tips and activities:

- This new Moon is good for psychic work and connecting with the Otherworld and the world of Fairy. It carries all the energy of the usual new Moon but perhaps with a little bit extra energy.
- It is a good time to work magic for new beginnings, new ventures and personal growth.
- However, to make room for new adventures you may need to cut some ties or have a clear out.
- The Sidhe Moon is perfect for spiritual death to enable rebirth.
- Do make an offering to the Otherworld and to the Fae at this time.

Black Moon

And then we have a black Moon. This usually refers to the third new Moon in a season that has four new Moons. This happens approximately once every thirty–three months. The modern interpretation is to call the second new Moon in a month a black Moon, which happens approximately once every twenty–nine months. And once every twenty years we get no new Moon in February, always February as it has less days than the other months. When this happens January and March will have a second new Moon. This can also happen with the full Moon.

Black Moon spell tips and activities:

- You also get an extra boost of super power with a black

Moon.

- The new black Moon brings extra opportunities along with heightened intuition and self–knowledge. A full black Moon is also super charged and extra good for inner work, divination and Otherworld connections.
- The black Moon is also excellent for releasing and banishing magic.

Super Moon

When the Moon is at its closest point to Earth in her monthly orbit, we call it a super Moon. Because she is at her closest point to the earth, she appears to be much bigger in the sky. It happens when the earth, the Moon and the Sun all align. This happens almost once a year (roughly every fourteenth full Moon). The term 'supermoon' seems to be fairly modern but it does what is says on the tin. A supermoon does seem to put out more power including creating stronger tides on the earth. From a magical stand–point super Moon power should be utilized to the max. Don't waste the opportunity of extra oomph in your workings. The energy and power will be much stronger and more intense. Everything will be heightened and amplified.

Super Moon spell tips and activities:

- Work with the super Moon by connecting with the element of water in all its forms.
- Any spell work will be increased so try working a magnifying glass into your spell work to 'amplify' the magic.
- The super Moon is an excellent time to work a dedication whether it is to your pathway, coven or a particular deity.
- Drawing down the Moon on a super Moon is uber powerful, mind you don't get knocked off your feet!
- You may want to work some serious grounding exercises after the super Moon.

- Super Moon water or Moon cords will store extra Moon magic energy. If you don't have time for making Moon water (seriously, it doesn't take much effort though) or a Moon cord, pop a crystal under the super Moon to charge with special energy.

Micro Moon

If there is a point when the Moon is at its closest to the earth and appears larger there must be an opposite. Yup, when the full Moon is at its farthest from the earth it...well, actually it won't look much different at all to the naked eye to be honest. It also happens almost yearly but is only really noticeable to those science bods with special equipment to see it. You may just think the Moon seems a little less bright than usual. The energy from a micro Moon will be gentle and kind.

Eclipses

A lunar eclipse is a full Moon eclipse. A solar eclipse is a new Moon eclipse.

When a celestial body moves into the shadow of another celestial body wholly or in part we get an eclipse. They are quite mystical events. I cannot even begin to imagine what ancient civilisations thought about an eclipse, it must have seemed pretty scary. In fact, even now when it happens with all our understanding of the event it does seem to cast an eerie feeling over everything.

Basically, you get the full Moon phase in a very short period of time, the Moon appears as waxing, waning and reappearing during an eclipse. Use this condensed whole Moon cycle to work some powerful magic. Your spell work is going to be super amplified.

Eclipse spell tips and activities:

- An eclipse definitely carries a huge amount of power. We

are talking full or new Moon magic 'go large'!

- Eclipses have the power of kicking us back onto our rightful paths, whether we want to go or not. Humans have a habit of wandering into the wilderness and being easily distracted…ooh look shiny things…An eclipse brings us back into line. This can be challenging because generally we don't like change especially sudden ones. We must learn to trust that the magic of the Moon knows best.
- An eclipse can also give us insight, clarity and a doorway to the Otherworld.
- Good for meditation, transformation, personal growth, spiritual development, changes and opportunity.
- Work spells for intuition, psychic abilities, divination, wisdom, healing, connection, divine, magical abilities.

Blood Moon

Such a cool name that conjures up ideas of vampires and werewolves. It is however just the term for a total lunar eclipse. When the Moon moves behind the earth's shadow completely. This happens almost once a year. The Moon appears to have a red hue that is caused by dust particles in the atmosphere, which makes it sound much more boring than actual blood. This again must have been scary to our ancestors; it may have felt like the end of the world.

Lunar Occultation

Every twenty–eight years or so the Moon moves into a position that obscures a few things from the sky. It actually hides Venus, Mars, Mercury and the star Regulus. This is called a lunar occultation.

A Monthly Moon Challenge

There have been a few monthly challenges floating around social media, some asking for photos, drawings or writing. We ran a witchy one recently that was focused around the Moon phases for a month. I have included the challenge below with some adjustments to make it suit any month. Enter the correct date and day in the chart once you have checked the Moon phases. Obviously, you may need to miss one out for a 30 day month or more if you are working this in February. Some Moon phase apps and calendars only give new, waxing, full and waning so I have included both those and the more refined options to include the dark Moon and quarters. It may need a little tweaking to fit the Moon phases of the month you choose but it gives you a base to start.

Start each day by stepping outside and taking a deep breath in. Feel the energy of the day. What feelings, thoughts or keyword do you feel for the day?

There are two choices of challenge – quick challenges if you are short of time and longer ones if you prefer. Work with either or both.

Date	Day	Moon phase	Quick Challenge	Challenge
		Waxing crescent	New/ Wear something bright today that makes you happy.	Colour magic - what colour clothes are you wearing today? Why? And what does the colour mean to you?
		Waxing crescent	Stand outside and place your palms onto the earth and feel the connection.	Think about the element of Earth, what chores or daily activities do you do that correspond to the element of Earth?

		Waxing crescent	Pick an ingredient from your kitchen spice rack and carry some in your pocket or purse today.	Take a look in your kitchen cupboard and spice rack. What ingredient grabs your attention? Research it and see what magical properties it has.
		Waxing crescent	Pick a magical book from your collection, flick through the pages and read anything that jumps out at you.	Pick a magical book from your collection, perhaps one you haven't read yet and some time working through it.
		First quarter First quarter/ Waxing gibbous	At night, stand outside and send a wish up to the waxing Moon. Leave a jar of water out over night to create waxing Moon water.	Create a waxing Moon spell or chant to bring something into your life. Leave a jar of water out over night to create waxing Moon Create a spell to use the water with.
		First quarter/ Waxing gibbous	Pick a flower from your garden, a weed from outside or just a fallen leaf and carry it with you today.	Choose a flower or plant that you haven't worked with before, maybe one that is in your garden or that you saw when you were out. Do some research, what magical properties does it have?
		Waxing gibbous	Look in the mirror and say to yourself "I am fabulous".	Write an affirmation. What do you need to boost about yourself? Self-esteem? Confidence? Strength? Work with this affirmation each day.

		Waxing gibbous	Stand outside and send a wish up to the Sun.	Work with the Sun today, go outside or look out of the window during the morning and write a chant or create a Sun spell to bring something into your life.
		Waxing gibbous	Pick up a pebble or leaf from outside and pop it on your altar.	Create a nature mandala outside using leaves, flowers, seed heads, pebble, shells, and twigs. Or make one inside using spices and herbs from your food cupboard.
		Waxing gibbous	Stand outside for a couple of minutes and take a few deep breathes in and out.	Think about the element of Air, what chores or daily activities do you do that correspond to the element of Air?
		Waxing gibbous	Pop outside and hug a tree.	Choose a tree that you haven't worked with before, maybe one that is in your garden or that you saw when you were out. Do some research, what magical properties does it have?
		Waxing gibbous/ Full Moon	Leave a jar of water out over night to create full Moon	Leave a jar of water out over night to create full Moon water. Create a spell to work with your Moon water.
		Full Moon	Take a look up at the full Moon, what images do you see on her surface?	Water scrying - fill a dish with water and drop a silver coin in the bottom. Allow the light of the full Moon to shine on the surface

			and read any images or symbols you see.
	Waning gibbous/ Full Moon	Keep an eye out today for any animals that may cross your path. In reality or on TV, in a book etc. Acknowledge them.	Choose an animal that you feel drawn to, do some research, and/or meditate to meet it. What animal was it and what did you find out?
	Waning gibbous	Light a candle and spend a few moments watching the flame.	Think about the element of Fire, what chores or daily activities do you do that correspond to the element of Fire?
	Waning gibbous	Pop outside and soak up the Sun rays for a few moments, allow the energy to fill your body.	Work with the Sun today, go outside or look out of the window at or around midday and write a chant or create a Sun spell to use the power of the full Sun.
	Waning gibbous	When you vacuum or dust this week, visualise any negative energy dispersing as you work.	Cleanse your home, write a chant to go with it. What medium do you use to cleanse? Smoke, water, scent?
	Waning gibbous	Send out a blessing to Mother Earth.	Pick a goddess to research, one you haven't worked with before. Who did you choose and why? What did you find out?
	Waning gibbous	When you shower or bath today allow the	Think about the element of Water, what chores or daily activities

			water to wash away any negative vibes.	do you do that correspond to the element of Water?
		Third quarter	At night pop outside and send a wish up to the waning Moon.	Create a waning Moon spell or chant to release something from your life.
		Waning crescent/ quarter	Leave a jar of water out over night to third create waning Moon water.	Leave a jar of water out over night to create waning Moon water. Create a spell to work with the Moon water.
		Waning crescent/ Third quarter	Sit in front of your altar for a few minutes today and connect...	Take a good look at your altar. Does it need clearing, cleansing, or tweaking? Something adding or taking away?
		Waning crescent	Stand outside your home and see if you can connect with the energy beneath your feet.	Research your local area. Are there any ley lines, sacred sites, or ancient monuments?
		Waning crescent	Step outside and send a wish up to the Sun this afternoon.	Work with the Sun today, go outside or look out of the window during the afternoon and write a chant or create a Sun spell to release something from your life.
		Waning crescent	Take note of any natural images you see when you are out, today acknowledge them.	When you are out and about take a look at nature, your surroundings, and the architecture. Can you see any symbols or magical shapes?

		Waning crescent/ Dark Moon	Send a blessing to Father Sky today.	Pick a god to research, one you haven't worked with before. Who did you choose and why? What did you find out?
		New Moon/ Dark Moon	What clouds do you see today?	Work with natural divination. See what forms you can find and work with them. Cloud, rain, or flame divination maybe?
		Waxing crescent/ Dark Moon	Keep an eye out for any birds you see today, acknowledge them.	Choose a bird that you feel drawn to, do some research, and/or meditate to meet it. What animal was it and what did you find out?
		Waxing crescent/ New Moon	Close your eyes for a few moments...what images do you see or words pop into your head?	Draw a tarot or oracle card, rune, or ogham. See how it relates to your day.
		Waxing crescent/ New Moon	When you eat your lunch or dinner today send a blessing for the food.	Food magic - take a look in your fridge or food cupboard, what ingredients do you have that catch your attention? What magical properties do they have?

Mercury Retrograde

Yep, I know – this phrase usually strikes terror into the heart of many a Pagan or planet follower. And I realise it isn't a Moon phase, but I thought I would include it. Mercury retrograde has a reputation for causing absolute chaos with machinery and equipment breaking down, computers going haywire and any mishap or accident gets blamed on this poor ole planet, but why?

Well...the science bit is to look at what Mercury Retrograde actually is. It means the planet appears to be in retrograde or 'directed or moving backwards' so it seems as if the planet is travelling backwards through the sky in regard to the zodiac. It is all to do with the way our own orbit interacts with the orbits of other planets. It happens three or four times each year for about three weeks at a time.

Mercury is the planet closest to the Sun, so its orbit is much shorter than Earth's. On the three or four occasions a year that the retrograde happens Mercury makes a mad dash past Earth. As Mercury gets faster it creates a bit of a wild wake which is apparently the disruptive affect we feel. From an astrological view point Mercury is pretty much asleep during a retrograde so it just isn't paying attention.

As Mercury rules communication, technology and travel whatever goes wrong in these areas during its retrograde gets blamed for it. It covers listening, speech, learning, researching, negotiations, selling and buying. All sorts of official paperwork such as contracts and leases are also included under Mercury. And of course, computers, transportation and machinery.

Personally, I will leave it up to you as to whether you believe Mercury is responsible for all the negative happenings during a retrograde. I think possibly a lot of it is just coincidence and some of it is just us feeding the myth. Not that I am suggesting you should ignore it completely... Just be prepared and make sure you are extra careful with backing up and mechanical items.

If you prefer to play safe when Mercury is retrograde stay flexible, avoid signing any important documents or contracts and give yourself extra time to travel anywhere and perhaps take a map as back up in case the GPS fails. Take the time to review anything serious but wait until the retrograde has passed before you make your final decisions. Double check everything, don't rely on your memory, write lists and check them twice. There may also be a lot of miscommunication, don't jump to conclusions, don't listen to gossip (you should never trust gossip anyway) and make sure you seek clarity in any situation before acting or reacting, but then that is also good advice at any time. Don't stop your entire existence dead, just maybe plan ahead a little when you know it is coming.

You may also find that a Mercury retrograde is strongest on the start and end date of its run.

There is a positive spin on Mercury retrograde because it brings with it the power of emotional healing. Your intuition should be heightened at this time as well. The retrograde is a time to reflect and dig out old hurts and emotional blockages. Forgive, forget and let go. Chuck out those negative emotions and move forward. If something untoward happens don't just blame it on the retrograde, sit back and have a think about it, ask yourself what underlying reasons there were for it and whether you need to readjust something in your life or the way your energy is being directed to avoid it happening again. Don't let the retrograde take all the blame.

A Mercury retrograde also brings change, but you often can't see it yet. All kinds of things are 'up in the air' and you will need to wait until the retrograde has passed for them to settle into place. It gives us an opportunity to sit back and take stock, to have a think about the direction we are going in and whether it is working or not. It can also help bring closure to situations or issues and can reignite relationships and make reconnections.

You may find that lost items suddenly appear as well.

Take time during a Mercury retrograde to reorganise and have a clear out. Think of it as a 'Retrograde Clean'. Sort your wardrobes, clear out your cupboards, donate what you don't want or use to charity. Make a clean sweep. Reassess your life and everything in it, redesign anything that doesn't work, repair all that is broken.

Working with the Moon and the Zodiac

We are familiar with the Zodiac and the cycle that the Sun makes through its signs, but the Moon (and all the planets) also travel through them. As the Moon moves around the zodiac the term used is 'transit'. The Moon passes through each entire sign in just over two days. The Moon's passage through the Zodiac signs takes slightly less than 28 days. There are 13 of these cycles in a year. This means that the full Moon appears in a different sign of the Zodiac each month. The Moon is always opposite the Sun when it is full, so if you know what sign the Sun is occupying, the full Moon will be in the opposite sign of the Zodiac. (The Moon moves faster than the Sun).

I use a phone app to know what the Moon phase is and what sign, but I also use a Moon calendar (of the paper variety) both give detailed information. They will give you the Moon phase detail and the times the Moon moves in and out of each sign as well. For example, today the Moon is waning crescent 24.4% and in the sign of Capricorn.

If you can work your magic when the Moon is in a specific sign of the Zodiac, it will add a lot of power to the working. If you add to that the correct Moon phase, then you will have huge amounts of oomph. You can also draw or inscribe the symbol of the zodiac onto candles or include in sigils to gain the magic.

THE MOON IN ARIES

♈

Magical properties: Action, taking risks, power, authority, initiative, leadership, rebirth, willpower, renewal, independence, new projects, job ventures, fast moving, opportunity, creativity, strength, courage, lust, new projects related to money.

Business: Trading, buying, selling, launching new ventures

For bringing in energy and enthusiasm to your plans or new ventures.

A good time to go on a shopping spree.

Watch out for impulsiveness, running out of steam and other people's bad moods.

Avoid: Divination, anything that requires patience, resolving conflicts, acting on impulse, skipping the essentials. Rushing things. Trying to get your own way.

Waxing Moon in Aries: Find a new challenge, begin a new exercise.

Waning Moon in Aries: Personal pampering.

Element: Fire

Colours: White, pink, red

Body: Head

Herbs, Spices and Plants to work with when the Moon is in Aries

These are my suggestions based on the plants that are associated

with Aries but trust your intuition.

Bay

(Laurus nobilis)

Bay Magical Properties:

Protection, purification, strength, power, healing, creativity, spirituality, psychic powers

Ruling planet – Sun

Element – Fire

Gender – Masculine

Cinnamon

(Cinnamomum zeylanicum, Cinnamomum verum)

Cinnamon Magical Properties:

Success, healing, power, psychic powers, protection, love, focus, lust, spirituality, changes

Ruling planet – Sun

Element – Fire

Gender – Masculine

Coriander

(Coriandrum sativum)

Coriander Magical Properties:

Health, healing, peace, love, release, wealth, protection, negativity

Ruling planet – Mars

Sign – Aries

Element – Fire

Gender – Masculine

Dragons blood

(Daemonorops draco, Daemonorops propinquos)

Dragon's Blood Magical Properties:

Power, protection, love, happiness, dragon magic

Ruling planet – Mars
Sign – Aries
Element – Fire
Gender – Masculine

Feverfew

(Tanacetum parthenium, Chrysanthemum parthenium)
Feverfew Magical Properties:
Protection, peace, health, purification
Ruling planet – Venus
Sign – Aries, Sagittarius, Libra
Element – Water
Gender – Masculine

Frankincense

Frankincense Magical Properties:
Purification, spirituality, relaxation, focus, love, abundance
Ruling planet – Sun
Sign – Aries, Leo, Aquarius
Element – Fire
Gender – Masculine

Juniper

(Juniperus communes)
Juniper Magical Properties:
Love, exorcism, healing, protection, justice, stolen items, purification, psychic powers, clarity
Ruling planet – Sun, Jupiter, Moon
Sign – Aries
Element – Fire
Gender – Masculine

Marjoram

(Origanum majorana)

Marjoram Magical Properties:
Love, happiness, health, protection, marriage, grief
Ruling planet – Mercury
Sign – Aries, Capricorn
Element – Air
Gender – Masculine

Myrrh

(Commiphora myrrha)
Myrrh Magical Properties:
Protection, purification, healing, Crone, Underworld, courage
Ruling planet – Mars, Sun
Sign – Aries, Aquarius
Element – Water
Gender – Feminine

Nettle

(Urtica dioica)
Nettle Magical Properties:
Healing, protection, lust, money, exorcism.
Ruling planet – Mars
Sign – Scorpio, Aries
Element – Fire
Gender – Masculine

Rosemary

(Rosemarinus officinalis)
Rosemary Magical Properties:
Protection, love, lust, mental powers, exorcism, purification, healing, sleep
Ruling planet – Sun
Sign – Aries
Element – Fire
Gender – Masculine

Crystals to work with when the Moon is in Aries

Below are my suggestions for crystals to work with then the Moon is in Aries based on the crystals that are associated with this sign but be guided by your intuition.

Apache tear

Apache tear magical properties

Grief, releasing, blockages, peace, acceptance, forgiveness, balance, emotions, change, insight, clarity, success, hope, healing, grounding, protection, meditation, dispel negative energy

Energy: Projective
Element: Fire
Planet: Saturn, Jupiter
Zodiac: Aries, Capricorn
Birthstone: November

Aventurine (green)

Aventurine (green) magical properties

Balance, decisions, motivation, leadership, dreams, visualisation, creativity, luck, money, anxiety, calm, opportunities, happiness, adventure, love, courage, truth, comfort, support, healing, peace, connection, perception, intellect, psychic abilities

Energy: Projective
Element: Air
Planet: Mercury, Mars
Zodiac: Aries

Bloodstone

Bloodstone magical properties:

Organisation, adaptability, anxiety, clarity, concentration, renewal, energy, self–confidence, connection, calm, protection, breaking barriers, selfishness, mysticism, insight, spirituality, truth, intuition, creativity, guidance, strength, healing, victory, wealth, money, power, invisibility, deception, negative energy, divine connection, past life, dreams

Energy: Projective
Element: Fire, Earth
Planet: Mars
Zodiac: Aries, Pisces, Scorpio
Birthstone: February, March

Garnet

Garnet magical properties

Organisation, warrior spirit, protection, love, commitment, passion, sexuality, sensuality, attraction, depression, spiritual healing, success, self–confidence, energy, inspiration, perception, strength, survival, fear, courage, clarity, challenges, past life work, truth, compassion, deflecting negative energy, gossip, ambition, motivation, goals, purification, cleansing, balance, inner strength, self–empowerment, creativity, confidence, meditation, spirit work, nightmares, journeying, abundance, support

Energy: Projective
Element: Fie
Planet: Mars
Zodiac: Aries, Virgo, Capricorn, Leo, Aquarius
Birthstone: January

Hematite

Hematite magical properties

Grounding, money, decisions, manifestation, finances, healing, focus, clarity, stability, protection, balance, divination, problem solving, emotions, self–esteem, productivity, doubt, anxiety, communication, strength

Energy: Projective
Element: Fire, Earth
Planet: Saturn
Zodiac: Aries, Aquarius

Kyanite

Kyanite magical properties

Balance, harmony, calming, connection, psychic abilities, healing, communication, grounding, transformation, meditation, relaxation, luck, growth, leadership, new beginnings, clarity, decisions, stability, truth, vitality, abundance, spirituality, channelling, understanding, dreams

Energy	Receptive
Element	Water
Planet	Jupiter, Venus, Mars
Zodiac	Aries, Libra, Taurus

Jade

Jade magical properties

Purification, harmony, friendship, luck, protection, clarity, manifestation, peace, courage, wealth, longevity, wisdom, prosperity, love, renewal, fertility, uplifting, calming, confidence, truth, psychic abilities, spirit work, dreams, past life work, healing, abundance, finances, creativity, manifestation, emotions

Energy	Receptive
Element	Water
Planet	Venus, Neptune
Zodiac	Pisces, Libra, Gemini, Taurus, Aries
Birthstone	March

Jasper (red)

Jasper (red) magical properties

General: Protection, balance, stability, healing, grounding, stress, peace, happiness, confidence, fears, comfort, relaxation, release, beauty, astral travel, motivation, determination, energy, focus, prosperity, organisation, honesty, trust

Zodiac	Scorpio, Aries, Virgo
Birthstone	August

Energy	Projective
Element	Fire
Planet	Mars

THE MOON ON TAURUS

♉

Magical properties: Practical matters, property, permanence, sex, determination, stability, organization, patience, connection, financial security, prosperity, love, creativity, inner peace, confidence to speak out. Growth of any kind.

Staying power, bringing love into your life.

Make sure you get value for money on any purchases made.

Business: Making investments, employing new staff, decorating, looking after your staff.

Be careful with greed here though. Spells may take time to work but will be stable and long lasting.

Avoid: Trying to change someone's mind, anything that requires speed or improvising. Don't sit on your laurels, you may miss opportunities. Over–eating. Being possessive.

Waxing Moon in Taurus: Try new recipes or crafts. Visit the arts. Do some gardening.

Waning Moon in Taurus: Sort your finances. Relax and do something you love.

Element: Earth

Colours: Red, green, yellow

Body: Neck, throat, shoulders

Herbs, Spices and Plants to work with when the Moon is in Taurus

These are my suggestions based on the plants that are associated with Taurus but trust your intuition.

Coltsfoot

(Tussilago farfara)
Coltsfoot Magical Properties:
Visions, love, energy, health, tranquillity, peace
Ruling planet – Venus
Sign – Taurus
Element – Water
Gender – Feminine

Dandelion

(Taraxacum officinale)
Dandelion Magical Properties:
Wishes, divination, love, abundance, psychic powers
Ruling planet –Jupiter
Sign – Taurus
Element – Air
Gender – Masculine

Lungwort

(Pulmonaria officinalis)
Lungwort Magical Properties:
Healing, cleansing, releasing, calming
Ruling planet – Mercury
Sign – Taurus, Pisces
Element – Earth
Gender – Masculine

Mandrake

(Mandragora officinale)

It's poisonous…enough said.
Mandrake Magical Properties:
Protection, love, prosperity
Ruling planet – Mercury
Sign – Taurus, Cancer, Virgo
Element – Fire
Gender – Masculine

Myrtle

(Myrtaceae communis)
Myrtle Magical Properties:
Love, protection, money
Ruling planet – Venus, Moon
Sign – Taurus
Element – Water
Gender – Feminine

Thyme

(Thymus vulgaris, Thymus serpyllum)
Thyme Magical Properties:
Healing, health, peace, psychic powers, love, purification, courage, releasing, sleep, beauty
Ruling planet – Venus
Sign – Gemini, Taurus, Libra
Element – Water
Gender – Feminine

Crystals to work with when the Moon is in Taurus

Below are my suggestions for crystals to work with then the Moon is in Taurus based on the crystals that are associated with this sign but be guided by your intuition.

Carnelian

Carnelian magical properties

Grounding, protection, calm, concentration, confidence, self–worth, success, courage, creativity, negative energy, direction, control, organisation, opportunity, planning, psychic protection, jealousy, hate, harmony, depression, doubt, patience, stability, vitality, motivation, stamina, passion, truth, love, faith, honesty, trust, luck, abundance

Energy: Projective
Element: Fire
Planet: Sun
Zodiac: Taurus, Leo
Birthstone: May, June, July, August

Chrysocolla

Chrysocolla magical properties

Wisdom, peace, patience, love, soothing, intuition, energy, calming, emotions, fear, strength, clarity, balance, negative energy, insight, releasing, spirituality, psychic abilities, guilt, divine, harmony, communication, meditation

Energy: Receptive
Element: Water
Planet: Venus
Zodiac: Taurus

Chrysoprase

Chrysoprase magical properties

Courage, strength, wisdom, releasing, selfishness, imagination, happiness, success, balance, break barriers, protection, truth, healing, luck, prosperity, marriage, negative energy, transformation, love

Energy: Receptive
Element: Earth
Planet: Venus
Zodiac: Taurus, Cancer

Jade

Jade magical properties

Purification, harmony, friendship, luck, protection, clarity, manifestation, peace, courage, wealth, longevity, wisdom, prosperity, love, renewal, fertility, uplifting, calming, confidence, truth, psychic abilities, spirit work, dreams, past life work, healing, abundance, finances, creativity, manifestation, emotions

Energy	Receptive
Element	Water
Planet	Venus, Neptune
Zodiac	Pisces, Libra, Gemini, Taurus, Aries
Birthstone	March

Kyanite

Kyanite magical properties

Balance, harmony, calming, connection, psychic abilities, healing, communication, grounding, transformation, meditation, relaxation, luck, growth, leadership, new beginnings, clarity, decisions, stability, truth, vitality, abundance, spirituality, channelling, understanding, dreams

Energy	Receptive
Element	Water
Planet	Jupiter, Venus, Mars
Zodiac	Aries, Libra, Taurus

Quartz (rose)

Quartz (rose) magical properties

Love, happiness, emotions, spirituality, growth, fears, healing, sexuality, passion, calming, soothing, stress, depression, sleep, luck, wisdom, inspiration, success, intuition, grounding, balance, prosperity, self–esteem, harmony, trust, jealousy, gossip, beauty, peace, cleansing, fertility

Energy	Receptive

Element	Earth, Water
Planet	Venus, Moon
Zodiac	Taurus

Rhodonite

Rhodonite magical properties

Protection, renewal, emotions, strength, soothing, clarity, happiness, love, balance, harmony, decisions, confidence, spirituality, peace, energy, passion, optimism, changes, vitality, anxiety, travel, psychic abilities, self–confidence, trust, calming, relaxation, patience, determination, releasing, stress, negative energy

Energy	Projective
Element	Fire
Planet	Mars, Venus
Zodiac	Taurus

THE MOON IN GEMINI

♊

Magical Properties: Playing with ideas, learning, communicating, Short distance travel, business communication, social, energy, multi–tasking, negotiations, personal connections, healing, uncrossing, deals and transactions, teaching, learning. Sorting out of disputes.

A good time to go window shopping with friends.

This is not a good time for permanent changes. Be careful, this can be unpredictable.

Business: Buying, selling, business travel, correspondence, reorganizing, new plans, presentations.

Avoid: Distractions, lying, fabricating the truth, spreading yourself too thinly. Starting a job before finishing off others.

Waxing Moon in Gemini: Correspond and communicate with family and friends. Write, read and learn.

Waning Moon in Gemini: It's all about books; read, write and visit the library and book stores. Relax and enjoy reading.

Element: Air

Colours: Red, blue, orange

Body: Lungs, hands, arms

Herbs, Spices and Plants to work with when the Moon is in Gemini

These are my suggestions based on the plants that are associated

with Gemini but trust your intuition.

Angelica

(Angelica archangelica)

Angelica Magical Properties:

Protection, healing, exorcism, divination, prosperity, luck, hex breaking, courage

Ruling planet – Sun, Venus

Sign – Gemini, Cancer, Leo, Libra

Element – Fire

Gender – Masculine

Bergamot

(Monarda didyma, Mondarda fistulosa)

Bergamot Magical Properties:

Abundance, meditation, sleep, dreams, clarity, friendship

Sign – Gemini, Libra

Element – Air

Gender – Feminine

Dill

(Anethum graveolens)

Dill Magical Properties:

Protection, love, lust, money, jealousy, balance, clarity, knowledge, magic

Ruling planet –Mercury

Sign – Cancer, Gemini, Leo

Element – Fire

Gender – Masculine

Honeysuckle

(Lonicera caprifolium, Lonicera japonica, Lonicera periclymenum)

Honeysuckle Magical Properties:

Prosperity, psychic powers, protection, balance, lust, meditation, memory
Ruling planet – Jupiter
Sign – Gemini, Cancer
Element – Earth
Gender – Masculine

Oregano

(Origanum vulgare)
Oregano Magical Properties:
Ruling planet – Mars, Venus, Mercury
Sign – Gemini
Element – Air
Gender – Masculine

Tansy

(Tanacetum vulgare)
Tansy Magical Properties:
Health, longevity, rebirth, cleansing, protection, travel
Ruling planet – Venus
Sign – Gemini
Element – Water
Gender – Feminine

Thyme

(Thymus vulgaris, Thymus serpyllum)
Thyme Magical Properties:
Healing, health, peace, psychic powers, love, purification, courage, releasing, sleep, beauty
Ruling planet – Venus
Sign – Gemini, Taurus, Libra
Element – Water
Gender – Feminine

Crystals to work with when the Moon is in Gemini

Below are my suggestions for crystals to work with then the Moon is in Gemini based on the crystals that are associated with this sign but be guided by your intuition.

Agate (banded)

Agate (banded) magical properties

Perception, wisdom, balance, spirituality, goodwill, peace, memory, concentration, stamina, truth, clarity, honesty, courage, protection, calming, sleep, dreams, strength, longevity, nature, love, anti–stress, energy

Energy: Projective
Element: Fire
Planet: Mercury
Zodiac: Gemini

Agate (moss)

Agate (moss) magical properties

Nature, happiness, prosperity, wealth, longevity, friendship, success, abundance, healing, renewal, fertility, creativity, confidence, strength, love, beginnings, self–esteem, communication, emotions, stress, releasing, hope, trust, depression, growth, finances, cleansing, support, peace, stability, fears, luck, divination

Energy Receptive
Element Earth
Planet Moon
Zodiac Virgo, Gemini

Jade

Jade magical properties

Purification, harmony, friendship, luck, protection, clarity, manifestation, peace, courage, wealth, longevity, wisdom, prosperity, love, renewal, fertility, uplifting, calming, confidence, truth, psychic abilities, spirit work, dreams, past life work, healing, abundance, finances, creativity, manifestation, emotions

Energy	Receptive
Element	Water
Planet	Venus, Neptune
Zodiac	Pisces, Libra, Gemini, Taurus, Aries
Birthstone	March

Quartz (clear)

Quartz (clear) magical properties

Purification, cleansing, healing, calming, emotions, strength, support, spirituality, energy, balance, psychic abilities, motivation, uplifting, decisions, anxiety, divine connection, amplifying, focus, meditation, manifestation, channelling, protection, negative energy, clarity, wisdom, concentration, learning, spirit work, communication, astral travel, divination, dreams, harmony

Energy	Projective, Receptive
Planet	Sun, Moon
Element	Fire, Water
Zodiac	Leo, Gemini, Capricorn

Serpentine

Serpentine magical properties

Meditation, peace, clarity, nature, fairy magic, emotions, calming, protection, negative energy, love, prosperity, manifestation, psychic protection, success, cleansing

Energy:	Projective
Element:	Fire
Planet:	Saturn
Zodiac:	Gemini

THE MOON IN CANCER

Magical properties: Home, hearth, nurturing, children and family, but watch for others' sensitivities, compassion. Motherhood, fertility, pregnancy, finding a new home, exploration of past lives, scrying, divination, psychic abilities. Finding household decorations that you would like.

Do your essentials shop, home purchases and presents for friends.

Business: Bringing projects to a successful conclusion, signing papers.

Avoid: Emotional over–eating, anything that requires objectivity. Don't be oversensitive, try not to take on other's emotions. Interfering in other people's business.

Waxing Moon in Cancer: Visit family. Decorate. Get in the kitchen and experiment.

Waning Moon in Cancer: Go for a walk or a swim. Get out into the garden. Reorganise.

Element: Water

Colours: Blue, green, brown

Body: Breasts, stomach

Herbs, Spices and Plants to work with when the Moon is in Cancer

These are my suggestions based on the plants that are associated

with Cancer but trust your intuition.

Angelica

(Angelica archangelica)

Angelica Magical Properties:

Protection, healing, exorcism, divination, prosperity, luck, hex breaking, courage

Ruling planet – Sun, Venus

Sign – Gemini, Cancer, Leo, Libra

Element – Fire

Gender – Masculine

Dill

(Anethum graveolens)

Dill Magical Properties:

Protection, love, lust, money, jealousy, balance, clarity, knowledge, magic

Ruling planet –Mercury

Sign – Cancer, Gemini, Leo

Element – Fire

Gender – Masculine

Honeysuckle

(Lonicera caprifolium, Lonicera japonica, Lonicera periclymenum)

Honeysuckle Magical Properties:

Prosperity, psychic powers, protection, balance, lust, meditation, memory

Ruling planet – Jupiter

Sign – Gemini, Cancer

Element – Earth

Gender – Masculine

Hyssop

(Hyssopus officinalis)

Hyssop Magical Properties:

Purification, protection, healing

Ruling planet – Jupiter, Moon

Sign – Cancer

Element – Fire

Gender – Masculine

Jasmine

(Jasminum grandiflorum, Jasminum officinale, Jasminum odoratissimum)

Jasmine Magical Properties:

Dreams, money, love, meditation, lust

Ruling planet – Moon, Venus

Sign – Cancer

Element – Water

Gender – Feminine

Mandrake

(Mandragora officinale)

It's poisonous…enough said.

Mandrake Magical Properties:

Protection, love, prosperity

Ruling planet – Mercury

Sign – Taurus, Cancer, Virgo

Element – Fire

Gender – Masculine

Mugwort

(Artemisia vulgaris)

Mugwort Magical Properties:

Strength, psychic powers, protection, dreams, healing, astral travel, feminine energy, cleansing

Ruling planet – Venus, Moon
Sign – Cancer
Element – Earth
Gender – Feminine

Violet

(Viola odorata)
Violet Magical Properties:
Love, lust, peace, healing, protection, commitment, death and rebirth
Ruling planet – Venus
Sign – Cancer, Libra
Element – Water
Gender – Feminine

Wormwood

(Artemisia absinthium)
Wormwood Magical Properties:
Vengeance, attack magic, protection, divination, dreams, meditation, psychic powers
Ruling planet – Mars, Moon
Sign – Cancer, Scorpio
Element – Fire
Gender – Masculine

Crystals to work with when the Moon is in Cancer

Below are my suggestions for crystals to work with then the Moon is in Cancer based on the crystals that are associated with this sign but be guided by your intuition.

Calcite (orange)

Calcite (orange) magical properties
Amplification, energy, protection, grounding, centring, purification, peace, calm, emotions, balance, fear, depression,

problems, power, potential, breaking patterns, changes, inspiration, creativity, positive energy, wealth, abundance, leadership, perseverance, finances, confidence, determination, money, opportunities, clarity, productivity, release

Energy: Receptive
Element: Earth
Planet: Sun
Zodiac: Cancer

Chrysoprase

Chrysoprase magical properties

Courage, strength, wisdom, releasing, selfishness, imagination, happiness, success, balance, break barriers, protection, truth, healing, luck, prosperity, marriage, negative energy, transformation, love

Energy: Receptive
Element: Earth
Planet: Venus
Zodiac: Taurus, Cancer

Moonstone

Moonstone magical properties

New beginnings, Moon magic, intuition, calming, psychic abilities, balance, harmony, wishes, cleansing, uplifting, hope, meditation, emotions, love, divination, spirituality, wealth, truth, healing, sensuality, insight, peace, wisdom, communication, confidence, abundance, prosperity, dreams, fertility, travel

Energy Receptive
Element Water
Planet Moon
Zodiac Cancer, Libra, Scorpio
Birthstone June, September

Opal

Opal magical properties

Inspiration, change, creativity, imagination, releasing, spirituality, invisibility, emotions, dream work, visualization, appreciation, astral projection, power, psychic abilities, past life work

Energy	Projective, Receptive
Element	Earth, Air, Fire, Water
Planet	Mercury
Zodiac	Cancer, Libra, Pisces, Scorpio
Birthstone	October, April

Selenite

Selenite magical properties

Clarity, psychic protection, cleansing, balance, stability, emotions, divine, connections, spirituality, psychic abilities, spirit work, protection, healing, breaking barriers, decisions, intuition, meditation, money, success, love

Energy	Receptive
Element	Water
Planet	Moon
Zodiac	Cancer

Silver

Silver magical properties

Healing, communication, cleansing, energy, intuition, stability, spirituality, patience, perseverance, Moon magic, negative energy, protection, balance, psychic abilities, manifestation, wealth, prosperity, abundance, travel, dreams, emotions, purification, love, peace, astral travel

Energy	Receptive
Element	Water
Planet	Moon
Zodiac	Cancer

THE MOON IN LEO

Magical properties: Vitality, the heart, success, creativity, dignity, strong feelings, entertainment, opportunity, authority, fertility, confidence, courage, strength, leadership abilities, fame, career.

Bringing money to you, but only if it is badly needed.

Any shopping trips during this phase will be expensive, be prepared.

Business: Money talks, controlling situations, property deals.

Avoid: Love or emotions spells, detailed work. Don't spend too much! Remember to treat your colleagues with respect, don't be so bossy…Resentment.

Waxing Moon in Leo: Creativity rules. Spend some time with your loved ones.

Waning Moon in Leo: Watch TV or go to the movies. Get some Sun on your skin.

Element: Fire

Colours: Orange, red, green

Body: Heart, solar plexus

Herbs, Spices and Plants to work with when the Moon is in Leo

These are my suggestions based on the plants that are associated with Leo but trust your intuition.

Angelica

(Angelica archangelica)

Angelica Magical Properties:

Protection, healing, exorcism, divination, prosperity, luck, hex breaking, courage

Ruling planet – Sun, Venus

Sign – Gemini, Cancer, Leo, Libra

Element – Fire

Gender – Masculine

Bay

(Laurus nobilis)

Bay Magical Properties:

Protection, purification, strength, power, healing, creativity, spirituality, psychic powers

Ruling planet – Sun

Element – Fire

Gender – Masculine

Burdock

(Arctium lappa)

Burdock Magical Properties:

Protection, healing, cleansing

Ruling planet – Venus

Sign – Leo, Libra

Element – Water

Gender – Feminine

Chamomile

(Chameamelum nobile, Anthemis nobilis)

Chamomile Magical Properties:

Sleep, dreams, love, calm, money, relaxation, purification, balancing

Ruling planet – Sun

Sign – Leo
Element – Water
Gender – Masculine

Dill

(Anethum graveolens)
Dill Magical Properties:
Protection, love, lust, money, jealousy, balance, clarity, knowledge, magic
Ruling planet –Mercury
Sign – Cancer, Gemini, Leo
Element – Fire
Gender – Masculine

Fennel

(Foeniculum vulgare)
Fennel Magical Properties:
Purification, protection, healing
Ruling planet – Mercury
Element – Fire
Gender – Masculine

Frankincense

Frankincense Magical Properties:
Purification, spirituality, relaxation, focus, love, abundance
Ruling planet – Sun
Sign – Aries, Leo, Aquarius
Element – Fire
Gender – Masculine

Rue

(Ruta graveolens)
Rue Magical Properties:
Protection, health, healing, purification, balance, clarity,

anxiety, hex breaking
Ruling planet – Mars, Sun
Sign – Leo
Element – Fire
Gender – Masculine

Sunflower

(Helianthus annuus)
Sunflower Magical Properties:
Wishes, fertility, truth, integrity, luck, protection, loyalty, happiness
Ruling planet – Sun
Sign – Leo
Element – Fire
Gender – Masculine

Crystals to work with when the Moon is in Leo

Below are my suggestions for crystals to work with then the Moon is in Leo based on the crystals that are associated with this sign but be guided by your intuition.

Amber

Amber magical properties:
Manifesting, energy, beauty, Sun magic, power, wishes, intellect, clarity, wisdom, balance, purification, protection, psychic abilities, healing, calm, patience, love, sensuality, good luck, marriage, abundance, success, vitality, joy, sexuality, cleansing, stress, harmony, creativity

Energy: Projective
Element: Fire, Spirit
Planet: Sun
Zodiac: Leo

Carnelian

Carnelian magical properties

Grounding, protection, calm, concentration, confidence, self–worth, success, courage, creativity, negative energy, direction, control, organisation, opportunity, planning, psychic protection, jealousy, hate, harmony, depression, doubt, patience, stability, vitality, motivation, stamina, passion, truth, love, faith, honesty, trust, luck, abundance

Energy: Projective
Element: Fire
Planet: Sun
Zodiac: Taurus, Leo
Birthstone: May, June, July, August

Garnet

Garnet magical properties

Organisation, warrior spirit, protection, love, commitment, passion, sexuality, sensuality, attraction, depression, spiritual healing, success, self–confidence, energy, inspiration, perception, strength, survival, fear, courage, clarity, challenges, past life work, truth, compassion, deflecting negative energy, gossip, ambition, motivation, goals, purification, cleansing, balance, inner strength, self–empowerment, creativity, confidence, meditation, spirit work, nightmares, journeying, abundance, support

Energy: Projective
Element: Fie
Planet: Mars
Zodiac: Aries, Virgo, Capricorn, Leo, Aquarius
Birthstone: January

Labradorite

Labradorite magical properties

Transformation, cleansing, breaking patterns, potential, psychic abilities, intuition, confidence, spirituality, focus, protection, imagination, relaxation, soothing, energy, healing, stress, anxiety, luck, abundance, success, decisions, trust, changes, strength, courage, self–confidence, inspiration, perseverance, journeying, clarity, insight, meditation, depression, jealousy, grounding

Energy	Projective
Element	Water
Planet	Earth, Moon, Uranus
Zodiac	Aquarius, Sagittarius, Scorpio, Leo

Pyrite

Pyrite magical properties

Releasing, breaking patterns, clarity, protection, support, decisions, growth, success, inspiration, grounding, vitality, learning, perception, memory, wisdom, psychic abilities, healing, cleansing, prosperity, wealth, abundance, luck, strength, motivation, manifestation, finances, energy, Sun magic, power, focus, perseverance, confidence, divination, communication, self–confidence, meditation

Energy	Projective
Element	Fire
Planet	Mars, Sun
Zodiac	Leo

Quartz (clear)

Quartz (clear) magical properties

Purification, cleansing, healing, calming, emotions, strength, support, spirituality, energy, balance, psychic abilities, motivation, uplifting, decisions, anxiety, divine connection, amplifying, focus, meditation, manifestation, channelling, protection, negative energy, clarity, wisdom, concentration, learning, spirit work, communication, astral travel, divination, dreams, harmony

Energy	Projective, Receptive
Planet	Sun, Moon
Element	Fire, Water
Zodiac	Leo, Gemini, Capricorn

Rhodocrosite

Rhodochrosite magical properties

Power, potential, strength, confidence, healing, new beginnings, breaking barriers, releasing, joy, happiness, creativity, determination, manifestation, prosperity, abundance, love, emotions, peace, renewal, connection, balance, spirituality, harmony, energy

Energy	Projective
Element	Fire
Planet	Mars, Jupiter
Zodiac	Scorpio, Leo

Tiger's eye

Tiger's eye magical properties

Amplification, balance, harmony, releasing, fears, anxiety, courage, strength, self–confidence, focus, creativity, optimism, self–worth, protection, psychic abilities, healing, wealth, money, opportunity, abundance, prosperity, luck, success, commitment, determination, support, clarity, vitality, motivation, grounding, patience

Energy	Projective
Element	Fire, Earth
Planet	Sun
Zodiac	Leo, Capricorn

THE MOON IN VIRGO

♍

Magical properties: Organisation, detail, health, hard work, focus, planning, reaping your just rewards, career, employment, details, education, healing and stability. Fitness, refining your diet, purification, acquiring or improving skills. Ensuring a good 'harvest' from a project.

Your eye is keen on detail in this phase.

Business: Buying, selling, business travel, negotiations, demonstrations and stock taking.

Avoid: Job interviews, being too picky or critical. Being over critical and being too judgmental.

Waxing Moon in Virgo: Take a look at your health and make adjustments to a healthier way of living. Make new plans.

Waning Moon in Virgo: Get rid of bad habits. Have a good clear out, get rid of anything you no longer need or use.

Element: Earth

Colours: Yellow, green, black

Body: Digestive system

Herbs, Spices and Plants to work with when the Moon is in Virgo

These are my suggestions based on the plants that are associated with Virgo but trust your intuition.

Bergamot

(Mentha citrate)

Bergamot (Orange) Magical Properties:

Money, uplifting, success, Sun magic, banishing, purification

Planet – Mercury, Sun

Sign – Virgo, Aquarius

Element – Air

Gender – Masculine

Fennel

(Foeniculum vulgare)

Fennel Magical Properties:

Purification, protection, healing

Ruling planet – Mercury

Element – Fire

Gender – Masculine

Mandrake

(Mandragora officinale)

It's poisonous…enough said.

Mandrake Magical Properties:

Protection, love, prosperity

Ruling planet – Mercury

Sign – Taurus, Cancer, Virgo

Element – Fire

Gender – Masculine

Patchouli

(Pogostemon)

Patchouli Magical Properties:

Grounding, Earth magic, prosperity, money, protection, sex magic, balance, calm

Ruling planet – Saturn

Sign – Virgo

Element – Earth
Gender – Feminine

Sandalwood

(White Sandalwood – Santalum album)
(Red Sandalwood – Pterocarpus santalinus)
Sandalwood (Red) Magical Properties:
Meditation, love
Ruling planet – Venus, Jupiter
Sign – Sagittarius, Virgo
Element – Water
Gender – Feminine
Sandalwood (White) Magical Properties:
Death rites, purification, wishes, psychic powers
Ruling planet – Moon, Mercury
Sign – Sagittarius, Virgo
Element – Water
Gender – Feminine

Scullcap

(Scutellaria)
Scullcap Magical Properties:
Faithfulness, restoring, prosperity, stress, peace
Ruling planet – Saturn
Sign – Virgo
Element – Water
Gender – Feminine

Valerian

(Valeriana officinalis)
Valerian Magical Properties:
Protection, purification, love, sleep, peace, animal spirit, stress
Ruling planet – Venus, Jupiter

Sign – Virgo
Element – Water, Earth
Gender – Feminine

Crystals to work with when the Moon is in Virgo

Below are my suggestions for crystals to work with then the Moon is in Virgo based on the crystals that are associated with this sign but be guided by your intuition.

Agate (moss)

Agate (moss) magical properties

Nature, happiness, prosperity, wealth, longevity, friendship, success, abundance, healing, renewal, fertility, creativity, confidence, strength, love, beginnings, self–esteem, communication, emotions, stress, releasing, hope, trust, depression, growth, finances, cleansing, support, peace, stability, fears, luck, divination

Energy	Receptive
Element	Earth
Planet	Moon
Zodiac	Virgo, Gemini

Aragonite

Aragonite magical properties:

Balance, insight, grounding, peace, meditation, understanding, connections, family, friendship, calming, emotional balance, energy, releasing, stabilizing, spiritual development, concentration, flexibility, tolerance, patience, acceptance, support, stress relief

Energy:	Projective, Receptive
Element:	Earth
Planet:	Sun, Earth
Zodiac:	Virgo, Capricorn

Amazonite

Amazonite magical properties

Courage, soothing, bravery, calming, determination, focus, clarity, insight, self–confidence, self–assurance, respect, grace, intuition, understanding, balance, communication, creativity, inspiration, spirituality, success, luck, money, stress relief, energy, worries, fears

Energy: Receptive
Element: Earth
Planet: Saturn
Zodiac: Virgo, Pisces

Garnet

Garnet magical properties

Organisation, warrior spirit, protection, love, commitment, passion, sexuality, sensuality, attraction, depression, spiritual healing, success, self–confidence, energy, inspiration, perception, strength, survival, fear, courage, clarity, challenges, past life work, truth, compassion, deflecting negative energy, gossip, ambition, motivation, goals, purification, cleansing, balance, inner strength, self–empowerment, creativity, confidence, meditation, spirit work, nightmares, journeying, abundance, support

Energy: Projective
Element: Fie
Planet: Mars
Zodiac: Aries, Virgo, Capricorn, Leo, Aquarius
Birthstone: January

Jasper (red)

Jasper (red) magical properties

General: Protection, balance, stability, healing, grounding, stress, peace, happiness, confidence, fears, comfort, relaxation, release, beauty, astral travel, motivation, determination, energy, focus, prosperity, organisation, honesty, trust

Zodiac	Scorpio, Aries, Virgo
Birthstone	August
Energy	Projective
Element	Fire
Planet	Mars

Sugilite

Sugilite magical properties

Spirituality, wisdom, clarity, insight, courage, truth, passion, inspiration, healing, strength, channelling, psychic abilities, amplification, confidence, focus, love, emotions, releasing, calming, peace, protection, connection, balance, understanding, stress

Energy	Receptive
Element	Water
Planet	Mercury, Jupiter
Zodiac	Virgo

THE MOON IN LIBRA

♎

Magical properties: Contracts, partnership, love, charm, artistic talent, eloquence, friendships, peace, diplomacy, compromise, fairness. Bringing balance and harmony into your relationships. Marriage, partnerships, business contracts and agreements. Legal matters, justice, increasing your social life. Attracting love into your life.

You might feel a bit indecisive, ask a friend to help with decisions.

Business: Making new partnerships and collaborations, marketing, signing documents, negotiations, office socials.

Avoid: Flakey people! Not taking your share of the workload or responsibilities. Be positive, don't dither on decisions. Getting too stressed.

Waxing Moon in Libra: Get romantic. Buy yourself something pretty. Meet up with friends.

Waning Moon in Libra: Find some peace and relaxation. Go on a dinner date. Seek out the arts.

Element: Air

Colours: Black, blue, purple

Body: Kidneys, back

Herbs, Spices and Plants to work with when the Moon is in Libra

These are my suggestions based on the plants that are associated with Libra but trust your intuition.

Angelica

(Angelica archangelica)

Angelica Magical Properties:

Protection, healing, exorcism, divination, prosperity, luck, hex breaking, courage

Ruling planet – Sun, Venus

Sign – Gemini, Cancer, Leo, Libra

Element – Fire

Gender – Masculine

Bergamot

(Monarda didyma, Mondarda fistulosa)

Bergamot Magical Properties:

Abundance, meditation, sleep, dreams, clarity, friendship

Sign – Gemini, Libra

Element – Air

Gender – Feminine

Burdock

(Arctium lappa)

Burdock Magical Properties:

Protection, healing, cleansing

Ruling planet – Venus

Sign – Leo, Libra

Element – Water

Gender – Feminine

Elder

(Sambucus nigra/Canadensis)

Elder Magical Properties:

Protection, healing, faeries, purification, intuition, exorcism, hex breaking, rebirth

Ruling planet – Venus

Sign – Sagittarius, Aquarius, Libra

Element – Water

Gender – Feminine

Feverfew

(Tanacetum parthenium, Chrysanthemum parthenium)

Feverfew Magical Properties:

Protection, peace, health, purification

Ruling planet – Venus

Sign – Aries, Sagittarius, Libra

Element – Water

Gender – Masculine

Saint John's Wort

(Hypericum perforatum)

Saint John's Wort Magical Properties:

Protection, health, strength, love, divination, happiness, abundance, truth

Ruling planet – Sun

Sign – Aquarius, Libra

Element – Fire

Gender – Masculine

Thyme

(Thymus vulgaris, Thymus serpyllum)

Thyme Magical Properties:

Healing, health, peace, psychic powers, love, purification, courage, releasing, sleep, beauty

Ruling planet – Venus

Sign – Gemini, Taurus, Libra

Element – Water
Gender – Feminine

Violet

(Viola odorata)
Violet Magical Properties:
Love, lust, peace, healing, protection, commitment, death and rebirth
Ruling planet – Venus
Sign – Cancer, Libra
Element – Water
Gender – Feminine

Crystals to work with when the Moon is in Libra

Below are my suggestions for crystals to work with then the Moon is in Libra based on the crystals that are associated with this sign but be guided by your intuition.

Jade

Jade magical properties
Purification, harmony, friendship, luck, protection, clarity, manifestation, peace, courage, wealth, longevity, wisdom, prosperity, love, renewal, fertility, uplifting, calming, confidence, truth, psychic abilities, spirit work, dreams, past life work, healing, abundance, finances, creativity, manifestation, emotions

Energy	Receptive
Element	Water
Planet	Venus, Neptune
Zodiac	Pisces, Libra, Gemini, Taurus, Aries
Birthstone	March

Kyanite

Kyanite magical properties

Balance, harmony, calming, connection, psychic abilities, healing, communication, grounding, transformation, meditation, relaxation, luck, growth, leadership, new beginnings, clarity, decisions, stability, truth, vitality, abundance, spirituality, channelling, understanding, dreams

Energy	Receptive
Element	Water
Planet	Jupiter, Venus, Mars
Zodiac	Aries, Libra, Taurus

Lepidolite

Lepidolite magical properties

Transformation, soothing, calming, stress, happiness, changes, emotions, psychic abilities, spirituality, depression, divination, connection, strength, uplifting, luck, hope, balance, peace, sleep, harmony, decisions, addiction, releasing, trust, goals, optimism, patience, dreams, opportunities, support, love

Energy	Receptive
Element	Water
Planet	Jupiter, Neptune
Zodiac	Libra

Moonstone

Moonstone magical properties

New beginnings, Moon magic, intuition, calming, psychic abilities, balance, harmony, wishes, cleansing, uplifting, hope, meditation, emotions, love, divination, spirituality, wealth, truth, healing, sensuality, insight, peace, wisdom, communication, confidence, abundance, prosperity, dreams, fertility, travel

Energy	Receptive
Element	Water
Planet	Moon
Zodiac	Cancer, Libra, Scorpio
Birthstone	June, September

Opal

Opal magical properties

Inspiration, change, creativity, imagination, releasing, spirituality, invisibility, emotions, dream work, visualization, appreciation, astral projection, power, psychic abilities, past life work

Energy	Projective, Receptive
Element	Earth, Air, Fire, Water
Planet	Mercury
Zodiac	Cancer, Libra, Pisces, Scorpio
Birthstone	October, April

Tourmaline

Tourmaline magical properties

Calming, harmony, balance, insight, spirituality, protection, negative energy, transformation, courage, grounding, fears, creativity, understanding, power, motivation, commitment, patience, stability, releasing, emotions, anxiety, strength, happiness, protection, relaxation, friendship, astral travel

Energy	Receptive (pink, green, blue, black, watermelon)
	Projective (watermelon, red)
Element	Water (pink, blue, watermelon)
	Fire (watermelon, red)
	Earth (green, black)
Planet	Venus, Mars
Zodiac	Libra
Birthstone	October

Tourmaline (black)

Black tourmaline magical properties:

Understanding, self–confidence, psychic abilities, dispel negative energy, fears, grief, concentration, communication, relaxation, compassion, serenity, balance, transformation, healing, strength, tolerance, protection, grounding

Energy:	Receptive
Element:	Earth
Planet:	Venus, Mars
Zodiac:	Libra
Birthstone:	October

THE MOON IN SCORPIO

♏

Magical properties: Loyalty, ownership, mysteries, occult, psychic development, magic, personal power, divination, sex magic, passion, transformation, renewal, banishing, secrets, energy. Matters requiring insight. Increasing your libido or to attract passionate love (be careful though as relationships with a Scorpio influence are likely to be transformational and not always predictable). Healing of the mind and emotions. Scrying. Concentration, single mindedness.

Your shopping mode will be shrewd and, on the ball, you won't be gullible to any old sales pitch.

Watch out for suspicion and anger.

Business: Property deals, signing documents, problem solving, making important deals.

Avoid: Trusting new people, family parties, manipulation. Keeping secrets, being arrogant and spiteful. Becoming too jealous or controlling (not easy for a Scorpio!).

Waxing Moon in Scorpio: Learn something new, take a course in a subject you have always been interested in. Look at the stars.

Waning Moon in Scorpio: Do some shadow work, dig deep and seek out the answers.

Element: Water

Colours: Brown, black, red

Body: Reproductive and eliminatory organs

Herbs, Spices and Plants to work with when the Moon is in Scorpio

These are my suggestions based on the plants that are associated with Scorpio but trust your intuition.

Basil

(Ocimum basilicum)

Basil Magical Properties:

Wealth, money, prosperity, love, exorcism, protection, happiness, peace

Ruling planet – Mars

Sign – Scorpio

Element – Fire

Gender – masculine

Blackthorn (Sloe)

(Prunus spinosa)

Blackthorn Magical Properties:

Protection, exorcism, divination, healing

Ruling planet – Saturn and Mars

Sign – Scorpio

Element – Fire

Gender – Masculine

Horehound

(Marrubium vulgare)

Horehound Magical Properties:

Exorcism, protection, healing, clarity, peace, love

Ruling planet – Mercury

Sign –Scorpio

Element – Air

Gender – Masculine

Ivy

(Hedera helix)

Ivy Magical Properties:

Protection, healing, binding, love, abundance, fidelity

Ruling planet – Saturn, Moon

Sign – Scorpio

Element – Water

Gender – Feminine

Lily

(Lilium spp)

Lily Magical Properties:

Goddess, witchcraft, hexes, uncrossing, protection

Ruling planet – Moon, Venus

Sign – Scorpio

Element – Water

Gender – Feminine

Nettle

(Urtica dioica)

Nettle Magical Properties:

Healing, protection, lust, money, exorcism.

Ruling planet – Mars

Sign – Scorpio, Aries

Element – Fire

Gender – Masculine

Pennyroyal

(Mentha/Mamentha pulegium)

Pennyroyal Magical Properties:

Strength, protection, peace, initiation, Goddess, business

Ruling planet – Mars, Venus

Sign – Scorpio, Libra

Element – Fire

Gender – Masculine

Wormwood

(Artemisia absinthium)

Wormwood Magical Properties:

Vengeance, attack magic, protection, divination, dreams, meditation, psychic powers

Ruling planet – Mars, Moon

Sign – Cancer, Scorpio

Element – Fire

Gender – Masculine

Crystals to work with when the Moon is in Scorpio

Below are my suggestions for crystals to work with then the Moon is in Scorpio based on the crystals that are associated with this sign but be guided by your intuition.

Amethyst

Amethyst magical properties

Peace, protection, success, good luck, hidden knowledge, legal issues, spirituality, contentment, soothing, relaxation, calm, hope, patience, transformation, changes, breaking patterns, grounding, guilt, overcoming addictions, business matters, judgement, clarity, courage, travel, psychic protection, sleep, anxiety, focus, understanding, happiness, justice, intuition, inspiration, channeling, meditation

Energy: Receptive
Element: Water
Planet: Jupiter, Neptune
Zodiac: Pisces, Scorpio, Sagittarius
Birthstone: February

Bloodstone

Bloodstone magical properties:

Organisation, adaptability, anxiety, clarity, concentration, renewal, energy, self–confidence, connection, calm, protection, breaking barriers, selfishness, mysticism, insight, spirituality, truth, intuition, creativity, guidance, strength, healing, victory, wealth, money, power, invisibility, deception, negative energy, divine connection, past life, dreams

Energy: Projective
Element: Fire, Earth
Planet: Mars
Zodiac: Aries, Pisces, Scorpio
Birthstone: February, March

Citrine

Citrine magical properties:

Happiness, joy, Sun magic, negative energy, optimism, abundance, depression, stress, success, wealth, healing, intuition, creativity, confidence, changes, self–esteem, protection, psychic powers, fears, clarity, stamina, nightmares

Energy: Projective
Element: Fire
Planet: Sun, Jupiter
Zodiac: Scorpio
Birthstone: November

Fluorite

Fluorite magical properties

Magic, imagination, discernment, aptitude, psychic protection, protection, purification, calming, relaxation, tension, anxiety, organisation, structure, challenges, declutter, releasing, support, breaking patterns, intuition, confidence, reassurance, comforting, communication, balance, spirituality, decisions, manifestation, peace, meditation, grounding, healing, cleansing, channelling, past life work, fairy realm, amplifying, memory, power, emotions, depression, stability

Energy:	Projective
Element:	Water, Air
Planet:	Neptune
Zodiac:	Scorpio, Aquarius, Pisces

Jasper (red)

Jasper (red) magical properties

General: Protection, balance, stability, healing, grounding, stress, peace, happiness, confidence, fears, comfort, relaxation, release, beauty, astral travel, motivation, determination, energy, focus, prosperity, organisation, honesty, trust

Zodiac	Scorpio, Aries, Virgo
Birthstone	August
Energy	Projective
Element	Fire
Planet	Mars

Labradorite

Labradorite magical properties

Transformation, cleansing, breaking patterns, potential, psychic abilities, intuition, confidence, spirituality, focus, protection, imagination, relaxation, soothing, energy, healing, stress, anxiety, luck, abundance, success, decisions, trust, changes, strength, courage, self–confidence, inspiration, perseverance, journeying, clarity, insight, meditation, depression, jealousy, grounding

Energy	Projective
Element	Water
Planet	Earth, Moon, Uranus
Zodiac	Aquarius, Sagittarius, Scorpio, Leo

Malachite

Malachite magical properties

Changes, transformation, clarity, emotions, protection, support, healing, peace, travel, fears, growth, creativity, renewal, energy, wealth, money, opportunity, abundance, new beginnings, finances, success, business, focus, strength, wisdom, releasing, prosperity, breaking barriers, psychic abilities, manifestation, soothing, stress, love, power

Energy	Receptive
Element	Earth
Planet	Venus
Zodiac	Capricorn, Scorpio

Moonstone

Moonstone magical properties

New beginnings, Moon magic, intuition, calming, psychic abilities, balance, harmony, wishes, cleansing, uplifting, hope, meditation, emotions, love, divination, spirituality, wealth, truth, healing, sensuality, insight, peace, wisdom, communication, confidence, abundance, prosperity, dreams, fertility, travel

Energy	Receptive
Element	Water
Planet	Moon
Zodiac	Cancer, Libra, Scorpio
Birthstone	June, September

Opal

Opal magical properties

Inspiration, change, creativity, imagination, releasing, spirituality, invisibility, emotions, dream work, visualization, appreciation, astral projection, power, psychic abilities, past life work

Energy	Projective, Receptive
Element	Earth, Air, Fire, Water
Planet	Mercury
Zodiac	Cancer, Libra, Pisces, Scorpio
Birthstone	October, April

Rhodocrosite

Rhodochrosite magical properties

Power, potential, strength, confidence, healing, new beginnings, breaking barriers, releasing, joy, happiness, creativity, determination, manifestation, prosperity, abundance, love, emotions, peace, renewal, connection, balance, spirituality, harmony, energy

Energy	Projective
Element	Fire
Planet	Mars, Jupiter
Zodiac	Scorpio, Leo

Unakite

Unakite magical properties

Love, happiness, growth, wealth, success, harmony, decisions, support, balance, emotions, stability, confidence, strength, anxiety, nature, courage, transformation, releasing, spirituality

Energy	Receptive
Element	Fire, Water
Planet	Mars, Venus, Pluto
Zodiac	Scorpio

THE MOON IN SAGITTARIUS

Magical properties: Philosophy, adventure, journeys, integrity, motion, study, honesty, imagination, new techniques, optimism. Long distance travel. Learning. Writing and publishing. Religion and philosophy.

Get to the shops, there are fabulous bargains to be had.

Business: Advertising, promotions, business travel and meetings, money and legal issues.

Avoid: Divination or psychic work, pointless arguments. Sloppy work. Boredom. Taking unnecessary risks. Over–indulging.

Waxing Moon in Sagittarius: Start a new course. Go on holiday, travel or just get away somewhere.

Waning Moon in Sagittarius: Read about other places in the world. Meditate. Go for a walk.

Element: Fire

Colours: Purple, red, yellow

Body: Thighs

Herbs, Spices and Plants to work with when the Moon is in Sagittarius

These are my suggestions based on the plants that are associated with Sagittarius but trust your intuition.

Beech

(Fagus sylvatica)

Beech Magical Properties:

Wishes, creativity, spirituality, divination, luck, success

Ruling planet – Saturn

Sign – Sagittarius

Element – Air and Earth

Gender – Feminine

Birch

(Betula pendula, Betula pubescens, Betula lenta, Betula alba)

Birch Magical Properties:

Purification, protection, exorcism, new beginnings, courage, fertility, love, release

Ruling planet – Venus, Moon, Jupiter

Sign – Sagittarius

Element – Water, Air

Gender – Feminine

Cedar

(Cedrus spp)

Cedar Magical Properties:

Purification, money, protection, Goddess

Ruling planet – Sun, Jupiter

Sign – Sagittarius

Element – Fire

Gender – Masculine

Elder

(Sambucus nigra/Canadensis)

Elder Magical Properties:

Protection, healing, faeries, purification, intuition, exorcism, hex breaking, rebirth

Ruling planet – Venus

Sign – Sagittarius, Aquarius, Libra
Element – Water
Gender – Feminine

Feverfew

(Tanacetum parthenium, Chrysanthemum parthenium)
Feverfew Magical Properties:
Protection, peace, health, purification
Ruling planet – Venus
Sign – Aries, Sagittarius, Libra
Element – Water
Gender – Masculine

Hawthorn

(Crataegus oxacantha/monogyna)
Hawthorn Magical Properties:
Happiness, fertility, love, protection, purification, forgiveness, faeries, hope
Ruling planet – Mars, Venus
Sign – Sagittarius
Element – Fire
Gender – Masculine

Nutmeg

(Myristica fragrans)
Nutmeg Magical Properties:
Money, luck, fidelity, protection
Ruling planet – Jupiter
Element – Fire
Gender – Masculine

Oak

(Quercus alba, Quercus robur, Quercus petraea)
Oak Magical Properties:

Healing, health, protection, money, fertility, luck, strength, vitality, power
Ruling planet – Sun, Jupiter, Mars
Sign – Sagittarius
Element – Fire, Water
Gender – Masculine

Rowan

(Sorbus acuparia)
Rowan Magical Properties:
Psychic powers, power, success, protection, love, spirituality, faeries, divination, healing, inspiration
Ruling planet – Sun, Mercury
Sign – Sagittarius
Element – Fire
Gender – Masculine

Sage

(salvia officinalis)
Sage Magical Properties:
Protection, wishes, wisdom, purification, stimulating, intuition, abundance, success.
Ruling planet – Jupiter
Element – Air
Gender – Masculine

Sandalwood

(White Sandalwood – Santalum album)
(Red Sandalwood – Pterocarpus santalinus)
Sandalwood (Red) Magical Properties:
Meditation, love
Ruling planet – Venus, Jupiter
Sign – Sagittarius, Virgo
Element – Water

Gender – Feminine
Sandalwood (White) Magical Properties:
Death rites, purification, wishes, psychic powers
Ruling planet – Moon, Mercury
Sign – Sagittarius, Virgo
Element – Water
Gender – Feminine

Crystals to work with when the Moon is in Sagittarius

Below are my suggestions for crystals to work with then the Moon is in Sagittarius based on the crystals that are associated with this sign but be guided by your intuition.

Amethyst

Amethyst magical properties
Peace, protection, success, good luck, hidden knowledge, legal issues, spirituality, contentment, soothing, relaxation, calm, hope, patience, transformation, changes, breaking patterns, grounding, guilt, overcoming addictions, business matters, judgement, clarity, courage, travel, psychic protection, sleep, anxiety, focus, understanding, happiness, justice, intuition, inspiration, channeling, meditation

Energy: Receptive
Element: Water
Planet: Jupiter, Neptune
Zodiac: Pisces, Scorpio, Sagittarius
Birthstone: February

Goldstone

Goldstone magical properties
Ambition, luck, goals, determination, persistence, achievements, success, calm, emotions, energy, enthusiastic, confidence, self–belief, inner self, personal development, possibilities, courage, direction, clarity, uplifting, optimism, protection,

deflects negative energy, knowledge, perception, manifestation, creativity, faith, energy flow, spirituality, abundance, wealth, grounding, perspective, ambition, drive, ingenuity, money, generosity, willpower, goals, emotions, divination (see also copper for additional magical properties)

Energy:	Receptive/Projective
Element:	Fire, Earth
Planet:	Jupiter, Venus
Zodiac:	Sagittarius

Labradorite

Labradorite magical properties

Transformation, cleansing, breaking patterns, potential, psychic abilities, intuition, confidence, spirituality, focus, protection, imagination, relaxation, soothing, energy, healing, stress, anxiety, luck, abundance, success, decisions, trust, changes, strength, courage, self–confidence, inspiration, perseverance, journeying, clarity, insight, meditation, depression, jealousy, grounding

Energy	Projective
Element	Water
Planet	Earth, Moon, Uranus
Zodiac	Aquarius, Sagittarius, Scorpio, Leo

Lapis lazuli

Lapis lazuli magical properties

Protection, manifestation, meditation, psychic protection, problem solving, knowledge, clarity, decisions, memory, spirituality, peace, energy, organisation, concentration, stress, luck, negative energy, wealth, abundance, success, love, confidence, truth, renewal, intellect, wisdom, leadership, legal issues, sleep, anxiety, harmony, understanding

Energy	Receptive
Element	Water

Planet	Venus, Jupiter
Zodiac	Sagittarius

Obsidian (black)

Obsidian (black) magical properties

Truth, healing, clarity, illusions, breaking barriers, integrity, grounding, centring, strength, courage, protection, cleansing, meditation, stress, calming, relaxation, depression, anxiety, wealth, luck, focus, emotions, power, determination, success, patience, perseverance, releasing, spirit work, spirituality, challenges, past life work, divination

Energy	Projective
Element	Fire, Earth, Water
Planet	Saturn, Jupiter
Zodiac	Sagittarius

Obsidian (snowflake)

Obsidian (snowflake) magical properties

Grounding, protection, birth & death, rebirth, connection, challenges, past life work, dispel negative energy, releasing, healing, centering, scrying

Energy	Projective
Element	Fire
Planet	Saturn, Jupiter
Zodiac	Sagittarius

Quartz (smoky)

Quartz (smoky) magical properties

Grounding, centring, focus, negative energy, decisions, cooperation, creativity, emotions, depression, anxiety, jealousy, nature, protection, calming, manifestation, wishes, divination, meditation, insight, guidance, uplifting, fears, relaxation, releasing, abundance, luck, prosperity

Energy	Receptive

Element	Earth
Planet	Saturn, Jupiter
Zodiac	Capricorn, Sagittarius

Sodalite

Sodalite magical properties

Creativity, communication, peace, friendship, clarity, truth, connection, knowledge, wisdom, emotions, balance, divination, psychic abilities, cleansing, confidence, fears, love, intuition, decisions, perseverance, anxiety, insight, organisation, self–esteem, releasing, understanding, harmony, learning, dreams, meditation

Energy	Receptive
Element	Water
Planet	Jupiter, Venus
Zodiac	Sagittarius

THE MOON IN CAPRICORN

♑

Magical properties: Building, rules and regulations, discipline. Career matters, ambition, logic, planning, recognition, business, determination, drive, politics, financial gain, spiritual matters, organization, stability.

Avoid the shops at this time, it will just be a headache.

Business: Work some extra hours (but not too much, it is all about balance), deal with money, organization, new ventures.

Avoid: Emotional relationships, conflict, being too strategic. Being inflexible and over working. Worrying about finances.

Waxing Moon in Capricorn: Do the housework. Start new ventures.

Waning Moon in Capricorn: Sort your finances. Talk to friends and family about your goals and desires.

Element: Earth

Colours: Red, brown, black

Body: Knees, bones

Herbs, Spices and Plants to work with when the Moon is in Capricorn

These are my suggestions based on the plants that are associated with Capricorn but trust your intuition.

Benzoin

(Styrax benzoin)

Benzoin Magical Properties:

Prosperity, purification, calming, confidence, love, lust

Ruling planet – Sun, Venus

Sign – Capricorn

Element – Air

Gender – Masculine

Comfrey

(Symphytum officinale)

Comfrey Magical Properties:

Money, travel, protection, healing, hex breaking, bringing together

Ruling planet – Saturn

Sign – Capricorn

Element – Water

Gender – Feminine

Marjoram

(Origanum majorana)

Marjoram Magical Properties:

Love, happiness, health, protection, marriage, grief

Ruling planet – Mercury

Sign – Aries, Capricorn

Element – Air

Gender – Masculine

Pine

(Pinus)

Pine Magical Properties:

Centring, focus, Dragon magic, protection, truth, abundance, purification, fertility, healing

Ruling planet – Mars, Saturn

Sign – Capricorn
Element – Air, Fire
Gender – Masculine

Plantain

(Plantago spp. Lanceolata, Plantago major, Plantago media)
Plantain Magical Properties:
Strength, protection, healing, energy, courage
Ruling planet – Venus
Sign – Capricorn
Element – Earth
Gender – Feminine

Poppy

(Papaver spp)
Poppy Magical Properties:
Love, sleep, money, luck, fertility, rebirth, grief
Ruling planet – Moon, Mars, Venus
Sign – Capricorn
Element – Water
Gender – Feminine

Solomon's Seal

(Polygonatum officinale)
Solomon's Seal Magical Properties:
Wisdom, knowledge, protection, exorcism, success, Elementals, purification
Ruling planet – Saturn
Sign – Capricorn
Element – Water
Gender – Feminine

Witch Hazel

(Hamamelis virginiea)

Witch Hazel Magical Properties:
Protection, divining, balance, grief
Ruling planet – Sun, Saturn
Sign – Capricorn
Element – Fire
Gender – Masculine

Crystals to work with when the Moon is in Capricorn

Below are my suggestions for crystals to work with then the Moon is in Capricorn based on the crystals that are associated with this sign but be guided by your intuition.

Apache tear

Apache tear magical properties
Grief, releasing, blockages, peace, acceptance, forgiveness, balance, emotions, change, insight, clarity, success, hope, healing, grounding, protection, meditation, dispel negative energy

Energy: Projective
Element: Fire
Planet: Saturn, Jupiter
Zodiac: Aries, Capricorn
Birthstone: November

Aragonite

Aragonite magical properties:
Balance, insight, grounding, peace, meditation, understanding, connections, family, friendship, calming, emotional balance, energy, releasing, stabilizing, spiritual development, concentration, flexibility, tolerance, patience, acceptance, support, stress relief

Energy: Projective, Receptive
Element: Earth
Planet: Sun, Earth
Zodiac: Virgo, Capricorn

Garnet

Garnet magical properties

Organisation, warrior spirit, protection, love, commitment, passion, sexuality, sensuality, attraction, depression, spiritual healing, success, self–confidence, energy, inspiration, perception, strength, survival, fear, courage, clarity, challenges, past life work, truth, compassion, deflecting negative energy, gossip, ambition, motivation, goals, purification, cleansing, balance, inner strength, self–empowerment, creativity, confidence, meditation, spirit work, nightmares, journeying, abundance, support

Energy: Projective
Element: Fie
Planet: Mars
Zodiac: Aries, Virgo, Capricorn, Leo, Aquarius
Birthstone: January

Jet

Jet magical properties

Protection, fears, dispel negative energy, psychic attacks, depression, solutions, psychic abilities, past life work, support, grief, divination

Energy Receptive
Element Earth, Spirit
Planet Saturn
Zodiac Capricorn

Malachite

Malachite magical properties

Changes, transformation, clarity, emotions, protection, support, healing, peace, travel, fears, growth, creativity, renewal, energy, wealth, money, opportunity, abundance, new beginnings, finances, success, business, focus, strength, wisdom, releasing, prosperity, breaking barriers, psychic abilities, manifestation, soothing, stress, love, power

Energy	Receptive
Element	Earth
Planet	Venus
Zodiac	Capricorn, Scorpio

Quartz (clear)

Quartz (clear) magical properties

Purification, cleansing, healing, calming, emotions, strength, support, spirituality, energy, balance, psychic abilities, motivation, uplifting, decisions, anxiety, divine connection, amplifying, focus, meditation, manifestation, channelling, protection, negative energy, clarity, wisdom, concentration, learning, spirit work, communication, astral travel, divination, dreams, harmony

Energy	Projective, Receptive
Planet	Sun, Moon
Element	Fire, Water
Zodiac	Leo, Gemini, Capricorn

Quartz (smoky)

Quartz (smoky) magical properties

Grounding, centring, focus, negative energy, decisions, cooperation, creativity, emotions, depression, anxiety, jealousy, nature, protection, calming, manifestation, wishes, divination, meditation, insight, guidance, uplifting, fears, relaxation, releasing, abundance, luck, prosperity

Energy	Receptive
Element	Earth
Planet	Saturn, Jupiter
Zodiac	Capricorn, Sagittarius

Tiger's eye

Tiger's eye magical properties

Amplification, balance, harmony, releasing, fears, anxiety, courage, strength, self–confidence, focus, creativity, optimism, self–worth, protection, psychic abilities, healing, wealth, money, opportunity, abundance, prosperity, luck, success, commitment, determination, support, clarity, vitality, motivation, grounding, patience

Energy	Projective
Element	Fire, Earth
Planet	Sun
Zodiac	Leo, Capricorn

THE MOON IN AQUARIUS

Magical properties: Inventions, social life, future goals, divination, personal choices, past life work, spirit work, innovation, creativity, independence, friendship and breaking bad habits. Technology, science, forming and maintaining friendships, establishing groups. Gaining more freedom or autonomy. Developing intuition.

Take a trip out to the more unusual stores, find something bizarre.

Be careful of bringing in rebellious energies though. Becoming more detached or overcoming being too emotional.

Business: Property deals, money issues, refurbishing, working with colleagues.

Avoid: Discussing personal issues. Being distracted and ignoring individuals. Breaking the rules and rebelling for the sake of it.

Waxing Moon in Aquarius: Decorate. Dance, socialize, do something that makes you happy.

Waning Moon in Aquarius: Volunteer for a local charity. Have lunch with friends. Reorganise your home.

Element: Air

Colours: Blue, green, white

Body: Calves, ankles, circulatory and glandular systems

Herbs, Spices and Plants to work with when the Moon is in Aquarius

These are my suggestions based on the plants that are associated with Aquarius but trust your intuition.

Bergamot

(Monarda didyma, Mondarda fistulosa)

Bergamot Magical Properties:

Abundance, meditation, sleep, dreams, clarity, friendship

Sign – Gemini, Libra

Element – Air

Gender – Feminine

Cypress

(Cupressus sempervirens)

Cypress Magical Properties:

Release, binding, grief, protection, healing

Ruling planet – Saturn

Sign – Aquarius

Element – Earth

Gender – Feminine

Elder

(Sambucus nigra/Canadensis)

Elder Magical Properties:

Protection, healing, faeries, purification, intuition, exorcism, hex breaking, rebirth

Ruling planet – Venus

Sign – Sagittarius, Aquarius, Libra

Element – Water

Gender – Feminine

Fennel

(Foeniculum vulgare)

Fennel Magical Properties:
Purification, protection, healing
Ruling planet – Mercury
Element – Fire
Gender – Masculine

Frankincense

Frankincense Magical Properties:
Purification, spirituality, relaxation, focus, love, abundance
Ruling planet – Sun
Sign – Aries, Leo, Aquarius
Element – Fire
Gender – Masculine

Myrrh

(Commiphora myrrha)
Myrrh Magical Properties:
Protection, purification, healing, Crone, Underworld, courage
Ruling planet – Mars, Sun
Sign – Aries, Aquarius
Element – Water
Gender – Feminine

Saint John's Wort

(Hypericum perforatum)
Saint John's Wort Magical Properties:
Protection, health, strength, love, divination, happiness, abundance, truth
Ruling planet – Sun
Sign – Aquarius, Libra
Element – Fire
Gender – Masculine

Crystals to work with when the Moon is in Aquarius

Below are my suggestions for crystals to work with then the Moon is in Aquarius based on the crystals that are associated with this sign but be guided by your intuition.

Aquamarine

Aquamarine magical properties:

Calming, soothing, serenity, sea magic, travel, intuition, wisdom, creativity, compassion, relaxation, truth, secrets, clarity, enlightenment, reasoning, flexibility, moderation, judgement, tolerance, order, spirituality, psychic abilities, peace, purification

Energy: Receptive
Element: Water
Planet: Moon, Neptune
Zodiac: Pisces, Aquarius
Birthstone: March

Fluorite

Fluorite magical properties

Magic, imagination, discernment, aptitude, psychic protection, protection, purification, calming, relaxation, tension, anxiety, organisation, structure, challenges, declutter, releasing, support, breaking patterns, intuition, confidence, reassurance, comforting, communication, balance, spirituality, decisions, manifestation, peace, meditation, grounding, healing, cleansing, channelling, past life work, fairy realm, amplifying, memory, power, emotions, depression, stability

Energy: Projective
Element: Water, Air
Planet: Neptune
Zodiac: Scorpio, Aquarius, Pisces

Garnet

Garnet magical properties

Organisation, warrior spirit, protection, love, commitment, passion, sexuality, sensuality, attraction, depression, spiritual healing, success, self–confidence, energy, inspiration, perception, strength, survival, fear, courage, clarity, challenges, past life work, truth, compassion, deflecting negative energy, gossip, ambition, motivation, goals, purification, cleansing, balance, inner strength, self–empowerment, creativity, confidence, meditation, spirit work, nightmares, journeying, abundance, support

Energy: Projective
Element: Fie
Planet: Mars
Zodiac: Aries, Virgo, Capricorn, Leo, Aquarius
Birthstone: January

Hematite

Hematite magical properties

Grounding, money, decisions, manifestation, finances, healing, focus, clarity, stability, protection, balance, divination, problem solving, emotions, self–esteem, productivity, doubt, anxiety, communication, strength

Energy: Projective
Element: Fire, Earth
Planet: Saturn
Zodiac: Aries, Aquarius

Labradorite

Labradorite magical properties

Transformation, cleansing, breaking patterns, potential, psychic abilities, intuition, confidence, spirituality, focus, protection, imagination, relaxation, soothing, energy, healing, stress, anxiety, luck, abundance, success, decisions, trust, changes, strength, courage, self–confidence, inspiration, perseverance, journeying, clarity, insight, meditation, depression, jealousy, grounding

Energy	Projective
Element	Water
Planet	Earth, Moon, Uranus
Zodiac	Aquarius, Sagittarius, Scorpio, Leo

Moldavite

Moldavite magical properties:

Transformation, changes, spiritual development, intuition, growth, healing, love, Otherworld communication, astral travel

Energy	Projective
Element	Fire
Planet	Uranus
Zodiac	Aquarius

THE MOON IN PICSES

♓

Magical properties: Spiritual and psychic matters, but guard against confusion and deception. Creativity, the arts, care, compassion, dream work, inner work, secrets, imagination, transitions, secrets, banishing, empathy, past life work, luck, magic in general. Enhance or develop psychic abilities. Letting life flow.

Any trips out should be interspersed with breaks, you might tire easily.

Business: Document signing, financial agreements, marketing, stock taking.

Avoid: Busy communal places. Being too easily influenced, self–doubt and being drawn into unrealistic expectations. Changing your mind.

Waxing Moon in Pisces: Enjoy the arts and be creative. Treat yourself to some luxury pamper time.

Waning Moon in Pisces: Listen to music, watch your dreams, look after yourself.

Element: Water

Colours: White, green, blue

Body: Feet

Herbs, Spices and Plants to work with when the Moon is in Pisces

These are my suggestions based on the plants that are associated with Pisces but trust your intuition.

Bladder wrack

(Fucus vesiculosus)

Bladder wrack Magical Properties:

Protection, sea magic, money, psychic powers, weather magic

Ruling planet – Moon

Sign – Pisces

Element – Water

Gender – Feminine

Dulse Magical Properties:

Lust, love, harmony, peace, protection

Ruling planet – Moon

Sign – Pisces

Element – Water

Gender – Feminine

Fern

(Pteridophyte)

Fern Magical Properties:

Spirit work, Underworld, Faerie, protection, love, invisibility

Ruling planet – Mercury

Sign – Taurus, Pisces

Element – Air

Gender – Masculine

Geranium

(Pelargonium maculatum/P.odoratissimum/Hortorum)

Geranium Magical Properties:

Protection, fertility, love, socialise, aura cleansing

Ruling planet – Venus
Sign – Pisces
Element – Water
Gender – Feminine

Lily of the Valley

(Convallaria majalis)
Lily of the Valley Magical Properties:
Happiness, cleansing, success, faeries, divination, magic
Ruling planet – Mercury
Sign – Pisces
Element – Air
Gender – Masculine

Lungwort

(Pulmonaria officinalis)
Lungwort Magical Properties:
Healing, cleansing, releasing, calming
Ruling planet – Mercury
Sign – Taurus, Pisces
Element – Earth
Gender – Masculine

Meadowsweet

(Spiraea filipendula, Filipendula ulmaria, Spirea ulmaria)
Meadowsweet Magical Properties:
Peace, happiness, love
Ruling planet – Jupiter
Sign – Gemini, Pisces
Element – Air
Gender – Masculine

Rose

(Rosa spp)

Rose Magical Properties:

Love, psychic powers, healing, luck, protection, peace, mysteries, knowledge, dreams, friendship, death and rebirth, abundance

Ruling planet – Venus, Moon

Sign – Pisces

Element – Water

Gender – Feminine

Willow

(Salix alba, Salix fragilis)

Willow Magical Properties:

Love, protection, healing, cleansing, wishes, release, inspiration, intuition

Ruling planet – Moon

Sign – Pisces

Element – Water

Gender – Feminine

Crystals to work with when the Moon is in Pisces

Below are my suggestions for crystals to work with then the Moon is in Pisces based on the crystals that are associated with this sign but be guided by your intuition.

Amethyst

Amethyst magical properties

Peace, protection, success, good luck, hidden knowledge, legal issues, spirituality, contentment, soothing, relaxation, calm, hope, patience, transformation, changes, breaking patterns, grounding, guilt, overcoming addictions, business matters, judgement, clarity, courage, travel, psychic protection, sleep, anxiety, focus, understanding, happiness, justice, intuition, inspiration, channelling, meditation

Energy: Receptive

Element: Water
Planet: Jupiter, Neptune
Zodiac: Pisces, Scorpio, Sagittarius
Birthstone: February

Amazonite

Amazonite magical properties

Courage, soothing, bravery, calming, determination, focus, clarity, insight, self–confidence, self–assurance, respect, grace, intuition, understanding, balance, communication, creativity, inspiration, spirituality, success, luck, money, stress relief, energy, worries, fears

Energy: Receptive
Element: Earth
Planet: Saturn
Zodiac: Virgo, Pisces

Bloodstone

Bloodstone magical properties:

Organisation, adaptability, anxiety, clarity, concentration, renewal, energy, self–confidence, connection, calm, protection, breaking barriers, selfishness, mysticism, insight, spirituality, truth, intuition, creativity, guidance, strength, healing, victory, wealth, money, power, invisibility, deception, negative energy, divine connection, past life, dreams

Energy: Projective
Element: Fire, Earth
Planet: Mars
Zodiac: Aries, Pisces, Scorpio
Birthstone: February, March

Fluorite

Fluorite magical properties

Magic, imagination, discernment, aptitude, psychic protection,

protection, purification, calming, relaxation, tension, anxiety, organisation, structure, challenges, declutter, releasing, support, breaking patterns, intuition, confidence, reassurance, comforting, communication, balance, spirituality, decisions, manifestation, peace, meditation, grounding, healing, cleansing, channelling, past life work, fairy realm, amplifying, memory, power, emotions, depression, stability

Energy: Projective
Element: Water, Air
Planet: Neptune
Zodiac: Scorpio, Aquarius, Pisces

Jade

Jade magical properties

Purification, harmony, friendship, luck, protection, clarity, manifestation, peace, courage, wealth, longevity, wisdom, prosperity, love, renewal, fertility, uplifting, calming, confidence, truth, psychic abilities, spirit work, dreams, past life work, healing, abundance, finances, creativity, manifestation, emotions

Energy Receptive
Element Water
Planet Venus, Neptune
Zodiac Pisces, Libra, Gemini, Taurus, Aries
Birthstone March

Larimar

Larimar magical properties

Peace, clarity, healing, inspiration, spirituality, understanding, calming, soothing, uplifting, emotions, fears, depression, patience, creativity, love, communication, friendship, guidance, happiness, decisions, relaxation, meditation, wisdom, divine, harmony

Energy:	Receptive
Element:	Water/Fire/Spirit
Planet:	Neptune
Zodiac:	Pisces

Opal

Opal magical properties

Inspiration, change, creativity, imagination, releasing, spirituality, invisibility, emotions, dream work, visualization, appreciation, astral projection, power, psychic abilities, past life work

Energy	Projective, Receptive
Element	Earth, Air, Fire, Water
Planet	Mercury
Zodiac	Cancer, Libra, Pisces, Scorpio
Birthstone	October, April

Turquoise

Turquoise magical properties

Purification, negative energy, protection, balance, relaxation, emotions, stress, spirituality, energy, depression, clarity, wisdom, understanding, psychic abilities, insight, intuition, past life work, communication, wealth, abundance, finances, prosperity, luck, decisions, friendship, uplifting, meditation, love, harmony

Energy	Receptive
Element	Earth
Planet	Venus, Neptune
Zodiac	Sagittarius, Pisces, Aquarius
Birthstone	December

Void Moon

When the Moon is void this refers to the Moon when it is moving from one astrological sign to another, it can take a whole day, or it can be just a few hours or even minutes. But during that time the Moon is not assigned to any particular astrological sign. It is a bit of a 'blind spot' when it comes to working magic. Probably best to sit this out before working any magic until the Moon meets up with its astrological friends again.

Your Personal Sign

We probably all know the answer straight away to the question "what sign are you?". But this usually refers to our Sun sign i.e. our sign of the Zodiac. But you also have a Moon sign, and it can have just as much influence on your life as your Sun sign, sometimes even more.

The date and time of your birth dictates your Sun, star or zodiac sign, it is the position of the Sun at that point when you entered the world. And the position of the Moon at the time of your birth dictates your Moon or lunar sign.

If you wondered why you are a Scorpio, say, and your friend is too but their personality is completely different it may be that you have different Moon signs.

Finding out your Moon sign can be done by hand but is a long and complicated process (just the thought of it makes my head explode). However, in today's techno world the internet offers much easier options. Do a browser search for 'free birth charts' or 'find my Moon sign' it should bring up several sites that will do all the work for you. However, you will need to input some details:

- Date of birth.
- The town or city you were born in, if it was out in the wilds then go for the nearest big town.
- The time you were born, this may be more difficult as some birth certificates don't have it noted. Hopefully a parent or family member can help you out. Go with your best guesstimate if the exact time isn't known. Put a time in rather than 'not known', a guess is better than nothing.

The site will then produce a chart for you with lots of information. It may look complicated but take some time to read through it.

Your Moon sign will be the zodiac mentioned next to the word 'Moon'. So, although my horoscope (Sun) sign is Scorpio, my Moon sign is '10° 15' Pisces'.

The chart will also show the sign that is your ascendant, mine is Libra. Your ascendant may well be the same as your Sun or Moon sign, but it could also be different like mine.

Each of these will play a part in adding their energy and characteristics to your personality.

Once you have your signs sorted, make a list of all the suggested qualities that are associated with them. Go through each one and be honest with yourself. Do they truly represent you? Do you identify with one sign more than another?

As the Moon travels through each astrological sign it brings different energies. If you keep an eye on each day and which sign the Moon is in as well as the Moon phase it will help you to understand your moods and emotions.

Sun or Star sign Zodiac

Here are the dates for your 'star sign' or what is actually your Sun sign. This is the date that you were born on. I have also given a very short description of the type of personality traits that come under each sign. It isn't definitive and as mentioned before, will also depend on what your Moon sign is as well along with many other planetary influences on the day you were born.

Aries – 21st March to 19th April

Ruled by Mars, impatient, competitive, fighting spirit, confident, bossy, attention, leader, adventurous, possible diva traits

Taurus – 20th April to 20th May

Ruled by Venus, sensual, romantic, luxury, relaxed or full head on, comfort, know your own mind, opinions, stubborn, loyal, dependable

Gemini – 21st May to 20th June

Ruled by Mercury, communication, technology, curiosity, adventure, changeable, busy, gossip

Cancer – 21st June to 22nd July

Ruled by the Moon, sensitive, intuitive, nurturing, psychic, loyal, family orientated, likes home comforts, can be moody

Leo – 23rd July to 22nd August

Ruled by the Sun, dramatic, showy, likes the spotlight, leadership, likes praise, big hearted, generous, helpful, protective, fun

Virgo – 23rd August to 22nd September

Ruled by Mercury, communication, analysing, opinions, judgements, helpful, good listener, always thinking, perfectionist, loves nature

Libra – 23rd September to 22nd October

Ruled by Venus, beauty, love, charmer, loves the arts and the finer things in life, fighter, balanced, justice, social, takes things at their own pace

Scorpio – 23rd October to 21st November

Ruled by Pluto, power, control, mysteries, likes the 'dark' side, sensitive, can read people well, intense, loyal

Sagittarius – 22nd November to 21st December

Ruled by Jupiter, happy, energetic, confident, big personality, travel, free spirit, optimistic, ambitious, busy, upbeat, wisdom, truth

Capricorn – 22nd December to 19th January

Ruled by Saturn, traditional, plays by the rules, ambitious, cautious, hard–working, strength, devoted, supportive, trustworthy

Aquarius – 20th January to 18th February

Ruled by Uranus, unique, original, authentic, team player, popular, social, connections, environmental, hardworking, tenacious

Pisces – 19th February to 20th March

Ruled by Neptune, prefers to escape reality, imagination, creative, loves the arts, moody, dreamer, compassion, healer, sensitive

Egyptian Zodiac

The Egyptian horoscope is one of the oldest calendars. Based on the ancient Egyptian gods it is laid out according to the birth date. It has twelve signs each one embodying the characteristics of the deity. The Egyptians halved the day into temporal hours, the length of those depended on the time of year. A summer hour was longer than that of a winter one. Although they did divide the day into twenty–four hours. Temporal hours were later adjusted to equinoctial hours to help the astronomers with their charts and drawings.

The dates shown here include the months used after influence from the ancient Greeks and the traditional dates based on the Decans (a decan is the subdivision of an astrological sign).

Thoth

The month of Thoth – 29th August to 27th September

Traditional dates – 1st–19th April, 8th–17th November

Keywords: Wisdom, learning, resourceful, creativity, balance, honest, enterprise, helping, enthusiasm, modesty, clarity.

Horus

The month of Horus – 29th September to 27th October

Traditional dates – 20th April to 7th May, 12th–19th August

Keywords: Influence, strength, stubbornness, vengeance, charisma, intelligence, courage, impatience, understanding, intense.

Wadjet

The month of Wadjet – 28th October to 26th November

Keywords: Ambition, caution, pessimism, helpful, careful, loyalty.

Sekhmet

The month of Sekhmet – 27th November to 26th December.

Traditional dates – 29th July to 11th August, 30th October to 7th November

Keywords: Optimism, morals, happiness, principles, protection, honesty, destruction, sensitivity, anger, impatience, vengeance, imagination.

Sphinx

The month of Sphinx: 27th December to 25th January

Keywords: Discipline, sensible, adaptable, discretion, discerning, humour, proud, haughty.

Shu

The month of Shu: 26th January to 24th February.

Keywords: Creativity, talent, success, fear, conscientious, hesitation, humour, warmth, principles.

Isis

The month of Isis: 25th February to 26th March.

Traditional dates: 11th–31st March, 18th–29th October, 19th–31st December.

Keywords: Ambition, dedication, passion, activity, honour, confidence, respect, outspoken, idealism, intuition, logic, generosity.

Osiris

The month of Osiris: 27th March to 25th April.

Traditional dates: 1st–10th March, 27th November to 18th December.

Keywords: Enthusiasm, directness, helpful, adventure, confidence.

Amun–Ra

The month of Amun–Ra: 26th April to 25th May.

Traditional dates: 8th–21st January, 1st–11th February.

Keywords: Helpful, generosity, success, love, power, warmth.

Hathor

The month of Hathor: 26th May to 24th June.

Keywords: Charm, healing, sensuality, romance, protection, cunning, beauty.

Phoenix

The month of Phoenix: 25th June to 24th July

Keywords: Optimistic, determination, flexibility, caring, adventure, strength, stubborn.

Anubis

The month of Anubis: 25th July to 28th August.

Traditional dates: 8th–27th May, 29th June to 13th July.

Keywords: Protection, truth, honesty, intelligence, cunning, sympathy.

Nile

Traditional dates: January 1st–7th/June 19th–28th/September

1st–7th/November 18th–26th

Keywords: Peace, logic, practical, caution, protection, beginnings, nurturing.

Mut

Traditional dates: 22nd–31st January, 8th–22nd September.

Keywords: Focus, determination, shy, patience, charm, irony.

Geb

Traditional dates: 12–29th February, 20th–31st August.

Keywords: Justice, fertility, beginnings, sensitivity, proud, grounding, danger, modesty.

Seth

Traditional dates: 28th May to 18th June, 28th September to 2nd October.

Keywords: Impulsive, perfection, challenges, darkness, weather, deceit, envy.

Bastest

Traditional dates: 14th–28th July, 23–27th September, 3rd–17th October

Keywords: Intuition, psychic abilities, kindness, anxiety, protection, truth, security, fertility, generosity, comfort, balance.

Chinese Zodiac

The Chinese zodiac has an animal for each year, rotating every twelve years. Pick the animal for the year you were born.

Rat: 2020, 2008, 1996, 1984, 1972, 1960, 1948, 1936

Keywords: Kindness, resourceful, versatility, quick witted

Ox: 2021, 2009, 1997, 1985, 1973, 1961, 1949, 1937

Keywords: Dependable, strength, determination, diligence

Tiger: 2022, 2010, 1998, 1986, 1974, 1962, 1950, 1938
Keywords: Competitive, confidence, bravery

Rabbit: 2023, 2011, 1999, 1987, 1975, 1963, 1951,1939
Keywords: Responsibility, kindness, elegance, quiet

Dragon: 2024, 2012, 2000, 1988, 1976, 1964, 1952, 1940
Keywords: Enthusiasm, intelligence, confidence

Snake: 2025, 2013, 2001, 1989, 1977, 1965, 1953, 1941
Keywords: Intelligence, wisdom, enigmatic

Horse: 2026, 2014, 2002, 1990, 1978, 1966, 1954, 1942
Keywords: Energy, activity

Goat/Ram: 2027, 2015, 2003, 1991, 1979, 1967, 1955, 1943
Keywords: Sympathy, gentle, calm

Monkey: 2028, 2016, 2004, 1992, 1980, 1968, 1956, 1944
Keywords: Curiosity, intelligence, sharp

Rooster: 2029,2017, 2005, 1993, 1981, 1969, 1957, 1945
Keywords: Courage, hard–working, observation

Dog: 2030, 2018, 2006, 1994, 1982, 1970, 1958, 1946
Keywords: Honesty, love, prudence

Pig: 2019, 2007, 1995, 1983, 1971, 1959, 1947
Keywords: Diligence, generosity, compassion

Native American Zodiac

You will find animals or representations of them throughout the

Native American culture and spiritual beliefs. Your date of birth will decide which animal is your zodiac sign. You could also work magic associated with these animals, corresponding to the month.

Jan 20th – 18th February: Otter

Keywords: Independence, loyal, fun, unconventional, goals, creativity, intuition, nurturing, wisdom, truth, friendship, curiosity, memory, enthusiasm

Feb 19th – 20th March: Wolf

Keywords: Compassion, family, love, consideration, solitude, balance, generosity, protection, intuition

March 21st – 19th April: Falcon

Keywords: Wisdom, vision, clarity, spirit, energy, grounding, decisions, leadership, challenges, adventure, observation, self–confidence, passion

April 20th – 20th May: Beaver

Keywords: Strategy, goals, love, tenacity, creativity, foundations, hard–working, security, self– assurance, home, calm

May 21st – 20th June: Deer

Keywords: Passion, social, communication, wisdom, energy, compassion, nurturing, peace, stability, organisation

June 21st – 21st July: Woodpecker

Keywords: Community, family, faithful, devotion, nurturing, intuition, money, nature

July 22nd – 22ndt August: Salmon

Keywords: Enthusiasm, generosity, passion, fun, success,

objectives, compassion, creativity

August 23rd – 22nd September: Bear

Keywords: Observations, deep thoughts, practical, heart, hard work, strength, truth, acceptance, sincerity, curiosity, comfort

September 23rd – 22nd October: Raven

Keywords: Magic, psychic abilities, truth, business, finances, charisma, perception, passion, new projects

October 23rd – 21st November: Snake

Keywords: Psychic abilities, healing, secrets, spirituality, calm, adaptable, flexibility, goals, cunning

November 22nd – 21st December: Owl

Keywords: Truth, wisdom, honesty, flexibility, patience, hope, optimism, focus, discovery, energy

December 22nd – 19th January: Snow Goose

Keywords: Spirituality, enlightenment, love, strategy, comfort, challenges, love, patience, home, friendship

Celtic Zodiac

As most cultures work with the Moon in some form or another, this zodiac draws upon Celtic beliefs working with the monthly Moons. Did they create a Celtic zodiac? I am not convinced as to the age of this system, but it is interesting nonetheless.

Work with your date of birth to find your sign or use the energy for working magic that corresponds.

December 24th – 20th January: Stag/Deer

Keywords: Leadership, integrity, solar magic, vision, persistence, patience, pride, hard work, leadership, honour, aspirations

January 21st – 17th February: Cat

Keywords: Psychic abilities, sensuality, quick witted, intelligence, independence, creativity

February 18th – 17th March: Snake/Adder

Keywords: Wisdom, power, healing, calm, mysteries, communication, flexibility, curiosity

March 18th – 14th April: Fox

Keywords: Sincerity, stealth, sexuality, adventure, cunning, fun, intelligence

April 15th – 12th May: Bull

Keywords: Loyal, humour, stubbornness, stability, grounding, strength, advice, truth, trust

May 13th – 9th June: Seahorse

Keywords: Fearless, imagination, shape shifting, resourceful, changes, memory, attention, intellect, money

June 10th – 7th July: Wren

Keywords: Charm, nurturing, creativity, inspiration, happiness, the arts, intuition, insight

July 8th – 4th August: Horse

Keywords: Passion, achievements, goals, power, direction, charisma, strength, competition

August 5th – 1st September: Salmon

Keywords: Intuition, goals, fun, wisdom, creativity, spirituality, dream work, meditation, inspiration

September 2nd – 29th September: Swan

Keywords: Honour, faithful, beauty, love, nobility, passion, organization, spirituality, expression

September 30th – 27th October: Butterfly

Keywords: Idealistic, peace, social, connections, dreams, movement, new ideas, happiness

October 28th – 24th November: Wolf

Keywords: Drive, survival, purpose, opinion, bravery, obstacles, ethics, honour, spirituality

November 25th – 23rd December: Hawk/Falcon

Keywords: Ambition, intuition, psychic abilities, focus, generosity, kindness, goals

Celtic Tree Moons

I am not sure how old the Celtic Tree calendar is, some say it is as ancient as the Ogham, others say it is a more modern invention, however it is a lovely calendar to follow and is based on thirteen months each named for trees, all based on the Ogham. You can use the added energy from the trees to enhance your Moon magic.

Birch Moon: 24th December – 20th January, new beginnings, goal setting, creativity and fertility

Rowan Moon: 21st January – 17th February, preparation, sowing the seeds, astral travel, protection

Ash Moon: 18th February – 17th March, travel, transformation, spiritual journeys

Alder Moon: 18th March – 14th April, balance and fertility

Willow Moon: 15th April – 12th May, healing and expressing the emotions

Hawthorn Moon: 13th May – 9th June, fertility, love and prosperity

Oak Moon: 10th June – 7th July, growth, success, blessings

Holly Moon: 8th July – 4th August, celebration, wishes, protection

Hazel Moon: 5th August – 1st September, inner wisdom, intuition

Vine Moon: 2nd September – 29th September, balance, bringing plans to fruition

Ivy Moon: 30th September – 27th October, strength and endurance

Reed Moon: 28th October – 24th November, connection with the ancestors, looking within

Elder Moon: 25th November – 23rd December, endings and beginnings

Moon Magic Grimoire

This section covers all kinds of information associated with the Moon, read through it for interest or use it as a reference guide.

Drawing down the Moon

Drawing down the Moon is a term used to call deity directly into your body. Performed in ritual usually by the High Priestess or Priest. The embodiment of the goddess in the form of Moon energy is drawn into the person's body. Once done the Goddess speaks through the Priest/ess. The strength of the experience can vary from a brief encounter to full possession, it is or should be an altered state of consciousness. The ritual is usually performed on or around the full Moon.

It is a beautiful ritual to perform but does take work and energy and can be quite overwhelming. I don't recommend attempting this until you are proficient in the Craft.

The High Priest/ess will stand in the centre of the circle with her feet shoulder width apart and raising her arms up and out, to welcome the Goddess.

They will then recite some words to invite the Goddess into them.

Often the Charge of the Goddess is used (attributed originally to Gerald Gardner and Aleister Crowley, but the familiar version is said to have come from Doreen Valiente), but you can use any words that you feel are appropriate.

The history of the ritual may have begun in ancient Greece, Thessalian witches were believed to have been in control of the Moon. There is also a poem within the Vangelo (The Gospel of the Witches) which defines drawing down the Moon. The ritual is now practiced by many Wiccan covens, but the modern version may have had its roots within Gardnerian Wicca.

I have taken inspiration from the Charge of the Goddess and created my own:

Words for Drawing Down the Moon by Rachel Patterson

Move your feet apart and raise your arms to welcome the Moon

When you feel the Moon's energy and the presence of her spirit, say:

I am the Mother of all life
I am the emotion of living
The beams of mystery
The spark of creation in the skies
I am the reflection on the water

Whenever you have need during the dark hours
Any day of the week
Look up to the skies and feel my power
I am the spirit within you

Whether on your own or gathered as a group
Look to me, learn from me
And honour my wisdom
I will share my knowledge, intuition and power

Celebrate under the night sky
Dance in the light of my beams
Eat, drink, sing and make merry
All in honour of my name

I am the spirit of knowledge and love for the earth
Share my love and emotion with all beings
Strive towards your wishes and desires
Keep your faith strong

Love and respect one another

My power and might will open doors for you
I will shine the light to guide your way
My spirit and energy will fill you with the power
And desire to keep you on the right pathway

I open my heart to the Goddess within me
Blessed be!

Listen and learn from the power and insight the Goddess provides for you. Please also remember to ground properly after including this in your ritual.

Moon Bathing

What is Moon bathing? It is exactly what it sounds like. Similar to sun bathing but without the need for lotion or health risks. You also don't even need to be outside. Lay or stand under the Moon outside or sit beside a window indoors and allow the Moonlight to bathe you in her beams. It doesn't even matter what the Moon phase is, although if you are finely tuned into her magic you may be able to tell a difference between the energy of the phases.

Literally just sit or stand quietly, look up at her or close your eyes and breath…

Soak up the energy she provides, allow it to wash over you and fill your soul. Moon bathing is relaxing, calming, refreshing, energizing, replenishing, nurturing, transforming, insightful and connecting.

Crystals under the full Moon

Social media is full of memes advising everyone to pop their crystals out to cleanse, purify and soak up the moonlight on a full Moon…but I don't…and it isn't because I don't like being told what to do…

I do put some crystals out on the full Moon but not all of them. There are some crystals that I think suit the Moonlight but others that I find work better by being put out in either the Sunshine or even the rain and wind. For instance, I put stones like moonstone (obviously!), quartz and blue lace agate out in the Moonlight.

But for stones such as sunstone, topaz, tiger's eye, carnelian, amber and all the fiery stones I like to put them in the sunshine so that they soak up the masculine energy instead.

And then we have watery stones, if it is raining then there are some stones that love being out in it such as amethyst, blue lace agate and lapis. (Note: Don't put porous stones out in the rain… they may not be there when you get back…).

You can even take it further and separate them into the four elements and put out air stones on a windy day and bury earth stones (carefully and mark where you put them) in the soil.

Air stones would be things like amethyst, citrine and turquoise. For earth these stones might be agate, jasper and jet.

Obviously, some of the stones will fit into a couple of the categories and I also go by colour; yellow, red and orange stones go in the Sun and white, blue and pale stones go under the Moon.

Trust your intuition…but I prefer not to lump all the stones under the Moon because it is incredibly powerful and I personally feel that some of my crystals work better with Sun, wind or water energy instead. Go with what feels right for you…

Programming and charging your crystals

When you want to work with a crystal within magic you will need to charge it with the energy of your intent. Basically, you need to tell it what you would like it to do. Do be polite and ask it nicely but make sure you really push that energy. The strength of your will and commitment to the outcome is paramount in any spell work. That crystal needs to be very, very clear about what you expect from it and what you would like it to do.

A lot of crystals also have lunar associations, below you will find a list of some of them.

Generally, most white stones have receptive energy and are associated with the Moon.

Moon crystals are useful for these magical workings: Sleep, psychic abilities, luck, fortune, purity, protection, truth, meditation, peace, sincerity, justice and to ward doubt and fear.

Use a crystal to make yourself a lunar charm to help keep you in synch with the Moon phases and the phases of your own life.

Moon Crystals

The list of crystals below are all strongly associated with the Moon.

Agate (moss)

Agate (moss) magical properties

Nature, happiness, prosperity, wealth, longevity, friendship, success, abundance, healing, renewal, fertility, creativity, confidence, strength, love, beginnings, self–esteem, communication, emotions, stress, releasing, hope, trust, depression, growth, finances, cleansing, support, peace, stability, fears, luck, divination

Energy Receptive
Element Earth
Planet Moon
Zodiac Virgo, Gemini

Howlite

Howlite magical properties

Understanding, wisdom, connection, truth, meditation, focus, stress, anxiety, calm, strength, peace, releasing, emotions, selfishness, communication, creativity, inspiration, motivation, concentration, support, patience, relaxation, courage, past life work, astral travel

Energy:	Projective
Element:	Earth
Planet:	Moon, Earth
Zodiac:	Gemini, Virgo

Jasper (grey)

Jasper (grey) magical properties

General: Protection, balance, stability, healing, grounding, stress, peace, happiness, confidence, fears, comfort, relaxation, release, beauty, astral travel, motivation, determination, energy, focus, prosperity, organisation, honesty, trust

Energy	Receptive
Element	Air
Planet	Moon
Zodiac	Scorpio, Aries, Virgo

Labradorite

Labradorite magical properties

Transformation, cleansing, breaking patterns, potential, psychic abilities, intuition, confidence, spirituality, focus, protection, imagination, relaxation, soothing, energy, healing, stress, anxiety, luck, abundance, success, decisions, trust, changes, strength, courage, self–confidence, inspiration, perseverance, journeying, clarity, insight, meditation, depression, jealousy, grounding

Energy	Projective
Element	Water
Planet	Earth, Moon, Uranus
Zodiac	Aquarius, Sagittarius, Scorpio, Leo

Moonstone

Moonstone magical properties

New beginnings, Moon magic, intuition, calming, psychic abilities, balance, harmony, wishes, cleansing, uplifting, hope, meditation, emotions, love, divination, spirituality, wealth, truth, healing, sensuality, insight, peace, wisdom, communication, confidence, abundance, prosperity, dreams, fertility, travel

Energy	Receptive
Element	Water
Planet	Moon
Zodiac	Cancer, Libra, Scorpio

Mother of pearl

Mother of pearl magical properties

Protection, calming, healing, stress relieving, relaxation, soothing, emotions, intuition, imagination, sensitivity, adaptability, harmony, fear, love, clarity, decisions, organization, endurance

Energy	Receptive
Element	Water
Planet	Moon, Neptune
Zodiac	Cancer, Gemini

Opal

Opal magical properties

Love, loyalty, consciousness, faithful, peace, emotions, moods, freedom, independence, psychic abilities, creativity, release, self–worth, memory, spontaneity

Energy	Receptive
Element	Water
Planet	Moon, Neptune
Zodiac	Cancer, Libra, Scorpio, Pisces

Pearl

Pearl magical properties

Honesty, innocence, purity, integrity, focus, concentration, meditation, tranquility, wisdom, faith, sincerity, truth

Energy	Receptive
Element	Water

Planet	Moon
Zodiac	Gemini, Cancer

Quartz (rose)

Quartz (rose) magical properties

Love, happiness, emotions, spirituality, growth, fears, healing, sexuality, passion, calming, soothing, stress, depression, sleep, luck, wisdom, inspiration, success, intuition, grounding, balance, prosperity, self–esteem, harmony, trust, jealousy, gossip, beauty, peace, cleansing, fertility

Energy	Receptive
Element	Earth, Water
Planet	Venus, Moon
Zodiac	Taurus

Quartz (clear)

Quartz (clear) magical properties

Purification, cleansing, healing, calming, emotions, strength, support, spirituality, energy, balance, psychic abilities, motivation, uplifting, decisions, anxiety, divine connection, amplifying, focus, meditation, manifestation, channelling, protection, negative energy, clarity, wisdom, concentration, learning, spirit work, communication, astral travel, divination, dreams, harmony

Energy	Projective, Receptive
Planet	Sun, Moon
Element	Fire, Water
Zodiac	Leo, Gemini, Capricorn

Selenite

Selenite magical properties

Clarity, psychic protection, cleansing, balance, stability, emotions, divine, connections, spirituality, psychic abilities, spirit work, protection, healing, breaking barriers, decisions, intuition, meditation, money, success, love

Energy	Receptive
Element	Water
Planet	Moon
Zodiac	Cancer

Silver

Silver magical properties

Healing, communication, cleansing, energy, intuition, stability, spirituality, patience, perseverance, Moon magic, negative energy, protection, balance, psychic abilities, manifestation, wealth, prosperity, abundance, travel, dreams, emotions, purification, love, peace, astral travel

Energy	Receptive
Element	Water
Planet	Moon
Zodiac	Cancer

Touchstone

You can keep a touchstone just for you. A unique personal power source of energy that is aligned with your own vibes. Pick a stone that resonates with you, it might correspond with your zodiac sign perhaps or just be a crystal that you love. Cleanse and charge it in the full Moon, then keep it by your bed for seven nights. This will create a powerful stone for you to draw personal energy from, one that is connected to you directly. Recharge it regularly under the full Moon.

Shells

Living near the sea I am lucky enough to be able to collect sea shells easily, I love walking along the beach and always come back with pockets full of shells. So how about the magical properties of the humble sea shell? Obviously, sea shells are associated with water, I often use a shell to represent west when

I am in ritual, I also use them in water element witch bottles. The Moon controls the tides of the ocean, so shells are also associated with the lunar magic. Being associated with water and the Moon I think the shell works perfectly in spells for emotions too.

Shells also have an association with the goddess Aphrodite, so can also be used for love spells. Use a shell as a love drawing talisman. In the past shells were used in some parts of the world as currency so they have the association of money and prosperity. Use in money drawing spell pouches (with a silver coin and some mint or basil) or pop a small shell in your purse.

Think about what a shell is, it is a protective covering for the creature inside making shells also good for protection. Use them in your witch bottles or strung on a necklace for this purpose. You can also pop a shell on the collar of your dog or cat to bring protection.

Shells can be used in divination, use in a set with pebbles, crystals and bones to cast a reading. Shells can have runes or symbols carved or painted on them.

Particular shells also have their own individual meanings:

Abalone – General use and containment of empowered herbs and stones. Very good for love spells, balance and affirmations. An abalone amulet will protect against negative energy. Abalone talismans will bring creativity. Wearing an abalone shell will bring protection against negative energy but also protection from depression, sorrow and fear. The abalone shell brings creativity and inspiration. Abalone make good tools to use for balancing your chakras because it carries the colours of the rainbow. Abalone shells make good holders for incense.

Auger - (And any long pointy shaped shells) due to their shape they bring a masculine energy…and can be used for fertility, strength, protection or courage.

Clam shells – Purification and love but also friendships.

Conch shell –This shell is used to make a loud noise when

blown so it works well for summoning spells, communication and clearing away confusion. It is a symbol of truthful speech and strength and love.

Cockles – Love, friendship, relationships and emotions.

Cone shells – Time to take charge and lead by example with this shell but it may also indicate a situation where you need to retreat or take cover.

Cowrie shell – Prosperity, money, love and fertility – if you look at a cowrie shell it looks very 'feminine' (i.e. yoni shaped). String cowrie shells onto red cord or a thread long enough to hang over your tummy for fertility and once you are pregnant to protect your unborn child. Make a necklace from charged cowrie shells to wear for general protection.

Whelks – Dramatic positive change and getting a grip on a situation. Also, useful for decision and direction spell work.

Limpets – Courage, confidence, endurance and strength.

Scallops – A good all–purpose shell but also for travel and movement.

Oysters – Good fortune, love and passion but also for banishing spell work.

Sand dollars (echinoids) – Wisdom and knowledge.

Moon snails – Lunar magic, psychic abilities, purification and peace.

If you are collecting your own sea shells please make sure that the creature is not still inside it, if you do pick up one with a living creature toss it back into the water. If you are purchasing your sea shells in a shop or from the internet do make sure they are from sustainable and viable sources.

If you collected the shells from the sea shore then I don't think they need any preparation, they have the energy of the sea and the Sun already in them. If, however you purchased your shells from a store you might like to sit them in a bowl of salt water for a few hours, or in the Sunlight or Moonlight.

Crystal Water

Water (or any liquid come to that, although water is generally pure and takes on the energy of the crystal well) can be charged with the magical power of a crystal. You can even get special water bottles that have crystal infills. But crystal water or crystal elixir as it is often called, is easy to make yourself. You will need to check that the crystal is SAFE to drop into water, make sure it won't disintegrate and that it isn't toxic, as that would be bad... very bad.

Crystal essence is water that has been imbued with the energy of a single specific crystal. An elixir is usually a mixture of essences blended with an intent in mind. The most straightforward way to create a crystal essence is to drop a crystal into a glass or bottle of water. Cover with a lid and leave in the Moonlight for a while, a few hours or overnight will be fine.

The safer method is to put the crystal inside a container before popping that into water. This way you make sure that no toxic elements leak out directly into the water. Place the crystal in a small glass or bottle and then place that into a larger container that has the water in. Your prepared crystal essence can then be mixed with another made from a different crystal to combine the energy or used on its own.

- The water can be drunk, add to the power by stating your intent before you sip the water.
- Use to bathe an area of your body or add to bath water.
- Anoint your pulse points, chakras, altars or magical tools.
- Dab onto candles and pouches for spell work.
- Feed your plants with the water.
- Sprinkle around your home to clear out negative energy.

Moon Deities

If you are planning a ritual to celebrate one of the Moon phases or need some extra power for a particular Moon spell, try calling upon a deity that is associated with the Moon. I would recommend doing some proper research on your chosen deity first if you have not worked with them before. Calling in random deities with no knowledge of them can be a dangerous past time. There are many Moon deities, but here is a list of some of them:

Aine – an Irish goddess of summer and the Moon, she looks after livestock and crops. She is also known as a Fairy Queen and a Sun goddess. Associated with midsummer/Litha and Lughnasadh. Call upon her for: Love, protection, fertility, wealth, sovereignty, Moon magic, Sun magic, fairy magic.

Andraste – a warrior goddess of Britain – she was invoked by Queen Boadicea/Boudicca. Call upon her for: Strength, courage, warrior, victory, battle, guidance, inspiration, honour.

Anu – a Mesopotamian/Sumerian sky god viewed as Father of the gods and ruler of the heavens, the stars, and the spirits. Call upon him for: Goals, wishes, spirituality.

Anuket – Egyptian goddess of the crescent Moon. She is responsible for the annual flooding of the river Nile. She watches over agriculture and all food growth along with wealth and prosperity. Call upon her for: Wealth, prosperity, growth, fertility, nourishment, contentment.

Aradia – An Italian goddess of the Moon, she is often referred to as Queen or Goddess of the Witches. Call upon her for: Moon magic, calling down the Moon, Witchcraft, Magic.

Arianrhod – Welsh goddess of the Moon. She forms the triple goddess triad with Blodeuwedd and Cerridwen. Her name translates as 'silver disc', she is often referred to as Goddess of the Silver Wheel. Arianrhod guides the dead to the other side and rules the sky and the sea as well as the Moon. She can shapeshift into an owl. She is also known as one of the goddesses of Avalon. Call upon her for: Moon magic, dream work, psychic abilities, divination, past lives, reincarnation, other realms, feminine power, retribution, karma.

Artemis – Greek goddess associated with the crescent Moon, she is goddess of the hunt and rules over forest and animals. Artemis protects those in childbirth and young girls. She is a strong, independent virgin goddess. Usually depicted holding a bow and arrow. Call upon her for: Warrior, strength, courage, night magic, protection, independence, defence, justice, nature.

Asherah – Ancient West Semitic goddess, often referred to as Queen of the Gods. Also known as 'She who walks on the sea' or 'holiness'. You will find her name in the Old Testament she is consort of Yahweh. Asherah is a goddess of the sea. Call upon her for: Divine wisdom, feminine energy, feminine issues, strength, self–esteem, self– confidence, courage, kindness, love, divination, insight, justice, fertility, compassion, healing, nurturing.

Athene/Athena – Greek goddess of weaving, a trait often connected with the Moon. She is a goddess of wisdom and a full on warrior gal complete with protection, defence and all the hero stuff. Her skills also cover cunning, metal work and weapons. Basically, don't mess with her. Call upon Athene for: protection, courage, leadership, victory, discipline, control, wisdom, defence, cunning.

Blodeuwedd – Welsh goddess, who has a connection with the Moon, and death and reincarnation (aspects of the Dark Moon). Her name translates as 'flower face' as she was created out of plants by magicians, who then later changed her into an owl (it was a whole punishment betrayal thing). As a maiden she forms part of the triad with Arianrhod and Cerridwen. A goddess of spring and one of the five goddesses of Avalon. Call upon her for: Beauty (temporary), spring, reincarnation, transformation, betrayal, manipulation, strength, power, love, wisdom, innocence.

Cerridwen – Welsh goddess usually shown hunched over her cauldron filled with Awen (inspiration and wisdom). Generally seen as the crone aspect of the triad with Blodeuwedd and Arianrhod. A goddess of the Moon she covers death, rebirth, magic, and divination of all kinds. Also, one of the five goddesses of Avalon. Call upon Cerridwen for: Inspiration, creativity, wisdom, death, rebirth, divination, prophecy, spiritual transformation, justice, fertility, luck.

Chang–O – Chinese goddess of the Moon. Banished from heaven along with her husband, destined to be mere mortals. Chang–O took a double dose of immortality pill, without sharing with her husband (rude). She floated up to the Moon, leaving her husband behind. Call upon her for: Love, partnership, courage, power, fertility, growth, manifesting, belief, self–confidence, new beginnings, transformation.

Coyolxauhqui – Aztec Moon goddess. Her name translates as 'painted with bells'. Apparently in most images she is wearing bells on her cheeks, which must be terribly uncomfortable. When the full Moon rises you can see the bells as rosy red. In a bit of a misunderstanding Coyolxauhqui had her head cut off, which was flung up into the sky, where it became the Moon. Call upon her for: Moon magic, family issues, balance,differences.

Cybele/Kybele –Phrygian goddess of the Underworld and associated with the dark Moon. Worshipped in ancient Greece and found in Romany mythology. Some associate her with the Greek/Minoan goddess Rhea. She is known as mother of the gods. Associated with mountains, caves, nature, and wild animals particularly hawks, lions and bees. Call upon her for: Love, victory, strength, relationships, humour, healing, health, fun, stability.

Demeter – Ancient Greek goddess of the full Moon. She is an Olympian goddess of agriculture, harvest, and fertility. Featuring in the Eleusinian mysteries alongside her daughter Persephone. She forms a triad with Persephone and Hecate, Demeter taking on the mother role. Equivalent to the Roman goddess Ceres. Call upon her for: Abundance, harvest, mysteries, fertility, marriage, relationships, life and death, rebirth, justice, grief, suffering, parenthood.

Diana – Goddess of the Moon, hunter, and Roman Queen of Witches. She is queen of the open skies and may also have been worshipped as a Sun goddess as well as the Moon. Call upon her for: Fertility, abundance, harvest, protection, children, nurturing, hunting, childbirth.

Epona – Celtic/Saxon/Gaulish goddess of horses. Ancient Britains gave her the title 'Rigantona' which translates as Great Queen. Call upon her for: Protection, animals, love, fertility, providence, leadership, authority.

Ereshkigal – A Sumerian Queen of the Underworld and in her aspect as the Crone is goddess of the Dark Moon. An excellent goddess to work with to seek your shadow side. She is a powerful deity. Call upon her for: Shadow work, justice, power, love, wisdom.

Freyja/Freya – although not called a Moon goddess, many of her attributes connect her with both the Full and Dark Moons. A Norse goddess of love, beauty, war, and fertility. She leads souls of dead warriors to the Otherworld. She rides a chariot driven by two cats, so she must be powerful to get cats to do what they are told! Call upon her for: Love, beauty, fertility, war, dearth, happiness, sex, sensuality, inspiration.

Hathor – Egyptian goddess of the Moon, associated with the dark Moon. Goddess of the Underworld but also ruler of the sky. She is a mother to all Egyptians. Definitely packing a powerful punch of feminine energy having given birth to the universe, she must have been exhausted.

Call upon her for: Love, feminine energy, beauty, sexuality, happiness, romance, music, the arts, protection (primarily for women).

Hekate – Greek goddess of the dark Moon. She covers new beginnings and magic of all kinds. She walks the ancient roads and pathways, particularly associated with crossroads, those where three roads cross. She forms a triad with Persephone and Demeter, she being the Crone aspect. She guards the spirit world and wields power over all realms. She is one seriously intimidating goddess, but wise beyond words. Call upon her for: Moon magic, witchcraft, herb magic, necromancy, protection, prosperity, new beginnings, decisions, mysteries, knowledge, learning, inner work, shadow work.

Hera – Greek Olympian Queen of gods, she covers marriage, childbirth and looking after women (she's got her hands full then). Although she can help when called upon, she has a jealous side and can be vengeful particularly when infidelity is involved. Call upon her for: Love, humour, forgiveness, romance, creativity, marriage, strength, courage, self– confidence, jealousy.

Hestia – Greek goddess of the hearth and home she is also a fire goddess. Her Roman equivalent is Vesta. The Greeks did not have statues of this goddess as it was believed she didn't take human form, instead she appeared as the flames of fire in the hearth. Hestia was the first born of the Olympian goddesses. She is absolutely about new beginnings and the start of all things. This goddess is the ultimate super house keeper and home maker, with added omnipotence. Call upon her for: Home life, domesticity, fire magic, devotion, wishes, manifesting, unity, new beginnings, spirituality, blessings.

Ilmatar/Luonnotar – A Finnish–Ugrian creation goddess of the air whose duck laid eggs on her knee. The eggs fell and the whites became the Moon, the yolks the Sun and the shell pieces became the stars. She is goddess of the crescent Moon. Call upon her for: New beginnings, creativity, inspiration, traditions, fertility, nature, the arts, magic.

Inanna – Sumerian goddess of the full Moon and the stars, also known as Ishtar in Babylon. She is Queen of heaven and earth. She has a reputation for being a little bit saucy which led her to be linked to fertility rituals. She does look after her followers, dishing out the rules and keeping them safe. Call upon her for: Love, fertility, warrior, strength, courage, seduction, sensuality, protection, justice.

Ishtar – Babylonian goddess of the full Moon, also known as Inanna in Sumeria. A goddess of love, sex, and war (pretty much covers it all then) she is a bit of a floozy, taking many lovers to bed (I don't judge). Call upon her for: Love, passion, sexuality, fertility, womanhood, independence, insight, inspiration, wishes.

Isis – Egyptian goddess Queen of Egypt. She is looked upon as Mother Moon, Queen of Sorcery, and the life force within the river Nile. Isis taught her people useful skills, those they would need to survive and flourish, no being high up in the sky for this one, she got down with her subjects (very practical woman). Call upon her for: Magic, dreams, divination, harvest, perspective, love, spirituality, faithfulness, destiny, revitalisation, fulfilment, inner beauty, spirituality, rebirth, feminine energy, knowledge, motherhood, healing, changes, manifesting.

Ixchel – Mayan goddess of the Moon, weaving, water, and childbirth. Mother of all Mayan deities she rules over life and death and bears the title of 'Keeper of Souls'. Her name translates as 'Lady Rainbow'. She spends her time constantly changing from a beautiful young woman into an old crone, it must be both exhausting and confusing. Call upon her for: Weather magic, fertility, health, healing, childbirth, water magic, rainbow magic, control, power, choices, assertion, self–confidence.

Juno – A Roman goddess, mother of all the gods. She protects Rome and all things feminine. She is a goddess of marriage, women, and young girls. She is a strong, confident business woman, she definitely has a modern approach to being a deity. Her Greek equivalent is Hera. Call upon her for: Romance, love, relationships, marriage, protection, leadership, time, feminine energy, safety, happiness.

Kali/Kali Ma – Hindu goddess of time, change and destruction and the Divine Mother. She has blue black skin, red eyes and four arms. Often seen with skulls hanging around her neck. This is a real kick butt, no messing kind of gal. She is a forceful destroyer but brings rebirth with it, she is the cycle of destruction and creation. Call upon her for: Death and rebirth, cycles, time, happiness, courage, hope, change, cleansing, transformation, destruction, fear, knowledge, creativity.

Kuan Yin – Chinese/Buddhist goddess of mercy who is probably one of the most chilled out and relaxed deities ever. This beautiful goddess hears all your prayers and responds to each and every request for help. She needs some kind of medal… Call upon her for: Kindness, magic, health, healing, fertility, children, sympathy, support, suffering, encouragement, enlightenment, spirituality, protection.

Levana – A Roman goddess of childbirth. Her name derives from the Latin 'levare' which means to raise or lift. She is present at the birth of every child. Call upon her for: New beginnings, protection of children, childbirth.

Lucina – Roman goddess of light. She also covers childbirth. Possibly later merged with Juno and/or Diana. She may even have been converted, becoming St Lucy. An ancient bronze mask believed to depict Juno Lucina shows her with a tiny crescent Moon engraved on her forehead. Call upon her for: Charity, protection, health, healing, kindness, banishing, fertility, well–being.

Luna – Roman goddess of the Moon. Depicted as a beautiful woman with the power to ease childbirth and bring about love. She carries a very strong feminine energy. If you want an answer to a problem, then call upon this lovely lady to bring you the answer in your dreams, it is her speciality. Her Greek equivalent is Selene. Call upon her for: Feminine energy, water magic, safety, travel, intuition, blue Moon magic, protection, illusion, truth, love, psychic abilities, dreams, solutions.

Ma'at – Egyptian goddess of the crescent Moon, order, and balance. Think 'strict school headmistress', she dishes out the justice as she sees fit, whether you are a deity or a mere mortal. Her name translates as 'truth/that which is straight'. If you are looking for balance between work and home life or any kind of justice, Ma'at should be on your speed dial. Call upon her for: Justice, balance, freedom, new beginnings, morals, organisation, law, promises, fairness, truth, oaths, harmony, honesty.

Mama Quila/Killa– Incan goddess of the full Moon, she cried silver tears. Lunar eclipses were said to be caused by a serpent or animal attacking Mama Quilla (ouch). She also covers marriage and the menstrual cycle. She is known as 'Mother Moon' and is responsible for the passage of time. Call upon her for: Time, Moon magic, feminine issues, protection of women, marriage, relationships, truth, deceit.

Mani – From the Norse pantheon, son of the giant Mundilfore. Mani is the god of the Moon and brother to the Sun goddess; Sol. Mani controls the phases of the Moon and guides it across the skies. He also helps humans learn to tell the time and date. Mani and Sol are both chased endlessly by a pair of wolves, who will catch and devour them at Ragnarok (the end of the world), let's hope they never get caught… Call upon him for: Moon magic, Moon phases, time.

Neith/Nit – Egyptian goddess of the crescent Moon and domesticity. She has an eclectic list of duties including war, hunting, and weaving. She is also considered to be the personification of the primordial waters of creation. Call upon her for: Home, marriage, protection, feminine energy, hunting, war, creativity, new beginnings.

Nephthys – Egyptian goddess of the dark Moon, the dead, darkness, and the shadows. She is the dark to the light of Isis. Call upon her for: Death and rebirth, night magic, protection, shadow work, grief, spirit work, devotion, reincarnation, power, magic.

Ops – Roman goddess of the full Moon and agriculture. If you are after abundance and prosperity then Ops is your 'go to' goddess. She can also teach you all kinds of practical skills to gain that abundance for yourself. Ain't nothing in this life for free! Call upon her for: Fertility, abundance, wealth, nurturing, prosperity, opportunity, growth.

Parvati – Hindu goddess of the crescent Moon. Oh, this goddess has all the feminine wiles and knows how to use them. She is maiden to the Mother Durga and Crone Kali. She can charm the secrets out of the trees. Call upon her for: Power, creativity, new beginnings, victory, feminine energy, beauty, charm, secrets, the arts, fertility, cleansing, devotion.

Rhiannon – if you aren't singing the Fleetwood Mac song right now, you need to… A Welsh goddess and great Queen of Wales. She brings peace, comfort, and patience. If you are looking for magical enchantments, then she has a bounty of them. Call upon her for: Patience, comfort, peace, magic, movement, relaxation, communication, fertility, leadership, spirit work, motivation, dream work.

Selene – From ancient Greece, she is a Titan Moon goddess, sister of Helios (the Sun). She drives a silver chariot drawn by two white horses, across the sky each night. The Roman equivalent is Luna. Call upon her for: Moon magic, dream work, sleep, Moon phases, magic, divination, sensuality.

Sin/Nanna – Sumerian Moon god with a long flowing beard sometimes depicted as being made of lapis lazuli. He rode upon a winged bull. He was represented by the number thirty, the days in a lunar month. Nanna is the Sumerian name for the Moon god, which may mean just the full Moon phase. 'Sin' being the name given to the crescent Moon. Call upon him for: Moon magic, fertility, prosperity, growth.

Thoth – Egyptian ibis headed Moon god. He is a seriously studious dude. God of writing and wisdom he is considered to be one of the most important gods of ancient Egypt (he didn't let it go to his head though). Call upon him for: Knowledge, Moon magic, wisdom, learning, intellect, meditation, logic, reason, magic, secrets, balance, judgement.

Venus – Roman goddess of love, passion, and sexuality. This goddess has more va va voom than she needs, so she likes to share it around. She also covers gardens and spring within her remit. Equivalent to the Greek Aphrodite. Call upon her for: Love, passion, sexuality, romance, beauty, self–esteem, happiness, relationships, charm, the arts.

Vesta – Roman goddess of the crescent Moon, the hearth and home. She rules domesticity with a flip of the feather duster and a whip of her apron. She keeps the house and family running like clockwork. She is known as Hestia in Greece. Call upon her for: Home, family, relationships, harmony, peace, love, fertility, fire magic, spirituality.

Moon Animals

Some animals immediately make you think of the Moon, others just because they are nocturnal. It may be that an animal is connected to the Moon by exhibiting lunar characteristics. Whatever the connection, there are a lot of interesting animals that correspond with the Moon. Call upon their energies to help you with your Moon magic and to lend you their individual characteristics. Here are my suggestions:

Alligator/Crocodile

The good ole croc can see incredibly well which has led to its association with clarity and clear thought. Although it has often been linked to a destructive kind of power it can show us great knowledge and how the cycle of life, death and rebirth works. They are a primordial force that has connections to the land and the water, their main role though being that of water guardians, defending and keeping the secret mysteries of the deep. Crocodiles shed tears, not real ones but just to lubricate their eyes (apparently) and this could be a sign that we aren't showing or acknowledging our true emotions.

Keywords: Clarity, truth, visions, cycle of life, rebirth, emotions, mysteries, and secrets.

Bat

The bat is synonymous with the dark of night and the light of the Moon. Some folklore stories suggest that bats were thought to be witches and if one flew close by you it was a witch checking up on you or sending a curse (I will pop by later, look out for me…). I think the bat gets a bit of bad press and the horror film industry has not helped. They are in fact beautiful highly sensitive creatures who bring intuition, dreams and visions. They also have really cool night vision which can help you to see through illusions and find the truth. The bat is very sociable and loves nothing more than a good ole chat with the rest of the group. Living in the dark caves of Mother Earth the bat brings rebirth as it emerges from the depths every night. Bat does however require a lot of commitment from you so be warned it doesn't work with slackers.

Keywords: Commitment, challenges, renewal, rebirth, communication, intuition, sensitivity, illusion, truth and dreams.

Cat

Not necessarily a nocturnal animal, but the cat does like to roam the streets and roof tops at night. Those with a cat at home will know that they are gods and should be worshipped and pampered in every way shape and form…Cat brings elegance, independence and intuition and I think it has a definite feminine energy. She is also full of mystery, wisdom and understanding (mostly on how to annoy humans) but she also brings healing and balance. And obviously curiosity, which apparently killed the cat. Cat also comes with good psychic abilities and always spirituality.

Keywords: Independence, healing, curiosity, mystery, psychic abilities, elegance, intuition, mystery, wisdom, understanding and balance.

Cow

A whole load of bull…or cow… Both the bull and the cow are symbolic of fertility, although the cow obviously brings mothering instincts into play as well. The bull is very masculine and embodies the solar energy of the Sun whereas the cow is feminine personified and signifies the energy of the Moon, they make a nice balance. I think both the cow and the bull have earthy connections. These are both all about being productive, starting new projects or feeling stubborn or even insecure.

Keywords: Fertility, motherhood, Sun and Moon magic,

stubbornness, insecurity, productive, earth magic, stability, aggression, defence, contentment and strength.

Crab

Creature of the ocean but also the shore, the crab can show us that taking detours, or a side step can give us clarity or take us in a better direction. With its hard shell the crab also offers protection, not just physically but on an emotional level too. And of course, crab also shows us that it is good to 'come out of your shell'. Some types of crab shed their shell on occasion and exchange it for another, showing us that life is a cycle and you can have rebirth at any time. Dump excess emotional baggage with crab and move forward.

Keywords: Protection, rebirth, emotions, trust, shielding, connections, directions, choices, home, life cycles, releasing, clarity, insight, curiosity, challenge, perseverance.

Crow

This is one very powerful animal spirit guide and a clever beggar as well. Crow brings wisdom, knowledge and magic from every dimension and helps us to learn to trust our own intuition. He is also mindful, not just of our own self but also in judging other's actions and words. Crow is very much an eccentric individual and he encourages that in those he chooses to walk with. Crow also brings change, creation, spiritual strength and the ability to see into the past and the future. He is a bit of a cheeky sly one though and deception is not beneath him in fact sometimes he revels in it. He does teach us to adapt, to look beyond the ordinary and to listen to what is going on around us.

Keywords: Mindfulness, truth, trust, intuition, integrity, individuality, change, past/present/future, spiritual strength, magic, wisdom, deception and awareness.

Deer/Stag

Beautiful, elegant and graceful creatures both the stag and the deer are royalty within the woods and are sacred in many cultures. A white hart is often depicted as a messenger from the Otherworld that can guide you on your spiritual quest. Stag is a creature of the hunt with strength, courage and power. Both like to graze during dawn and dusk and these are in between times when the veil between our world and the Otherworld is hazy.

Keywords: Grace, reaching your goals, alertness, hunt, intuition, listening, transformation, observation, decisions, Otherworld, spirituality, messages, gentleness, innocence and adventure.

Dog

A dog animal spirit guide is for life, not just for Yule...definitely man (or woman's) best friend and so jam packed with loyalty you couldn't fit in another wet slobbery lick. Dog is devoted but also a protector, a companion, faithful and hardworking. Dog is also good with communication, especially if he needs a walk...he can also provide healing and support. The 'black dog' is a creature that foretells impending doom and a term used for depression so this dark side of dog can also be a warning system.

Keywords: Loyalty, devotion, protection, companion, faithful, hard work, communication, healing, support and warning.

Dolphin

It might be a mammal, but it lives in the sea, they were often thought to be an indication that storms were coming, and sailors believed that dolphins charmed the winds. They are incredibly intelligent and very playful, enjoying life on the ocean waves but they also bring healing and balance.

Keywords: Wisdom, playfulness, healing, balance, freedom, change, communication, trust, harmony, emotions and water magic.

Dragon

Phewy, this is a huge area and needs an entire book to itself. However, if dragon has come to you then it will probably be a particular colour or type, whether it is an elemental dragon (earth, air, fire, water), a region one (ice, sand, snow etc) or a cultural one (Chinese, Welsh etc) the range of them is endless. Each one will bring its own very special and unique characteristics and qualities. The basic qualities of a dragon are strength and courage, but they can bring all kinds of messages and magical properties to aid us in life. They are a very primordial energy and incredibly powerful.

Keywords: Strength, courage, energy – other meanings are specific to the type of dragon.

Fox

The wily cunning ole fox has appeared in myths and legends for centuries bringing his shape shifting and healing abilities with him. He is skilful, creative and full of the mystical dawn/dusk in between magic that is also often associated with the world of Faerie. He can teach us his cunning and clever ways using camouflage, agility and the art of shape shifting. He doesn't out run…he observes plans, plots and schemes, anticipating the next move and outwitting those that chase him. He is smart and crafty, but he does go over the top sometimes and becomes unbearably so.

Keywords: Cunning, stealth, courage, observation, persistence, wisdom, magic, shape shifting and invisibility.

Frog/Toad

It was once believed that toads were witches who had shape shifted…seriously if I was going to shape shift it wouldn't be into a toad…but it does mean that toad brings cauldrons full of magic and witchcraft with it. Both creatures have very similar magical properties; the frog is just slightly damper.

They are a representation of rebirth and new life and a symbol of awakening…have you kissed any frogs lately? Patience is definitely one of the virtues frog brings as they spend hours sitting still waiting for their prey. The tadpole into frog scenario also creates the powers of transformation and water brings emotions and intuition.

Keywords: Magic, witchcraft, rebirth, new life, awakening, patience, transformation, emotions and intuition.

Hare/Rabbit

Rabbits and hares like to make lots of baby rabbits and hares… so fertility is key here. They also have a strong connection to the seasons and the Moon. They like to live in burrows which also gives them an earthy grounded energy. Rabbits and hares are both nocturnal linking them to intuition, emotions and reflection. They are very sociable animals and love a bit of a rabbit get together, but they can also show aggression and jealousy when provoked– much the same as any family or community. They are alert and sensitive to the environment around them and very cautious, but they also like to have a good hop and a skip.

Keywords: Fertility, seasons, Moon magic, earth energy, intuition, emotions, reflection, social, community, jealousy, sensitivity, caution and joy.

Mole

A big part of mole medicine is the ability to trust your senses and your instincts and to be able to 'feel' the truth or a lie. Mole lives under the ground so makes an excellent guide to the Underworld and to mysteries and secrets. Mole has faith and can guide you on your spiritual journey.

Keywords: Trust, senses, instincts, truth, guidance, Underworld, mysteries, faith and spirituality.

Moth

Winged insect of the night, drawn to any light that shines in the darkness. As a nocturnal creature the moth can give us a connection to the Otherworld and its mysteries. Moth relies on his inner guidance and uses his intuition and instincts to find the way. Even when it might seem pointless, the moth continues onwards (how many times does a moth crash into the lightbulb?). He brings faith, but not blind faith, teaching us to adjust and react when necessary. Moth is also a master of disguise, he suggests you might just be trying to hide yourself away or disguising your true emotions, have faith and trust in yourself.

Keywords: Transformation, confusion, light and dark, messages, movement, sensitivity, clarity, psychic abilities, optimism, opportunity, faith, determination, secrets, releasing, power, happiness, Otherworld, intuition, emotions, dreams, instincts.

Owl

There are lots of myths and legends about this beautiful bird of the night and some conflict between good and bad. Owl will defend itself and the nest of its young, but it also has an offbeat approach to parenting where some chicks may starve due to lack of food or be killed off by siblings. It is a creature of the between times choosing to fly at dawn, dusk and during the dark of the night so it tends to have connections to gods of death in many cultures. Some say that to hear an owl screech means impending doom…Owl is another creature that was said to be a witch that had shape shifted.

Keywords: Protection, witchcraft, magic, death and rebirth, silence, swiftness, deception (uncovering), Underworld, wisdom, dreams, shape shifting, messages, secrets and omens.

Panther/Leopard

This category covers panthers, leopards, jaguars and cougars as they all have the same or very similar characteristics. They are extremely fierce, treacherous, malicious and savage but they are also intelligent and quick to learn. These animals bring bravery, courage, boldness and a beautiful grace. Panther can teach you how to pace yourself and allow time to rest and play in between getting the job done. However, panther is always the first and fastest to respond to any situation and deals well with deadlines and pressure. Panther can also give guidance within your personal and professional life. Panther is a feminine energy, the dark goddess and the dark of the Moon and is a symbol of death and rebirth.

Keywords: Malice, fierceness, bravery, courage, grace, pacing yourself, pressure, timeframes, life, death and rebirth.

Raven

A very mystical and magical bird which appears in myths and legends connected with the occult and dark gods and goddesses across the globe. They were often feared because of their habit of feeding on the corpses of the dead hanging from the gallows (ewwww). However, raven was just doing its bit in the natural cycle of life. Raven has the power to help you shift consciousness and enter other realms and dimensions; he is also a shape shifter himself. Keeper of secrets, magic and transformation the raven can help you uncover and work with your inner fears. He brings lightness to the dark helping to resolve inner conflicts. Raven will bring changes to your life and put the spark back into your magical and spiritual world.

Keywords: Introspection, courage, magic, healing, rebirth, secrets and shape shifting.

Snail

The snail probably wouldn't be your first choice for an animal spirit guide, but if it comes your way don't argue...go with it, there will be a reason. One of the main purposes for snail's arrival is to bring you patience by the slime load. Snail knows that good things come to those that wait and anything important is worth doing properly and at a steady pace, life is all too fast, and we should all slow down and give ourselves time to smell the roses. Snails are generally quite small so it also brings the message that you might need to focus on the detail and take notice of the smaller things. And of course, the snail is protected by an outer shell, so it brings protective qualities as well as the idea that sometimes you need to withdraw and have some 'me time'. Associated with the Moon because they like to do their best work at night and by 'best work' I mean eating all my plants.

Keywords: Patience, protection, spiral of life, letting go of deadlines, slowing down, paying attention to details, inner work and withdrawal.

Snake

Quite often a shadow guide, the snake has so many wonderful qualities that will help and guide you. It sheds its skin which reminds us that we can shed our illusions and any self–imposed limitations or ideas and brings a link to astral travel. Snake also brings fertility, creation and transformation. He is also seen as a symbol of sexuality and linked with many deities for that same reason. Snake is energy, raw power and our inner spark of spirituality but he also brings healing and wisdom.

Keywords: Transformation, fertility, astral travel, creativity, sexuality, power, spirituality and healing, wisdom.

Unicorn

A mythical creature (or not…) stories about the unicorn can be found throughout the world. Usually the unicorn is depicted as pure white with a long spiral horn (the alicorn) on its forehead but it has been described as being many other colours. Unicorn is pure and innocent which is why children will often connect very well with this animal spirit guide. They are full of magic and enchantment and often linked with the Faerie world. They are said to be so fast that no one can ever catch one if you chase it, but if it comes to you it can bring transformation, prosperity, strength, success, spirituality, changes, and valour.

Keywords: Purity, innocence, magic, enchantment, Faerie, speed, transformation, prosperity, strength, success, spirituality, changes and valour.

Wolf

Wolf spirit animal guide is a teacher, a pathfinder and a guardian who helps us to understand about ourselves and others. He brings new ideas and steers us in the right direction to learn new things and gain the knowledge and wisdom that we seek. Wolves are usually found in packs taking on the responsibilities of family and they are territorial prepared to protect themselves. Due to their sensitive and intuitive nature they can also spot deceit or hidden agendas straight away. Of course, they love to be outside hunting by the light of the Moon.

Keywords: Teacher, pathways, guardian, understanding, new ideas, knowledge, wisdom, community, responsibilities, protection, sensitivity, intuition and truth.

Meditation to find your Moon animal.

Work with this meditation to find a spirit animal guide associated with the Moon. They may just pop by with a message, you might find they stay for a while and you never know, you may even discover a lift long spirit guide. Be open to whatever comes your way. Find a space where you won't be disturbed and make yourself comfortable. Focus on your breathing, deep breaths in and deep breaths out.

As your world around you dissipates you find yourself standing in the dark of night, the area around you being lit by the bright light of a full Moon hanging above you. The sky is a dark indigo blue and sprinkled with stars. The air has a chill to it, but you are dressed well and feeling warm and comfortable. You start to investigate your surroundings. The Moon provides just enough light for you to see where you are going. There are tall stone pillars stretching upwards as far as your eye can see, some disappearing into the darkness, others broken and crumbling. The grass is littered with pieces of broken stonework, some having lain so long on the ground that nature has taken over. Roses rambling over fallen pillars and wild flowers pushing up through pieces of crumbled wall. It seems as if Mother Nature has claimed the derelict temple for herself. Because a temple is exactly what it used to be, long ago. All that remains now is a broken shell of a structure.

Walk around and take a look, see what you can find…

As you are wandering around the temple remains you catch movement from the corner of your eye. Did it fly in from above, climb over the stones or creep in from below the soil?

You stand still, listening and watching.

A creature slowly makes its way out into a pool of light thrown down by the full Moon.

What animal is it?

It stops and looks directly at you; your eyes meet and there is a connection.

Listen for any messages, ask questions. Why is the animal here? What does it need to share with you?

Take as much time as you need conversing with the Moon animal.

When you are finished, in a quick movement the animal is gone, and you are once again alone in the fallen remains of the temple. You call out your thanks.

But you notice something in the spot where the animal was, walk over and take a look. It has left a gift for you. Pick it up, what is it? And what does it mean to you?

Take a last look around the area and then look up to the Moon, send her your blessing.

Now slowly and gently come back to this reality. Wriggle your fingers and toes and open your eyes. Have a drink and something to eat. Jot down any messages, things you saw or heard and what your gift was. It may help to refer back to this at a later date.

Flowers and Plants Ruled by the Moon

When you want to work with a herb or plant within magic it helps to charge it with the energy of your intent. Basically, you need to tell it what you would like it to do. Do be polite and ask it nicely but make sure you really push that energy. The strength of your will and commitment to the outcome is paramount in any spell work. That plant material needs to be very, very clear about what you expect from it and what you would like it to do.

The plants and flowers listed below are all ruled by the Moon and can be used in magical workings or grown in your garden to impart her lunar magic. You can also journey to meet with the spirit of plants and herbs. They can help give you guidance and insight into situations and provide you with energy for your magic.

Aloe

(Aloe vera)
Aloe Magical Properties:
Luck, protection, calming, Moon magic, psychic abilities
Ruling planet – Moon, Saturn
Sign – Sagittarius
Element – Water
Gender – Feminine

Birch

(Betula pendula, Betula pubescens, Betula lenta, Betula alba)
Birch Magical Properties:
Purification, protection, exorcism, new beginnings, courage, fertility, love, release
Ruling planet – Venus, Moon, Jupiter
Sign – Sagittarius
Element – Water, Air

Gender – Feminine

Bladder wrack

(Fucus vesiculosus)

Bladder wrack Magical Properties:

Protection, sea magic, money, psychic powers, weather magic

Ruling planet – Moon

Sign – Pisces

Element – Water

Gender – Feminine

Calamus

(Acorus calamus)

Caution: some varieties of Calamus are poisonous so please be very careful and make sure you have identified it correctly if you are intending to ingest it.

Calamus Magical Properties:

Money, protection, healing, luck

Ruling planet – Moon, Sun

Element – Water

Gender – Feminine

Camellia

(Camellia japonica)

Camellia Magical Properties:

Abundance, prosperity, spirituality

Ruling planet – Moon

Element – Water

Gender – Feminine

Chickweed (Starwort)

(Stellaria media)

Chickweed Magical Properties:

Love, fidelity, dreams, protection, fertility, Moon magic

Ruling planet – Moon
Element – Water
Gender – Feminine

Dittany

(Dictamnus albus)
Dittany Magical Properties:
Fire, Samhain
Ruling planet –Moon
Element – Fire
Gender – Feminine

Dulse

(Palmaria palmate)
Dulse Magical Properties:
Lust, love, harmony, peace, protection
Ruling planet – Moon
Sign – Pisces
Element – Water
Gender – Feminine

Eucalyptus

(Eucalyptus spp)
Eucalyptus Magical Properties:
Moon magic, Sun magic, divination, dreams, healing, purification
Ruling planet – Moon, Sun
Element – Water, Air
Gender – Feminine

Evening Primrose

(Oenothera)
Evening Primrose Magical Properties:
Feminine energy, Moon magic, faerie, hunting

Ruling planet – Moon
Element – Water
Gender – Feminine

Gourd

(Cucurbitaceae)
Gourd Magical Properties:
Protection, cleansing
Ruling planet – Moon
Element – Water
Gender – Masculine

Honesty

(Lunaria spp)
Honesty Magical Properties:
Money, monsters, truth
Ruling planet – Moon
Element – Earth
Gender – Feminine

Hyssop

(Hyssopus officinalis)
Hyssop Magical Properties:
Purification, protection, healing
Ruling planet – Jupiter, Moon
Sign – Cancer
Element – Fire
Gender – Masculine

Iris

(Iris spp)
Iris Magical Properties:
Wisdom, purification, Moon magic, divination, dreams, love
Ruling planet – Moon, Venus

Sign – Taurus, Aquarius
Element – Water
Gender – Feminine

Ivy

(Hedera helix)
Ivy Magical Properties:
Protection, healing, binding, love, abundance, fidelity
Ruling planet – Saturn, Moon
Sign – Scorpio
Element – Water
Gender – Feminine

Jasmine

(Jasminum grandiflorum, Jasminum officinale, Jasminum odoratissimum)
Jasmine Magical Properties:
Dreams, money, love, meditation, lust
Ruling planet – Moon, Venus
Sign – Cancer
Element – Water
Gender – Feminine

Juniper

(Juniperus communes)
Juniper Magical Properties:
Love, exorcism, healing, protection, justice, stolen items, purification, psychic powers, clarity
Ruling planet – Sun, Jupiter, Moon
Sign – Aries
Element – Fire
Gender – Masculine

Lemon Balm

(Melissa officinalis)

Lemon Balm Magical Properties:

Success, healing, anti–depression, memory, love, anxiety

Ruling planet – Moon, Venus

Sign – Cancer

Element – Water

Gender – Feminine

Lily

(Lilium spp)

Lily Magical Properties:

Goddess, witchcraft, hexes, uncrossing, protection

Ruling planet – Moon, Venus

Sign – Scorpio

Element – Water

Gender – Feminine

Mallow

(Malva spp, Lavatera)

Mallow Magical Properties:

Love, Samhain, protection

Ruling planet – Moon, Venus

Element – Water

Gender – Feminine

Mugwort

(Artemisia vulgaris)

Mugwort Magical Properties:

Strength, psychic powers, protection, dreams, healing, astral travel, feminine energy, cleansing

Ruling planet – Venus, Moon

Sign – Cancer

Element – Earth

Gender Feminine

Myrtle

(Myrtaceae communis)

Myrtle Magical Properties:

Love, protection, money

Ruling planet – Venus, Moon

Sign – Taurus

Element – Water

Gender – Feminine

Poppy

(Papaver spp)

Poppy Magical Properties:

Love, sleep, money, luck, fertility, rebirth, grief

Ruling planet – Moon, Mars, Venus

Sign – Capricorn

Element – Water

Gender – Feminine

Rose

(Rosa spp)

Rose Magical Properties:

Love, psychic powers, healing, luck, protection, peace, mysteries, knowledge, dreams, friendship, death and rebirth, abundance

Ruling planet – Venus, Moon

Sign – Pisces

Element – Water

Gender – Feminine

Sandalwood

(White Sandalwood – Santalum album)

Sandalwood (White) Magical Properties:

Death rites, purification, wishes, psychic powers
Ruling planet – Moon, Mercury
Sign – Sagittarius, Virgo
Element – Water
Gender – Feminine

Sweetpea

(Lathyrus odoratus)
Sweetpea Magical Properties:
Courage, strength, friendship, peace, happiness, truth, spirituality, psychic abilities, protection, sleep
Ruling planet – Venus, Moon, Mercury
Element – Water
Gender – Feminine

Willow

(Salix alba, Salix fragilis)
Willow Magical Properties:
Love, protection, healing, cleansing, wishes, release, inspiration, intuition
Ruling planet – Moon
Sign – Pisces
Element – Water
Gender – Feminine

Wormwood

(Artemisia absinthium)
Wormwood Magical Properties:
Vengeance, attack magic, protection, divination, dreams, meditation, psychic powers
Ruling planet – Mars, Moon
Sign – Cancer, Scorpio
Element – Fire
Gender – Masculine

Meditation to meet your Moon plant spirit guide

Find a space where you won't be disturbed and make yourself comfortable. Close your eyes and focus on your breathing. Deep breaths in and deep breaths out.

As your world around you dissipates you find yourself standing at the edge of a large rambling and seemingly untidy garden. It is twilight, the Sun has disappeared below the horizon but the last rays of Sun are still peeking out. Soon to disappear to plunge the sky into darkness, as the Moon makes an appearance.

There is a dusty dirt path beneath your feet that disappears into the plant life of the garden. The pathway is overgrown with plants hanging across and above it. You are drawn to follow it…

As you walk take a look at the plants on either side of you, gently push those out of the way that hang over the pathway.

What you notice is a scent beginning to emerge, a beautiful heady perfume rising up from the garden. Breathe in deeply, it is intoxicating.

As the sky gets darker and the last rays of Sun disappear, you see small lights appearing within the foliage. Flickering dots of light, zipping and dancing around. You realise they are fire flies jumping from plant to plant.

Then very slowly white flowers begin to open, their beautiful bright petals seemingly providing light for you to find your way.

A direction seems to be lighting up for you to follow, you head in the direction of the scent and the glowing flowers…

To a small clearing, once a beautiful stone fountain surrounded by a marble floor with stone benches at the edges. The water is no longer running, and the fountain is filled with plants and wild flowers tumbling over the edges.

You sit on one of the benches and your eye is drawn to a particular plant growing from the fountain in front of you.

Reach out and touch the plant, a connection is made…

What does it look like? What shape and colour are the leaves? Does it have flowers? What scent does it have?

Listen carefully to any messages the plant spirit may have for you. It may tell you its name, it may not. Ask any questions you might have.

When you are ready thank the plant and turn back, heading the way you came.

Make your way through the foliage, following the path to the point where you came in.

Know that you can always come back to this point.

Slowly and gently come back to this reality, wriggle your fingers and toes and open your eyes. Drink and eat something. Jot down any notes or messages to refer back to later.

Cooking with the Moon Cycle

The power of the Moon is incredibly strong and affects our moods and emotions. By working with the cycles of the Moon rather than against them, going with the flow so to speak can make our lives much easier. We can also tailor the foods we eat to the phases of the Moon to tap into that power and to work with the rhythm of our bodies and emotions too.

Obviously, the Moon phases span the seasons so we will eat differently on a spring full Moon than on a winter one.

Spring Moons – this is a season of new beginnings, growth and awakening so eat the foods that inspire you to connect with the energies of spring.

Summer Moons – summer is a time for sitting outside and eating whether it is dinner in your back garden or a picnic on the beach. It is a time for celebrating life and all that we have.

Autumn Moons – harvest time, we start to think about warming, hearty foods and giving thanks to the land for all that she has supplied us with.

Winter Moons – it is cold and dark (and probably wet) so eating with the Moon phases at winter will involve foods that warm us, keep us strong and maintain our bodies through the winter season.

The Moon for each month also has its own magical properties and energies, go with your intuition and how you feel and how the energies around you make you feel and cook accordingly. Take a look at the individual Moon phase and month sections within this book for more ideas on eating with the Moon phases.

Foods, Herbs and Spices ruled by the Moon

These herbs, spices and foods are all ruled by the Moon.

Blueberries

(Vaccinium Cyanococcus)

Blueberries Magical Properties:

Calm, peace, protection, passion, fertility

Ruling planet – Moon

Element – Earth, water

Gender – Feminine

Broccoli

(Brassica oleracea)

Broccoli Magical Properties:

Strength, protection

Ruling planet – Moon

Element – Water

Gender – Feminine

Brussels sprouts

(Brassica oleracea)

Brussels Sprouts Magical Properties:

Stability, endurance, protection

Ruling planet – Moon

Element – Water

Gender – Feminine

Butter

Butter Magical Properties:

Peace, spirituality, Faerie

Ruling planet – Moon

Element – Earth

Gender – Feminine

Cabbage

(Brassica oleracea/var.)

Cabbage Magical Properties:

Moon magic, protection, prosperity, fertility, love
Ruling planet – Moon
Element – Water
Gender – Feminine

Cauliflower

(Brassica oleracea)
Cauliflower Magical Properties:
Emotions, Moon magic, protection
Ruling planet – Moon
Element – Water
Gender – Feminine

Caviar

Caviar Magical Properties:
Emotions, passion
Ruling planet – Moon
Element – Water
Gender – Feminine

Coconut

(Cocos nucifera)
Coconut Magical Properties:
Protection, purification, chastity
Ruling planet – Moon
Element – Water
Gender – Feminine

Crab

Crab Magical Properties:
Spirituality, hex breaking
Ruling planet – Moon
Element – Water
Gender – Feminine

Cucumber

(Cucumis sativus)

Cucumber Magical Properties:

Fertility, emotions, chastity, meditation, spirituality, purification, healing

Ruling planet – Moon

Element – Water

Gender – Feminine

Eggs

Eggs Magical Properties:

Fertility, creation, life, new beginnings, divination

Element – Water, Earth, Air, Fire

Gender – Masculine/Feminine

Grapes

(Vitis vinifera)

Grapes Magical Properties:

Spiritual, fertility, Moon magic

Ruling planet – Moon

Element – Air, Water

Gender – Feminine

Gravy

Gravy Magical Properties:

Calming, emotions, healing, cleansing, purification

Ruling planet – Moon

Element – Water

Gender – Feminine

Ice Cream

Ice Cream Magical Properties:

Love, spirituality, various depending on what flavours you add

Ruling planet – Moon
Element – Water
Gender – Feminine

Kiwi Fruit

(Actinidia deliciosa)
Kiwi Fruit Magical Properties:
Love, romance
Ruling planet – Moon
Element – Water, Earth
Gender – Masculine

Lemon

(Citrus x lemon)
Lemon Magical Properties:
Purification, Moon magic, happiness, decisions, uplifting, love, protection, friendship, fidelity
Ruling planet – Moon
Element – Water
Gender – Feminine

Lettuce

(Lactuca sativa)
Lettuce Magical Properties:
Fertility, meditation, astral travel, calm
Ruling planet – Moon
Element – Water
Gender – neutral

Melon

Melon Magical Properties:
Love, chaos, healing, purification
Ruling planet – Moon
Element – Water

Gender – Feminine

Milk

Milk Magical Properties:

Feminine power, goddess energy, Moon magic, nurturing, offerings, love, spirituality, Faeries

Ruling planet – Moon

Element – Water

Gender – Feminine

Mushrooms

Mushrooms Magical Properties:

Strength, courage, magic, balance

Ruling planet – Moon

Element – Earth

Gender – Feminine

Oysters

Oyster Magical Properties:

Passion, balance

Ruling planet – Moon

Element – Water

Gender – Masculine & feminine

Papaya

(Carica papaya)

Papaya Magical Properties:

Love, protection

Ruling planet – Moon

Element – Water

Gender –Feminine

Poppy Seeds

(Papaver somniferum)

Poppy Seeds Magical Properties:
Calm, peace, luck, protection, invisibility, prosperity
Ruling planet – Moon
Element – Air, Water
Gender – Feminine

Potato
(Solanum tuberosum L)
Potato Magical Properties:
Energy, magic, grounding, prosperity, healing
Ruling planet – Moon
Element – Earth
Gender – Feminine

Pumpkin
(Cucurbita spp)
Pumpkin Magical Properties:
Prosperity, Crone magic, healing
Ruling planet – Moon
Element – Earth
Gender – Feminine

Soya Bean
(Glycine max)
Soya Bean Magical Properties:
Fertility, passion, prosperity, luck, psychic powers, spirituality
Ruling planet – Moon
Element – Earth
Gender – Feminine

Water
Water Magical Properties:
Emotions, cleansing, purification

Ruling planet – Moon
Element – Water
Gender – Feminine

White Wine

White Wine Magical Properties:
Spirituality, offerings, happiness, love
Ruling planet – Moon (white wine)
Element – Earth, Fire
Gender – Feminine

Yogurt

Yogurt Magical Properties:
Spirituality, creativity, depression
Ruling planet – Moon
Element – Water, Air
Gender – Feminine

Moon Spell Craft

In this section you will find ideas and inspiration, with things to do, create or work with all associated with the Moon. I share with you some of my favourite spell working items. I have also given suggested correspondences and ingredients to use, but as always go with your intuition and the items that you have to hand. Spell work and witchcraft should not cost lots of money. Don't spend huge amounts of cash importing exotic ingredients from the other side of the globe. Use whatever you have growing in your garden, found in your kitchen cupboards or purchased from your local farmers market, supermarket or Asian grocery store.

Moon Diary

I am, I confess, absolutely rubbish at keeping a journal. However, if you can give it a go and stick with it, a Moon diary is an excellent record to keep. It can track each Moon phase and astrological position and how they affect your moods and wellbeing. It can help you to understand your own cycle (no matter what gender you are) and to live in harmony with the energy of the Moon rather than fighting against it.

Diaries and calendars have the Moon phases included or there are some good phone apps and printable charts downloadable from the net.

If you are really serious about getting down and dirty with Moon magic, then a detailed Moon journal is a good idea.

A ring binder/loose leaf folder is my method of choice because it gives flexibility to take bits out, add things and move them around. But you may prefer a bound journal or even to keep it all typed up on your laptop. The choice is yours. Also see the phenology wheel in this book.

I am going to give you some suggestions on how to use it, but it isn't set in stone, keep it fluid and add what feels right to you.

- Your Moon sign – Once you have worked out your Moon sign from your date of birth jot down the details; personality traits and habits and those that resonate with you. Include those that you don't think are relevant at first, you may make discoveries along the way.
- There are some good online sites that will help you work out your Moon sign. You may also like to add details of your Sun sign as well.
- Moon cycle journal with all the phases noted on. You can also add the signs the Moon is in to give a more detailed basis.
- Areas of your life – Relationships, love, family, work, school, health and social life. This will give you a section to add how each of these are affected by the different phases of the Moon.
- A general/daily section to chart your movements and general mood and wellbeing.
- Add to your journal by putting in drawings and images of the Moon, yourself and anything that takes your fancy. Decorate it with paint, pen, stickers or fancy designs if you are taken to do so.
- This is also a good place for those that want to keep a record of menstruation, it often seems to tie in with the Moon phases.

This will be your personal journal so make it yours.

You may find it tricky to keep up with our journal regularly if it is a new practice to you (or you are rubbish at journaling like me). Find a system that works for you. It might just be a case of setting a regular time each day to sit for a few minutes and write up your notes. If you do lapse, don't beat yourself up about it. Just jump back in and start again. You don't have to write volumes, pages or even paragraphs. Just a sentence or two each day is perfectly acceptable.

Using your journal on a regular basis will not only help you keep in tune with the Moon but also to learn a lot about yourself in the process. It really is a personal journey of discovery.

Phenology Wheel

I am including what is referred to as a phenology wheel here. Personally, I find the spaces way too small to write in, I prefer to write it in list format. But this will give you some sort of guide to begin with.

A phenology is a type of journal or calendar that encourages you to observe and log what is happening with nature and the earth around you. It records seasonal and cyclic phenomena.

We use this in our Kitchen Witch School lessons. We have provided a template for you to experiment with or you might like to create your own design. You can begin at any point you wish; my suggestion is to start at the full or new Moon.

- The outer ring tracks the phases of the Moon.
- The second ring can be used to log the weather on that particular day. You could draw a Sun or a cloud with rain for example. If you aren't very artistic you can either write or devise a symbol to represent the weather.
- The third and the largest ring is for logging natural phenomena; how you might be feeling, your energy levels or for those that menstruate it can be used to track your cycle.
- The inner ring can be used to write the date.

I have added boxes at the bottom for additional notes and drawings you might like to add. There isn't a lot of space on the wheel for writing so you may want to use it as a reference and write your findings on a separate piece of paper or journal.

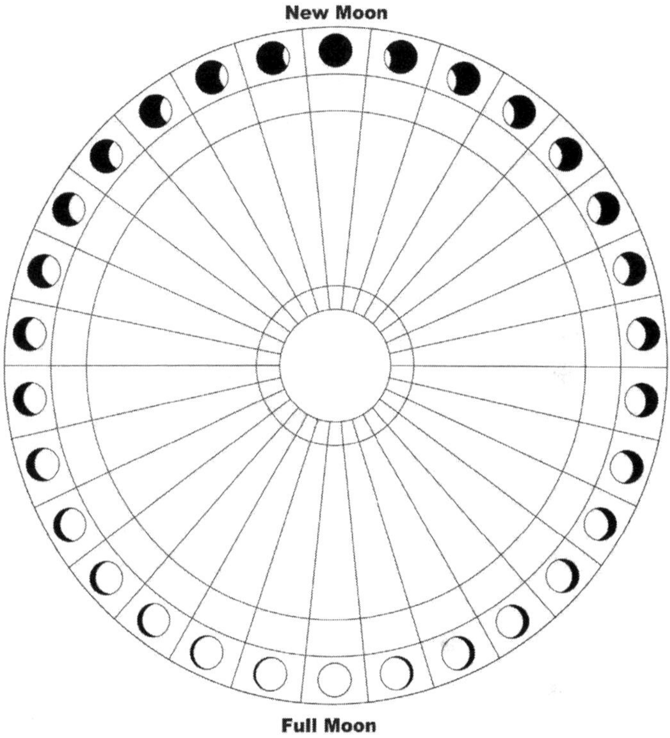

Animal & Plant Activity	Notes

Moon Altar

If you want to work regularly with the magic of the Moon, then setting up a dedicated Moon altar might be a good idea. It can be a focal point for your Moon meditations or Moon magical workings. Where you put it will be dictated by what room you have, but just a window sill would work, especially if it gets the Moonlight shining through it. A tray that you can put inside a cupboard works if you aren't 'out of the closet'. A table top, sideboard, shelf or occasional table – it doesn't have to be grand. The most important part is to make it yours.

If you have a safe place in your garden where pets, animals and children won't disturb it or eat the offerings, that works well too.

How you decorate it or what you put on it is up to you. I believe an altar is a very personal space and should reflect your personality. Be guided by your intuition and allow it to be fluid. Start with an empty space and see what happens. I often find space left on an altar allows for movement of energy.

- A dark cloth to represent the sky or even one with Moons or stars on.
- Candles of course, I prefer to stick with white to represent the Moon or different colours for each phase.
- Moon pictures, ornaments or statues, you can get some lovely ones in shops, online or often in charity/thrift stores. Or make your own from clay or salt dough.
- Crystals, herbs, spices or flowers that are associated with the Moon.
- Images of Moon gods and goddesses.
- Crystal balls or scrying dishes tie in nicely and leaving them on your Moon altar will add to the energy.
- Incense or an oil burner. You can change the scent to match the Moon phase.
- An offering dish is useful.
- You might like to place an image or something that represents you somewhere on the altar to make the personal connection.
- There are some lovely lamps available now that are in the shape and image of the Moon.

- Divination tools can be kept on your Moon altar to cleanse and recharge.
- A house plant or fresh flowers that need attention help you to focus regularly on your altar.
- Any spells that are in progress can be left on your altar.
- Any petitions, contracts or letters particularly ones of employment or new projects can be rolled or folded and popped on your altar to keep the positive energy working.
- Natural items such as pebbles, shells and leaves can all be used to decorate your altar.

Once your altar is set up, I suggest doing a very short ceremony to cleanse and dedicate it. Sprinkle it with Moon water or waft incense around each item to clear the energy. Then sit quietly and look carefully at each object you have placed there. Acknowledge why it is there and what it means to you. Then finish by dedicating it to the Moon or even to a specific Moon deity if you prefer.

Just say a few words, use your own thoughts and say it from the heart. It doesn't need to be fancy, something like:

I dedicate this altar to the powers of the Moon, blessed be.

Any altar benefits from being cleared and re–set regularly, a Moon one really sets its own timetable, once a month on a particular Moon phase works well. Whether it is each full Moon or maybe on the new Moon for fresh starts each month.

If you can't have an obvious altar on display, then you can use a shelf or cupboard top and put a vase of flowers on it. Keep it simple, it doesn't have to look like a corner of Merlin's cave, it can be an altar in disguise. Use everyday objects and only you will know the meaning.

If you don't have space for an altar or can't have one on display, then use the power of your mind. Visualise a Moon altar or even a sacred space you can visit when in meditation. There are no limits with this, you can be anywhere, anytime and fill it with as much junk as you want to.

Offerings

Whenever you work a spell or ask something of the Moon, the Sun or any of the planets. Or when you request energy or guidance from deity, the elements or animal spirit guides. It is only good manners to say thank you. I like to do that in the form of offerings.

It doesn't have to be extreme, just a little water for a tree that gifted you some leaves. Or feeding the birds to say thank you to Mother Nature. If you want to be specific, then giving an offering is a good way of doing so.

Create your offering to correspond with the deity and their likes or dislikes. Or if you are working magic with a particular Moon phase then tailor your offering to that intent.

Offerings can be made in small dishes on your altar. This is good for indoor use and keeps items out the way of wildlife, pets and small children. Although if you have cats, they have a tendency to investigate altars.

If you have an outside altar you can give offerings to the earth and the elements. If you are leaving offerings outside, please make sure they are biodegradable and not poisonous to wildlife.

I know it is a custom to tie blessings and offerings to trees, but please don't. Most of the ties seem to be plastic or manmade and don't break down. Even biodegradable twine or ribbon can restrict the growth of a tree or even cause damage or infection. And don't even get me started on leaving tealights out in the wild. Just don't do it.

Better to leave some flowers, herbs, bird seed or plant food outside as an offering. Even pretty pebbles, feathers or shells can work.

Indoors, well you aren't limited by anything except perhaps

space. I have seen a lot of different offerings from chocolate covered peanuts to menstrual blood. Trust your intuition and if in doubt ask the deity, the element or the planet what it would like as a thank you gift.

Here are some ideas:

- Create a herb and spice blend
- Fresh flowers
- A little tipple such as coffee, wine, rum or mead
- Sweets and chocolates
- Fruit and vegetables
- Feathers
- Bones (animal, not human…)
- Twigs, seed heads, leaves and berries
- Crystals
- A portion of your meal
- Milk, butter, cheese, honey, sugar or jam

My matron goddess The Cailleach is partial to a boiled sweet, but then all old ladies like boiled sweets, don't they?

Moon Vision Board

You may have heard or even worked with vision boards before. They are a way of manifesting things into our lives in a very visual way. The classic vision board is created on a sheet of paper or card. Cut out images from magazines or print off pictures from the net that represent your intent, your goals and dreams. Pin them to the board. This works well on a cork noticeboard. The techies amongst you may prefer to use the computer and make a collage on your laptop or even your phone. Pinterest is also a good online vision board option.

If you are manifesting, then the waxing Moon is a good time to create your board, but it can be used for anything. Don't be tempted to throw everything on one board. As with any magical working keep it clear and simple, focus on one intent at a time. Cluttering up your board with a mish mash of desires can confuse the energy and who knows what you could end up with?

But what about creating a Moon phase vision board? Section it into phases and add images that represent your intent, pop them into the corresponding Moon phase section. You could add images of the Moon phases too.

Take care when overlapping your images, think about what they represent and how they interact with each other.

Put the board where you will see it regularly. Each time you look at it say or think a positive thought and add energy to it. On each Moon phase spend some time meditating with the board as a visual focus point. Visualise your goals being reached. On the full Moon take some extra time and add the power it brings. On the waning Moon visualize letting go of anything that is stopping you from reaching your goal.

It may take some time and it will require some attention from you. Don't forget to give thanks when it all falls into place.

Making Magical Moon Water

Blessed, charged or magical water – whatever you want to call it is super simple to make. Blessed water can be used for all sorts of things such as anointing (yourself, candles or magical tools), for consecrating and cleansing tools, adding to spell workings, ritual baths or even to drink.

You start with water (unsurprisingly) and it is your choice whether you use filtered, spring, tap water or collected rain water. If you are worried about using tap water and all the icky stuff that is supposed to be in it, you can boil it first and allow it to cool. Then you need to put it in a container, I find that a glass jar works very well. At this point if you feel the urge you could charge and cleanse the water by holding your hand over the top and sending your intent into the water or you could waft some sage or incense over the top. Then you need to place the jar in the light of the Moon, you can put it outside but I would put a lid on the jar. However, you can also sit it indoors on a window sill, it just needs to be able to catch the light of the Moon. The full Moon works well for this, but you could put water out in each phase of the Moon and then you have different types for different spell workings. (See the Herbal Moon Water for more ideas).

You can tailor your Moon water by charging it when the Moon is in a specific astrological sign. Use it for magic associated with the astrological sign. Don't forget to label it!

Moon Circles

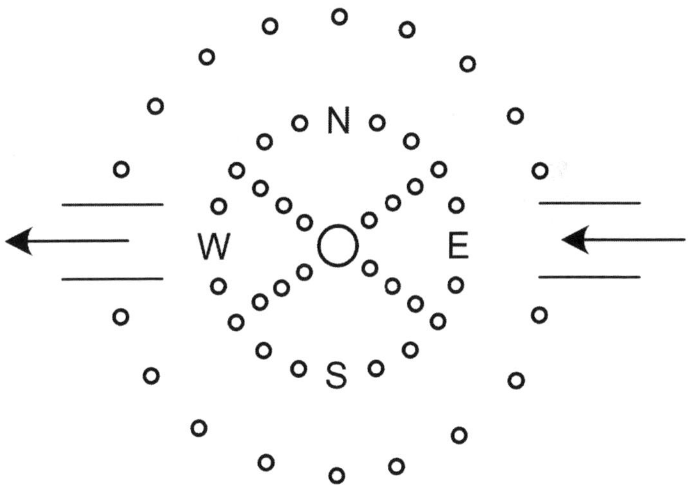

This idea is the mish mash child from the union of a ritual circle and a labyrinth. It can be quite powerful but is really simple to make. You will need some space to create one and items such as cord, pebbles, shells, flower heads, pine cones, tealights, large crystals or similar items to mark out your circle. The circle can be used as a solitary or within a group and is a place for meditation, cleansing, divination, recharging and connecting with the divine.

You have an outer circle with an entrance and exit then an inner circle that is divided into four sections to represent the elements (or a number and subjects that you choose) and a small central circle inside that. You could if you prefer, divide the inner circle into three areas to represent past, present and future. Or keep with four and have them as maiden, mother, matriarch and crone. These areas represent the wisdom and insight you can gain whilst inside them.

Create the circles as large as you need or within the space you have. You will need to be able to walk around the circle and sit inside it.

I like to start in the centre with a large crystal or something to use as a focal point, a crystal ball, chalice or cauldron would also work well depending on the energy you want it to lend to the circle.

Put your focal point down on the ground and make a small circle of pebbles, tealights or whatever you are using around it. Then create a circle around that big enough for you to divide into sections that you can stand or sit within. Three or four sections work well. Mark what each section represents with the directions, tarot cards, crystals or whatever works for your purpose.

Lastly you need to create an outer circle with a small space for the entrance in the east and an exit in the west and room for you to walk around inside it. If you have the space, you can put cushions or stools in the sections to sit on. Preferably, you want to enter in the east and exit the circle in the west. This follows the Sun rising in the east and setting in the west.

You may like to smudge people/yourself before you enter the circle. This works well at night time if you lay out the circles using tealights or lamps but make sure you have enough space so that you don't accidentally sit on a candle or set fire to your clothes...

When you are ready enter the circle in the east and walk

clockwise around it at least three times or multiples of three to raise the energy. Stop when you feel ready and sit in the section by you and face the centre. Spend some time in that section and be open to whatever messages are given to you. Ask any questions you would like. Once you feel the time is right stand up and if you feel the need you can walk the circle again otherwise walk around to the exit. There is no right or wrong, be guided by your intuition.

Remember to send your thanks for any wisdom or insight you have been given.

Lunar Incense

I love to create blends especially for loose incense, I encourage you to experiment with ingredients and see what works for you. I have given some blend suggestions throughout this book, play around with the quantities but my usual 'rule of thumb' is equal parts of each. If using essential oil in the incense blends just add in 2 or 3 drops to start, you can always add more. I like to include a resin and a wood as a base for my incense blends, it helps the mixture to burn for a longer period of time.

I love incense, well actually I love scent of all kinds. Certain smells can evoke all kinds of wonderful feelings, emotions and memories. White musk takes me back to the mid 80's and the perfume I used to wear. Anything with sandalwood reminds me of my husband and his aftershave. Frankincense is the scent I associate mostly with Glastonbury. Cinnamon and cloves are the scents of the festive season (my favourite time of the year). Each one individual and unique. However, incense can not only set off smoke detectors in the house but can also cause issues with those that suffer from asthma. I often get asked what other options people can use, here are some of my suggestions.

Smokeless incense oven

This is just pure genius. Discovered on a recent trip to

Glastonbury. Beautiful glass incense oven. You pop a tealight in the bottom, a small amount of sand in the top and sprinkle the loose incense in. The heat from the tealight warms the incense and releases the scent without the smoke. One was added to my collection…and I have used it regularly ever since.

Oil burner

You are probably all familiar with the oil burner. A tealight goes underneath and essential oil in the top. The heat from the tealight warms the oil and releases the scent. The first time I used one, it burnt. Lesson learnt, I then added water in the top with the oil in. Although the water evaporates quite quickly too. Further experimentation and I now pop a bit of candle wax in the top and add the essential oil to that.

Wax melts

Used in the oil burner mentioned above. A lot less fuss and no worry about it burning. There are some lovely scented wax melts out there. Be wary of purchasing those with synthetic fragrance. They smell of chemicals and I am pretty sure they are full of them, you don't want to be inhaling that.

Smokeless oil burner oven

A homemade version of the smokeless incense oven. Using an oil burner, pop your tealight at the bottom as usual. Then sprinkle a thin layer of sand in the top dish, pop loose incense on the top and et voila!

Scented spray

You can make your own cleansing and purifying mist by using a spray bottle filled with distilled water (boil the water in your kettle and let it cool) and adding a few drops of essential oil to it and popping a rosemary, sage or lavender sprig into the bottle.

Microwave incense

Let's get techie...pop a heat proof bowl of water in your microwave, add a good dash of something like lemon juice and heat for a couple of minutes. It fills the room with a gorgeous scent. You can add lots of different ingredients, cinnamon and clove work well too. Just make sure you have plenty of water.

Simmering incense

Using the same principal as microwave incense, fill a saucepan with water and add your ingredients. Items such as cinnamon sticks and slices of citrus fruit work well. Simmer gently to fill the house with a lovely scent.

Diffuser

A piece of kit you will need to purchase, it has a water reservoir that you add a few drops of essential oil to, you plug it in and switch it on and vapour/mist is released into the air.

Scented candles

A good reliable option to get scent into a room. As with the wax melts, I would personally check to make sure the scents are natural.

Essential Oils

If you are creating essential oil blends start with a base oil such as almond oil and add in your essential oil choices. I usually start with 10ml of base oil and add in around 20 drops of essential oil in total. Fabulous as these essential oils smell, some of them can be damaging if placed straight onto the skin. Please be careful. If using in a massage or anointing oil, please dilute the essential oils with a base oil such as coconut, almond, jojoba, sunflower or olive oil. Start with simple blends, less is usually more.

Test a few drops in a dish mixed together before you make up a whole batch. Two or three different oils in one blend is a good start. Once you become more experienced you can start playing around with more. Although if you pass seven oils in one blend it may become confusing.

Perfume scents have 'notes' – top, middle and base. Good fragrances have a balance of the three.

- Top notes are light, refreshing and often citrusy.
- Middle nots are herbal and flowery.
- Base notes are deep, rich and often woody.

Most oil blends once mixed will store for up to three months if kept in a dark place. Make sure any storage pots, jars and bottles have been thoroughly sterilised before use.

Oils can be used to dress candles for spell work, dabbed on your pulse points as anointing oil or sprinkled onto magical tools or into magic pouches. They can also be transformed into many different types of body lotions and potions.

Making your own Herbal Oils

Herbal oils are different to essential oils which are made with a more complicated process. These are herbal oils you can easily make for culinary use (provided the plant matter is edible obviously) or for magical use such as anointing candles.

There are various methods, here is the simplest:

Tear or roughly chop your plant matter, whether it is herbs, plant leaves or flowers.

Pop them in a clean, dry jar. How much plant matter you use will depend on the size of the jar.

Fill it loosely with the plant matter but leave a couple of inches open space above the herbs.

Pour in your oil, making sure you cover the plant matter by at least an inch, or even a little more.

Make sure the herbs are all fully covered.

Put a lid on and give the jar a good shake.

Place in a warm place, preferably on a window sill where it can catch the Sun. Shake the jar once a day. Leave it there for two weeks or even three.

Now strain out the plant matter from the oil, use a piece of cheesecloth for a better sieving or you can use a mesh strainer.

Pour the oil into a clean jar.

Label and date.

The oil should keep for up to a year in a cool, dark place.

Some pieces of the plant matter may float in the oil after saturation, this is perfectly normal, even if they start to decay just skim them off.

The Body Care Basics

I have included some body care recipes within each Moon phase, with ingredients specific to that phase. But here are the basic recipes if you want to experiment. A note about salt; most bath salt and body care recipes use Epsom or sea salt. These are larger grain type salts. You can use expensive Himalayan salt if you have money to waste, but honestly, supermarket sea salt or even table salt works just as well. The larger flaked salt will take longer to dissolve. Use whatever suits your budget.

Room Spritz

Spray around your room or sacred space.

You will need:

2 tablespoons vodka

2 tablespoons distilled water (boiled then cooled water)

20–30 drops essential oil (mixture of your choosing)

Mix all the ingredients together and pour into a sterilised spritzer bottle. Shake well before use. Will keep for up to six months.

Bath Melts

Add a melt to your warm bath or use in the shower.

Makes 10 melts.

You will need:

50g/2 oz shea nut butter

50g/2 oz cocoa butter

2 tablespoons solid coconut oil

20 drops essential oil (mixture of your choosing)

Melt the shea butter and cocoa butter in a bowl over a pan of simmering water. Add the coconut oil and stir. Add the essential oils and mix together. Pour into mini cupcake moulds or ice cube trays. Leave to cool and set. Keep in the fridge for up to three months.

Bath Infusion

Add the infusion to your bath water, as a foot bath, or add to a bucket of warm water for a floor or surface wash.

You will need:

500ml/16 fl oz water

10 drops essential oils (mixture of your choosing)

1 tablespoon sea salt

2 tablespoons dried herbs/dried flowers

Boil the water then pour over the dried herbs/flowers. Leave to infuse for ten minutes.

In a separate bowl add the essential oils to the salt and mix to a paste.

Strain the herb/flower water.

Add the oil and salt paste to the strained water infusion.

Stir until the salt has dissolved.

Body Scrub

Scoop some out into your hand and massage into the skin,

then rinse off. It clears out the skin pores and leaves your skin soft.

You will need:

1 tablespoon oats

2 tablespoons base oil

1 teaspoon dried herbs/flowers

8 to 10 drops essential oils (mixture of your choosing)

Grind the oats and dried herbs/flowers to a powder in a pestle and mortar, blender or use the end of a rolling pin in a dish.

Mix the essential oils with the base oil.

Combine it all together to form a paste.

Store in an airtight jar for up to three months.

Body Oil

Massage into the skin.

You will need:

3 tablespoons base oil such as almond or jojoba

20 drops essential oil (mixture of your choosing)

Mix the oils together.

Store in an airtight bottle for up to three months.

Bath salts

Add a couple of tablespoons of these bath salts to your bath.

You will need:

450g/16 oz sea salt

225g/8 oz Epsom salt

6 drops essential oils (mixture of your choosing)

1 teaspoon of dried herbs/flower

Mix together, keep in an air–tight jar.

Body Butter

Use as you would a moisturiser.

You will need:

225g/8 oz shea butter or cocoa butter (or a mixture of both)
110g/4 oz coconut oil
110g/4 oz carrier oil such as almond or jojoba
20 drops of essential oils (mixture of your choosing)

Put the butters, coconut oil and carrier oils into a bowl over a pan of simmering water. Stir continuously until all the ingredients are melted. Remove from the heat and allow to cool slightly. Add in your essential oils. Put the mixture in the fridge to cool for about an hour, it should still be soft but starting to harden around the edges. Now whisk the mixture for about ten minutes, until it is light and fluffy. This is best done using an electric mixer. Spoon into glass jars and seal with lids.

Put back into the fridge to set for about fifteen to twenty minutes.

Body Spritz

Spray all over for a lovely refreshing and hydrating scent.

You will need:

75ml/2 ½ fl oz distilled water, or you could use rose water
2 tablespoons aloe vera juice or gel (this isn't essential but helps make the spray more hydrating)
25 drops essential oil (mixture of your choosing)

Combine everything together and pour into a sterilised spray bottle. This will keep for up to six months. Sake well before use.

Perfume Oil

Keep this in a roll on bottle or jar to dab onto your skin.

You will need:
10ml/0.3 fl oz base oil such as almond or jojoba
10–12 drops essential oil (mixture of your choosing)

Combine the base oil with the essential oils. Shake the bottle before use.
Note: Remember a scent smells better if you use a balance of the three notes; base, mid and top.

Body powder

Body powders are easy to make and to customise.
You will need:
2 tablespoons baking soda
5 tablespoons arrowroot or corn starch
6 teaspoons of powdered herbs and/or flower petals
12 drops essential oil

Mix the essential oil with the dried herbs and allow it to dry. Then combine with the baking soda and arrowroot/corn starch.

Spell Pouches

Spell bag, spell pouch, medicine bags, gris gris or mojo bags are fabulous to work with. (All different names for pretty much the same thing).

A spell pouch contains items that are charged with your intent. Your pouch once it is put together is essentially 'alive' with energy and it will need to be looked after and 'fed' with magic powder (instructions in this book). You will need to feed it periodically to maintain its energy force.

A spell pouch can contain all sorts of items – herbs, roots, spices, crystals, feathers, bones, shells, dirt, pebbles, coins – what you put in your medicine bag is up to you. You can also add a petition slip; a piece of paper with your intent written on.

Traditional gris gris bags use red flannel for the bag itself but I like to add colour magic to my spell pouch, I use orange material a lot as this is the colour for success, but also using green for prosperity, blue for healing etc works really well. If you are working with a particular Moon phase or zodiac sign you could use a colour that corresponds with that.

You don't even have to be good at sewing, just use a handkerchief, a scarf, or felt is good as it doesn't fray, or just use a scrap of material. They can be tied with string or ribbon, but remember you need to get into it regularly to feed it. You can also use the chiffon bags that craft shops sell for wedding favours. If all else fails, then use an envelope! Be creative…

Absolutely trust your intuition and be guided by it with making your own spell pouches, but here are some suggestions for each Moon phase (all suggestions for herbs and plant material are dried, any fresh plant material put in a bag will go mouldy). For the crystals you only need to use a crystal chip or a small tumble stone.

How to create your spell pouch

Choose your bag and the items you want to put inside it. Charge each one with your intent and add it to the bag. You could say a chant or state your intent out loud once you are finished. Charge the whole bag under the corresponding Moon phase. Keep the pouch with you or place on your altar. Feed it regularly with magic powder to recharge it or give it a shake occasionally and restate your intent. Once the pouch has finished its job you can dispose of it in the trash or bury it. Crystals can be removed, cleansed and used again if you wish.

New Moon

Bag colour: Green, orange of white

Plant content: Acorns, basil, bay, cardamom, cherry stones, chilli seeds, cinnamon bark, egg shells, jasmine flowers, nettle, nutmeg, oak leaves, orange peel, pasta, peach stone, sage, tomato pips, walnut shells

Crystal: Amethyst, citrine, clear quartz, labradorite, moonstone, smoky quartz

Other: Silver coins, new pins

Waxing Crescent Moon

Bag colour: Orange, pink, blue

Plant content: Basil, beans, cedar bark or leaves, chicken bones, cinnamon bark, coriander seeds, fennel seeds, fish bones, garlic (the white outer skin), honeysuckle flowers, juniper berries, pine needles, rosemary, thyme

Crystal: Amber, amethyst, banded agate, carnelian, citrine, malachite, rose quartz, tiger's eye

Other: Horseshoe charm (obviously not a life size horseshoe…)

First Quarter Moon

Bag colour: Yellow, purple, blue

Plant content: Almonds, ash bark or leaves, beech bark or leaves, black peppercorns, cinnamon bark, dandelion flowers or seeds, elder bark or leaves, fennel seeds, peach stone, rowan bark, leaves or berries, sage, sunflower seeds, turkey bones, walnut shells, willow bark or leaves

Crystal: Agate (moss), amber, aventurine (green), carnelian, citrine, fluorite, goldstone, labradorite, lapis lazuli, pebble, pyrite, quartz (clear)

Other: Sea shells, silver charms

Waxing Gibbous Moon

Bag colour: Blue, red, orange

Plant content: Cashew shells, chilli seeds, cinnamon bark, coffee beans, curry leaves, elder bark or leaves, elm bark or leaves, grapefruit peel or pips, lime peel or pips, orange peel or pips, pansy flowers, poppy seeds, primrose flowers, rose petals, saffron, sesame seeds, tansy flowers, violet flowers

Crystal: Amber, amethyst, bloodstone, calcite (orange), citrine, goldstone, labradorite, lepidolite, malachite, obsidian (black), quartz (clear), rhodochrosite, rhodonite, tiger's eye.

Other: Paper clips (for organisation)

Full Moon

Bag colour: White, purple, red, silver

Plant content: Basil, black pepper corns, chilli seeds, cocoa nibs, cinnamon bark, egg shells, fish bones, garlic (white outer skin), hyssop, jasmine flowers, mint (a peppermint sweet works well), oregano, pasta, rose petals, rose hips, sandalwood, thyme, tomato seeds, yarrow

Crystal: Amethyst, chrysocolla, quartz (clear), kyanite, moonstone, moss agate, selenite, quartz (smoky)

Other: Silver charms, sea shells

Waning Moon

Bag colour: White, black, pale blue

Plant content: Bay, bean, coriander seeds, eucalyptus leaves or bark, fish bones, hyssop, jasmine flowers, lemon peel or pips, lime peel or pips, marjoram, mint, orange peel or pips, pasta, rice, rosemary, sage, sandalwood, star anise, yarrow

Crystal: Black tourmaline, bloodstone, citrine, clear quartz, obsidian, smoky quartz, snowflake obsidian

Other: Incense cones, sea salt flakes

Third Quarter Moon

Bag colour: White, pale blue, pink

Plant content: Alyssum, birch leaves or bark, carnation, chamomile, cinnamon bark, coriander seeds, elm bark or leaves, holly leaves or bark, honeysuckle, lemon peel or pips, liquorice root, mushrooms (dried definitely), plum stone, self–heal, thyme, turkey bones, willow leaves or bark, witch hazel leaves or bark, woodruff

Crystal: Agate (banded), amber, green aventurine, carnelian, chrysoprase, fluorite, garnet, goldstone, lepidolite, moonstone, black obsidian, rose quartz, rhodochrosite, sodalite, tiger's eye, unakite

Other: Small pieces of mirror, oyster shell

Waning Crescent Moon

Bag colour: Blue, pale green, pale yellow

Plant content: Ash leaves or bark, bay, burdock, carnation, coriander seeds, dock, elder leaves or bark, fennel seeds, fish bones, garlic (outer white skin), hazelnut shells, hyssop, juniper berries, lime peel or pips, lungwort, melon seeds, mint, mugwort, nettle, pine needles, rosemary, star anise, tansy, thyme, violet

Crystal: Amethyst, bloodstone, hematite, labradorite, larimar, lepidolite, malachite, black obsidian, pyrite, selenite, sugilite, tiger's eye

Other: Beer bottle caps

Dark Moon

Bag colour: Black, dark purple, dark blue

Plant content: Apple seeds, ash leaves or bark, bay, burdock, dandelion, elder leaves or bark, fennel seeds, garlic (outer white skin), hawthorn berries, leaves or flowers, hazel leaves, flowers, bark or nut shells, foxglove, heather, jasmine, mugwort, nutmeg, oak leaves, bark or acorns, rosemary, rue, sage, sandalwood, star anise, tansy, tobacco, thistle, willow leaves or bark, wormwood

Crystal: Apache tear, chrysocolla, fluorite, labradorite, obsidian, red jasper, selenite

Other: Photograph of yourself

Aries

Bag colour: White, pink, red

Plant content: Bay, cinnamon bark, coriander seeds, feverfew, juniper berries, marjoram, nettle, rosemary

Crystal: Apache tear, aventurine (green), bloodstone, hematite, kyanite, red jasper

Other: Draw the zodiac symbol on a slip of paper, a disc of wood or paint it on a pebble

Taurus

Bag colour: Red, green, yellow

Plant content: Coltsfoot, dandelion, lungwort, myrtle, thyme

Crystal: Carnelian, chrysocolla, chrysoprase, kyanite, rose quartz, rhodonite

Other: Draw the zodiac symbol on a slip of paper, a disc of wood or paint it on a pebble

Gemini

Bag colour: Red, blue, orange

Plant content: Angelica, bergamot, dill, honeysuckle, oregano, tansy, thyme

Crystal: Banded agate, moss agate, clear quartz, serpentine

Other: Draw the zodiac symbol on a slip of paper, a disc of wood or paint it on a pebble

Cancer

Bag colour: Blue, green, brown

Plant content: Angelica, dill, honeysuckle, hyssop, jasmine, mugwort, violet, wormwood

Crystal: Orange calcite, chrysoprase, moonstone, opal, selenite, silver

Other: Draw the zodiac symbol on a slip of paper, a disc of wood or paint it on a pebble

Leo

Bag colour: Orange, red, green

Plant content: Angelica, bay, burdock, chamomile, dill, fennel seeds, rue, sunflower seeds, leaves or petals

Crystal: Amber, carnelian, labradorite, pyrite, clear quartz, rhodochrosite, tiger's eye

Other: Draw the zodiac symbol on a slip of paper, a disc of wood or paint it on a pebble

Virgo

Bag colour: Yellow, green, black

Plant content: Bergamot, fennel seeds, sandalwood, scullcap, valerian

Crystal: Moss agate, aragonite, amazonite, red jasper, sugilite

Other: Draw the zodiac symbol on a slip of paper, a disc of wood or paint it on a pebble

Libra

Bag colour: Black, blue, purple

Plant content: Angelica, bergamot, burdock, elder leaves or bark, feverfew, Saint John's Wort, thyme, violet

Crystal: Kyanite, lepidolite, moonstone, tourmaline (all colours)

Other: Draw the zodiac symbol on a slip of paper, a disc of wood or paint it on a pebble

Scorpio

Bag colour: Brown, black, red

Plant content: Basil, blackthorn leaves, bark or thorns, horehound, ivy, nettle, pennyroyal, wormwood

Crystal: Amethyst, bloodstone, citrine, fluorite, red jasper, labradorite, malachite, moonstone, rhodochrosite, unakite

Other: Draw the zodiac symbol on a slip of paper, a disc of wood or paint it on a pebble

Sagittarius

Bag colour: Purple, red, yellow

Plant content: Beech leaves or bark, birch leaves or bark, cedar leaves or bark, elder leaves or bark, feverfew, hawthorn leaves, bark or thorns, nutmeg, oak leaves, bark or acorns, rowan leaves, bark or berries, sage, sandalwood

Crystal: Amethyst, goldstone, labradorite, lapis lazuli, black obsidian, snowflake obsidian, smoky quartz, sodalite

Other: Draw the zodiac symbol on a slip of paper, a disc of wood or paint it on a pebble

Capricorn

Bag colour: Red, brown, black

Plant content: Comfrey, marjoram, pine needles, plantain, poppy seeds, Solomon's seal, witch hazel leaves or bark

Crystal: Apache tear, aragonite, malachite, clear quartz, smoky quartz, tiger's eye

Other: Draw the zodiac symbol on a slip of paper, a disc of wood or paint it on a pebble

Aquarius

Bag colour: Blue, green, white

Plant content: Bergamot, cypress leaves or bark, elder leaves or bark, fennel seeds, Saint John's wort

Crystal: Fluorite, hematite, labradorite, moldavite

Other: Draw the zodiac symbol on a slip of paper, a disc of wood or paint it on a pebble

Pisces

Bag colour: White, green, blue

Plant content: Bladder wrack, dulse, fern, geranium, lily of the valley, lungwort, meadowsweet, rose petals, willow bark or leaves

Crystal: Amethyst, amazonite, bloodstone, fluorite, larimar, turquoise

Other: Draw the zodiac symbol on a slip of paper, a disc of wood or paint it on a pebble

January

Bag colour: White, violet, black

Plant content: Alyssum, basil, bay, betony (wood), birch leaves or bark, black pepper, cardamom, cinnamon bark, cloves, coriander seeds, crocus, cumin seeds, fennel seeds, garlic (white outer skin), holly leaves, bark or berries, honeysuckle, horehound, juniper berries, lavender, marjoram, mint, mustard seeds, nutmeg, rosemary, rue, sage, star anise, witch hazel bark or leaves, woodruff

Crystal: Agate (moss), amber, fluorite, hematite, kyanite, quartz (clear), rhodonite, selenite, sugilite, sunstone, tiger's eye, turquoise

February

Bag colour: Light blue, violet, pale green, pink

Plant content: Avocado stone, basil, bay, birch leaves and bark, cherry stones, cinnamon bark, dock, fennel seeds, fish bones, hawthorn bark, leaves or thorns, hazel leaves or bark, hyssop, juniper berries, lime peel or pips, melon seeds, mistletoe leaves, olive stones, peach stones, pine needles, poppy seeds, rose petals, rosemary, rowan leaves, bark or berries, rue, strawberry leaves, vervain

Crystal: Agate (moss), amber, aventurine (green), chrysoprase, fluorite, larimar, malachite, moonstone, pebble, quartz (clear), quartz (rose), selenite, sugilite, sunstone, turquoise

March

Bag colour: Pink, pale green, pale blue, yellow, white, lilac

Plant content: Birch leaves or bark, bluebell, cloves, cornflower, cyclamen, egg shells, fennel seeds, hawthorn bark, leaves or thorns, hazel leaves, bark or nuts, honesty, horsetail, mustard seeds, parsley, pasta, pine needles, primrose, rice, Saint John's Wort, snapdragon, sunflower, sweet pea, walnut shells

Crystals: Agate (moss), agate (blue lace), celestite, chrysocolla, fluorite, howlite, kyanite, larimar, moonstone, pyrite, quartz (rose), sodalite, turquoise

April

Bag colour: Red, gold, green

Plant content: Bay, beech leaves or bark, bergamot, black pepper, chilli seeds, cinnamon bark, clover, cumin seeds, holly leaves, bark or berries, lemon balm, lily of the valley, pasta, primrose, rowan leaves, bark or berries, Solomon's seal, tomato seeds

Crystals: Agate (moss), aventurine (green), calcite (orange), carnelian, citrine, goldstone, labradorite, lepidolite, malachite, rhodochrosite, rhodonite, sodalite, tiger's eye

May

Bag colour: Green, brown, pink, orange, red

Plant content: African violet, alexanders, almond, ash leaves or bark, bay, beech leaves or bark, camellia, cinnamon bark, cornflower, elder leaves or bark, grape seeds, heliotrope, mustard seeds, parsley, rowan leaves, bark or berries, self–heal, star anise, sweetpea, willow bark or leaves

Crystals: Amethyst, bloodstone, chrysocolla, citrine, fluorite, goldstone, kyanite, labradorite, lapis lazuli, moonstone, quartz (rose), rhodochrosite, selenite, sunstone, turquoise

June

Bag colour: Orange, gold, green

Plant content: Bay, blackthorn leaves, black pepper, bark or thorns, carnation, daisy, delphinium, garlic (the white outer skin), horsetail, lavender, lemon peel or pips, mugwort, mushrooms (very definitely dried ones), oak leaves, bark or acorns, pennyroyal, pine nuts, plantain, raspberry leaves, Saint John's Wort, sesame seeds, sunflower, sweetpea, tea leaves (black)

Crystals: Agate (blue lace), fluorite, hematite, labradorite, lapis lazuli, lepidolite, pyrite, quartz (clear), quartz (smoky), rhodonite, selenite, sunstone, turquoise, unakite

July

Bag colour: Silver, blue, grey

Plant content: Ash leaves or bark, bergamot, chamomile, cinnamon bark, cramp bark, cumin seeds, date stones, eucalyptus leaves or bark, heather, heliotrope, holly leaves, bark or berries, honeysuckle, jasmine, plum stones, rose petals, rowan leaves, berries or bark, sage, sandalwood, star anise, tea leaves (black)

Crystals: Agate (blue lace), amethyst, fluorite, howlite, kyanite, labradorite, larimar, moonstone, black obsidian, quartz (clear), quartz (smoky), turquoise

August

Bag colour: Yellow, gold, orange

Plant content: Bergamot, carnation, chilli seeds, coffee, coltsfoot, elm bark or leaves, grapefruit peel or pips, heather, hyssop, lemon peel or pips, lime peel or pips, orange peel or pips, lemon balm, plantain, rose petals or thorns, rosemary, saffron, sesame seeds, sweet pea, tansy

Crystals: Agate (moss), amber, bloodstone, labradorite, larimar, malachite, pyrite, quartz (clear), rhodochrosite, sodalite, sunstone, turquoise

September

Bag colour: Brown, green, yellow

Plant content: Alexanders, agrimony, chamomile, cramp bark, dill, dock, elm leaves or bark, fish bones, honeysuckle, geranium, liquorice root, lungwort, mint, mushrooms (dried), plum stone, rue, salt flakes, self–heal, tansy, witch hazel leaves or bark

Crystals: Agate (blue lace), amber, amethyst, fluorite, hematite, kyanite, labradorite, rhodonite, selenite, sugilite, turquoise

October

Bag colour: Dark blue, orange, black

Plant content: Almond, apple pips, ash leaves or bark, bay, cinnamon bark, dittany, elder leaves or bark, fern, grapefruit peel or pips, heather, morning glory, mugwort, parsley, pasta, periwinkle, saffron, sage, star anise, thistle, thyme, willow bark or leaves

Crystals: Bloodstone, fluorite, labradorite, lepidolite, malachite, black obsidian, tourmaline, turquoise, unakite

November

Bag colour: Grey, deep green, dark blue

Plant content: Almond, bay, bergamot, bladder wrack, borage, cinnamon bark, coriander seeds, elm leaves or bark, grass, hazel leaves, bark or nuts, juniper berries, marigold, mustard seeds, mugwort, pasta, rowan leaves, bark or berries, saffron, sage, sandalwood (white), yarrow

Crystals: Chrysocolla, citrine, kyanite, labradorite, lepidolite, malachite, moonstone, quartz (clear), rhodonite, selenite, sodalite, sugilite, turquoise

December

Bag colour: Red, white, green, silver, gold

Plant content: Alyssum, basil, cocoa nibs, cumin seeds, borage, horehound, lavender, meadowsweet, orange peel or pips, pennyroyal, poppy seeds, saffron, sweet pea, thyme, vervain, violet, yarrow

Crystals: Agate (blue lace), agate (moss), amethyst, fluorite, howlite, larimar, lepidolite, rhodochrosite, rhodonite, quartz (rose), sunstone, tourmaline

Magic Powders

Magic powders have lots of uses, although they do work well to 'feed' your spell pouches. They can be used to roll candles in for spell work, to sprinkle around your house for protection, to add oomph to rituals and any spells, to add to poppets and witches' bottles or to wear in a small bottle as a charm.

To make a magic powder the ingredients you use must be ground so you will need either a pestle and mortar or the end of a rolling pin and a solid bowl. As you add each ingredient to the bowl charge it first with your intent. I also like to charge the powder as a whole once it is complete too. This can then be fed to your spell pouch each week, just a sprinkle; you can even boost the power by feeding it on the corresponding day of the week to your intent. Or keep it in an airtight bottle or jar and use for all sorts of other spell work.

I like to use a base for my magic powders, I usually use either salt or sugar, as it grinds well and adds its own qualities to the mix too.

New Moon

Plant content: Basil, bay, cardamom, chamomile, chilli seeds, ground cinnamon, egg shells, jasmine flowers, myrrh, nettle, ground nutmeg, oak leaves, orange peel, paprika, rue, sage, tomato pips, wheat flour

Base: Sugar

Waxing Crescent Moon

Plant content: Basil, bergamot, cedar bark or leaves, ground cinnamon, coriander seeds, fennel seeds, garlic (the white outer skin), honeysuckle flowers, juniper berries, myrrh, pine needles, rosemary, sandalwood (white), thyme

Base: Sugar

First Quarter Moon

Plant content: Alexanders, almonds (ground), ash bark or leaves, beech bark or leaves, benzoin, black peppercorns, ground cinnamon, cleavers, dandelion flowers or seeds, elder bark or leaves, fennel seeds, hazel bark or leaves, rowan bark, leaves or berries, sage, sandalwood (white), sunflower seeds, violet, willow bark or leaves, wheat flour

Base: Sugar

Waxing Gibbous Moon

Plant content: Baking powder/soda, cashew nuts, chilli seeds, cinnamon bark, cleavers, coffee, coltsfoot, cramp bark, curry leaves, elder bark or leaves, elm bark or leaves, grapefruit peel, lime peel, orange peel, pansy flowers, paprika, plantain, poppy seeds, primrose flowers, rose petals, saffron, sesame seeds, scullcap, tansy flowers, violet flowers

Base: Sugar

Full Moon

Plant content: Basil, bergamot, black pepper corns, chilli seeds, cocoa, ground cinnamon, egg shells, garlic (white outer skin), hyssop, jasmine flowers, mint, myrtle, oregano, rose petals, rose hips, sandalwood, thyme, tomato seeds, yarrow

Base: Sugar and salt mix

Waning Moon

Plant content: Bay, coriander seeds, cypress leaves or bark, eucalyptus leaves or bark, frankincense, hyssop, jasmine flowers, lemon peel, lime peel, marjoram, mint, myrtle, orange peel, parsley, rice, rosemary, sage, sandalwood, star anise, yarrow

Base: Salt

Third Quarter Moon

Plant content: Alexanders, alyssum, birch leaves or bark, carnation, celandine, chamomile, ground cinnamon, coriander seeds, cypress bark or leaves, dill, elm bark or leaves, holly leaves or bark, honeysuckle, lemon peel, liquorice root, lungwort, mushrooms (dried definitely), rue, self–heal, thyme, wheat flour, willow leaves or bark, witch hazel leaves or bark, woodruff

Base: Salt

Waning Crescent Moon

Plant content: Angelica, ash leaves or bark, bay, burdock, carnation, comfrey, coriander seeds, dock, elder leaves or bark, fennel seeds, feverfew, garlic (outer white skin), hazelnut, hyssop, juniper berries, lime peel, lungwort, melon seeds, mint, mugwort, myrrh, nettle, pine needles, rosemary, star anise, tansy, thyme, violet

Base: Salt

Dark Moon

Plant content: Apple seeds, ash leaves or bark, bay, benzoin, burdock, cypress leaves or bark, dandelion, dittany, dragon's blood, elder leaves or bark, fennel seeds, frankincense, garlic (outer white skin), ground ginger, hawthorn berries, leaves or flowers, hazel leaves, flowers, bark or nuts, foxglove, heather, jasmine, mugwort, myrrh, nutmeg, oak leaves or bark, paprika, rosemary, rue, sage, sandalwood, star anise, tansy, tobacco, thistle, willow leaves or bark, wormwood

Base: Salt

Aries

Plant content: Bay, ground cinnamon, coriander seeds, dragon's blood, feverfew, frankincense, juniper berries, marjoram, myrrh, nettle, rosemary

Base: Sugar

Taurus

Plant content: Coltsfoot, dandelion, lungwort, myrtle, thyme

Base: Salt

Gemini

Plant content: Angelica, bergamot, dill, honeysuckle, oregano, tansy, thyme

Base: Salt

Cancer

Plant content: Angelica, dill, honeysuckle, hyssop, jasmine, mugwort, violet, wormwood

Base: Sugar

Leo

Plant content: Angelica, bay, burdock, chamomile, dill, fennel seeds, frankincense, rue, sunflower seeds, leaves or petals

Base: Sugar

Virgo

Plant content: Bergamot, fennel seeds, sandalwood, scullcap,

valerian
Base: Salt

Libra

Plant content: Angelica, bergamot, burdock, elder leaves or bark, feverfew, Saint John's Wort, thyme, violet
Base: Salt

Scorpio

Plant content: Basil, blackthorn leaves, bark or thorns, horehound, ivy, nettle, pennyroyal, wormwood
Base: Sugar

Sagittarius

Plant content: Beech leaves or bark, birch leaves or bark, cedar leaves or bark, elder leaves or bark, feverfew, hawthorn leaves, bark or flowers, ground nutmeg, oak leaves or bark, rowan leaves, bark or berries, sage, sandalwood
Base: Sugar

Capricorn

Plant content: Benzoin, comfrey, marjoram, pine needles, plantain, poppy seeds, Solomon's seal, witch hazel leaves or bark
Base: Salt

Aquarius

Plant content: Bergamot, cypress leaves or bark, elder leaves or bark, fennel seeds, frankincense, myrrh, Saint John's wort
Base: Salt

Pisces

Plant content: Bladder wrack, dulse, fern, geranium, lily of the valley, lungwort, meadowsweet, rose petals, willow bark or leaves

Base: Sugar

January

Plant content: Alyssum, basil, bay, betony (wood), birch leaves or bark, black pepper, cardamom, ground cinnamon, cloves, coriander seeds, crocus, cumin seeds, fennel seeds, garlic (white outer skin), holly leaves, bark or berries, honeysuckle, horehound, juniper berries, lavender, marjoram, mint, mustard seeds, ground nutmeg, rosemary, rue, sage, star anise, witch hazel bark or leaves, woodruff

Base: Salt

February

Plant content: Basil, bay, birch leaves and bark, cherry leaves, ground cinnamon, dock, fennel seeds, hawthorn bark, leaves or thorns, hazel leaves or bark, hyssop, juniper berries, lime peel, melon seeds, mistletoe leaves, olive leaves, peach leaves, pine needles, poppy seeds, rose petals, rosemary, rowan leaves, bark or berries, rue, strawberry leaves, vervain

Base: Salt

March

Plant content: Birch leaves or bark, bluebell, cloves, cornflower, cyclamen, egg shells, fennel seeds, hawthorn bark, leaves or thorns, hazel leaves or bark, honesty, horsetail, mustard seeds, parsley, pine needles, primrose, rice, Saint John's Wort, snapdragon, sunflower, sweet pea

Base: Sugar

April

Plant content: Bay, beech leaves or bark, bergamot, black

pepper, chilli seeds, ground cinnamon, clover, cumin seeds, holly leaves, bark or berries, lemon balm, lily of the valley, primrose, rowan leaves, bark or berries, Solomon's seal, tomato seeds

Base: Sugar

May

Plant content: African violet, alexanders, almond, ash leaves or bark, bay, beech leaves or bark, camellia, ground cinnamon, cornflower, elder leaves or bark, grape seeds, heliotrope, mustard seeds, parsley, rowan leaves, bark or berries, self–heal, star anise, sweetpea, willow bark or leaves

Base: Salt

June

Plant content: Bay, blackthorn leaves, bark or thorns, black pepper, carnation, daisy, delphinium, garlic (the white outer skin), horsetail, lavender, lemon peel, mugwort, mushrooms (very definitely dried ones), oak leaves or bark, pennyroyal, pine nuts, plantain, raspberry leaves, Saint John's Wort, sesame seeds, sunflower, sweetpea, tea leaves (black)

Base: Salt

July

Plant content: Ash leaves or bark, bergamot, chamomile, ground cinnamon, cramp bark, cumin seeds, eucalyptus leaves or bark, heather, heliotrope, holly leaves, bark or berries, honeysuckle, jasmine, rose petals, rowan leaves, berries or bark, sage, sandalwood, star anise, tea leaves (black)

Base: Sugar

August

Plant content: Bergamot, carnation, chilli seeds, coffee, coltsfoot, elm bark or leaves, grapefruit peel, heather, hyssop, lemon peel, lime peel, orange peel, lemon balm, plantain, rose petals, rosemary, saffron, sesame seeds, sweet pea, tansy

Base: Sugar

September

Plant content: Alexanders, agrimony, chamomile, cramp bark, dill, dock, elm leaves or bark, honeysuckle, geranium, liquorice root, lungwort, mint, mushrooms (dried), rue, self–heal, tansy, witch hazel leaves or bark

Base: Salt

October

Plant content: Almond, apple pips, ash leaves or bark, bay, ground cinnamon, dittany, elder leaves or bark, fern, grapefruit peel, heather, morning glory, mugwort, parsley, periwinkle, saffron, sage, star anise, thistle, thyme, willow bark or leaves

Base: Salt

November

Plant content: Almond, bay, bergamot, bladder wrack, borage, ground cinnamon, coriander seeds, elm leaves or bark, grass, hazel leaves or bark, juniper berries, marigold, mustard seeds, mugwort, rowan leaves, bark or berries, saffron, sage, sandalwood (white), yarrow

Base: Sugar

December

Plant content: Alyssum, basil, cocoa powder, cumin seeds, borage, horehound, lavender, meadowsweet, orange peel, pennyroyal, poppy seeds, saffron, sweet pea, thyme, vervain, violet, yarrow

Base: Sugar

Witches Bottles

Something I have made for years are witch bottles. I always keep a couple in the house and renew them regularly. Their purpose in my home is to soak up negative energy and keep the house full of happy positive vibes. However, witch bottles can be made for any intent. These are so easy to make, you don't need special pretty bottles you can just use old clean jam jars.

Generally speaking, the modern day witch bottles are very similar to historical witch bottles in their basic structure, even though their intended purpose has changed. The most common purpose for constructing a witch bottle today is to capture negative energy and send it back out as positive. The basic structure of witch bottles can be used for purposes other than protection such as prosperity, healing and love.

Basically, a witch bottle is a container of some sort, usually a jar or a bottle, which is filled with objects that correspond to a given intent. The items are magically charged as they are added and can also be recharged with energy for as long as is needed, provided the bottle does not get broken.

Traditionally a witch bottle would have contained nails, earth, stones, knotted threads, herbs, spices, resin, flowers, candle wax, salt, vinegar, oil, coins, ashes and quite often urine.

Originally witch bottles were used to keep witches away. They also used to contain all sorts of bodily fluids, hair and finger nail clippings – you can add these if you want to.

Start with your jar or bottle, then as charge each item before you add it, layering up the 'ingredients' as you go.

It really is up to you what you put in. I like to put in three nails to attract negativity and for protection, I also put in a piece of string with three knots in, knotting in my intent with each tie.

If it is for prosperity, I often drop in a silver coin. I usually put salt in for protection, cleansing and purification. I also like to add some kind of dried pulse – lentils or beans to 'soak' up any negative energies. Garlic is good for protection too. Then add any herbs, spices and flowers that correspond with your intent – rose petals for love, cinnamon for success, mint and basil for prosperity etc. Keep filling the jar or bottle up until you reach the top then put the lid on. If you are using a jam jar, I like to draw a pentacle on the lid. If I am using a bottle with a cork, I like to seal the cork lid with dripped wax.

If you are making the witch bottle for protection for your own home I like to put in a pebble from the garden, a couple of fallen leaves from the tree in my yard and a bit of cobweb from inside the house, it makes it all more personal and ties the bottle to the energies of the home. our witch bottle can be charged under the light of the Moon.

A twist on the witches' bottle is a money jar: Use a clean, cleansed jar and half fill it with rice or seeds. As you half fill the jar visualise prosperity and abundance. Then every day add a pinch of seeds to the jar, visualising prosperity as you do. When the jar is full bury the seeds whilst sending up a request to deity that your desire will be fulfilled. Start this jar on a new or waxing Moon for added oomph.

You can also do this with a jar and your loose change, each time you drop a couple of coins in the jar visualise prosperity, every so often sprinkle in a few herbs that correspond with prosperity such as basil or mint. When the jar is full you can count it up and use it for something special.

Below I have given some suggestions for witch bottles to correspond with the various Moon phases and months.

New Moon

Candle wax: Green orange or white

Plant content: Acorns, basil, bay, cardamom, cherry stones, chilli seeds, cinnamon bark, egg shells, jasmine flowers, nettle, nutmeg, oak leaves, orange peel, pasta, peach stone, sage, tomato pips, walnut shells

Crystal: Amethyst, citrine, clear quartz, labradorite, moonstone, smoky quartz

Other: Silver coins, new pins, knotted string (with your intent tied in), bent nails, hair, nail clippings, cobwebs, sugar

Waxing Crescent Moon

Candle wax: Orange, pink, blue

Plant content: Basil, beans, cedar bark or leaves, chicken bones, cinnamon bark, coriander seeds, fennel seeds, fish bones, garlic (the white outer skin), honeysuckle flowers, juniper berries, pine needles, rosemary, thyme

Crystal: Amber, amethyst, banded agate, carnelian, citrine, malachite, rose quartz, tiger's eye

Other: Horseshoe charm (obviously not a life size horseshoe…) silver coins, new pins, knotted string (with your intent tied in), bent nails, hair, nail clippings, cobwebs, sugar

First Quarter Moon

Candle wax: Yellow, purple, blue

Plant content: Almonds, ash bark or leaves, beech bark or leaves, black peppercorns, cinnamon bark, dandelion flowers or seeds, elder bark or leaves, fennel seeds, peach stone, rowan bark, leaves or berries, sage, sunflower seeds, turkey bones, walnut shells, willow bark or leaves

Crystal: Agate (moss), amber, aventurine (green), carnelian, citrine, fluorite, goldstone, labradorite, lapis lazuli, pebble, pyrite, quartz (clear)

Other: Sea shells, silver charms, silver coins, new pins, knotted string (with your intent tied in), bent nails, hair, nail clippings, cobwebs, sugar

Waxing Gibbous Moon

Candle wax: Blue, red, orange

Plant content: Cashew shells, chilli seeds, cinnamon bark, coffee beans, curry leaves, elder bark or leaves, elm bark or leaves, grapefruit peel or pips, lime peel or pips, orange peel or pips, pansy flowers, poppy seeds, primrose flowers, rose petals, saffron, sesame seeds, tansy flowers, violet flowers

Crystal: Amber, amethyst, bloodstone, calcite (orange), citrine, goldstone, labradorite, lepidolite, malachite, obsidian (black), quartz (clear), rhodochrosite, rhodonite, tiger's eye.

Other: Paper clips (for organisation), silver coins, new pins, knotted string (with your intent tied in), bent nails, hair, nail clippings, cobwebs, sugar

Full Moon

Candle wax: White, purple, red, silver

Plant content: Basil, black pepper corns, chilli seeds, cocoa nibs, cinnamon bark, egg shells, fish bones, garlic (white outer skin), hyssop, jasmine flowers, mint (a peppermint sweet works well), oregano, pasta, rose petals, rose hips, sandalwood, thyme, tomato seeds, yarrow

Crystal: Amethyst, chrysocolla, quartz (clear), kyanite, moonstone, moss agate, selenite, quartz (smoky)

Other: Silver charms, sea shells, silver coins, new pins, knotted string (with your intent tied in), bent nails, hair, nail clippings, cobwebs, sugar, salt

Waning Moon

Candle wax: White, black, pale blue

Plant content: Bay, bean, coriander seeds, eucalyptus leaves or bark, fish bones, hyssop, jasmine flowers, lemon peel or pips, lime peel or pips, marjoram, mint, orange peel or pips, pasta, rice, rosemary, sage, sandalwood, star anise, yarrow

Crystal: Black tourmaline, bloodstone, citrine, clear quartz, obsidian, smoky quartz, snowflake obsidian

Other: Incense cones, sea salt flakes, new pins, knotted string (with your intent tied in), bent nails, hair, nail clippings, cobwebs

Third Quarter Moon

Candle wax: White, pale blue, pink

Plant content: Alyssum, birch leaves or bark, carnation, chamomile, cinnamon bark, coriander seeds, elm bark or leaves, holly leaves or bark, honeysuckle, lemon peel or pips, liquorice root, mushrooms (dried definitely), plum stone, self–heal, thyme, turkey bones, willow leaves or bark, witch hazel leaves or bark, woodruff

Crystal: Agate (banded), amber, green aventurine, carnelian, chrysoprase, fluorite, garnet, goldstone, lepidolite, moonstone, black obsidian, rose quartz, rhodochrosite, sodalite, tiger's eye, unakite

Other: Small pieces of mirror, oyster shell, sea salt flakes, new pins, knotted string (with your intent tied in), bent nails, hair, nail clippings, cobwebs

Waning Crescent Moon

Candle wax: Blue, pale green, pale yellow

Plant content: Ash leaves or bark, bay, burdock, carnation, coriander seeds, dock, elder leaves or bark, fennel seeds, fish bones, garlic (outer white skin), hazelnut shells, hyssop, juniper berries, lime peel or pips, lungwort, melon seeds, mint, mugwort, nettle, pine needles, rosemary, star anise, tansy, thyme, violet

Crystal: Amethyst, bloodstone, hematite, labradorite, larimar, lepidolite, malachite, black obsidian, pyrite, selenite, sugilite, tiger's eye

Other: Beer bottle caps, sea salt flakes, new pins, knotted string (with your intent tied in), bent nails, hair, nail clippings, cobwebs

Dark Moon

Candle wax: Black, dark purple, dark blue

Plant content: Apple seeds, ash leaves or bark, bay, burdock, dandelion, elder leaves or bark, fennel seeds, garlic (outer white skin), hawthorn berries, leaves or flowers, hazel leaves, flowers, bark or nut shells, foxglove, heather, jasmine, mugwort, nutmeg, oak leaves, bark or acorns, rosemary, rue, sage, sandalwood, star anise, tansy, tobacco, thistle, willow leaves or bark, wormwood

Crystal: Apache tear, chrysocolla, fluorite, labradorite, obsidian, red jasper, selenite

Other: Photograph of yourself, sea salt flakes, new pins, knotted string (with your intent tied in), bent nails, hair, nail clippings, cobwebs

Aries

Candle wax: White, pink, red

Plant content: Bay, cinnamon bark, coriander seeds, feverfew, juniper berries, marjoram, nettle, rosemary

Crystal: Apache tear, aventurine (green), bloodstone, hematite, kyanite, red jasper

Other: Draw the zodiac symbol on a slip of paper, a disc of wood or paint it on a pebble, sugar, new pins, knotted string (with your intent tied in), bent nails, hair, nail clippings, cob webs

Taurus

Candle wax: Red, green, yellow

Plant content: Coltsfoot, dandelion, lungwort, myrtle, thyme

Crystal: Carnelian, chrysocolla, chrysoprase, kyanite, rose quartz, rhodonite

Other: Draw the zodiac symbol on a slip of paper, a disc of wood or paint it on a pebble, salt, new pins, knotted string (with your intent tied in), bent nails, hair, nail clippings, cob webs

Gemini

Candle wax: Red, blue, orange

Plant content: Angelica, bergamot, dill, honeysuckle, oregano, tansy, thyme

Crystal: Banded agate, moss agate, clear quartz, serpentine

Other: Draw the zodiac symbol on a slip of paper, a disc of wood or paint it on a pebble, salt, new pins, knotted string (with your intent tied in), bent nails, hair, nail clippings, cob webs

Cancer

Candle wax: Blue, green, brown

Plant content: Angelica, dill, honeysuckle, hyssop, jasmine, mugwort, violet, wormwood

Crystal: Orange calcite, chrysoprase, moonstone, opal, selenite, silver

Other: Draw the zodiac symbol on a slip of paper, a disc of wood or paint it on a pebble, sugar, new pins, knotted string (with your intent tied in), bent nails, hair, nail clippings, cob webs

Leo

Candle wax: Orange, red, green

Plant content: Angelica, bay, burdock, chamomile, dill, fennel seeds, rue, sunflower seeds, leaves or petals

Crystal: Amber, carnelian, labradorite, pyrite, clear quartz, rhodochrosite, tiger's eye

Other: Draw the zodiac symbol on a slip of paper, a disc of wood or paint it on a pebble, sugar, new pins, knotted string (with your intent tied in), bent nails, hair, nail clippings, cob webs

Virgo

Candle wax: Yellow, green, black

Plant content: Bergamot, fennel seeds, sandalwood, scullcap, valerian

Crystal: Moss agate, aragonite, amazonite, red jasper, sugilite

Other: Draw the zodiac symbol on a slip of paper, a disc of wood or paint it on a pebble, salt, new pins, knotted string (with your intent tied in), bent nails, hair, nail clippings, cob webs

Libra

Candle wax: Black, blue, purple

Plant content: Angelica, bergamot, burdock, elder leaves or bark, feverfew, Saint John's Wort, thyme, violet

Crystal: Kyanite, lepidolite, moonstone, tourmaline (all colours)

Other: Draw the zodiac symbol on a slip of paper, a disc of wood or paint it on a pebble, salt, new pins, knotted string (with your intent tied in), bent nails, hair, nail clippings, cob webs

Scorpio

Candle wax: Brown, black, red

Plant content: Basil, blackthorn leaves, bark or thorns, horehound, ivy, nettle, pennyroyal, wormwood

Crystal: Amethyst, bloodstone, citrine, fluorite, red jasper, labradorite, malachite, moonstone, rhodochrosite, unakite

Other: Draw the zodiac symbol on a slip of paper, a disc of wood or paint it on a pebble, sugar, new pins, knotted string (with your intent tied in), bent nails, hair, nail clippings, cob webs

Sagittarius

Candle wax: Purple, red, yellow

Plant content: Beech leaves or bark, birch leaves or bark, cedar leaves or bark, elder leaves or bark, feverfew, hawthorn leaves, bark or thorns, nutmeg, oak leaves, bark or acorns, rowan leaves, bark or berries, sage, sandalwood

Crystal: Amethyst, goldstone, labradorite, lapis lazuli, black obsidian, snowflake obsidian, smoky quartz, sodalite

Other: Draw the zodiac symbol on a slip of paper, a disc of wood or paint it on a pebble, sugar, new pins, knotted string (with your intent tied in), bent nails, hair, nail clippings, cob webs

Capricorn

Candle wax: Red, brown, black

Plant content: Comfrey, marjoram, pine needles, plantain, poppy seeds, Solomon's seal, witch hazel leaves or bark

Crystal: Apache tear, aragonite, malachite, clear quartz, smoky quartz, tiger's eye

Other: Draw the zodiac symbol on a slip of paper, a disc of wood or paint it on a pebble, salt, new pins, knotted string (with your intent tied in), bent nails, hair, nail clippings, cob webs

Aquarius

Candle wax: Blue, green, white

Plant content: Bergamot, cypress leaves or bark, elder leaves or bark, fennel seeds, Saint John's wort

Crystal: Fluorite, hematite, labradorite, moldavite

Other: Draw the zodiac symbol on a slip of paper, a disc of wood or paint it on a pebble, salt, new pins, knotted string (with your intent tied in), bent nails, hair, nail clippings, cob webs

Pisces

Candle wax: White, green, blue

Plant content: Bladder wrack, dulse, fern, geranium, lily of the valley, lungwort, meadowsweet, rose petals, willow bark or leaves

Crystal: Amethyst, amazonite, bloodstone, fluorite, larimar, turquoise

Other: Draw the zodiac symbol on a slip of paper, a disc of wood or paint it on a pebble, sugar, new pins, knotted string (with your intent tied in), bent nails, hair, nail clippings, cob webs

January

Candle wax: White, violet, black

Plant content: Alyssum, basil, bay, betony (wood), birch leaves or bark, black pepper, cardamom, cinnamon bark, cloves, coriander seeds, crocus, cumin seeds, fennel seeds, garlic (white outer skin), holly leaves, bark or berries, honeysuckle, horehound, juniper berries, lavender, marjoram, mint, mustard seeds, nutmeg, rosemary, rue, sage, star anise, witch hazel bark or leaves, woodruff

Crystal: Agate (moss), amber, fluorite, hematite, kyanite, quartz (clear), rhodonite, selenite, sugilite, sunstone, tiger's eye, turquoise

Other: Write the month name on a slip of paper, a disc of wood or paint it on a pebble, salt, new pins, knotted string (with your intent tied in), bent nails, hair, nail clippings, cob webs

February

Candle wax: Light blue, violet, pale green, pink

Plant content: Avocado stone, basil, bay, birch leaves and bark, cherry stones, cinnamon bark, dock, fennel seeds, fish bones, hawthorn bark, leaves or thorns, hazel leaves or bark, hyssop, juniper berries, lime peel or pips, melon seeds, mistletoe leaves, olive stones, peach stones, pine needles, poppy seeds, rose petals, rosemary, rowan leaves, bark or berries, rue, strawberry leaves, vervain

Crystal: Agate (moss), amber, Aventurine (green), chrysoprase, fluorite, larimar, malachite, moonstone, pebble, quartz (clear), quartz (rose), selenite, sugilite, sunstone, turquoise

Other: Write the month name on a slip of paper, a disc of wood or paint it on a pebble, salt, new pins, knotted string (with your intent tied in), bent nails, hair, nail clippings, cob webs

March

Candle wax: Pink, pale green, pale blue, yellow, white, lilac

Plant content: Birch leaves or bark, bluebell, cloves, cornflower, cyclamen, egg shells, fennel seeds, hawthorn bark, leaves or thorns, hazel leaves, bark or nuts, honesty, horsetail, mustard seeds, parsley, pasta, pine needles, primrose, rice, Saint John's Wort, snapdragon, sunflower, sweet pea, walnut shells

Crystals: Agate (moss), agate (blue lace), celestite, chrysocolla, fluorite, howlite, kyanite, larimar, moonstone, pyrite, quartz (rose), sodalite, turquoise

Other: Write the month name on a slip of paper, a disc of wood or paint it on a pebble, sugar, new pins, knotted string (with your intent tied in), bent nails, hair, nail clippings, cob webs

April

Candle wax: Red, gold, green

Plant content: Bay, beech leaves or bark, bergamot, black

pepper, chilli seeds, cinnamon bark, clover, cumin seeds, holly leaves, bark or berries, lemon balm, lily of the valley, pasta, primrose, rowan leaves, bark or berries, Solomon's seal, tomato seeds

Crystals: Agate (moss), aventurine (green), calcite (orange), carnelian, citrine, goldstone, labradorite, lepidolite, malachite, rhodochrosite, rhodonite, sodalite, tiger's eye

Other: Write the month name on a slip of paper, a disc of wood or paint it on a pebble, sugar, new pins, knotted string (with your intent tied in), bent nails, hair, nail clippings, cob webs

May

Candle wax: Green, brown, pink, orange, red

Plant content: African violet, alexanders, almond, ash leaves or bark, bay, beech leaves or bark, camellia, cinnamon bark, cornflower, elder leaves or bark, grape seeds, heliotrope, mustard seeds, parsley, rowan leaves, bark or berries, self–heal, star anise, sweetpea, willow bark or leaves

Crystals: Amethyst, bloodstone, chrysocolla, citrine, fluorite, goldstone, kyanite, labradorite, lapis lazuli, moonstone, quartz (rose), rhodochrosite, selenite, sunstone, turquoise

Other: Write the month name on a slip of paper, a disc of wood or paint it on a pebble, salt, new pins, knotted string (with your intent tied in), bent nails, hair, nail clippings, cob webs

June

Candle wax: Orange, gold, green

Plant content: Bay, blackthorn leaves, black pepper, bark or thorns, carnation, daisy, delphinium, garlic (the white outer skin), horsetail, lavender, lemon peel or pips, mugwort, mushrooms (very definitely dried ones), oak leaves, bark or acorns, pennyroyal, pine nuts, plantain, raspberry leaves, Saint John's Wort, sesame seeds, sunflower, sweetpea, tea leaves (black)

Crystals: Agate (blue lace), fluorite, hematite, labradorite, lapis lazuli, lepidolite, pyrite, quartz (clear), quartz (smoky), rhodonite, selenite, sunstone, turquoise, unakite

Other: Write the month name on a slip of paper, a disc of wood or paint it on a pebble, salt, new pins, knotted string (with your intent tied in), bent nails, hair, nail clippings, cob webs

July

Candle wax: Silver, blue, grey

Plant content: Ash leaves or bark, bergamot, chamomile, cinnamon bark, cramp bark, cumin seeds, date stones, eucalyptus leaves or bark, heather, heliotrope, holly leaves, bark or berries, honeysuckle, jasmine, plum stones, rose petals, rowan leaves, berries or bark, sage, sandalwood, star anise, tea leaves (black)

Crystals: Agate (blue lace), amethyst, fluorite, howlite, kyanite, labradorite, larimar, moonstone, black obsidian, quartz (clear), quartz (smoky), turquoise

Other: Write the month name on a slip of paper, a disc of wood or paint it on a pebble, sugar, new pins, knotted string (with your intent tied in), bent nails, hair, nail clippings, cob webs

August

Candle wax: Yellow, gold, orange

Plant content: Bergamot, carnation, chilli seeds, coffee, coltsfoot, elm bark or leaves, grapefruit peel or pips, heather, hyssop, lemon peel or pips, lime peel or pips, orange peel or pips, lemon balm, plantain, rose petals or thorns, rosemary, saffron, sesame seeds, sweet pea, tansy

Crystals: Agate (moss), amber, bloodstone, labradorite,

larimar, malachite, pyrite, quartz (clear), rhodochrosite, sodalite, sunstone, turquoise

Other: Write the month name on a slip of paper, a disc of wood or paint it on a pebble, sugar, new pins, knotted string (with your intent tied in), bent nails, hair, nail clippings, cob webs

September

Candle wax: Brown, green, yellow

Plant content: Alexanders, agrimony, chamomile, cramp bark, dill, dock, elm leaves or bark, fish bones, honeysuckle, geranium, liquorice root, lungwort, mint, mushrooms (dried), plum stone, rue, salt flakes, self–heal, tansy, witch hazel leaves or bark

Crystals: Agate (blue lace), amber, amethyst, fluorite, hematite, kyanite, labradorite, rhodonite, selenite, sugilite, turquoise

Other: Write the month name on a slip of paper, a disc of wood or paint it on a pebble, salt, new pins, knotted string (with your intent tied in), bent nails, hair, nail clippings, cob webs

October

Candle wax: Dark blue, orange, black

Plant content: Almond, apple pips, ash leaves or bark, bay, cinnamon bark, dittany, elder leaves or bark, fern, grapefruit peel or pips, heather, morning glory, mugwort, parsley, pasta, periwinkle, saffron, sage, star anise, thistle, thyme, willow bark or leaves

Crystals: Bloodstone, fluorite, labradorite, lepidolite, malachite, black obsidian, tourmaline, turquoise, unakite

Other: Write the month name on a slip of paper, a disc of wood or paint it on a pebble, salt, new pins, knotted string (with your intent tied in), bent nails, hair, nail clippings, cob webs

November

Candle wax: Grey, deep green, dark blue

Plant content: Almond, bay, bergamot, bladder wrack, borage, cinnamon bark, coriander seeds, elm leaves or bark, grass, hazel leaves, bark or nuts, juniper berries, marigold, mustard seeds, mugwort, pasta, rowan leaves, bark or berries, saffron, sage, sandalwood (white), yarrow

Crystals: Chrysocolla, citrine, kyanite, labradorite, lepidolite, malachite, moonstone, quartz (clear), rhodonite, selenite, sodalite, sugilite, turquoise

Other: Write the month name on a slip of paper, a disc of wood or paint it on a pebble, sugar, new pins, knotted string (with your intent tied in), bent nails, hair, nail clippings, cob webs

December

Candle wax: Red, white, green, silver, gold

Plant content: Alyssum, basil, cocoa nibs, cumin seeds, borage, horehound, lavender, meadowsweet, orange peel or pips, pennyroyal, poppy seeds, saffron, sweet pea, thyme, vervain, violet, yarrow

Crystals: Agate (blue lace), agate (moss), amethyst, fluorite, howlite, larimar, lepidolite, rhodochrosite, rhodonite, quartz (rose), sunstone, tourmaline

Other: Write the month name on a slip of paper, a disc of wood or paint it on a pebble, sugar, new pins, knotted string (with your intent tied in), bent nails, hair, nail clippings, cob webs

Poppets

It is a shame the poppet has had so much bad press. When most people think of a poppet, they automatically think of the Voodoo doll, thanks to this item's negative portrayal in movies and on television. However, the original use was for healing. Although obviously they were used for bindings and curses too.

I like to think of a poppet as a person shaped spell holder and use them for love, luck, protection, prosperity and healing.

Remember that poppets have a long tradition behind them, and that tradition is influenced by the magical practices of a wide range of cultures. Treat your poppets well, and they will do the same for you.

As for design, well it is really up to you. You can make a simple poppet from twine tied together right up to detailed material poppets with hair and glass eyes and of course anywhere in between. You can even use dollies or Barbie dolls. I have also made poppets by just using a potato, it really doesn't need to be complicated or fancy.

I like to use felt when making poppets basically because I am a lazy sewer. With felt you don't have to hem. And of course, felt comes in all sorts of colours so you can correspond the colour of felt used to the intent.

I cut out two felt shapes, a bit like a gingerbread man shape or a simple cross shape.

Then I sew one button on for one eye and a cross for the other eye, followed by a mouth. Then I sew on a little red felt heart.

Next, I sew with neat but not fancy stitches around the edges of the figure, again you can use coloured thread to correspond with your intent.

I leave a gap and then stuff the poppet with some off cuts of felt, cut up pieces of old tights/pantyhose or strips of old t shirt material. I leave a space in its tummy to fill with herbs and spices; occasionally I will add a crystal too. You can use all sorts of herbs, woods, plants, roots and spices even salt and rice – go with what suits your intent or what feels right for you. Salt, rice and dried pulses are good if your poppet is larger as they fill up the space nicely and also work for purification, protection, negative energy and in the case of rice, prosperity too. Charge each item as you add it. Then when your poppet is full, sew him up and I like to charge him with my intent again once he is whole.

Your poppet can be left out under the Moon to charge with the corresponding Moon phase. I like to set the poppet on my altar and recharge him occasionally with my intent.

Some people choose to bury the poppet once he is made, allowing the universe to work the magic, the choice is yours.

To make your poppet, use the fillings and colour guide as suggested for the spell pouches in this book. Match the colour to the material used to make the poppet or add coloured ribbon.

Candle Magic

Using herbs for candle magic is really simple and easy. You can anoint the candle with essential oil first and then roll the candle in dried herbs or you can sprinkle the dried herbs on the top of the candle (this works well with tea lights). If I sprinkle the herbs on top of a pillar candle, I like to then seal it by dripping candle wax from another candle over the top of the herbs.

Anointing your candle with essential oils adds to the power of your intent and aligns them with your energy or that of the Moon phase. You can also use magic powders on your candles too. If you use the rolled beeswax candles, you can carefully unroll the beeswax sheet and sprinkle herbs or magic powder onto it and carefully roll it back up again.

Decide on your intent; select the candle you wish to use and then use corresponding herbs and oils whose magical properties align with your magical intent. The finished candle can also be set out to charge in the Moonlight.

Then light your candle and visualise your intent, if you are using a crystal place it in front of the candle so that it soaks up the magic. Once finished dispose of any wax remains and keep the crystal with you or place on your altar.

New Moon

Candle colour: Green, orange of white

Anointing oils: Basil, bay, cardamom, cinnamon, jasmine, nettle, nutmeg, orange, peach, sage, walnut

Plant content: Basil, bay, cardamom, chamomile, chilli seeds, ground cinnamon, egg shells, jasmine flowers, myrrh, nettle, ground nutmeg, oak leaves, orange peel, paprika, rue, sage, tomato pips

Crystal: Amethyst, citrine, clear quartz, labradorite, moonstone, smoky quartz

Waxing Crescent Moon

Candle colour: Orange, pink, blue

Anointing oils: Basil, cedar, cinnamon, coriander, fennel, honeysuckle, juniper, pine, rosemary, thyme

Plant content: Basil, bergamot, cedar bark or leaves, ground cinnamon, coriander seeds, fennel seeds, garlic (the white outer skin), honeysuckle flowers, juniper berries, myrrh, pine needles, rosemary, sandalwood (white), thyme

Crystal: Amber, amethyst, banded agate, carnelian, citrine, malachite, rose quartz, tiger's eye

First Quarter Moon

Candle colour: Yellow, purple, blue

Anointing oils: Almond, black pepper, cinnamon, dandelion, elder, fennel, peach, rowan, sage, sunflower, walnut, willow

Plant content: Alexanders, almonds (ground), ash bark or leaves, beech bark or leaves, benzoin, black peppercorns, ground cinnamon, cleavers, dandelion flowers or seeds, elder bark or leaves, fennel seeds, hazel bark or leaves, rowan bark, leaves or berries, sage, sandalwood (white), sunflower, seeds, violet, willow bark or leaves

Crystal: Agate (moss), amber, aventurine (green), carnelian, citrine, fluorite, goldstone, labradorite, lapis lazuli, pebble, pyrite, quartz (clear)

Waxing Gibbous Moon

Candle colour: Blue, red, orange

Anointing oils: Cinnamon, elder, grapefruit, lime, orange, pansy, poppy, primrose, rose, sesame, violet

Plant content: Cashew nuts, chilli seeds, cinnamon bark, cleavers, coffee, coltsfoot, cramp bark, curry leaves, elder bark or leaves, elm bark or leaves, grapefruit peel, lime peel, orange peel, pansy flowers, paprika, plantain, poppy seeds, primrose flowers, rose petals, saffron, sesame seeds, tansy flowers, violet flowers

Crystal: Amber, amethyst, bloodstone, calcite (orange), citrine, goldstone, labradorite, lepidolite, malachite, obsidian (black), quartz (clear), rhodochrosite, rhodonite, tiger's eye.

Full Moon

Candle colour: White, purple, red, silver

Anointing oils: Basil, black pepper, cinnamon, hyssop, jasmine, mint, oregano, rose, sandalwood, thyme, yarrow

Plant content: Basil, bergamot, black pepper corns, chilli seeds, cocoa, ground cinnamon, egg shells, garlic (white outer skin), hyssop, jasmine flowers, mint, myrtle, oregano, rose petals, rose hips, sandalwood, thyme, tomato seeds, yarrow

Crystal: Amethyst, chrysocolla, quartz (clear), kyanite, moonstone, moss agate, selenite, quartz (smoky)

Waning Moon

Candle colour: White, black, pale blue

Anointing oils: Bay, coriander, eucalyptus, hyssop, jasmine, lemon, lime, marjoram, mint, orange, rosemary, sage, sandalwood, star anise, yarrow

Plant content: Bay, coriander seeds, cypress leaves or bark, eucalyptus leaves or bark, frankincense, hyssop, jasmine flowers, lemon peel, lime peel, marjoram, mint, myrtle, orange peel, parsley, rosemary, sage, sandalwood, star anise, yarrow

Crystal: Black tourmaline, bloodstone, citrine, clear quartz, obsidian, smoky quartz, snowflake obsidian

Third Quarter Moon

Candle colour: White, pale blue, pink

Anointing oils: Alyssum, birch, carnation, chamomile, cinnamon, coriander, holly, honeysuckle, lemon, thyme, willow, witch hazel, woodruff

Plant content: Alexanders, alyssum, birch leaves or bark, carnation, celandine, chamomile, ground cinnamon, coriander seeds, cypress bark or leaves, dill, elm bark or leaves, holly leaves or bark, honeysuckle, lemon peel, liquorice root, lungwort, rue, self–heal, thyme, willow leaves or bark, witch hazel leaves or bark, woodruff

Crystal: Agate (banded), amber, green aventurine, carnelian, chrysoprase, fluorite, garnet, goldstone, lepidolite, moonstone, black obsidian, rose quartz, rhodochrosite, sodalite, tiger's eye, unakite

Waning Crescent Moon

Candle colour: Blue, pale green, pale yellow

Anointing oils: Bay, carnation, coriander, elder, fennel, hazelnut, hyssop, juniper, lime, mint, nettle, pine, rosemary, star anise, tansy, thyme, violet

Plant content: Angelica, ash leaves or bark, bay, burdock, carnation, comfrey, coriander seeds, dock, elder leaves or bark, fennel seeds, feverfew, garlic (outer white skin), hazelnut, hyssop, juniper berries, lime peel, lungwort, mint, mugwort, myrrh, nettle, pine needles, rosemary, star anise, tansy, thyme, violet

Crystal: Amethyst, bloodstone, hematite, labradorite, larimar, lepidolite, malachite, black obsidian, pyrite, selenite, sugilite, tiger's eye

Dark Moon

Candle colour: Black, dark purple, dark blue

Anointing oils: Apple, bay, dandelion, elder, fennel, hawthorn, heather, jasmine, Mugwort, nutmeg, rosemary, rue, sage, sandalwood, star anise, tansy, thistle, willow

Plant content: Apple seeds, ash leaves or bark, bay, benzoin, burdock, cypress leaves or bark, dandelion, dittany, dragon's blood, elder leaves or bark, fennel seeds, frankincense, garlic (outer white skin), ground ginger, hawthorn berries, leaves or flowers, hazel leaves, flowers, bark or nuts, foxglove, heather, jasmine, mugwort, myrrh, nutmeg, oak leaves or bark, paprika, rosemary, rue, sage, sandalwood, star anise, tansy, tobacco, thistle, willow leaves or bark, wormwood

Crystal: Apache tear, chrysocolla, fluorite, labradorite, obsidian, red jasper, selenite

Aries

Candle colour: White, pink, red

Anointing oils: Bay, cinnamon, coriander, feverfew, juniper, marjoram, nettle, rosemary

Plant content: Bay, ground cinnamon, coriander seeds, dragon's blood, feverfew, frankincense, juniper berries, marjoram, myrrh, nettle, rosemary

Crystal: Apache tear, aventurine (green), bloodstone, hematite, kyanite, red jasper

Other: Inscribe the zodiac symbol into the side of the candle

Taurus

Candle colour: Red, green, yellow

Anointing oils: Coltsfoot, dandelion, lungwort, myrtle, thyme

Plant content: Coltsfoot, dandelion, lungwort, myrtle, thyme

Crystal: Carnelian, chrysocolla, chrysoprase, kyanite, rose quartz, rhodonite

Other: Inscribe the zodiac symbol into the side of the candle

Gemini

Candle colour: Red, blue, orange

Anointing oils: Angelica, bergamot, dill, honeysuckle, oregano, tansy, thyme

Plant content: Angelica, bergamot, dill, honeysuckle, oregano, tansy, thyme

Crystal: Banded agate, moss agate, clear quartz, serpentine

Other: Inscribe the zodiac symbol into the side of the candle

Cancer

Candle colour: Blue, green, brown

Anointing oils: Angelica, dill, honeysuckle, hyssop, jasmine, mugwort, violet

Plant content: Angelica, dill, honeysuckle, hyssop, jasmine, mugwort, violet

Crystal: Orange calcite, chrysoprase, moonstone, opal, selenite, silver

Other: Inscribe the zodiac symbol into the side of the candle

Leo

Candle colour: Orange, red, green

Anointing oils: Angelica, bay, burdock, chamomile, dill, fennel, rue, sunflower

Plant content: Angelica, bay, burdock, chamomile, dill, fennel seeds, frankincense, rue, sunflower seeds, leaves or petals

Crystal: Amber, carnelian, labradorite, pyrite, clear quartz, rhodochrosite, tiger's eye

Other: Inscribe the zodiac symbol into the side of the candle

Virgo

Candle colour: Yellow, green, black

Anointing oils: Bergamot, fennel, sandalwood, scullcap, valerian

Plant content: Bergamot, fennel seeds, sandalwood, valerian

Crystal: Moss agate, aragonite, amazonite, red jasper, sugilite

Other: Inscribe the zodiac symbol into the side of the candle

Libra

Candle colour: Black, blue, purple

Anointing oils: Angelica, bergamot, burdock, elder, feverfew, Saint John's Wort, thyme, violet

Plant content: Angelica, bergamot, burdock, elder leaves or bark, feverfew, Saint John's Wort, thyme, violet

Crystal: Kyanite, lepidolite, moonstone, tourmaline (all colours)

Other: Inscribe the zodiac symbol into the side of the candle

Scorpio

Candle colour: Brown, black, red

Anointing oils: Basil, blackthorn, horehound, ivy, nettle, pennyroyal

Plant content: Basil, blackthorn leaves, bark or thorns, horehound, ivy, nettle, pennyroyal

Crystal: Amethyst, bloodstone, citrine, fluorite, red jasper, labradorite, malachite, moonstone, rhodochrosite, unakite

Other: Inscribe the zodiac symbol into the side of the candle

Sagittarius

Candle colour: Purple, red, yellow

Anointing oils: Beech, cedar, elder, feverfew, hawthorn,

nutmeg, oak, rowan, sage, sandalwood

Plant content: Beech leaves or bark, birch leaves or bark, cedar leaves or bark, elder leaves or bark, feverfew, hawthorn leaves, bark or flowers, ground nutmeg, oak leaves or bark, rowan leaves, bark or berries, sage, sandalwood

Crystal: Amethyst, goldstone, labradorite, lapis lazuli, black obsidian, snowflake obsidian, smoky quartz, sodalite

Other: Inscribe the zodiac symbol into the side of the candle

Capricorn

Candle colour: Red, brown, black

Anointing oils: Comfrey, marjoram, pine, plantain, poppy, Solomon's seal, witch hazel

Plant content: Benzoin, comfrey, marjoram, pine needles, plantain, poppy seeds, Solomon's seal, witch hazel leaves or bark

Crystal: Apache tear, aragonite, malachite, clear quartz, smoky quartz, tiger's eye

Other: Inscribe the zodiac symbol into the side of the candle

Aquarius

Candle colour: Blue, green, white

Anointing oils: Bergamot, cypress, elder, fennel, Saint John's wort

Plant content: Bergamot, cypress leaves or bark, elder leaves or bark, fennel seeds, frankincense, myrrh, Saint John's wort

Crystal: Fluorite, hematite, labradorite, moldavite

Other: Inscribe the zodiac symbol into the side of the candle

Pisces

Candle colour: White, green, blue

Anointing oils: Fern, geranium, lily of the valley, lungwort, meadowsweet, rose, willow

Plant content: Bladder wrack, dulse, fern, geranium, lily of the valley, lungwort, meadowsweet, rose petals, willow bark or leaves

Crystal: Amethyst, amazonite, bloodstone, fluorite, larimar, turquoise

Other: Inscribe the zodiac symbol into the side of the candle

January

Candle colour: White, violet, black

Anointing oils: Basil, bay, betony, birch, black pepper, cardamom, cinnamon, clove, coriander, fennel, holly, honeysuckle, juniper, lavender, marjoram, mint, nutmeg, rosemary, rue, sage, witch hazel, woodruff

Plant content: Alyssum, basil, bay, betony (wood), birch leaves or bark, black pepper, cardamom, ground cinnamon, cloves, coriander seeds, crocus, cumin seeds, fennel seeds, garlic (white outer skin), holly leaves, bark or berries, honeysuckle, horehound, juniper berries, lavender, marjoram, mint, mustard seeds, ground nutmeg, rosemary, rue, sage, star anise, witch hazel bark or leaves, woodruff

Crystal: Agate (moss), amber, fluorite, hematite, kyanite, quartz (clear), rhodonite, selenite, sugilite, sunstone, tiger's eye, turquoise

February

Candle colour: Light blue, violet, pale green, pink

Anointing oils: Basil, bay, birch, cherry, cinnamon, fennel, hawthorn, hyssop, juniper, lime, peace, pine, poppy, rose, rosemary, rowan, rue, strawberry, vervain

Plant content: Basil, bay, birch leaves and bark, cherry leaves, ground cinnamon, dock, fennel seeds, hawthorn bark, leaves or thorns, hazel leaves or bark, hyssop, juniper berries, lime peel, melon seeds, mistletoe leaves, olive leaves, peach leaves, pine needles, poppy seeds, rose petals, rosemary, rowan leaves, bark or berries, rue, strawberry leaves, vervain

Crystal: Agate (moss), amber, aventurine (green), chrysoprase, fluorite, larimar, malachite, moonstone, pebble, quartz (clear), quartz (rose), selenite, sugilite, sunstone, turquoise

March

Candle colour: Pink, pale green, pale blue, yellow, white, lilac

Anointing oils: Birch, clove, cornflower, fennel, hawthorn, honesty, horsetail, pine, primrose, Saint John's Wort, snapdragon, sunflower, sweet pea, walnut

Plant content: Birch leaves or bark, bluebell, cloves, cornflower, cyclamen, egg shells, fennel seeds, hawthorn bark, leaves or thorns, hazel leaves or bark, honesty, horsetail, mustard seeds, parsley, pine needles, primrose, rice, Saint John's Wort, snapdragon, sunflower, sweet pea

Crystals: Agate (moss), agate (blue lace), celestite, chrysocolla, fluorite, howlite, kyanite, larimar, moonstone, pyrite, quartz (rose), sodalite, turquoise

April

Candle colour: Red, gold, green

Anointing oils: Bay, beech, bergamot, black pepper, cinnamon, clover, holly, lemon balm, lily of the valley, primrose, rowan, Solomon's seal

Plant content: Bay, beech leaves or bark, bergamot, black pepper, chilli seeds, ground cinnamon, clover, cumin seeds, holly leaves, bark or berries, lemon balm, lily of the valley, primrose, rowan leaves, bark or berries, Solomon's seal, tomato seeds

Crystals: Agate (moss), aventurine (green), calcite (orange), carnelian, citrine, goldstone, labradorite, lepidolite, malachite, rhodochrosite, rhodonite, sodalite, tiger's eye

May

Candle colour: Green, brown, pink, orange, red

Anointing oils: Almond, ash, beech, camellia, cinnamon, cornflower, elder, heliotrope, rowan, self–heal, star anise, sweet pea, willow

Plant content: African violet, alexanders, almond, ash leaves or bark, bay, beech leaves or bark, camellia, ground cinnamon, cornflower, elder leaves or bark, grape seeds, heliotrope, mustard seeds, parsley, rowan leaves, bark or berries, self–heal, star anise, sweetpea, willow bark or leaves

Crystals: Amethyst, bloodstone, chrysocolla, citrine, fluorite, goldstone, kyanite, labradorite, lapis lazuli, moonstone, quartz (rose), rhodochrosite, selenite, sunstone, turquoise

June

Candle colour: Orange, gold, green

Anointing oils: Bay, blackthorn, black pepper, carnation, daisy, delphinium, horsetail, lavender, lemon, Mugwort, oak, pennyroyal, plantain, Saint John's wort, sesame, sunflower, sweet pea

Plant content: Bay, blackthorn leaves, bark or thorns, black pepper, carnation, daisy, delphinium, garlic (the white outer skin), horsetail, lavender, lemon peel, mugwort, mushrooms (very definitely dried ones), oak leaves or bark, pennyroyal, pine nuts, plantain, raspberry leaves, Saint John's Wort, sesame seeds, sunflower, sweetpea, tea leaves (black)

Crystals: Agate (blue lace), fluorite, hematite, labradorite, lapis lazuli, lepidolite, pyrite, quartz (clear), quartz (smoky), rhodonite, selenite, sunstone, turquoise, unakite

July

Candle colour: Silver, blue, grey

Anointing oils: Ash, bergamot, chamomile, cinnamon, cramp bark, eucalyptus, heather, heliotrope, holly, honeysuckle, jasmine, rose, rowan, sage, sandalwood, star anise

Plant content: Ash leaves or bark, bergamot, chamomile, ground cinnamon, cramp bark, cumin seeds, eucalyptus leaves or bark, heather, heliotrope, holly leaves, bark or berries, honeysuckle, jasmine, rose petals, rowan leaves, berries or bark, sage, sandalwood, star anise, tea leaves (black)

Crystals: Agate (blue lace), amethyst, fluorite, howlite, kyanite, labradorite, larimar, moonstone, black obsidian, quartz (clear), quartz (smoky), turquoise

August

Candle colour: Yellow, gold, orange

Anointing oils: Bergamot, carnation, coltsfoot, elm, grapefruit, heather, hyssop, lemon, lime, orange, lemon balm, plantain, rose, rosemary, saffron, sesame, sweet pea, tansy

Plant content: Bergamot, carnation, chilli seeds, coffee, coltsfoot, elm bark or leaves, grapefruit peel, heather, hyssop, lemon peel, lime peel, orange peel, lemon balm, plantain, rose petals, rosemary, saffron, sesame seeds, sweet pea, tansy

Crystals: Agate (moss), amber, bloodstone, labradorite, larimar, malachite, pyrite, quartz (clear), rhodochrosite, sodalite, sunstone, turquoise

September

Candle colour: Brown, green, yellow

Anointing oils: Alexanders, agrimony, chamomile, cramp bark, dill, dock, elm, honeysuckle, geranium, lungwort, mint, rue, self–heal, tansy, witch hazel

Plant content: Alexanders, agrimony, chamomile, cramp bark, dill, dock, elm leaves or bark, honeysuckle, geranium, liquorice root, lungwort, mint, mushrooms (dried), rue, self–heal, tansy, witch hazel leaves or bark

Crystals: Agate (blue lace), amber, amethyst, fluorite, hematite, kyanite, labradorite, rhodonite, selenite, sugilite, turquoise

October

Candle colour: Dark blue, orange, black

Anointing oils: Almond, apple, ash, bay, cinnamon, dittany, elder, fern, grapefruit, heather, mugwort, periwinkle, saffron, sage, star anise, thistle, thyme, willow

Plant content: Almond, apple pips, ash leaves or bark, bay, ground cinnamon, dittany, elder leaves or bark, fern, grapefruit peel, heather, morning glory, mugwort, parsley, periwinkle, saffron, sage, star anise, thistle, thyme, willow bark or leaves

Crystals: Bloodstone, fluorite, labradorite, lepidolite, malachite, black obsidian, tourmaline, turquoise, unakite

November

Candle colour: Grey, deep green, dark blue

Anointing oils: Almond, bay, bergamot, borage, coriander, elm, hazel, juniper, marigold, mugwort, rowan, saffron, sage, sandalwood, yarrow

Plant content: Almond, bay, bergamot, bladder wrack, borage, ground cinnamon, coriander seeds, elm leaves or bark, grass, hazel leaves or bark, juniper berries, marigold, mustard seeds, mugwort, rowan leaves, bark or berries, saffron, sage, sandalwood (white), yarrow

Crystals: Chrysocolla, citrine, kyanite, labradorite, lepidolite, malachite, moonstone, quartz (clear), rhodonite, selenite, sodalite, sugilite, turquoise

December

Candle colour: Red, white, green, silver, gold

Anointing oils: Alyssum, basil, borage, horehound, lavender, meadowsweet, orange, pennyroyal, poppy, saffron, sweet pea, thyme, vervain, violet, yarrow

Plant content: Alyssum, basil, cocoa powder, cumin seeds, borage, horehound, lavender, meadowsweet, orange peel, pennyroyal, poppy seeds, saffron, sweet pea, thyme, vervain, violet, yarrow

Crystals: Agate (blue lace), agate (moss), amethyst, fluorite, howlite, larimar, lepidolite, rhodochrosite, rhodonite, quartz (rose), sunstone, tourmaline

Witches Ladder

You could create a witch's ladder with twine, wool or ribbon and insert feathers each one for intent, such as luck, prosperity, love, healing or success. A witch ladder can also be used for curses.

The basic structure is that of braiding three, nine or twelve cords together, they can be made from string, ribbon or twine. But the idea is to weave your spell into the cords as you plait, chanting as you go if you wish. Colour magic can be added in if you want to with the use of coloured ribbon, beads or feathers. Charms, buttons and bells can also be added in. Once your plait is done you can pop feathers or sprigs of herbs in between the threads to add intent to your spell.

If you want to charge your ladder with a particular Moon phase you could either make the ladder whilst sitting the in light of the Moon and/or leaving it to charge under Moonlight.

Instructions:

You can make the process your own, but here is how I create a witch ladder.

You will need:

9 pieces of twine, of equal length
2 short pieces of twine or ribbon
3 feathers
Any herbs you wish to add, but make sure they can be poked into the plaits

Plait three pieces of twine together, three times – so that you have three plaits, put a knot in the top and bottom of each.

As you plait, visualise your intent and say a chant or state your intent out loud.

Now tie the tops together with your ribbon or twine.

Plait the three plaits together, visualising your intent, saying your chant or stating your intention out loud.

Now tie the bottoms together with your ribbon or twine.

Insert each feather into the finished plait, stating your intention out loud and sending energy into it.

Next add your herbs, slotting them into the plait and stating your intention.

Your ladder is now complete, pop it on your altar or hang it by your front door.

New Moon

Ribbon/twine/feather colour: Green, orange of white
Plant content: Bay, dried chillies, cinnamon bark, nettle, nutmeg, oak leaves, orange peel, sage,

Waxing Crescent Moon

Ribbon/twine/feather colour: Orange, pink, blue
Plant content: Cedar bark or leaves, chicken bones, cinnamon bark, fish bones, pine sprigs, rosemary, thyme

First Quarter Moon

Ribbon/twine/feather colour: Yellow, purple, blue
Plant content: Ash bark or leaves, beech bark or leaves,

cinnamon bark, dandelion leaves, elder bark or leaves, rowan bark or leaves, sage, turkey bones, willow bark or leaves

Waxing Gibbous Moon

Ribbon/twine/feather colour: Blue, red, orange

Plant content: Dried chillies, cinnamon bark, curry leaves, elder bark or leaves, elm bark or leaves, grapefruit peel, lime peel, orange peel, dried roses

Full Moon

Ribbon/twine/feather colour: White, purple, red, silver

Plant content: Dried chillies, chocolate wrappers, cinnamon bark, fish bones, hyssop, mint, oregano, dried roses, rose hips, sandalwood, thyme, yarrow

Waning Moon

Ribbon/twine/feather colour: White, black, pale blue

Plant content: Bay, eucalyptus leaves or bark, fish bones, hyssop, lemon peel, lime peel, marjoram, mint, orange peel, rosemary, sage, sandalwood, yarrow

Third Quarter Moon

Ribbon/twine/feather colour: White, pale blue, pink

Plant content: Birch leaves or bark, carnation, cinnamon bark, elm bark or leaves, holly leaves or bark, lemon peel, liquorice root, thyme, turkey bones, willow leaves or bark, witch hazel leaves or bark

Waning Crescent Moon

Ribbon/twine/feather colour: Blue, pale green, pale yellow

Plant content: Ash leaves or bark, bay, carnation, dock, elder leaves or bark, fish bones, hyssop, lime peel, lungwort, mint, mugwort, nettle, pine sprigs, rosemary, tansy, thyme

Dark Moon

Ribbon/twine/feather colour: Black, dark purple, dark blue

Plant content: Apple leaves, ash leaves or bark, bay, burdock, elder leaves or bark, hawthorn leaves or flowers, hazel leaves or bark, heather, mugwort, oak leaves or bark, rosemary, rue, sage, sandalwood, tansy, thistle, willow leaves or bark

Aries

Ribbon/twine/feather colour: White, pink, red

Plant content: Bay, cinnamon bark, feverfew, juniper sprigs, marjoram, nettle, rosemary

Taurus

Ribbon/twine/feather colour: Red, green, yellow

Plant content: Coltsfoot, dandelion, lungwort, myrtle, thyme

Gemini

Ribbon/twine/feather colour: Red, blue, orange

Plant content: Angelica, bergamot, dill, oregano, tansy, thyme

Cancer

Ribbon/twine/feather colour: Blue, green, brown

Plant content: Angelica, dill, honeysuckle, hyssop, mugwort

Leo

Ribbon/twine/feather colour: Orange, red, green

Plant content: Angelica, bay, burdock, dill, rue, sunflower

Virgo

Ribbon/twine/feather colour: Yellow, green, black

Plant content: Bergamot, fennel, sandalwood, scullcap, valerian

Libra

Ribbon/twine/feather colour: Black, blue, purple

Plant content: Angelica, bergamot, burdock, elder leaves or bark, feverfew, Saint John's Wort, thyme

Scorpio

Ribbon/twine/feather colour: Brown, black, red

Plant content: Basil, blackthorn leaves, bark or thorns, horehound, ivy, nettle, pennyroyal, wormwood

Sagittarius

Ribbon/twine/feather colour: Purple, red, yellow

Plant content: Beech leaves or bark, birch leaves or bark, cedar leaves or bark, elder leaves or bark, feverfew, hawthorn leaves, bark or thorns, oak leaves or bark, rowan leaves or bark, sage, sandalwood

Capricorn

Ribbon/twine/feather colour: Red, brown, black

Plant content: Comfrey, marjoram, pine, plantain, Solomon's seal, witch hazel leaves or bark

Aquarius

Ribbon/twine/feather colour: Blue, green, white

Plant content: Bergamot, cypress leaves or bark, elder leaves or bark, fennel, Saint John's wort

Pisces

Ribbon/twine/feather colour: White, green, blue

Plant content: Bladder wrack, dulse, fern, geranium, lily of the valley, lungwort, meadowsweet, dried roses, willow bark or leaves

January

Ribbon/twine/feather colour: White, violet, black

Plant content: Bay, birch leaves or bark, cinnamon bark, fennel, holly leaves or bark, lavender, marjoram, mint, rosemary, rue, sage, witch hazel bark or leaves

February

Ribbon/twine/feather colour: Light blue, violet, pale green, pink

Plant content: Bay, birch leaves and bark, cinnamon bark, dock, fennel, fish bones, hawthorn bark or leaves, hazel leaves or bark, hyssop, lime peel, mistletoe leaves, olive sprigs, pine needles, dried roses, rosemary, rowan leaves or bark, rue, strawberry leaves, vervain

March

Ribbon/twine/feather colour: Pink, pale green, pale blue, yellow, white, lilac

Plant content: Birch leaves or bark, fennel, hawthorn bark or leaves, hazel leaves or bark, honesty, horsetail, pine needles, Saint John's Wort, sunflower, sweet pea

April

Ribbon/twine/feather colour: Red, gold, green

Plant content: Bay, beech leaves or bark, bergamot, dried chillies, cinnamon bark, holly leaves or bark, lemon balm, rowan leaves or bark, Solomon's seal

May

Ribbon/twine/feather colour: Green, brown, pink, orange, red

Plant content: Alexanders, ash leaves or bark, bay, beech leaves or bark, cinnamon bark, elder leaves or bark, heliotrope, rowan leaves or bark, self–heal, willow bark or leaves

June

Ribbon/twine/feather colour: Orange, gold, green

Plant content: Bay, blackthorn leaves or bark, carnation, delphinium, horsetail, lavender, lemon peel, mugwort, mushrooms (very definitely dried ones), oak leaves or bark, plantain, raspberry leaves, Saint John's Wort, sunflower, sweet pea

July

Ribbon/twine/feather colour: Silver, blue, grey

Plant content: Ash leaves or bark, bergamot, chamomile, cinnamon bark, cramp bark, eucalyptus leaves or bark, heather, heliotrope, holly leaves or bark, dried roses, rowan leaves or bark, sage, sandalwood

August

Ribbon/twine/feather colour: Yellow, gold, orange

Plant content: Bergamot, carnation, dried chillies, coltsfoot, elm bark or leaves, grapefruit peel, heather, hyssop, lemon peel, lime peel, orange peel, lemon balm, plantain, dried roses, rosemary, sweet pea, tansy

September

Ribbon/twine/feather colour: Brown, green, yellow

Plant content: Alexanders, agrimony, chamomile, cramp bark, dill, dock, elm leaves or bark, fish bones, geranium, liquorice root, lungwort, mint, mushrooms (dried), rue, selfheal, tansy, witch hazel leaves or bark

October

Ribbon/twine/feather colour: Dark blue, orange, black

Plant content: Ash leaves or bark, bay, cinnamon bark, dittany, elder leaves or bark, fern, grapefruit peel, heather, mugwort, parsley, periwinkle, sage, thistle, thyme, willow bark or leaves

November

Ribbon/twine/feather colour: Grey, deep green, dark blue

Plant content: Bay, bergamot, bladder wrack, borage, cinnamon bark, elm leaves or bark, grass, hazel leaves or bark, marigold, mugwort, rowan leaves or bark, sage, sandalwood (white), yarrow

December

Ribbon/twine/feather colour: Red, white, green, silver, gold

Plant content: Alyssum, basil, borage, horehound, lavender, meadowsweet, orange peel, thyme, vervain, yarrow

Moon Herb Water/Candles

You can use charged Moon water for this and add to the energy by popping in plant matter, herbs and spices that correspond to the phase. I like to put the Moon water in a jar, add the herbs and plants and then float a tealight on the top. This transforms it into a jar candle spell. You can create similar jar spells using regular tap water if you don't have Moon water. You don't have to put a candle on the top. Just add the plant material and then use the water to anoint candles for magic, splash the water on ritual tools or dab on your pulse points to impart the Moon phase magic.

I use dried or fresh plant matter or spices, but you can also add essential oils if you prefer. Be careful with the candle if you add essential oils to the water! And it goes without saying... don't drink the water...

These are my suggestions for the Moon phases, but trust your own intuition and the items you have to hand:

New Moon Herbal Water

Add any of these to your water: Beech bark, leaves or seeds, birch bark or leaves, cherry blossom, leaves or stones, cinnamon bark, crocus flowers or leaves, dandelion seeds, hawthorn leaves, blossom or thorns, pomegranate seeds, primrose flowers or leaves, sage, willow leaves or bark

Waxing Crescent Moon Herbal Water

Add any of these to your water: Acorns, birch bark or leaves, blueberries, cherry blossom, leaves or stones, chickweed, corn, cucumber, daffodil, fennel seeds, hawthorn leaves, seeds or bark, mistletoe, mustard seeds, oak leaves or acorns, oats, parsley, peach pits, pine needles poppy seeds, rice (bear in mind this will swell in the water), sunflower seeds

First Quarter Moon Herbal Water

Add any of these to your water: Bay, beech leaves or bark, black peppercorns, chilli seeds or dried chillies, cleavers, dandelion seeds, fennel seeds, hazel leaves or bark, paprika, pasta (bear in mind this will swell in the water), peach pits, pomegranate seeds, sage, sunflower seeds, vanilla, violet flowers, willow bark or leaves

Waxing Gibbous Moon Herbal Water

Add any of these to your water: Cashew nuts, chilli seeds or dried chillies, cinnamon bark, cleavers, coffee, coltsfoot, cramp bark flowers or leaves, lime slices, peel or pips, orange slices, peel or pips, pansy flowers, plantain, plum stones, pomegranate seeds, poppy seeds primrose flowers, rose petals, leaves or thorns, sesame seeds, tansy, violet flowers

Full Moon Herbal Water

Add any of these to your water: Alexanders, almond, bay, beech leaves or bark, blackthorn blossom, leaves or thorns, borage, cherry blossom, leaves or stones, cinnamon bark, coffee, cranberries, cucumber, dandelion, grass, hazelnut, juniper berries, leaves or thorns, lemongrass, mustard seeds, pasta (bear in mind this will swell in the water), rose leaves, petals or thorns, rowan leaves, berries or bark, saffron, sage, star anise, thyme, witch hazel leaves or bark, yarrow

Waning Gibbous Moon Herbal Water

Add any of these to your water: Alexanders, apple slices, peel or pips, bergamot, birch leaves or bark, carnation, celandine, chamomile, chives, coriander seeds or leaves, cramp bark leaves or blossom, cypress leaves or bark, frankincense, garlic, hazel leaves or bark, hazelnuts, iris, lemongrass, lung wort, plum stones, sage, self–heal, thyme, willow leaves or bark

Third Quarter Moon Herbal Water

Add any of these to your water: Alexanders, alyssum, birch leaves or bark, carnation, celandine, chamomile, chives, coriander leaves or seeds, cypress leaves or bark, dill, holly leaves, bark or berries, honeysuckle, lemon slices, peel or pips, liquorice root, lungwort, rue, self–heal, thyme, willow leaves or bark, woodruff, witch hazel or bark

Waning Crescent Moon Herbal Water

Add any of these to your water: Agrimony, apple slices, peel or pips, ash leaves, seed or bark, bay, blackthorn leaves, blossom or thorns, burdock, caraway seeds, carnation, cinnamon bark, coltsfoot, comfrey, coriander seeds or leaves, cramp bark leaves or blossom, cucumber, dock, echinacea, eucalyptus leaves or bark, fennel seeds, garlic, hazel leaves or bark, hyssop, ivy, juniper leaves, berries or thorns, lemon balm, lime slices, peel or pips, marjoram, mint, myrrh, nettle, oak leaves, bark or acorns, pine needs, rose petals, leaves or thorns, rosemary, tansy, thyme, willow bark or leaves

Dark Moon Herbal Water

Add any of these to your water: Alexanders, apple slices, peel or pips, bergamot, betony, cardamom, columbine/aquilegia, clove, coffee, dill, echinacea, juniper leaves, berries or thorns, knotweed, lavender, mustard seeds, myrrh, orange slices, peel or pips, rosemary, rue, self–heal, walnut

Moon in Aries Herbal Water

Add any of these to your water: Bay, cinnamon bark, coriander seeds or leaves, dragon's blood, feverfew, frankincense, juniper leaves, berries or thorns, marjoram, myrrh, nettle, rosemary

Moon in Taurus Herbal Water

Add any of these to your water: Coltsfoot, dandelion, lungwort, mandrake, myrtle, thyme

Moon in Gemini Herbal Water

Add any of these to your water: Angelica, bergamot, dill, honeysuckle, oregano, tansy, thyme

Moon in Cancer Herbal Water

Add any of these to your water: Angelica, dill, honeysuckle, hyssop, jasmine, mandrake, mugwort, violet, wormwood

Moon in Leo Herbal Water

Add any of these to your water: Angelica, bay, burdock, chamomile, dill, fennel seeds, frankincense, rue, sunflower seeds

Moon in Virgo Herbal Water

Add any of these to your water: Bergamot, fennel seeds, mandrake, patchouli, sandalwood, scullcap, valerian

Moon in Libra Herbal Water

Add any of these to your water: Angelica, bergamot, burdock, elder bark or leaves, feverfew, Saint John's Wort, thyme, violet

Moon in Scorpio Herbal Water

Add any of these to your water: Basil, blackthorn bark, leaves or thorns, horehound, ivy, lily, nettle, pennyroyal, wormwood

Moon in Sagittarius Herbal Water

Add any of these to your water: Beech bark or leaves, birch bark or leaves, cedar bark or leaves, elder bark or leaves, feverfew, hawthorn blossom, bark or thorns, nutmeg, oak leaves, bark or acorns, rowan leaves, berries or bark, sage, sandalwood

Moon in Capricorn Herbal Water

Add any of these to your water: Benzoin, comfrey, marjoram, pine, plantain, poppy, Solomon's seal, witch hazel bark or leaves

Moon in Aquarius Herbal Water

Add any of these to your water: Bergamot, cypress leaves or bark, elder leaves or bark, fennel seeds, frankincense, myrrh, Saint John's Wort

Moon in Pisces Herbal Water

Add any of these to your water: Bladder wrack, dulse, fern, geranium, lily of the valley, lungwort, meadowsweet, rose petals, leaves or thorns, willow bark or leaves

January Herbal Water

Add any of these to your water: Alyssum, basil, bay, betony, birch bark or leaves, black pepper corns, cardamom, cinnamon bark, clove, coriander seeds or leaves, crocus, cumin seeds, dill, fennel seeds, garlic, ginger, honeysuckle, horehound, juniper berries, bark or thorns, lavender, marjoram, mint, mustard seeds, nutmeg, parsley, patchouli, rosemary, rue, sage, star anise, turmeric, witch hazel bark or leaves, woodruff

February Herbal Water

Add any of these to your water: Avocado stone, basil, birch leaves or bark, bay, cherry stones, cinnamon bark, cucumber, dock, fennel seeds, fish bones, fig stones, frankincense, ginger, hawthorn blossom, leaves or thorns, hazel bark or leaves, hyssop, juniper leaves, berries or thorns, lime slices, peel or pips, melon seeds, mistletoe, myrrh, olive stones, peach pits, pine needles, poppy seeds, rose petals, leaves or thorns, rosemary, rowan berries, leaves or bark, rue, strawberry leaves, thyme, vervain

March Herbal Water

Add any of these to your water: Birch bark or leaves, clove, cornflower, cranberries, cyclamen, egg shells, fennel seeds, hawthorn leaves, blossom or thorns, hazel bark or leaves, honesty, horsetail, mustard seeds, parsley, pasta (bear in mind this will swell in the water), pine needles, pomegranate seeds, primrose, rice (bear in mind this will swell in the water), Saint John's Wort, snapdragon, sunflower seeds, sweetpea, walnut

April Herbal Water

Add any of these to your water: Bay, beech bark or leaves, benzoin, bergamot, black pepper corns, chilli seeds or dried chillies, cinnamon bark, clover, cumin seeds, ginger, holly leaves, bark or berries, lemon balm, lily of the valley, pasta (bear in mind it will swell in the water), primrose, rowan bark, leaves or berries, Solomon's seal, tomato seeds or slices, vanilla

May Herbal Water

Add any of these to your water: African violet, alexanders, almond, ash bark or leaves, bay, beech bark or leaves, camellia, cinnamon bark, cornflower, cucumber, elder bark or leaves, frankincense, grapes, heliotrope, mustard seeds, orchid, parsley, rowan leaves, bark or berries, self–heal, sweet pea, star anise, vanilla, willow bark or leaves

June Herbal Water

Add any of these to your water: Bay, blackthorn leaves, bark or thorns, black pepper, carnation, chestnut, daisy, delphinium, dragon's blood, garlic, horsetail, lavender, lemon peel, slices or pips, oak leaves, bark or acorns, pennyroyal, pine nut, plantain, raspberry, Saint John's wort, sesame seeds, sunflower seeds, sweetpea, tea leaves (black)

July Herbal Water

Add any of these to your water: Ash leaves or bark, bergamot, chamomile, cinnamon bark, cramp bark leaves or flowers, cumin seeds, date pits, eucalyptus leaves or bark, frankincense, ginger, heather, heliotrope, holly leaves, bark or berries, honeysuckle, jasmine, plum stones, rose petals, leaves or thorns, rowan bark, leaves or berries, sage, sandalwood, star anise, tea leaves (black)

August Herbal Water

Add any of these to your water: Bergamot, carnation, chilli seeds or dried chillies, coffee, coltsfoot, elm bark or leaves, grapefruit peel or pips, heather, hyssop, lemon peel or pips, lemon balm, lime peel or pips, orange peel or pips, passion flower, plantain, rose petals, leaves or thorns, rosemary, saffron, sesame seeds, sweetpea, tansy

September Herbal Water

Add any of these to your water: Alexanders, agrimony, chamomile, cramp bark leaves or flowers, dill, dock, elm bark or leaves, fish bones, ginger, honeysuckle, geranium, liquorice root, lungwort, mint, oyster shell, patchouli, plum stone, rue, self–heal, tansy, witch hazel bark or leaves

October Herbal Water

Add any of these to your water: Almond, apple slices or pips, ash, bay, cinnamon bark, dittany, elder bark or leaves, fern, grapefruit peel or pips, heather, myrrh, morning glory, mugwort, parsley, pasta (bear in mind this will swell in the water), periwinkle, saffron, sage, star anise, thistle, thyme, willow bark or leaves

November Herbal Water

Add any of these to your water: Almond, bay, bergamot, bladder wrack, borage, chives, cinnamon bark, coriander leaves or seeds, elm bark or leaves, grass, hazelnut, juniper leaves, berries or thorns, marigold, mugwort, mustard seeds, pasta (bear in mind this will swell in the water), rowan bark, leaves or berries, saffron, sage, sandalwood (white), wormwood, yarrow

December Herbal Water

Add any of these to your water: Alyssum, basil, blueberries, borage, cocoa nibs, cumin seeds, frankincense, horehound, hyacinth, lavender, meadowsweet, orange peel, slices or pips, pennyroyal, poppy seeds, saffron, sweetpea, thyme, vervain, violet, yarrow

Moon Phase Month Spell

If you are really serious about something and are happy to spend some time working the magic for it then building the spell up over a month of Moon phases can be very effective.

- Start on a dark Moon and spend some quiet time thinking about what you really need or want to achieve.
- On the new Moon write down your intention, just the basics.
- On the waxing Moon add some details and work your magic spell.
- For the full Moon celebrate it coming together or use the full Moon power to add a boost to your intent.
- At the waning Moon release anything that is getting in the way of your goal.
- By the next dark Moon reflect on how it all went and what

changes, if any, would need to be made the next time around.

This works nicely if you have a large taper candle, burn a section of it on each Moon phase to add to your intent. On the phase where you work your magic add in crystals and herbs if you wish.

You can swap this around and work releasing magic on the waning Moon and add in positive energy on the waxing. Any void of energy you create must be filled with positive energy otherwise the negative cycle has a habit of repeating itself.

And remember to follow your intuition, if you plan to work a particular spell on a set Moon phase but when it comes to it you don't feel like it, don't do it. Be flexible, work around it, work with it or postpone it. Don't work against it because it will either fizzle out or go off in the wrong direction. The Moon will be there next time.

And once the magic is worked don't forget your manners, give thanks to the Moon and maybe even an offering too.

Moon Cords

One way of 'collecting' and keeping Moon energy is by making a Moon cord.

The cord is made on a particular phase of the Moon and the energy is trapped in each knot and kept there until needed.

We don't always have the time, opportunity or inclination to work magic on a specific Moon phase. If you create Moon cords then no matter what the Moon phase it is, you always have the corresponding Moon energy to work your spell.

Of course, it is easier and better to do any working on the actual Moon phase but sometimes it just isn't possible, so if you have Moon cords to hand you don't have to wait.

To make a Moon cord; use wool, string, cord or thread about two feet long. It helps if you have different colours then you can use a different colour for each phase of the Moon, to help identify them afterwards.

You will need to be able to see and feel the Moon to make your cord.

Here, the choice is yours – you can cast a full circle if you wish. But I prefer to just light a candle and invoke a suitable lunar deity and ask them to lend their power.

Face the Moon and hold your cord up towards it.

You can say prepared words then, or just ask for what you need – the power of that particular phase of the Moon to be drawn down into your cord for safe keeping until you need it.

You can also use the following:

By knot of ONE, the spell's begun
By knot of TWO, it cometh true
By knot of THREE, so mote it be
By knot of FOUR, this power I store
By knot of FIVE, the spell's alive
By knot of SIX, this spell I fix
By knot of SEVEN, events I'll leaven
By knot of EIGHT, it will be Fate
By knot of NINE, what's done is mine

As you visualise the power entering your cord, start tying knots.

You will need to tie nine in total each an equal distance apart.

If you don't use the chant above, on your last knot it is an idea to finish with something that completes the spell such as 'so mote it be'. Being a bit of a Trekkie I like to use the phrase 'make it so'.

Thank the deity and the Moon for their energies.

Keep the cord safe. When you need the energy from that particular Moon phase place it on your altar, around your candle or wherever you are working your spell.

There are two modes of thought on using the cord, you can either keep using it and just recharge it at the next Moon phase or you can actually undo one of the knots each time you need that energy to 'release' it.

Once you have used all the knots you can reuse the cord, or I prefer to start with a new cord so that there is no confusion with the magical energy.

This type of knot magic can also be used for spell working of any kind, tie your intent into each knot whether it is for prosperity, love, banishing, healing or any number of other ideas that you might have.

Simple Spells

As a Kitchen Witch I like to keep things simple and straight forward. I have given a lot of spell working ideas above such as spell pouches, candle magic and witch bottles. If you want to keep it even simpler here are my suggestions, work on the corresponding Moon phase and you are all set.

- The simplest spell of all is to stand outside, look up at the Moon and ask for what you want or need.
- Write your wish or desire on a slip of paper and burn it, bury it or wash it away.
- Light a candle, it doesn't have to be fancy, just a birthday cake candle will do and sit in front of it, visualize your needs or desires, sit with the candle until it burns out.
- Hold a pebble in your hand, send your negative vibes into it and throw it away.
- Write your wish or desire on a pebble and bury it.
- Send your wishes into a seed and plant it.
- Send your wishes into a flower or herb, bury it, burn it or offer it to running water.

Working magic hints and tips

Moon Meditation

One of the easiest ways to work with the Moon and soak up her energy, whatever the Moon phase is to meditate. It helps if you can see the dark night sky when you do, but you can work with a photo or a picture or even just visualize. Work your intent into the Moon phase and design your meditation around it.

Intent

When I say intent, I am referring to your intention, the reason you are meditating or holding a ritual or working a spell. What is your goal? What do you seek? What do you want to achieve?

My advice is to keep it simple. Don't work with lots of requests all at the same time. Be clear and concise and remember that what you want isn't always what you need, the Universe has a habit of stepping in and making changes on your behalf.

- Set your intention
- Set a time frame
- Be specific
- Focus
- Will – you must put the effort in, if you aren't really that fussed about it then the energy to push it forward won't be there.
- Boost it – by working your magic on the corresponding Moon phase, day of the week, using colours and herbs that tie in with your intent you can give it more oomph.

Remember that you don't have to ask for anything to work with the magic of the Moon. You could just sit and 'be'. Having quiet alone time is very precious especially in today's busy world. Even if you can grab five minutes to stand and look up at the

Moon it will be special. Just be still and silent, open up your senses and listen, she may have some wisdom or guidance to share with you.

Energy of the days

Each day of the week has its own specific energies and I would suggest you check first thing each morning to find out what the energy is for you.

Take a step outside your house and breathe in, relax and allow your mind to connect with what the day has in store. See what words pop into your head or what feelings, emotions or insight the universe can throw your way. Taking just those few moments each morning will hopefully give you guidance for the rest of the day and point you in the right direction for what kind of magic will work best at that time.

Monday Magic – Let's have a sneak peek at Monday…

It was the good ole Babylonians that set up the seven–day week for us, which in turn was based on the Sumerian calendar. Seven days relating to the transition of the Moon phases.

Then the Romans took on the tradition installing the Julian calendar in the first century BC. Before that they used the nundinal cycle which had eight days.

The ancient Greeks named the days of the week after the planets and in turn their gods. The Romans then substituted their gods as did the Germanic people. Monday of course is named after the Moon. In old English it was named Mōnandæg which translates as 'day of the Moon'. For any Pagan, Monday has a huge amount of possibilities, we tend to work very closely with the Moon and her phases.

There are memes about Mondays, there are songs about Mondays…what is it that people don't like about Monday? I suspect the general feeling is because Monday is the first day of the working week after the weekend for a lot of people. Having had two days of not getting up early and mooching about or partying, Monday arrives with a wakeup call…literally.

Actually, I don't mind Monday. For me it is the fresh start to a new week, full of potential and possibilities, albeit that the alarm is not always a welcome beginning.

If you want some kind of structure, then the days of the week have particular magical intents that are specific and traditional to work with on those days, but as always be guided by your own intuition. Below are some suggestions for Monday:

Work magic on a Monday for:

- Fertility – and I am not just talking about the pitter patter of tiny feet (whether in human or animal form) but fertility of new projects, ideas and plants.
- Intuition – get your spidey senses working at full speed.
- Emotions – take a look inside and see why you are feeling how you do, give your emotions a bit of an overhaul.
- Clarity – get a clear head and see things from a fresh new perspective.
- Wisdom – time to do some research or learn about something new.
- Dreams – take a look at your dreams, what do they mean to you. Or set some dreams, desires and goals in motion.
- Travel – make plans…explore…
- Feminine energy – the Moon has heap loads of feminine vibes, tap into them and see what she can help you with.
- Peace – and breathe…ahhhhhhh. Find that inner (or outer peace) even if it is just for a few moments, relish it.
- Moon magic – well on a Monday that makes perfect sense, right?
- Illusions – the Moon can cause some big ole confusing illusions, take a step back and see through the veil.

Whatever you do on a Monday, be thankful for what you have and that you are seeing in another day. Make the most of what you have and work with the energies around you.

Week day suggestions:

Monday – fertility, intuition, emotions, clarity, wisdom, dreams, travel, feminine energy, peace, Moon magic and illusions.

Tuesday – success, strength, defense, protection, courage and challenges.

Wednesday – communication, fortune, luck, changes, creativity, wild magic, cunning and the arts.

Thursday – healing, strength, prosperity, wealth, abundance, protection and good health.

Friday – romance, friendships, passion, fertility and love.

Saturday – protection, wisdom, spirituality, cleansing and banishing.

Sunday – prosperity, success, wealth, promotion, fame, personal achievements and acknowledgement.

These are just for guidance...trust your own intuition and go with what works for you.

Magical times of the day

There are some time points during the day that lend themselves to magic, you don't have to work in tune with them but I encourage you to give it a try and see what you get from it.

Dawn

When the Sun rises over the horizon and a new day begins. As a working wife and mother I don't often have time to go and sit on the beach or on top of a hill to experience the Sunrise, it just doesn't fit in with school runs and work schedules but…if you get a free morning it is worth making the effort even if you just watch it from your back garden.

This is a time of day when things move slowly (well for most of us that is true until after the first cup of coffee right?). Dawn does not have a sense of hurry about it, dawn likes to move gently. The Sunrise lends itself to gentle magic that brings renewal, rebirth and restoration.

If you don't have the time or means to sit and watch the Sunrise how about greeting the Sun when you get up in the morning? Whether the Sun has been awake for a few minutes or a few hours it feels good to give it a nod of appreciation and a greeting to start your day.

Noon

The Sun is now at the height of its travel and the clock strikes the day time witching hour of twelve. It is an energy filled time of the day so make the most of it. Stand outside and shout to the world, the universe and the divine let them know what your hopes, dreams and desires are…put it out there! It is a time of strength, passion and creativity.

The middle of the day has a really strong earth and fire energy to it, use that in your spell working to the best advantage. If you don't have any workings to do, then maybe get out your drum and join the Sun in some energetic drumming and dancing.

Dusk

At the twilight of the day we are surrounded in a much calmer somehow mysterious type of energy. It makes me think of the mists coming down onto the moors with a shadowy magic about it. This is a time of the day to look inwards for insight and inspiration but also to connect with the Otherworld to gain clarity.

Take some time to look, listen and think; map out your web of life in front of you and follow the threads so that you know what adjustments need to be made.

Dusk is a very personal spiritual time of the day.

At the midnight hour

Midnight...the witching hour when all around us is in darkness. The midnight hours are perfect for spirit communication on a deep level to seek answers to mysteries of life, the universe and everything.

Scrying, divination, meditation and candle magic work well in the dark hours and of course, if the Moon is not dark, we can see and work with her beautiful face in full view.

A few ritual notes

Rituals should be personal to you whether they are ceremonial, freeform or otherwise. Work them to suit you. I have given ritual 'scripts' here but do feel free to tweak them. Change the words, the spells or ingredients used if your intuition tells you too or be guided by the contents of your cupboard. I call upon the elements in each ritual, but you might want to work with animal energy for each quarter or not call on them at all. What I have provided is a guide, use it as is or make it your own.

Circle Casting

Walk the circle or if you are limited for space turn around on the spot. Use your visualisation skills and 'see' a circle forming but also allow your circle to expand so that it forms a bubble. You are then protected above and below. You may like to mark your circle if you have the room by sprinkling salt, dried herbs or flowers.

Quarter Calls

I work with the four elements and start in the North but begin in whatever direction you feel is right for you. To finish I thank the elements by working in reverse order, again do what works for you. Lighting a candle in each direction as you call the quarter works well. If you have the room, you may also like to place a representation at each compass point. A dish of soil or salt at north for earth, incense or a feather at east for air, a candle or matches at south for fire and a dish of water or a shell at west for water. Be creative if you wish, place images of corresponding animals at each quarter or dishes of herbs or flowers. We even had a Kitchen Witch ritual where we had four types of cake, one at each direction.

Deity

I have chosen a deity for each ritual, aligned with their characteristics and the energy they can offer you. Often, I work with just one deity in ritual, but I have worked with two or more on occasion. Calling a male and a female deity does bring about a certain balance to a ritual, if you prefer. You may like to just call upon Mother Earth or Father Sky or not request the presence of deity at all. Go with what works for you. As you call deity into ritual you might like to light a central candle in their honour.

Grounding and centring

Grounding yourself before and after any ritual or energy work is advisable. The simplest method beforehand is to take a few deep breathes in and out, focus on your breathing to calm and steady yourself. Now visualise roots growing from your feet into the earth, let them search downwards through the soil. When you reach the centre allow the earth energy to flow through the roots and into your body. Take what you need to balance. When you feel grounded and centered slowly bring your roots back up. After a ritual to release excess energy place the palms of your hands on the ground and let any energy you don't need flow back into the earth. Clapping your hands and stamping your feet also works, as does eating something. Do not leave a ritual or any energy work without grounding yourself, it will leave you with a cracking headache.

Basic Ritual Script

Below is the basic ritual script I have used in the Moon phase rituals within this book. It gives a general circle casting, quarter calls and closing. If you would like to use it as a starting point for a Moon ritual, you can add in your own deity calls and spell work.

Cast the circle

Walking deosil (clockwise) around the circle.

> With the power of the Moon
> *I cast this circle to attune*
> *Magic creating a boundary to last*
> *This Moon circle is now cast*

Call the quarters

Facing North

> *I call upon the element of earth*
> *May you bring your energy of grounding and stability to this rite*
> *Earth, I welcome you*

Facing East

> *I call upon the element of air*
> *May you bring your energy of intellect and inspiration to this rite*
> *Air, I welcome you*

Facing South

> *I call upon the element of fire,*
> *May you bring your energy of passion and power to this rite*
> *Fire, I welcome you*

Facing West

I call upon the element of water,
May you bring your energy of emotions and cleansing to this rite
Water, I welcome you

Invite Deity

Spell work

Feast: Eat and drink something to celebrate your ritual and to help you ground. Sprinkle some of the drink and food onto the earth after the ritual as an offering to deity.

Thank Deity

Release the quarters

Facing West

I thank the element of water,
For bringing your energy of emotions and cleansing to this rite
Water, I bid you farewell

Facing South

I thank the element of fire,
For bringing your energy of passion and power to this rite
Fire, I bid you farewell

Facing East

I thank the element of air
For bringing your energy of intellect and inspiration to this rite
Air, I bid you farewell

Facing North

I thank the element of earth
For bringing your energy of grounding and stability to this rite
Earth, I bid you farewell

Close the circle

Walking widdershins (anti clockwise) around the circle

I thank the power of the Moon
I uncast this circle but stay in tune
Magic unties the boundary to last
This Moon circle is now uncast

Moon Divination

We are spoilt for choice with types of divination, some of them work better on the full Moon such as water scrying but they can all be used for Moon magic. The dark Moon is also an excellent time to work forms of divination that don't require the light of the Moon. Here I have included some of my favourites:

Tarot

Probably one of the most recognised forms of divination. If you aren't familiar with reading the cards, I encourage you to just open up a pack, shuffle and pick a few cards. Trust your intuition and 'say what you see'. Don't over think it, just go with the images from the cards that jump out at you. And of course, the tarot has its very own Moon card:

The Moon tarot card

The Moon is all about intuition, dreams and your unconscious so this card embodies all of that and more. It is about illusions, fear and anxiety. That which is unseen and that which we don't understand. A card of mysteries. We often project past experiences of fear onto our present, although not always consciously. Any previous pain or anxiety is often repressed and shoved to the back of our minds and not dealt with. Where it sits and festers and escapes on occasion through our daily lives in unexpected ways. To prevent this, issues and fears need to be acknowledged and released. This is a card of illusions when things may not appear as they really are. Don't make quick judgements or decisions without doing proper research and finding out the truth. This card also has a strong feminine energy and can help you with your intuition and inner work.

Tarot cards and oracle cards can be used as a focal point for meditation or as a key component to spell work. Below I have listed some general correspondences with cards but trust your intuition about which ones to use.

Abundance: The Empress, The Star, The World, Ace of Pentacles, Six of Pentacles, Nine of Pentacles, Ace of Cups.

Action/to set things in motion: The Chariot, The Empress, Ace of Wands, Eight of Wands.

Bad habits, to overcome: Strength, Temperance, Judgement, The World.

Balance: The Lovers, Justice, Temperance, Two of Swords, Four of Wands, Two of Cups.

Binding spells: Temperance, Two of Swords, Eight of Swords, Hanged Man.

Business prosperity: Three of Wands, The Sun, Ace of Pentacles.

Challenges: The Magician, Queen of Swords, Two of Wands.

Changes: Wheel of Fortune, The Magician, Hanged Man, Death, The Tower, Judgement, The World, Knight of Swords, Eight of Wands.

Commitment: The Lovers, Three of Pentacles, Three of Wands, Two of Cups.

Communication: The Magician, Page of Swords.

Confidence: The Emperor, The Chariot.

Courage and strength: The Star, Strength, The Chariot, The Fool, Ace of Swords, Knight of Swords, Seven of Wands, Nine of Wands.

Decisions: Justice, The Hermit, The Star, The Lovers, The Hanged Man, The Devil, Judgement, Two of Pentacles, Two of Swords, Seven of Swords, King of Swords, Seven of Cups.

Dreams: The Star, The Moon, Ace of Cups, High Priestess.

Emotions: The Empress, Queen of Cups.

Employment: Justice, The Emperor, Judgement, Page of Wands, Two of Wands, Eight of Pentacles, Ace of Pentacles, Ace of Wands, Three of Wands, Four of Wands.

Fertility: The Sun, The Fool, The Empress, Ten of Cups, Ace of Wands.

Friendship: Three of Cups, Two of Cups, Knight of Cups.

Goals: The Emperor, The Chariot, Strength.

Growth: The Empress, The Hermit.

Happiness and positive energy: The Sun, The Empress, The World, The Star, Ten of Pentacles, Ace of Cups, Four of Wands, Queen of Wands, Ten of Cups.

Healing and good health: Strength, The World, The Magician, The Sun, The Star, The Empress, The Chariot, Judgement, Three of Cups.

Inspiration, ideas and creativity: The Magician, The Moon, The Star, The Fool, The Empress, The World, The Hierophant, Temperance, Ace of Cups, Ace of Wands, Queen of Wands, Page of Cups, Knight of Cups.

Intuition: The High Priestess, The Devil, The Moon.

Knowledge and Wisdom: The Hermit, High Priestess, The Moon, The Magician, The Hierophant, Wheel of Fortune, Two of Pentacles, Ace of Swords, Page of Pentacles.

Leadership: The Emperor, The Chariot, King of Swords, King of Cups.

Love: The Lovers, Knight of Cups, The Star, Two of Cups, Ace of Cups, Four of Wands.

Luck: The World, The Star, Wheel of Fortune.

Magic: The Magician, The High Priestess, The Moon.

New beginnings: The Fool, The Emperor, The World, The Chariot, The Hermit, Death, The Sun, Two of Pentacles, Ten of Swords, Ace of Wands, Knight of Wands, Four of Cups, Eight of Cups.

New business/project success: The Magician, The Sun, Ace of Wands, The Empress, Seven of Pentacles.

Opportunities: The Magician, Wheel of Fortune, The Devil, The Star, The World, Knight of Cups, Seven of Cups.

Overcoming obstacles: The Chariot, Strength, Death, Temperance, Ace of Swords, Six of Swords, Six of Wands, Three of Cups.

Power: The Emperor, The Chariot, Strength, Temperance, Ace of Swords.

Protection: The Empress, The Emperor.

Potential: The Fool.

Prosperity and money: Wheel of Fortune, Ten of Pentacles, Knight of Pentacles, Page of Pentacles, Six of Pentacles, Ace of Pentacles, Two of Pentacles, Four of Pentacles, Queen of Pentacles.

Protection: The Star, The Chariot, Temperance, Four of Wands.

Releasing: Hanged Man, Death, The Devil, The Tower, Four of Swords, Six of Swords.

Self–improvement and transformation: Temperance, The World, Judgement, The Magician, Strength, High Priestess, The Chariot.

Spirituality: The High Priestess, The Hermit, The Sun, The Moon, The Star, The Hierophant, The Hermit, The Tower, The World.

Stress relief: Hanged Man, Ace of Cups, Temperance, Four of Cups.

Success: The Chariot, Wheel of Fortune, Justice, The Star, The Moon, The Sun, The World, Ace of Pentacles, Queen of Pentacles, King of Pentacles, Ace of Swords, Two of Swords, Six of Swords.

Travel: The Chariot, Eight of Wands.

Truth: The High Priestess, The Lovers, Justice, The Tower, The Moon, Ace of Swords, Knight of Wands, Seven of Cups, Queen of Cups.

Oracle Cards

We are spoilt for choice with oracle cards of all kinds of designs (including my own Flower Magic deck). There are also some decks specifically designed as Moon magic cards. Take a look around and see which ones take your fancy. They all work in pretty much the same way, pick a card for the day or do a full spread reading as you would with tarot. Unlike tarot they don't have set meanings, each deck will have its very own stories.

Mirror Scrying

Scrying on a reflective surface is an ancient practice. The Romans and ancient Egyptians all make mention of scrying and magic mirrors. Mirrors have been used but also highly polished dark stone surfaces and black crystals.

I like to use a black mirror. I have a couple that I have been gifted over the years, a small one and a large one. The large one is quite overwhelming sometimes though.

There are some beautiful black mirrors available to purchase, the really expensive ones are made from highly polished obsidian. But you can make your own very cheaply.

You will need:

A picture frame (doesn't need to be new or fancy) with a glass front.
Black paint

All you do is paint the piece of glass from the frame on one side. Then fit it back into the frame with the painted side inwards. Then you have a smooth shiny black mirror. It is that easy.

I like to light a candle and sit in the dark with the full Moon shining through onto the surface of the mirror. But you can do this with just a candle flame. Ground and centre yourself and take a few deep breaths in and out. Then look into the dark mirror, I think it helps to slightly unfocus your eyes.

Make a note of any images, shapes, symbols or patterns that you see. You may also find words form in your head. Finish once you feel ready or when your mind starts to wander. Allow some time for your subconscious to process the messages.

A dark mirror benefits from cleansing regularly, wafting with incense smoke works well.

Water Scrying

This one is incredibly easy to set up and you don't need any special tools. Find a bowl or dish, preferably one that has a darker inside. Fill it with water. I like to drop a silver coin into the dish to help with reflections. A few drops of ink on the water surface or a sprinkle of herbs also works well.

Now position the dish so that light from the full Moon shines onto the surface of the water. Ground and centre yourself so that your energy is calm and focused. Take a few deep breaths in and out. Now look across the top of the surface of the water, I think it helps to unfocus your eyes and not look directly into the water, just over the top of it. You might get images, symbols or patterns, you may even feel words forming in your mind.

Take your time. Make a note of the things you see and hear so that you can look back at them later to translate. Stop when you feel ready or if you lose focus or your mind begins to wander. Pour the water onto the ground as an offering. Let the experience rest for a couple of days, allow yourself time to process it. Then read through your notes and see what it means to you.

Scrying can be done with any body of water such as a lake or a pond. I have even read messages in puddles.

If you want to scry and there is no full Moon, or visible Moon you can set a candle in front of the dish and allow the reflection from the flame to fall upon the surface of the water.

Lunomancy

Lunomancy is the practice of telling the past, present and the future by looking at the shadows created by the Moon onto a person's face. Full Moon is best for this form of Moon divination. You need to ask the person to sit still and just see what random shadows fall. The depth of the shadow, the length, shape and where it falls on the face can all be read as part of the meaning. Sometimes a silver dust is used, this is spread on the readers hands and then onto the person's face before the reading begins.

Selenomancy

Divination by observing the phases and appearance of the Moon. 'Selene' is the Greek word for 'Moon' and 'manteia' means 'prophecy'. You can read the patterns that appear on the surface of the Moon, any colours or reflections, the phase the Moon is in and how much you can see through cloud cover.

Crystal Ball/Crystallomancy

Crystallomancy is the art of divination using a shiny surface such as a crystal ball but also polished quartz or crystal stones. Any shiny, reflective surface can be used really. Position your crystal so that the light of the Moon, full Moon preferably, shines onto the crystal surface. You can use a crystal ball without the aid of Moonlight, in this case it helps to set a lit candle near to the crystal ball. You need to gaze 'unfocused' just across the surface of the crystal and interpret what images, shapes or colours you see.

Pendulum

Pendulums are really easy to make, you just need a piece of thread, string or leather thong, add a small heavy object to the end such as a hag stone, piece of wood or a shell and you have a readymade pendulum. Hold the thread loosely over your finger and thumb, allow the pendulum to hang and steady itself. Ask it to give you a yes, see which way it swings, it may be clockwise or side to side. Then ask it to give you a no, it may swing anti clockwise or up and down. Each pendulum is individual, and you will need to discover which way it swings for yes and no. Once you have that sorted you can ask it simple questions. Obviously make sure the answers can be just a yes or no, it isn't going to get more complicated.

Tea leaves

One of the traditional ways of divination. Using loose leaf tea, the reader will swirl the leaves in the bottom of the cup to see how they move and tip them out on to a saucer to see what images arise. The official name for reading tea leaves is tasseography. You can also do this using coffee grounds.

Wax shapes

Officially called ceroscopy, a reader will light a candle, ask a question and then drip wax from it onto a bowl of cold water. The answer to the query can be read in the shapes and images of the wax.

Gardening by the Moon

Planting or gardening by the Moon is an old tradition to help plan when you plant and harvest your crops. The idea being that the phases of the Moon affect how a plant grows and even how much moisture there is in the soil. Seeds are believed to absorb more water during a new and full Moon because the energy of the Moon pulls moisture upwards to the surface of the soil. This results in faster and better germination. The growth of a plant is said to be affected by geotropism; this is how a plant grows in relation to gravity. Roots are pulled downwards by the gravitational pull and stems are directed upwards. If you chose to plant and harvest by the Moon, also consider where you are in the world, weather and seasons also play a part.

An easy to follow general guide is:

From the day of the new Moon through the waxing period up to full – plant annual flowers and vegetables that crop above ground.

New Moon or first quarter – seeds planted now will take up lots of water, swell and burst open (which is a good thing). This Moon phase is said to help with balance growth. Best plants to start off on this phase are things such as pumpkins, tomatoes, kale, spinach, cabbage, lettuce and broccoli.

Second quarter – the Moon still gives out lots of light but there is less gravitational pull. This is a good time for the leaves to really develop. Planting at the end of the second quarter and just before the full Moon is a perfect time to harness the full light of the Moon and the moisture in the soil. Plant things like beans, melon and squashes.

From the day after the full Moon through the waning period until it is new again – plant flowering bulbs, biennial and perennial flowers and vegetables that crop below ground.

Full Moon or third quarter – Gravity is pulling its very hardest on the full Moon and obviously there is optimum Moonlight levels, this helps with root development. Plant your root crops such as beetroot, carrots and parsnips. Bulbs also benefit from being planted on a full Moon. If you have any perennials to transplant, now is the time to do it.

Fourth quarter – The gravitational pull and light is lower now. The moisture levels are at their lowest, so it is not the best time for planting, better to work on other things such as pruning and harvesting.

Astrological days also affect how you garden, depending on what sign the Moon is in:

When the Moon is in Aries: Weed, plant flavourful vegetables, till the soil, mow the lawn. Harvest crops. Prune.

When the Moon is in Taurus: Plant bulbs, sow vegetable seeds, annuals and flowering plants. Don't plant any vines.

When the Moon is in Gemini: Weed, prune and control pests and diseases. Till the soil. Don't plant, sow seeds or move plants. Harvest crops.

When the Moon is in Cancer: Sow plants and flowers, watery vegetables and fruit. Make sure the garden is well watered.

When the Moon is in Leo: Avoid any planting, seed sowing or moving of plants. Weed and control pests and diseases, prune. Harvest crops.

When the Moon is in Virgo: Avoid any planting, seed sowing or moving of plants. Prune. Weed and control pests and diseases. Till the soil.

When the Moon is in Libra: Plant flowers, vines and climbers. Avoid planting vegetables.

When the Moon is in Scorpio: Sow, plant and move fruit, flowers and vegetables. Plant vines and climbers.

When the Moon is in Sagittarius: Plant flavourful fruit and vegetables. Till the soil. Mow the lawn. Harvest crops. Prune.

When the Moon is in Capricorn: This is a growing and hardening period for most plants. Don't do any weeding. Get on with some garden maintenance.

When the Moon is in Aquarius: Till the soil, mow the lawn. Avoid planting, sowing or moving plants. Harvest crops.

When the Moon is in Pisces: Good for general planting and root growth. Sow low growing plants.

If you want to find out more details look for a Farmer's Almanac, they have a host of information about planting and harvesting by the Moon.

Moon Garden

Moon gardens can have many facets. Using all white and silver plants works well but also plants that flower or release their scent at night. There are many plants that are also associated with the energy of the Moon.

Creating Moon shaped flower beds and using white and grey stones, pebbles, crystals and shingle can also be effective. Reflective surfaces can be included, whether it is mirrors, dark pools of water or white candles.

Suggested white or silver plants, these all come in white varieties:

Artemisia, astilbe, acanthus, agapanthus, agave, alstroemeria, anemone, angelica, lilies, heliotrope, petunia, scabiosa, wisteria, dianthus, hibiscus, hydrangea, daffodil, magnolia, jasmine, camellia, datura (Moonflower), hyacinth, peony, aquilegia/columbine, lilac, chrysanthemum, hellebore, yarrow, cosmos, begonia, ferns, centaurea, cardoon, sea holly, helichrysum, heuchera, brunnera, lungwort, dusty miller, melianthus, curry plant, sedum, dicentra alba, evening primrose, honeysuckle, hosta, maiden grass, Moonflowers, nicotiana, sage, clematis, rhododendron, viburnum, cistus, lunaria annua, convolvulus, roses, primula, foxglove, phlox, dahlia, echinacea, tulips, allium, stachys, lavender, grasses, delphinium and white daisies.

Moon Predictions, Folklore & Myths

Our ancestors looked to the skies and nature to help them predict the weather. It was important to know what was coming as their lives depended on the crops and livestock. The Moon was often used to predict the weather.

A circle around the Moon warned of bad weather. This was usually followed by rain or storms. It is fairly factual, the circle we see is caused by ice crystals within the clouds. These clouds are the ones that often bring rain with them.

Wolves are said to howl at the full Moon when in reality I suspect it is just because they are more likely to be out hunting in the light it casts. It helps them see their prey and they are shouting to their wolfie mates to tell them supper is on the table.

A bright new Moon will bring rain but also a bountiful harvest.

A red tinted Moon warns of a dry year ahead.

A red Moon rising means rain the next day.

If you dream of a new Moon it is a prediction of wealth or a happy marriage.

Dreaming about a red or blood Moon is a sign of very bad luck or even war.

A young lady dreaming of the Moon growing dim should keep a hold on her tongue otherwise she will be miserable.

Make sure you have a silver coin in your pocket on the new Moon, it will ensure you have money for the coming month.

If you are looking for a happy marriage, the best day to get married is on the first full Moon in June.

Dreaming of a Moon eclipse predicts disease will follow.

Corn planted during a waning Moon will grow slower but will have larger ears.

Babies born a day after the full Moon will be successful in life.

If you hear an owl calling under the full Moon it predicts a death in the local area.

Frost that arrives in the dark of the Moon will kill fruit buds and blossom, but if the frost arrives in the light of the Moon it will do no harm.

If you wash new clothes during a full Moon, they will not last long.

If you catch a glimpse of a new Moon over your right should, it will bring you good luck.

Start new projects during the new Moon for the greatest success (us witches know that one!).

For the best chance of a good marriage accept a proposal during a full Moon.

If you like to do a bit of crabbing, shrimping or clam digging then the full Moon is the best time.

Show your newborn baby to the waxing Moon to bring strength to the child.

When moving house try and arrive at your new residence during the new Moon, it will bring prosperity.

If you point nine times in one night at the Moon you will not go to Heaven…hmm, reckon there is a connection to witches with this one?

Seeing the first sliver of a new Moon in a clear sky without trees or foliage in view is lucky.

A lucky rabbit's foot will be even luckier if it was killed in a cemetery by a cross eyed man on the dark of the Moon (seriously where do they get this stuff from?).

Hold a moonstone in your mouth on the full Moon, it will reveal the future (please do not choke on it).

A full Moon arriving on a Monday is said to be lucky.

Mushrooms that are collected on a full Moon are said to be cursed by the Fae and should not be eaten.

A fairy ring of mushrooms is most dangerous under a full Moon.

A full Moon arriving on a Sunday is thought to be unlucky.

If you see the first sliver of a new Moon through a window it will bring bad luck and you will break some crockery.

Washing new clothes on a full Moon means the items will not wear well.

Apparently, it is unlucky to sleep in the Moonlight.

Never point at the new Moon or view any Moon over your shoulder, it will bring bad luck.

According to the ancient Greeks the full Moon is apparently the best time to consummate a marriage.

Do not venture outside on the dark Moon, you risk falling foul to the Devil…ruh roh, that's me scuppered then.

If a child is born when the Moon is one day old, it will have a long and prosperous life.

If a child is born when the Moon is waning the child will be unhealthy.

If a child is born on a full Moon, they will have a strong personality.

A child born on a dark Moon will need special care.

Sleeping for any length of time in Moonlight will send you blind or crazy.

And avoid vampires on the waning Moon, it is apparently the time when they feel the greatest need to feed…

Moon Goddess Ritual

I am very honoured to include the script from one of our open Kitchen Witch rituals. Written by our lovely team: Vanessa Armstrong, Sue Perryman, Joshua Petchey, Heather Dewhurst, Gwyneth Sangster and Samantha Leaver.

On this occasion we did things a little differently. We are blessed to have both a yew tree grove, a beech grove and open fields at the Queen Elizabeth Country Park in Hampshire where we hold our rituals.

Introduction:

You will be used to the usual ritual format, even though at Kitchen Witch we have often strayed from the norm, this one is somewhat different even for us. There will be no circle casting and no quarter calls, in fact there will be very little that resembles a traditional ritual. We are instead going to take a journey together through the phases of the Moon, working a little magic as we go.

We will start in the yew tree grove and move eventually to the beech trees, stopping twice on the way.

There will not be any hail and welcomes or farewells, but there will be several occasions where you can repeat 'Blessings to the goddess'. We also won't be sending the goddesses on their way in the traditional format, we are asking for their assistance so we will thank them with offerings.

Start at the Yew grove:

We are in the dark Moon, a time of purification, for releasing and letting go. May we call upon assistance from the great goddess Hekate...

Hecate daughter of Perses and Asteria,

Goddess of witchcraft, magic, the Moon, doorways, and dreams,
As You wrap us in Your power
We release to You our worries, fears and egos.
Cocoon us safely within the darkness which is Your womb,
To rest surrounded by Your Blessings.

Healing Temple Meditation

Take several deep breaths in and out...

As your world around you dissipates you find yourself in what looks to be a temple, there are stone pillars all around you with beautiful carvings, the floor beneath your feet is a breath taking mosaic made up from tiny pieces of brightly coloured tiles creating an amazing swirling pattern.

You then look up and realize that although you are surrounded by walls the top of the temple is open to the sky which is a deep midnight blue and littered with bright sparkling stars. It is then that you notice each of the stone pillars has a large flaming torch to light up the room you are in.

Then you hear a beautiful sound, the soft soothing strings of a harp...so you follow the notes through the temple to a large room that is the colour of a bright blue summer sky. In the centre of the room is a Sunken bath filled with the clearest, brightest blue water and floating with pink and red rose petals, the scent of the bath water is captivating and on the side of the bath is a huge fluffy towel and you just know that it is meant for you.

Stepping into the bath the warm scented water draws you in further until you are lying comfortably submerged in its healing soothing waters. You can still hear the harp music and the combination of the beautiful sound, the scents and warm water starts to heal your mind, your body and your soul...

You can feel your worries, grief, pain and any emotional troubles just melting away...

You lay in complete bliss and allow the temple bath to work its healing magic...

You step out from the water and wrap yourself in the large welcoming towel that feels like a big soft hug.

When you are ready you leave the bath and walk back through the temple giving a word of thanks for the healing received.

Then slowly come back to this reality, wriggling your fingers and toes and gently open your eyes.

We offer you earthy mugwort in your name Lady Hecate (Hekate) with gratitude for the gifts of the darkened womb. Blessings of the dark.

Move to just outside the Yew grove:

> *We have now moved into the new Moon, a time for wishes and weaving of hopes and dreams. May we call upon the great goddess Freyja...*
> *Freyja, Goddess of ambition and courage,*
> *Weaver of magic, Vanquisher of enemies.*
> *You are the energy, forever building within us;*
> *The love, the rage, the passion, boiling beneath the surface.*
> *Your golden chariot, riding forth, leading a procession of fire–spirited warriors;*
> *The glory of battle, made so by the inspiration you instil.*
> *The Earth, coming to life in the spring,*
> *The Moon, waxing towards it brightest day.*
> *You too bestow upon us the exhilaration of possibility; the wonder of what is to come and the ambition to strive for the future.*
> *Blessings to Freyja!*

ALL:

Spiral dance with drumming

ALL:

Take a handful of rose petals and throw them to the wind with a wish.

We offer fresh lemon balm in your name Freya with gratitude for the gifts of inspired ambition. Blessings of the New.

Move to the middle of the field:

And now we move into the full Moon phase, one of creating a spark and igniting your inner passion. May we call upon the great Goddess Aine.
Aine, Goddess of Love, Fertility, the heady days and warm nights of Summer
which invokes passions, love and romance.
Your name means brightness, joy, radiance and splendour.
You bring us the Sun's power, together with the hopes of fruitfulness and abundance and the Moon's mystery, with intuition and regeneration.
We ask for your assistance today as we look to light the fires of our own passions and claim our powers!
Blessings to Aine!

ALL:

Each person takes an incense stick and lights it from a central candle, takes a moment to focus on the smoke and think about their passions and goals.

We offer you fiery rosemary in your name Aine with gratitude for the gifts of intuitive regeneration. Blessings of the full.

Beech grove:

And finally, for this cycle at least we move into the waning Moon, a time of harvest and feasting. May we call upon the great Goddess Demeter.

Lady Demeter, daughter of Cronus and Rhea

Sister Olympian and matriarchal mother.
You carry the cornucopia of our wishes,
You allow us to reap the bounty of spring's growth
And summer's passion
Now we feast.

Blessings to the goddess

ALL:
Extinguish incense sticks in water.

Take a cake and a drink and focus on what you are thankful for and your achievements.

Feast and drink.

We offer you hearty cake in your name Demeter with gratitude for the gifts of banishment through release. Blessings of the Waning.

As the Moon goes down...

This is your journey and your pathway. Work with the magic of the Moon in a way that suits you. Make it happen for you in a way that feels right. There is no right or wrong, just the magic of the Moon available to all.

Sources/Further reading:

Pagan Portals Animal Magic by Rachel Patterson
A Kitchen Witch's World of Magical Plants and Herbs by Rachel Patterson
A Kitchen Witch's World of Magical Food by Rachel Patterson
Kitchen Witchcraft: Crystal Magic by Rachel Patterson
Musesrealm.net
Histmyst.org
Drikpanchang.com
Learnreligions.com
Britannica.com
Ancient.eu.com
UCL.ac.uk
Thaliatook.com
Theoi.com
Timeanddate.com
Moonphases.co.uk
Almanac.com
Earthsky.org
Astro.cafeastrology.com
Astrostyle.com
Sunsigns.org
Astrology for Dummies – Orion
Complete Book of Astrology by Caitlin Johnstone
Whats-your-sign.com

MOON
BOOKS

PAGANISM & SHAMANISM

What is Paganism? A religion, a spirituality, an alternative belief system, nature worship? You can find support for all these definitions (and many more) in dictionaries, encyclopaedias, and text books of religion, but subscribe to any one and the truth will evade you. Above all Paganism is a creative pursuit, an encounter with reality, an exploration of meaning and an expression of the soul. Druids, Heathens, Wiccans and others, all contribute their insights and literary riches to the Pagan tradition. Moon Books invites you to begin or to deepen your own encounter, right here, right now.

If you have enjoyed this book, why not tell other readers by posting a review on your preferred book site.

Recent bestsellers from Moon Books are:

Journey to the Dark Goddess
How to Return to Your Soul
Jane Meredith
Discover the powerful secrets of the Dark Goddess and transform your depression, grief and pain into healing and integration.
Paperback: 978-1-84694-677-6 ebook: 978-1-78099-223-5

Shamanic Reiki
Expanded Ways of Working with Universal Life Force Energy
Llyn Roberts, Robert Levy
Shamanism and Reiki are each powerful ways of healing; together, their power multiplies. *Shamanic Reiki* introduces techniques to help healers and Reiki practitioners tap ancient healing wisdom.
Paperback: 978-1-84694-037-8 ebook: 978-1-84694-650-9

Pagan Portals – The Awen Alone
Walking the Path of the Solitary Druid
Joanna van der Hoeven
An introductory guide for the solitary Druid, *The Awen Alone* will accompany you as you explore, and seek out your own place within the natural world.
Paperback: 978-1-78279-547-6 ebook: 978-1-78279-546-9

A Kitchen Witch's World of Magical Herbs & Plants
Rachel Patterson
A journey into the magical world of herbs and plants, filled with magical uses, folklore, history and practical magic. By popular writer, blogger and kitchen witch, Tansy Firedragon.
Paperback: 978-1-78279-621-3 ebook: 978-1-78279-620-6

Medicine for the Soul

The Complete Book of Shamanic Healing

Ross Heaven

All you will ever need to know about shamanic healing and how to become your own shaman...

Paperback: 978-1-78099-419-2 ebook: 978-1-78099-420-8

Shaman Pathways – The Druid Shaman

Exploring the Celtic Otherworld

Danu Forest

A practical guide to Celtic shamanism with exercises and techniques as well as traditional lore for exploring the Celtic Otherworld.

Paperback: 978-1-78099-615-8 ebook: 978-1-78099-616-5

Traditional Witchcraft for the Woods and Forests

A Witch's Guide to the Woodland with Guided Meditations and Pathworking

Mélusine Draco

A Witch's guide to walking alone in the woods, with guided meditations and pathworking.

Paperback: 978-1-84694-803-9 ebook: 978-1-84694-804-6

Wild Earth, Wild Soul

A Manual for an Ecstatic Culture

Bill Pfeiffer

Imagine a nature-based culture so alive and so connected, spreading like wildfire. This book is the first flame...

Paperback: 978-1-78099-187-0 ebook: 978-1-78099-188-7

Naming the Goddess

Trevor Greenfield

Naming the Goddess is written by over eighty adherents and scholars of Goddess and Goddess Spirituality.

Paperback: 978-1-78279-476-9 ebook: 978-1-78279-475-2

Shapeshifting into Higher Consciousness

Heal and Transform Yourself and Our World with Ancient Shamanic and Modern Methods

Llyn Roberts

Ancient and modern methods that you can use every day to transform yourself and make a positive difference in the world.

Paperback: 978-1-84694-843-5 ebook: 978-1-84694-844-2

the neck to the shoulder, are common in LBA levels at the inland site of Beycesultan, though these are regularly provided with either ring or flattened bases and have pronounced trefoil mouths.[25] Two examples of jugs closely resembling the larger reddish-brown burnished jugs from Kommos in fabric, profile, and size, although lacking either a lug or a handle on the lower body, were part of a ship's cargo recovered some 25 km east of Bodrum near the mouth of Şeytan Deresi (Devil's Creek) and provisionally dated to the early Shaft Grave period, or very end of the local Middle Bronze Age.[26] Finally, the very distinctive knobbed decoration of jug C8689 from Kommos (fig. 13) has distant parallels on large jars of shape 26 and cooking bowls of shape 31 from Beycesultan levels V and IVC, respectively.[27] Although the parallels so far published are by no means close enough to enable one or more specific southwest Anatolian production centers of the reddish-brown burnished jugs from LM II–IIIB contexts at Kommos and other contexts on Crete to be identified, in combination they serve to mark the coastal regions between the Gulf of Izmir and the Gulf of Kerme as the probable source area of these imports. Features such as the thickened horizontal or sloping lips, the burnished reddish-brown and often somewhat mottled exteriors, the emphasis on articulated bases, the distinct but usually not sharply offset necks on closed forms, and the penchant for multiple fine grooves at the transition from neck to shoulder are all aspects of the reddish-brown burnished jugs from Kommos that are very difficult to parallel in Minoan pottery but that seem quite common in that of west-central and southwest Anatolia at this time.

The unusually high frequency of jugs of a particular size in this reddish-brown burnished class as it is so far attested on Crete suggests that these vessels may have been used to transport a particular product from coastal Anatolia to Minoan ports.[28] The possible provision for the attachment of a lid on one of the jug necks from Kommos (figs. 2a, 9b) may be a further indication of such a transport function for these medium-sized vessels. They are nowhere near as large as the contemporary Canaanite jars of the Levant or the coarse-ware stirrup jars of the Aegean, much less of Cypriot pithoi. Indeed, they are even smaller than the transport container that Watrous christened the short-necked amphora, which was produced in large numbers at or around Kommos.[29] But their reduced size may be a

25. Mellaart and Murray 1995, 4, 7, 13, fig. P.5.1, 3, 8, pl. IIIb.4 [Beycesultan III], 24, 29, 41, fig. P.19.5–9, pl. VIb [Beycesultan II].

26. Bass 1976, 298–9, fig. 5B–C.

27. Lloyd and Mellaart 1965, 91, 98, fig. P.9.4, 7 [Beycesultan V], 115, fig. P.22.10, 116, fig. P.23.1, 117 [Beycesultan IVC]. I am grateful to Peter Pavuk for drawing these parallels to my attention.

28. Ceramic versions of the jug form thus far attested on Crete are noticeably smaller on average than copper versions of either LM/LH I or LM II/LH IIB–LM/LH IIIA date (Matthäus 1980, 163–8, 172–3).

29. Rutter 2000. The capacities of short-necked amphorae range from c. 9.5–10.5 liters, roughly twice those of the reddish-brown burnished jugs.

function of the product they were designed to carry, whatever that may have been. In any case, if the suggestion that these reddish-brown burnished jugs from Kommos and other Minoan sites are western Anatolian imports is correct, these vessels would at last provide evidence from the Anatolian side for the kind of intense interaction between the coastal regions of southwest Anatolia and Crete that sites such as Knidos, Iasos, and above all Miletos, to name but a few, have long provided from the Minoan side.[30]

The distribution of these imported, reddish-brown burnished jugs on Crete is rather unusual. Unlike the quantities of Egyptian and Sardinian vessels found at Kommos,[31] they are by no means peculiar to that site. At the same time, unlike both Cypriot and Syro-Palestinian imports, they are not limited to coastal sites on Crete.[32] Yet there are several well-explored Minoan sites that have produced substantial evidence for occupation during LM IIIA but no examples of either jugs or any other shapes in this reddish-brown burnished class. These sites include coastal locales in both western (e.g., Chania) and eastern (e.g., Mochlos, Gournia) Crete, as well as important centers at some remove from the sea (e.g., Hagia Triada, just an hour's brisk walk from Kommos). So why do these jugs turn up where they do?

Moreover, in view of how little is known of the LM II period throughout the island of Crete, it is striking how many of these jugs appear for the first time at their respective sites in contexts of that period. This is, of course, precisely when copious artifactual evidence for Mycenaeans on Crete shows up for the first time. Is there some connection between reddish-brown burnished jugs and Mycenaean overlordship on Crete?[33] To my knowledge, nothing remotely resembling these coil-made, medium-coarse, burnished jugs has been found on the Greek mainland at the time in question. Nor is there anything similar from the richly furnished Mycenaean cemeteries on Rhodes. On Kos, however, there are a number of monochrome red-burnished jugs from the Langada tombs that seem broadly

30. Niemeier and Niemeier 1997; Niemeier 1999.

31. Watrous 1992, 162–8; Rutter 1999, 142–4, 173–5 table 3, 177–9 table 5; 2006.

32. Rutter 1999, 141–2, 147–8; 2006.

33. The more developed shape of the copper version of such jugs, Matthäus' shape 21 (1980, 172–3, pl. 68A), is above all characteristic of the so-called "burials with bronzes" on Crete (e.g., Zapher Papoura Tombs 14 and 36 at Knossos, Archanes Tholos A, and Kalyvia Shaft Grave 4 at Phaistos) that are often identified as the tombs of a Mycenaean ruling aristocracy (Popham et al. 1974, 253–4; Matthäus 1980, 68–74; Driessen and Macdonald 1984; Kilian-Dirlmeier 1985; Löwe 1996, 52–4; Whitley 2002, 222–3). Of the four examples of shape 21 published before 1980 from the mainland, at least two and perhaps three were found at Dendra, one at Asine. Although these later metal jugs, or hydrias, as Matthäus and Catling term them, are often smaller and exhibit more care in their manufacture than the earlier ones of Matthäus' shape 20 (1980, 174–5), they never feature a lug on the lower body as do ceramic versions of the type from Kommos, Knossos' Kephala Tholos, and Chondros Viannou. Contemporary examples of essentially the same shape from Sellopoulo Tomb 4 at Knossos that lack a horizontal handle on the lower body are described by Catling and Matthäus as jugs (Matthäus 1980, 196 [shape 26]; Popham et al. 1974, 236–8 nos. 31–2, 251).

similar.[34] Unfortunately, these have been published without profiles and exclusively in black-and-white photographs, so it is difficult to assess how closely they resemble the reddish-brown examples from Crete. The earliest of these jugs from Kos, however, is no earlier than LH IIIA, so they postdate the sudden appearance of reddish-brown burnished jugs at Kommos and in the Knossos area in LM II. If the presence of these jugs in LM II contexts marks a new stage in contacts between Crete and the Arzawa lands of western Anatolia at precisely the time when a Mycenaean administration came to power at Knossos, one may reasonably ask whether this new relationship might have any connection with the initial mention shortly thereafter of Ahhiyawa in the Hittite texts in connection with the activities of Madduwatta and Attarisiya, the "Man of Ahhiya."[35] Could it be, for example, that the name Ahhiya or Ahhiyawa was originally applied by the Hittites to the LM II–IIIA2 Early kingdom centered at Knossos, by far and away the most powerful polity in the southern Aegean during the period c. 1450–1375 B.C.?[36] If this had been the case, one might have expected the destruction of Knossos c. 1375 B.C. to have resulted in the disappearance of Ahhiyawa from Hittite documents. But perhaps the name was adopted by a successor power on the Greek mainland. Alternatively, the earlier term Ahhiya may have been applied to Mycenaean Knossos in LM II–IIIA2 Early, while the later term Ahhiyawa was used by the mainland Greek (probably Argive) successor to Knossian dominance in the Aegean during the period c. 1375–1200 B.C.[37]

Further speculation on historical questions of such potential importance is unquestionably premature in the light of our limited understanding at present of contacts between Crete and southwestern Anatolia during the fifteenth and fourteenth centuries B.C. But the recognition that the reddish-brown burnished class of pottery surveyed here is imported to Crete rather than locally produced, as well as being far more common at some key sites in LM II–IIIA1 central Crete than previously realized, may open up some interesting avenues of future research on several different fronts in the years to come.

34. Morricone 1965–1966, 107 no. 15, fig. 315.2 [Tomb 10], 124 no. 1, fig. 108.5 [Tomb 16], 151 no. 4, fig. 143.2 [Tomb 25], 202–3 no. 2, fig. 214.5 [Tomb 44], 209 no. 7, fig. 221.6 [Tomb 45], 271 no. 3, fig. 315.3 and 276 no. 1, fig. 314 [sporadic finds without context].

35. Bryce 1998, 59–63, 140–9; Cline 1994, 68–77, 121–5.

36. I owe this provocative suggestion to Sturt Manning, to whom I am also grateful for some intriguing initial discussions of this possibility.

37. For the notion that the name Ahhiyawa might have been applied to different regions within the Aegean at different periods, albeit with different candidates for those locations than those suggested here, see Cline 1994, 69. For two recent discussions of the "Ahhiyawa question," see Georgiadis 2003, 112–3 and Hope-Simpson 2003, the latter with a comprehensive bibliography.

WORKS CITED

Alexiou, S. 1967. *Υστερομινωικοί Τάφοι Λιμένος Κνωσσού (Κατσαμπά)*. Βιβλιοθήκη τῆς ἐν Ἀθήναις Ἀρχαιολογικῆς Ἑταιρείας 56. Athens: En Athenais Archaiologike Hetaireia.

Bass, G.F. 1976. "Sheytan Deresi: Preliminary Report." *IJNA* 5, 4: 293–303.

Bayne, N. 2000. *The Grey Wares of North-West Anatolia in the Middle and Late Bronze Age and the Early Iron Age and their Relation to the Early Greek Settlements*. Asia Minor Studien 37. Bonn: Rudolf Habelt.

Betancourt, P.P. 1990. *Kommos*. Vol. 2, *The Final Neolithic through Middle Minoan III Pottery*. Princeton, NJ: Princeton University Press.

Betancourt, P.P., G.H. Myer and J.B. Rutter. 1988. "The Ceramic Petrography of Early Helladic Pottery from Lerna." In *A Pot for All Reasons: Ceramic Ecology Revisited, Papers Dedicated to Frederick R. Matson, 1986*, edited by C.C. Kolb and L.M. Lackey, 73–80. Philadelphia: Laboratory of Anthropology, Temple University.

Betancourt, P.P., G.H. Myer and S.J. Vaughan. 1995. "Petrography." In *Lerna. A Preclassical Site in the Argolid*. Vol. 3, *The Pottery of Lerna IV*, by J.B. Rutter, 666–710. Princeton, NJ: American School of Classical Studies at Athens.

Bryce, T. 1998. *The Kingdom of the Hittites*. Oxford: Clarendon.

Cadogan, G. 1967. "Late Minoan IIIC Pottery from the Kephala Tholos Tomb near Knossos." *BSA* 62: 257–65.

Cline, E.H. 1994. *Sailing the Wine-Dark Sea: International Trade and the Late Bronze Age Aegean*. *BAR-IS* 591. Oxford: Tempus Reparatum.

Driessen, J. and C. Macdonald. 1984. "Some Military Aspects of the Aegean in the Late Fifteenth and Early Fourteenth Centuries B.C." *BSA* 79: 49–74.

Evans, A. 1921. *The Palace of Minos at Knossos*. Vol. 1. London: Macmillan.

Georgiadis, M. 2003. *The South-Eastern Aegean in the Mycenaean Period: Islands, Landscape, Death and Ancestors*. *BAR-IS* 1196. Oxford: Archaeopress.

Günel, S. 1999a. *Panaztepe*. Vol. 2, *Die Keramik von Panaztepe und ihre Bedeutung für Westkleinasien und die Ägäis im 2. Jahrtausend*. Ankara: Türk Tarih Kurumu.

———. 1999b. "Vorbericht über die mittel- und spätbronzezeitliche Keramik vom Liman Tepe." *IstMitt* 49: 41–82.

Hawkins, J.D. 2002. "The Historical Geography of Western Anatolia in the Hittite Texts," 94–101. In "Troy in Recent Perspective," by D.F. Easton, J.D. Hawkins, A.G. Sherratt and E.S. Sherratt. *AnatSt* 52: 75–109.

Hope Simpson, R. 2003. "The Dodecanese and the Ahhiyawa Question." *BSA* 98: 203–37.

Kilian-Dirlmeier, I. 1985. "Noch einmal zu den 'Kriegergräbern' von Knossos." *JRGZM* 32: 196–214.

Knapp, A.B. and J.F. Cherry. 1994. *Provenience Studies and Bronze Age Cyprus: Production, Exchange and Politico-Economic Change*. Monographs in World Archaeology 21. Madison, WI: Prehistory Press.

Lloyd, S. and J. Mellaart. 1965. *Beycesultan*. Vol. 2, *Middle Bronze Age Architecture and Pottery*. Occasional Publications of the British Institute of Archaeology at Ankara 8. London: British Institute of Archaeology at Ankara.

Löwe, W. 1996. *Spätbronzezeitliche Bestattungen auf Kreta*. *BAR-IS* 642. Oxford: Tempus Reparatum.

Marinatos, S. 1974. *Excavations at Thera*. Vol. 6, *1972 Season*. Βιβλιοθήκη τῆς ἐν Ἀθήναις Ἀρχαιολογικῆς Ἑταιρείας 64. Athens: En Athenais Archaiologike Hetaireia.

Matthäus, H. 1980. *Die Bronzegefässe der kretisch-mykenischen Kultur*. Prähistorische Bronzefunde. Vol. 2, Part 1. Munich: C. H. Beck.

Mellaart, J. and A. Murray. 1995. *Beycesultan*. Vol. 3, Part 2, *Late Bronze Age and Phrygian Pottery and Middle and Late Bronze Age Small Objects*. Occasional Publications of the British Institute of Archaeology at Ankara 12. London: British Institute of Archaeology at Ankara.

Morricone, L. 1965–1966. "Eleona e Langada: Sepolcreti della Tarda Età del Bronzo a Coo." *ASAtene* 43–44 (n.s. 27–28): 5–311.

Niemeier, B. and W.-D. Niemeier 1997. "Milet 1994–1995. Projekt 'Minoisch-mykenisches bis protogeometrisches Milet': Zielsetzung und Grabungen auf dem Stadionhügel und am Athenatempel." *AA*: 189–248.

Niemeier, W.-D. 1999. "Mycenaeans and Hittites in War in Western Asia Minor." In *POLEMOS: Le contexte guerrier*

en Égée à l'Âge du Bronze. Actes de la 7e Rencontre égéenne internationale Université de Liège, 14–17 avril 1998, edited by R. Laffineur, 141–55. *Aegaeum* 19. Liège: Université de Liège.

Nixon, L.F. 1996. "The Oblique House and the Southeast Rooms." In *Kommos*. Vol. 1, *The Kommos Region and Houses of the Minoan Town*. Part 2, *The Minoan Hilltop and Hillside Houses*, edited by J.W. Shaw and M.C. Shaw, 59–76. Princeton, NJ: Princeton University Press.

Platon, L. 1997. "Caractère, morphologie et datation de la bourgade postpalatiale de Képhali Chondrou Viannou." In *La Crète Mycénienne. Actes de la Table Ronde Internationale organisée par l'École française d'Athènes*, edited by J. Driessen and A. Farnoux, 357–73. *BCH* Suppl. 30. Paris: École Française d'Athènes.

Popham, M.R. 1964. *The Last Days of the Palace at Knossos: Complete Vases of the Late Minoan IIIB Period. SIMA* 5. Lund: Carl Bloms.

———. 1984. *The Minoan Unexplored Mansion at Knossos. BSA* Suppl. 17. Oxford: British School of Archaeology at Athens and Thames and Hudson.

Popham, M.R., E.A. Catling and H.W. Catling. 1974. "Sellopoulo Tombs 3 and 4, Two Late Minoan Graves near Knossos." *BSA* 69: 195–257.

Rutter, J.B. 1999. "Cretan External Relations During Late Minoan IIIA2–B (ca. 1370–1200 BC): A View from the Mesara." In *The Point Iria Wreck: Interconnections in the Mediterranean ca. 1200 B.C. Proceedings of the International Conference, Island of Spetses, 19 September 1998*, edited by W. Phelps, Y. Lolos and Y. Vichos, 139–86. Athens: Hellenic Institute of Marine Archaeology.

———. 2000. "The Short-Necked Amphora of the Post-Palatial Mesara." In *Πεπραγμένα Η' Διεθνούς Κρητολογικού Συνεδρίου. Προϊστορική και Αρχαία Ελληνική Περίοδος*, Vol. A3, edited by T. Detorakes and A. Kalokairinos, 177–88. Heraklion: Hetaireia Kretikon Istorikon Meleton.

———. 2006. "Ceramic Imports at Kommos." In *Kommos*. Vol. 5, *The Monumental Buildings at Kommos*, edited by J.W. Shaw and M.C. Shaw, 646–88. Princeton, NJ: Princeton University Press.

Sackett, L.H., M.R. Popham, P.M. Warren and L. Engstrand. 1965. "Excavations at Palaikastro VI." *BSA* 60: 248–315.

Shaw, J.W. and M.C. Shaw. 1993. "Excavations at Kommos (Crete) during 1986–1992." *Hesperia* 62: 129–90.

Watrous, L. V. 1992. *Kommos*. Vol. 3, *The Late Bronze Age Pottery*. Princeton, NJ: Princeton University Press.

Watrous, L.V., P.M. Day and R.E. Jones. 1998. "The Sardinian Pottery from the Late Bronze Age Site of Kommos in Crete: Description, Chemical and Petrographic Analyses, and Historical Context." In *Sardinia and Aegean Chronology: Towards the Resolution of Relative and Absolute Dating in the Mediterranean*, edited by M.S. Balmuth and R.H. Tykot, 337–40. Studies in Sardinian Archaeology 5. Oxford: Oxbow.

Whitley, J. 2002. "Objects with Attitude: Biographical Facts and Fallacies in the Study of Late Bronze Age and Early Iron Age Warrior Graves." *CAJ* 12: 217–32.

ELENI S. BANOU received her degree in History and Archaeology from the University of Athens and studied Classical Archaeology at the University of Pennsylvania where she received a Ph.D. Her dissertation is entitled "Pottery Groups from the West Side of Area A at Pseira, Crete." She was a staff member of the Pseira excavations and has contributed to many of the Pseira publications. Banou is a member of the Greek Archaeological Service and has been directing excavations since 1993 at the site of Pera Galenoi, located just west of Fodele on the north coast of Crete. [ebanou@freemail.gr]

KOSTANDINOS S. CHRISTAKIS studied Classical and Near Eastern Archaeology at the University of Rome "La Sapienza" and received his Ph.D. at the University of Bristol. He currently teaches in the Department of Education at the University of Crete. Christakis is collaborating with G. Rethemiotakis in the investigation of the site Galatas Pediados, Crete, and he is responsible for the publication of the stratified deposits from the sanctuary of Kato Simi Viannou. His published works (articles and two monographs) focus on staple storage, subsistence economy and the politics of the past. He is currently working on a book examining the storage technologies and the palatial and domestic economy of the settlement of Knossos. [christakis@her.forthnet.gr]

PETER M. DAY received his B.A. in Archaeology from the University of Southampton. After his introduction to Aegean archaeology as Research Fellow in Ceramic Petrology at the Fitch Laboratory, British School at Athens, he carried out doctoral research at the University of Cambridge, where his dissertation "A Petrographic Approach to the Study of Pottery in Neopalatial East Crete" was based on the archaeological and ethnographic study of pottery manufacture. His postdoctoral research at the MacDonald Institute of Archaeological Research, Cambridge, and at the Laboratory of Archaeometry, NCSR "Demokritos" in Athens, concentrated on the Early Bronze Age of Crete. Since 1994 he has taught at the Department of Archaeology, University of Sheffield, and is the author or coauthor of over 60 articles and monographs, many concerning the methodology and application of ceramic analysis. [p.m.day@sheffield.ac.uk]

EDWARD W. FABER was awarded a B.Sc. in Archaeological Science from the University of Sheffield. Following this he spent time as a graduate researcher in the Laboratory of Archaeometry, NCSR "Demokritos" in Athens, including participation in the European Union TMR project GEOPRO. He has recently submitted a Ph.D. thesis to the University of Sheffield entitled "Middle Minoan Polychrome Pottery: An Integrated Microstructural, Geochemical and Mineralogical Investigation of its Production Technology and Provenance." [edwardwfaber@yahoo.co.uk]

MARIA RELAKI was awarded a B.A. in Archaeology and Art History from the University of Athens, and an M.A. in Archaeology and Prehistory from the University of Sheffield. After having worked briefly for the Greek Archaeological Service in eastern Crete, she went on to gain her Ph.D. with a dissertation entitled "Social Arenas in Minoan Crete: A Regional History of the Mesara from the Final Neolithic to the End of the Protopalatial Period" from the University of Sheffield. She has used ceramic petrography to study ceramic assemblages from Mochlos, Kavousi and Poros in Crete and Rhodes in the Dodecanese, resulting in several publications. She is currently a Post-doctoral Research Associate at the University of Sheffield, working on ceramics of the Early Bronze II southern Aegean. [m.relaki@sheffield.ac.uk]

JEREMY B. RUTTER received his Ph.D. from the University of Pennsylvania and is now the Sherman Fairchild Professor of the Humanities, Dartmouth College. He is the author of *The Transition to Mycenaean* (1976, with Sarah H. Rutter), *Ceramic Change in the Aegean Early Bronze Age* (1979) and *Lerna*. Vol. 3, *The Pottery of Lerna IV* (1995), as well as numerous journal articles and reviews. [Jeremy.B.Rutter@Dartmouth.edu]

ELENI TSIVILIKA studied History and Archaeology at the University of Thessaloniki. She is a member of the Greek Archaeological Service and since 1993 has codirected, with Eleni Banou, excavations at the site of Pera Galenoi, Crete.

ALEYDIS VAN DE MOORTEL received an M.A. in Classics from the Catholic University of Leuven, an M.A. in Anthropology with a specialty in Nautical Archaeology from Texas A&M University and an M.A. and Ph.D. in Classical and Near Eastern Archaeology from Bryn Mawr College. Her dissertation was entitled "The Transition from the Protopalatial to the Neopalatial Society in South-Central Crete: A Ceramic Perspective." She is currently Assistant Professor of Classics at the University of Tennessee. From 1992–2003 she worked as a pottery analyst at Kommos in southern Crete, and she is publishing the Protopalatial pottery from the civic center. She is now codirector of the Greek-American excavations of the Bronze Age and Early Iron Age site of Mitrou, in East Lokris. [avdm@utk.edu]

MALCOLM H. WIENER has published numerous papers dealing with the Eastern Mediterranean world in the Bronze Age, focusing in particular on the external relations of Minoan Crete and the chronology of the Middle and Late Bronze Age. His publications include "Crete and the Cyclades in LM I: The Tale of the Conical Cups," "Trade and Rule in Palatial Crete," "The Isles of Crete? The Minoan Thalassocracy Revisited," "The Nature and Control of Minoan Foreign Trade," "Present Arms / Oars / Ingots: Searching for Evidence of Military or Maritime Administration in LM IB," "The White Slip I of Tell el-

Dab^ca and Thera: Critical Challenge for the Aegean Long Chronology," "The Absolute Chronology of Late Helladic IIIA2 Revisited," "Times Change: The Current State of the Debate in Old World Archaeology," "Time Out: The Current Impasse in Bronze Age Archaeological Dating," "Chronology Going Forward (With a Query about 1525/4 B.C.)" and "Egypt and Time." [mhwiener@villacandia.com]

Printed on Cougar Opaque paper
from Bembo types, with design
and typography by
Jerry Kelly.

NEW YORK · MMVI